Fact-Finding in Civil Litigation

A Comparative Perspective

R.R. Verkerk

Fact-Finding in Civil Litigation

A Comparative Perspective

intersentia

METRO

Ius Commune Europaeum

Remme Verkerk
PhD thesis

Fact-Finding in Civil Litigation. A Comparative Perspective

ISBN 978-94-000-0074-2
D/2010/7849/83
NUR 822

Antwerp - Oxford - Portland
www.intersentia.com

ACKNOWLEDGEMENTS

Dit boek vormt de afsluiting van een project waar ik meerdere jaren aan heb gewerkt. Een bijzondere periode, waarin ik veel heb mogen leren. Een periode waarin ik vrijwel zonder uitzondering met plezier 's ochtends mijn kantoor binnenstapte. De rust van het onderzoek werd vaak afgewisseld met de gezellige drukte van het onderwijs.

Tijdens de afgelopen jaren heb ik mijn werkzaamheden met veel collegae besproken. Ik heb veel mogen leren van de talloze gesprekken die in formele en informele settings plaatsvonden. Een speciaal dankwoord voor mijn beide promotoren is hier zeker op zijn plaats. Jaap en Remco, jullie hebben me beiden gesteund, vertrouwen gegeven en me gevraagd en ongevraagd van advies voorzien. Eveneens wil ik alle andere collegae aan de faculteit bedanken, met velen heb ik samen onderwijs verzorgd, congressen bezocht en regelmatig een praatje gemaakt. Door jullie aanwezigheid is werken zoveel meer geweest dan het verrichten van werkzaamheden. Ik hoop jullie ook in de toekomst nog vaak te treffen.

I also would like to address the many colleagues that have provided me with very valuable assistance writing this book. First of all, I thank the members of the Assesment Committee, that have put a lot of effort reading the manuscript. Their comments and suggestions have improved the quality of this book. I would like to thank colleages at the University of Vienna and those at Wayne State University for their assistance. I would like to express gratitude to the many American academics and practitioners that have helped me to understand the American procedural system. Without their assistance, it would not have been possible to understand the operatation of the American procedural system.

Verder een woord van dank aan de vele anderen die dit werk mogelijk gemaakt hebben. Een woord van dank aan de Rechtbank Maastricht, waar ik een unieke mogelijkheid gekregen heb het Nederlands burgerlijk procesrecht zelf toe te passen. Eveneens wil ik hen bedanken die mij hebben bijgestaan met de afronding en opmaak van dit boek.

Tot slot een woord van dank aan mijn vrienden, ouders en familie. In het bijzonder een woord van dank aan Femmie: de rust en liefde die ik thuis ervaren heb, is mijn werk enkel ten goede gekomen. Verder nog een vriendelijk woord voor Lucas en Thijs: zonder jullie was dit boek veel eerder afgerond, maar had mijn werk veel minder betekenis.

Remme Verkerk
Maastricht, maart 2010

TABLE OF CONTENTS

LIST OF ABBREVIATIONS

ABA	American Bar Association
AcP	Archiv für de civilistische Praxis
ALI	American Law Institute
BlgNr	Beilage(n) zu den stenografischen Protokollen des Nationalrates
C.	Codex (Justinian, 533 A.D.)
CJRA	Civil Justice Reform Act
CPR	Civil Procedural Rules (England)
CEPEJ	The European Commission for the Efficiency of Justice
D.	Digest (533 A.D.)
ECJ	European Court of Justice
ECtHR	European Court of Human Rights
EGZPO	Einführungsgesetz zur Zivilprozessordnung
FRCP	Federal Rules of Civil Procedure
FRD	Federal Rules Decisions
FRE	Federal Rules of Evidence
HNJV	Handelingen Nederlandse Juristen Vereniging
JBl	Juristische Blätter
JZ	Juristenzeitung
LJN	Landelijk Jurisprudentie Nummer
NCSC	National Center for State Courts
NJ	Nederlandse Jurisprudentie
NJB	Nederlands Juristenblad
NTBR	Nederlands Tijdschrift voor Burgerlijk Recht
NUCCUSL	National Conference of Commissioners on Uniform State Laws
ÖJZ	Österreichische Juristenzeitung
RGBl	Reichsgesetzblatt
Rv	Wetboek van Burgerlijke Rechtsvordering
RvdW	Rechtspraak van de Week
TCR	Tijdschrift voor Civiele Rechtspleging
Trema	Tijdschrift voor de Rechterlijke Macht
Unidroit	International Institute for the Unification of Private Law

W.	Weekblad van het Recht
WODC	Wetenschappelijk Onderzoek- en Documentatiecentrum
WPNR	Weekblad voor Privaatrecht Notariaat en Registratie
ZPO	Zivilprozessordnung
ZZP	Zeitschrift für Zivilprozess
ZZPInt	Zeitschrift für Zivilprozess international

Chapter 1

INTRODUCTION

1. The Subject Matter of this Book: Fact-finding in Civil Litigation

This book is on civil litigation which could be defined as 'a process before a court of law, voluntarily initiated by a plaintiff acting in what he sees as his own interest and opposed by a defendant who refuses, in what he, in his turn, sees as his interest, to meet the plaintiff's claim against him'.[1] In order to determine whether or not a claim or defense should be granted, the facts of the case are often decisive. In many court procedures, both issues of law and matters of fact are debated. This book focuses on the factual debates that take place in the litigation process. Debates on matters of fact generally are at the heart of the litigation process. As Blackstone put it: '(e)xperience will abundantly show, that above a hundred of our lawsuits arise from disputed facts, for one where the law is doubted of'.[2]

Procedural Rules and the Stages in the Process of Fact-finding

The factual debate that takes place in a court of justice roughly consists of three stages: the fact-gathering stage, the evidence stage and the decision-making stage. Together these stages constitute the process of fact-finding. This book discusses the rules on fact-finding. This implies that it discusses rules that regulate how information is gathered, evidence is presented and how a decision on matters of fact is made.

During the fact-gathering stage a search for relevant information is conducted. In addition, information is shared, such that relevant information is available to both parties and the judge. In this stage, the parties generally first provide a written statement which contains their claim or defenses as well as a short account of the

1 Jolowicz 2000, p. 22.

2 Blackstone 1768, Vol. 3, p. 330: 'Experience will abundantly show, that above a hundred of our lawsuits arise from disputed facts, for one where the law is doubted of. About twenty days in the year are sufficient, in Westminster-hall, to settle (upon solemn argument) every demurrer or other special point of law that arises throughout the nation: but two months are annually spent in deciding the truth of facts, before distinct tribunals, in the several circuits of England (...)'.

relevant facts. Such written statements will be referred to as 'pleadings'. In addition, most systems have rules that require the parties to share relevant information with their opponent and the court out of their own motion. I will use the term 'disclosure' to refer to the *sua sponte* sharing of information.[3] Moreover, mostly on the European Continent, relevant facts are discussed at preparatory hearings. During these hearings, the judge will freely discuss the facts of the case with the parties and their lawyers. I will often use the term 'personal appearance of the parties' to refer to such preparatory hearings. Lastly, there are procedural mechanisms that enable the parties to request each other to provide relevant information. These mechanisms are jointly referred to as 'discovery'. Common discovery devices used in the United States include interrogatories, depositions and requests for the production of documents. Interrogatories are written questions that can be put to the opponent, who is bound to answer under oath. A deposition is the taking of an out-of-court testimony of a witness or a party in the fact-gathering stage of litigation. Requests for the production of documents enable one party to inspect or copy documents held by the other party.

The case will proceed to the second stage, the evidence stage, if there is a genuine disagreement between the parties on a particular question of fact. In the evidence stage, parties have the opportunity to present evidence in order to convince the decision maker that their version of the facts is the most plausible. Witness' testimony, expert findings, written documents and exhibits may all serve to provide evidence.

In the decision stage, the decision maker will weigh the evidence and render a decision on matters of fact. Procedural systems commonly make use of a set of rules that prescribe how a decision should be reached. There are rules that determine how evidence ought to be evaluated and weighed. Other rules prescribe what ought to be done when it is not possible to determine the veracity of a fact after all evidence has been evaluated (rules on the burden of proof).

Comparative Method and Aims of this Book

This book describes the common features and differences in the fact-finding arrangements of different legal systems. The core of this book consists of a 'horizontal' comparison between the fact-finding arrangements of three different modern jurisdictions: Austria, the Netherlands and the United States.

A comparative approach may serve a number of purposes.[4] Some comparative literature provides an all encompassing overview of the black letter law of different procedural systems that may be of use to lawyers who handle transnational cases.[5]

3 Note that I will use the U.S. terminology in this respect. This may deviate from the terminology (presently) used in England; see the definitions used in CPR Part 31.

4 On the objectives of comparative law, see Zweigert & Kötz 1998, Chapter 2 and Merryman 1999b, p. 483.

5 There are encyclopedic works that provide a detailed description of the rules of evidence in different jurisdictions (e.g Lebre de Freitas 2004 and Nagel & Bajons 2003). There also have been a number of comparative books on discovery (e.g. Yoshida 2001 and Van den Reek →

A comparative approach is sometimes part of a greater effort towards the international unification and approximation of law.[6] This book serves a single purpose. It compares systems in order to enhance the understanding of procedural law in general. Procedural rules and practices that are self-evident to a Dutch or American lawyer become less evident once they are contrasted with regulations used abroad. By comparing the rules in one jurisdiction with those of another jurisdiction, one is able to identify the distinctive features of a legal system. Comparative law is thus much like learning classical languages. I was taught Latin and Greek in high school to enhance my understanding of modern languages, not for the purpose of being able to communicate with people that died approximately 2000 years ago. Although the primary aim of this book is to increase knowledge, it may also be used for a second purpose. Comparative law can serve as an heuristic instrument to generate a 'range of model solutions' to problems encountered within a particular jurisdiction.[7] It is generally prudent to consider the legal ideas that have been tried and tested with satisfaction elsewhere. If one would like to derive insights from the study of comparative law, one should however realize that a rule transplanted from one system into another, might function wholly differently in its new environment.[8]

In this book, a deliberate choice has been made to focus on the differences between legal systems. Thereto, special attention is devoted to jurisdictions that could be labeled as exceptional. In addition, I have chosen to focus in particular on those areas of procedural law where jurisdictions have opted for different solutions. This book is therefore lopsided and distinctions may have been overdrawn. I have probably not paid sufficient attention to areas where a broad international consensus exists. Likewise, I will not discuss the numerous jurisdictions that flocked to the middle ground.

This book primarily compares the Austrian, Dutch and the United States federal system. The federal American fact-finding arrangements are of particular interest as these contain a large number of highly exceptional features, including the use of the civil jury, party driven discovery and exclusionary rules of evidence. The Austrian procedural system is of interest as it has traditionally placed an extraordinary emphasis on the role of the court and the pursuit of truth. It is also highly relevant from an historical perspective. Austrian legislation of the late 19th century has been influential in many other jurisdictions. This book focuses primarily on the historical and theoretical aspects of Austrian law. As the author is most familiar with the Dutch fact-finding arrangements, these will be discussed in greater depth. The Dutch procedural system is particularly of interest as it has recently been reformed. In addition, there seems to be a growing body of empirical literature in the Netherlands that is of great help in assessing recent reforms and understanding how the law operates in legal practice.

1997). General works on comparative civil litigation include Carey-Miller & Beaumont 1993, Chase, Herschkoff, Silberman, Taniguchi & Varano 2007 and Snijders 1996.

6 See for instance Storme 1994; American Law Institute & UNIDROIT 2006 and Lang 1999.

7 Zweigert & Kötz 1998, p. 15.

8 Lowenfeld 1997 and Damaska 1997b.

It is common in comparative literature to make a distinction between common law and civil law systems of procedure. Such a taxonomy is useful as an intellectual aid. It is indeed often possible to extend the findings of this study to differences between continental and common law systems in general. References to other jurisdictions will often be made to illustrate this point. Nevertheless, there are restrictions on the external validity of the findings of this book. Categorization can induce one to make unjustified generalizations that oversimplify reality. Properly speaking, this book should hence be primarily understood as an inquiry into the rules and practices of three jurisdictions, not as an attempt to contrast all civil law systems with all common law jurisdictions.

2. Research Questions and General Overview

This book is not an encyclopedia. Many relevant aspects of the fact-finding process, such as the distinctive rules in family law procedures, special rules for taking evidence abroad, remedies, privileges to refuse to testify and rules on the burden of proof will not be discussed in great detail. After all, there are plenty of doctrinal works that provide an excellent description of the law in a particular jurisdiction.[9] This book gives an overview of the distinctive features of the jurisdictions discussed. The details of the rules are only discussed if relevant to understand differences between jurisdictions.

In order to understand statutes, codes or case law, knowledge of the bare text of a rule seldom suffices. Rules are not well understood in isolation, but should be regarded as components of an entire system.[10] Thus this book places fact-finding regulations in a broader context. First, legal history is useful to elucidate the legal tradition that has shaped the mindset of legal practitioners and legislators (See Chapters 2, 3 and 6). In addition, this book shows how specific rules on fact-finding constitute a (coherent) system (Chapters 7 and 8). Moreover, the political and constitutional setting is relevant to understand how the procedural rules operate (Chapter 9). Last, empirical research is useful to move beyond the black letter law and gain some understanding of how the rules on fact-finding operate in legal practice.

The Rules of Fact-finding: A concise History

The first chapters of this book provide an historic introduction to the different fact-finding arrangements in Austria, the Netherlands and the United States. A brief description of the historic development of procedural rules provides for a series of comparisons in time (vertical comparison). The vertical comparison helps to enhance our understanding of procedural law in at least three ways. First, a (vertical) comparison between contemporary legal systems and previously existing procedural regimes may help us to understand the legal tradition that has shaped

9 For Austria, see Rechberger & Simotta 2009. For the Netherlands see Snijders, Klaassens & Meijer 2007 and Van Hooijdonk & Eijsvoogel 2009. For the United States see Yeazell 2008.

10 Ewald 1994, p. 2106. Ewald refers to the 'context principle' in this respect.

the minds and habits of those that apply and design procedural legislation. Second, the history of procedural law helps to understand the nature of the development of the law.[11] Third, the history of procedural law reveals that procedural systems often are interrelated.[12]

In Chapter 2, the history of Austrian and Dutch fact-finding arrangements will be outlined. The starting point for the historical analysis is the medieval Romano-Canonical model of procedure. Both the Dutch and the Austrian system are historically rooted in the medieval learned procedure. Although vestiges of the old system have remained, a new fact-finding system is currently in place. In Austria, the 1895 Code of Civil Procedure departed from the main principles of the learned procedure. In the Netherlands, the system was reformed gradually. To a large extent, the gradual changes in the Netherlands were similar to those brought about by the 1895 Austrian Code.

In Chapter 3, the history of U.S. fact-finding arrangements will be discussed. The rules on fact-finding in most American jurisdictions are rooted in medieval English law. The English fact-finding rules were gradually replaced. In the 19th century, the first codifications of procedural law were enacted in the United States and new rules of evidence were developed. In the 20th century, the introduction of the Federal Rules of Civil Procedure radically altered the process of fact-gathering.

In Chapter 4, it will be argued that there have been many examples of cross influences between the Netherlands, Austria and the various U.S. jurisdictions. Mostly, these took the form of borrowing. Cross-influences between Continental and American jurisdictions have been rare since the 1930s. I will conclude that the legal systems of the Netherlands and Austria and those in the United States have grown further apart since the 1930s.

Summarizing the above, the following main research question is addressed in Chapters 2 and 3:

1. What is the historical background of the fact-finding rules that are currently in place in Austria, the Netherlands and the United States?

To answer this question, the following sub-questions will be addressed.

1.1 When were the current fact-finding rules in Austria, the Netherlands and the U.S. developed?
1.2 What have been the main reasons to implement specific rules on fact-finding?
1.3 Do the jurisdictions studied have common roots?
1.4 Have there been cross-influences between the procedural systems of Austria, the Netherlands and the U.S.?
1.5 Has there been a divergence or convergence of the procedural rules on fact-finding?

11 Ewald 1995 and Watson 1993, p. 7.

12 Watson 1978, p. 316: '[the] relationship between one legal system and another which is the result of borrowing is, I believe, the heart of comparative law'.

Fact-finding Rules and Practices: A Comparison
Chapters 2 and 3 conclude with a description of the main fact-finding arrangements presently in force in Austria, the Netherlands and the federal system of the United States. In Chapter 4, the main differences between these systems will be described briefly. The important stages in the process of fact-finding in each of the jurisdictions studied will be identified. In addition, the different roles of parties, lawyers and judges in the process of fact-finding will be discussed.

Chapters 5 and 6 explore two specific topics in greater detail. They serve as examples that illustrate the more general patterns set out in Chapters 2, 3 and 4. These chapters highlight some of the clearest differences between the Austrian, Dutch and American jurisdictions. Chapter 5 describes the different ways in which expert evidence is utilized. This chapter illustrates the great differences that exist across jurisdictions in the evidence stage. Subsequently, in Chapter 6, the different procedural mechanisms to put questions to the litigants are discussed. It reveals that there are large differences between Continental and American jurisdictions in the process of fact-gathering.

Together, Chapter 4, 5 and 6 serve to identify the distinctive features of the three jurisdictions studied. Sometimes black letter laws differ greatly. At other times, the laws are similar across jurisdictions but operate differently in practice. Two main questions will be addressed:

2a What are the main differences between the black letter fact-finding rules in Austria, the Netherlands and the U.S. federal system?
2b What are the main differences in the ordinary modes of fact-finding in legal practice in Austria, the Netherlands and the United States?

To address these questions adequately, I will answer the following sub-questions:

2.1 What are the important stages in the process of fact-finding in Austria, the Netherlands and the United States?
2.2 Who is primarily responsible for the process of fact-gathering, the presentation of evidence and decision making?
2.3 What are the rules that regulate the involvement of experts in the litigation process in Austria, the Netherlands and the U.S.? How do these rules operate in legal practice?
2.4 What are the rules that regulate the interrogation of the parties? How do these rules operate in legal practice?

Understanding Different Fact-finding Rules and Practices
In Chapters 7, 8 and 9, I aim to provide a partial explanation for the different fact-finding arrangements that apply across jurisdictions. Therefore, I will identify the underlying objectives, principles and ideas that explain and justify seemingly unrelated rules of civil procedure. It will be argued that rules constitute a system and should not be considered in isolation.

Chapter 7 deals with the objectives and leading principles of the Austrian Code of Civil Procedure. The views of Franz Klein, who drafted the Austrian Code, are discussed in greater depth. Klein argued that fact-finding rules primarily serve the efficient enforcement of substantive law. In Chapter 8, I shall identify two fundamental features of the U.S. procedural model: the adversarial system and the civil jury. It will be shown that specific fact-finding rules that are typically American serve either the civil jury or the implementation of the adversarial principle.

In Chapter 9, it will be argued that political theory provides an adequate framework to understand the objectives and fundamentals of procedural law and the differences between procedural systems. I will conclude that the prevailing views on democracy and the role of the state in society impact the design of procedural rules on fact-finding.

Summarizing the above, the following two main questions will be addressed in Chapters 7, 8 and 9.

3a What are the main objectives and principles of the fact-finding process in both Austria and the United States?
3b What is the rationale behind the objectives and principles of the process of fact-finding in Austria and the United States?

Good Fact-finding Processes: On the Effectiveness of Legal Rules
Legislators commonly design a system of rules that aims to provide for an accurate, fair, legitimate and efficient process of fact-finding. Whether the desired results are attained depends on a multitude of factors. Although it is difficult to make conclusive comparative judgments on the success of procedural rules, an attempt will be made to discuss the most significant arguments as well as the available empirical data. On the basis of these, it is possible to draw some careful conclusions on the legitimacy, fairness, efficiency and accuracy of fact-finding rules.

Throughout this book, several attempts will be made to assess the fairness of specific fact-finding arrangements. In particular, studies will be discussed that have measured the litigant's perception of fairness. It will be shown that procedural arrangements influence the perceived fairness of the litigation process.

Furthermore, the degree in which rules and practices are an effective means to foster the accuracy of the process of fact-finding will be discussed. Some empirical data are available on the degree to which all relevant information is identified (see for instance (Section 6.2.1.2). In addition, theoretical models that predict whether specific fact-finding arrangements are likely to generate correct outcomes are addressed (Chapter 10).

In Chapter 4, comparative statistics on the duration of litigation are briefly discussed. These data illustrate that it is difficult to make conclusive comparative judgments on the efficiency of fact-finding processes. Nevertheless, largely on the basis of economic theory (Chapter 10), I will draw some general conclusions on the efficiency of the fact-finding rules in Austria, the Netherlands and the U.S.

The last main question that will be touched upon is:

4 To what extent are the Austrian, Dutch and U.S. rules successful in ensuring a fair, accurate, legitimate and efficient process of fact-finding?

PART I

GENERAL HISTORIC AND COMPARATIVE INTRODUCTION

INTRODUCTION

The following chapters describe the historical background of the fact-finding rules that are currently in place in Austria, the Netherlands and the United States. Chapters 2 and 3 respectively describe the history of Continental and Angelo-American fact-finding arrangements. The historical inquiry in these chapters gradually evolves into a comparative analysis. A discussion of recent historical developments provides the starting point for a discussion of the main differences between systems in Chapter 4.

Chapter 2

A CONCISE HISTORY OF FACT-FINDING ON THE EUROPEAN CONTINENT

1. Procedure in Medieval and Early Modern Times

1.1. *The Romano-Canonical Model*

Introduction

Beginning at the 11th century, the renewed interest in Roman law led to a revolution in the medieval study and practice of law. A learned system of law emerged based on a large collection of legal texts from Antiquity: the *Corpus Iuris Civilis* of the Roman emperor Justinian. Partly under influence of the Church, the systematic and scholastic study of Roman law became a European enterprise.[1] Roman law itself had never regarded civil procedure as a separate discipline. A systematic approach to procedural law was absent and procedural texts and rules were scattered throughout the *Corpus Iuris Civilis*. From the 12th century onwards, the Ecclesiastical Courts increasingly turned to the Roman legal texts in their need for more professional procedural regulations. Procedural law was first studied systematically as an independent branch of law. Roman law and Canon law provided the building blocks for the new Romano-Canonical procedural model. A variety of learned treatises were devoted to the subject of civil procedure, of which the encyclopedic *Speculum Judiciale* (1271-1276) of Durantis was the culmination.[2] These treatises outlined the structure of the court procedure (*ordines judiciarii*).[3]

The procedural regime of the *ius commune* left room for some degree of variation between the courts. Each court developed its own practice based on the learned procedural model (*stylus curiae*). Nevertheless, the main features of the Romano-Canonical model were widely used throughout large parts of Europe. In the *ius commune* courts, the number of available actions was never limited. A number of claims could be handled in a single law suit.[4] Once a case was filed, there

1 A concise overview of the most relevant medieval sources is provided by Nörr 1973.

2 On the influence of the work of Durantis see Van Rhee 2000a, p. 596.

3 See in general Van Caenegem 1971, No. 10; Cappelletti 1970; Helmholz 2004, Chapter 5 and Von Bethmann-Hollweg 1874.

4 Endemann 1891, p. 227.

was not much flexibility in the procedural steps to be followed. Most of the stages were necessarily handled in a fixed order.[5] The procedure was mainly a written procedure. Each stage in the procedure was well documented. The Romano-Canonical procedure did not adhere to the principle that all evidence had to be presented as directly as possible to the decision-maker (principle of immediacy).[6] Often, a final decision was primarily based on the written case file. The final decision on both factual and legal matters was always made by one or more professional judges. Juries or lay judges were not used. The phases of the Romano-Canonical procedure relevant to the process of fact-finding are described below.

Identifying the Issues

The written statement whereby the plaintiff first presented his case was referred to as the *libellus* (libel).[7] The libel contained a brief statement of the plaintiff's claim and the main grounds on which the claim was based. A detailed account of the underlying facts was often not required.[8] The Romano-Canonical model usually required the defendant to raise possible defenses in a fixed order. It was a general rule that the defendant first had to introduce preliminary defenses which did not go to the merits of the case (*exceptiones*). There were many possible *exceptiones* that were often subdivided into different categories.[9] These included objections against the jurisdiction of the court or the legal capacity of a party as well as the exception that another court had already ruled on the issue. If these preliminary defenses failed, the defendant could subsequently defend his case on the merits. The moment that the defendant had contested the case on the merits was referred to as the *litis contestatio*.[10] The defendant could in his pleading allege new legal grounds that could 'defeat' the libel. The parties could continue to raise new grounds in successive pleadings. If a preliminary defense was raised, but the defendant did not discuss the case on the merits, this did not imply that the facts related to the merits were acknowledged.[11]

This system, whereby (preliminary) defenses could be raised one by one, provided the defendant with many possibilities to delay the proceedings. To avoid delay, there have been deviations from the general model in which defenses were raised one by one. Many courts required the defendant to raise all his defenses at once. If a defendant failed to introduce defenses or matters of fact before the procedure advanced to the next stage, the defendant lost the right to raise this

5 In modern German terminology: *Prinzip der Gesetzlichen Reihenfolge,* see Millar 1923, §5.

6 Millar 1923, §6.

7 Other terms, e.g. *'petitio'*, were also used. See Litewsky 1999, p. 229 and Endemann 1891, p. 193.

8 Litewsky 1999, p. 230 *et seq.*; Helmholz 2004, p. 321 and Langdell 1907, Sections 5-24.

9 Defenses were commonly subdivided in two larger categories: *exceptiones dilatoriae* and *exceptiones peremptoiriae*. Often a separate category of *exceptiones declinatoria* was distinguished. See Litewsky 1999, p. 299, 304-309 and Endemann 1891, p. 214-222. As a general rule these *exceptiones* had to be raised in a fixed order and before the *litis contestatio*, see Litewsky 1999, p. 304, p. 309-310 and Helmholz 2004, p. 323.

10 Endemann 1891, p. 228-229 and Litewsky 1999, p. 335.

11 D. 44.1.9.

defense or plead these facts. In later procedural doctrine, this was referred to as the principle of contingent cumulation (*Eventualmaxime*).[12] Throughout the 16th and the 17th centuries, some courts in the Low Countries adhered to the *Eventualmaxime*.[13] Similarly, the Austrian General Judicial Ordinance (1781) required the parties to raise all their defenses at once.[14]

Contrary to the procedure before the English common law courts, the pleading stage of the Romano-Canonical procedure did not reduce the dispute to a single issue. After the exchange of pleadings a number of factual issues could remain disputed. These facts required further evidence. An example may clarify the system of pleading. The plaintiff John, in his libel, could claim the payment of 100 florins based on the fact that John had lent 100 florins to Susan and she had failed to repay the money. Susan could make three challenges: she could deny the existence of the original agreement. She could also argue that the loan had been agreed upon years ago and plead the statute of limitations in her answer. At the same time, Susan could argue that she had repaid the money at an earlier point in time. Though the arguments are mutually inconsistent, Susan could raise all three of them. Unlike the traditional common law system, Susan is not forced to choose between either one of the three arguments. If Susan succeeds in proving either one and John does not come up with a new legal argument, she will win her case.

At some point after the '*litis contestatio*', the parties and the lawyers were required to take 'the Calumnia oath' in which they swore to be truthful and to refrain from any form of vexatious litigation.[15] The wording of the Calumnia oath was: 'I swear that the claim and defenses are just; I shall assure that the truth will not be distorted; I shall not present false testimony or forge evidence; and I will not cause undue delay'.[16] The oath was used in Austria in medieval times without any modifications.[17] Equally, an almost literal translation of the Latin phrases was used in courts in the Low Countries.[18]

12 Millar 1923, p. 25: 'the so-called "*Eventualmaxime*" or principle of "eventuality", which may be more conveniently designated in English as the *principle of contingent cumulation*. This might also be termed the principle of mass attack or mass defense, since what it insists upon is that the party at a given stage bring[s] forwards simultaneously, and not consecutively, all items of allegation or proof pertaining to that stage, whether consistent or inconsistent with each other, even though the disposition of one of these items would render unnecessary consideration of the others'.

13 Van Rhee 1997, p. 111 and De Damhouder 1626, p. 357. However, some preliminary defenses had to be raised before the *litis contestatio*.

14 Sections 7, 40-42 General Judicial Ordinance.

15 Litewsky 1999, p. 335-344.

16 Litewsky 1999, p. 342: 'Illud iuretur, quod lis sibi iusta videtur, Et si quaeretur, verum non inficietur, Nil promittetur, nec falsa probation detur, Ut lis tardetur dilatio nulla petetur'. Also see Endemann 1891, p. 236, who quotes Durantis, l.c. §4.

17 See Rosbach (Prax. Civ., tit L n. 11) as quoted by Klein 1885, p. 111.

18 E.g. De Damhouder 1626, p. 383-385, CAP. CLIX: 'Die van calumnie sweert moet vijf dingen hebben 1) Dat hy gelooft dat hy, so int eysschen als verweeren, een goede sake heeft. 2) Dat hy warachtige vrage niet ontkennen en sal. 3) Dat hij geen valsche preuven gebruyken en sal. 4) Dat hy geen dilayen calunieuselijk eysche sal. 5) Dat hy den Rechter met gene giften gecorrumpeert heeft, noch corrumperen sal'.

After the exchange of pleadings the parties were required to indicate under oath which facts they acknowledged and which facts they denied (see Section 6.1).[19] The aim of these party statements was to avoid the taking of unnecessary evidence. Roman law and the Romano-Canonical model both required an express admission. The system, unlike the common law and Germanic procedure, did not accept the rule that facts that were not admitted were considered to be denied.[20] An express admission of facts provided evidence against a party.[21] Remainders of the idea that an admission of a party provides 'full evidence' against him have continued to exist for a long time. The 1781 Austrian General Judicial Ordinance contained four provisions on 'proof by admission' (*Beweise durch Eingeständniss*). In the Netherlands, an admission was considered to provide full evidence until 1988.[22] In France, it is still considered to be the case that an admission provides full evidence against a party.[23]

Limited Means of Discovery

Discovery is a modern Angelo-American term that refers to a set of procedural instruments available to litigants to obtain and preserve information in the early stages of litigation (see Section 6.1.1.2). Such instruments were scarcely available in the learned procedure. Although the Calumnia oath required the litigants to refrain from behavior that would distort the truth and the litigants were required to affirm or deny facts under oath (*interrogationes/positiones*), the Romano-Canonical procedure provided hardly any means to compel an opponent to produce adverse evidence. The so-called *nemo tenetur edere contra se* principle, sometimes also referred to as the *nemo contra se edere cogitur* principle, was sometimes applied in the Romano-Canonical model.[24] This principle holds that a party is not obliged to provide an opponent with the means to win his case. Certain passages of Roman law have been quoted in support of this principle. Codex 4.20.7 for instance states:

> 'The demand which you make, namely, that the adverse party shall be compelled to produce the persons by whom the business was transacted, is entirely too strong. Therefore, understand that you yourself should introduce your own evidence in the case, and that your adversaries cannot be obliged to furnish testimony against themselves'.[25]

19 This could also happen before the *litis contestatio,* Endemann 1891, p. 224, p. 238.

20 Millar 1926, §5.

21 Endemann 1891, p. 247-252 and Litewsky 1999, p. 376-377.

22 Under the present rules in the Netherlands and some other Continental jurisdictions, an admission on fact is not evidence itself, but has as a result that there is no need to examine evidence.

23 Former Articles 1960-1965 Dutch Civil Code, Sections 107-110 Austrian General Judicial Ordinance and Articles 1354-1356 French Civil Code.

24 Kohl 1971, Chapter 1.

25 Translation: S.P. Scott, 1932, Cincinatti, the Central Trust Company: 'Nimis grave est quod petitis, urgueri ad exhibitionem partem diversam eorum, per quos sibi negotium fiat. Unde intellegitis, quod intentioni vestrae proprias adferre debeatis probationes, non adversum se ab adversariis adduci'.

Especially with regard to the discovery of documents, the learned procedure contained very limited possibilities to compel the parties to produce documents.[26] Discovery of documents in the learned procedure was possible if based on a reinterpreted version of the *actio ad exhibendum*. This allowed the discovery of documents if a document was 'common' to both parties.[27] Apart from this rule, it was held that parties were always obliged to produce the documents they wished to rely on for their own claim or defense.[28] Conversely, the parties had no duty to provide their opponent with documents that would support their opponent's claim or defense.[29] This implied that parties could generally not be compelled to produce adverse documents.[30]

Evidence

Only disputed facts required evidence.[31] The presentation of evidence would take place in the order of the taking of the pleadings.[32] First, the plaintiff would be given the opportunity to provide evidence for the facts alleged in the libel. If the defendant had rebuttal, he could adduce it subsequently.[33] The judge would then render a decision on the libel upon the evidence presented. If the libel was not proven, the plaintiff lost his action. If the facts in the libel were proven, the case would proceed to the next stage: the defendant's answer. This time the defendant would be the first to present evidence, after which the plaintiff could present rebuttal. If there was not enough proof for the defendant's answer, he or she lost the case. If the defendant managed to prove the facts in his answer, the plaintiff would be required to present new evidence for the plaintiff's next pleading. This process would continue until a pleading in the series was found not proven or the last pleading was proven.

The Romano-Canonical model had modernized the previously employed methods of evidentiary proof. The means of proof that were used in the early Middle Ages, such as the 'proof by fire and water', the 'duel', the use of 'oath helpers' and the 'ordeal' were abolished.[34] The 'rationalization' of evidence had started under influence of the Church long before the 11th century but culminated in the 12th and 13th centuries.[35] The new rules largely were the product of scholastic

26 Litewsky 1999, p. 426.

27 C. 2.1.7 and D. 10.4.3.9.

28 D. 2.13.1.3.

29 Durantis l.c. §6, Nos. 16, 22: '1. ut actor fundet intentionem vel reus exceptionem et tunc non cogitur quid edere, si ipse non utator; 2. si ipse utator, tunc editor adversario sine die et consule; 3. ut de falso arguetur, et tunc editor cum die et consule'. As quoted by Endemann 1891, p. 279.

30 Endemann 1891, p. 280: 'Im Ganzen wird der Richter eher einen Dritten, als die Gegenpartei zur Herausgabe zwingen'.

31 Litewsky 1999, p. 356.

32 Langdell 1907, Section 8 and Litewsky 1999, p. 325.

33 The court exceptionally *ex officio* ordered the presentation of evidence, such as the taking of the supplementary oath. See Litewsky 1999, p. 361.

34 See in general Levy 1965.

35 Schmoekel 2000 and Von Bethmann-Hollweg 1874, §130.

precision and the mistrust of both judges and parties. A detailed system of rules regulated the presentation and weighing of evidence (i.e., the principle of 'formal or legal proof').[36] These rules mostly shifted the burden of proof to the plaintiff.[37] The Romano-Canonical procedure recognized a long list of means of proof (*argumenta*), the most significant were: witnesses, documents, presumptions, *notoria* (self-proving issues), and the formal party oaths.[38]

There were restrictions on the admissibility of evidence. Hearsay was not admissible in the learned procedure.[39] Various individuals were not able to testify, such as non-Christians and the close relatives of the parties.[40] Many of these restrictions continued to exist on the European Continent throughout much of the 19th and 20th centuries.

The presentation of evidence, such as the hearing of witnesses or the production of documents, was subject to detailed rules. The parties would suggest suitable witnesses and formulated the questions - often referred to as *articuli* or *capitula* - that were to be put to the witnesses.[41] The witnesses were generally not heard in open court and the parties were mostly not allowed to be present during the examination of witnesses.[42] The secrecy of the procedure aimed at reducing the odds that the testimony would be biased or partial. It was possibly also the result of a misinterpretation of Roman sources.[43] The examination of the witness was originally done by a judge, often not the judge who would ultimately decide the case.[44] Sometimes, the examination of witnesses was delegated to other court officials.[45] The examination was thus frequently not in the presence of the judge who decided the case, in violation of the English common law 'principle of immediacy'. Judges based their decision on a written summary that listed the most significant findings of the witness examination.[46] The written account of the testimony would generally only be made known to the parties after all evidence had been presented. After the taking of evidence was completed and the parties had been provided with the written summaries of the testimonies of witnesses, the cause was ready for an oral hearing. The attorneys of both parties could then orally argue their case before the court.[47]

A complex system of rules determined the hierarchical order of the different means of proof. The probative value of each of the different means of proof was

36 Millar 1923, p. 94.

37 The basic rule was: 'Actore non probante absolvitur reus'. See Endemann 1891, p. 253 *et seq.* and Litewsky 1999, p. 362.

38 Durantis for example listed no less than 13 means of proof. See Endemann 1891, p. 255; Engelmann 1927, p. 479 and Litewsky 1999, p. 371.

39 Herrmann 1995, p. 36.

40 Litewsky 1999, p. 390-392.

41 Litewsky 1999, p. 402-403 and Van Rhee 1997, p. 171-172.

42 Litewsky 1999, p. 366, p. 401.

43 See in particular C. 4.20.14.

44 I.e. the judge at the place of the witness' residence. Litewsky 1999, p. 406.

45 Langdell 1907, p. 763 and Millar 1923, p. 152.

46 Cappelletti 1970, p. 850 and Millar 1923, §8.

47 Litewsky 1999, p. 446 *et seq.*

partly determined by law. There were different categories of documents, which had a different evidential value.[48] There were detailed rules with respect to witnesses. Normally witness statements would provide 'half' proof, which implied that the declarations of a single witness could never suffice to prove a matter of fact. A witness statement would have to be backed by another witness statement, a supplementary oath, or some other means of proof, such that the total amount of evidence would amount to full proof. Many authors proposed more detailed rules to classify the credibility of witnesses according to age, social ranking or sex. The evidential value of proof was hence sometimes even subdivided into a quarter or an eighth of full proof.[49] In the end, this system required the judge to make a calculation; only if full proof had been presented, the court could establish the facts accordingly. The learned procedure also had rules to determine what would happen if both parties had adduced equal and contradictory means of proof. In such cases, the judge could ask one of the parties to take a supplementary oath (see Section 6.1.3).[50] These rules differed strongly from those in the English common law courts (Section 3.1).

It can be concluded that a complex set of rules reduced the role of the judge in the Romano-Canonical procedure to a minimum.[51] To the extent that the procedural rules provided some leeway, the parties, rather than the court, determined the course of the proceedings. Using modern terminology, one may conclude that the principles of party-disposition and party-presentation were leading principles of the Romano-Canonical procedure (see Section 7.2).

1.2. *The Influence of the Romano-Canonical Model*

The Roman-Canonical model was influential in large parts of Europe, partly because of its widespread use in Church Courts.[52] In those parts of southern Europe where traces of 'vulgar' Roman law had survived, the Roman-Canonical procedure was generally smoothly adopted. Political authorities like the kings in Castile, Hungary, Portugal and Bohemia implemented elements of the Romano-Canonical model in their own courts and territories. In England, the influence of the learned procedure was rather small as the creation of a centralized and professional procedure had preceded the reception of Roman law on the Continent. As set out in Section 3.1, elements of the Romano-Canonical model did have some influence on

48 Litewsky 1999, p. 369-370, p. 420.
49 Litewsky 1999, p. 410-413; Van Caenegem 1971, p. 17 and Cappelletti 1970, p. 849.
50 See e.g. De Damhouder 1626, p. 478-480.
51 Endemann 1891, p. 272: 'Der Richter, weit entfernt von freier Erforschung der Wahrheit, war für das Verfahren in äusserster Anspannung der Verhandlungsmaxime gebunden durch das Thun und Lassen der Parteien, für die Beurtheilung bis zu einem fast arithmetischen Herausrechnen der Ergebnisse; durch die Sätze der juridischen Beweislehre die Parteien bei ihrem Verhalten, Schritt für Schritt gebunden durch Vorschriften, die mit ihrem Formalismus jede freiere Bewegung erdrücken und damit das Augenmerk von der Herstellung materieller Wahrheit vollständig ablenken mussten'.
52 Van Caenegem 1971, Nos. 12, 27.

the English equity procedure.[53] The learned procedure was also influential in Scotland.[54] A brief description of the influence of the Romano-Canonical procedure on French, Dutch and Austrian civil procedural practices will be presented below.

In the United Provinces, the Romano-Canonical model influenced the 'style' of most superior courts.[55] As the United Provinces remained politically divided, considerable differences between regions continued to exist until the late 18th century. Earlier attempts to unify the procedural legislation and practices had failed.[56] A single set of procedural legislation never applied throughout the area. There was no unified court structure. In Holland, Zeeland and West-Friesland, the High Council of Holland Zeeland and West-Friesland served as the court of last instance.[57] The Council of Brabant was the court of last resort in much of Brabant until 1795.[58] In Drenthe, the *Etstoel* was the court of first and last resort until the 1790s.[59] In other territories, court structures were even more dispersed.[60] In some courts, the influence of the Romano-Canonical procedure was more thorough than in others.[61] The Dutch procedural traditions came to an end with the introduction of French legislation in the early 19th century. The French influence would be lasting; a study of the roots of the Dutch procedure is hence impossible without a basic understanding of the French developments.

Under King Louis IX (1214-1270), elements of the Romano-Canonical model had already found their way into the French courts.[62] Initially, courts implemented local variations of the Romano-Canonical procedure. A Royal Ordinance of 1667, also known as the *Code Louis*, was an early attempt to unify procedural law throughout France.[63] Though the Ordinance of 1667 was not an innovative Code, the merit of the Ordinance was that it created a systematic compilation of the existing rules. The Ordinance retained many elements of the Romano-Canonical model, such as the use of 'half-proof' (*semi-pleine preuve*), the examination of witnesses in secrecy and the decisory oath.[64]

53 See Helmholz 2004, Chapter 5, on the influence of the learned procedure in the ecclesiastical courts.

54 Mark characterised the 16th century Scottish Court of Session as 'Romano-Canonical' and 'a typical European *ius commune* court'. See Mark 2004.

55 See Wedekind 1971, §2, 3 and Van Caenegem 1971, No. 51. For a description of the 'style' of the Great Council of Malines, see Van Rhee 1997.

56 Van Caenegem 1971, p. 66-68.

57 Le Bailly & Verhas 2005, Chapter 1.

58 Broers 2000, p. 11.

59 Becker 2005.

60 One could for instance travel 50 miles in what is presently the (Dutch) province of Limburg and pass through many jurisdictions. See Berkvens 2010a; Berkvens 2010b and Berkvens 2006.

61 In Drenthe for example, the influence of the Romano-Canonical procedure was much less pronounced than in other localities. See Becker 2005, Chapters 5 and 6.

62 Millar 1937, p. 276.

63 Van Caenegem 1971, Nos. 47-48.

64 See for example Article 15, Title 22, 'Des enquêtes' for the provisions on the secrecy of the examination of witnesses. On the decisiory oath see Section 6.1.3.

Until the 15th century, the Romano-Canonical procedure did not get a foothold in the German lands.[65] Ordeals and judicial combat had been used to resolve civil disputes until the 13th century and oath helpers had remained important until the 15th century.[66] Roman-Canonical Law was, however, almost entirely adopted in the *gemeine Recht* of the German lands from the 15th century onwards and would remain very influential during the era of codification.[67] The process of fact-finding in the German lands was also constructed along Romano-Canonical lines. To some extent, the procedure became even more formalistic than the Romano-Canonical procedure as it strongly adhered to the segmentation of the procedure in stages. A particular step had to be taken at a particular point in time.[68] This implied that facts had to be alleged by the parties before the judge would give an interim judgment (*Beweisurteil/Beweisinterlokut*) that ordered the taking of evidence. This further implied that new factual allegations and newly suggested means of proof were only admissible after the interlocutory judgment in exceptional cases. The main modes of proof were by witnesses, documents, formal oaths (Section 6.1.3), experts and inspections of real property.[69] The detailed rules of formal proof of the Romano-Canonical procedure regulated whether or not evidence was admissible and sufficient. The *gemeine Recht* would deeply influence the developments in Austria. The Habsburg Empire contributed to the increased influence of the learned procedure throughout many countries like Hungary, Poland, Northern Italy and Croatia.[70]

The influence of the Romano-Canonical procedure on the different procedural systems of Continental Europe explains the similarities between the national codifications enacted in the era of codification. Even now, many provisions in the procedural codifications are rooted in the learned procedure. Often, these rules fulfill a different function than they did in the past. Rules on the interrogation of parties provide one example of how the learned procedure affected procedural rules throughout the Continent (Chapter 6). Traces of Romano-Canonical model law can also be found when we look at the rules on the discovery of documents in modern codifications. Different modern Continental systems still use a translation of the word *communia* in Codex 2.1.7.[71] Despite the fact that the meaning of the word is unclear and ill-defined, many codifications have continued to hold that documents are discoverable if these are 'common to both parties'. Section 810 of the German Civil Code uses the word '*gemeinschaftlichen*'. Section 304(1)(3) Austrian Code of Civil Procedure and Section XLIII of the Law Enacting the Austrian Code of Civil

65 Van Caenegem 1971, No. 12.

66 Also see the short introduction in Fasching 1990, Chapters 2.3-2.4.

67 Van Caenegem 1971, No. 32.

68 Millar 1923, §5.

69 Van Caenegem 1971, No. 44.

70 Van Caenegem 1971, No. 47.

71 The word 'communia' can be translated as 'common'. C. 2.1.7: 'Procurator privatae rationis instrumentorum, quae communia tibi esse dicis cum fisco, describendorum facultatem secundum morem fieri iubebit: et si quando res exegerit ad fidem petitionis tuae apud alium iudicem praebendam aliquid eorum proferri, desiderante eo qui convenitur, ut id fiat, praecipiet'.

Procedure (*EGZPO*) also allow for the discovery of a document that is '*gemeinschaftlich*'. The Dutch Code of Civil Procedure, until the 1988 Civil Evidence Act, also specified that documents that were '*gemeen*' to both parties were discoverable.[72]

The use of similar wording is no coincidence, as all provisions mentioned can be traced back to the Roman *actio ad exhibendum*. De Damhouder, describing practices in the Low Countries in the 16th century, argues that parties could not be compelled to produce adverse documents that could help the opposing party. One exception to the latter rule existed: a party could be compelled to produce a document if the document was 'common' to both parties.[73] Roman-Dutch Law continued to hold that only 'common' documents were discoverable.[74]

The Romano-Canonical rules on document discovery also influenced the *gemeine Recht* and early German codifications. Parties were, in general, not obliged to produce adverse documents. Only those documents that were identified as '*gemeinschaftlichen Urkunden*' were held to be discoverable.[75]

Although no direct influence could be traced, the similarities with the English common law in the 18th century are striking.[76] At common law, the parties in a lawsuit had no general duty to produce documents in their possession.[77] Nevertheless, partly under the influence of Lord Mansfield, the regime was somewhat more liberal with regard to 'common documents'. In *Ward v. Apprice* (1705), the lack of rules on discovery was held to be 'mischievous' if parties had one common book for their transactions and one initiated an action against the other.[78]

2. The Early Codification of Procedural Law

During the era of codification, a general tendency on the European Continent could be perceived in which the European Romano-Canonical Procedure made place for national procedures with nationally codified laws. The French royal Ordinance of 1667 provides an early example of 'nationalized law'. Many legislative texts mainly codified existing practices, thereby demonstrating a strong influence from the learned Romano-Canonical procedure. Exceptions did exist: the 1781 Prussian Code generally referred to as the *Corpus Juris Fridericianum*, was designed to reform and

72 Articles 1922-1923 of the 1838 Civil Code.

73 De Damhouder 1626, p. 257, CAP. CXIII: 'Van brieven van titel over te leggen, naer dat den eysch geexhibeert is'. *(...)* 'beyde de parthijen ghemeen'.

74 See Anema 1940, p. 244 for a concise history of the provisions of the 1838 Dutch Civil Code.

75 Dilcher 1959, p. 476-477.

76 I could find no direct references to Roman law. It is generally known that Lord Mansfield was Scottish and familiar with Roman law. See Plucknett 1956, p. 299-300.

77 Wigmore 1940, §1858.

78 *Ward v. Apprice*, 6 Mod 264, 87 Eng. Rep. 1011. In *Ward v. Apprice* the court did not order the production of documents but allowed the defendant seeking discovery to give notice to the plaintiffs to produce the books 'and thereby raise a presumption against them if they refuse'. See Millar 1952, p. 219.

improve upon the existing justice system.[79] Influential codifications in Austria and the Netherlands are discussed below.

2.1. *Early Austrian Codifications*[80]

In 1753, Maria Theresia appointed a commission to draft uniform civil procedural legislation that would apply throughout her empire. The Austrian General Judicial Ordinance (*Allgemeine Gerichtsordnung*) was not enacted until 1781. The new Code was Austria's first codification in the field of civil procedure. It was conservative insofar as it did not aim to create new or better law. It merely codified the existing *gemeine Recht*. The 1781 Ordinance would be one of the influential early codifications in Europe. The Ordinance would eventually enter into in Lombardy, Hungary, Slovenia and Croatia, but failed to be successful in other parts of the Empire such as the Habsburg Low Countries.[81] Some other jurisdictions enacted legislation based on the Ordinance and newer versions of the Ordinance were later enacted in Venice and Tirol.[82]

The General Judicial Ordinance adhered to a number of central principles that were clearly inspired by the Romano-Canonical procedure. First, the Ordinance embraced the principle of party-presentation (*Verhandlungsmaxime*, see Section 7.2). The court was passive; both with regard to the gathering of facts and the presentation of evidence.[83] Judges were not competent to decide on procedural questions and had to refer questions to the Courts of Appeal if they doubted the rationale of the Ordinance.[84] Second, the Ordinance favored a written over an oral procedure.[85] As the procedure was well documented, the judge who was involved in the process of fact-finding could very well be a different judge than the one that would draft the final decision.[86] The Ordinance accordingly did not embrace the principle of immediacy. A third feature of the Ordinance was that the proceedings were not public *(Nichtöffentlichkeit)*.

The structure of the proceedings, and thereby the process of identifying the factual issues that divided the parties, differed from the Romano-Canonical model.[87] Normally, parties would exchange two pleadings. Subsequently, the court would

79 See in general, Engelmann 1927, p. 591.

80 General works on Austrian procedural history include Schoibl 1987 and Schwartz 1898. Works in English include Engelmann 1927 and Van Caenegem 1971.

81 Van Caenegem 1971, Nos. 51, 64, 69.

82 Jelinek 1991, p. 50.

83 Oberhammer 1993, p. 36. 'Die totale Vernachlässigung der diskretionären Gewalt des Richters, desses ausgeprägt passive Stellung im Hinblick auf die Stoffsammlung im Verfahren zieht sich wie ein roter Faden durch das ganze Gesetz'.

84 Section 437 General Judicial Ordinance.

85 There were special and exceptional proceedings which incorporated more oral elements, see Sections 15-33 General Judicial Ordinance. These exceptional proceedings were used frequently: see Schwartz 1898, p. 674.

86 See for instance Sections 155-158 General Judicial Ordinance.

87 Schwartz 1898, p. 676.

give an interlocutory proof judgment after which evidence could be taken.[88] The General Judicial Ordinance implemented the principle of contingent cumulation (*Eventualmaxime*). This implied that the defendant had to allege all his defenses in his first pleading. Any defenses not raised in the first pleading would not be considered afterwards.[89] The principle also implied that new facts alleged by either party after the first pleading would in principle be disregarded by the judge.[90] If one did not immediately and explicitly deny a fact raised by the opposing party, the judge had to consider that fact to be true.[91] Parties were also bound to indicate the means of proof they had available to prove their contentions of fact in their pleadings.[92]

The 1781 Ordinance did not recognize a general duty for the parties to exchange relevant information and case related means of proof. There was no duty for a party to aid his opponent by providing him with the adverse evidence he had at hand. If one party had the burden of proof, the other was free to withhold documents or remain silent with respect to the names of potential adverse witnesses.[93]

The evidentiary rules of the Ordinance were those of the *gemeines Recht* and were clearly inspired by the Romano-Canonical procedure.[94] As in the Romano-Canonical procedure, the hearing of witnesses was done on the basis of *written* questions formulated by the parties (*Weisartikel, articuli*). The parties were generally not present when the witness had to respond to these written questions.[95] After the examination of all witnesses, the parties would receive *written* summaries of the witness examination. They were entitled to adduce a *written* opinion on the implications of the witnesses' answers.[96]

The General Judicial Ordinance made use of the medieval theory of formal proof. Accordingly, different means of proof had a different evidential value and one often needed several means of proof to provide 'full proof'. For example: the Ordinance made distinction between reliable, unreliable and contested witnesses (*unbedenkliche, bedenkliche und verwerfliche Zeugen*). The testimony of witnesses belonging to either of these categories would respectively provide half proof, less

88 Sections 2 and 136 General Judicial Ordinance.

89 Section 42 General Judicial Ordinance; Van Caenegem 1971, No. 69 and Millar 1923, §5.

90 Sections 47, 48, 53, 54 and 174 General Judicial Ordinance. An exception was made if a party, under oath, would testify that the newly alleged fact was not known to him when the pleading was made or if a party had to allege new facts in reaction to the pleading of the other party.

91 Section 11 General Judicial Ordinance.

92 Section 12 General Judicial Ordinance.

93 Klein 1891, p. 44: 'Dass man heute noch von einer allgemeine Ueberzeugung reden kann, welche die wechselweise Unterstützungspflicht leugnet (...)'. Also see Heimerl 1857, p. 44-45: 'Bei der Verfolgung ihres Zweckes sind sie zwar nicht verpflichtet, sich wechselweise in der Erreichung ihres regelmäßig collidirenden Zieles zu unterstützen und sich im Prozesse die Beweisführung zu erleichtern; (...)'.

94 Schwartz 1898, p. 673.

95 Sections 146-148, 165 General Judicial Ordinance. Also see Oberhammer 1993, p. 37.

96 Section 173 General Judicial Ordinance.

than 'half proof' or would not be admissible at all.[97] One discriminatory rule held that two Jewish witnesses testifying in favor of a Jew who litigated against a Christian were considered unreliable witnesses.[98] In a case in which two Jewish witnesses provided an extremely convincing testimony and no other evidence was available, the judge could not determine that the disputed fact was proven. Equally, the judge could not establish a fact on the basis of the opinion of a single expert; only two experts could provide full proof.[99]

The Austrian General Judicial Ordinance of 1781 led to a practice in which parties and their lawyers had ample opportunities to hamper the swift resolution of disputes. The resulting excessive costs and delay created by the parties convinced Leopold II to aim for additional civil procedural reform only shortly after the enactment of the Ordinance. Leopold II hence pushed for another codification: the West Galician Ordinance of 1796 (*Westgalizische Gerichtsordnung*). This new Code replaced the Code of 1781 in different regions of Austria between 1797 and 1817. The general principles of the West Galician Ordinance did not deviate from those of the General Judicial Ordinance, but did limit the strict application of the principle of party-presentation (*Verhandlungsmaxime*).[100] In some regards the new Ordinance was more 'modern' than the 1781 Ordinance. The West Galician Ordinance for instance did allow the court to orally discuss matters of fact with the parties.[101]

2.2. *The 1806 French Code of Civil Procedure*

In the first years of the French Revolution, the replacement of the *Ancien Régime* and its judicial institutions had led to revolutionary changes in the French court structure. Nevertheless, the procedural rules had not been subject to lasting and successful reform during the first decade after the Revolution. In these first years, the Ordinance of 1667 would remain the most influential source of procedural law although it was briefly and unsuccessfully replaced by revolutionary legislation.[102] The rise of Napoleon cleared the way for the 1806 Code of Civil Procedure.[103] The 1806 Code was amongst the most influential Codes on the European Continent and would remain influential in countries like Belgium, Italy, the Netherlands, Poland, Switzerland and Russia.[104]

With respect to its contents, the Code was far from revolutionary. The 1667 Ordinance was the most authoritative source during the drafting process and the starting point for the new Code.[105] However, in some areas the new Code of 1806

97 Sections 133-145 General Judicial Ordinance. The spouse of a party could for instance not testify at all whereas those hostile to one of the parties were considered to be 'bedenklich'.

98 Section 142 General Judicial Ordinance.

99 Section 196 General Judicial Ordinance.

100 Van Caenegem 1971, No. 69.

101 Sections 21-22 West Galician Ordinance; on the oral procedure, see Schwartz 1898, p. 678.

102 Wijffels 2008, p. 7-8.

103 Wijffels 2008, Part I.

104 Van Rhee 2006 and Van Caenegem 1971, No. 63.

105 Wijffels 2008, p. 18-19.

deviated from former legislation, such as no longer prescribing that witnesses had to be heard in secrecy. In addition, it introduced more oral elements to the procedure. The codification of 1806 also enlarged the role of the judge in the evaluation of evidence. It started from the premise that the 'inner conviction of the judge' (*conviction intime*) rather than the theory of formal proof was decisive in the evaluation of evidence. Nevertheless, the Code of 1806 and the Civil Code of 1804, although less stringent than earlier legislation, still contained many restrictions on the free evaluation of evidence. For instance, many potential witnesses were not qualified to testify and rules continued to prescribe that some documents provided full proof.[106]

2.3. *The 1838 Dutch Code of Civil Procedure*

From 1795 onwards, Dutch law underwent a strong French influence. After the Netherlands was completely annexed by the French in 1810, the French legal codifications entered into force throughout the country. Although the Netherlands soon regained its independence, it was not until 1st of October 1838 that Dutch national codifications were enacted. Even though this was a Dutch national Code of Civil Procedure, it clearly stood in the Romano-Canonical Continental tradition and was strongly inspired by French law. A majority of the Code's provisions were nothing but translations of French provisions that had previously been in force. A new substantive Dutch Civil Code, based on the French Code Napoleon, was enacted in the same year.[107]

The Code of Civil Procedure inherited its primary features from the French Code of 1806.[108] The principle that both parties ought to be heard was of central importance (*hoor en wederhoor, principe de contradictoire*). The proceedings according to the 1838 Code would take place in open court and were accessible to both the parties and the public. Gauged by modern standards, the procedural rules and practices under the 1838 Code were fairly formalistic. To ensure a 'professional' mode of process, the rules required the parties be represented by a lawyer in all cases pending before the District Court, the Courts of Appeal and the Court of Cassation. The most significant features of the process of fact-gathering and fact-finding will be discussed below.

Pleading and the Structure of Litigation

It is complicated to understand the ordinary course of litigation under the 1838 Code of Civil Procedure as practice soon deviated from the written laws. The Code recognized several different procedures: an 'ordinary' procedure, a written procedure, a County Court procedure and two different sorts of summary

106 See e.g. Article 283 of the Code of Civil Procedure. Similarly, Article 1341 of the Civil Code provided that witnesses could not testify to provide evidence for the existence of a document or contract if the value of the underlying transaction exceeded 150 francs.

107 Moorman van Kappen 1994. Articles 1902-2030 of the Civil Code were on evidence.

108 See Van Boneval Faure 1893, p. 20, p. 107 and Haardt 1951.

procedures.[109] One of the summary procedures was almost exclusively used in the District Courts a couple of decades after the enactment of the Code.[110] The procedures that were identified as the written and the ordinary procedures in the Code of Civil Procedure, were hardly used in legal practice.

The procedure was generally initiated when the writ (*dagvaarding*) was served on the defendant by a bailiff.[111] The writ summoned the defendant to appear before the court at a certain date and time and notified the defendant about the plaintiff's claim. The law required the *dagvaarding* to contain 'the means and the matter of the claim and a clear conclusion'.[112] The provision aimed at assuring that the defendant knew *what* the plaintiff demanded and *why* he believed he was entitled to that claim.[113] What exactly was meant by 'means' and 'matter' gave rise to some discussion.[114] It was clear, however, that a brief statement of facts was required and that parties were not required to argue matters of law. According to Van Boneval Faure, the plaintiff had to provide sufficient factual details such that the claim could follow from these statements of fact and a legal rule by logical deduction.[115]

Unless the written procedure was specifically chosen, the Code of Civil Procedure required that the pleadings be presented orally.[116] In practice this requirement was often neglected and oral pleading was widely replaced by an exchange of written documents.[117] The law specified that the normal procedure allowed both parties to present two pleadings; in summary proceedings parties were only allowed to file a single pleading. Courts often allowed the parties to file additional pleadings, for instance, after the examination of witnesses.[118]

If the defendant intended to appear to defend his case, the first pleading was the plaintiff's complaint. Because the Dutch Code of 1838 did not adhere to the *Eventualmaxime*, the preliminary defenses and other defenses of the defendant could subsequently be alleged in stages. The Code of Civil Procedure of 1838 made a distinction between preliminary defenses (*excepties*) and defenses on the merits (*verweren ten principale*).[119] First preliminary defenses had to be raised in a certain order, and then by means of the answer the remaining exceptions and defenses on the merits were raised. This implied that there was a possibility of a number of

109 All procedures are listed in Chapters 2 and 3 of the first Book of the 1838 Code of Civil Procedure.

110 A procedure originally designed for simple and urgent cases (*summiere behandeling*), former Artss 137-140 Code of Civil Procedure. On its use in practice see Van Boneval Faure 1900, p. 117, §68-69.

111 Article 1 Code of Civil Procedure. Non-contentious cases were however initiated by petition. In County Court cases, the parties could also jointly initiate proceedings without a writ.

112 Article 5(3) of the 1838 Dutch Code of Civil Procedure: '...de middelen en het onderwerp van de eis met eene duidelijke en bepaalde conclusie'.

113 Van Rossum 1907, p. 35.

114 Van Rossum 1907, p. 35, p. 36.

115 Van Boneval Faure 1900, §55, p. 16.

116 The Code uses the verb 'voordragen', see for instance former Article 139 Code of Civil Procedure.

117 Van Boneval Faure 1900, p. 124.

118 Meijers 1918, p. 159-164.

119 Articles 159-161 of the 1838 Code of Civil Procedure. See Star Busmann 1955, Nos. 227-233.

small procedures before the actual case was judged on its merits. Parties could also lodge appeal after an interlocutory judgment had been rendered. If a party would abuse the rules, it could take a while before the case was judged on the merits.[120] This procedure was justified by the idea that if an exception was granted, one had saved the costs and difficulties of a detailed study and discussion of the defenses on the merits.

After the exchange of the pleadings, the judge could formally determine that matters of fact were disputed and that evidentiary hearings were necessary. After the pleadings and the taking of evidence, parties were allowed to argue their case by means of an oral closing plea. Although the parties were free to plead their own case, the oral plea was usually presented by counsel. During the closing plea, parties were not allowed to raise new factual issues.[121] Afterwards, the judge would render his final judgment. In the absence of oral closing pleas, the court could render a final judgment after the exchange of pleadings and the taking of evidence.[122] In practice, the judge seldom rendered a judgment straight away, but would set a date by which the written judgment would be due.[123]

The Adversarial System

The 1838 Code adhered to the principle referred to as *'lijdelijkheid van de rechter,'* which literally translates as 'the passiveness of the judge'. This principle has similarities to the adversarial principle under Anglo-American law, the German *Dispositionsmaxime* and *Verhandlungsmaxime* and the French *principe dispositif.* The principle as such was not explicitly codified; it was first recognized and described by Van Boneval Faure in the 19th century.[124] According to him, the principle of *lijdelijkheid,* implied that the parties decide whether or not to start litigation and that the parties determine what the subject-matter of their case will be. The judge may not intervene in these matters *ex officio*. The principle also states that the parties determine the course of the proceedings. A judge may not compel parties to proceed to the next stage in the procedure. This interpretation of *lijdelijkheid* clearly opposes the modern notion of judicial 'case management'. The principle of *partijautonomie* (party autonomy) addresses the very same tension between the tasks of the parties on the one hand and the judge's role on the other. Though it stresses this topic from the parties' perspective, both principles can be seen as two sides of the very same coin.

Compared to the 1781 Austrian Ordinance, the Dutch Code of 1838 was less adversarial with regard to the gathering and examination of evidence. The official

120 Star Busmann 1955, No. 222.

121 Van Boneval Faure 1900, p. 126.

122 Referred to as 'recht op de (overgelegde) stukken', Van Rossum 1907, p. 74.

123 Articles 45-47 of the 1838 Code of Civil Procedure and Van Rossum 1907, p. 74.

124 Van Boneval Faure 1893, p. 110-113: 'Het voeren van een rechtsgeding is, èn wat het aanleggen daarvan betreft èn wat betreft den omvang van den aan 's rechters beslissing onderworpen strijd, afhankelijk van de partijen. De rechter treedt daarbij niet ambtshalve op. (...) Het beginsel van 's rechters lijdelijkheid vindt ook ten aanzien van de voortzetting van het geding zijne toepassing. De rechter is niet bevoegd aan de partijen de voortzetting van het geding te bevelen'.

doctrine held that the parties framed the factual issues. But once a factual matter was disputed, the court could become more actively involved in the gathering and examination of evidence. The Dutch Code of Civil Procedure granted the judge a wide range of powers to request evidence for disputed facts. A judge could *ex officio* order parties to present witness testimony, order a local visit to a scene of the dispute (*descente*), order the parties to affirm a matter of fact under oath or determine that experts would be appointed. The judge could, however, not summon a specific witness or appoint a specific expert if this witness or expert had not been suggested by a party.[125] The influential proceduralist Van Boneval Faure argued that the powers of the judge to actively order the production of evidence if facts were disputed did not infringe upon the principle of *lijdelijkheid van de rechter*.[126]

Party autonomy and *lijdelijkheid* were undisputed principles in Dutch legal thinking during the heyday of liberalism in the second half of the 19th century.[127] The judge left the initiative to the parties. In many ways, legal practice adhered to these principles more rigidly than the legislator had intended. Judges hardly ever made full and effective use of the powers granted to them by the Code of Civil Procedure.[128]

Remnants of the System of Formal Proof

The 1838 Dutch Civil Code, much like the French Code Napoleon, inherited much of the Romano-Canonical system of formal proof. It recognized the following five means of proof: documents, witnesses, presumptions, admissions and the judicial oath.[129] This list is not exclusive, as the Code of Civil Procedure additionally mentioned expert evidence and local visits to a scene of the dispute as distinct means of proof.[130] Many technical elements of the medieval system were preserved; the Civil Code, for example, still contained the complex rule on the *capitula connexa*.[131] It attached great value to documentary evidence and distrusted the testimony of witnesses, often excluding witness testimony altogether. Written evidence was occasionally exclusively held admissible.[132] The Civil Code also specified that certain categories of documents provided full proof.[133] It contained a rule (of French origin) that banned the use of witnesses if the value of the claim exceeded 300 guilders.[134] The most notable restriction on the admissibility of

125 Articles 103, 199, 219 and 222 of the 1838 Code of Civil Procedure. On the supplementary oath, see Article 1977 of the 1838 Civil Code. Before 1988, the court could not decide *ex officio* which expert to appoint. See De Groot 2008, p. 130.

126 Van Boneval Faure 1893, p. 112.

127 Bosch-Boesjes 1991, p. 23 and Verkerk 2005a.

128 Anonymous 1891, p. 384 and Meijers 1918, p. 146-170.

129 Article 1903 of the 1838 Civil Code, see also Van Rhee 2008c.

130 Articles 219, 222 (1838) Code of Civil Procedure.

131 Article 1961 of the 1838 Civil Code, 'onsplitsbare bekentenis', see Anema 1940, p. 430-440.

132 Articles 202, 1719, 1888 of the 1838 Civil Code and Former Articles 38 and 255 of the Commercial Code, see also Van Bell 1866, p. 15.

133 Articles 1907 and 1912 of the 1838 Civil Code.

134 Articles 1933 and 1937 of the 1838 Civil Code.

witness testimony was that parties and their close family were not allowed to take the stand.[135] The Civil Code restricted the probative value of the testimony of witnesses. It retained the medieval *Unus testis nullus testis* rule, which specified that the testimony of a single witness would not suffice to provide full proof.[136] In part, the Code did not depart from the secrecy of the medieval procedure: the examination of witnesses was not accessible to the general public.[137]

Discovery and the 'Nemo tenetur edere contra se' Principle

In the Dutch legal system of 1838, the *nemo tenetur edere contra se* principle was of great significance. This principle held that parties in a civil case were protected against self-incrimination. The 1838 Codes were drafted in a way that gave little opportunity for opposing parties or the judge to compel a party to provide adverse information. Similar to the Romano-Canonical procedural system, each party was free to withhold relevant evidence that would be detrimental to his case.

The rules, case law and legislative history on the discovery of documents provide the clearest example of the influence of the *nemo tenetur edere contra se* principle. An early government draft of the Civil Code had proposed a relatively wide rule that allowed for the discovery of documents. The government had argued that the draft provision 'aimed to discover the truth'.[138] But members of Parliament considered it a 'cruelty' to allow the parties to search for evidence in possession of the opposing party.[139] In 1833, an amended draft passed through Parliament again. In its Explanatory Memorandum, the government explained why it had amended the draft in this regard:

> 'Although one would like to praise the intentions of the drafters of this provision, which aimed to track down the truth, it has been proposed on the other hand, that men have always under all legislations been hesitant to search for means of proof *e domo adversarii* (literally: in the opponents home RRV), because the plaintiff should find support for his claim himself and, if he lacks documents or witness testimony, he can resort to the decisory oath,(...) For that reason the aforementioned provision of the law has been limited to documents that are common to the parties...'.[140]

135 Article 1947 of the 1838 Civil Code.

136 Article 1942 of the 1838 Civil Code.

137 Article 205 of the 1838 Code of Civil Procedure.

138 Article 19 of an 1830 draft of the second Section of the fourth Book of the Civil Code had provided the parties with almost unlimited powers to compel their opponent to produce case-related documents. See Noordziek 1892, p. 240, p. 257: 'In elken stand van het geding kan de eene partij van de andere vorderen, dat dezelve onder eede die stukken overlegge, welke onder hare berusting zijn en de zaak in geschil betreffen. (...) Men heeft de bepaling als hoogst zedelijk en billijk beschouwd omdat dezelve strekt tot ontdekking der waarheid'.

139 Noordziek 1892, p. 257.

140 Erkelens & Jungmann 1892, p. 614: 'Hoezeer men gaarne hulde doet aan de bedoelingen van de opstellers van deze wetsbepaling, welke strekking leidde om op het spoor der waarheid te geraken, zo heeft men echter aan den anderen kant voorgesteld, dat men steeds onder alle wetgevingen huiverig is geweest, om de bewijsmiddelen e domo adversarii op te zoeken, vermits de aanlegger verplicht is zijnen eisch op zichzelf te staven en hij bij gebreke van →

This clarification has been criticized as it is neither true nor consistent with other parts of the Explanatory Memorandum.[141] The legislative history of this provision (Article 1923 of the 1838 Civil Code) does illustrate the legislators underlying motives: one cannot be compelled to provide the opposing party with the evidence he needs. The Court of Cassation was asked to decide upon the scope of this provision on the 12th of November 1875. The Court of Cassation refused to order a landlady to produce a copy of the rental contract to the tenant that had signed the contract. The document was not considered to be 'common' to both parties. The Court elaborated:

> 'Taking into consideration that the word "common" linguistically means "being the property of more than one person" and that the word is used in that meaning in various provisions of our Civil Code (...) because one (i.e. the legislator RRV) did not want that parties would search for means of proof *e domo adversarii*, one has, strictly in line with the *nemo contra edere cogitur*, only recognized the duty of parties to hand over documents if a request for the production of a document can be based on a right (i.e. property right RRV) of the party that requests production of a document'.[142]

Van Boneval Faure concluded that no person can be compelled to hand over documents in his possession, to his opponent in the proceedings or to a third person involved in another law suit, only because the other person has a procedural interest in the production of a document.[143]

The legislative history of the interrogation on facts and articles (see Section 6.1), provides another example of the influence of the *nemo tenetur edere contra se* principle. The Explanatory Memorandum of the draft Articles 201-211 recognized that the provisions could be useful to clarify the facts. Nevertheless, the government recognized the difficulties with the provision and specified that the interrogation 'should never be used by the parties to pull a fast one on each other or to supplement the lack of evidence of one party by a testimony of the other party against that other party's interests'.[144] During the Parliamentary deliberations on the

schriftelijk of testimoniaal bewijs zijne toevlucht kan nemen tot den beslissenden eed. (...) Om die reden heeft men de voorzeide wetsbepaling beperkt tot stukken, die aan de partijen gemeen zijn...'.

141 See e.g. Opzoomer & Levy 1902, p. 63.

142 Court of Cassation, 12 November 1875, W. 3917: 'Overwegende toch, dat het woord "gemeen" taalkundig betekent "het aan meerdere in eigendom behorende" en dat het bij die beteekenis wordt gebruikt in onderscheidende artikelen van het Burgerlijk Wetboek; (...) Omdat men niet wilde dat partijen hunne bewijsmiddelen e domo adversarii zouden opzoeken, zoodat men, streng vasthoudende aan het nemo contra edere cogitur, de verplichting tot overlegging alleen heeft willen erkennen waar zij op het recht van degene die zo vordert gegrond is'. For a detailed description of the case, see Kuyk 1921.

143 See Van Boneval Faure 1896, p. 205: 'Niemand kan gedwongen worden hem toebehoorende stukken, bij welker kennisneming zijne wederpartij in een geding of een derde in een door dezen tegen een ander gevoerd geding enkel en alleen belang mocht hebben, uit te leveren'.

144 *Handelingen der Staten Generaal* 1836-1837, p. 224: '(...) dit middel (...) nimmer behoort gebezigd te worden, om elkander te vergaauwen of het gebrek aan bewijs aan de zijde van de eene partij door de wederpartij door een getuigenis tegen haar zelve te doen aanvullen,...'.

20th of February 1837 it was reported that: 'it seems that virtually everything has been done in order to take away the disadvantages such a hearing could have for one of the parties'.[145] It was feared that the rules, which *inter alia* required that the questions put to the interrogated party would be communicated to that party in advance, would not function as an effective tool to discover the truth.[146] This criticism later appeared to be justified.[147]

The 1838 Fact-finding Arrangements: Possible Consequences
The combination of a passive judge, a system of formal proof and the *nemo tenetur edere contra se* principle led to rulings that were generally considered to be unfair. It is important to understand the possible consequences of the principles of some of the older Continental codifications as well as the old common law system to understand the increased cry for 'truth' and an 'active judiciary' between the 1880s and the 1930s. An 1869 Dutch case of an injured cabin boy provides a sad illustration.[148] A cabin boy fell on a journey overseas and got sick. As a result of his sickness he became deaf, making him unsuitable for the labor market. When the ship returned to the docks, he demanded compensation from his employer. According to substantive law, he was entitled to damages if the accident happened on board of the ship (Article 423 of the Commercial Code). The employer refused to pay compensation, after which the cabin boy filed a law suit. The cabin boy argued that the accident took place on board of the ship. His employer denied the allegation. The law did not require the employer to explain his denial. Neither did the Code of Civil Procedure require a party to be truthful. The cabin boy had the burden of proof pursuant to Article 1902 of the Civil Code. The evidence rules excluded witness statements as a means of proof under Article 1937 of the Civil Code (the rule held that witness evidence was inadmissible if the claim exceeded an amount of 300 guilders). The cabin boy wished to provide evidence by means of the ship's logbook. However, the court could not order the production of the document, as it was not the 'common' property of the cabin boy and the company (Article 1923 of the Civil Code). The judge could not make use of adverse inferences against the employer because the law specified that the judge could not make use of 'factual presumptions' if the testimony of witnesses was inadmissible (Article 1959 Civil Code). The cabin boy failed to present evidence for a fact that was self-evident: he could perfectly hear when he boarded the ship, yet was deaf when the ship returned to the docks. He lost his case.

145 *Handelingen der Staten Generaal* 1836-1837, p. 232: '(...) men schijnt er dan ook alles aangewend te hebben, om, zoo mogelijk, het nadeel hetwelk uit zulk een verhoor voor eene partij kan ontstaan, weg te nemen...'.

146 *Handelingen der Staten Generaal* 1836-1837, p. 246.

147 See Denijs 1936 and Weve 1878.

148 District Court of Rotterdam 22 March 1869, as discussed by Ledeboer 1888.

3. Modern Codifications of Procedural Law

3.1. *The 1895 Austrian Code of Civil Procedure*

3.1.1. Introduction of the Austrian Code of Civil Procedure

Early Attempts to reform the Austrian procedural System: Bagatellverfahren 1873
Throughout the 19th century, discontent with the existing General Judicial Ordinance and West Galician Ordinance was widespread. Unsuccessful attempts to reform Austrian civil procedural rules include legislative proposals in 1816, 1820, 1858, 1862, 1876, and 1881.[149] These reform proposals often aimed to depart from the leading principles of the General Judicial Ordinance. The 1862 legislative draft proposed to introduce an oral and public procedure inspired by the French legislation of 1806. It aimed to reduce procedural formalities and increase the powers of the judge. It also proposed to introduce provisions that required the parties to speak the truth. The 1876 draft also proposed many innovations that would ultimately be introduced roughly two decades later.[150]

Although these attempts failed to modify the general procedural framework, reforms that were more modest in scope were successful. Most notable was the introduction of a Law on the Proceedings in Petty Causes (*Bagatellverfahren*) by Minister of Justice Julius Glaser in 1873.[151] Prior to his appointment as a Minister of Justice, Glaser had argued for a fundamental reform of the proceedings in simple cases with small amounts in dispute.[152] The Law on the Proceedings in Petty Causes was very different from the Ordinances of 1781 and 1796. It introduced a public and oral procedure, embraced the principle of immediacy, empowered the judge to hear the parties *ex officio*, empowered the judge to order the parties to produce evidence *ex officio* and held that all evidence had to be freely evaluated.[153] The Law on Proceedings in Petty Causes would clear the way for the new Austrian Code of Civil Procedure in 1895.

The Introduction of the 1895 Code of Civil Procedure
Procedural legislation and procedural methods often result from a long historical process where incremental changes gradually shaped and adjusted the procedural regime. The Dutch procedural rules and practices are the result of many centuries of gradual and incremental reform.[154] The result of such a piece-meal approach is that one cannot really speak of 'one model' or 'one ideology' that served as a blueprint for the Code of Civil Procedure. The idea of 'one Code, one model' did exist in Austria. The founding father of the 1895 Austrian *Zivilprozessordnung* was Franz

149 Schoibl 1987, p. 40.
150 Jelinek 1991, p. 53.
151 Law of 27 April 1873, *Official State Journal* (RGBl.) 66, *über das Verfahren in geringfügigen Rechtssachen* (*Bagatellverfahren*).
152 See Glaser 1859.
153 Sections 1, 16-17, 20, 31-33, 53 and 70 of the Law on the Proceedings in Petty Causes.
154 Van Nispen 1993 and Eshuis 1998, p. 12.

Klein.[155] As an academic, Klein criticized the Austrian practice of his time, making suggestions to reform the rules of civil procedure.[156] Later, Klein was employed by the Ministry of Justice where he prepared the draft of the Code of Civil Procedure that would eventually be enacted in 1895.[157] After that, Klein was appointed as Minister of Justice, where he served for several years. This position allowed him to effectively implement his ideas in legal practice.

The 1895 Civil Procedural Code could be considered a break with the Austrian codifications that had relied heavily on the Romano-Canonical procedure.[158] Contrary to earlier codifications, the 1895 Code was an example of legislation that aimed to invoke social change and improve existing practices. It came into existence in a period in which legislation was increasingly regarded as a tool for 'social engineering' by leading procedural academics.[159] The introduction of the Code was carefully prepared to ensure a smooth transition to a new procedural regime. The codification was enacted and published in August 1895 and entered into force in 1898.[160] Between 1895 and 1898, the Ministry of Justice organized instructional meetings for judges and hired new judges in greater numbers. Monitoring and inspection teams were also created to promote the correct application of the Code once it entered into force.[161]

The Influence of the Austrian Code of Civil Procedure

The Austrian Civil Procedural Code of 1895 has been referred to as 'the most influential modern procedural codification'.[162] Some jurisdictions would adopt legislation (virtually) identical to the Austrian Code, many other jurisdiction only adopted some key elements of the Austrian legislation.

The Austrian Code was influential in many countries that were once under Habsburg rule. After the First World War, Austrian procedural legislation remained in force in parts of Czechoslovakia (until 1950) and parts of Italy (until 1928).[163] Codifications enacted in nations that were once (partly) part of the Austrian-Hungarian empire, such as the 1911 Hungarian Code of Civil Procedure, the 1932 Polish Code of Civil Procedure and the 1929 Yugoslavian Code of Civil Procedure were strongly inspired by the Austrian Code of Civil Procedure.[164]

155 For an overview of the life and works of Franz Klein, see Sprung 1988.

156 Klein 1891.

157 On the work of Klein at the Ministry of Justice, see Reindl 1988.

158 Schwartz, wrote on procedural codification between 1495 and 1895. The last Chapter on the Austrian reform of 1895 is called 'Umkehr?'. Schwartz 1898. Also see Van Rhee 2008a.

159 Parker & Lewisch 1998, Chapter 2.

160 The Code was enacted on the 1st of August and published on the 9th of August, *Reichsgesetzblatt* 1895, LX. Stück, No. 113, p. 365.

161 Klang 1948, p. 84-86.

162 Erik Wolf, as quoted in Damrau 1988: 'die einflussreichste moderne Zivilprozesskodifikation überhaupt'. Also see Satter 1936 and Baur 1970, p. 446.

163 Jelinek 1991, p. 72 and Weitz 2006, Section 1.

164 The 1895 Code was already introduced in the Austrian part of Poland. See Van Caenegem 1971, No. 69 and Jelinek 1991, p. 58, p. 75. It has continued to influence the present codifications in (parts of) former Yugoslavia. See for instance on Croatia: Uzelac 2004, p. 288.

Many other Continental jurisdictions were clearly inspired by the Austrian legislation; examples include the 1905 Code of Montenegro, the 1918 Code of the Swiss canton Bern and the 1912 Code of Liechtenstein.[165] In Denmark (1916) and Norway (1915), codifications were enacted in the beginning of the 20th century that were inspired by the Austrian Code.[166] The Swedish Code of 1942 was also inspired by the works of Klein.[167] The Austrian Code thoroughly influenced the German procedural legislation as well. The Austrian provisions on judicial case management, the interrogation of parties and the duty of parties to provide a complete and truthful account of the facts were almost literally copied to the German Civil Procedural Code in the reforms of 1909, 1924 and 1933.[168]

In other countries the influence of the 1895 Code was present, but less overwhelming. In Greece and Romania, the Austrian Code and the works of Klein initiated a number of amendments to the Code of Civil Procedure.[169] In the Netherlands, legislative drafts were written that reveal a strong Austrian influence.[170] In other countries like France, Austrian developments contributed to a renewed debate on the reform of civil litigation, though they failed to directly influence legislative change.[171] The influence of Klein's work has not been limited to European jurisdictions. Klein's work was influential in Japan (1926) and the Chinese Codes of 1921 and 1935 were inspired by the Austrian Code of 1895.[172]

Although the influence of the Austrian Code of Civil Procedure has not always been decisive and lasting, this (incomplete) overview illustrates that developments in Austria have invoked changes elsewhere. The fundamentals of the Austrian system have been exported to other major Continental jurisdictions. Hence it is often possible to generalize and extend observations on Austrian law to a larger number of jurisdictions.

3.1.2. The Leading Principles and Innovations of the Austrian Code

Klein's doctrinal works on the nature and purposes of legal process are in essence utilitarian. There is a clear resemblance between the works of Jeremy Bentham and the Code of Civil Procedure drafted by Klein. Both Bentham and Klein are

165 Jelinek 1991, p. 58-59.

166 See Munch-Petersen 1926, p. 627 and Van Caenegem 1971, p. 101. A new Norwegian Code has been enacted more recently which still contains many 'Austrian' features, such as Section 11-5 on the court's duty to give guidance, Section 21-2 on the free evaluation of evidence and Section 21-4 on the parties' duties of truth and disclosure. An English translation of the Norwegian Code is available at <www.ub.uio.no/ujur/ulovdata/lov-20050617-090-eng.pdf>, last consulted in February 2010.

167 Ginsburg 1965, p. 341 and Jelinek 1991, p. 77.

168 Damrau 1988.

169 Jelinek 1991, p. 75.

170 For Italy and Czechoslovakia see: Satter 1936, p. 280 and Jelinek 1991 p. 61. For the Netherlands see Van Rhee 2005a and Van Rhee 2000b.

171 See e.g. Tissier 1906, p. 649. Tissier discusses Austrian law to argue in favor of a stronger managerial judge. Also see Wijffels 2005b.

172 Sprung 1988, p. 35 and Van Caenegem 1971, No. 69.

proponents of what Twining coined the 'rationalist tradition' of procedure and evidence.[173] The utilitarian theory and principles underlying the 1895 Code of Civil Procedure will be set out in greater detail in Chapter 7. In the Sections below the main features of the 1895 Austrian Code will be described briefly. The 1895 Code of Civil Procedure would deviate from its 18th century predecessors in almost every respect.

The Austrian Code of Civil Procedure favored oral over written procedures. Franz Klein had, in his earlier writings, been positive about the experiences with oral proceedings pursuant to the enactment of the Law on Petty Causes.[174] The 1895 Code of Civil Procedure, in accordance with the views of Klein, considered the oral hearing(s) to form the most important and significant phase of the proceedings.[175] Section 176 Code of Civil Procedure specifies that the parties should discuss their case orally.[176] Section 177 specifies that parties are not allowed to read out written accounts instead of arguing their case orally.[177] At the oral hearing, the parties are heard, factual and legal issues are addressed and evidence is presented and discussed.[178] Written pleadings could be exchanged before the oral hearings, yet the Code specified that these only served to prepare for oral hearings.[179]

The Austrian Code of Civil Procedure adhered to the principle of immediacy (*Unmittelbarkeit*). The new Code, like the 1873 Law on the Proceedings in Petty Causes, prescribed that the judge present at the oral hearings should also render the final judgment.[180] Exceptions to the general rule do exist, which have led most commentators to believe that the principle of immediacy is not a leading principle of the Code but rather a pragmatic means to improve the efficiency of litigation.[181]

The 1895 Austrian Code favored proceedings in open court. Both the parties and the general public, in principle have a right to access the oral hearings.[182] Witnesses were no longer heard in secrecy.

Another distinctive feature of the Code of Civil Procedure was that it favored a concentrated proceeding over a procedure split up into a number of preset stages. Regardless of the number of actual hearings, the Code specified that the oral phase was always considered to be a single stage in the proceedings.[183] Judges had to schedule as few hearings as possible. Preferably all matters of fact should be dealt with at a single and uninterrupted hearing (*Verfahrenskonzentration*).[184] Thereby the

173 Twining 2006, p. 76.
174 Klein 1891, Chapter 6, p. 88.
175 Rechberger & Simotta 2009, No. 734, p. 379: 'Die mündliche Streitverhandlung (§§171ff ZPO) bildet den wichtigsten Teil des erstinstanzlichen Verfahrens'.
176 'Vor dem erkennenden Gerichte verhandeld die Parteien über den Rechtstreit mündlich (...)'.
177 '(...) Das ablesen schriftlicher Aufsätze statt mündlichen Vorbringens ist unzulassig'.
178 Sections 177 and 259 Austrian Code of Civil Procedure.
179 The pleadings are referred to as 'vorbereitende Schriftsätze', Section 176 Code of Civil Procedure.
180 Section 70 Law on the Proceedings in Petty Causes and Section 412 Code of Civil Procedure.
181 See e.g. Fasching 1990, No. 671.
182 Section 171 Code of Civil Procedure and Fasching 1990, No. 681.
183 Section 193(2) Code of Civil Procedure.
184 Rechberger 2001.

Austrian system, at a very early point in time, introduced what has been coined 'the main hearing model'. If it was necessary for a fair disposal of the case, the single oral phase of the proceeding could consist of more than one hearing. Klein was inspired by the German Code of Civil Procedure of 1877 that had refuted the strict application of the principle of contingent cumulation (*Eventualmaxime*).[185] By recognizing only a single oral stage in the proceeding, the 1895 Code of Civil Procedure departed from a strict application of this principle.[186] Under the older Codes that were in force before 1898, a failure to allege facts or suggest evidence in the proper stage of the proceedings could deprive parties of the right to allege the fact or present the evidence. According to the Code of 1895, until the end of the oral phase, parties could raise new matters of fact or suggest new means of proof. Only if parties belatedly alleged facts and thereby caused delay, could the court refuse to take into account newly presented facts and evidence.[187]

An interesting feature from a comparative perspective was the introduction of discovery in the Code of Civil Procedure of 1895. Klein had been inspired by the English regulations on discovery that had been in force since the Judicature Acts.[188] The Austrian Code of 1895 accordingly introduced a general duty that required the parties to provide a complete and truthful account of the facts (*Wahrheitspflicht*, Section 178). The Code also contained more specific rules, such as Section 184 of the Code which empowered the parties to question their adversary at an oral hearing about all relevant factual issues, including the availability and existence of documentary evidence and other means of proof (see Section 6.1.2.4). The Code further empowered the parties to request the court to order an opponent to produce documents or exhibits. Sections 303-305, and 318 Code of Civil Procedure indicate that the judge could refuse to order a party to produce evidence only in case of weighty reasons (*wichtige Gründe*). In addition, it was possible to compel third parties to produce relevant evidence (Section 308 Code of Civil Procedure, see Section 7.3.2).

Another very innovative feature of the Austrian Code of Civil Procedure was that the Code strengthened the role of the court in the process of fact-gathering and fact-finding. Although the Code of Civil Procedure continued to adhere to the principle of party disposition, it did refute the principle of party-presentation (see Chapter 7.2).

The last significant feature of the 1895 Code of Civil Procedure was that it adhered to the principle of the free evaluation of evidence. The Law on the Proceedings in Petty Causes (*Bagatellverfahren 1873*) first introduced the free evaluation of evidence in Austria.[189] The 1895 Code followed this example and thereby departed from the Romano-Canonical system of formal proof. Section

185 Klein 1891, Part V., p. 72. Klein argued the *Eventualmaxime* had to be abandoned as in Germany.

186 Rechberger 2001, Part 6.

187 Section 179 Code of Civil Procedure. In exceptional circumstances, a lawyer who had wrongfully caused undue delay could be fined.

188 Klein 1891, p. 47 *et seq.* and Kralik 1988, p. 92-93.

189 Sections 31-33 Law on the Proceedings in Petty Causes.

272(1) of the Code specifies that the judge should 'after a careful examination of the proceeding and the examination of all evidence, led by his free conviction, decide whether or not a certain factual statement should be held true'.[190] The 1895 Code of Civil Procedure recognized fewer exceptions to the free evaluation of evidence than the 1806 French Code and the 1838 Dutch Code of Civil Procedure. The Code of Civil Procedure no longer banned close family and those convicted of certain crimes to testify as witnesses. Inspired by developments in England and the Law on the Proceedings in Petty Causes, the Code also enabled the parties to give a testimony under oath (see Chapter 6).

3.1.3. The Austrian Procedural System since 1895

Although the 1895 Civil Procedural Code has been amended to a considerable extent, it is still in force today. In the 1970s, the Austrian legal aid scheme was widened, which led to small changes in existing civil procedural legislation.[191] Recent amendments to the Code of Civil Procedure include the introduction of provisions on mediation and a full revision of the law on arbitration.[192] There is an abundance of accessible literature on the reform of procedural law in Austria since 1895.[193] The reforms of 1983 and 2002, that amended the rules on fact-finding, are discussed below.

The most significant procedural reform since the enactment of the Code in 1895 was the 1983 Reform Act.[194] The aim of the Reform Act was twofold: it aimed to make the procedure more simple and time efficient and it tried to improve access to justice. These basic aims of the reform fit well into the general objectives of the 1895 Code of Civil Procedure. Klein had clearly favored simple, accessible and swift proceedings.[195] The many changes to the Code of Civil Procedure that resulted from the 1983 Reform Act did not reveal that the legislator made use of a consistent underlying theory that linked the specific changes to these aims.[196] Some of the changes to the Code did fit better in the existing procedural model than others.[197]

The reform included a variety of changes on matters like the jurisdiction of the courts, small claims proceedings before the County Courts, the availability of

190 Section 272(1) Code of Civil Procedure: 'Das Gericht hat, soferne in diesem Gesetze nicht etwas anderes bestimmt ist, unter sorgfältiger Berücksichtigung der Ergebnisse der gesamten Verhandlung und Beweisführung nach freier überzeugung zu beurteilen, ob eine tatsächliche Angabe für wahr zu halten sei oder nicht'.

191 Schoibl 1987, Chapter 5.

192 See for a description of this Mediation Act: Hopf 2004. On arbitration see Rechberger 2006.

193 On the changes of Austrian law since 1895, see Fasching 1998; Schoibl 1987; Fasching 1990, Chapter 2.8 and Bajons 2005.

194 Law of 2 February 1983, *Official State Journal* (BGBl) 135.

195 Fasching 1982, p. 70.

196 Schoibl 1987, p. 77: '...Bei dieser Vielzahl von Änderungen lässt sich ein einheitliches Konzept des Gesetzgebers nicht immer klar erkennen...'.

197 Schoibl 1987, Chapter 7.

remedies and arbitration.[198] The reform widened the possibilities of amending the pleadings by supplementing information that was lacking in the initial pleading.[199] The 1983 reform also loosened the very strict application of the principle of immediacy for reasons of efficiency. Evidence that was examined in another proceeding, for instance, did not have to be reexamined for the sole reason of fulfilling the requirement of immediacy.[200] Another relevant change brought about by the Act affected the rules on the interrogation of parties (*Parteivernehmung*). The interrogation of parties would no longer be regarded as a subsidiary means of proof and the 1983 reform made it possible to interrogate both parties under oath (see Chapter 6).

The Austrian 2002 Reform Act affected the structure of litigation and the rules on fact-gathering. The 2002 Reform Act entered into force on the 1st of January 2003 and was introduced to combat delays in civil litigation.[201] The Explanatory Memorandum explicitly referred to the works of Klein to stress the importance of swift proceedings.[202] The 2002 Reform *inter alia* addressed the order for payment procedure (*Mahnverfahren*) and default judgments.

Three important novelties of the 2002 Procedural Reform are mentioned below.[203] First, the structure of the procedure was changed to ensure a swifter resolution of the dispute. The 'first hearing' (*erste Tagsatzung*), at which the merits of the case were not addressed, was abolished.[204] Instead, a 'preparatory hearing' (*vorbereitende Tagsatzung*) is scheduled after the defendant files his answer (*Klagebeantwortung*). The preparatory hearing serves to promote settlement, to discuss factual and legal matters and to set a time-table for further proceedings.[205] In connection with this the formal order for the production of evidence (*Beweisbeschluss*) has been abolished as the production of evidence is to be planned at the preparatory hearing.[206] These changes are in line with the views of Klein. Klein had clearly favored pragmatism and efficiency with respect to the discussion of factual issues and the taking of evidence.[207]

198 For a short accessible summary of the reform see Schoibl 1987, p. 77-87. More detailed contributions on the Reform Act include Fasching 1982 and König 1982.

199 Section 84(3) Code of Civil Procedure, see Konecny 1984. The provision has been criticized. König referred to it as 'the worst provision' of the reform proposal, König 1982, p. 411.

200 See the newly introduced Section 281a Code of Civil Procedure. Fasching 1982, p. 124.

201 962 BlgNr GP XXI, p. 15-16. Die *Zivilverfahrens-Novelle* 2002, *Official State Journal* (BGBl) I,76.

202 962 BlgNr GP XXI, p. 16. Also see P. Böhm, Bundesrat, Stenographisches Protokoll, 686. Sitzung, Seite 94: '(...) die Zivilverfahrens-Novelle 2002. Sie bildet zweifellos einen Meilenstein in der neueren Geschichte der österreichischen Zivilprozessreform. In zeitgemäßer Form kehrt sie nämlich zum leider zwischenzeitig oft verwässerten Grundkonzept Franz Kleins von 1895 zurück'.

203 See for concise summaries: *AnwBl* 2002/4, p. 184 and *AnwBl* 2002/10, p. 500-501.

204 962 BlgNr GP XXI, p. 17, in 1983 Section 243(4) was introduced which already allowed the judge to skip the first hearing if it was known that the defendant would defend his case. Fasching 1982, p. 126.

205 Sections 257, 258 Code of Civil Procedure and 962 BlgNr GP XXI, p. 18, p. 33.

206 Former Section 277 Austrian Code of Civil Procedure, see 962 BlgNr GP XXI, p. 36.

207 See e.g. Klein 1900, p. 148.

The 2002 Reform also codified a duty for the parties to ensure a swift resolution of the dispute (*Prozessförderungspflicht*, Section 178(2) Code of Civil Procedure). The Code of Civil Procedure thereby explicitly stated what had already been part of Austrian law. Before 2002, the Code had specified that if a party causes delay by culpably alleging information or evidence at a late point in the proceedings, the judge could disregard that information or evidence.[208] A similar provision had existed with respect to evidence. In practice, the court does not frequently refuse to admit facts or evidence alleged by the parties. It happens more frequently that the party that caused delay is ordered to pay a larger share of the costs of litigation.[209] The legislator specified that the procedural duty for the parties to allege information as early as possible was not an attempt to reintroduce the '*Eventualmaxime*'.[210] A last central tenet of the 2002 reform was an increased focus in the Code of Civil Procedure on the right to be heard. Amendments to the Code require the judge to hear the parties on specific issues more frequently.[211] These changes codified existing case-law that had held that court decisions should never surprise the parties.[212]

It may be concluded that in spite of the many changes to the Code of Civil Procedure, the provisions related to fact-finding have largely remained untouched.[213] The amendments of 1983 and 2002 have not infringed upon the basic principles of the Code. The fundamentals of the process of fact-gathering and fact-finding of the 1895 Code remain as important today as they were shortly after its enactment. Some features have even been reinforced, rather than abolished. The position of the judge has been strengthened since the introduction of the Code and Klein's writings on this topic are still read and quoted.[214]

208 Sections 179 and 275(2) Code of Civil Procedure.

209 Bajons 2003, No. 28, p. 446 and Sections 44 and 48 Code of Civil Procedure.

210 962 BlgNr GP XXI, p. 22: 'Die Prozessförderungspflicht darf keinesfalls im Sinne einer Eventualmaxime verstanden werden (...)'. Also see Section 179 Code of Civil Procedure.

211 See e.g. Sections 182a, 208(2a) and 259 Code of Civil Procedure.

212 962 BlgNr GP XXI, p. 25. Also see decisions after 2002 on this issue, such as Supreme Court 25 May 2005, 7Ob83/05i, EF-Slg 2005, 112.104-112.108: 'Die Rechtsmeinung, wonach nur eine Rechtsansicht, wenn sie bis zum Schluss der Verhandlung erster Instanz von keiner der Parteien ins Treffen geführt wurde und daher keine Gelegenheit zur Stellungnahme bestand, als überraschend angesehen werden kann, kann nach der ZVN 2002 nicht aufrecht erhalten bleiben'. Supreme Court 14 June 2005, 2Ob101/04Y, Miet-Slg 2005, 57.636 (2005): 'Das Gericht darf die Parteien in seiner Entscheidung nicht mit einer Rechtsauffassung überraschen'.

213 Fasching 1988, p. 102-103.

214 Fasching 1988, p. 102-103: 'Dementsprechend hat auch der Gesetzgeber diesen Kleinschen Grundgedanken nicht nur nicht abgeschwächt, sondern mehrfach ganz deutlich verstärkt'. Fasching *inter alia* refers to the increased duties of the court to instruct litigants in person (Section 39 Abs 2 Z 1 ASGG). Rechberger 1998, p. 57: 'Hier (zurückdrängung des Verhandlungsmaxime) ist slicht alles, was Klein vor 100 Jahre zu sagen wusste, bis zum letzten Beistrich auch heute noch aktuell'.

3.1.4. The Operation of the Austrian Code in Legal Practice

Statistical information on the operation of the Austrian justice system is scarce and it is difficult to make general remarks on the operation of the Code in practice.[215] On the basis of the available data and the remarks made in literature by practitioners; I will try to make some general observations on the role of the court, the efficiency of litigation and the pursuit of truth in the Austrian system since the 1895 Code of Civil Procedure entered into force.

A couple of years after the Austrian Code was adopted, Klein described its operation in practice. According to Klein, the introduction of the new legislation was a great success; judges and lawyers were praised as they effectively implemented the general ideas behind the Code.[216] Klein was especially positive about the concentrated oral hearings during which judges effectively managed the proceedings.[217] Shortly after the enactment, courts were often making use of their powers to order the parties to appear before the court.[218] Klein claimed that judges had successfully managed the process of fact-finding (*materielle Prozessleitung*).[219] He might not be the most objective source, yet his positive evaluation of the first decade after the enactment of the Code is generally shared in literature.[220]

After the first decades, Austrian practice started to face some difficulties and challenges not uncommon to other European jurisdictions.[221] External factors like wars, high inflation and the economic depression gave rise to an increase in the case load of the courts. This put much pressure on the Austrian system and gave rise to less active case management by the courts. It led to fewer oral elements in the proceedings, longer written pleadings and undue delay. Eventually it led to a growing discrepancy between black letter law and legal practice. But from the 1950s onwards, the system seemed to recover and judges actively managed cases, most notably during the oral hearings.

215 Most available information on the Austrian justice system is retrieved from the Information System of the Ministry of Justice, a source of data not properly made accessible to the general public *(Betriebliches Informationssystem der Justiz)*.

216 Klein 1900, p. 5: '(...) hat die Praxis nicht bloß erfüllt, sondern in manchen Beziehungen weit übertroffen was man von ihr und vom Gesetze erwarten könnte. Mit Elan und großem Geschick haben Richter- und Anwaltstand das Gesetz modern erfasst und ausgeführt und damit das Gelingen des Reformwerkes entschieden'.

217 Klein 1900, p. 5-6: 'Mit Hilfe der im Ganzen richtig erfassten Prozessleitung hat die Praxis bald eine Unmittelbarkeit herzustellen und eine Concentration der Verhandlung zu erreichen gewusst, wie man sie bisher im Zivilverfahren eigentlich kaum für möglich gehalten hat'.

218 Section 183(1) Code of Civil Procedure and Klang 1948, p. 87.

219 Klein 1900, p. 12: 'Die Prozessleitung könnte manchmal - hauptsächlich im einzelrichterlichen Verfahren - zielbewusster und kraftvoller sein. Aber hiervon abgesehen, wird sie mit Erfolg und durchwegs mit richtigem Takte gehandhabt und hat sich - wie eben erwähnt - als eine außerordentlich erfolgreiche Waffe gegen die Prozesschicane bestens bewährt. (...) Wohl aber sind zahlreiche Beweise für den oft verblüffenden Effect eines schlagfertigen Gebrauches der materiellen Prozessleitungs-befugnisse bekannt geworden'.

220 See e.g. Fasching 1988, p. 99.

221 Klang 1948, p. 87-94 and Fasching 1988.

The strong role of the judge in the Austrian legal system has been criticized both before and after the introduction of the Code. It has been argued that a strong judge and an imprecise Code of Civil Procedure reduce legal certainty and equality.[222] It was argued that strong judicial powers endanger the neutrality of the judge and can lead to abuse of power. According to Fasching, a leading Austrian proceduralist, Austrian experiences have shown that these objections have not proven to be genuine problems in Austrian practice.[223]

As it is not easy to untangle cause and effect, it is extremely difficult to determine whether the Austrian procedural rules have increased the efficiency of the proceedings. There are reasons to assume that judicial case management has contributed to the efficient resolution of disputes.[224] A skillful Austrian judge can quickly identify the relevant issues, avoid the unnecessary taking of evidence and freely evaluate evidence. A judge has sufficient tools to detect and sanction inappropriate behavior of the parties. An experienced judge can use her discretion to assure a fair, efficient and effective process of fact-finding. It is difficult to operationalize, measure and quantify effects of judicial case management.

Shortly after the enactment of the Austrian Code, the Austrian legal system proved to be extremely efficient. In Austria proceedings were concluded much swifter than in the surrounding countries. It was common to conclude a case at first, second and third instance within one year.[225] Klein had gathered detailed statistics which nicely show how swiftly the system operated. Statistics show that in 1898 a large majority of cases were concluded within half a year and hardly any cases were pending before the Austrian courts for longer than one year.[226] More detailed statistics exist about the duration of litigation in both 1900 and 1910. These show that in small claims cases (*Bagatellverfahren*), over 90% of all cases were concluded within one month and the number of small cases not concluded within 6 months was between 0.1 and 0.4%.[227] Similarly, over 80% of the cases were concluded in the County Courts (*Bezirksgericht*) within one month and the number of cases not concluded within 6 months was between 0.3 and 2.6%. Before the District Courts (*Gerichtshof*), about half of the cases were concluded in one month and in most courts over 80% of the cases were concluded within 3 months. Only a very small percentage of cases before the District Courts were not concluded within one year.[228] Although precise statistics are not widely available, the Austrian legal system has managed to assure a fairly quick resolution of disputes in the more recent past as well (Section 4.3).

There is no reason to believe that the efficiency in Austria in the early years was achieved at the expense of judicial quality or fairness. As the number of quashed decisions had not significantly increased in any of the Courts of Appeal

222 Baur 1970, p. 447.
223 Fasching 1988, p. 102-103.
224 Also see in this respect Oberhammer & Domej 2010.
225 Klang 1948, p. 85.
226 Klein 1900, p. 7-8.
227 Klein & Engel 1927, p. 331.
228 Klein & Engel 1927, p. 331-333.

after the introduction of the Code, Klein argued that the 1895 Code had not negatively affected the rectitude of the final decision.[229]

Empirical data on the average costs of litigation in Austria do not seem to be available. Separate statutes do specify some of the costs of litigation. For instance, the court fees are fixed by statute and the size of the fee depends on the value of the claim.[230] These court fees cover a fairly large share of the expenses of the court system.[231] Equally, a statute provides for a nonbinding system of flat rates to determine the fees of attorneys.[232]

As set out in greater detail in Chapter 7, the pursuit of truth is one of the central tenets of the Austrian procedural model. Since the enactment of the Code, the judiciary has been hesitant to actively search for the truth beyond the bare allegations of the litigants.[233] The duty of parties to speak the truth (*Wahrheitspflicht*) is rarely enforced. The provision was clearly meant to create a legal duty for both parties. Since the introduction of the Code, most have regarded it to be merely an 'ethical postulate'.[234]

Similarly, judges have often been hesitant to base their decision on facts not pleaded by the parties. If during the presentation of evidence new facts become known that were previously not raised by the parties (*Überschießende Beweisergebnisse*), the judge may, according to the Code of Civil Procedure, base her decision on these facts.[235] The judge must provide the parties an opportunity to be heard. Nevertheless it is in line with the judicial duty to establish the facts truthfully that the final judgment is based on all relevant facts known. The Austrian Supreme Court has at times also drawn this conclusion.[236] However, the Supreme Court and

229 Klein 1900, p. 12-13. The new rules restricted the availability of appeal. This may have affected the ratio of quashed decisions.

230 *GerichtsGebührenGesetz* of 27 November 1984.

231 Bundesministerium 2009, Chapter 6.1.

232 The *Rechtsanwaltstarifgesetz* provides for non-binding flat rates for the filing of the complaint, for the filing of additional pleadings or motions and for attending oral hearings etc. A party who wins the case cannot recover expenses beyond the rates set out in the aforementioned Act.

233 Also see in this respect: Kralik 1988, p. 93.

234 The Explanatory Memorandum spoke of an 'Anerkennung einer Rechtspflicht der Parteien zu wahrheitsgemäßer und erschöpfender Sachverhaltsangabe', Materialien 1897, p. 260. In literature this view is also defended, see for instance Fasching 1990, No. 654: 'Die Wahrheitspflicht ist kein bloß ethische Verpflichtung sondern eine Rechtspflicht', Fucik in Rechberger 2000, §178 and Kralik 1988, p. 191-192: '... ist die Wahrheitspflicht der Parteien, nicht erst bei ihrer Vernehmung im Beweisverfahren, sondern schon bei ihrem Vorbringen. Die Erfüllung dieser Pflicht ist freilich in der Praxis eher ein ethisches Postulat geblieben'.

235 Section 272 Code of Civil Procedure, see Rechberger in Fasching & Konecny 2002-2005, §266, No. 78.

236 Austrian Supreme Court, 8 September 1948, SZ 21/123, Ob 271/48. See Rechberger in Fasching & Konecny 2002-2005, §266, No. 79. That these new facts should be relevant follows from various decisions by the Austrian Supreme Court such as Supreme Court, 12 October 1960, *JBl* 1961, 123: 'Bei der Beweisaufnahme hervorgekommene Umstände sind nur dann zu berücksichtigen, wenn sie in einem entsprechenden Parteienvorbringen Deckung finden', and Supreme Court, 21 September 2006, Geschäftszahl 2Ob179/06x: 'Nach ständiger Rechtsprechung setzt die Berücksichtigung "überschießender Beweisergebnisse" bei der →

other courts have gone further at times and have held that a judge must wait for parties to explicitly plead newly found relevant facts after they have been discovered before the judge can use them.[237] Thereby the principle of party-presentation effectively prevails over the pursuit of truth. This view finds no support in the Civil Procedural Code. It could force the judge to base his decision on facts which are known to be incomplete or incorrect.[238]

Austrian courts have also been (too much) at guard to avoid fishing expeditions. Judges have frequently refused to allow the examination of evidence aimed at eliciting new facts (*Ausforschungsbeweis*).[239] Judges have thereby often denied parties possibilities to conduct a search for facts.

The examples above illustrate that judges have not always actively tried to establish the facts correctly. Another related issue is that some provisions of the Code related to fact-finding played a much less prominent role in practice than Klein had envisaged. To a large extent, it must be admitted that some theoretical discussions about the rules have had very few practical consequences. Academics and politicians have spent considerable effort in discussing principles, guidelines and theories concerning the pursuit of truth that had little or no practical significance. First, there has been quite some discussion concerning the extent to which the judge could *ex officio* order the taking of evidence against the will of both parties. Against Klein's advice, Parliament added a provision in the Austrian Code of 1895 that the judge could not *ex officio* order the production of documents and the hearing of witnesses if both parties were opposed.[240] The discussion had little practical relevance. Today, judges rarely make use of their powers to order the *ex officio* taking of evidence not suggested by the parties.[241]

Klein had stressed the importance of rules on discovery. It seems that the rules on discovery in the Code did not have a great impact in legal practice.[242] While

rechtlichen Beurteilung voraus, dass diese im Parteienvorbringen Deckung finden, sich also im Rahmen des geltend gemachten Klagsgrundes oder der erhobenen Einwendungen halten'.

237 See for instance Austrian Supreme Court 2 July 1968, 8Ob173/68, SZ 41/87: 'Wenn der Beklagte der Ansicht war, daß der Anspruch des Klägers trotz des Vorliegens dieser Umstände aus einem besonderen Gründe ausgeschlossen sei, dann hätte er diesen Grund behaupten müssen. Daß dies von Seite des Beklagten im Verfahren erster Instanz nicht geschehen ist, hat das Berufungsgericht richtig erkannt. Denn die Frage an einen Sachverständigen kann ebensowenig das Vorbringen der Partei ersetzen wie eine Parteiaussage'. A similar position is defended by Schragel in Fasching & Konecny 2002-2005, §178, No. 6.

238 Fasching 1990, No. 661 and Rechberger in Fasching & Konecny 2002-2005, §266, No. 80.

239 Kralik 1988, p. 93 and Rechberger in Fasching & Konecny 2002-2005, p. 266, No. 82.

240 Section 183(2) Code of Civil Procedure.

241 Fucik in Rechberger 2000, §183, No. 1. Fucik claims the provision is of 'geringer praktischer Bedeutung'. In a private conversation with an Austrian judge, I learned that he had only once ordered the hearing of a witness not suggested by the parties in more than 15 years.

242 Also see Rechberger 1998, p. 65: 'Die "gegenseitige Unterstützung der Prozessparteien", (...) hat schon in die Zivilprozessordnung nicht in jenem Umfang Eingang gefunden, den sich Klein ursprünglich vorstellte. Sie erweist sich in der heutigen Prozessrechtspraxis aber auch deshalb als nicht so eminent wichtiges Anliegen, weil sich die Parteien(vertreter) nur selten →

much attention has been paid to the regulations that allow a party to request the production of documents in possession of the opposing party, these detailed provisions in the Code of Civil Procedure are not frequently used.[243] Within a system in which judges actively discuss matters of fact and the availability of evidence with both parties, there is little need for party-driven discovery. If a judge thoroughly examines the parties at the first preparatory hearing and it becomes apparent that relevant documents exist, yet a party fails to suggest using the document as evidence, the judge could take additional measures. The court could inquire why the document has not been produced, order its production, or simply take the failure to produce the document into account when freely evaluating all evidence.

3.2. *The Incremental Reform of the Dutch Code of Civil Procedure*

The Dutch Code of Civil Procedure of 1838 is still in force at present, although it has been revised frequently. Van Nispen, in this respect, speaks of a 'gradual recodification' of the Code of Civil Procedure.[244] Eshuis counted 19 serious attempts to improve civil procedural rules between 1855 and 1998, of which only four have led to a change of the law.[245] Many small changes were made throughout the last two centuries and countless commissions have written reports on the civil justice system. In the 1990s, no less than nine official government reports of civil litigation were written within a single government term.[246] The broad lines of the Dutch developments since 1838 are discussed in the subsequent Sections.

3.2.1. Many Proposals, Few Changes, 1838-1959

In the second half of the 19th century, the 1838 Code of Civil Procedure was increasingly criticized. It was argued that the codes enacted in 1838 contained many flaws.[247] Nevertheless, no serious amendments to the Code of Civil Procedure were made before 1896. Complete new drafts and substantial suggestions for revision of the law had been made in 1855, 1865, 1877 and 1893. None of these projects made its way through Parliament. The minor legal changes that were enacted prior to 1896 were of little significance.[248] A.F.K. Hartogh, lawyer and Member of Parliament, initiated the first serious revision of the Code of Civil Procedure in 1896. The 1896

als völlig unkooperativ erweisen. Diese Erfahrung wird auch durch die Tatsache verifiziert, dass die ausführliche Regelung der ZPO über die Urkundenedition nur geringe praktische bedeutung besitzen'.

243 See Sections 303-309 Code of Civil Procedure. Unfortunately I have failed to find statistics on the matter. If one however searches databases on case law or literature on these provisions, one finds very few references. In private conversations with practitioners, I was told these provisions were only used sporadically.

244 See Van Nispen 1993.

245 Eshuis 1998, p. 12.

246 Van Mierlo 1998.

247 See for instance Caroli 1907, p. 3 *et seq.*

248 For all amendments to the Code prior to 1893, see Van Boneval Faure 1893, §5.

Reform introduced a new ordinary procedure applicable to almost all civil cases, limited oral elements in the proceedings and limited possibilities for appeal of interlocutory decisions.[249]

The first half of the 20th century was much like the end of the 19th century: there were plenty of proposals for law reform but few of these proposals were successful.[250] In 1901, the *Staatscommissie Feith* presented a legislative proposal to revise all provisions on evidence.[251] Government had presented the draft with minor amendments to Parliament in 1903 and 1907.[252] The drafts were never accepted. In 1911, the Dutch Association of Jurists (*Nederlandse Juristen Vereniging*) formed a committee that drafted a new Code of Civil Procedure. A year later the Liberal-Democratic Union (*VDB*), also drafted a new Code of Civil Procedure.[253] Neither of these drafts would be enacted. In 1911, the government formed a Committee to address the discontent with the existing civil procedural laws. The Committee, chaired by Gratama, was mainly composed of individuals that had helped to draft the Codes of 1911 and 1912. The Committee presented its final draft Code of Civil Procedure in 1920. The 1920 Gratama Draft met fierce opposition.[254] A last serious attempt to revise the fundamentals of the Code of Civil Procedure was the 1948 Report of a State Committee chaired by Dorhout Mees. The report provided guidelines for the reform of civil procedural law and practice.[255] The proposal met wide resistance, most particularly from the bar. It failed to initiate significant legal reform.[256] The reform proposals between 1901 and 1948 basically identified the same problems. In addition, the solutions they proposed were very similar.

Civil litigation was also at the heart of the debate amongst attorneys, judges and academia. The very influential Dutch Association of Jurists (*Nederlandse Juristen Vereniging*) frequently made the civil procedural regulations on fact-finding and evidence the subject of its annual conference. It discussed the interrogation on facts and articles in 1878, the (free) evaluation of evidence in 1879, the adversarial role of the judge in 1881 and 1891. The 1907 conference of the Association was dedicated to

249 See Jongbloed 2005 for a brief history of the Dutch procedural system in English.

250 For an overview of this period see Van Rhee 2000b. Not all legislative proposals between 1900 and the 1950s have been discussed. An unsuccessful proposal to change the ordinary mode of hearing witnesses has for instance remained undiscussed, see on this topic: Köster 1956 and Van Tuyll van Serooskerken 1956. Modest proposals for reform have not all been discussed either, e.g. the 1938 reform proposals of the Bar, see *Advocatenblad* 1938, 123-187 and Hoogenbergh 1938.

251 Feith Committee 1901, Preface, iv.

252 *Tweede Kamer* 1903-04, Bijlagen, No. 70; Feith Committee 1901 and Government Draft 1907. The legislative proposal was ultimately withdrawn in 1928.

253 See on both drafts: Trenité 1914 and the editorial of *Weekblad van het Recht*, 26 July 1912, W. 9336.

254 The Gratama Draft was praised by the Dutch Association of Jurists (*HNJV* 1924). The Dutch Bar Association was critical. Lawyers feared that their role in the proceedings would decrease, see Star Busmann 1921 and Kuyk 1923.

255 Staatscommissie Dorhout Mees 1948.

256 Most critics refuted the report on the grounds that it was 'too radical'; see *inter alia* Haardt 1949, p. 317; Veegens 1948, p. 489-490 and Schenk 1948.

a discussion of the general principles of civil litigation and the duties of the litigants to be truthful. In 1915 the duty of the parties to disclose information was discussed. The minutes of these conferences, at which the members were often asked to vote on a particular issue, provide a good overview of the central issues and prevailing opinions of judges, attorneys and scholars around 1900.

If one combines the legislative drafts, the notes of the aforementioned conferences and the many journal articles devoted to civil litigation, a clear picture emergences. There was a consensus on the causes of dissatisfaction with the procedural arrangements of the early 20th century. The system was widely believed to be outdated,[257] too adversarial,[258] too formalistic[259] and too inefficient.[260] Moreover, all suggestions to improve the system seemed to point in the same direction. The influence of Austrian ideas and Austrian solutions was considerable.[261] Explicit references to Austrian law were common. The drafts of 1901, 1911, 1912 and 1920 often contained provisions thoroughly inspired by those in the Austrian Code of 1895. Austrian ideas were discussed widely. In 1907, the Dutch Association of Jurists discussed the fundamentals of the justice system. Both main speakers at the conference, Caroli and Hartzfeld, were clearly inspired by and familiar with the Austrian Code of Civil Procedure and the Austrian doctrinal works.[262] A large majority of the members of the Association held the opinion that the judge should cooperate with the parties and intervene in the course of the proceedings.[263]

All drafts written in the early 20th century emphasized the importance of the pursuit of truth and an active judiciary.[264] Many specific measures were taken to avoid excessive formalism and to ensure that the law would not obstruct the pursuit of truth. The 1901 Feith draft enhanced the free evaluation of evidence by the court, eliminated restrictions on the admissibility of evidence and abolished other rules

257 Complaints on the outdated provisions on party interrogation were common. See Van Creveld 1940; Denijs 1936 and De Vrieze 1943.

258 Hartzfeld 1907, p. 159. Hartzfeld argued that the Dutch judges were more adversarial than English or French judges.

259 The Dutch Association of Jurists discussed the issue of free evaluation of evidence in 1879. The members of the Association were generally positive towards the free evaluation of evidence, see *HNJV* 1879, vraagpunt 2. Complaints that the procedure contained too few oral elements were also common. See Caroli 1907, p. 3 and Gratama Committee 1921a, p. 3.

260 The Dorhout Mees Report identified undue formalism, unsatisfactory processes of fact-gathering and fact-finding and the inefficiency of the litigation process as the main evils in the Dutch litigation practice: Staatscommissie Dorhout Mees 1948. For complaints on excessive delay in the procedure see Nolen 1941 and Van Deinse 1941.

261 On the influence of Austrian law see Van Rhee 2005a and Post 1907.

262 Hartzfeld 1907, p. 136-137 and Caroli 1907, p. 49.

263 *HNJV* 1907.

264 The Gratama Committee favored 1) a greater emphasis on the pursuit of truth; 2) direct communication between the parties and the judge at oral hearings; 3) wider judicial powers; 4) adjudication on the merits (i.e. not formalism); 5) an efficient allocation of judicial resources and 6) lower costs of litigation. Gratama Committee 1921a and Gratama Committee 1921b. Very explicit on the pursuit of truth: Hartzfeld 1907, p. 146 and Caroli 1907, p. 10, p. 53, p. 56.

that obstructed the pursuit of truth.[265] Other proposals explicitly used the Feith draft as a starting point for reviewing the rules of evidence.[266] Furthermore, it was increasingly argued that parties had a duty to be truthful.[267] Most legislative drafts also proposed to widen the rules on the discovery of documents as had been done in Austria.[268]

All drafts proposed enhancing the powers of the judge to see to it that information and evidence was forthcoming. Judicial powers to order *ex officio* the examination of evidence were enhanced.[269] As in Austria, the unsuccessful Dutch reform proposals empowered the court to order a personal appearance of the parties before the court. It was argued that the oral hearing at which the court could discuss the case with the parties should be at the heart of the litigation process.[270]

Often, practitioners argued that the reform proposals were 'too radical'.[271] If one retrospectively examines the Feith Draft of 1901, the Gratama Draft of 1920 and the recommendations of the Dorhout Mees Committee, their content is certainly 'modern' in the eyes of present day lawyers and judges. It is remarkable that many of the unsuccessful ideas and suggestions were ultimately implemented between 1988 and 2002. Legislative changes between 1838 and the 1950s were very few in number. Three general trends could be perceived between 1838 and the 1950s.

First, the Code was amended to specify more explicitly that the judge was empowered to hear the parties in order to ask them to clarify their statements in the written pleadings. In 1896, the *Lex Hartogh* specified that the judge could ask the parties during the oral closing pleas to clarify their allegations.[272] In 1923, Article 19a Code of Civil Procedure was newly introduced. This provision stated that the judge

265 Feith Committee 1901, Preface. The draft *inter alia* suggested abolishing the provision that determined that witness testimony was inadmissible if the claim exceeded 300 guilders, the rules on the burden of proof, the rule on the *capitula connexa*, and rules that limited or fixed the probative value of certain means of proof.

266 The 1920 Gratama Draft took the 1901 Feith Draft as a starting point. The 1948 guidelines in turn suggested to reform the provisions on evidence in accordance with the 1920 Draft. Staatscommissie Dorhout Mees 1948, Section 14, p. 148.

267 In 1915 the Dutch Association of Jurists discussed truthfulness in litigation. De Brauw, Simons and A. Levy were of the opinion that a party should not have a legal duty to speak the truth, see *HNJV* 1915, p. 46, p. 48, p. 58. Starr Busmann, Nolst Trinité, S. Gratama, Levy Sr. and P. Scholten were of the opinion that parties should be legally bound to be truthful, *HNJV* 1915, p. 10-92, p. 85, p. 158.

268 Articles 1926-1927 of the Feith Draft, see Feith Committee 1901, p. 105. Also see Article 246 of the 1920 Gratama Draft. In 1907 Caroli and Hartzfeld had also argued that the Austrian rules on the discovery of documents would be useful in the Dutch context. Caroli 1907, p. 52-53 and Hartzfeld 1907, p. 149-150.

269 See Feith Committee 1901, p. 37. The Gratama Draft empowered the court to order the parties to disclose exhibits and to request public bodies for information (Articles 133, 160 and 170 Gratama Draft).

270 See for instance Staatscommissie Dorhout Mees 1948, Section 8.

271 In three front-page contributions in 1912, the editor of an influential legal journal *Weekblad van het Recht* (1912, W. 9268, 9270, 9336), gave a critical reflection on the 1911 and 1912 Draft Codes of Civil Procedure. The editor claimed the drafts were lopsided as they focused too much on the pursuit of truth and the role of the court.

272 Former Article 144 Code of Civil Procedure.

was entitled to order the parties to attend an oral hearing and to ask the parties to clarify their statements of fact.[273] Only in the last decades of the 20th century judges did use these powers in a large scale. Second, by laws in 1923 and 1934, some of the most severe restrictions on the use of witness evidence were removed.[274] Third, in 1937, the *rolrechter*, a judge who has the broad responsibility of supervising the progress of all cases pending before (a division of) the court, was introduced. This Act affected the division of labor within the courts.[275]

Apart from minor legislative changes, there were also minor changes in the interpretation and application of the law. In 1921 for example, the Court of Cassation rendered an important decision that slightly widened the possibilities of discovering documents. The Court broadened its interpretation of the phrase 'common to both parties' in Article 1923 of the Civil Code. The decision implied that a contract signed by both parties was generally discoverable.[276] More significant was a gradual development in the case law of the Court of Cassation from 1900 onwards that required the parties to substantiate the allegations in the written pleadings (see Section 2.4).[277] This gradual change would have a great impact on legal practice, as it required the parties to disclose more information and empowered the court to draw adverse inferences if parties failed to do so.

3.2.2. The Incremental Reform of Dutch Civil Procedure

Since the 1950s, numerous attempts have been made to adjust and improve the fact-finding arrangements in civil cases. Often, these changes were part of a broader legislative scheme aimed at improving the court organization and judicial procedures in criminal, civil and administrative matters. The most significant changes since 1959 with regard to the process of fact-gathering and fact-finding are discussed below.

273 Act of 5 May 1923, *Official State Journal* (Stb.), 189.

274 Act of 22 June 1923, *Official State Journal* (Stb.), 280 (Article 1933 was repealed and the possibility to challenge witnesses was abolished); Act of 16 May 1934, *Official State Journal* (Stb.), 253 (The possibilities for relatives of parties to testify was widened) and Act of 2 July 1934, *Official State Journal* (Stb.), 347 (Articles 1934, 1935 and 1940 were repealed and the distinction between commercial and non-commercial cases was removed).

275 Act of 9 December 1937, *Official State Journal* (Stb.), 208.

276 Court of Cassation, 20 May 1921, W. 10776, *NJ* 1921, 788 and Court of Appeal 's Gravenhage, 7 January 1921, W. 10689. The presiding judge of the Court of Cassation was S. Gratama.

277 Court of Cassation, 13 November 1914, *NJ* 1915, 107 and Court of Cassation, 18 December 1925, *NJ* 1926, 228.

The Civil Evidence Act of 1988

Discontent with the law on evidence was widespread. In particular there was dissatisfaction with 1) the adversarial role of the court; 2) the rule on the burden of proof; 3) limits to the admissibility of evidence and 4) the limitations on the free evaluation of evidence. Most commentators and practitioners agreed that all unsuccessful attempts to improve the system of civil evidence in the first half of the 20th century had provided good solutions, yet had been too radical.[278]

In 1947, E.M. Meijers was asked to review the 1838 Civil Code. There was consensus in literature and amongst practitioners that it would be advisable to transfer the law on evidence from the Civil Code to the Code of Civil Procedure, as was the case in Germany and Austria. As the new Civil Code would not contain provisions on evidence, the Minister of Justice appointed a State Committee to redraft the rules of evidence such that these could all be transferred to the Code of Civil Procedure. The State Committee presented its draft in 1959.[279] The draft was well received by academics and practitioners.[280] Nonetheless, it would take another 10 years until the 1959 draft was, with slight modifications, presented to Parliament. It was widely discussed and generally received well.[281] An Advisory Committee that represented the judiciary and the bar commented the proposal. This Committee was generally positive, but proposed abolishing the rule that unqualified the parties to testify as witnesses.[282] This suggestion initiated a fierce debate that delayed the swift enactment of the legislative proposal. The Civil Evidence Act eventually entered into force on the 1st of April 1988. Since that date, the rules of evidence have been subject to only a few minor amendments.[283]

278 See Haardt 1951, p. 108. In 1924 and 1951, the Dutch Association of Jurists had discussed the law on civil evidence. A question addressed in 1924 and 1951 was: 'Should there be a general provision in the law of evidence on the burden of proof?', *HNJV* 1924, p. 153, Question 1 and *HNJV* 1951, p. 79, Question 3. Contrary to the recommendations of the Dorhout Mees Committee and the Gratama Draft, a majority of the members, both in 1924 and 1951, voted 'yes'. Similarly, a majority of the members in 1951 believed, contrary to the Dorhout Mees recommendations, that an admission of fact and documents made to serve as proof of a transaction *(akten)* should provide *prima facie* evidence *(beslissende bewijskracht) HNJV* 1951, Questions 5 and 7.

279 Staatscommissie voor de Nederlandse Burgerlijke Wetgeving, 'Bewijsrecht: Ontwerp van Wet met Memorie van Toelichting', s'Gravenhage, 1959, Staatsdrukkerij en uitgeverijbedrijf. Also see Stein 1970 and Van Creveld 1959.

280 Haardt claimed it provided a 'salutary' set of rules and qualified the draft as 'modern', yet without 'excessive experimental provisions'. Haardt 1959, p. 502. Beekhuis praised the draft as a 'realistic draft' that proposed only those changes that were generally believed to be necessary and salutary. Beekhuis 1960, p. 575. A Committee of lawyers, appointed by the Dutch Bar Association to comment on the draft, was in general very pleased with the draft. See Dirkzwager 1960.

281 See e.g. Beekhuis 1970 and Stein 1970.

282 *Commissie van advies, ingesteld door de Nederlandse Vereniging voor de Rechtspraak en de Nederlandse Orde van Advocaten, Rapport aangaande het Ontwerp van Wet houdende nieuwe regeling van het bewijsrecht in burgerlijke zaken,* published as an Appendix to *Advocatenblad,* 15 June 1970, p. 5-6. Also see Section 6.1.3.

283 The text of the 1988 Civil Evidence Act has been translated into English, see Hebly 1992.

The Contents of the Civil Evidence Act[284]

The Civil Evidence Act changed both the form and the structure of the law. Some of the most archaic elements of the old codifications, such as the provisions on the decisory oath, the *capitula connexa*, tally sticks and the interrogation on facts and articles, were abolished.[285] The number of provisions was significantly reduced: the 71 Articles in the Civil Code and 81 Articles in the Code of Civil Procedure would eventually be replaced by less than 60 new provisions on evidence. The new provisions on evidence were systematically structured; a number of general provisions on evidence preceded the rules on specific means of proof and rules on the (provisional) examination of evidence prior to the commencement of the action.

The Civil Evidence Act applied to all civil cases, but made a distinction between issues parties could freely dispose of and issues parties could not freely dispose of.[286] In most tort and contract cases, parties may freely dispose of matters of fact. In these cases the judge must respect contractual agreements between the parties on matters of evidence and the court may not request evidence for undisputed issues. In other cases, such as family law cases, the parties may not freely stipulate on the factual issues and the outcome of the procedure. In such cases the judge may order evidence for undisputed facts and is not bound by the agreements between the parties.[287] A good example of a contractual agreement that would generally bind the court is a mediation agreement in which quarrelling neighbors agree that the mediation sessions remain confidential. If the mediation is unsuccessful, and litigation follows the judge will have to respect the confidentiality agreement.

The 1988 Civil Evidence Act explicitly preserved the adversarial system. In issues the parties can freely dispose of, the Code continued to hold that an admission of fact binds the court. In addition, Article 149(1) of the Code clarifies that the judge should not search for facts beyond those alleged by the parties:

> 'Article 149 (1) Unless the law specifies differently, the judge may only base his decision on facts or rights that have become known to the judge in the course of the proceeding or have been alleged (by the parties) and that have been established in accordance with this Section of the Code. Facts or rights that have been alleged by one party and have not been denied or not been adequately denied by the other party, shall be held to be true by the court, save for the powers of the court to order the production

284 See for an overview Gras & Wiersema 1986 and Stein 1988.

285 See Chapter 6. The *Capitula Connexa* (*onsplitsbare bekentenis*) was codified in former Article 1961 of the Civil Code. A 'kerfstok' (split tally stick) is a wooden stick that would be split into two parts. Carvings were made when both parts were kept together. Each party would keep one of the parts. Whenever a shopkeeper, for example, provided a customer with a product bought on credit, the customer and the shopkeeper would both bring their part of the stick and both parts of the wooden stick could be held together such that one or more carvings could be made. The number of carvings indicated the quantity sold on credit. As wood carvings were unique and both parties had a stick with 'matching' carvings, the sticks were a reliable means of proof.

286 See *HNJV* 1951, p. 79-81, Questions 1 and 10.

287 Articles 176, 180 and 182 of the 1988 Code of Civil Procedure. See current Articles 149, 153 Code of Civil Procedure (*Bewijsovereenkomst*).

of evidence in cases in which the parties cannot freely dispose of the subject matter of the case'.[288]

Prior to the introduction of the Civil Evidence Act, there was much discussion as to whether the Code of Civil Procedure should contain a provision regulating the burden of proof.[289] Article 1902 of the 1838 Dutch Civil Code was considered unsatisfactory as it lacked clarity. The approach of the Austrian Code of Civil Procedure, which simply did not contain any rule on the burden of proof, was also rejected.[290] After initial drafts had been amended, a compromise was found that was similar to German law.[291] This implied that substantive law would play a pivotal role in determining which party had the burden of proof.[292] The provision that was eventually enacted in 1988 read as follows: 'A party that wishes to obtain a certain legal result based on specific facts or rights has the burden to prove these facts or rights, unless there is either a specific legal rule or a requirement of reasonableness and fairness that gives reason to allocate the burden of proof differently'.[293]

The Civil Evidence Act abolished restrictions on the admissibility of evidence. Most significant was that rules that banned parties and their close family from testifying were not retained in the new rules (see Chapter 6.1.3). Therefore the Dutch Code, like the Austrian Code of 1895, virtually abolished all restrictions on the admissibility of relevant evidence. The Civil Evidence Act specified that 'the evaluation of evidence is left to the decision of the judge, unless the law determines

288 This provision was Article 176(1) of the 1988 Code of Civil Procedure. 'Tenzij uit de wet anders voortvloeit, mag de rechter slechts die feiten of rechten aan zijn beslissing ten grondslag leggen, die in geding aan hem ter kennis zijn gekomen of zijn gesteld en die overeenkomstig de voorschriften van deze afdeling zijn komen vast te staan. Feiten of rechten die door ene partij zijn gesteld en door wederpartij niet of niet voldoende zijn betwist, moet de rechter als vaststaand beschouwen, behoudens zijn bevoegdheid bewijs te verlangen, zo vaak aanvaarding van stellingen zou leiden tot een rechtsgevolg dat niet ter vrije bepaling van partijen staat'. See Court of Cassation, 20 November 2009, *LJN* BJ8340 for a recent example of a case in which the Court of Cassation quashed a decision because a lower court had wrongfully determined that an undisputed fact was not true.

289 A distinction is commonly made between the burden of persuasion and the burden of production. This coincides with the German distinction between the 'objective Beweislast' on the one hand and the 'subjektive Beweislast' or 'Behauptungslast' on the other hand. The former addresses the question 'Who will loose the case if the judge remains undecided? (i.e. *non liquet*) the latter terms address the question 'Who should (first) present evidence?' This terminology was introduced in German literature by Wehli 1896. Also see Klicka 1995, p. 12-17.

290 The Austrian Code of Civil Procedure contains no general rule on the burden of proof. Case law 'filled the gap' and has introduced rules similar to the Dutch provision enacted in 1988. See Fasching 1990, Nos. 878-892.

291 Article 177 of the 1959 Draft proposed a halfway solution between strict rules (i.e. rules of substantive law) and wide judicial discretion. See Stein 1970, p. 337 and Beekhuis 1960, p. 580.

292 The government stressed that it adhered to the 'objectiefrechtelijke theorie'. See Hidma & Rutgers 2004, No. 25, p. 45. Compare Rosenberg, Schwab & Gottwald 2004, §114.

293 Article 177 of the 1988 Code of Civil Procedure, current Article 150 Code of Civil Procedure. 'De partij die zich beroept op de rechtsgevolgen van door haar gestelde feiten of rechten, draagt de bewijslast van die feiten of rechten, tenzij uit enige bijzondere regel of uit de eisen van redelijkheid en billijkheid een andere verdeling van de bewijslast voortvloeit'.

otherwise'.[294] Many restrictions on the free evaluation of evidence that had existed before, such as the *unus testis nullus testis* rule, were abolished. The Civil Evidence Act nevertheless continued to recognize a few important exceptions to the free evaluation of evidence. Most notable is that certain documents, such as most contracts signed by both parties,[295] provide *prima facie* evidence.[296] The Civil Evidence Act even added a new restriction to the free evaluation of evidence: Article 188 Code of Civil Procedure specified that final and conclusive judgment on matters of fact in a defended criminal action in a Dutch court provided *prima facie* evidence of that fact. Another notable exception to the free evaluation of evidence is that if a party has been examined as a witness, his or her testimony cannot serve to provide full evidence for the allegations that party is required to prove, unless the examination serves to supplement other incomplete evidence.[297]

The 1988 Civil Evidence Act widened the possibilities for the provisional examination of evidence prior to the commencement of the action.[298] The Act widened the existing possibilities for hearing witnesses before the initiation of the action. The Act also introduced provisions that enabled investigations by a court appointed expert and a local visit to a scene of the dispute prior to the commencement of the proceedings.

The 2002 Reform Act: Legislative History and Objectives

The 2002 Reform Act was one of the most influential reforms of the Code of Civil Procedure. As part of a larger legislative attempt, that also aimed to reform the judicial organization and to improve the administration of justice in administrative cases, plans were launched in the 1990s to amend the Code of Civil Procedure.[299] In 1996 a proposal to review the whole judicial structure was submitted to Parliament.[300] The proposal aimed to merge the County Courts *(kantongerechten)* and District Courts (*(arrondissements)rechtbanken*) such that there would be only a single court of first instance. This proposal was unsuccessful and repealed in 1998. However, many civil procedural elements of the proposal were received positively. Separate legislative proposals were subsequently presented to Parliament. On the 1st of January 2002, laws that affected both the judicial organization and the

294 Article 179(2) of the 1988 Code of Civil Procedure, current Article 152(2) Code of Civil Procedure. 'De waardering van het bewijs is aan het oordeel van de rechter overgelaten tenzij de wet anders bepaalt'.

295 Articles 183-188 of the 1988 Code of Civil Procedure, current Articles 156-161 Code of Civil Procedure.

296 Article 178 of the 1988 Code of Civil Procedure, current Article 151 Code of Civil Procedure, reads as follows: '1) *Prima facie* evidence (*dwingend bewijs*) implies that the judge is bound to consider the contents of evidence to be true or to give the evidence the weight prescribed by law. 2) Rebuttal is admissible, also against *prima facie* evidence, unless the law prescribes that rebuttal is not admissible'.

297 Article 213 of the 1988 Code of Civil Procedure, current Article 164 Code of Civil Procedure.

298 Articles 202-207 Code of Civil Procedure and Section 6.1.3.

299 For English literature on the Reform, see Jongbloed 2005, Section 5. Jongbloed discusses some of the influential reports preceding legislative change, such as the findings of the *Leemhuis Committee*.

300 *Kamerstukken II* 1995-1996, 24 651.

proceedings at first instance entered into force.[301] The 2002 Reform Act, or rather Reform Acts, changed both the structure and the numbering of the Articles of the Code of Civil Procedure.

It must be noted that the 2002 Reform Act formed a part of a major overhaul of the system of civil justice between 1996 and 2003.[302] Other changes include: 1) the introduction of uniform court rules *(landelijk rolreglement)* that supplement the Code of Civil Procedure;[303] 2) the attempt to deal with delay by the temporary creation of a 'court' that wrote judgments on behalf of District Courts that had significant backlogs (*Vliegende Brigade*); 3) changes on the jurisdiction of the County Courts;[304] 4) the introduction of a new mechanism to finance the courts on the basis of the number of cases resolved rather than on the basis of the number of incoming cases and 5) a significant increase in the staff and budget of the District Courts.[305]

The 2002 Reform Act aimed to revise the proceedings before the courts of first instance.[306] According to the Explanatory Memorandum, the reform aimed for simplification of the procedural laws, a decrease in the number of unnecessary procedural formalities, a 'modernized' relationship between the judge and the parties, greater efficiency and the harmonization of the different civil, administrative and criminal court procedures.[307] For present purposes, the third and fourth points are most significant.

The Explanatory Memorandum to the Reform Act noted that the importance of the adversarial principle had diminished.[308] The Act further increased the judge's powers to manage the process of fact-gathering.[309] Primarily however, the Act aimed to adjust the role of the parties. The Explanatory Memorandum stressed the importance of increasing the duties of parties to disclose information.

> 'Parties are, briefly put, not free to remain silent with respect to facts relevant for the opposing party in the proceedings. If a party nevertheless does so, the case can be reopened and the judgment can be annulled (Court of Cassation, 4 October 1996, *NJ* 1998, 45). By increasing the duties of parties to disclose information and thereby

301 *Legislative Documents* 27181, 27182, 26855, 27748 and 27824. See Van Mierlo & Bart 2002.

302 Eshuis 2007. Eshuis describes each of these changes and their effects on the duration of litigation.

303 These uniform court rules replaced the local court rules that previously existed in each of the District Courts.

304 Before 1999 the County Courts were competent to hear most cases of which the value did not exceed 5.000,- guilders, in 1999 and 2002 this amount was raised to 10.000 guilders and 5.000,- Euro.

305 Between 1995 and 2004 there has been an increase in the staff of the District Courts by 50%. The court budget almost doubled in the same period of time. Civil litigation did cost the taxpayer 10 Euro per capita in 1995 and 19 Euro per capita in 2004. Van Erp 2006, Chapter 5.

306 See in general, Salomons 2002; Wieten 2002 and Jongbloed 2002.

307 Van Mierlo & Bart 2002, p. 4-9. *Kamerstukken II* 1999-2000, 26 855, No. 3.

308 Van Mierlo & Bart 2002, p. 5. See in general on the 'demise' of the strict adversarial model before 2002: Bosch-Boesjes 1991.

309 Dammingh 2009, p. 12-15.

> reducing the autonomy of the parties, one can prevent that the judge will intervene actively to gather facts and thereby loose his passive and adversarial stance'.[310]

In order to increase procedural efficiency, judges and lawyers were required to cooperate to assure swift and cheap proceedings. The Explanatory Memorandum stressed the need for an early exchange of information. The personal appearance of the parties, a preparatory hearing that would be scheduled after the defendant had filed his answer, was considered the most important vehicle to reduce costs and delay (see Sections 2.4 and 4.3).[311] Before 2002, it was common for attorneys to be very brief in their first pleading and only provide the full factual details in their last written pleading.[312] The 2002 Reform Act restructured the ordinary course of litigation such that parties would be 'forced' to put their cards face up on the table in the beginning of the proceedings. Since 2002, parties file a single pleading only before the case is orally discussed during a personal appearance of the parties.

The 2002 Reform Act : Specific Articles

As was common in many modern Codes of Civil Procedure, such as the New French Code of Civil Procedure of 1975, the revised Dutch Code of Civil Procedure contains provisions outlining the Code's guiding principles (Articles 19-35).[313] These provisions codified the right to be heard (Article 19), the duty of judge and the parties to avoid undue delay (Article 20), the principle *ius curia novit* (Article 25) and the principle that the proceedings take place in open court and are accessible to the public (Articles 27-28). Most relevant for the process of fact-finding are Articles 21, 22 and 24 of the Code.

As indicated above, the 1838 Code contained no general duty for the parties to be truthful and disclose relevant information. Throughout the second half of the 20th century, most commentators concluded that parties had a legal duty to be truthful.[314] Star Busmann, for instance, argued that a general duty to be truthful could be derived from existing duties to produce documents (former Articles 8, 11 Commercial Code and former Articles 1638e, 1923 Civil Code) and the rules that enabled cases to be reopened in case of deceit (*herroeping*, Article 382 Code of Civil Procedure).[315] The newly introduced Article 21 Code of Civil Procedure, modeled after Section 178 Austrian Code of Civil Procedure, codified the duty to be

310 Van Mierlo & Bart 2002, p. 6: 'Zo staat het een partij niet vrij om, kort gezegd, in een procedure voor de wederpartij gunstige feiten te verzwijgen. Doet zij dat toch, dan kan het vonnis vernietigd worden in een requeste-civiel procedure (HR 4 oktober 1996, *NJ* 1998, 45). Met een aanscherping van processuele mededelingsplichten - en daarmee een beperking van de autonomie van partijen -, kan juist voorkomen worden dat de rechter zich in het proces van feiten- en waarheidsvinding (nog) actiever (en minder lijdelijk) moet gaan gedragen'.

311 Van Mierlo & Bart 2002, p. 7.

312 This observation was made by a number of government committees. See Eshuis 2007, p. 73.

313 On the role of the general principles in French law, see Cadiet 2005, Section 4.1.1.

314 Van der Wiel 2004, Nos. 23-24, p. 24-26. Van der Wiel refers to a large number of doctrinal works of legal scholars that held that a duty to be truthful existed before 2002.

315 Star Busmann 1955, No. 208.

truthful.[316] The provision reads: 'The parties have a duty to present a complete and truthful account of all relevant facts. If a party does not comply with this duty, the judge may draw the conclusions he deems fit'.

Article 22 Code of Civil Procedure specified that the judge could request the parties to provide relevant information or documents. Judges may, for instance, give case-specific instructions prior to the personal appearance. Such instructions could include ordering a party to produce a document prior to a hearing.[317] Article 22 reads:

> 'The judge may in all situations, during any stage of the proceedings, order both or one of the parties to clarify statements of fact or to hand over specified and case related documents. Parties may refuse to comply with these orders in case of weighty reasons. The judge will decide whether or not the refusal is justified. If the refusal is not justified, the judge may draw the conclusions he deems fit'.[318]

The introduction of Article 22 of the Code marked an endpoint in a long process of increasing judicial control over the process of fact gathering. Previously, judges were only allowed to ask the parties to clarify their factual allegations. Judicial powers to order the production of documents had long been limited by the *nemo tenetur edere contra se* principle. Since the enactment of the Code in 1838, judicial powers to order the production of documents were mainly restricted to the 'account books of merchants' (*koopmansboeken*).[319] In 1989, the judicial powers at a personal appearance of the parties had been widened, as the judge could order parties to produce specific, case-related documents.[320] In 1991, County Court judges (*kantonrechter*) were empowered to order the production of documents during any stage of the proceedings.[321]

Article 24 Code of Civil Procedure codified the principle of party autonomy (*partij autonomie*). The provision preserves the general division of tasks between the court and the parties: the parties alone gather and allege matters of fact. As

316 Kremer 2003 and Klaassen 2002.

317 As regulated by Article 89 Code of Civil Procedure and Article 2.12. Landelijk Rolreglement (Uniform Court Rules). For empirical data that illustrate that judges sometimes, but not too frequently, order the production of documents prior to a court hearing. See Van der Linden 2008, Section 3.1 and Eshuis 2007, p. 110-112, Table 3, Figure 19. These data illustrate that the differences between courts regarding case specific instructions are large.

318 'De rechter kan in alle gevallen en in elke stand van de procedure partijen of één van hen bevelen bepaalde stellingen toe te lichten of bepaalde, op de zaak betrekking hebbende bescheiden over te leggen. Partijen kunnen dit weigeren indien daarvoor gewichtige redenen zijn. De rechter beslist of de weigering gerechtvaardigd is, bij gebreke waarvan hij daaruit de gevolgtrekking kan maken die hij geraden acht'.

319 Former Articles 12, 13 Commercial Code. See Van Boneval Faure 1896, §113. In 1922, the provisions were transferred to Article 8 Commercial Code. In 2002 the provision was moved to Article 162 Code of Civil Procedure. There were also possibilities to request the production of specific documents such as public records and data contained in the municipal Registry of births, deaths and marriages. Articles 833-843 of the 1838 Code of Civil Procedure.

320 *Official State Journal* (Stb.), 1989, No. 483, which altered Article 19a Code of Civil Procedure.

321 Former Article 110 Code of Civil Procedure, *Official State Journal* (Stb.), 1991, No. 50.

specified above in Article 22, the judge may demand that parties clarify their contentions of fact or hand over documents. Article 24 states: 'The judge investigates and decides the case on the basis of the issues parties have based their claim, request or defense on, unless the law specifies otherwise'.[322]

More specific provisions in the Code of Civil Procedure related to fact-finding generally had to be interpreted in the light of more general provisions such as Articles 21, 22 and 24 of the Code. The 2002 Reform Act introduced many specific changes; those relevant to the fact-finding process will be discussed below.[323]

The 2002 Reform Act introduced a couple of interrelated rules that changed the ordinary course of litigation. First, a single document (*dagvaarding*) replaced the writ (*dagvaarding*) and the complaint (*conclusie van eis*), two separate procedural documents that generally had identical content prior to 2002. Second, parties are required to supply each other and the court with more information in their first pleadings than before.[324] As had long been the case in Austria, the plaintiff in his complaint and the defendant in his answer are required to identify the evidence they could allege in support their statements of fact (*bewijsaandraagplicht*, Articles 111(3) and 128(5) Code of Civil Procedure). Article 111(3) of the Code also requires the plaintiff to specify the objections to the claim raised by the defendant prior to the action and the grounds thereof.[325] The latter rule aims to assist the court in quickly identifying the nature of the dispute. Third, pursuant to a fairly successful 'speedy process experiment' in a number of District Courts, the 2002 Reform Act emphasized the personal appearance of the parties before the court.[326] Since 2002 the judge should schedule a hearing after the defendant files an answer, unless there are reasons not to do so (Article 131 Code of Civil Procedure, Chapter 6). Fourth, the use of written pleadings and oral closing pleas was restricted. Before 2002, the parties had a right to exchange a second set of pleadings and present an oral closing plea.[327] Article 132(2) of the Code specified that if a personal appearance of the parties had been ordered, parties were only entitled to file a reply and a rebuttal if the court believed such was salutary or necessary. Similarly, the court may determine that counsel will not be given an opportunity to give an oral closing plea if a personal appearance of the parties was held earlier in the proceedings. In the absence of a personal appearance, parties do have a right to oral closing pleas.[328]

The aforementioned changes increased the importance of the personal appearance of the parties: prior to 2002 this hearing was an 'intermezzo' between

322 'De rechter onderzoekt en beslist de zaak op de grondslag van hetgeen partijen aan hun vordering, verzoek of verweer ten gronde hebben gelegd, tenzij uit de wet anders voortvloeit'. If new facts are discovered during litigation, the judge may generally give parties an opportunity to allege additional facts. For recent case law on this provision see Court of Cassation, 14 March 2008, *LJN* BC1231 and Court of Cassation, 11 December 2009, *LJN* BJ7329. Also see Klaassen 2009, p. 64.

323 Also see Asser 2002.

324 Van Mierlo & Bart 2002, p. 276.

325 On the degree in which parties actually comply with this requirement, see Novakovski 2006.

326 *Versneld regime experiment*, see Eshuis 2007, Section 3.2 and Verschoof 2004.

327 Van Mierlo & Bart 2002, p. 4. Article 132 Code of Civil Procedure.

328 Article 134 Code of Civil Procedure.

the first two and the last two written pleadings. Now the personal appearance is in many cases the last stage before the judge renders a(n) (interim) judgment. As noted before, these changes in the ordinary structure of litigation aimed to create an incentive for the parties to exchange as much information as possible at an early stage in the proceeding.

The 2002 reform made some modest changes to the rules on (the gathering of) evidence that had been introduced by the 1988 Civil Evidence Act. Firstly, the Reform Act slightly widened the provision on party-driven document discovery (Article 843a Code of Civil Procedure).[329] Since 2002 this provision reads as follows:

> '1) Anyone who has a lawful interest therein may, at his own expense, demand inspection, a copy of, or an extract from, a properly identified document regarding a legal relationship to which he or his legal predecessors are a party, from the person who has such a document at his disposal or in his custody. Documents encompass information stored on any device designed to contain information. 2) The court shall, if necessary, decide on the way in which inspection is to be arranged, or copies or extracts are to be produced. 3) Those who have a duty to treat information with confidentiality because of their profession, are not bound to fulfill the demand of paragraph 1 if the document in question is held solely for these professional purposes. 4) The person who has a document at his disposal or in his custody is not bound to fulfill the demand of paragraph 1 if there are weighty reasons not to do so, neither is that person obliged to fulfill the demand if it can reasonably be expected that justice can properly be done without inspection of the documents'.[330]

The Dutch provision on document discovery has been widened substantially since the enactment of the 1838 Civil Code, but is fairly restrictive when compared to Anglo-American rules on document discovery. Unlike Anglo-American rules, the rules require leave of the court and demand that documents be sufficiently identified. The Explanatory Memorandum to the 2002 Reform Act specified that the latter requirement was aimed at preventing so-called 'fishing expeditions'.[331] A request for discovery of documents should sufficiently clarify what specific

329 For a more in depth discussion on the increased possibilities for the disclosure of documents in the Netherlands, see Ekelmans 2007 and Sijmonsma 2007.

330 '1) Hij die daarbij rechtmatig belang heeft, kan op zijn kosten inzage, afschrift of uittreksel vorderen van bepaalde bescheiden aangaande een rechtsbetrekking waarin hij of zijn voorgangers partij zijn, van degene die deze bescheiden te zijner beschikking of onder zijn berusting heeft. Onder bescheiden worden mede verstaan: op een gegevensdrager aangebrachte gegevens. 2) De rechter bepaald zo nodig de wijze waarop inzage, afschrift of uittreksel zal worden verschaft. 3) Hij die uit hoofde van zijn ambt, beroep of betrekking tot geheimhouding verplicht is, is niet gehouden aan deze vordering te voldoen, indien de bescheiden uitsluitend uit dien hoofde te zijner beschikking staan of onder zijn berusting zijn. 4) Degene die de bescheiden te zijner beschikking of onder zijn berusting heeft is niet gehouden aan deze vordering te voldoen, indien daarvoor gewichtige redenen zijn, alsmede wanneer redelijkerwijs aangenomen kan worden dat een behoorlijke rechtsbedeling ook zonder verschaffing van de gevraagde gegevens is gewaarborgd'.

331 See Van Mierlo & Bart 2002, p. 552. Case law also refutes fishing expeditions. See for example District Court of Amsterdam, 5 October 2006, *LJN* AZ0951 and the opinion of J. Spier in Court of Cassation 22 February 2008, *LJN* BB5626.

documents are to be disclosed.[332] A party cannot request the judge to order the disclosure of a document if one merely suspects that a document could possibly exist.[333] Neither will the court grant a request for the production of 'all documents in the administration of a corporation related to the contractual agreement'.[334] A third restriction on the discovery of documents is that only documents 'with respect to a legal relationship in which the person that requests the document is a party' are discoverable. This restriction, a remnant of the old rule that only documents that were 'common' to both parties were discoverable, is presently applied with leniency by the (lower) courts.[335] The Explanatory Memorandum indicates that in tort cases there is a 'legal relationship' between the parties.[336] Nevertheless, case law of the Court of Cassation before 2002 illustrates that the requirement may be very restrictive.[337]

In the recent years, since the 2002 Reform Act, it has become possible to obtain provisional measures to preserve (documentary) evidence.[338] Gradually, courts have granted requests for the attachment documents held by the opponent party or third parties, even without the other party having been heard (*bewijsbeslag*).[339]

The 2002 Reform Act also led to a number of minor changes to the rules of evidence.[340] These completed a silent and virtually unnoticed development in Dutch law towards the gradual adoption of the principle of immediacy.[341] Article 155 Code of Civil Procedure, introduced by the Reform Act, specifies that the judge who was

332 See e.g. District Court Zwolle, 8 February 2005, *LJN* AS9413.

333 See e.g. District Court 's-Gravenhage, 27 July 2005, *LJN* AU5178 and District Court of Middelburg, 5 April 2006, *LJN* AZ0931.

334 See e.g. District Court of Breda, 2 February 2004, *JOR* 2004, 90.

335 Sijmonsma 2007, p. 44.

336 Van Mierlo & Bart 2002, p. 554.

337 Court of Cassation, 18 February 2000, *NJ* 2001, 259. News International claimed that Clinger had committed fraud and had taken money. News International had reason to believe that money disappeared into a bank account of a certain bank. News International requested that the bank be compelled to produce bank statements (of Clinger's account) on the basis of Article 843a Code of Civil Procedure. The District Court refused to allow such disclosure as these bank statements could not be qualified as documents regarding 'a legal relationship between News International and the Bank'. The Court of Cassation upheld the decision. Similarly, a debtor who claims not to posses any money cannot be forced by the creditor to produce a stack of paperwork to 'prove' that he indeed does not have any money. Court of Cassation, 20 September 1990, *NJ* 1992, 552. For additional examples, see Ekelmans 2005, p. 60. It has been argued that the provision should be interpreted less restrictive today. See Ekelmans 2005 and Ekelmans 2007, p. 12-23.

338 Before 2002 judges did not allow for the attachments of documents in order to preserve these. Dutch law had no equivalent to the English Pillar orders. Nevertheless it was argued that a legal basis for the attachment of documents exited. See Barendrecht & Van Den Reek 1994.

339 See in this respect Article 7 of Directive 2004/48/EC of the European Parliament and the Council of 29 April 2004, on the enforcement of intellectual property rights; Articles 1019a-1019c Dutch Code of Civil Procedure; Wesseling-van Gent 2006, p. 107-109; Ekelmans 2007, p. 56-61 and Linssen 2009.

340 See Asser 2002 for a concise overview.

341 Immediacy is in Dutch legal literature, other than in German literature, not mentioned as a 'principle of civil procedure'. One searches in vain in the index of textbooks on civil procedure for the word 'onmiddelijkheid'.

present during the presentation of evidence shall, to the extent it is possible, also render the court's decision. The 1838 Code of Civil Procedure had not codified the principle of immediacy, but before 2002 a more limited provision had held that the judge present at the examination of witnesses was (save exceptions) required to render the final decision.[342]

Recent Developments and the Fundamentals of the Justice System

Academics, as well as members of Parliament had argued that there was a need for a fundamental review of the entire civil justice system.[343] In 2001, the Government appointed a Committee composed of the proceduralists Asser, Groen and Vranken. The Committee published its interim report in 2003, a note on the progress of the project in 2004, and its final report in 2006.[344] These reports covered a broad number of topics, including alternative forms of dispute resolution and appellate procedure.

The authors stress in both reports that parties and the judge should cooperate and have a joint responsibility for the proceeding.[345] Such a joint responsibility is based on the general principle that parties should take into account the valid interests of others. Asser, Groen and Vranken conclude that parties have a duty to cooperate in the process of fact-gathering.[346] This also implies that parties have a duty to disclose the information and evidence they have available. Parties should, according to the committee, 'put their cards face up on the table'.[347] The duty of parties to provide information goes beyond the duty to support and provide evidence for their own statements.[348] On the basis of these general principles, the authors propose to make the discovery of documents more widely available.[349] The authors propose to introduce discovery rules like those in the English legal system.[350]

342 Former Article 203 Code of Civil Procedure (before 1988) and former Article 212 of the Code of Civil Procedure (after 1988).

343 Asser & Vranken 1999 and Van Mierlo & Bart 2002, p. 30-35. p. 30. 'In de literatuur wordt juist de laatste tijd steeds nadrukkelijker gepleit voor een fundamentele herbezinning op het procesrecht'. For a discussion in English see Van Rhee 2008b.

344 Asser, Groen, Vranken & Tzankova 2003; *Handelingen Tweede Kamer* 27 October 2004, No. 14, p. 848. Asser, Groen, Vranken & Tzankova 2006, p. 203-212.

345 Asser, Groen, Vranken & Tzankova 2006, Chapter 5.

346 Asser, Groen, Vranken & Tzankova 2006, p. 48-49: 'De grondslag van deze gezamenlijke verantwoordelijkheid van de procesdeelnemers is gelegen in de algemene maatschappelijke norm dat men over en weer rekening houdt met elkaars gerechtvaardigde belangen. Wederzijdse informatie en communicatie ten aanzien van de feiten en de juridische standpunten is de daaruit voortvloeiende gedragsnorm voor partijen en rechter'.

347 Asser, Groen, Vranken & Tzankova 2003, p. 80: 'De medewerkingsverplichting van partijen brengt in concreto voor hen een verplichting tot opening van zaken mee. Het principe van de kaarten op tafel, (...) heeft ook bij ons als leidend beginsel te gelden. De verplichting tot openheid hebben partijen ook ten opzichte van elkaar'. Also see Asser, Groen, Vranken & Tzankova 2006, p. 46.

348 Asser, Groen, Vranken & Tzankova 2006, p. 73: '(...) dat partijen informatieplichten jegens elkaar hebben die verder gaan dan het onderbouwen en bewijzen van de eigen stellingen'.

349 Asser, Groen, Vranken & Tzankova 2006, Section 6.5.3.2.

350 Asser, Groen, Vranken & Tzankova 2006, p. 74.

Another tenet of the proposals of Asser, Groen and Vranken is that they emphasize the role of the court. They argue that a judge should not remain passive during the process of fact-finding. The authors clearly refute a sporting theory of justice and argue that the autonomy of parties can no longer be the guiding principle of Dutch civil procedural law.[351] Asser, Groen and Vranken wish to introduce further forms of case management, *inter alia* by further strengthening the role of the personal appearance of the parties.[352] Most revolutionary is their suggestion of deviating from the principle of party disposition. They suggest that the judge should be allowed to allege facts *ex officio*. In their final report they argue:

> 'Though the parties should allege facts upon which they base their claim, request or defense, the judge should be entitled - in case he is in doubt - to investigate also undisputed statements of fact. The introduction of a provision similar to Article 8:69(3) Code of Administrative Procedure (which allows the judge in administrative cases to "supplement" facts RRV) seems the obvious solution'.[353]

Another interesting suggestion of Asser, Groen and Vranken is to regulate the stage preceding the commencement of the action. On the basis of positive results obtained in English and French law, Asser, Groen and Vranken concluded that various procedural tools could successfully be applied to resolve disputes before an action is filed.[354] Asser, Groen and Vranken therefore suggest the adoption of specific sets of rules for specific cases, akin to the English pre-action protocols.[355]

The recommendations of Asser, Groen and Vranken have received a lot of attention in the literature.[356] In 2007, the Minister of Justice gave its reaction to their findings and recommendations. The Minister initiated a programme for legislative action, which may in time lead to a revision of (parts of) the Code of Civil Procedure.[357] A proposal to redraft the rules on the discovery of documents has already been launched.[358] If these newly proposed rules are accepted, it would mark an endpoint in a gradual development towards a liberal rather than a very restrictive policy on party directed discovery of documents.

351 Asser, Groen, Vranken & Tzankova 2006, p. 49: '(...) in dit verband hebben wij afstand genomen van het begrip 'partijautonomie' en geconcludeerd dat dit niet meer als richtinggevend beginsel kan dienen'.

352 Asser, Groen, Vranken & Tzankova 2006, Section 7.1.2.

353 Asser, Groen, Vranken & Tzankova 2006, p. 46 and Asser, Groen, Vranken & Tzankova 2003, p. 81: 'Ook al zijn het de partijen die de feiten stellen als grondslag van hun vordering, verzoek of verweer, de rechter dient de bevoegdheid te hebben om, waar hij twijfelt, ook onbestreden feitelijke stellingen nader te onderzoeken. Invoering van een bevoegdheid als neergelegd in art. 8:69 lid 3 Awb ligt (aanvulling van feiten) voor de hand'.

354 Asser, Groen, Vranken & Tzankova 2003, p. 115.

355 Asser, Groen, Vranken & Tzankova 2006, Chapter 6.

356 E.g. the last issue of the *Tijdschrift voor Civiele Rechtspleging* in 2006 and Ingelse 2004.

357 The Ministers reaction, entitled 'Visie op het civiele proces: reactie fundamentele herbezinning burgerlijk procesrecht' is available at <www.justitie.nl>, last consulted in February 2010.

358 Adviescommissie Burgerlijk Procesrecht 2008.

4. The Present Continental Procedural Landscape

The changes made to the forms and modes of fact-gathering and fact-finding since the 19th century in Austria and the Netherlands have been fairly similar. The 1895 Austrian Code of Civil Procedure paved the way and set the example for reform elsewhere. Changes to the Dutch system of civil litigation in 1988 and 2002 resemble the changes brought about in the Austrian system a century earlier. Three broader trends can be perceived if one studies the changes to the process of fact-finding in Austria and the Netherlands. I believe these broader developments can be perceived in other (Continental) European jurisdictions as well. In both the Netherlands and Austria, there seems to be a new general structure of the proceedings in which a single set of pleadings is followed by a lengthy preparatory oral hearing at which the parties are generally present. Parties are increasingly required to disclose relevant information and to produce (adverse) evidence. There has been a general trend in both the Netherlands and Austria to abolish the formalism and rigidity that had dominated the law on evidence since medieval times. These three trends in turn have contributed to the changed role of the different actors in the legal process. In the subsequent Sections these changes will be explored in greater depth.

4.1. *The Renewed Structure of the Proceedings*

Changes in the general structure of litigation have had a significant impact on the process of fact-finding, most notably on the process of fact-gathering. It will be argued below that the centre of the process of fact gathering has shifted from the written pleadings to the oral hearing.

A Limited Number of Preparatory Written Pleadings

The Austrian General Judicial Ordinance of 1781 allowed both parties to file two pleadings. The plaintiff was entitled to file a complaint and a reply (*Klage und Replik*), the defendant could file an answer and a rebuttal (*Einrede und Duplik*).[359] The general procedure described by the Austrian Code of 1895 reduced the total number of pleadings to two: the complaint (*Klage*) and the answer (*Klagebeantwortung*).[360] In proceedings before the County Courts (*Bezirksgerichten*) however, the defendant was not required and not expected to file an answer.[361] In the present day Austrian system there is occasionally only a single pleading: the plaintiff's complaint. Therefore, it is obvious that in the Austrian system the significance of the pleadings has decreased since the introduction of the 1895 Code of Civil Procedure.

359 Section 2 of the 1781 Austrian General Judicial Ordinance.

360 Sections 226, 243 of the 1895 Austrian Code. Since 2002, see Section 239 Code of Civil Procedure.

361 Section 440(2) Code of Civil Procedure. This Section specifies that the defendant is not required to file a statement of defense. Also see Fasching 1990, Nos. 1620, 1623 and Rechberger & Simotta 2009, Nos. 690, 948.

In the Netherlands, the 1838 Code did not adhere to *Eventualmaxime* and allowed the exchange of a number of pleadings. The defendant could raise his exceptions and defenses separately.[362] Since the 1896 *Lex Hartogh*, the parties have no longer been allowed to raise exceptions one by one in procedures pending before the District Courts. The *Lex Hartogh* further prescribed that there should be a 'concentration of defenses' in the answer.[363] A party had to raise all his defenses on the merits in the answer. A failure to raise exceptions or defenses in the answer could deprive the defendant of the right raise these defenses.[364] Throughout the 19th and 20th centuries, it was common for the parties to file two pleadings each. Thereby parties occasionally were very brief in their complaint or answer, and more detailed in their reply and rebuttal (*conclusies van repliek en dupliek*).[365] Since 2002, if a personal appearance has been scheduled, leave of the court is required if attorneys wish to file additional written pleadings.

On the basis of data obtained at four Dutch District Courts, the percentage of defended cases in which the plaintiff filed a reply was significantly reduced between 1996 and 2003. Although the differences between the four courts were large; the percentage of defended cases in which a reply was filed dropped on average from roughly 55% in 1996 to roughly 40% in 2003.[366] A questionnaire filled out by members of the Judiciary in 2004 showed that 141 out of 190 judges estimated that attorneys asked the court whether they could file an additional pleading (after a personal appearance had been scheduled) in less than a quarter of all cases. 121 out of 141 judges indicated that they generally denied requests of attorneys who wished to file an additional pleading.[367]

As noted above, the 2002 Reform Act increased the duties of the parties to identify the means of proof in support of the facts they relied upon. The plaintiff was required to mention objections raised by the defendant prior to litigation. In those courts where judges actively enforced these rules and gave case specific instructions, empirical data show that it took longer before the personal appearance was scheduled, yet the overall time to disposition was considerably shorter.[368]

The Oral Hearing as the Main Stage of the Legal Process

In the Austrian system before 1898, the plaintiff was entitled to raise his complaint either orally or in writing. In cases in which the pleadings were presented orally, the court would make a written summary of the pleading (*Protokol*).[369] Many parts of the procedure were in writing; the hearing of witnesses for example, was preceded by a *written* interlocutory judgment, and both parties would formulate *written*

362 Van Rossum 1907 and Star Busmann 1955, p. 200. See Former (i.e. after 1896) Articles 140 and 141 Code of Civil Procedure.

363 Former Article 141 Code of Civil Procedure. Quote in Dutch: 'concentratie der verdediging'.

364 Former Article 141 Code of Civil Procedure.

365 This general observation is often made by practitioners; see for instance Verschoof 2004, p. 339.

366 Eshuis 2007, p. 225, Table 52.

367 Verschoof 2004, p. 340.

368 Eshuis 2007, p. 224.

369 See Chapter 2 of the General Judicial Ordinance, Sections 17-33.

questions that would be put to the witness in the absence of the parties. A *written* transcript of the examination would be communicated to the parties.[370] After evidence had been examined, the parties were entitled to file a *written* document in which they interpreted and reacted to the evidence that had been presented and all materials that had been gathered.[371]

As noted above, the 1895 Code of Civil Procedure, like the 1873 Law on the Proceedings in Petty Causes, made the oral hearing the centre stage of the legal process. The Code, for instance, replaced the written modes of examining witnesses by a free oral interrogation of witnesses whereby parties could orally react upon these findings.[372]

Initially, the first oral hearing (*erste Tagessatzung*) would take place right after the complaint had been served on the defendant. At this first hearing, exceptions raised by the defendant could be discussed, but the merits of the case were not addressed until the defendant had filed his answer. Since 2002, this first hearing has been abolished. Only after the defendant has filed an answer, will the court schedule a preparatory hearing (*Vorbereitende Tagessatzung*). If the inquiry at this hearing shows that there is no genuine dispute of fact and no further evidence is needed, the court is able to render a judgment after the hearing. Judges will often try to convince the parties to settle. In either case, the preparatory hearing marks the final stage in the process of litigation.

In the Netherlands, the 2002 Reform Act aimed to change the ordinary course of litigation. The Reform Act seems to have contributed to an increase in the number of cases in which the court ordered a personal appearance of the parties. In the early 1990s, such a hearing was scheduled in only 15% of the defended cases nationwide.[373] Large differences between the District Courts existed in the 1980s and 1990s.[374] In the District Court of Breda, for example, a personal appearance of the parties was ordered in 44% of all cases concluded in 1989.[375] Since the early 1990s, the number of cases in which hearings were scheduled has increased. Data from cases handled by 10 out of the 19 District Courts, between the 1st of May and the 31st of August 2002, show that a personal appearance of the parties was scheduled in 60% of all defended cases. Differences between the 10 District Courts were fairly large, ranging from 29% to 100%.[376] Data from the District Courts of Utrecht and 's-Hertogenbosch in 2006 and 2007 indicate that in these courts a personal appearance of the parties is scheduled in 90-95% of all cases.[377]

370 Sections 136-175 General Judicial Ordinance.

371 Section 173 General Judicial Ordinance. The provision allowed the parties to file a '*Beweisschrift*' after the examination of witnesses. Also see Sections 238-246 General Judicial Ordinance on the 'final compilation of the case file' (*Inrotulirung der Akten*).

372 See e.g. Section 278(2) Code of Civil Procedure which notes that the discussion on the evidence that was presented should take place at the oral hearing.

373 Groeneveld & Klijn 2002, Paragraph 1.1.

374 Also see Eshuis 2007, p. 125, on differences between courts in 1994-1996 and 2003.

375 Duin, Warnaar & Leijten 1990, p. 405.

376 Groeneveld & Klijn 2002, Paragraph 1.1.

377 Van der Linden 2008, Paragraph 1.5.

The Reform Act also increased the time needed for the personal appearance of the parties (*comparitie van partijen*). Additional time was needed to accommodate for the fact the lawyers no longer had a right to file an additional pleading or make an oral closing plea. With regard to the time reserved for a personal appearance, there are large differences between the District Courts. A survey of members of the judiciary in 2002 revealed that more than a third of the respondents believed that the new regime had increased the length of the hearings. In several courts the time reserved for a personal appearance was increased from 60-90 minutes to more than 90 minutes. The study showed that since January 2002, six out of ten hearings took longer than 90 minutes. A hearing was rarely concluded within an hour.[378] A 2004 survey of Dutch judges showed that most Dutch courts schedule 90 minutes for a personal appearance of the parties. A significant number of courts scheduled 2 hours for such a hearing. In those courts where 90 minutes were reserved for a hearing, 72% of the judges claimed that most hearings could be properly resolved within the 90 minutes.[379]

Since 2002, judges more often render a (dispositive) judgment after the personal appearance of the parties.[380] Data based on 150 personal appearances before the District Courts of Utrecht and 's-Hertogenbosch in 2006 and 2007 show that in 32% of all cases a settlement is reached at the personal appearance of the parties. In 60% of all cases, the judge renders a(n) (interim) judgment after the personal appearance of the parties. Only in the remaining 8% of cases are other steps taken pursuant to the personal appearance, such as a continuation of the hearing at a later point in time or the exchange of additional written pleadings.[381]

Empirical research has shown that the use of a personal appearance of the parties after the filing of the answer has contributed to a significant reduction of the time to disposition. The increased use of personal appearances before the court did not lead to more settlements, but successfully encouraged the parties to settle their case at an earlier point in time.[382] Data based on cases concluded between 1994 and 1996 already showed that cases in which a personal appearance of the parties was ordered were resolved considerably more quickly.[383] The median time to disposition decreased since the 2002 Reform Act. Between 1994 and 1996, the median time in defended cases was 525 days; in 2003 it was 336 days and in 2005 it was 294 days.[384] Courts that used more personal appearances were, as shown in Table 2.1, better able to reduce the median time to disposition.

378 Groeneveld & Klijn 2002, Paragraph 2.3.

379 'Handleiding Regie vanaf de Conclusie van Antwoord', 2008, Paragraph 16, available at <www.rechtspraak.nl>, last consulted in February 2010.

380 Surveys reveal that a personal appearance is now more often followed by a judgment, see Groeneveld & Klijn 2002, Paragraph 2.1.

381 Van der Linden 2008, Paragraph 3.7.

382 Eshuis 2007, p. 214-216.

383 Eshuis 1998, p. 92.

384 Van Erp, Niemijer, Ter Voert & Meijer 2007, p. 50.

Table 2.1. Changes in the use of the personal appearance of the parties and the median time to disposition in defended cases between 1994 and 2003[385]

District Courts	Changed Use of the Personal Appearance of the Parties	Changes in the Median Time to Disposition
Almelo, Amsterdam, Breda, Den Bosch, Middelburg, Utrecht	Increased use of less than 40%	Average Decrease of 11%
Alkmaar, Arnhem, Assen, Den Haag, Haarlem, Roermond, Rotterdam, Zutphen, Zwolle	Increased use between 40% and 60%	Average Decrease of 34.4%
Dordrecht, Groningen, Leeuwarden, Maastricht	Increased use of more than 60%	Average Decrease of 44.5%

One would expect that the increased importance of the personal appearance would lead to a decrease in the frequency in which attorneys and parties make use of oral closing pleas. The Code of Civil Procedure has specified since 2002 that the judge may refuse to grant a party the right to an oral closing plea if a personal appearance of the parties has been scheduled.[386] I have failed to find empirical data on the use of oral closing pleas.

4.2. *The Rise of Disclosure and Discovery*

4.2.1. Demise of the *nemo tenetur edere contra se* Principle

In the Austrian system before 1898, a party did not have to provide his opponent with the means to win his case. Klein had written near the end of the 19th century that parties were not required to provide an opponent any assistance throughout the legal process.[387] In contrast, the Law on the Proceedings in Petty Causes (*Bagatellverfahren*) of 1873 explicitly refuted the practice whereby parties could withhold relevant information and evidence. The Explanatory Memorandum to Section 38 of the Law on the Proceedings in Petty Cases noted that it 'aimed to counter all attempts of parties to withhold evidence from their adversary'.[388] The 1895 Austrian Code of Civil Procedure refuted the *nemo tenetur edere contra se* principle. This followed indirectly from the rules on document discovery as well as from the fact that the Code specified that the financial interest of the parties did not provide a justification for them to refuse to answer questions.[389] Thus, in the

385 Eshuis 2007, Table 41, p. 211.

386 Article 134 Code of Civil Procedure.

387 Klein 1891, p. 44.

388 Klein 1891, p. 48: 'Die Gesetzgebung sollte aber auch die Neuerung des §. 38 Bag.-Verf., (...), treu bleiben. Die Motive zum Entwurfe des Gesetzes über das Bagatellverfahren erklärten sie damit, dass jedem Bestreben entgegenzutreten sei, „das darauf abzielt, der Gegenpartei die Beweismittel vorzuenthalten". Das ist an herrlicher Gedanke; (...)'.

389 Sections 321 and 380 Austrian Code of Civil Procedure. It follows from the former provision that the court could decide that a refusal to answer a question was justified if it would create an immediate financial disadvantage to a witness. Although most provisions on the →

Austrian legal system there is no privilege that protects parties from their duty to disclose information on the ground that the information is unfavorable. In line with the Code of Civil Procedure, the Austrian Supreme Court has held that in cases where a party has insufficient evidence available to prove his case, the opposing party certainly has a duty not to withhold the evidence which he has at his disposal.[390]

In the Netherlands, the *nemo tenetur edere contra se* principle was widely contested in the beginning of the 20th century.[391] The principle was not only applied to the discovery of documents and the interrogation of parties, but had also allowed parties to refuse to cooperate with court appointed experts.[392] The 1953 'blood test decision' of the Court of Cassation reversed earlier case law and led to the general refutation of the *nemo tenetur edere contra se* principle. In this case the Court of Cassation quashed the decision of the Court of Appeal by arguing that:

> 'The Court of Appeal's decision is apparently based on the general statement that one cannot expect a party to provide his opponent with data that could subsequently be used as evidence against him. (…) It is, on the contrary, not uncommon in the Code of Civil Procedure that a party is requested to cooperate in the process of fact-finding'.[393]

Since the 1950s, many amendments to the Dutch Code of Civil Procedure have increased the parties' duties to produce (adverse) information.[394] Since 2002, Article 198 Paragraph 3 Code of Civil Procedure codified the conclusion that could be drawn from the 'blood test decision'. This provision specifies that parties are bound to cooperate with the investigation of a court appointed expert. If parties do not sufficiently cooperate with the expert's investigation, the judge may draw the conclusions he deems fit (i.e. draw adverse inferences).[395]

examination of witnesses also apply to parties, parties may not refuse to answer questions if such information would (be detrimental to their case and thereby) harm their financial position.

390 Austrian Supreme Court, 14 September 1982, 5 Ob 677/82: 'Allerdings ist im Falle eines Beweisnotstandes der Gegner verpflichtet, ihm zur Verfügung stehende Beweismittel dem Beweispflichtigen nicht vorzuenthalten (…)'.

391 See e.g. Article 246 of the 1920 Gratama Draft. At the 1915 conference of the Dutch Association of Jurists Arnold Levy argued that it was about time for the legislator to depart from the rule: *nemo cogi potest edere contra se* (i.e. the *nemo tenetur* principle), *HNJV* 1915, p. 59.

392 Court of Cassation, 7 March 1952, *NJ* 1953, 402 and Court of Appeal Arnhem, 31 October 1939, *NJ* 1940, 231.

393 Court of Cassation, 12 June 1953, *NJ* 1954, 61 (*Bloedproefarrest*). In the underlying case the Court of Appeal upheld a decision of a District Court, and argued that it could not be expected of a party to provide evidence that was detrimental to his case. The Court of Cassation held: 'dat 's Hofs beslissing kennelijk steunt op de algemene stelling, dat van een partij niet kan worden verlangd, dat zij aan haar wederpartij in de procedure de door deze verlangde gegevens voor tegenbewijs tegen zichzelf verschaft (...) dat integendeel in dit Wetboek niet onbekend is de figuur, dat van een partij medewerking aan een gerechtelijke verrichting wordt verlangd…'.

394 See in general Van den Reek 1997.

395 The Explanatory Memorandum specified that this provision is a specific rule that specifies the more general principle newly introduced in Article 21 Dutch Code of Civil Procedure. See →

In civil cases, the *nemo tenetur edere contra se* principle is now widely rejected throughout Continental Europe.[396] In Italy, this principle was abolished with the introduction of a new Code of Civil Procedure in 1942.[397] In Belgium and in France, the principle was abandoned in the 1960s as part of a greater overhaul of the procedural regime.[398] The European Court of Justice, to provide another example, held that:

> 'neither a comparative analysis of national laws, nor Article 6 of the European Convention for the Protection of Human Rights and Fundamental Freedoms of 4 November 1950, nor Article 14 of the International Covenant on Civil and Political Rights of 19 December 1966 (United Nations Treaty Series, Volume 999, p. 171) enabled the conclusion to be reached that there was a general principle of Community law giving a legal person the right not to give evidence against itself in the case of infringements in the economic sphere, in particular in matters of competition law'.[399]

A 2004 European Directive on the enforcement of intellectual property rights in the European Union provides a good example of legislation that requires Member States of the Union to provide at least some means of discovery. The intellectual property directive required all Member States to ensure that 'on application by a party which has presented reasonably available evidence to support its claims, and has, in substantiating those claims, specified evidence which lies in the control of the opposing party, the competent judicial authorities may order that such evidence be presented subject to the protection of confidential information'.[400]

Germany currently seems to be taking an exceptional position. In Germany the *nemo tenetur edere contra se* principle is still rather influential. In 1990, the German Supreme Court based a decision on the general principle that no party is obliged to provide his opponent with the materials that opposing party needs to win his case.[401] Recent literature continues to hold that the *nemo tenetur edere contra se*

Van Mierlo & Bart 2002, p. 372. On Article 198 also see Court of Cassation 22 February 2008, *LJN* BB5626.

396 Most extensive on the demise of the *nemo tenetur* principle is Kohl 1971. Also see Stürner 2005, footnote 163.

397 See for instance Articles 210-213 of the Italian Code of Civil Procedure (*ordine di esibizione*). A colleague recommended the introductory pages of Andrea Graziosi, *L'Esibizione Istruttoria Nel Processo Civile Italiano*, Milano, Giuffrè (2003) for an historic introduction of the principle in Italy.

398 Kohl 1971, Chapter 2, Section 1 and Kohl 1984, p. 75.

399 ECJ, 10 November 1993, C-60/92, par. 11, in which the ECJ summarizes its decision in Case 374/87 Orkem v. Commission [1989] ECR 3283.

400 Article 6, par. 1 of Directive 2004/48/EC of the European Parliament and the Council of 29 April 2004 on the enforcement of intellectual property rights.

401 BGH, *NJW* 1990, 3151: 'Es bleibt vielmehr bei dem Grundsatz, dass keine Partei gehalten ist, dem Gegner für seinen Prozesssieg das Material zu verschaffen, über das er nicht schon von sich aus verfügt'.

principle is still part of the German legal system, despite the widened possibilities for the court to order the production of documents.[402]

4.2.2. Increased Duties to Provide Information

In Austria and the Netherlands, parties are increasingly required to disclose information. Many Continental systems codified a general duty for the parties to provide a complete and truthful account of the facts. Judges now frequently refuse to determine that evidence was needed if facts were disputed but one of the parties had not sufficiently substantiated its factual allegations. With the rise of oral hearings before the court, the parties were increasingly questioned directly by the court.

The 1895 Austrian Code of Civil Procedure specified that the parties, during the oral hearings, had a duty to provide a complete and truthful account of the facts.[403] The Austrian provision was influential and was transplanted, with minor changes, into other legal systems, such as Germany, Sweden, Croatia, Norway and the Netherlands.[404] It was not a new invention. Klein was certainly influenced by earlier Austrian legislation with a similar content.[405] Before the era of codification, under the Romano-Canonical model of procedure, the parties would take a Calumnia oath in which they swore to refrain from vexatious litigation. Thereby parties also confirmed under oath that they would not distort the truth.[406] The General Judicial Ordinance of 1781 and the West Galician Ordinance of 1796 did not prescribe the taking of the Calumnia oath. Nevertheless, similar provisions directed against vexatious litigation existed. Section 409 of the General Judicial Ordinance ordered the judge to give a party (and that party's lawyer) an appropriate sanction if a party had acted in bad faith or in violation of the law. Section 540 of the West Galician Ordinance was almost identical but explicitly identified untruthfulness as vexatious litigation. [407]

402 See Katzenmeier 2002, p. 534; Rosenberg, Schwab & Gottwald 2004, §108-8 and Hess 1999, p. 169. A different opinion is held by Stürner 1976.

403 It is surprising that the Austrian rule does not state that it also applies to the contents of the written pleadings. See Sections 226 and 243 Code of Civil Procedure.

404 Section 178 Austrian Code of Civil Procedure; Section 138 German Code of Procedure, Chapter 43; Section 6 Swedish Code of Judicial Procedure; Sections 21-4 Norwegian Code of Civil Procedure; Article 21 Dutch Code of Civil Procedure and Article 9 of the 2003 Croatian Civil Procedure Act.

405 See in general Klein 1885.

406 See in this regard Oberhammer 1993, p. 60.

407 Section 409 General Judicial Ordinance: 'Wenn der Richter in dem abgeführten Prozesse, oder in der ergriffenen Appelazion, oder Revision bey einer, oder anderer Parthey eine offenbare Widerrechtlichkeit, und besondern Muthwillen bemerkte, hat derselbe die betreffende Parthey, und ihren bestellten Rechtsfreund mit einer angemessenen Strafe an Gelde, oder Leibe anzusehen'. Section 540 West Galician Ordinance: 'Wenn der Richter in dem abgeführten Prozesse, oder in der ergriffenen Appelation, oder Revision bey einer, oder anderer Parthei eine offenbare Widerrechtlichkeit, zumal in Widersprechung wahrhafter oder angebung unwahrhafter Umstände bemerkte, hat derselbe die betreffende Parthei, und →

The codification of a duty to be truthful is a powerful political statement that indicates that parties are not merely possessors of a right, but also carry a duty to allege facts in good faith. But as a legal rule, the duty to provide a complete and truthful account of the facts is not precise and very difficult to enforce. It is generally believed by authorities that more specific rules that require parties to provide information are needed.

A second development that required the parties to disclose more information was that a mere denial of the facts adduced by the other party no longer sufficed. Under the Romano-Canonical model, one could often respond to the allegations of the opposing party by a brief '*non credo*' after which the opponent was required to produce evidence. Currently, in most Continental systems a bare denial of fact does generally not suffice. A denial should 'fairly meet the substance of the averments denied'.[408] In the 19th century Dutch system, if a party clearly denied a fact alleged by the opposing party, the fact was considered disputed and the party who had the burden of proof was obliged to provide evidence.[409] It was not required to explain why one denied the facts adduced by the opposing party. Throughout the 19th and the beginning of the 20th century, the Court of Cassation quashed various decisions of Courts of Appeal that requested more than a clear denial of fact.[410] This led to a practice whereby vexatious defendants denied all allegations of the plaintiff without any further explanation, hoping the plaintiff would fail to provide evidence for at least one matter of fact.

In 1901 the Dutch Court of Cassation held that a defendant may not deny a whole list of statements in a single sentence (i.e. 'The defendant denies all facts alleged by the plaintiff unless these are explicitly acknowledged hereafter').[411] Such general denials should be ignored by the courts. The Court of Cassation has confirmed this decision since.[412] In 1914, a Court of Appeal had decided that if the plaintiff had argued the defendant's income was 6.000,- guilders, the defendant could not merely deny that fact, but also had to tell what his income was. The Court of Cassation upheld the decision.[413] It was the first decision that held that a mere denial of facts did not suffice and that a further motivation was required. Meijers, in his much quoted annotation of a 1923 decision of the Court of Cassation, summarizes the new doctrine as follows:

ihren bestellten Rechtsfreund mit einer angemessenen Strafe an Gelde, oder Leibe anzusehen'.

408 This is the language of FRCP Rule 8.

409 Court of Cassation, 18 December 1925, *NJ* 192 6, 228. m.nt. E.M.M.

410 Court of Cassation, 1 February 1889, W. 5674; Court of Cassation 11 May 1900, W. 7453; Court of Cassation 28 December 1902, W. 7850 and Court of Cassation 8 May 1903, W. 7924. See the case note under Court of Cassation, 18 December 1925, *NJ* 1926, 228.

411 Court of Cassation, 3 May 1901, W. 7604.

412 Such as Court of Cassation, 22 March 1907, W. 8513; Court of Cassation 30 April 1915, *NJ* 1915, 785; Court of Cassation 27 January 1921, *NJ* 1921, 352.

413 Court of Cassation, 13 November 1914, *NJ* 1915, 107. See also Starr Busmann, *HNJV* 1915, p. 69.

> 'One can presently without doubt conclude that in our proceedings there is a duty for parties to provide information; according to which, every time the judge is convinced that a party knows more about the debated issues than he has noted in his written pleadings, the judge may set aside the statements in the pleading as these are insufficiently substantiated'.[414]

Since the introduction of the Civil Evidence Act in 1988, the case law of the Court of Cassation has been codified. Article 149(1) Code of Civil Procedure states that '(...) Facts or rights that have been alleged by one party and have not been denied *or not been adequately denied* by the other party, shall be considered true by the court(...)'.[415] In Dutch legal literature it is widely recognized that parties have 'a duty to allege facts' (*stelplicht*). If parties are aware of relevant details, these ought to be mentioned in the pleadings or at the personal appearance of the parties. Case law of the Court of Cassation has set more precise standards in this regard.[416] Case law has pointed out that certain parties have an extended duty to plead facts with particularity and substantiate their denials (*verzwaarde stelplicht*). If a patient sues a doctor for medical negligence, the doctor has control over most means of proof and has more knowledge concerning the medical details (information asymmetry). At the same time, the patient generally has the burden of proof. This creates a difficult position for the patient which is partly overcome by the fact that a doctor has an extended duty to substantiate his factual allegations (*verzwaarde stelplicht*). The judge will more easily than in other cases disregard the doctor's denial of facts as 'insufficiently substantiated'.[417] Similarly, there have been labor law cases in which the Court of Cassation determined that an employer had an extended duty to plead facts with particularity.[418]

In the Netherlands, lack of knowledge or information to form a belief does not always have the effect of a denial. For example: the District Court of Leeuwarden held in a case in which a tenant could not remember whether or not he received the

414 Court of Cassation, 18 December 1925, *NJ* 1926, 228, m.nt. E.M.M: 'Men kan thans zonder twijfel constateeren, dat in onze procedure een mededeelingsplicht voor partijen bestaat, krachtens welke telkens als de rechter de overtuiging heeft, dat een partij meer van de geschilpunten afweet, dan hij in zijn conclusie neerschrijft, hij de conclusie als onvoldoende gemotiveerd ter zijde kan stellen'. This decision was upheld in later decisions, such as Court of Cassation, 7 January 1926, *NJ* 1926, 259.

415 'Tenzij uit de wet anders voortvloeit, mag de rechter slechts die feiten of rechten aan zijn beslissing ten grondslag leggen, die in het geding aan hem ter kennis zijn gekomen of zijn gesteld en die overeenkomstig de voorschriften van deze afdeling zijn komen vast te staan. Feiten of rechten die door de ene partij zijn gesteld en door de wederpartij niet of niet voldoende zijn betwist, moet de rechter als vaststaand beschouwen, behoudens zijn bevoegdheid bewijs te verlangen, zo vaak aanvaarding van de stellingen zou leiden tot een rechtsgevolg dat niet ter vrije bepaling van partijen staat'. Before 2002, this provision was contained in Article 176(1) Code of Civil Procedure.

416 See *inter alia* Court of Cassation, 12 May 1989, *NJ* 1989, 596.

417 Court of Cassation, 20 November 1987, *NJ* 1988, 500. Also see Giesen 1999.

418 Court of Cassation, 6 April 1990, *NJ* 1990, 573.

general terms which applied to a rental contract, that the tenant's denial had to be set aside as 'insufficiently substantiated'.[419]

It can be concluded that if a party in the Dutch legal system (or in the Austrian system) is not sufficiently forthcoming with relevant information, the judge may establish the facts contrary to that party's interests without examining any evidence.[420] Even if parties have suggested evidence in support of their factual statements, the court may set their allegations aside as 'inadequately denied' or 'insufficiently substantiated'.[421] Especially in cases in which the value of the claim is limited and the number of disputed facts is relatively large, a Dutch judge will frequently make use of phrases like 'as stated by the plaintiff and inadequately denied by the defendant, the court assumes that…'.[422] Judging whether or not facts are adequately denied involves a balancing act in which courts should avoid two evils. On the one hand the court wishes to avoid the waste of resources that results from unnecessary examination of evidence. On the other hand, the court should not too swiftly determine that a fact is inadequately denied when a genuine dispute on matters of fact does exist.

A third development that required the parties to disclose more information was the introduction of an oral procedure in which they could be questioned in person at a hearing. The oral hearing was much more effective than the older, mostly written, mechanisms of party interrogation. Paper does not blush and an answer orally given by a party differs greatly from a well prepared answer drafted by an attorney. The Austrian system envisaged an active judge who would orally question the parties in open court in order to establish the facts truthfully (see Chapters 6 and 7). The Austrian system also provided for rules that enabled the parties to put questions to each other.

4.2.3. Orders to Produce Evidence

Increased Judicial Powers to order the Parties to produce Evidence

Under the earlier Continental codifications, the judge sometimes had powers to order the production of evidence but was not entitled to adduce facts *ex officio*. In accordance with the principle of party disposition, the parties were generally exclusively entitled to frame the issues; the judge could only order the production of

419 County Court Section District Court Leeuwarden, 18 May 2006, *LJN* AX3651.

420 In Austria, the General Judicial Ordinance already refused to accept general statements that categorically denied facts stated by the opponent party. General Judicial Ordinance Section 5 '(...) daher soll Beyrückung einer allgemeinen Verneinungsklausel verboten, und ohne Wirkung sein'. The 1895 Code of Civil Procedure accepted that facts that were admitted by the opponent party did not require proof. Section 267 of the Code added the rule that 'in the absence of an explicit admission by a party, the judge has to determine, carefully taking into account all the statements of that party, whether or not a fact should be considered to have been admitted'.

421 See e.g. Court of Cassation, 30 June 2006, *LJN* AX3410.

422 At the site <www.rechtspraak.nl>, the search phrases 'onvoldoende gemotiveerd betwist' and 'onvoldoende gemotiveerd weersproken' lead to over 1,000 hits, last consulted in February 2010.

evidence for disputed facts.[423] The precise scope of the judicial powers to order the production of evidence differed throughout the Continent. Only expert evidence could be ordered by the judge *ex officio* under the Austrian General Judicial Ordinance of 1781.[424] As noted previously, the 1838 Dutch Code of Civil Procedure granted the judge a wider range of powers to request evidence for disputed facts. A judge could *ex officio* order parties to present witness testimony, order a local visit to a scene of the dispute, order the parties to take an oath or determine that an expert had to be appointed.[425]

Generally speaking, since the late 19th century most Continental systems have gradually increased the judicial powers to order the production of evidence. The 1895 Austrian Code of Civil Procedure empowered the court to examine the litigants (see Chapter 6). It also allowed the judge to order the production of a document, drawings or exhibits a party had referred to. Furthermore, the court could order a local visit to a scene of the dispute, appoint an expert or hear witnesses *ex officio*.[426] In the Netherlands, legislative changes in 1989, 1991 and 2002 strengthened the powers of the court to order the parties to produce documents. Similar developments can be seen elsewhere on the European Continent. Newly introduced codifications such as the Swedish Code of Judicial Procedure of 1942 and the Belgian Judicial Code of 1967 contain a provision that empowers the court to order the parties to produce case related documents.[427] The French Code of Civil Procedure of 1975 contains a general provision that enables the court to conduct a factual investigation and order the litigants and third parties to produce evidence.[428] Since 2002, German judges may order litigants or a third party to produce documents 'which a party had made reference to'.[429]

Throughout most of the European Continent, judges now have powers to order the production of evidence *ex officio*. The details of the rules differ greatly.[430] For example, a German judge is presently not entitled to hear witnesses *ex officio*; only upon motion of a party, a witness may be summoned to testify.[431] A German judge may order a local visit *ex officio*.[432] In Austria, the judge may summon a witness *ex officio*, unless both parties would oppose the examination of that witness. The Austrian judge may also *ex officio* order a visit of the *locus quo*, regardless of

423 See e.g. for the Netherlands, Van Boneval Faure 1893, p. 112.

424 See Section 187 Austrian General Judicial Ordinance. Even if the judge wished to order a supplementary oath, the judge could only do so upon the request of a party. See Section 6.1.3.

425 Former Articles 103, 199, 219 and 222 Dutch Code of Civil Procedure. On the supplementary oath, see Article 1977 of the 1838 Civil Code. The judicial powers to order the production of documents were however very limited in the Netherlands.

426 Section 183 Austrian Code of Civil Procedure.

427 See Chapter 38 of the Swedish Code of Judicial Procedure and Article 877 of the Belgian Judicial Code.

428 Articles 10 and 11 of the French Code of Civil Procedure.

429 Section 142 Code of Civil Procedure: '(...) Urkunden (...) auf die siche eine Partei bezogen hat(...)'.

430 Also see the many small differences with respect to the appointment of experts in Section 5.1.

431 Rosenberg, Schwab & Gottwald 2004, p. 812-857.

432 Section 144 German Code of Civil Procedure.

whether or not both parties would oppose the local visit.[433] In the Netherlands a judge may *ex officio* order a party to present witness evidence. A judge may however not decide to hear a specific witness not suggested by either one of the parties.[434] Judges may *ex officio* order a local visit.[435] In addition a contractual agreement on the admissible means of proof between the litigants may bind a Dutch court.[436]

Party Driven Discovery

Quite often, one reads in comparative literature that Continental systems do not have discovery provisions. Hazard and Huang for instance claim:

> 'In contrast to common law jurisdictions, a word is sufficient about document discovery under civil-law systems. There is none. Under the civil law, a party has a right only to request the court to require the opposing party to produce a document. This arrangement is a corollary to the general principle in the civil law system that the court, rather than the parties, is in charge of the development of evidence'.[437]

> '(...) the party under Continental civil procedure does not have the right to compel his opponent or a third party to produce evidentiary materials or relevant information. In so far as evidence-gathering is concerned, the only resort the party has is to move for judicial taking of evidence (...)'.[438]

These statements are inaccurate, incorrect and probably a result of unjustified generalizations. Many Continental systems have enacted rules that allow a party, with leave of the court, to request the production of (properly identified) documents. The 1895 Austrian Code of Civil Procedure, as noted before, seems to have been the first Continental jurisdiction to adopt rules on party driven discovery (see Section 7.3.2). The Austrian rules provided for extensive and detailed regulations that enabled parties to request the production of documents (as well as other means of proof) in possession of the other party. Other countries, such as Sweden, have also been more liberal in widening the rules on document discovery.[439] In France, since 1975 the parties may request the court to compel a party or a third person to produce (precisely identified) documents. The French Code of Civil Procedure specifies that the court 'will order the production of the

433 Section 183 Austrian Code of Civil Procedure.

434 Article 166 Dutch Code of Civil Procedure. Although judges may indicate that they wish to hear certain witnesses, the judge may ultimately only examine those witnesses suggested by the parties. Rutgers, Flach & Boon 1988, p. 234. Court of Cassation, 2 May 1952, *NJ* 1952/422. In some (non contentious) cases judges may *ex officio* decide to hear a witness not suggested by the parties, Article 284 Code of Civil Procedure.

435 Article 201 Code of Civil Procedure.

436 Article 153 Code of Civil Procedure; Asser 2009, p. 36.

437 Hazard 1997, p. 1682.

438 Huang 2003, p. 44. Huang's book in general portrays very little knowledge of Continental European systems, wrongly assumes all Continental systems are more or less the same and hardly refers to non-English literature.

439 Chapter 38 of the Swedish Code of Judicial Procedure.

document if the request is well founded'.[440] The Dutch developments since the early 20th century illustrate that party driven discovery of documents was initially indeed very restrictive. Many early attempts to widen the rules on party driven discovery failed. At present, it is nevertheless much easier to obtain documentary evidence held by an opponent than it was a century ago.[441]

4.3. *The Deformalization of the Law of Evidence*

A third general trend which can be perceived in the Netherlands and Austria, as well as in many other Continental jurisdictions, is that the law on evidence has become increasingly less complex and less rigid. Many Continental jurisdictions have gradually departed from the learned Romano-Canonical Procedure that had suffered from misplaced scholastic mathematization. Early codifications had retained the basic elements of the Romano-Canonical system of formal proof and *inter alia* contained provisions 1) that restricted the admissibility of evidence and 2) rules that limited the probative value of evidence.

Rules that restrict the admissibility of evidence are a stringent species of rules that restrict the probative value of evidence (i.e. the probative value of inadmissible evidence is zero). Older codifications set a number of restrictions on the admissibility of evidence. In the Netherlands and Austria, as set out in the preceding Sections and Chapter 6, rules that restricted the admissibility of witness testimony have virtually all been abolished. Parties and their close family, as well as those convicted of crimes, are now competent to give testimony under oath. Hearsay (as well as double or triple hearsay), is no longer inadmissible.[442] The starting point for modern Continental codifications seems to be that all relevant evidence is admissible. Article 152(1) Dutch Code of Civil Procedure specifies that save exceptions set by the law, proof can be provided by all possible means. Even evidence that has been illegitimately obtained, such as a document stolen by one of the parties, is generally admissible in civil cases in both the Netherlands and Austria.[443] A judge however generally may refuse to examine evidence suggested by the parties if the evidence seems to be irrelevant.[444]

In both Austria and the Netherlands, judges have increasingly been allowed to evaluate all evidence freely. Rules that restrict the probative value of certain means of proof and specify that a fact cannot be established unless 'full' proof is alleged, have almost all been abolished. The Dutch rule that specifies that the testimony of a

440 Articles 138-142 of the French Code of Civil Procedure. Article 139(2) reads as follows: 'Le juge, s'il estime cette demande fondée, ordonne la délivrance ou la production de l'acte ou de la pièce, en original, en copie ou en extrait selon le cas, dans les conditions et sous les garanties qu'il fixe, au besoin à peine d'astreinte'.

441 See Ekelmans 2007 for an extensive overview of the case law in this area.

442 See e.g. on the '*testimonium de auditu*', Dutch Court of Cassation, 26 November 1948, *NJ* 1949, 149.

443 For Austria see Kodek 2001; for the Netherlands see Kremer 1999 and Asser 2009, footnote 137.

444 Section 275 Austrian Code of Civil Procedure: '(...) unerheblich scheinende Beweise sind ausdrücklich zuruck zu weisen'.

party cannot provide full proof in support of that party's allegations, is a rare modern remnant of rules of formal proof. Similarly, in the present Austrian and Dutch rules of evidence, there are only few rules that prescribe that certain means of proof, mostly specified categories of documents, provide *prima facie* evidence (*vollen Beweis/dwingend bewijs*).[445] Recently, partly under the influence of European legislation, the rules of evidence also allow for the use of electronic documents that provide *prima facie* evidence.[446]

4.4. *The Demise of the Adversarial System*

The changes discussed in Sections 2.4.1-2.4.3 have led to considerable changes in the role of the different actors in the process of fact-finding. The free evaluation of evidence provides a very effective tool in the hands of judges to ensure that information is forthcoming and parties are cooperative. Parties are encouraged to be disclose relevant information and should be at guard not to convey the impression that relevant information is withheld. The oral hearing in open court has become the new center stage in the legal process. As judges are fairly active at oral hearings, this transition in the structure of litigation has clearly led to a situation in which the judge is increasingly involved in the process of fact-gathering. At the same time, party driven stages in the legal process, such as written pleadings, the drafting of written questions (*articuli*) for witnesses and oral closing pleas are less significant than before.

The 1895 Austrian Code of Civil Procedure broke with a strict adversarial judicial process in which the parties dominated the process of fact-gathering and the presentation of evidence. Since 1895 the role of the judiciary in the legal process has been significantly enhanced. The changes in Austria were often adopted at a later point in time in other European countries. Presently in the Netherlands and Austria, both the models of litigation as organized warfare and the model of an inquisitive judiciary that imposes a decision upon the parties are rejected. Both in Austria and the Netherlands, the ideal relationship between the actors in the legal process is not a competitive game but rather a cooperative venture. Klein, in his 1927 book on the Austrian system of civil litigation, had spoken of an *Arbeitsgemeinschaft* between litigants, attorneys and the court.[447] Throughout the 20th century, notions of 'cooperation' and 'joint responsibility' seem to have been central tenets underlying legislative change. German scholars accordingly identified a new procedural principle underlying newly introduced rules that give the parties and the court joint responsibilities: the *Kooperationsmaxime*.[448] French laws that widened the court's powers to manage the process of litigation in 1965 stressed that civil proceedings

445 Articles 151, 157 Dutch Code of Civil Procedure; Sections 292-294 Austrian Code of Civil Procedure and Fasching 1990, No. 821.

446 See Directive 1999/93/EC of the European Parliament and of the Council, 13 December 1999. Also see Sections 292-294 Austrian Code of Civil Procedure, Article 15a Dutch Civil Code and Section 156a Dutch Code of Civil Procedure, that will enter into force in 2010.

447 Klein & Engel 1927, p. 197.

448 Rosenberg, Schwab & Gottwald 2004, §77(5).

had to be governed by effective cooperation between judges and attorneys in the interest of litigants.[449] The recent Dutch reports by Asser, Groen and Vranken provide a last example of the increased focus on 'cooperation'.

Central to many procedural debates in the late 19th and early 20th century was the ideological debate on the dichotomy between strict adversarial and inquisitorial modes of adjudication. In more recent times it seems that the discussion has shifted to ensuring different objectives, such as access to justice, litigant satisfaction and efficiency. Cooperation and joint responsibilities are believed to be suitable instruments to reach these objectives. Attempts to improve the efficiency of the legal process have affected the rights and duties of the parties and the court. The new rules that require the parties (and the judge) to ensure that a swift resolution of the dispute is possible, provide a good example.[450]

449 Wijffels 2005c, p. 274.

450 This rule, known as the *Prozessförderungspflicht*, was codified in Germany in 1933 (and was strengthened in 1977 and 2001), in the Netherlands in 2001 (Article 20 Dutch Code of Civil Procedure) and in Austria in 2002, (Section 178(2) Austrian Code of Civil Procedure).

Chapter 3

FACT-GATHERING AND EVIDENCE IN ANGLO-AMERICAN LEGAL HISTORY

1. The English Roots of the United States' Procedural System

The direct ancestor of the American legal system is English law.[1] The basic elements of the American procedural regime can be traced back to medieval England. From the 12th century onwards, the English royal courts had developed a complex body of law. It was these rules that eventually influenced procedural law and practice throughout the vast British Empire. Although legal diversity existed in the early colonial days, the influence of the English legal system in Northern America increased as legal complexity increased in the 17th and 18th centuries. The fundamentals of the English common law system, such as the civil jury, the writ, written pleadings and oral testimony in open court were in use in the colonies in the 17th and 18th centuries. After the American Revolution, a system based on the English common law was formally adopted by the various states of the Union.[2] The fundamentals of English procedure later also influenced newly acquired territories of the Union, such as Louisiana and Texas, which had no common law tradition.[3] We will address the basic elements of the fact-finding process in the English common law courts, and the fact-finding procedure before the English Court of Chancery below. A history of English law is useful to understand the legal tradition that has brought about and shaped the present American fact-finding arrangements.

1 For a very general, short and accessible introduction see Berman 1961.
2 For an overview of American law in colonial times, see Friedman 1985, Chapter 1, p. 56-58.
3 Friedman 1985, Chapter 2.

1.1. *Fact Gathering and Evidence in Early English Law*

1.1.1. The English Common Law

The Writ and the Forms of Action

Originally, the English Kings were only occasionally involved in the administration of justice. In ordinary cases, feudal lords traditionally dealt with disputes. The Kings would hear civil disputes only in matters of state and certain cases of special difficulty. The few classes of cases in which the King's Court was competent were routinely handled by means of standardized procedures. The standardized forms both limited the jurisdiction of Court and allowed for the efficient resolution of these disputes. Over time, the jurisdiction of the royal courts widened and the role of the traditional feudal courts declined. The number of cases that were resolved by the royal courts gradually increased, as well as the number of standardized forms of action. From the 12th and 13th centuries onwards, the King's Bench, the Court of Common Pleas and the Exchequer developed a complex body of law generally referred to as 'the common law' or simply 'law'.[4]

Until the 18th century, the procedure at law was not considered to be an issue that could be separated from the substance of the law.[5] Much more than on the European Continent, the focus was on actions, procedures and legal remedies rather than substantive rights. Substantive rights were to be understood in terms of procedure. Procedure itself was not systematic; but a diverse collection of actions, all designed to address a specific wrong. The standardized forms of action created a system only comparable to the ancient *legis actiones* procedure of classical Roman law.

The first step in the litigation process was the issuing of the original writ.[6] A writ was an official document written in the King's name, issued by the King's Chancery on payment of a standard fee. The original writ worked like a 'license to litigate' for the plaintiff, and at the same time conferred the power on the court to try the case. Different writs were issued for different purposes. The increased jurisdiction of the royal courts led to the introduction of new forms of action and new original writs. In the 13th century, a more or less fixed list of writs could be identified. Each writ was directed against a particular wrong, and the plaintiff could choose the writ which most suited his demands. A plaintiff had to choose one writ and thereby one standardized form of action. The choice of writ determined which court would be competent, the rules that applied to the pleadings, and what form the trial would take. This way, procedure and substantive law were inseparably linked. One could not combine two or more forms of action in a single lawsuit. The choice of one form of action limited the scope of the dispute and required a party to make a difficult choice right at the outset of litigation. If the plaintiff chose an

4 See in general Baker 2002; Plucknett 1956; Van Caenegem 1971 and Van Rhee 2005c.

5 Plucknett 1956, p. 381-382.

6 In the earlier days, the writs did not officially mark the commencement of the action. They were rather 'commands' which the defendant had to follow. Only if the defendant refused, would an action be truly initiated.

inappropriate form of action he was required to purchase a second writ.[7] The system can be clarified by means of an example. Suppose Edward's land has been wrongly and aggressively occupied by his neighbor John. If Edward wants to take legal measures, he has to choose between the available forms of action. He may opt for a very old fashioned *praecipe writ* which - if successful - would result in a duty for John to render the land to Edward. In this case, the trial could be by battle. Edward can also bring one of the *trespass actions;* this is a broad category of actions directed against the 'wrongs' of the defendant. Some *trespass actions* enabled Edward to obtain damages through a jury trial, but would not compel John to return the land to Edward. Another good option would be an *assize of novel disseisin,* which allowed for the rapid ejection of John, yet could not be used to determine the ultimate issue of ownership. In order to determine the issue of ownership, Edward can make use of a *writ of right.* In short, Edward must make an important choice at the outset of litigation which impacts his claim and the further course of litigation.[8]

After the original writ had been issued, the plaintiff was to take the writ to the appropriate court with jurisdiction to try the case, such as the King's Bench. An officer of the court subsequently issued 'judicial writs', documents that would ensure the appearance of the defendant.

Common Law Pleading[9]

The wording of the original writ was very general and provided very few details about the nature of the case. Before the case could proceed to trial, both parties were to attempt to identify the issue that divided them. This was done by means of 'pleadings'. The basic objective of the 'pleadings' was to filter out a single issue that was in controversy and to omit all other issues. Originally, the pleadings were presented orally. A clerk would subsequently translate these pleadings into Latin and put them on what was called the 'plea roll'. The rules were strict in the sense that the written plea rolls were binding and unalterable. The oral pleading was gradually replaced by an exchange of written pleadings during the 14th, 15th and the 16th centuries. The written pleadings put forward by members of the bar gradually replaced the written accounts of the clerks.

The plaintiff would first present his opening pleading which would reveal the grounds of the claim and the particular action. In the medieval royal courts, the opening pleading of the plaintiff was referred to as the 'count'. The precise content of the count was dictated by the chosen form of action. Generally, the plaintiff had to limit his action to a single claim or cause as it was often not allowed to join two or more causes of action.

The defendant could choose from several available pleas in response to the plaintiff. Again, the precise content of the plea would depend on the form of action.[10] Four options were generally available. Firstly, the defendant could tackle

7 Maitland 1909, Lecture 1.

8 Baker 2002, p. 57-67; Plucknett 1956, p. 357-360 and Subrin 1986, p. 915.

9 See in general Van Rhee 2005c; Baker 2002, Chapter 5; Plucknett 1956, Chapter 3; Holdsworth 1907; Reppy 1954, Section 3 and Clark 1947.

10 For a Table containing all different pleas, see Hale 1713, p. 152.

the general issue this was referred to as a *general traverse*. The scope of this 'defense' is very wide, possibly leaving many factual issues to be resolved at trial. In a debt case the defendant would plea *nil debet,* denying the existence of the debt. In a trespass case, the defendant would plea 'not guilty', implying that he had not committed the alleged wrong. Secondly, the defendant could plead a *special traverse,* whereby he denied one fact alleged by the plaintiff. This would result in one factual question to be resolved at trial. Thirdly, the defendant could rest his case with regard to the facts, but challenge the claim on legal grounds, referred to as a *demurrer.* A demurrer implied that the defendant admitted the facts stated by the plaintiff but denied that these facts amounted by law to a claim against the defendant. The last option for the defendant was the so-called *confession and avoidance.* This involved an admission of the facts stated by the plaintiff combined with the introduction of new facts. The confession and avoidance required the plaintiff to submit a new pleading and choose amongst the four options here listed in reaction to the issues newly raised.

Once one of the parties had chosen one of the first three pleas mentioned above, the exchange of pleadings terminated. The result was that either an issue of law or an issue of fact was disputed. The parties thereby used the pleadings to conclusively define the disputed issue. If the last pleading was a demurrer, the issue was a legal question for the judge to resolve. If the last pleading was a general or a special traverse, the issue was factual, often tried by a jury. Matters of fact not raised in the pleadings could not be put to the jury.

An example may clarify the common law system of pleading. Suppose John has claimed the payment of 100 pounds, based on the fact that John had lent 100 pounds to Susan and she had failed to repay the money. Susan must make a choice out of one of the four options above. She could opt for the special traverse, arguing that she did repay the money. She had the possibility of pleading the general traverse, denying the existence of the debt. Susan could argue that, based on the facts adduced by John, the law did not entitle John to the claim (demurrer). She could also choose a 'confession and avoidance', for instance by arguing that Susan and John had later made an agreement in which John would grant a full acquittal if Susan provided him with 5 head of cattle. Susan could argue she indeed did provide John with 5 head of cattle. If Susan chose the 'confession and avoidance', John would in turn have to make a choice for either the demurrer, the special traverse (e.g. by denying that he received 5 head of cattle), the general traverse (denying the existence of the second agreement) or a 'confession and avoidance' (which would again require Susan to make a choice). The distinctive element of common law pleading is that Susan had to make a single choice. She could not both argue that she repaid the debt and argue that the debt did not exist, as in the Continental model of pleading.

In Continental systems the parties were free to allege a collection of factual and legal arguments, as the judge could be relied upon to untangle chaotic pleadings, eliminate irrelevant matters and unravel the remaining issues.[11] The

11 Millar 1926.

distinctive nature of common law pleading is that it would always produce a single legal or factual issue.[12] In order to ensure that the pleadings produced a single issue, additional rules were needed. At common law it was not allowed to allege facts in the alternative. Neither was it allowed to make 'hypothetical pleadings' or 'double pleadings'.[13]

In the 17th century, the system of pleading became increasingly complex, technical and formalistic. Although the technical details of English common law pleading were never fully adopted in the New World, many technical aspects found their way to the United States.[14]

The Trial[15]

If the pleadings resulted in a factual issue to be resolved, the pretrial phase was concluded and the case could proceed to trial. Blackstone distinguished seven forms of trial that were available to resolve factual questions in civil cases: trial by record, trial by inspection or examination, trial by certificate, trial by witnesses without the intervention of the jury, trial by wager of battle, trial by wager of law and trial by jury.[16] The trial by jury gradually became predominant. At first, juries consisted of 12 people that lived within the vicinity of the parties. Such neighbors often were well-acquainted with the circumstances of the case and decided both questions of law and fact. Under King Edward I (1272-1307), the distinction between factual and legal issues was gradually recognized. At the same time, jurors were increasingly seen as a body of neutral fact-finders rather than a group of people with first hand knowledge of the case.

Before the jury, oral argument was opened by counsel of the party who held the affirmative of the question in issue. The witnesses of that party would be called one by one and would be orally examined by counsel of both parties. Subsequently, the opposing party would present his evidence. After the presentation of evidence and the oral arguments by counsel, the judge would sum up the case for the jury. The judge would identify the main issue in controversy, give an opinion on matters of law, and would make other comments which he believed necessary to direct the jury.[17] The jury would render its decision directly after the judge's instructions. The

12 Langdell 1907, p. 772: 'The object of pleading at common law is not, as in the civil law, to give notice to the parties respectively and to the court of the of the facts intended to be proved, but to separate the law from the facts and to narrow the latter down to a single issue, with a view to a trial by jury'.

13 See Clark 1947, §42. An example of pleading in the alternative is: 'the defendant wrote and published, *or* caused to be written and published a libel'. An example of hypothetical pleading is '*if* the defendant denies that he wrote and published a libel, *then* the plaintiff alleges that the defendant caused the libel to be written and published'. An example of double pleading is: 'The plaintiff is entitled to his claim because the defendant wrote and published a libel. The plaintiff *is also entitled to his claim* because defendant had breached a contract'.

14 Millar 1952, p. 40.

15 See in general: Van Rhee 2005c; Van Caenegem 1971 and Baker 2002, Chapter 5.

16 Blackstone 1768, p. 330.

17 Blackstone 1768, p. 375.

jury could freely evaluate the evidence that had been presented at trial (*principle of free evaluation of proof*).

The Emergence of Rules of Evidence

The English common law developed detailed and restrictive rules of evidence. Rules of evidence were only developed in the 1500s, when trial by jury had gradually become predominant and witnesses had emerged as the chief source of evidence.[18] Throughout the 16th and the 17th centuries, foundations were laid for a number of basic principles for the rules of evidence. Rules on privileges, the right to compulsory attendance of witnesses, and the rules that incapacitated various categories of witnesses all found their origin in this period. Rules on the admissibility of witness evidence were largely established in the 16th century.[19] Those who refused to take the (Christian) oath for religious reasons (Quakers, Jews and Hindus) were disqualified from testifying. Others were incapacitated to testify because they had a financial interest in the outcome of the case. The latter rule also excluded parties and their spouses from testifying in court.[20]

At the beginning of the 18th century, the right to question witnesses by means of cross-examination was established. The adversarial presentation of evidence would become a distinctive feature of the Anglo-American mode of fact-finding. Cross-examination was often believed to be a powerful and effective tool to investigate the facts.[21]

A substantial amount of literature on evidence was not written until the late 18th century.[22] According to early commentators, most of the rules of evidence were justified by the so-called 'best evidence rule'.[23] This rule held that 'original' evidence was preferred, and 'secondary' evidence should be held inadmissible. For example: a (hand-written) copy of a document should be excluded as the original document provides more reliable evidence. The 'best evidence' principle has been of less

18 See in general Holdsworth 1907.

19 See Ladd 1942, p. 332-336 and Twining 2006, p. 37.

20 It was held by Tindal CJ in *Worrall v. Jones* (1831), 7 Bing 395, that the exclusion of parties and their spouses was based on the fact that they had an interest in the outcome of the case. See Allen 1997.

21 Well known is the view of Wigmore, who stated that '(...) the right of cross-examination by counsel, (...) gave to our law of evidence the distinction of possessing the most efficacious expedient ever invented for the extraction of truth (although, to be sure, like torture, -that great instrument of the Continental system,- it is almost equally powerful for the creation of false impressions)'. Holdsworth 1907, p. 694. Similar and older statements exist, see Langbein 2003, p. 246.

22 Twining 2006, p. 35-75.

23 See Twining 2006, p. 41. *Omychund v. Barker* (1745) 1 Atk, 21, 49; 26 ER 15, 33, per Lord Harwicke, held that no evidence was admissible unless it was 'the best that the nature of the case will allow'. The 18th century treatise of Gilbert entitled 'The Law of Evidence' considered the 'Best Evidence' rule as the most important element of the law of evidence. See Landsman 1990, p. 1152.

importance in England over the recent decades but still has some influence in the United States.[24]

1.1.2. The Court of Chancery

Since the 14th century, the petitioning of the King was a common phenomenon if the common law failed to provide justice in the eyes of the litigants. During the second half of the century, such complaints and petitions were commonly referred to the Chancellor, an important Crown minister at the head of the Chancery. The Chancery began as a royal secretariat that issued writs. By 1400 many complaints were directly addressed to the Chancellor. The Chancellor often dealt with the complaints by means of a decree that was only binding upon the parties to the suit. The Chancellor's decisions were not intended to create a new system, but rather to reinforce the law by correcting defects in the regular administration of justice. It is commonly argued that the Court of Chancery initially served to provide a remedy for the rigidity and sclerosis of the common law. The Court of Chancery put more emphasis on general fairness or justice (it was referred to as a court of conscience) and less on the letter of the law.[25]

From the early 15th century until the late 17th century, the Court of Chancery became increasingly popular. Around 1600, the Court ceased to be a Court that exclusively handled extraordinary litigation. The one-judge court was soon overburdened.[26] Faced with thousands of petitions, standardization was needed, and general notions of 'fairness', 'justice' and 'conscience' gradually hardened into law. The Court of Chancery created its own binding precedent generally referred to as 'equity'.[27] Equity supplemented the common law, and enforced obligations that were not recognized under common law. Equity, unlike the common law, recognized trusts and mortgages. The Court of Chancery could also order a party to do something or to refrain from doing something whereas the courts of common law generally only award pecuniary compensation. The proceedings before the Court of Chancery were more flexible than under common law. The Court of Chancery did not require the plaintiff to choose one *form of action*. The Court of Chancery further allowed for means of discovery that were unavailable at law.

To a large extent, the Court of Chancery was influenced by the Romano-Canonical model of litigation. The first Chancellors had an ecclesiastical background and were trained in the canon law.[28] The equity procedure was not a

24 *Garton v. Hunter* [1969] 1 All ER 451, [1969] 2 QB 37 per Lord Denning MR held that 'The old rule, that a party must produce the best evidence that the nature of the case will allow, and that any less good evidence is to be excluded, has gone by the board long ago. (...) Nowadays we do not confine ourselves to the best evidence. We admit all relevant evidence'. In the United States, FRE Rule 1002 (which requires the production of original documents or photographs) provides a clear example of a remnant of the Best Evidence Rule in the federal American system.

25 For a more detailed account on the origins of equity see: Macnair 2007, Part 4.

26 Langbein 1974, Part 2. Langbein argues that the Chancery was in essence a one judge court.

27 Van Rhee 2005c.

28 Millar 1952, p. 25.

copy of the ecclesiastical system. Some aspects of the Romano-Canonical model, such as the detailed rules on proof, were not adopted in full in the procedure at the Court of Chancery.[29] Direct Continental influences were most pronounced before King Henry VIII broke with the Catholic Church in the early 16th century.[30] The Romano-Canonical influence subsequently ceased to be of great significance after the procedures at the Court of Chancery became more settled.[31]

In two areas the influence of the Romano-Canonical model on the fact-finding arrangements of the equity procedure was both thorough and lasting.[32] The concepts of proof and the presentation of evidence in equity were strikingly similar to the Romano-Canonical model of proof.[33] In equity, there was also a preference for written evidence.[34] The testimony of witnesses in equity was taken in secrecy and the methods of interrogation were almost identical to the procedures followed in the ecclesiastical courts.[35] The Chancery had adopted rules that allowed the parties to put questions to each other by means of the bill of complaint. The interrogation part of the chancery Bill was largely modeled after the 'positions' in the Romano-Canonical procedure.[36]

1.2. *Early Modes of Fact Gathering and Evidence in the United States*

1.2.1. The Early United States Court System

The 13 American colonies that became independent states in 1783 all had their own judicial systems. The way in which equity cases were dealt with illustrates the diversity of state court structures of the late 18th century. Pennsylvania, for example, lacked a separate court of equity. Common law courts partly compensated for the omission, by sometimes allowing equitable defenses. Other states like New Jersey and New York did have a separate court of equity, and law and equity cases were decided by different judges. In Delaware, one common law court sat four times a year as an equity court; whereas in North Carolina each superior court of law was empowered to act as a court of equity in the same district.[37] The typical state system consisted of a pyramid of courts with a Supreme Court at its apex. In spite of diversity in court structure, states each had some sort of trial court of general jurisdiction. These courts go by various names such as 'Circuit Court', 'Superior

29 Millar 1952, p. 26. Some limits to the free evaluation of evidence did exist. If the defendant for instance positively denied a statement of the plaintiff under oath, the testimony of a single witness would not suffice to prove the statement. See in general on the similarities between the Romano-Canonical system of evidence and evidence in equity: Macnair 1999 and Millar 1937, p. 439-440.

30 Kessler 2004, p. 1200.

31 Millar 1952, p. 27.

32 Langdell 1907, p. 773.

33 Macnair 1999, p. 291.

34 Macnair 1999, p. 164.

35 Macnair 1999, p. 169, p. 177.

36 See Section 6.1.

37 Friedman 1985, p. 54, p. 147; Millar 1936, p. 11 and Millar 1952, p. 40.

Court' or 'District Court'. Differences between the court structures of states exist today, but lower state courts still are the courts of general jurisdiction.

The third Article of the 1787 U.S. Constitution specified that the (federal) judicial power was vested in the Supreme Court and that it would be left to Congress to decide whether or not there would be lower federal courts. Congress soon after established such lower courts of limited jurisdiction by means of the 1789 Judiciary Act. The jurisdiction of the federal courts increased over the course of time. State courts and the federal courts might have concurrent jurisdiction. It was - and still is - an important tactical decision for a lawyer to determine where to bring an action if several courts are competent to try the case.[38]

During the 18th century and the early 19th century, the English distinction between law and equity was retained in many states as well as in the federal courts. Gradually most states abolished separate equity courts. Often the same courts and the same judges would handle both cases at law and in equity. Both law and equity had their own body of substantive law as well as their own procedural rules. The procedural regimes of both legal systems were very different. At law the facts could for instance be tried by a jury whereas cases in equity were tried by the court.

During the first decades after American independence, in both equitable cases and cases at law, the proceedings continued to be closely linked to the English legal system. English legal literature, in particular Blackstone's 'Commentaries on the Laws of England', was widely read and used throughout the United States. Many lawyers and judges were trained in the English legal system. Nevertheless, some technicalities such as the classical English system of pleading were soon abandoned. The strong link between American and English law was recognized in legal texts as well. The 1822 Federal Rules of Equity specified that in 'all cases where the rules prescribed by this court, or by the Circuit Court, do not apply, the practice of the Circuit Courts shall be regulated by the High Court of Chancery of England'.[39]

1.2.2. Fact-Finding during the late 18th and the early 19th Century

Fact-finding in the Common Law Procedure

As noted earlier, the specific mode of the proceedings in the courts at law depended to a large extent on the particular *'form of action'* chosen by the plaintiff. These forms of action were also used in the New World. In New York prior to 1848, ten forms of action were in use at the courts of law.[40] Despite the differences between the forms of action, it is possible to make more general assertions about the proceedings at law. Prominent features of the (late 18th century) procedure at law are listed below.

Common law pleading was designed to force the parties to reduce the 'issue' to a single question of law or fact. After the exchange of the pleadings, the common law traditionally provided very few possibilities for the discovery of information. When compared to present day standards, one could argue that discovery was virtually non-existent. The lack of discovery and the existence of detailed rules that

38 See e.g. Friedenthal, Kane & Miller 2005, Chapter 2.

39 Rule 33, as cited by Kessler 2004, p. 1206.

40 Clark 1993, p. 82.

excluded relevant evidence often hindered proper access to information.[41] Another distinctive feature of the common law procedure was that the right to a civil jury was preserved in the U.S. Constitution as well as many state Constitutions (see Section 8.3). The use of the jury as a trier of fact would have large implications for the process of fact-finding (see Section 8.3). It *inter alia* required the oral presentation of evidence in open court.

A last distinctive feature is that the courts at law adopted the adversarial system. From the 17th century onwards, more and more adversarial mechanisms found their way into the English and American legal system. By the end of the 1700s the adversarial system had been firmly established in both England and the United States.[42]

Fact finding in Equity Proceedings

The traditional equitable procedure differed greatly from the proceedings at law, and it was generally accepted that the equitable procedure was more flexible. Yet there had been complaints that the equitable procedure in the United States during the 19th century consumed vast amounts of time and money.[43] With regard to the process of fact-finding, four distinctive features of the equity procedure are prominent.

Pleading in equity was largely based on the pleading practices in the ecclesiastical courts.[44] The pleadings did not need to result in a single disputed issue. The equity procedure provided some means of discovery and thereby could 'correct' for the lack of access to information under control of one's adversary at law.[45] The procedure before the courts of equity was traditionally initiated by a bill of complaint, which required the defendant to answer under oath. Subsequently, the plaintiff could file a reply.[46] In the bill of complaint the plaintiff could add an 'interrogating part' in which the defendant was asked to answer certain questions under oath. This allowed the plaintiff to ask whether or not documentary evidence existed. If the defendant admitted that a document existed, the court could order the inspection of the document (Section 6.1).

The testimony of witnesses at the Court of Chancery was not taken in open court but by means of written depositions. The party who requested the witness testimony would formulate interrogatories which were to be put to the witness. Court appointed officers were to hear the witnesses outside the courtroom in the absence of the parties. Although the Judiciary Act of 1789 had provided for oral testimony in federal equity cases, the traditional written practice continued to exist in the United States until the early 20th century.

A last feature of the equity procedure was that the court played a rather large role in equitable proceedings. Judges and masters had wide powers to manage and

41 Wigmore 1940, Vol. 6, §1845.
42 Landsman 1988, p. 15.
43 Kessler 2004, p. 1227 and Millar 1936, p. 14.
44 Langdell 1907.
45 Macnair 2007, Part 6.
46 Kessler 2004, p. 1207.

direct the mode of the proceedings such as determining the way in which evidence was presented.[47] Furthermore, the proceedings in equity never made use of the civil jury. This implied that the judge would make the final decision on both factual and legal issues.

1.2.3. Evidence in the Late 18th Century and the Early 19th Century

In the 18th century the law of evidence was largely centered on the best evidence rule and the disqualification of certain persons to testify as a witness.[48] The doctrinal and judicial focus throughout the 18th century was largely on pleading. From the late 18th century throughout most of the 19th century, the law of evidence would be the centerpiece of judicial attention.[49] The best evidence rule was no longer considered the leading principle. Other rules, such as those on relevance and hearsay became more prominent.[50]

Courts - most notably the appellate courts - controlled developments in the law of evidence. The case *Crease v. Barett* (1835) introduced the so-called 'Exchequer Rule', which presumed that an error in the application of the evidence rules was prejudicial and reversible.[51] This implied that new trials were often ordered if the rules of evidence were violated.[52] At the same time, rules of evidence increasingly became subject to legislation. New rules of evidence came into existence and some existing rules were refined, adjusted or abolished. A full system of evidence was gradually developed. Detailed evidence rules restricted the freedom of the judge and the jury to discuss and decide on matters of fact. These rules demonstrate distrust in both the judge and the jury and have perhaps been developed as a counterweight to both.[53]

Throughout the 18th and the 19th centuries, two general developments could be identified.[54] The first development was that rules on the admissibility of witness evidence were loosened. The second development was that more and more rules were developed to safeguard the passivity and neutrality of the trier of fact. Both developments will be discussed below.

47 See in general: Kessler 2004.

48 See Langbein 1996, p. 1176 on the work of Gilbert and 18th century sources on the law of evidence. Langbein argues that the law of evidence dealt with three broad topics: proof of writings, disqualification of witnesses and the sufficiency of proof.

49 Yeazell 1994, p. 642-643 and Lettow Lerner 2000, p. 263.

50 See, in general Landsman 1990.

51 149 Eng. Rep 1353 (Ex. 1835) as quoted and discussed by Yeazell 1994, p. 644-645.

52 The rule was repealed by congress in 1919, see Yeazell 1994, p. 647.

53 Friedman 1985, p. 153.

54 The same distinction is made by Landsman 1988, p. 17.

The Admissibility of Witness Testimony

The rules of evidence - including those newly developed - met heavy criticism throughout the 18th and 19th centuries.[55] Jeremy Bentham is most renowned for his criticism of the rules of evidence of the common law. Bentham basically opposed all rules of evidence and had lamented that '(i)n the map of science, the department of evidence remains to this hour a perfect blank'.[56] Most particularly, Bentham challenged rules that excluded relevant evidence.[57] Bentham, in summarizing his own five volume work on evidence, held that a central proposition in his work was 'that, merely with a view to rectitude of decision, to the avoidance of the mischiefs attached to undue decision, no species of evidence whatsoever, willing or unwilling, ought to be excluded (...)'.[58] Bentham thus argued that the rules that banned witnesses on grounds of imbecility, interest or infamy, or in principle all common law rules that banned certain categories of evidence, had to be abolished.[59] Despite this criticism, American courts continued to insist that evidence should be subject to judicial screening before it would be presented to the jury. Partly because of Bentham's criticism, some of the restrictions on the admissibility of evidence were however abolished throughout the 18th and 19th centuries in both England and the United States.[60]

A significant development in the 18th and 19th centuries was the elimination of restrictions on the admissibility of witnesses. A 1744 English case, *Omychund v. Barker*, held that a deposition of a witness who had been sworn according to Hindu oaths ought to be admitted as evidence. The case effectively made it possible for all those that were not willing to take a (Christian) oath to testify in court.[61] Similarly, the rule that anyone with a financial interest in the case could not testify was gradually abolished.[62] Also the rule that disqualified parties to take the stand was gradually abandoned (see Chapter 6). Although there was a general tendency to relax the rules on admissibility of witness evidence, some fresh restrictions were added. The doctor-patient privilege was introduced in New York in 1828. This example was followed by other states, such as Missouri in 1835.[63]

55 Long before Bentham, it was argued that exclusionary rules had to be construed narrowly. Landsman 1990, p. 1166.

56 Bentham 1827, p. 22.

57 Twining 2006, p. 43-44 and Landsman 1990, Part III.

58 Bentham 1827, p. 1.

59 Bentham 1827, p. 3. 'Willing or unwilling, witnesses of all descriptions ought to be heard: the willing not to be excluded on any grounds such as imbecility, interest or infamy; the unwilling not be excused on any such ground as that of their unwillingness, either established or presumed (...)'.

60 On the influence of Bentham see Allen 1997, Introduction.

61 *Omychund (Ormichund) v. Barker* (1744) 1 Atk 21, 40, per Parker LCB. As discussed by Allen 1997, p. 51 and Landsman 1990, p. 1165.

62 See in general: Bodanksy 1981.

63 See Friedman 1985, p. 154.

Cross-Examination and the passivity and neutrality of the trier of fact

The second development in the law of evidence in the 18th and 19th centuries was linked to the rise of the adversarial system.[64] The right to cross-examination by counsel was established in the early 18th century. The strong emphasis on cross-examination in the period that followed contributed to the passivity of the trier of fact. It was believed to be of utmost importance that the trier of fact - especially the jury - would remain both neutral and passive.

The Passive Role of the Jury

To ensure that the jury would remain passive, new rules were introduced throughout the 19th century. In the 18th century, the jury would be active, often asking questions of the witnesses or parties. Sometimes jurors even requested the parties to summon specific witnesses.[65] Jurors that had personal knowledge of the case could be sworn to testify.[66] Gradually however, it was held inappropriate for the jury to ask questions, take notes or to discuss the case prior to the evaluation of all evidence.[67] The jurors were to remain passive as 'potted courtroom plants'.[68]

The Independence of the Jury: Judicial Comments on Evidence and Facts

To ensure neutrality of the jury, judges could no longer directly persuade or advise the jury on the merits of the case. As jurors are untrained, inexperienced and are not required to provide reasons for their decisions, the jury has always been subject to control and guidance. Traditionally the main technique to exercise some form of control over the jury was that the judge would provide informal guidance by commenting on the merits of the case. As in England, American judges initially tended to control the jury by providing comments on both matters of fact and law. Thereby judges were capable of 'dominating' the decision of the jury.[69] Partly under the influence of the bar, it was gradually believed to be improper for the judge to comment on matters of fact. In the late 18th and throughout the 19th century many American states - mostly in the South and the West - took away the right of the judge to comment on evidence.[70] Judicial discretion in speaking to jurors was replaced by a formalized system of rules on jury instruction.[71] Additionally, a trend could be observed in which judges gradually had fewer opportunities to 'correct' the verdict of the jury once it was rendered.[72]

64 See Landsman 1990 on the relationship between the adversarial system and evidence.

65 Langbein 2003, p. 318.

66 Blackstone 1768, p. 375.

67 Note 1964.

68 This metaphor is used by Damaska 1997a, p. 90.

69 See Langbein 1996, p. 1190-1193 for examples of how the judge at times 'dominated' the jury. Lettow Lerner 2000, p. 205-209.

70 Some states enacted a statute, in other cases the matters were dealt with in the constitution. Sometimes Supreme Courts of state jurisdiction held that it was improper for the trial judge to comment on evidence. See Lettow Lerner 2000, Part III and Langbein 2003, p. 321-323.

71 The formalized rules on jury instruction are still influential today. Rule 51 of the FRCP allows parties to be heard and object to the judge's instructions.

72 Langbein 2003, p. 330.

The constitutional right to a jury trial and rules that prevented judges from commenting on matters of fact would be vital for the preservation of the jury in the United States. In other common law countries, the jury has effectively been abolished. In England, the County Court Act of 1846 and the Common Law Procedure Act of 1854 had made trial by jury optional. This laid the groundwork for the disappearance of the English civil jury. As English judges could comment on matters of fact, they often dominated the English civil jury. Judges commented so frequently on both matters of fact and law that judicial instructions rather than the 'conscience of the jury' was the true determinant of the jury verdict.[73] In addition, throughout the 19th century the judiciary increasingly became independent of the Crown, such that the role of the civil jury as a bulwark against an oppressive government became less significant. As the English jury almost always followed the instructions of an independent judge, it took only a small step to conclude that the jury served no useful purpose.

New Mechanisms of Jury Control

The jury was regarded with suspicion. A new system of jury control was developed that emphasized prevention of jury error rather than the correction of errors or guidance of the jury.[74] One of the main elements of the modern laws on evidence is a set of rules that regulates what evidence may be presented to the jury. The doctrinal basis for exclusion of improper evidence and its mechanisms to enforce and implement exclusionary rules had not been elaborated by the late 18th century.[75] Exclusionary rules would ensure that the jury would not be misled by misleading or prejudicial material.[76] Precepts of judicial practice hardened into rules of evidence in the early 19th century.[77] This way judicial discretion was replaced by rules that empowered attorneys to demand the exclusion of evidence.

Another way in which the system of jury control was reshaped was through the increased use of directed verdicts and new trial orders.[78] Directed verdicts, now known as 'judgment as a matter of law', effectively allowed the judiciary to decide the case without awaiting the jury verdict. The court would use directed verdicts if the judge believed no reasonable jury would find that there were enough facts to grant a party relief.[79] New trial orders were also used increasingly if the rules of evidence had been violated.

73 Hanly 2005, p. 258-259.

74 The thesis that the rules of evidence were developed to account for the use of lay jurors is the classic, yet not undisputed, theory on the origins of the law of evidence. See in this regard Macnair 1999, Chapter 1.

75 Langbein 2003, p. 248.

76 Landsman 1988, p. 17.

77 Langbein 2003, p. 251.

78 Yeazell 1994, p. 642-644. Also see Lettow Lerner 2000, p. 259, who describes that when judges were no longer allowed to comment on evidence they increasingly resorted to ordering new trials.

79 Compare FRCP Rule 50.

The Development of the Hearsay Rule
One of the most important rules of evidence that developed during the late 18th century and the 19th century was the hearsay rule. According to the hearsay rule, a statement not made by the declarant while testifying before the court, is in principle not admissible as evidence.[80] On the one hand, the rule that excluded hearsay was introduced to ensure that the jury would not take into account declarations of those that could not be cross-examined. This is in line with the rise of the adversarial system and the increased focus on the neutrality of the trier of fact. On the other hand, many new exceptions to the rule were added that effectively widened the admissibility of witness evidence. The result of both developments was an increased complexity of the law of evidence that exists to the present day.

Throughout the 18th century, hearsay was often admitted.[81] Only in the last decades of the 18th century did the hearsay rule become firmly established as one of the most important rules of evidence.[82] The rule could be rationalized by pointing out that 1) original evidence was preferred over derived evidence (best evidence rule); 2) evidence before the court and under oath was preferred over out of court evidence and 3) testimony ought to be subject to cross-examination. In the early 18th century, the best evidence rule and the significance of oath taking were the main reasons to argue that hearsay was 'no evidence'. In the late 18th century, the idea that the hearsay rule was needed to ensure counsel's right to cross-examine a witness became predominant.[83]

The hearsay rule was relaxed by many exceptions that were introduced throughout the 19th century.[84] These exceptions made more evidence admissible, yet also increased the complexity of the rule. Most of the newly introduced exceptions on hearsay appeared in England; some (i.e. the business-entry rule) originated in America.[85]

The hearsay rule has been abolished in England but is still of great significance in the United States.[86] One will search in vain to find an equivalent of the hearsay rule in Continental Codes of Civil Procedure.[87] On the Continent, the principle of free evaluation of evidence generally entails that hearsay evidence is admissible and ought to be freely weighed by the judge. There are however rules that demonstrate

80 For a more precise definition, see e.g. FRE Rules 801 and 802.

81 Langbein 1996, p. 1187.

82 Twining 2006, p. 37 and Langbein 2003, Chapter 4, p. 234-235. Langbein argues that the origin of the hearsay rule is often wrongly situated in the 17th century.

83 See Landsman 1990, p. 1156-1157. The origins of the rule have also been linked to the criminal law confrontation right, see Friedman 2002.

84 Some exceptions were old and based on rules that predated the hearsay rule, such as the 'dying declaration' exception. See Langbein 2003, p. 249.

85 Friedman 1985, p. 153-154.

86 Legislation of 1938 and 1968 weakened the hearsay rule in civil cases in England. Eventually it was abolished by the Civil Evidence Act 1995 (c. 38; see Sections 1 *et seq.* of this Act). Now hearsay is treated in CPR Part 33. On the United States, see Rules 801-807 of the FRE.

87 The principle of free evaluation of evidence opposes the exclusion of hearsay evidence. For the Netherlands see on the *testimonium de auditu*: Court of Cassation, 26 November 1948, *NJ* 1949, 149.

a preference of 'original' over 'derived' evidence or require that parties should have the possibility to comment on all relevant evidence.[88]

2. The Codification of Procedural Law

The procedural regime of the 19th century was much criticized for its complexity and technicalities. Legal source materials had grown rapidly and concerns were expressed that lawyers would be 'buried alive' in the 'labyrinths of the law'.[89] Chief complaints were the myriad of forms of actions at law, the complexity of common law pleading, the restrictions on joining of parties and actions and the existence of two procedural regimes - law and equity - alongside each other.[90] Throughout the 19th century, there were attempts to reform the common law by legislation. It was argued by many that codification would reduce the technicality and complexity of the legal process. Jeremy Bentham was well known for his criticism of the English law of procedure and evidence and strongly argued in favor of codification.[91]

2.1. *The Early Codifications*

2.1.1. The 1805 Louisiana Code of Procedure

The 1805 Louisiana Code of Procedure was the first codification of civil procedure in the United States. Although it was not implemented in other states of the Union and was replaced by a new Code of Practice in 1825, it deserves attention for two reasons.[92] First, the Code of Procedure was interesting as it stood in the civil law traditions of Spain and France while at the same time being subject to the constitutional and public law framework of the United States. The 1805 Code of Civil Procedure was drafted by Edward Livingston, who was strongly inspired by the French codifications and the works of Bentham.[93] Federal legislation however required the establishment of the civil jury and that witnesses were heard in open court.[94]

Second, the Louisiana Code of Procedure is of interest as it has had a significant impact on the 1848 New York Field Code, which is discussed below. Both with regard to form and content, the 1848 Field Code much resembled the 1805 Louisiana Code of Procedure.[95] Combining both these issues, it has been argued by

88 Damaska 1991. Damaska provides an historic account of Continental rules similar to the hearsay rule. The present day 'principle of immediacy' (*Grundsatz der Unmittelbarkeit*) in Austria also provides a good example of the preference of original over derived evidence.

89 See the views of Story, as described by Clark 1993, p. 66.

90 See Millar 1952, p. 204 and Blackstone 1768, Vol. 3, p. 382.

91 See in general Bentham 1843, Vol. III.

92 For a more detailed discussion of both codes see McMahon 1960 and Herman 2008.

93 McMahon 1960 and Clark 1993, p. 68-69.

94 McMahon 1960, p. 7.

95 Clark 1993, p. 81-85.

Clark that the Louisiana Code of Procedure formed the 'cultural intermediary' between Continental jurisdictions and the New York Field Code of 1848.[96]

2.1.2. The New York Field Code

The most successful early American Code of Civil Procedure was the New York Code of Procedure enacted in 1848.[97] Pursuant to the New York Constitution of November 1846, three commissioners were appointed to 'revise, reform, simplify, and abridge the rules and practice, pleadings, forms, and proceedings of the courts of record of this state, and to report thereon to the legislature'.[98] David Dudley Field (1805-1894) was one of the three commissioners. Due to his prominent role, the New York Code of Procedure has often been referred to as 'the Field Code'.

Field complained that the common law had created a system that 'obscured facts and legal issues instead of clarifying them'.[99] He primarily aimed to create legal certainty. Field argued that the law had to be accessible for ordinary people. According to his biographer, the writings of Livingston had contributed much to his ideas on codification.[100] In addition, Field had made 59 trips to Europe in his lifetime and spent a considerable amount of time studying Continental legal systems. The 1848 Field Code was simple and contained 391 Articles. It was inspired by continental legislation and therefore rightly referred to as a 'code in the French sense'.[101] An 1849 amended version of the Code was substantially larger as it also contained provisions on the organization of the judiciary and on evidence.[102] Field attached much value to a Code that would be both simple enough to be accessible, yet precise and clear enough to cover a significant number of cases.

The Field Code was soon revised and replaced by another much more detailed Code of Remedial Justice in 1876.[103] It would however remain influential outside the state of New York. It was soon adopted with amendments in Missouri, California, Iowa and many other states.[104] By 1873, a Code of Procedure based on the 1848 New York Code had been implemented in 27 American states.[105] Outside the United States, the Field Code would prove to be influential in Hong Kong, India and England. In England, procedural reform took place throughout the 19th century. Some earlier attempts like the 1832 Uniformity of Process Act, the 1834 'New Rules of Court' and the 1852 Common Law Procedure Acts had tried to remedy and address the most pressing difficulties of the legal system.[106] True reform was only

96 Clark 1993, p. 86.
97 See on this topic amongst others Field Code 1850, Van Rhee 1999 and Coe & Morse 1941.
98 1856 N.Y. Constitution, Article VI, §27.
99 See Field as quoted by Subrin 1988, p. 318.
100 Clark 1993, p. 73.
101 Friedman 1985, p. 391.
102 The amended 1849 version of the Field Code was substantially larger and contained 1884 provisions.
103 See for a more detailed description of this Code, Holdsworth 1907, p. 664 *et seq.*
104 For the history of its implementation in California see Blume 1965.
105 Field 1891, p. 523, Field Code 1850, p. ix. and Holdsworth 1907, p. 646-647.
106 On the changes in England see: Holdsworth 1907, p. 654, p. 674-679 and Van Rhee 2005c.

achieved by the Judicature Acts of 1873-1875 that had been inspired by the 1848 Field Code.[107]

The Field Code and the Fusion of Law and Equity

Throughout the 18th century and in the early 19th century, some American jurisdictions had eliminated a number of differences between the procedures of law and equity.[108] Several states, like Georgia, had extended the right to a jury trial to equity cases.[109] The true fusion between procedures of law and equity was not introduced until the 1848 Field Code. The Code abolished the forms of action and introduced a single set of civil procedural rules for all cases.[110] As equity and common law proceedings were merged, the Field Code took elements from both systems to build a new procedure.

As in the courts at law, the Field Code was positive about the use of juries and expanded the right to a jury.[111] In accordance with the common law, the Code of 1848 adopted the taking of evidence in open court. In addition, strict rules of the common law procedure were preferred over the wide judicial discretion and flexibility of the equity procedure.[112] Although the Field Code relied heavily on the procedure of the common law courts, it was also inspired by the equity procedure.[113] Like in equity, the Code provided possibilities for discovery.[114] By current American standards, discovery under the Field Code was relatively limited. It had no provisions on interrogatories. The Field Code empowered the judge to order one party to allow the other party to inspect or copy documents.[115] The 1848 New York Code also introduced the possibility to take an in court deposition of the opposing party in the pretrial stage of litigation.[116]

107 Millar 1952, p. 63; Van Rhee 2005c, Section 5 and Field Code 1850, p. ix. See Clark 1947, §6 for a short summary of the 19th century developments in England.

108 A clear exception was Texas which in line with its Spanish tradition never introduced separate procedures of law and equity. Millar 1936, p. 16.

109 Millar 1936, p. 20.

110 Section 118 of the 1848 Field Code and Section 636 of the 1849 Field Code state: 'All the forms of pleading heretofore existing, are abolished; and hereafter (...)' Section 62 of the 1848 Field Code and Section 554 of the 1849 Field Code state: 'The distinction between actions at law and suits in equity, and the forms of all such actions and suits, heretofore existing, are abolished; and, there shall be in this state, hereafter, but one form of action, for the enforcement or protection of private rights and the redress or prevention of private wrongs, which shall be denominated a civil action'.

111 Field Code, Section 208; see Subrin 1988, p. 333.

112 Subrin 1986, p. 934.

113 Subrin 1986, Part C, p. 931 argued the Field Code was predominantly inspired by the common law procedure.

114 Subrin 1988, p. 332. 'They provided, by our current standards, extremely limited discovery (...) There were no interrogatory provisions in the Field Code. One side could request permission to inspect and copy "a paper" in the other's possession or control "relating to the merits of the action, or the defence therein"'.

115 See on this topic Subrin 1988, p. 332 and Sections 1223-1224 of the 1849 Field Code.

116 Millar 1952, p. 211 and Subrin 1988, p. 333.

The merger of law and equity was never without problems. The worst was that the constitutional preservation of the jury in common law cases was 'a circumstance constantly militating against the completeness of fusion'.[117] In order to determine whether the parties had a constitutional right to a jury it was required to know whether the action would previously have been an action at law. This led to a variety of difficulties if the plaintiff had not confined the claim to a single legal rule or if the plaintiff sought a remedy which combined legal and equitable issues. This difficulty will probably continue to exist as long as the 'historical test' plays a role in the interpretation of the U.S. Constitution.[118]

The Field Code and the Rise of Code Pleading[119]

Common law pleading often obscured both matters of fact and law. Although the general 'groundwork' of the system was both simple and sound, many rigorous rules had increased its complexity. The system was easily abused; defendants often pleaded the 'general traverse' in order to keep the plaintiff in the dark about the actual arguments and evidence that would be alleged at trial.[120] By doing so, the whole objective of the pleading system to reduce the dispute to one simple and clear issue was circumvented. Complaints about pleading in equity were also common. The chancery bill was often criticized as it would involve too much repetition and was considered to constitute 'a tale thrice told'.[121]

Pleading reform was therefore a central element of the Field Code. The Code introduced 'fact pleading', at times also referred to as 'code pleading'.[122] The plaintiff was obliged to state in his complaint the: 'facts constituting the cause of action, in ordinary and concise language, without repetition' and a 'demand of the relief, to which the plaintiff supposes himself entitled'.[123] Equally, the defendant's answer had to contain a:

> 'denial of each allegation of the complaint controverted by the defendant, or of any knowledge or information thereof, sufficient to form a belief' and 'a statement of any new matter, (...), in ordinary and concise language, without repetition, and in such a manner as to enable a person of common understanding to know what is intended'.[124]

117 Millar 1936, p. 19.

118 On the present role of the 'historical test' see Friedenthal, Kane & Miller 2005, Chapter 11.

119 See in general, Holdsworth 1907.

120 Reppy 1954, p. 31-33 and Clark 1993, p. 82.

121 Millar 1936, p. 9, p. 14.

122 See Friedenthal, Kane & Miller 2005, Chapter 5, on code and notice pleading in the U.S. today.

123 Section 142 of the 1848 Field Code and Section 639 of the 1849 Field Code: 'The complaint shall contain: (...) 2. A statement of the facts constituting the cause of action, in ordinary and concise language, without repetition, and in such a manner as to enable a person of common understanding to know what is intended. 3. A demand of the relief, to which the plaintiff supposes himself entitled. If the recovery of money be demanded, the amount thereof must be stated'.

124 Section 149 of the 1848 Field Code, Section 645 of the 1849 Field Code.

The aim of fact pleading was clear: Field wanted the litigants to give a precise factual account about what had happened without worrying about legal technicalities and formalities. To ensure veracity and prevent meritless lawsuits, the Field Code required the parties to verify the pleadings by oath.[125]

Code pleading rules based on the Field Code effectively replaced the common law rules on pleading in the majority of American jurisdictions by 1873.[126] States like Maryland, Tennessee, Georgia, Mississippi and Texas did not adopt the Field Code yet enacted statutory systems based on the common law. These systems were often quite similar to the system of 'code pleading' of the Field Code.[127] The system of pleading has some resemblance with the Dutch and Austrian system of pleading. These similarities are not coincidental. Field was most likely influenced by the Louisiana Code of Procedure which in turn was inspired by Continental traditions.[128] Article 172 of the Louisiana Code of Procedure required the plaintiff's petition to contain a 'clear and concise statement of the object of the demand, as well as the nature of the title, or the cause of action on which it is founded'. The wording seems to have much in common with Article 61(3) of the 1806 French Code of Civil Procedure which required the plaintiff to provide *'L'objet de la demande'* and *'l'exposé sommaire des moyens'*. The French provision in turn would inspire a number of jurisdictions, it was for instance transplanted to the Dutch Code of Civil Procedure of 1838.[129]

2.2. *The Codification of Federal Law*

2.2.1. The Procedure in the Federal Courts Prior to 1938

In the Federal Courts, the distinction between law and equity would continue to exist until the 1938 Federal Rules on Civil Procedure. The United States District Court exercised jurisdiction according to two different systems of procedure: each court had a 'law side' and an 'equity side'. On the 'law side' courts were generally required to adjust their procedure to that of state jurisdictions.[130] An 1872 Act of Congress held that:

> 'the practice, pleadings, and forms and modes of proceeding in other than equity and admiralty causes in the circuit and district courts of the United States shall conform, as near as may be, to the practice, pleadings, and forms and modes of proceeding existing

125 Section 157 Field Code. This rule had some similarities to Rule 11 of the FRCP which requires attorneys to sign the pleadings.

126 See Clark 1947, p. 24-25 for a history of the 'rise of code pleading' up till 1947.

127 Holdsworth 1907, p. 672.

128 Clark 1993, p. 82, p. 83.

129 Former Article 5(3) Dutch Code of Civil Procedure: '(...) de middelen en het onderwerp van de eis met eene duidelijke en bepaalde conclusie (...)'.

130 The Process Acts of 1789 (1 stat. 93), 1792 (1 stat. 275) and 1828 (4 Stat. 278, Section 1) already held that state law was to be applied in Federal Courts. See Millar 1952, p. 57-58.

> at the time in like causes in the courts of record of the State within which such circuit or district courts are held (...)'.[131]

This so-called 'Conformity Act' led to diverse procedural regimes before the different United States District Courts. The aim of the Conformity Acts was obvious: it aimed to take away the inconvenience for the bar of having to study two different forms of procedure.[132] It is doubtful whether this objective was met.[133] Despite the fact that many states adopted legislation based on the Field Code, there was a wide variation of procedural methods between states.[134] Although the case law of the Supreme Court had set some minimum standards of fairness that applied to all federal courts, further harmonization of the different procedural regimes was limited.[135]

On the equity side, there was a little more uniformity as the Supreme Court had been empowered to promulgate federal procedural rules.[136] The first Federal Equity Rules were adopted in 1822, followed by the more influential 1842 General Rules on Equity which were amended several times. These Federal Equity Rules were explicitly based on the Equity practices in England, and therefore did not represent a serious departure from the existing equity procedures.[137] Although local courts remained free to enact additional rules on procedure in equity cases, the Equity Rules had ensured a large degree of harmonization between the U.S. District Courts.

On November 4, 1912, the Supreme Court promulgated new Federal Equity Rules that reflected the departure from the traditional procedure in equity that had been taking place since the 19th century.[138] These new Federal Equity Rules aimed to reduce complexity and increase the efficiency of litigation.[139] Later, it was concluded that the rules had generally functioned well.[140] In several ways, the Federal Equity Rules brought the equity procedure closer to the common law procedure. Most relevant was that the 1912 rules specified that witnesses were to be heard in open court rather than by a special examiner who would question the witness in the absence of the judge and the parties.[141] The oral examination of witnesses under the new rules and the adoption of the (adversarial) Field Code in a large number of

131 See Act of 1 June 1872, Chapter 255, Section 5, 196, 197 available though the statutes at large at <http://memory.loc.gov/ammem/amlaw/lawhome.html>, last consulted in October 2009.

132 See *Nudd v. Burrows*, 91 US 426, 441, 442, 1875 U.S. LEXIS 1385.

133 The ABA had concluded that the Conformity Act had produced no real convergence between state and federal practice. See Reppy 1954, p. 39 and the sources there quoted.

134 Millar 1952, p. 56-57.

135 This case law was largely based on the 14th Amendment of the Constitution. Gradually the case law on the 'due process of law' clauses became more developed. See in general for an historic account: Hough 1918.

136 Dietrich 1913.

137 Millar 1952, p. 60.

138 These Rules have been published in 18 Va. L. Reg. 641 1912-1913. See Dietrich 1913.

139 Lane 1932, p. 640.

140 Lane 1932, p. 659.

141 Rule 46. This rule was the result of a series of incremental changes, Kessler 2004, Part VI.

state jurisdictions had triggered the gradual introduction of adversarial elements in equity proceedings.[142] Nevertheless, Section 62 of the Federal Equity Rules illustrates that in the early 20th century, the rules still envisaged an active role of the court in the process of fact-finding:

> 'Section 62, Power of the Master
> The master shall regulate all the proceedings in every hearing before him, upon every reference; and he shall have full authority to examine the parties in the cause, upon oath, touching all matters contained in the reference, and also to require the production of all books, papers, writings, vouchers, and other documents applicable thereto; and also to examine on oath, *viva voice*, all witnesses produced by the parties before him, or by deposition, according to the acts of Congress, or otherwise, as here provided; and also to direct the mode in which the matters requiring evidence shall be proved before him; and generally to do all other acts, and direct all other inquiries and proceedings in the matters before him, which he may deem necessary and proper to the justice and merits thereof and the rights of the parties'.

In line with English developments, the 1912 Rules limited the role of the pleadings and expanded the scope of discovery (also see Section 6.1.2).[143] From then on, pleadings only had to contain a 'narrative' and a 'prayer'.[144] The Equity Rules of 1912 extended the use of interrogatories. After the defendant filed the answer, both parties could separately file interrogatories without leave of the court.[145] This change was innovative for two reasons: First, it separated interrogatories from the pleadings and second it placed the defendant on an equal footing with the plaintiff who was not able to file interrogatories under the old system. Additionally the Federal Equity Rules of 1912 allowed the taking of depositions with leave of the court when statutes specified so or in exceptional circumstances.[146] The Equity Rules also provided for the inspection and production of documents as well as the possibility to request one's opponent to admit in writing the execution or genuineness of any document.[147]

2.2.2. The 1938 Federal Rules on Civil Procedure

The 1934 Rules Enabling Act authorized the Supreme Court to promulgate rules of 'pleading and practice'.[148] Congress had retained the authority to amend or reject rules of procedure, yet the underlying philosophy of the Rules Enabling Act was

142 Kessler 2004, Part IV.
143 Millar 1937, p. 449.
144 See Rule 18 and 15 of the 1912 Federal Equity Rules.
145 Millar 1952, p. 212, Rule 58 of the 1912 Federal Equity Rules.
146 Rule 47 of the 1912 Federal Equity Rules.
147 Rule 58 of the 1912 Federal Equity Rules. On the proof of execution of documents in equity see Macnair 1999, p. 126.
148 See U.S.C. 28 Sections 2071-2077. In 1988, Congress further regulated the federal rulemaking process, see 28 U.S.C. Sections 2072-2074, as amended by Pub. L. 100-702, Title IV, Section 401(a), 102 Stat. 4648 (1988). See Clark 1947, p. 41-45 for an accessible description of the Rules Enabling Act.

that amendments to the rules of practice would largely be a judicial function with little intervention from Congress.[149] Shortly after the Act was passed, the debate on procedural reform was launched and the Supreme Court appointed an Advisory Committee to draft Rules of Procedure. After preliminary drafts had been made available for discussion by the bench and the bar, rules were adopted and ultimately promulgated by the Supreme Court in 1937. As a result of congressional inaction, the Federal Rules of Civil Procedure (FRCP) took effect on September 16, 1938.

To a large extent, the FRCP drew on the diverse legal systems that had developed within the United States. There were little or no traces of Continental influences.[150] The influence of the Federal Equity Rules was most significant; these were considered to be a good example of rules that were concise, simple and without unnecessary technicalities.[151] Charles E. Clark, the main architect of the FRCP, believed that the Federal Equity Rules of 1912 were a good starting point to draft the FRCP.[152] Like in equity, the FRCP granted the court discretion to make decisions on the course of litigation and to decide upon motions raised by the parties.[153] Formalism made way for disposing of cases on the merits, and thus judges - rather than strict rules - were to decide on procedural issues.[154] Pleading requirements, the joinder of parties and claims and the rules on discovery deviated from the previous practice at law and were construed more broadly than under the Federal Equity Rules. Although the FRCP were largely inspired by existing legal systems, the rules could certainly not be seen as a codification of existing law. Parts of the rules were certainly revolutionary.

The FRCP were, in the first decades after their introduction, considered a great success. Clark claimed that the success of the rules had been 'extraordinary in the history of procedural reform'[155] and that the rules, 'thoroughly tried', have not been found 'wanting'.[156] Since their promulgation, the FRCP have been a source of inspiration for the procedural rules and practices in state courts.[157] By 1960, 20 state jurisdictions had copied the rules in full. Another 6 or 7 states had adopted a number of rules that are largely identical to the FRCP without adopting the rules *in toto*.[158] Additionally a number of states had adopted only a couple of rules that were based on the Federal Rules. By now, a majority of states apply Procedural Rules based on the FRCP. State Rules of Civil Procedure typically lag somewhat behind. Amendments to the Federal Rules are often not introduced in the State Rules or are introduced at a much later point in time. For instance, the Michigan Court Rules of

149 Also see Stempel 2001, Part 2 for a very short introduction to the history of the FRCP.
150 Stiefel & Maxeiner 1994, p. 150. and Langbein 1995.
151 Subrin 1986, p. 954, p. 970 and Millar 1952, p. 62.
152 Subrin 1986, p. 973 and Clark 1947, p. 16-17: '(...) it was to equity that the codifiers went for most their modifications of the common law'.
153 Sunderland 1938, p. 7 and the details there mentioned.
154 Subrin 1986, Part III. Subrin discusses the views of Pound, Shelton and Clark.
155 Clark 1947, p. 39-40.
156 Clark 1958, p. 435.
157 Millar 1952, p. 217.
158 Clark 1961, p. 214; Wright 1959 and Clark 1947, p. 51-54.

1985 on discovery much resemble the FRCP of 1970. Many of the amendments to the FRCP have not been introduced by the Michigan Supreme Court. One will not find rules on disclosure in the Michigan Court Rules.[159]

The 1938 FRCP, still in force today, have been changed several times. In 1970 for example, the FRCP were revised extensively. Other changes to the Rules were 'style only' amendments. For instance, the 2007 Amendments were a 'comprehensive, style only revision' of a large number of rules, aimed at simplifying and modernizing the rules, without changing their meaning.[160] In the Sections below those parts of the FRCP that are most significant for the process of fact-finding will be outlined briefly.

The Federal Rules of Civil Procedure: The Merger of Law and Equity

Like the Field Code, the FRCP broke with the 'forms of action' and recognized only a single 'civil action'.[161] Thus, the FRCP replaced the regulations previously in place on both the law side of the federal courts (Conformity Act) and the equity side of the federal courts (Federal Rules on Equity). The distinction between different procedures on the 'law side' and the 'equity side' of federal courts would cease to exist.

The creation of a single 'civil action' was generally successful yet not without problems. First, the FRCP continued to make a distinction between jury cases and non-jury cases. Whether or not the 'civil action' was previously classified as an action at law or an equitable action, would continue to be of importance to determine whether or not the constitution granted parties the right to a trial by jury. Second, a separate procedure for suits in Admiralty continued to exist up till 1966.[162] Third, the application of the FRCP was not always uniform and local rules continued to fill 'gaps' in the FRCP.[163] Fourth, although the procedures have been merged, the difference between law and equity in substantive law have - despite the many 'fusion debates' - continued to exist to this present day.[164]

Pleading Under the FRCP

The Field Code required the plaintiff to state the 'facts constituting the cause of action' in ordinary language. Judges were generally unsympathetic to the Code's innovations. It has been argued that in legal practice judges were therefore not inclined to apply the law in line with the objectives of the Code.[165] Probably

159 For the Michigan Rules see <http://coa.courts.mi.gov/rules/>, last consulted in October 2009.

160 See a letter by the Committee on Rules of Practice and Procedure Of The Judicial Conference Of The United States, Washington, D.C. 20544, 1 November 2006. Available at <www.uscourts.gov/rules/congress0407.htm>, last consulted in February 2010.

161 FRCP Rule 2.

162 The Federal Rules were amended in 1966. Since then they also apply to Admiralty suits.

163 Rosenberg 1988b, p. 2209 and the references there mentioned.

164 For an overview of equity in modern law see Birks 1996.

165 Millar 1936, p. 200. '(...) the fact has often been emphasized that the judges upon whom devolved the early administration of the New York Code were generally unsympathetic to its →

contrary to the intentions of Field, the notions 'facts' and 'cause of action' gave rise to a whole body of literature and case law concerning the precise meaning of these notions. It was common to make a technical and somewhat vague distinction between 'evidentiary facts', 'ultimate facts' and 'conclusions of law'.[166] There was also a debate on the degree to which the phrase 'cause of action' required the plaintiff to plead matters of law or identify one or more legal rules on which the plaintiff based her claim.[167] Technical distinctions could lead to dismissal of cases due to pleading mistakes.

In the first decades of the 20th century, the criticism of the fact pleading rules and their technicalities led to the recognition of a new approach to pleading: 'notice pleading'. Notice pleading is a more liberal version of code pleading. It was argued that pleadings have a double function. On the one hand, they aim to identify with precision the issue or the issues that were disputed between the parties. On the other hand, a pleading, such as the complaint, serves to give the defendant notice of the nature of the claim such that the defendant is informed about the action she is called upon to defend. 'Notice pleading' stressed the latter function of the pleadings. The Michigan Judicature Act of 1915 provides an early example of legislation that embraced 'notice pleading'. The Act empowered the Supreme Court of Michigan to enact Rules to 'simplify (...) the pleadings' and to abolish 'all unnecessary forms and technicalities in pleading and practice'.[168] The Act further specified that 'no declaration shall be deemed insufficient which shall contain such information as shall reasonably inform the defendant of the nature of the case he is called upon to defend'.[169] The 1933 Illinois Civil Practice Act contained a similar provision stating that 'no pleading shall be deemed bad in substance which shall contain such information as shall reasonably inform the opposite party of the nature of the claim or defense which he is called upon to meet'.[170]

The Federal Rules desired that cases would be judged on the merits, and aimed to remove formal and technical requirements that could lead to decisions unrelated to the specifics of the underlying controversy. FRCP Rule 61 was most explicit as it required the court to 'disregard any error or defect in the proceeding which does not affect the substantial rights of the parties'. The FRCP were based on the belief that if pleadings aimed to narrow down the issues, this would require

innovations and construed its provisions so narrowly as to prevent it from fully accomplishing the objects at which it was aimed'.

166 Ultimate facts where those essential for the action or defense, whereas evidentiary facts were said to be the particular events of the case.

167 For a general overview of the somewhat confusing debates on fact pleading see Friedenthal, Kane & Miller 2005, §5.4 and §5.5; Millar 1936, §4, p. 201-202 and Clark 1947, §19. Clark argues that the most convenient interpretation is 'to consider a cause of action as an aggregate of operative facts giving rise to a right or rights (...) which will be enforced by the courts'. For an account of the use of pleadings as a means to identify legal rules that limit the scope of the dispute, see Maxeiner 2006, p. 558-569.

168 Judicature Act, Chapter I, Section 14 as quoted by Sunderland 1916, p. 551.

169 Judicature Act, Chapter XIV, Section 2 as quoted by Sunderland 1916, p. 551.

170 Section 42 of the Illinois Civil Practice Act as quoted by Millar 1936, p. 203.

strict pleading rules, which in turn would lead to formalism, costs and delay.[171] The federal rules therefore chose the approach that would be least formalistic: notice pleading.

The new FRCP were inspired by the pleading rules of the 1912 Federal Rules on Equity.[172] The drafters of the rules avoided the use of phrases like 'the cause of action' and 'ultimate facts' which had previously led to confusion. Instead, the rules required parties to provide 'a short and plain statement of the claim showing that the pleader is entitled to relief'.[173] The phrase abolished the requirement that the plaintiff identify the precise legal rule on which the claim was based. Relief in the alternative could be demanded by the parties. Contrary to the rules in a number of American jurisdictions, alternative and hypothetical statements of claim or defense were allowed, as were inconsistent counts and defenses.[174] Only a certain number of factual issues had to be pleaded 'with particularity'.[175] Equally, the rules on the amendment of pleadings were liberal.[176] The Supreme Court, in *Conley v. Gibson* (1957), specified that the basic requirement of the pleadings was that the opposing party had been sufficiently notified to meet the claim. The Supreme Court held in *Conley* that:

> '(...) the Federal Rules of Civil Procedure do not require a claimant to set out in detail the facts upon which he bases his claim. To the contrary, all the Rules require is "a short and plain statement of the claim" that will give the defendant fair notice of what the plaintiff's claim is and the grounds upon which it rests. The illustrative forms appended to the Rules plainly demonstrate this. Such simplified "notice pleading" is made possible by the liberal opportunity for discovery and the other pretrial procedures established by the Rules to disclose more precisely the basis of both claim and defense and to define more narrowly the disputed facts and issues. Following the simple guide of Rule 8 (f) that "all pleadings shall be so construed as to do substantial justice," we have no doubt that petitioners' complaint adequately set forth a claim and gave the respondents fair notice of its basis. The Federal Rules reject the approach that pleading is a game of skill in which one misstep by counsel may be decisive to the outcome and accept the principle that the purpose of pleading is to facilitate a proper decision on the merits'.[177]

In *Bell Atlantic Corp. v. Twombly* (2007) the Supreme Court addressed the common interpretation of *Conley v. Gibson*. The common interpretation was that a complaint could not be dismissed unless there was 'no set of facts' upon which relief could be granted. The Court argued that this reading of *Conley v. Gibson* had 'earned its

171 Clark 1947, p. 55.

172 Clark 1935, p. 1299: 'In general these rules *(i.e the Federal Equity Rules RRV)* (...) set forth not merely the best thought in English and American procedure of the date when they were adopted, but even of the present time. (...) The new rules dealing with pleading (...) practically follow the federal equity rules of pleading of 1913 with slight changes'. Also see Sunderland 1938, p. 10. On the drafting of the rules see Subrin 1986, p. 976.

173 FRCP Rule 8(a).

174 FRCP Rule 8(e); Millar 1936, p. 199 and Clark 1947, §42.

175 FRCP Rule 9.

176 FRCP Rule 15, also see Sunderland 1938, p. 15.

177 *Conley v. Gibson*, 355 U.S. 41, at 47-48 (1957).

retirement'.[178] In interpreting FRCP Rule 8, the Court introduced a new standard to determine whether or not the complaint showed that 'the plaintiff was entitled to relief' and gave 'the defendant fair notice'. Under the new standard, the court should critically assess whether the claim has some degree of plausibility. This standard is more stringent and therefore it is to be expected that under this standard a motion to dismiss will be granted more readily. The Supreme Court stressed in its decision that the new standard should avoid the possibility that companies would be subject to expensive discovery in unmeritorious cases.[179]

The concept of notice pleading was also applied to the defendant's answer. The FRCP specified that for both the plaintiff and the defendant 'each averment of a pleading shall be simple, concise and direct'.[180] The defendant was required to admit or deny the averments upon which the adverse party relied or to state that the defendant is without knowledge or information sufficient to form a belief as to the truth of a statement alleged by the plaintiff.[181] The FRCP held on to the general common law approach that 'averments in a pleading to which a responsive pleading is required, (...), are admitted when not denied'.[182]

The FRCP often allows the parties to amend and supplement their pleadings without leave of the court. When leave of the court is required to amend pleadings, the FRCP hold that 'leave shall be freely given if justice so requires'.[183]

In line with the Field Code, many states had resorted to sworn pleadings to ensure candor in pleading. The rule was often criticized, because it offered an obstacle to the presentation of inconsistent defenses.[184] The FRCP used a similar technique and tried to avoid abusive pleading by requiring attorneys to sign pleadings, written motions and other papers. It is doubtful whether the rule - and its amendments in 1983 and 1993 - have been effective to deter abuse.[185]

The Rationale behind the Discovery Arrangements of the 1938 FRCP

After the demise of common law pleading, some jurisdictions implemented new discovery devices (see Section 6.1.2.2). The 1938 FRCP rules on discovery would form the 'striking and imaginative departure from tradition'.[186] The new rules on discovery would have a massive impact on the process of fact-gathering in the decades after the introduction of the new rules.

Clark, who is generally considered to be the main architect of the FRCP, originally had not intended to include broad rules on discovery. It was Sunderland, professor at the University of Michigan, who managed to convince Clark and the other drafters of the rules of the benefits of broad rules on discovery. According to

178 *Bell Atl. Corp. v. Twombly*, 127 S. Ct. 1955, 2007 U.S. LEXIS 5901, at 1969.
179 *Bell Atl. Corp. v. Twombly*, 127 S. Ct. 1955, 2007 U.S. LEXIS 5901, at 1967.
180 FRCP Rule 8(e).
181 FRCP Rule 8(b).
182 FRCP Rule 8(d).
183 FRCP Rule 15(a)(2).
184 Millar 1936, p. 199.
185 Rule 11, See Rosenberg 1988b, p. 2201 for a discussion of empirical studies on Rule 11.
186 The Advisory Committee's Explanatory Statement Concerning 1970 Amendments to Discovery Rules, General Introduction to the Amendments of Rules 26-37.

Sunderland, discovery would offer a multitude of advantages: it would eliminate surprise at trial, lead to the preservation of evidence, reveal the main points in controversy and encourage informed settlement.[187] Sunderland was asked to prepare the first draft rules on discovery.[188]

Sunderland, in an article in the Yale Law Journal of 1932, was positive towards broadening the scope of discovery.[189] Both Sunderland and Clark believed that pleadings were inadequate to provide a basis for trial.[190] Common law pleading, that had forced the parties to define the issue, had been abandoned. In a less formalistic system, Sunderland believed that parties would be inclined to draft their pleadings such that they conveyed little information. American systems were hence in need of new procedural devices to assure proper preparation for trial. According to Sunderland, the traditional discovery in equity did not suffice to prepare for trial as it provided only discovery for 'attack' (i.e. assembling one's own case and evidence) and not for 'defense' (preparing to meet the evidence of the adversary party). New rules on discovery could fill this gap. Many states had broadened the scope of discovery and made it possible to learn from the adverse party what evidence he proposed using at trial.[191]

In order to avoid surprise at trial, Sunderland favored broad and liberal rules on discovery. A second reason to introduce broad and liberal rules was to prevent litigation from becoming a game of 'hide the ball'. Without such broad and liberal rules, Sunderland feared that lawyers would be inclined to withhold information detrimental to their client's case.[192] Restrictions on discovery were regarded with suspicion. On the basis of discovery practices in a number of states, it was concluded that restrictions on the free use of discovery were unnecessary and would create an enormous amount of trouble to the courts and parties in construing and applying them.[193] Experiences with the Federal Rules of Equity and discovery in state jurisdictions had already shown that discovery rules could be abused and could lead to increased costs. Prior to the introduction of the new FRCP, fears were expressed that the introduction of liberal discovery rules would lead to 'over discovery' and 'abuse'.[194] Additionally, it was argued that the wide range of discovery devices would favor richer over poorer litigants.[195] Sunderland recognized that there was a widespread fear of liberal discovery. He was of the

187 Subrin 1997, p. 716. For a more theoretical account of how discovery could increase the information available to both parties and thereby aid settlement, see Priest & Klein 1984.

188 Sunderland was much inspired by the work of Ragland. Ragland published a book in 1932 entitled *Discovery before Trial*, see Subrin 1994, p. 29 and Subrin 1997, p. 702.

189 Sunderland 1932. Sunderland quoted at length authors that had favored the broadened discovery and refuted objections against wider discovery.

190 According to Sunderland pleadings 1) left the parties ignorant of the evidence to be used by the other party 2) allowed the parties to conceal the real issues and 3) would not disclose a basis upon which settlement could be reached. Sunderland 1932 and Clark 1947, p. 576.

191 Sunderland 1932, p. 70.

192 Subrin 1994, p. 30.

193 Sunderland as quoted in Subrin 1997, p. 176.

194 Subrin 1994, p. 33-34.

195 Subrin 1997, p. 730-734.

opinion that hostility to fishing expeditions formed a 'powerful taboo' that had to be overcome.[196]

The Federal Rules of Civil Procedure: A Discovery Revolution

The rules initially drafted by Sunderland included every type of discovery known in the United States. Most of these discovery devices would be adopted in the FRCP that entered into force in 1938.[197] Although each of the discovery devices was used in state jurisdictions, no state had implemented all devices alongside each other. In addition, the FRCP had removed 'practically all restrictions as to the right of discovery'.[198] It was the combination of liberal rules on discovery which made the 1938 Rules revolutionary.[199]

The discovery devices that would be used most extensively were interrogatories, depositions and the production of documents.[200] In addition, the rules provided for the physical and mental examination of parties, the inspection of objects and (real) property, and requests for admissions.[201] The rules were fairly flexible and parties could agree to change procedures on discovery or limitations on discovery, except for those limitations set on time (Rule 29). The rules allowed the parties to use any combination of discovery devices to obtain information from the opposing party. It is for instance common in current legal practice to file a number of interrogatories in April in order to prepare for the deposition of one's adversary in June.[202]

The judiciary has not always been willing to comply with the newly introduced FRCP, and restricted the use of the new and liberal discovery devices on a number of different grounds. In the first decades after the enactment of the rules, the amendments to the rules and decisions of the Supreme Court moved towards broadening the scope of discovery and weakening the role of the court in pretrial discovery. Both trends will be discussed below.

The scope of discovery was gradually widened in the decades after the introduction of the FRCP.[203] In 1946, the Supreme Court promulgated a number of amendments that led to a further liberalization of the rules on discovery. It was made clear that discovery does not only serve to avoid surprise at trial: it is also meant to enable a 'broad search for facts'. A new, overarching provision on the scope of discovery was added that specified that: 'It is not ground for objection that the testimony will be inadmissible at the trial if the testimony sought appears

196 Subrin 1997, p. 697.

197 See Subrin 1997, p. 719-729 for the discussion within the Advisory Committee on the scope of discovery.

198 Sunderland 1938, p. 22.

199 Dobie 1938, p. 279 writes: 'Discovery, (...), now (for the first time) assumes a role of real importance in the federal courts'.

200 For data on the use of the different discovery devices see the findings of the FJC Discovery Study as discussed by Mullenix 1993, p. 1435. and Willging, Stienstra, Shaphard & Miletich 1998.

201 FRCP Rules 26-37.

202 Sunderland 1938, p. 24.

203 For a short introduction to the Federal Rules of Discovery see Stempel 2001, Part II.

reasonably calculated to lead to the discovery of admissible evidence'.[204] The Advisory Committee Note on the scope of depositions states:

> 'The amendments (...) make clear the broad scope of examination and that it may cover not only evidence for use at the trial but also inquiry into matters in themselves inadmissible as evidence but which will lead to the discovery of such evidence. The purpose of discovery is to allow a broad search for facts, the names of witnesses, or any other matters which may aid a party in the preparation or presentation of his case. (...)'.[205]

The 1946 Amendments also widened the scope of interrogatories. The Advisory Committee saw 'no reason why interrogatories should be more limited than depositions'.[206]

A year later, in *Hickman v. Taylor* the Supreme Court decided on the precise scope of discovery. The Supreme Court held that the various instruments of discovery aim to ascertain that 'civil trials in the federal courts no longer need be carried on in the dark'.[207] Thus, the court held that it was essential to litigation that the discovery rules were accorded 'a broad and liberal treatment'.[208] At the same time, the court held that there were limits to the scope of discovery. In *Hickman v. Taylor* the Supreme Court introduced the so-called 'work-product' rule that held that the files and mental impressions of an attorney could not be subject to discovery.[209] The rule aimed to ensure that attorneys can investigate their own case, without having to fear that materials prepared in anticipation of litigation or trial would be made available to the opposing party. In 1970, the work-product rule was codified in FRCP Rule 26(b)(3).

The first comprehensive amendments to the discovery rules were made in 1970.[210] Some of the changes were mainly technical; Rule 26 was rewritten to form a

204 FRCP Rule 26(b)(1).

205 Advisory Committee Note to the 1946 Amendment of Rule 26.

206 Advisory Committee Note to the 1946 Amendment of Rule 33.

207 *Hickman v. Taylor*, 329 U.S. 495 (1947) at 501: 'The various instruments of discovery now serve (1) as a device (...) to and clarify the basic issues between the parties, and (2) as a device for ascertaining the facts, or information as to the existence or whereabouts of facts, relative to those issues. Thus civil trials in the federal courts no longer need be carried on in the dark'.

208 *Hickman v. Taylor*, 329 U.S. 495 (1947) at 507: '(...) the deposition-discovery rules are to be accorded a broad and liberal treatment. No longer can the time-honored cry of "fishing expedition" serve to preclude a party from inquiring into the facts underlying his opponent's case. Mutual knowledge of all the relevant facts gathered by both parties is essential to proper litigation'.

209 *Hickman v. Taylor*, 329 U.S. 495 (1947) at 510: 'Not even the most liberal of discovery theories can justify unwarranted inquiries into the files and the mental impressions of an attorney'. At 514: 'When Rule 26 and the other discovery rules were adopted, this Court and the members of the bar in general certainly did not believe or contemplate that all the files and mental processes of lawyers were thereby opened to the free scrutiny of their adversaries. And we refuse to interpret the rules at this time so as to reach so harsh and unwarranted a result'.

210 A concise summary of the Amendment is provided by The Advisory Committee's Explanatory Statement Concerning 1970 Amendments to Discovery Rules, General Introduction to the Amendments of Rules 26-37.

'general' rule that applied to all discovery devices. With regard to content, one of the central elements of the 1970 amendments was that the scope of discovery was widened. The contents of insurance policies became discoverable and the showing of good cause was no longer necessary for discovery of documents, things and entry upon land. The discovery of information held by experts was widened, it was made more difficult to object to interrogatories or requests for admissions, and medical examinations became available as to certain non-parties.[211]

The second trend in the first decades after the enactment of the 1938 FRCP was that the Rules were amended to allow the discovery process to operate more and more without court intervention. Leave of the court was no longer required for most discovery instruments. The 1946 Amendment eliminated the requirement for leave of the court to take a deposition unless the plaintiff sought the deposition within 20 days after the commencement of the action.[212] The 1970 Amendment specified that leave of the court for the filing of interrogatories and the requests for production of documents, things and entries upon land was also no longer required.[213] At the same time, the machinery of discovery was altered to ensure that the court would not be overburdened with motions related to discovery. The 1970 Amendments changed the mechanics of interrogatories to reduce the need for court intervention.[214]

In American practice, judges usually do not get involved in discovery. Often judges do not wish to hear discovery motions and therefore frequently delegate this task to a magistrate judge. In spite of recent attempts to urge courts to manage discovery, 'success of judicial supervision in checking discovery abuse has been on the modest side'.[215] Lawyers generally believe that more involvement of the court in the process of discovery would be desirable and that sanctions ought to be imposed more frequently. In a survey of 177 Chicago lawyers in 1979, Brazil asked if 'there were any problems with the current system' of discovery.[216] The 'Negative Impact, Role or Attitudes of Judges or Magistrates' was mentioned by 71% of all lawyers and was thereby considered the single biggest problem in the operation of discovery (Table 3.1). Lawyers emphasized 'the court's inhospitality to hearing discovery disputes, the poor quality of decisions about discovery matters by trial judges and magistrates, and the underuse and ineffectiveness of sanctions'.[217] A Chicago litigator complained that 'Courts want nothing to do with discovery and never use sanctions. Rule 37 is really Rule Zero'.[218] Most lawyers favored more judicial involvement in discovery. An overwhelming majority of them favored more

211 These five changes respectively correspond to changes in Rule 26(b)(2), Rule 34(a), Rule 26(b)(4), Rules 33(b) and 36(a), and Rule 35(a).

212 FRCP Rule 26(a).

213 FRCP Rules 33(a), 34(b).

214 See the Advisory Committee Notes to 1970 Amendments of Rule 33. A significant change was that the interrogating party, rather than the interrogated party, would have to move for court intervention if the interrogated party objected to an interrogatory.

215 *Bell Atl. Corp. v. Twombly*, 127 S. Ct. 1955, 2007 U.S. LEXIS 5901, at 1967.

216 Brazil 1980, p. 825.

217 *Ibidem.*

218 Brazil 1980, p. 824.

frequent use of sanctions by the court.[219] Empirical studies reveal that judges hardly ever impose sanctions.[220] Brazil's study showed that lawyers believed that judges should be more active in resolving discovery disputes and sanctions had to be imposed more frequently and severely. According to a 1992 survey by the Federal Judicial Centre, two thirds of the judges moderately or strongly supported an increase in sanctions for bad faith discovery responses.[221]

The Federal Rules of Civil Procedure and Summary Judgments on the Merits

After the breakdown of common law pleading, the demurrer no longer existed. As the pleadings no longer narrowed down the dispute to a single issue, Anglo-American systems were increasingly faced with so-called 'sham pleas', pleadings that were unfounded in fact and could be used for the purpose of delay. In the late 19th and early 20th century, summary judgments were introduced in England and several American States to swiftly dispose of cases in which no genuine issue of fact existed.[222] The use of summary judgments was traditionally confined to certain categories of cases and often only available to the plaintiff.[223]

The FRCP adopted a provision on summary judgments which was construed broadly. The Rule was drafted by Sunderland and inspired by the Michigan Rules of Civil Procedure.[224] The new rule was 'bold' and 'revolutionary'. First, the procedure was made available in every civil action. Second, the Federal Rules explicitly made the motion for summary judgment available to both parties.[225] Although summary judgments may legally be ordered *sua sponte*, summary judgments are usually granted upon a motion raised by either one of the parties.[226] After the complaint is filed, the defendant may file a motion to dismiss for failure of the complaint to state a claim on which relief can be granted.[227] But usually motions for summary judgment are not made until each side has engaged in some form of discovery.[228]

The FRCP specified that a summary judgment shall be rendered if the pleadings, discovery findings and relevant documents 'show that there is no genuine issue as to any material fact and the moving party is entitled to a judgment

219 Brazil 1980, p. 866-867.

220 See Sofaer 1982, p. 703-706 for an overview of empirical data on the use of sanctions under Rule 37.

221 Federal Judicial Centre, Planning for the Future: Results of a 1992 Federal Judicial Center Survey of United States Judges 35 (1994) as discussed by McKenna & Wiggins 1998, p. 805.

222 The summary judgment originated in the 1855 English Bill of Exchange Act. See for an historic account: Millar 1952, Chapter 16; Clark 1951, p. 567-568; Miller 2003, p. 1016 and Burbank 2004, Part II.

223 Clark 1951, p. 569.

224 For a description of the history of the Federal Rules, see Burbank 2004, Part II.

225 FRCP Rule 56(a) and (b).

226 Whether the court may render a summary judgment without a prior motion by either of the parties was not clear from the rules. Clark 1951, p. 570-571. Courts have often held that a summary judgment can be rendered *sua sponte* if parties are properly heard. See Friedenthal, Kane & Miller 2005, p. 470.

227 See Rule 12(b)(6) and 12(c). This rule is substantially the same as the old demurrer.

228 Friedenthal, Kane & Miller 2005, p. 469.

as a matter of law'.[229] Minor facts, factual issues of little importance or feigned factual debates do not prevent the court from rendering a summary judgment. Only if the facts central to the claim or a defense are truly disputed, will a summary judgment not be rendered.[230] In deciding upon a motion, the judge is thus required to consider the merits of the case. Since the implementation of the FRCP, the legal standards for granting a motion for summary judgment or a motion to dismiss seem to have shifted in favor of granting rather than denying such a motion. Throughout the history of FRCP Rules 12 and 56 there has been a debate on how broadly the rules should be construed. Shortly after the enactment of the FRCP, courts seemed to hold that summary judgments were to be rendered sparingly, so as not to deprive the parties of their day in court.[231] Under the influence of a number of Supreme Court decisions, the standard for rendering a summary judgment was lowered.[232] In *Anderson v. Liberty Lobby* (1986) the Supreme Court seemed to introduce a different standard; arguing that the judge ought to inquire 'whether reasonable jurors could find by a preponderance of the evidence that the plaintiff is entitled to a verdict'.[233] In *Bell v. Twombly* (2007) the Supreme Court held that a judge had to determine whether the complaint had some degree of plausibility when deciding on a motion to dismiss.[234]

If the court does not grant a dispositive summary judgment, the judgment can still be of significance as a means to narrow down the issue. The court should 'ascertain what material facts exist without substantial controversy and what material facts are actually and in good faith controverted'.[235]

2.2.3. The Codification of the Law on Evidence

Since the late 18th century, Anglo-American literature has considered evidence as a separate branch of the law. Although differences between civil and criminal cases exist, statutes, case law and jurisprudence on evidence often cover both criminal and civil cases.[236] The typology in Anglo-American legal thinking is different from the Continental typology of the law. On the European Continent, evidence is generally considered to be either part of 'civil law', 'criminal law' or even 'administrative law'. In countries like Germany, Austria and the Netherlands the Codes of Civil Procedure contain most provisions on evidence. In countries like

229 FRCP Rule 56(c).

230 Friedenthal, Kane & Miller 2005, p. 474-475.

231 Miller 2003, p. 1019-1022.

232 Three important 1986 Supreme Court Decisions on summary judgments are *Matsushita Electric Industrial Co. v. Zenith Radio Corp.* 475 U.S. 574 (1986); *Anderson v. Liberty Lobby, Inc.* 477 U.S. 242 (1986) and *Celotex Corp. v. Catrett* 477 U.S. 317. See Miller 2003, p. 1026 *et seq.*

233 *Anderson v. Liberty Lobby, Inc.* 477 U.S. 242 (1986) at 252. This decision seems to apply the standard se by Federal Rule of Procedure 50(a) on directed verdicts.

234 *Bell Atl. Corp. v. Twombly,* 127 S. Ct. 1955, 2007 U.S. LEXIS, at 5901.

235 FRCP Rule 56(d).

236 In the U.S., rules of evidence commonly cover evidence in both criminal and civil cases. Differences between civil evidence and criminal evidence do exist, *inter alia* because of the different constitutional impact on criminal and civil evidence.

France, Italy and Belgium parts of the law of evidence are found in a separate chapter of the Civil Code.

In the U.S. until the second part of the 20th century, the rules of evidence were a product of common law. Although some uniformity existed between federal and state jurisdictions, the rules of evidence had not been codified. Throughout the 20th century it had been argued that codification was needed to simplify and clarify the rules of evidence. Although some unsuccessful attempts were made in the first decades of the 20th century, it was only in the second half of the 20th century that the first codifications were adopted.[237]

The 1942 Model Code of Evidence

The first influential attempt in the United States to codify the law of evidence was the 1942 American Law Institute's Model Code of Evidence. It aimed to serve as a blueprint that was to be studied by state committees with a view towards adopting the Model Code. Because of opposition from practitioners and esteemed academics like Wigmore, the Model Code has not been adopted by any state.[238] Nevertheless, it played a significant role as it inspired other codifications, most notably the 1953 Uniform Rules of Evidence and the 1975 Federal Rules of Evidence (FRE).

The Model Code was drafted by a Committee chaired by Edmund M. Morgan, professor at Harvard University.[239] The Code was relatively concise (113 rules) as the Committee had tried to find a middle way between a long 'catalogue' of rules and a 'creed' containing only general principles.[240]

The Model Code simplified and codified the existing common law. Three prominent features of the Model Code will be discussed here. First, the Model Code strengthened the role of the court and limited the adversarial control over the presentation of evidence. Morgan recognized the merits of the adversarial system, yet did not wish to regard the presentation of evidence as a 'battle between the great champions of the contending parties'.[241] While limiting the role of the parties, the Model Code stressed the role of the judge. As Morgan put it: 'the Code leaves no room for doubt as to the power of the trial judge'.

The Model Code adopted the starting point that 'all relevant evidence is admissible'.[242] In line with the developments of the previous centuries, there were no rules that barred witnesses who had an interest in the case or were not willing to take a Christian oath from giving testimony. It also departed from the common law by a further liberalization of the hearsay rule.[243]

A third remarkable feature of the Model Code was that Morgan downplayed the importance of the pursuit of truth in civil litigation. Neither did he focus on the

237 An example of an early attempt to codify the law is Wigmore's 1910 'Code of Evidence'. See Ariens 1992, Section 2D.

238 Ariens 1992, p. 234.

239 Ladd 1942.

240 Ladd 1942, p. 13.

241 Ladd 1942, p. 11.

242 Ladd 1942, p. 11.

243 Ladd 1942, Chapter 6 and general introduction.

enforcement of substantive law. It was the resolution of disputes which Morgan considered the true end of civil litigation. Morgan argued that the court's 'final determination is binding only between the parties and their privies. It does not pronounce upon the facts for any purpose other than the adjustment of the controversy before it'.[244]

The 1953 Uniform Rules of Evidence[245]
In 1948, the National Conference of Commissioners on Uniform State Laws (NCCUSL) decided to aim for a greater uniformity of state laws on evidence and convened a committee that would draft a codification. The Committee partly consisted of former members of the Model Code of Evidence committee and took the Model Code as a starting point. In 1953, the NUCCUSL passed the Uniform Rules of Evidence that were soon endorsed by the American Bar Association (ABA). The Uniform Rules of Evidence were influential. Several states, including California, Kansas, New Jersey and Utah, adopted a Code based on the Uniform Rules of Evidence.[246]

The Conference Committee claimed that the Uniform Rules were a modest reform, not a radical reformation of the law of evidence.[247] In many ways, the content of the Uniform Rules was similar to that of the Model Code. More authority was put in the hands of the court and less in the hands of counsel . The Uniform Rules began with the principle that all relevant evidence should be admissible and removed some restrictions on the admissibility of evidence.[248] For instance, the 'dead man's statute', a rule that prevailed in a large number of states, was not retained.[249] Unlike Morgan, the Conference Committee did not suggest that a trial was not primarily a search for truth.[250]

The Federal Rules of Evidence
In 1961, the Judicial Conference of the United States appointed a Special Committee to inquire whether the codification of the rules of evidence in federal courts would be feasible and advisable. The report was positive and led to the appointment of an Advisory Committee on Rules of Evidence in 1965. The legislative process leading towards the final enactment of the Federal Rules of Evidence (FRE) in 1975 was lengthy due to many revisions before approval by the Supreme Court and the fact that Congress stepped in to amend and revise the rules.[251]

The FRE have been subject to a number of incremental amendments since. The FRE are fairly concise, consisting of less than 70 rules and are therefore comparable

244 Ladd 1942, p. 3-4.
245 Jacobs 1955 and Ariens 1992, Section 2G.
246 Saltzburg, Martin & Capra 1998, Part 1.
247 Ariens 1992, p. 247.
248 Uniform Rules of Evidence, Rule 7.
249 See Section 6.1.3.
250 Ariens 1992, p. 247.
251 For a short introduction on its legislative history see: Saltzburg, Martin & Capra 1998, p. 3.

to Continental codifications.[252] The FRE could rightly be considered a codification as they totally supplanted the common law previously developed.[253] The FRE were to a very large extent inspired by the Uniform Rules of Evidence and state laws (i.e. the Codes of California and New Jersey). The Advisory Committee referred to the Uniform Rules in its notes to almost all of the newly proposed rules.[254]

Like the FRCP, the FRE claim that the rules should be construed to promote fairness, eliminate costs and delay, and to ascertain the truth.[255] With respect to content, the FRE could for the larger part be considered 'evolutionary' rather that 'revolutionary'.[256] The FRE led to a further simplification of the common law of evidence and sometimes deviated from the common law rules. The changes brought about by the FRE were pragmatic and incremental in nature.[257] The doctrines and rules that were developed throughout the 18th and the 19th centuries, such as rules on relevance, the cross-examination of witnesses, hearsay and the best evidence rule, continued to be prominent in the FRE.

Within a dozen years after the adoption of the FRE, a total of 31 states had codified their State law of evidence based wholly or substantially on the FRE.[258] Today, only a couple of states have not codified the law of evidence. In addition, the interpretations and amendments of the FRE have continued to influence legislation at the state level. The Michigan Rules of Evidence, adopted on January 5, 1978, provide an example of state laws based on the FRE. Save some small amendments in terminology, most provisions were identical to the FRE. Some provisions were based on the Uniform Rules of Evidence; occasionally one of the Michigan Rules of Evidence was based on Michigan Common Law.[259]

252 The Dutch Code of Civil Procedure has 59 Sections on evidence (Articles 149-207) and the Austrian Code contains 124 provisions (Sections 266-389). However, a pure numerical comparison is misleading. In the Federal system provisions on evidence are codified in the FRCP and the FRE. In Austria and the Netherlands all provisions form a part of the Code of Civil Procedure.

253 *United States v. Abel*, 469 U.S. 45 (1984), at 51: 'In principle, under the Federal Rules no common law of evidence remains'.

254 Very often the notes of the Advisory Committee contain phrases like: 'For Rules of similar import, see Uniform Rules 52 and 53, California Evidence Code §§1152, 1154; Kansas Code of Civil Procedure §60-452, 60-453; New Jersey Evidence Rules 52, 53'.

255 FRCP, Rule 1 and FRE, Rule 102.

256 Leonard & Gold 2004, p. 6.

257 Twining 2006, p. 72. 'Although this movement towards codification represents the general trend in the direction of simplification and further narrowing of the scope of the formal rules of evidence, these codes represent achievements of pragmatic, incremental change based on compromise rather than a clear victory for Thayerism, let alone Bethamism'.

258 These states are listed in Lilly 1987, p. xxv.

259 Michigan Rules of Evidence Rules 101, 202 and 1101 were for instance based on the Uniform Rules of Evidence whereas Rule 803(A) was based on Michigan Common Law.

3. Recent Developments

3.1. *Critique of the Inefficiency of American Litigation*

In the 1970s, the initial positive attitude towards the procedural rules and their application made way for criticism. For a couple of decades, the system of procedure was criticized for discovery abuse, high costs, delays, unpredictability, litigiousness, excessive judicial power and inequality between the parties.[260] A large number of reports were published to address the evils of the system and to call for action.[261] Stiefel and Maxeiner conclude that all but one of the reports 'agree that there is a crisis in the U.S. civil justice system brought on by excessive cost and delay'.[262] The American scholar Langbein wrote an influential comparative journal article in which he argued that German system of civil litigation was much more efficient than the American system.[263] In 1991, Vice President Dan Quayle argued that the American legal system provided the national economy a 'self inflicted competitive disadvantage'.[264]

It was commonly argued that American society was 'the most litigious' in the world.[265] It was believed that litigation rates were soaring rapidly and too many resources were spent on litigation. It is hard to judge indeed, whether there was a 'litigation explosion'. It is true that throughout the 20th century, there was a large increase in divorces and tort law cases. But there is no convincing evidence that there has been a large increase in the number of civil disputes. There has been a significant increase in spending on legal services in the United States.[266] However, the total number of cases filed is not excessive when compared to litigation rates in other jurisdictions.[267]

Discovery abuse, discussed in the next Section, was generally believed to be the biggest single cause of excessive costs and litigation delays. Many suggestions to improve the mechanics of the procedural rules were introduced. More fundamental were two other solutions that were constantly brought forward to combat costs and

260 See Subrin 1986, p. 911 and the literature there cited.

261 These reports include two ABA reports: ABA, 'Attacking Litigation Costs and Delay, Final Report of the Action Commission to Reduce Court Costs and Delays' (1984) and ABA, 'ABA Blueprint to Improve the Civil Justice System' (1992), a report by the Brookings Institution: 'The Brookings Institution, Justice for All, Reducing Costs and Delay in Civil Litigation, Report of a Task Force' (1989), a report by a Congressional Committee, 'U.S. Congress, Report of the Federal Courts Study Committee' (1990), and a Presidential Report, often referred to as the Quayle Report, 'U.S. President, Report from the Presidents Council on Competitiveness, Agenda for Civil Justice Reform in America' (1991). These reports are summarized by Stiefel & Maxeiner 1994.

262 Stiefel & Maxeiner 1994, p. 152.

263 Langbein 1985. See Stiefel & Maxeiner 1994 for a summary of the discussion that it triggered.

264 Quayle's views as discussed by Mullenix 1993, Part I.

265 For a critical assessment see Mullenix 1993, Part I; Stempel 2001 and Miller 2003, Part 1A.

266 See in this respect Friedman 2008, p. 178-181 and the studies there quoted.

267 See the empirical studies quoted in Section 3.4.3.

delay.[268] First, it was believed that an increased use of alternative dispute resolution methods would provide a remedy against flaws in the civil justice system. Second, it was believed that increased judicial case management could successfully cut costs, reduce the time to disposition and increase the settlement rate. Some empirical studies partly confirmed these beliefs.[269] The rise of case management will be discussed in Section 3.3.3.

3.2. *The Recent History of Discovery: A History of Abuse*

The Alleged Problem of Abuse

For the first decades after their enactment, the rules on discovery were generally believed to be sound.[270] The 1970 Amendments to the FRCP were based on the so-called 'Columbia Survey', a study whereby interviews and questionnaires of lawyers led to 2000 sets of responses on the basis of approximately 1200 cases concluded in 1962.[271] The Advisory Committee, in a preamble to the 1970 amendments of the discovery rules, summarized the findings of the survey as follows:

> 'The Columbia Survey concludes, in general, that there is no empirical evidence to warrant a fundamental change in the philosophy of the discovery rules. No widespread or profound failings are disclosed in the scope or availability of discovery. The costs of discovery do not appear to be oppressive, as a general matter, either in relation to ability to pay or to the stakes of the litigation. Discovery frequently provides evidence that would not otherwise be available to the parties and thereby makes for a fairer trial or settlement. On the other hand, no positive evidence is found that discovery promotes settlement'.

Gradually, pretrial discovery had become the most important phase in civil litigation. Complaints about over-discovery, abuse, lack of sanctions and lack of court intervention became more frequent in the late 1970s. Most reforms of the FRCP discovery rules can be understood against the background of discovery abuse. The history of the amendments to the FRCP is largely the history of its alleged abuse.

268 Subrin 1986, p. 912 and Miller 2003, Parts 1B and 1C. Stiefel & Maxeiner 1994, p. 153 conclude that all reports on the justice system seem to agree that case management would provide the solution.

269 See Rosenberg 1988a, Part 4 and Flanders 1978. For a critical discussion see Resnik 1984 and Resnik 1982, p. 417-418.

270 See Note 1961, p. 942: 'Nevertheless, it is generally agreed that discovery, as a complement to modern liberal pleading, has improved the operation and administration of our judicial system and has advanced the purposes it was designed to serve. It seems therefore that it is not discovery itself, but rather the details of its functioning, that require evaluation'. Schwarzer 1989, p. 704: 'For the first thirty years the Federal Rules appear to have worked to the satisfaction of the bar and the bench'.

271 The survey itself has not been published. For a description of its findings see Rosenberg 1988a, p. 25; Rosenberg 1969, p. 488 and Glaser 1968.

Some have coined a 1976 Pound conference as the 'inaugural event of the counter revolution' against broad discovery.[272] The American Bar Association appointed a Special Committee for the Study of Discovery Abuse that presented its findings in 1977. The Committee proposed limiting the scope of discovery and the number of interrogatories that could be served without a court order.[273] A Second Report of the Special ABA Committee for Study of Discovery Abuse was published in 1980.[274] Discovery abuse was considered one of the major problems in civil litigation for at least two decades. A survey of 1000 judges conducted in the late 1980s showed that judges rated abusive discovery as the main reason for the high costs of litigation.[275] A 1979 study conducted by Brazil was very influential with regard to discovery abuse.[276] Brazil interviewed 177 Chicago lawyers to understand the problems and abuses in the operation of discovery. The survey revealed differences between smaller and more complex cases. Lawyers involved in smaller cases were much more positive towards discovery than those involved in big cases.[277] Discovery in large cases was considered to be 'in serious trouble'. According to Brazil, such differences indicate that it might be wise to tailor different sets of discovery rules for different categories of cases.[278]

The study also revealed that tactical considerations influence the decisions of attorneys in conducting discovery. Lawyers believed that in 28% of all cases discovery is used as a means to shift a work burden to an opponent.[279] Discovery was frequently used as a tactical weapon to slow down the proceedings, to impose work burdens and economic pressure on the opposing party and to obscure the issues.[280] Examples of tactical (ab)use of discovery include the following: 1) One can react to a request to produce documents by 'bombarding' the opponent with loads of documents, such that the opponent will need to find the relevant documents somewhere halfway inside a big stack of paperwork; 2) lawyers can deliberately mislead the other party such that the other party prepares to meet arguments that will not be used; 3) In order to increase travel expenses of the opposing party, some lawyers have noticed depositions for remote places or requested the deposition of witnesses who live abroad; 4) attorneys have deliberately asserted unjustified objections to discovery such that the opponent has to request the court to compel discovery; 5) attorneys may instruct experts not to draft a report until just before trial; 6) discovery devices can be abused to obtain redundant or irrelevant

272 Stempel 2001, p. 207.

273 'Report of the Special Committee for Study of Discovery Abuse', as discussed by Rosenberg & King 1981, p. 580.

274 See Rosenberg & King 1981, p. 585 for a discussion of the Report.

275 'Judges Polled', 6 *Alternatives* 149 (1988) as cited by Rosenberg 1988b, p. 2205.

276 Brazil 1980, a study quoted by the Advisory Committee when it revised the FRCP in 1983 and 1993.

277 Brazil 1980, p. 802.

278 Brazil 1980, Part IX.

279 Brazil 1980, p. 857.

280 For statistical data see Brazil 1980, Part VI.

information; 7) rich litigants can 'over discover' and thereby threaten to drive their poorer opponent into bankruptcy to enforce an 'unfair' settlement.[281]

There may be doubts as to the extent of the abuse problem. In most cases, there is little or no discovery. Discovery abuse does seem to exist in a small proportion of all cases, and there is a general consensus that problems and abuses are more frequent in large and complex cases. The Columbia Survey, briefly mentioned in the previous paragraph, concluded that complaints about the other side's use of discovery occurred in over half the cases. Only one fourth of those who complained brought the behavior of an opponent to the attention of the court.[282] The study showed that depositions appeared to be generating most difficulties.[283]

In the aforementioned study by Brazil, lawyers were asked if 'there were any problems with the current system' of discovery. The problems most frequently encountered are listed below, along with the percentage of lawyers who mentioned the problem.

Table 3.1. Most frequently reported discovery problems[284]

Discovery Problems Reported	% of Lawyers
Negative Impact, Role or Attitudes of Judges or Magistrates	71%
Evasive Responses, Withholding Information, or Noncompliance	61%
Over Discovery	49%
Delay	43%
Cost	41%
Harassment	40%
Problems with Interrogatories	28%

Evasion of discovery requests was considered the second biggest problem. It was often associated with the use of interrogatories.[285] When asked whether evasive or incomplete responses have ever made discovery more difficult or caused lawyers not to uncover or pursue information, lawyers indicated that this problem occurred in 60% of all cases. Lawyers also reported that dishonesty or bad faith was a problem in a much smaller proportion of all cases they were involved in (14%).[286]

Other studies, often including data from more than a single district, were less negative concerning the scope of abuse. As mentioned above, a large majority of cases have little or no formal discovery; therefore discovery abuse has probably never been universally pervasive.[287] A 1997 survey by Willging *et al*, showed that out of those attorneys that reported one or more problems, 44% said problems occurred with document production, 37% said they occurred in initial disclosure, 26% said they occurred in expert disclosure and 26% said they occurred in

281 Brazil 1980, Part VI.
282 Rosenberg 1969, p. 490.
283 Rosenberg 1969, p. 487.
284 Brazil 1980, p. 825.
285 Brazil 1980, p. 829.
286 Brazil 1980, p. 838.
287 See Mullenix 1993, who discusses a number of empirical studies that draw this conclusion.

depositions. Overall, attorneys believed that 4% of litigation expenses are attributable to discovery problems.[288] The most frequently mentioned problems with regard to the production of documents was failure of the other party to respond adequately and timely.[289] More than half of the attorneys cited intentional delays and complications as a cause of problems.[290] Problems were far more likely to be reported by attorneys who handled very complex cases that had high stakes.[291]

The alleged discovery abuse was at the heart of the debate on procedural reform. The first Amendment to the FRCP to address the issue of abuse was very modest. The 1980 Amendment failed to include serious restrictions to discovery as it was believed that abuse of discovery 'while very serious in certain cases, is not so general as to require such basic changes in the rules that govern discovery in all cases'.[292] The 1983 amendments to the FRCP aimed to counter the problems of evasion and resistance to discovery, excessive discovery and counter-productive lawyer tactics. The Advisory Committee Notes to the 1983 Amendments claimed that discovery rules have been 'exploited to the disadvantage of justice'.[293] Since 1990, the prime concerns have focused on lowering costs and delays in the process of discovery. The 1990 Civil Justice Reform Act and the 1993 Amendments to the FRCP are examples of reforms that aimed to ensure a cheaper and swifter exchange of information. The aforementioned reforms offered four main solutions to problems of abuse, costs and delays in the process of discovery: 1) judicial case management to ensure speedy and inexpensive discovery; 2) the encouragement of parties to reach an agreement on time and cost efficient modes of conducting discovery; 3) limiting the scope of discovery and 4) the introduction of disclosure to supplement discovery.

Increased judicial case management was one of the main instruments to address abuse and excessive costs and delay in discovery (see Section 3.3.3).[294] Judges were increasingly encouraged to discuss formal discovery at pretrial conferences, enter a scheduling order, ensure that a discovery plan is made, regulate the scope of discovery in accordance with the needs of the case and - if necessary - impose sanctions. The 1980 amendments took the first modest step in the direction of using conferences as a means to manage discovery. The possibility of scheduling a discovery conference was introduced to provide a party faced with abusive discovery a means for obtaining judicial intervention. As contemplated, these discovery conferences were rarely used and were changed drastically in 1993.[295] The 1983 and 1993 Amendments introduced more far-reaching rules to accommodate the judicial management of discovery. The 1993 Amendments encouraged the use of

288 Willging, Stienstra, Shaphard & Miletich 1998, p. 532-533.
289 Willging, Stienstra, Shaphard & Miletich 1998, p. 540.
290 Willging, Stienstra, Shaphard & Miletich 1998, p. 540.
291 Willging, Stienstra, Shaphard & Miletich 1998, p. 582.
292 Advisory Committee Notes to the 1980 Amendment of Rule 26(f).
293 Advisory Committee Notes to the 1983 Amendments of Rule 26.
294 See *inter alia* Stempel 2001, p. 198.
295 Advisory Committee Notes to the 1980 Amendment of Rule 26(f): 'It is not contemplated that requests for discovery conferences will be made routinely'. See Advisory Committee Notes to the 1993 Amendment of Rule 26(f): 'the device has been used only sparingly'.

pretrial conferences as a means to manage discovery. The Advisory Committee Notes to the 1993 Amendments stressed that a pretrial scheduling and planning conference, whereby the parties and a judicial officer meet in person, should, 'to the extent practical, be held in all cases that will involve discovery'.[296]

A second solution to address some of the evils of discovery was to require the parties to cooperate in ensuring a smooth exchange of information. 1993 Amendments to the FRCP particularly stressed the role of parties in planning discovery, reaching agreements as to the modes of discovery that will be used and resolving discovery disputes. Since 1993, formal discovery cannot take place until the parties have conferred to construct a 'discovery plan'.[297] The meeting of both parties at a discovery conference should, in principle, take place in all cases and should be held prior to a regular pretrial conference where the judge may further manage discovery by setting timetables and defining limits to the scope and extent of discovery.[298] Additionally, FRCP Rule 29 was amended in 1993 to give greater opportunities to the litigants to agree upon modifications of procedural rules regulating the process of fact-finding. The Advisory Committee put it as follows: 'counsel are encouraged to agree on less expensive and time-consuming methods to obtain information, as through voluntary exchange of documents, use of interviews in lieu of depositions, etc'.[299] The 1993 Amendments further required the parties try and resolve discovery disputes in good faith before filing a motion for a protective order.[300]

The third method employed to make discovery more efficient and less vulnerable to abuse was to curb its scope. The 1983, 1993 and 2000 Amendments departed from the premise of the 1938 FRCP that 'more discovery is better'.[301] In 1983 the scope of discovery was limited by adding the requirement that discovery had to be proportional. Discovery could be limited: 1) if it was unreasonably cumulative, duplicative or if information could be obtained in more convenient ways; 2) if the party seeking information has had ample opportunity during the action to obtain the information sought or 3) if the burden and expense of discovery outweighs the likely benefits of discovery.[302] Limitations on the scope of discovery were to be understood in conjunction with increased resort to judicial case management. The Advisory Committee envisaged greater judicial involvement in the discovery process in order to restrict the scope of discovery. It was considered appropriate for the court to address matters of proportionality at its own initiative during a pretrial conference.[303]

In 2000, the scope of discovery was curbed by limiting discovery to things relevant to a 'claim or defense' rather than issues relevant to the 'subject matter' of

296 Advisory Committee Notes to the 1993 Amendments of Rule 16(b).
297 FRCP Rule 26(d).
298 Advisory Committee Notes to the 1993 Amendments of Rules 16 and 26(f).
299 Advisory Committee Notes to the 1993 Amendment of Rule 29.
300 FRCP Rule 26(c).
301 Rosenberg & King 1981, p. 581.
302 FRCP Rule 26(b)(2) (i.e. former Rule 26(b)(1)).
303 Advisory Committee Notes to the 1983 Amendments of Rule 26(b).

the controversy. The change aimed to 'signal' to judges that they have the 'authority to confine discovery' and to 'signal' to the parties that they are not entitled to use discovery 'to develop new claims or defenses'.[304] It is doubtful whether this change has had any effect in limiting the scope of discovery.[305]

The 1993 Amendments further limited the use of discovery by placing presumptive restrictions on the number of depositions (no more than 10) and interrogatories (no more than 25). Additional depositions or interrogatories were only allowed with leave of the court or stipulation of the other party.[306] The court was given greater power to limit the scope and extent of discovery. The court could adjust the maximum number of interrogatories or depositions, such that the maximum number would be proportionate to the needs and specifics of the case.[307] Equally, the court was empowered to set limits on the length of depositions and to limit the number of requests for admissions.[308] To depose a witness more than once required leave of the court.[309] The 2000 Amendments to the FRCP introduced a similar rule by setting a presumptive limit on the length of depositions of one day or seven hours. Although some recent amendments have tried to curb the scope of discovery, many other amendments have continued to accord the rules a 'broad and liberal treatment'. In 2006, FRCP Rule 34(a) was further amended to confirm that discovery of electronically stored information stands on an equal footing with the discovery of documents (e-discovery).

The fourth instrument for reform was the introduction of disclosure. In literature it had been argued that a move from 'discovery' to 'disclosure' would be a fruitful way to improve the system of pretrial exchange of information.[310] Disclosure rules require both parties to exchange information spontaneously. Discovery rules only require a party to provide information pursuant to a formal discovery request.[311] Disclosure had already been introduced in England with respect to documents in 1962. Under the English rule, the parties were required to make a list describing all relevant documents in their possession or control. Without waiting for an order or request, parties were required to produce the list to their

304 Advisory Committee Notes to the 2000 Amendments of Rule 26(b)(1).

305 Miller 2003, p. 1015: 'It does not appear that the change has been used to alter the ambit of discovery in any meaningful way'. For a critical assessment of the changes see Stempel 2001, Part VI.

306 FRCP Rules 30(a)(2)(A), 31 and 33(a).

307 Advisory Committee Notes to the 1993 Amendments of Rule 30(a): 'Leave to take additional depositions should be granted when consistent with the principles of Rule 26(b)(2), and in some cases the ten-per-side limit should be reduced in accordance with those same principles'.

308 Advisory Committee Notes to the 1993 Amendments of Rule 26(a).

309 FRCP Rule 30(a)(2)(B).

310 See e.g. Schwarzer 1989 and Schwarzer 1991. Sunderland, in his first draft of the federal rules, had included a provision that held that a party could be required to furnish descriptive lists of documents, books, and other tangible evidence known to that party and relevant to the case. The provision never entered into force. Subrin 1997, p. 726. Also see Issacharoff 1995 on the introduction of disclosure.

311 Schwarzer 1989, Part V.

opponent.[312] After the 1990 Civil Justice Reform Act (CJRA), many U.S. District Courts introduced rules that required parties to disclose information at the outset of litigation. The 1993 Amendments imposed upon the parties a duty to disclose information, needed to prepare for trial or make an informed decision on settlement, without awaiting a discovery request. Amended FRCP Rule 26(a) required both parties, at the outset of litigation, to disclose information regarding potential witnesses, documentary evidence, damages and insurance (initial disclosure). At a later stage, parties were required to inform the opposing party about the evidence that would be offered at trial. If parties intend to use expert witnesses at trial, they should disclose a mandatory expert report in advance (Chapter 5). The introduction of disclosure did not preclude the use of traditional discovery devices.[313] The 2000 Amendments changed the scope and application of initial disclosure. The most relevant amendment in this respect was that a party is now only required to disclose information that supported that parties' claim or defense rather than all information relevant to the matter.

It is doubtful whether legislative action has led to improvements. A 2008 survey of members of the American College of Trial Lawyers paints a very bleak picture of discovery in the U.S. District Courts.[314] The survey results confirm that there are serious problems with the procedural rules, especially the rules governing discovery.[315] 45% of all lawyers believe that there is discovery abuse in almost every case. 85% of the lawyers thought that litigation in general and discovery in particular was too expensive. The survey also provides a gloomy perspective on the advent of e-discovery. A large majority of lawyers believes e-discovery rules are abused and have led to a disproportional increase of discovery costs, as a share of total litigation costs.[316]

3.3. *Case Management*

Federal Courts have inherent powers to manage their own proceedings. [317] The 1938 FRCP supplemented these powers by granting the court discretion in a number of

312 R.S.C. Ord. 26, r.2.

313 Advisory Committee Notes to the 1993 Amendments of Rule 26(a).

314 ACTL & IAALS 2008, in this study 3,812 members of the American College of Trial Lawyers were surveyed (1,494 responded).

315 ACTL & IAALS 2008, p. 4.

316 ACTL & IAALS 2008, A-4.

317 See for instance *Chambers v. NASCO, Inc.*, 501 U.S. 32, 42–51 (1991), at 44: 'It has long been understood that "certain implied powers must necessarily result to our Courts of justice from the nature of their institution", powers "which cannot be dispensed with in a Court, because they are necessary to the exercise of all others". *United States v. Hudson*, 11 U.S. 32, 7 Cranch 32, 34, 3 L. Ed. 259 (1812); see also *Roadway Express, Inc. v. Piper*, 447 U.S. 752, 764, 65 L. Ed. 2d 488, 100 S. Ct. 2455 (1980) (citing Hudson). For this reason, "Courts of justice are universally acknowledged to be vested, by their very creation, with power to impose silence, respect, and decorum, in their presence, and submission to their lawful mandates". *Anderson v. Dunn*, 19 U.S. 204, 6 Wheat. 204, 227, 5 L. Ed. 242 (1821); see also Ex parte Robinson, 86 U.S. 505, 19 Wall. 505, 510, 22 L. Ed. 205 (1874). These powers are "governed not by rule or statute but by the control necessarily vested in courts to manage their own affairs so as to achieve the →

areas to allow a case-by-case approach towards the course of litigation.[318] Sunderland claimed that the rules covered 'the main features of the procedure by explicit rules' and left 'a great many details to be determined by judges in their discretion'.[319] Most particularly, the 1938 FRCP introduced pretrial conferences and preliminary hearings primarily aimed at improving the preparation for trial. Rule 16 of the 1938 FRCP stated that:

> 'In any action, the court may in its discretion direct the attorneys for the parties to appear before it for a conference to consider (1) The simplification of the issues; (2) The necessity or desirability of amendments to the pleadings; (3) The possibility of obtaining admissions of fact and of documents which will avoid unnecessary proof; (4) The limitation of the number of expert witnesses; (5) The advisability of a preliminary reference of issues to a master for findings to be used as evidence when the trial is to be by jury; (6) Such other matters as may aid in the disposition of the action'.

FRCP Rule 16 was inspired by the existing English summons for directions and American experiences in state courts.[320] Such conferences were a relatively new phenomenon in Anglo-American procedure. In England, 'summons for directions' were introduced in 1883.[321] New Jersey adopted a rule similar to the English rules in 1912, yet the rule had little practical impact.[322] Pretrial conferences were not effectively introduced in the United States until experiments were conducted in 1929 by the Circuit Court of Wayne County, Michigan sitting in Detroit. Without any particular legal basis or reference to English practice, the Court made it compulsory for attorneys to appear after pleadings were exchanged to see whether matters could be eliminated from the dispute or whether a settlement could be reached.[323] The Detroit practice was adopted by the Superior Court of Suffolk County, Massachusetts, sitting in Boston in 1935.

Federal judges were slow to exercise the powers which the law had granted them.[324] From the 1940s onwards, judges increasingly took a more pro-active stance in litigation.[325] The idea that judges should actively be involved in pretrial processes spread and (new) judges were increasingly taught to 'manage' cases in the pretrial phase.[326] Managerial techniques were diverse and often based on local rules or personal preferences of individual judges. In addition, much of the court's management techniques took place outside the reach of appellate control. The

orderly and expeditious disposition of cases". *Link v. Wabash R. Co.*, 370 U.S. 626, 630-631, 8 L. Ed. 2d 734, 82 S. Ct. 1386 (1962)'.

318 See in general Subrin 1986.

319 Sunderland 1938, p. 7.

320 The Advisory Committee Notes to Rule 16 refer to both English law and early American experiences.

321 For an historic account on the pretrial hearings, see Millar 1952, Chapter 15 and Sunderland 1937, p. 220. For a more recent comparative work see Jolowicz 2000, p. 45-51.

322 Sunderland 1937, p. 221.

323 Sunderland 1937, p. 224.

324 Burbank 1997, p. 700.

325 Resnik 1982, p. 377-379 and Flanders 1978, p. 147-150.

326 Resnik 1999, p. 943.

diversity between the different courts was relatively large. Courts and judges exercised a wide variety of different controls and scheduling techniques.[327] According to Flanders, some general consensus did exist; most federal judges in the late 1970s agreed that court supervision should take place from an early point in time until the resolution of the case.[328]

Gradually, more procedural rules have been implemented to encourage and aid further case management by the court. Early examples of rules on case management are the 1969 Manual for Complex and Multidistrict Litigation and the 1975 FRE. The Manual was developed to aid judges in managing larger and more complex cases.[329] The FRE granted the court considerable discretion to control the procedure to ensure the swift, fair and cheap ascertainment of truth.[330] The amendments to the FRCP have also shown an increased interest in case management techniques. The 1983 Amendments explicitly aimed 'to encourage pretrial management that meets modern litigation'.[331] The number of issues that could be addressed at pretrial conferences was expanded. The FRCP explicitly stated that the court should consider that pretrial conferences could be used to facilitate settlement and that the judge could consider to use the pretrial conference to formulate or simplify the issues.[332]

The best known legislative attempt to introduce and encourage case management techniques by means of regulation is perhaps the Civil Justice Reform Act of 1990 (CJRA).[333] According to the Act's sponsor U.S. Senator Biden, surveys conducted of more than one thousand participants of the justice system had shown that a majority of litigants, judges and lawyers agreed that delay and excessive cost significantly restrict access to the courts.[334] The CJRA required courts to actively address the excessive costs and delays in civil litigation.[335] Each U.S. District Court had to implement a 'Civil Justice Expense and Delay Reduction Plan' under the direction of an advisory group comprising attorneys and other persons who are representative of major categories of litigants in the courts.[336] Judicial case management formed the core of these plans. The Act specified that each advisory group had to consider, and could include, the following six case management principles.

327 Flanders 1978, p. 151.

328 Flanders 1978, p. 149-150.

329 A revised version of the Manual is still in use today: the 2004 fourth Manual for Complex Litigation, available at <www.fjc.gov>, last consulted in February 2010.

330 See e.g. Rule 611(a).

331 Advisory Committee Note to the 1983 Amendment of Rule 16, Introduction.

332 FRCP Rule 16(c)(9).

333 The Act had a sunset provision which specified that it would expire in 1997. It is uncertain to what extent the main parts of the CJRA indeed expired. See Tobias 1998.

334 Biden 1992, p. 2 referred to the study by L. Harris and Assoc., 'Procedural Reform of the Civil Justice System' (1989). For a critical assessment of the methodology of this study see Mullenix 1993.

335 28 U.S.C. Sections 471-482.

336 See in general: Biden 1992.

> '1) (...) differential (...) case specific management (...) (2) early and ongoing control of the pretrial process through involvement of a judicial officer (...) (3) for all cases that (...) are complex (...) careful and deliberate monitoring through a discovery-case management conference or a series of such conferences (...) (4) encouragement of cost-effective discovery through voluntary exchange of information among litigants and their attorneys and through the use of cooperative discovery devices; (5) (...) prohibiting the consideration of discovery motions unless accompanied by a certification that the moving party has made a reasonable and good faith effort to reach agreement with opposing counsel (...); and (6) authorization to refer appropriate cases to alternative dispute resolution programs (...)'.[337]

Some have been skeptical about the effects of the CJRA.[338] The effects of the Act have been measured and evaluated thoroughly by the RAND Corporation.[339] The evaluation compared ten U.S. District Courts that were required to adopt plans that incorporated the aforementioned case management principles (pilot programme) with ten other District Courts that had not implemented a programme based on case management principles. The main findings of the evaluation were that the pilot programme had little effect on time to disposition, litigation costs and attorney's satisfaction and views on the fairness of case management.[340] The evaluation did conclude that some specific forms of management were effective.[341] Early judicial case management involving an early trial schedule and planning settlement conferences reduced time to disposition, yet increased the number of attorney work hours. The study also demonstrated that shortening the discovery cutoff time proved to be an effective mechanism to reduce lawyer work hours and time to disposition.[342] A more recent empirical study could not confirm this finding.[343] Another interesting finding was that case management policies did not seem to affect attorney's satisfaction or views of fairness.

The legislative recognition of case management did not resolve the diversity in the case management techniques applied in the U.S. District Courts. On the contrary, the 1990 CJRA led to a 'balkanization' of the rulemaking process and promoted further diversity between the different courts.[344] Similarly, the 1993 Amendments to the FRCP discovery rules allowed local courts to deviate from the disclosure requirements. A 1997 survey showed that a clear majority of attorneys

337 28 U.S.C. Section 473.

338 Resnik 1984 and Mullenix 1993. Mullenix argues that the CJRA was not based on sound empirical data but on 'collectively shared myths'.

339 Kakalik, Hensler, McCaffrey, Oshiro, Pace & Vaiana 1996 and Kakalik, Dunworth, Hill, McCaffrey, Oshiro, Pace & Vaiana 1996. Both are available at <www.rand.org>, last consulted in February 2010.

340 Kakalik, Dunworth, Hill, McCaffrey, Oshiro, Pace & Vaiana 1996, p. 1.

341 Kakalik, Dunworth, Hill, McCaffrey, Oshiro, Pace & Vaiana 1996, p. 2.

342 Kakalik, Hensler, McCaffrey, Oshiro, Pace & Vaiana 1996, p. 61. If early case management is combined with an early discovery cutoff point, the increase of the costs of the former is offset by the decrease of the costs of the latter measure. Other findings seem to support this idea. Flanders 1978, p. 155, on the basis of a study conducted by 6 district courts, concluded that 'controls on time could be considerably more stringent'.

343 Willging, Stienstra, Shaphard & Miletich 1998, p. 533.

344 Mullenix 1993, p. 1443.

(60%) believed such a lack of uniformity created moderate or serious problems.[345] To some extent the 2000 Amendments to the FRCP have tackled the great diversity between the District Courts. Nevertheless, courts continue to make local rules supplementing the FRCP that create some degree of diversity between District Courts.[346]

There is reason to believe that the changes to the FRCP regarding discovery have contributed to increased activity by the judiciary. A 1997 study by Willging *et al.*, showed that meeting and conferring with regard to a discovery plan took place in most cases. A discovery plan or scheduling order was also entered in a majority of cases.[347] In 81% of all cases, judges were involved in discovery, mostly in the planning phase.[348] Even though more case management principles have been adopted over the years, it is generally believed that more judicial intervention is still needed. The study by Willging *et al.* showed that lawyers generally believed that further 'case management' would provide a solution to (some of the) discovery problems.[349] In response to a list of 13 changes that might reduce costs, lawyers opted for the following four solutions most frequently:[350] 1) The availability of judges to resolve discovery disputes (54%); 2) Adopting a uniform rule requiring initial disclosure (44%); 3) Imposing sanctions more frequently and severely (42%); 4) The introduction of a civility code (42%). To the extent case management was applied, this was generally appreciated by lawyers. The study of Willging *et al* showed that the vast majority of lawyers (83%) found no problems with the court's management of disclosure or discovery.[351] Lawyers were generally positive towards the use of pretrial conferences and conferences of parties and believed that they had contributed to reduced costs and time to disposition.[352]

We may conclude that since the enactment of the 1938 FRCP judges have self-consciously shifted roles from adjudicator to case-manager.[353] Judges no longer decide cases but have also become increasingly involved in planning, mediation and negotiation.[354] Although empirical evidence is not always convincing, the change towards case management was often justified on grounds of efficiency.

4. The New Procedural Landscape

The FRCP have been in force since 1938. Although the Rules have been subject to a number of Amendments, their general principles remained unchanged. What is

345 Willging, Stienstra, Shaphard & Miletich 1998, p. 542 *et seq*.

346 For an example of such rules see the rules that apply in Michigan, available at <www.mied.uscourts.gov/Rules/LocalRules/civilRules.cfm>, last consulted in February 2010.

347 Willging, Stienstra, Shaphard & Miletich 1998, p. 544.

348 Willging, Stienstra, Shaphard & Miletich 1998, p. 541.

349 Willging, Stienstra, Shaphard & Miletich 1998, p. 543.

350 Willging, Stienstra, Shaphard & Miletich 1998, p. 542.

351 Willging, Stienstra, Shaphard & Miletich 1998, p. 541.

352 Willging, Stienstra, Shaphard & Miletich 1998, p. 538.

353 Resnik 1986, discussed by Rosenberg 1988b, p. 2208.

354 Resnik 1982, p. 379.

relevant for present purposes is that American practice has changed. As explained below, pleadings are now of little importance, discovery has become the centerpiece of the process of fact-finding, and trials have become rare. It is difficult to determine to what extent changes in legal practice are a result of changes in the law. Often information is lacking and changes in the law have occurred alongside other developments.[355] Nevertheless, I will argue that the FRCP have contributed to the emergence of a new procedural landscape.

4.1. *Developments in Pleading*

American litigation witnessed a development in which common law pleading was gradually replaced by code pleading and later by notice pleading. These changes were primarily aimed to reduce technicalities and formalism but had two important side effects.

The new approach to pleading produced a very broad issue. Common law pleading would narrow down the dispute to a single issue of fact or law. Fact pleading would narrow down the issue to a number of facts. Notice pleading functioned solely to give reasonable notice of the pleader's case to the opponent and the court. Thus, notice pleading does not serve to narrow down the issues. Thereby it possibly produces a great number of disputed factual issues.[356] This has massive implications for the next stage in the civil process. The pleadings 'define the universe of relevance within which the discovery rules operate'.[357] If pleadings produce a broad issue, discovery will be much broader as well.

Second, pleading rules were no longer a procedural hurdle.[358] More cases would reach the next phase in litigation and parties had fewer incentives to provide an abundance of factual details in their pleadings.

As pleading no longer narrowed down the issues and did not present a procedural hurdle, notice pleading created the need for a new 'middle phase' in the process of litigation. In American practice, pleading once was at the heart of the common law procedure. After the enactment of the new FRCP, pleadings became a relatively unimportant step in litigation.

Current American pleading rules are more similar to the Continental rules on pleading. Established American scholars, who wrote on pleadings shortly after the introduction of the FRCP, argued that pleading under the FRCP had moved towards Continental pleading practices. In his handbook on pleading, Clark drew the comparison between Anglo-American and Continental pleadings, noting that '(u)nder the civil law little is expected of pleading' and that the 'Continental jurist

355 On methodological difficulties, see Rosenberg 1988b, p. 2198-2200.

356 Clark was well aware of the impact of reform. Clark 1947, p. 56: 'So notice pleading, giving some facts, presents a very broad issue'. Presently, American lawyers are of the opinion that notice pleading insufficiently narrows down the issues. See ACTL & IAALS 2008, A-3.

357 Hazard 1997, p. 1679.

358 An important exception is that 'a substantial number of cases (about a quarter of contested cases and about 7% of all terminated cases) end with jurisdictional dismissals'. Yeazell 1994, p. 694.

need not insist on the enforcement of pleading rules'.[359] Millar wrote that on the Continent the parties were

> 'allowed a free rein in advancing their respective pretensions, since the judge can be depended upon to make the necessary eliminations, adjustments and reduction to logical order as a preliminary of decision'. (...) 'we are bound to admit that the inexorable logic of events is approximating our procedural institutions more and more to those in use of the Continent'.[360]

Upon reading the American federal rules on pleading and comparing these to Continental rules, it seems that the rules on pleading are fairly similar. In both systems the pleader needs to allege sufficient facts such as that there is a legal rule which will entitle the party to his claim or defense. In both systems, issues like fraud need to be pleaded with particularity. In addition, on both sides of the Atlantic there has been a tendency to reduce formalism and to let 'substance' prevail over 'formalism'. For example: in the Netherlands Article 111(2) sub d Code of Civil Procedure specifies that the writ should contain the 'claim and the grounds of the claim'.[361] This requires that the facts alleged by the plaintiff, if proven, are sufficient to invoke a legal rule which entitles the plaintiff to his claim.[362] If the facts, if proven, do not entitle the plaintiff to his claim the court can rule that the complaint is inadmissible, proclaim the nullity of the complaint or refuse to grant the claim.[363] Case law has long shown that the most important question in understanding the pleading requirements is whether the defendant is sufficiently capable to defend his case on the basis of what the plaintiff has stated.[364] To the extent that the plaintiff fails to meet pleading requirements, the plaintiff will generally be able to correct the mistakes made.[365]

4.2. *The New Middle Phase in Litigation*

In the original common law procedure there were basically two stages: pleading and trial. As set out in the previous Section, pleadings became increasingly less significant. Instead, the drafters of the FRCP greatly expanded the menu of pretrial processes available to the litigants. Joinder of parties and issues, discovery and summary judgments became much more widely available under the new FRCP. Lawyers increasingly used these newly-created procedural tools. Discovery

359 Clark 1947, p. 55.

360 Millar 1926, p. 401, p. 407.

361 '(...) *de eis en de gronden daarvan*'. Also see Section 2.2.3.

362 The 19th century proceduralist Van Boneval Faure had already argued that the statements of fact in the complaint need to be so extensive that the claim follows from these statements of fact and a rule of law by logical deduction. Van Boneval Faure 1900, §56 p. 16. More recent: Van Mierlo & Van Dam-Lely 2003, p. 105, Section 2.1.11.1.

363 Court of Cassation 24 May 1957, *NJ* 1959, 10. See Van den Reek 1997, p. 15.

364 Star Busmann 1955, No. 187.

365 Article 120 Dutch Code of Civil Procedure. There has been a general trend in the Netherlands to 'deformalize' procedural rules and requirements. See for instance the Explanatory Memorandum to the 2001 Reform, Van Mierlo & Bart 2002, p. 4, p. 5.

requests, motions for joinder of issues and motions for a summary judgment currently frequently take place between the pleading phase and trial. A new middle phase in litigation was created, a phase which now dominates the process of fact-finding. Very prominent in the new middle phase are discovery and summary judgments.

Beyond doubt, the liberalization of discovery has been the single biggest innovation of the FRCP. Its impact has been massive. In the decades after the FRCP entered into force, discovery has expanded from 'a useful tool to a combination of lawyer's industry and litigator's religion'.[366] Discovery has become the centre of gravity of the modern civil process. A 1977 study by the Federal Judicial Center showed that discovery could be relatively time consuming. The study showed that in six districts the median time needed for completion of discovery varied between 113 and 302 days.[367] Another study was based on 1,812 interviews related to 1,649 'middle range disputes' resolved in 1978 at 5 U.S. District Courts.[368] The study showed that the median time spent on a case was 30.4 hours (mean: 72.9 hours). Discovery was the activity that consumed the biggest proportion of the time of lawyers devoted to the case: 16.7%. The time needed for discovery was slightly larger than time spent on conferring with the client (16%) and settlement discussions (15.1%).[369] A 1996 RAND report showed that in cases that lasted longer than 270 days, the average total lawyer work hours per litigant equaled 232, of which most hours were spent on discovery (83 hours, i.e. 36% of all work done).[370] The 1997 national survey, conducted by Willging *et al*, made use of a questionnaire send to 2000 lawyers who had worked on 1000 cases that were likely to have discovery.[371] The study showed that the median total costs of litigation reported by attorneys were $13.000 per client. About half of these costs were related to disclosure and discovery.[372]

That discovery would become important in the litigation process was not unintended or unforeseen. The drafters of the rules believed that pleadings were inadequate to provide a basis for trial.[373] They willingly construed broad rules to avoid surprises. Discovery has largely succeeded in providing a basis for trial and avoiding surprise.[374] Discovery has made the fact-gathering process in U.S. civil litigation much more thorough than fact-gathering on the European Continent.

366 Rosenberg 1988b, p. 2203: 'No change in litigation practice resulting from the Rules has had as great an impact as the liberalization of pretrial discovery. In the half century since the Rules gave discovery its modern look, this procedure for gathering information before trial has expanded from a useful tool to a combination lawyer's industry and litigator's religion. Discovery practice in federal litigation has taken on a life of its own. The first principle is "when in doubt, discover!"'.

367 Flanders 1978, see Tables 2, 3 and 4.

368 Cases in which the claim was smaller than $1,000 and 'mega cases' were excluded.

369 Trubek, Sarat, Felstiner, Kritzer & Grossman 1983, p. 90-91.

370 Kakalik, Hensler, McCaffrey, Oshiro, Pace & Vaiana 1996, Table 2.3.

371 Willging, Stienstra, Shaphard & Miletich 1998.

372 Willging, Stienstra, Shaphard & Miletich 1998, p. 548, Table IV.

373 Sunderland 1932 and Clark 1947, p. 576.

374 Yeazell 2004, p. 949.

The new FRCP made summary judgments more widely available. The change would have a massive impact on the practice in courts. A couple of decades after the introduction of the FRCP, the filing of motions for summary judgments seemed to have become the rule rather than the exception. More frequently, a failure to successfully defend a motion for summary judgment abruptly ended litigation. Summary judgments have been granted in increasingly larger numbers since the 1970s.[375] The percentage of cases in which a FRCP Rule 56 motion was granted increased from 6% in 1975 to 12% in 2000.[376] The percentage of cases terminated by a summary judgment seems to have increased from 1.8% in 1960 to 7.7% in 2000.[377] Although the drafters of the Federal Rules never intended to 'substitute trial by affidavit for trial by jury'[378] there have been complaints that Rule 56 effectively became a 'docket clearing instrument' that sometimes wrongfully deprived litigants of 'their day in court'.[379]

The growing importance of the middle phase of litigation required more court attention and resources. Motions to compel discovery, motions for a protective order, motions to impose sanctions on the other party or to grant summary judgment became more numerous. Judges were gradually forced to devote the bulk of their time to decide upon such motions.[380] In discussing statistical data on judicial rulings, Yeazell concluded that data suggests 'that today's federal judges have moved their focus away from trial to earlier stages of litigation'.[381]

It is not surprising that a development in which judges were given new tasks went hand in hand with the rise of case management. Case management techniques should largely be understood as newly developed professional good practices to tackle newly created judicial tasks. The development in which judges shifted roles from adjudicators to case managers is linked to a development in which judges are increasingly called upon to devote time to the newly created middle phase in litigation.

4.3. *The Decline of Trials*

Figures on the Decline of Trials

In the United States, the right to a jury trial in civil cases is constitutionally guaranteed and still enjoys massive support. Nevertheless, civil juries and civil bench trials are much less common than before. Many experienced lawyers have not been to trial for years. Empirical studies show that there is a gradual decrease in the number of trials both in state and federal courts. Over the last 70 years, the numbers

375 Burbank 2004, p. 621. Burbank argues that the increase in summary judgment is a result of increased case loads and more extensive use of discovery rather than the legal changes brought about by 1986 Supreme Court decisions.

376 Cecil, Miletich & Cort 2001 as discussed by Miller 2003, p. 1048-1052.

377 See Burbank 2004.

378 See Burbank 2004, p. 601, quoting Donworth, a member of the Advisory Committee.

379 Miller 2003 and Burbank 2004.

380 Yeazell 1994, p. 639.

381 Yeazell 1994, p. 637.

of cases that are resolved by means of a trial have been reduced to a very small proportion of the total number of actions filed (see Table 3.2).

Table 3.2. Civil (jury)trials in the United States District Courts[382]

Year	Civil Disposition	Trials	Jury Trials[383]	Trials/Disposition[384]
1962	50,320	5,802	47.7%	11.5%
1972	90,177	8,168	41.1%	9.1%
1982	184,835	11,280	42.3%	6.1%
1992	230,171	8,029	53.3%	3.5%
2002	258,876	4,569	65.8%	1.8%
2008	233,826	4,723	47.0%	2.0%

The decline in the number of trials as a percentage of the number of civil dispositions started long before 1962. When the Federal Rules entered into force, 18.9% of all dispositions were by means of a trial.[385] Earlier data from state courts indicate that trials were even more common in the late 19th century.[386] In the 1960s, the bulk of cases that went to trial were tort cases; currently civil rights cases account for more than a third of all civil trials.[387]

A similar decline in the number of trials exists in state courts. Aggregate data from 22 states show that the number of filings terminated by trials dropped from 36.1% in 1976 to 15.8% in 2002.[388] The differences between states are large and there is reason to believe that the decline of trials started long before the 1970s, as is illustrated by data from Massachusetts in Table 3.3.

382 Galanter 2004, Table 1. Also see Higginbotham 2002, p. 1408, Chart 2. On the 2008 data, see Duff 2008, Table C4A. Civil cases terminated during the 12-month period ending 30 September 2008.

383 The number of jury trials as a percentage of the total amount of trials.

384 This column lists the number of trials started as a percentage of the total number of civil dispositions.

385 Yeazell 1994, p. 633.

386 Galanter 2004, p. 466-469.

387 Galanter 2004, p. 464-465.

388 For a number of references to statistical data on the decline of trials in state courts see Ostrom, Strickland & Hannaford-Agor 2004 and Galanter 2004, Table 4, p. 507.

Table 3.3. Jury trials in the Massachusetts Superior Courts[389]

Year	Civil Jury Trials	Civil cases filed	Jury Trials/filings
1930	2684	39028	6,88%
1940	2647	29595	8,94%
1950	2549	30115	8,46%
1960	1331	39233	3,39%
1970	1792	41047	4,37%
1980	610	31786	1,92%
1990	741	37914	1,95%
2000	571	21555	2,65%

In other common law countries the proportion of cases that are disposed of through trials has also declined.[390] Trial by civil jury is virtually abolished in other common law jurisdictions.[391]

Causes of the Decline of the Number of Trials

There are various causes for the decline of trial. In this Section, I will argue that changes in the last 70 years have created incentives for both the parties and the judiciary to avoid trials. At the same time, alternatives to trial have become increasingly attractive to parties and judges. Parties and judges have gradually opted for fewer trials and more mediation, arbitration, settlement and summary judgments.

For several reasons, trials have become more complex. One reason is the increased complexity of our society in general. With the advance of science and technology, more technologically complex questions arise in a courtroom setting. Parties have increasingly resorted to expert witnesses to provide evidence for matters of fact. Lawyers have also increasingly turned to scientific experts to assist in the legal process itself. A good example is the newly developed 'scientific jury selection' methods that became popular in the last decades of the 20th century.[392] Such 'new' methods of jury selection have clearly led to an increase in the complexity and costs of jury trials.

To a large extent, the changes in procedural rules have contributed to the increased complexity of the factual basis of disputes. Under the old common law system, the issues were automatically narrowed down to a single factual issue. The gradual liberalization of pleading rules and the widening of discovery increased the number of disputed facts that could be addressed at trial. The abolition of mechanisms to narrow down the dispute and the introduction of instruments that allow a thorough search for facts has made trial factually much more complex. Moreover, the judge has become more passive during trial since the late 19th

389 Data are obtained from Murray 2004, Tables 1-2. The data for 1980 are based on the linear interpolation of the number of trials in 1979 and 1981. In interpreting the data one should take into account important factors like changes in the jurisdiction of the court. Between 1925 and 2000 the population of Massachusetts increased from 4.1 million to 6.3 million.

390 Kritzer 2004.

391 See Section 8.3.

392 Galanter 2004, p. 480.

century. The development led to a situation where it was increasingly inappropriate for the judge to interrupt and urge counsel to 'speed up' trial in the presence of the jurors.[393] The factors mentioned above have contributed to an increase in the time needed to conclude trials.[394] An increase in the duration of trial has in turn a direct impact on the costs of trial. Empirical data well illustrate the increase in time. Between 1915 and 1949, 60% of all civil trials in the Los Angeles Superior Court lasted no longer than one day. Between 1950 and 1979, only 20% of all trials at that court took one day or less.[395] Of all 3,387 trials terminated by a verdict in the U.S. District Courts between September 2006 and September 2007, 836 were resolved in one day, 560 were resolved in two days, 543 in three days, 1,227 in four to nine days, 196 in ten to 19 days and 25 in 20 days or more.[396]

Trials have always been costly, uncertain and in essence zero-sum games.[397] For those reasons the parties, in the majority of cases, have always only chosen to go to trial in a minority of cases. The increased costs, duration and complexity of trial have made trial more costly and have made the outcome of trial even more uncertain. Therefore, trials are less attractive for parties than they were roughly 70 years ago.

In 1962, Federal District judges handled on average 39 trials per year. In 2002, there were only 13 trials per judge per year.[398] Part of the reason why the number of trials has declined was that judges are no longer able to handle as many trials today as they could 70 years ago. First, as discussed before, trials today take longer than they did before. Second, the number of civil filings per judge per year more than doubled between 1962 and 2002.[399] At the same time the number of criminal cases per judge also increased.[400] The increase in the number of cases per judge per year clearly limits the percentage of cases that can proceed to trial. The number of non-

393 See the discussion above. In 2008 I attended a cross-examination of an expert witness at a jury trial in a Michigan state court. Attorneys of both sides put a large number of questions to the witness. The cross-examination took hours, yet could have been conducted much quicker. Some of the jurors dozed off. The judge did not interrupt often to ask the lawyers 'to speed it up' or to decide that a question was 'asked and answered'. The passive role of the trial judge stood in sharp contrast with the active and time-efficient stance of U.S. (magistrate) judges hearing motions.

394 Galanter 2004, p. 477 *et seq.*

395 See Galanter 2004, p. 477, who discusses a 1984 study by Molly Selvin & Patricia A. Ebener.

396 Duff 2008, Table T2, p. 393.

397 A zero-sum game is a situation in which the gains for one party are equal to the losses of the other party and *vice versa.*

398 Galanter 2004, p. 521, Figure 33. These numbers include both civil and criminal trials.

399 Galanter 2004, Figure 29, p. 501. In 1962 the case load per judge was 196 civil filings, in 2002 it was 443. In 1990 an individual judge was on average required to handle more than twice as many filings as a judge in 1940. There were 34,734 filings in federal courts in 1940 and 217,879 filings in 1990; there were 185 district court judges in 1940 and 564 in 1990. The caseload increased from 188 to 386 civil filings per judge per year. Especially as federal courts are not specialized and the civil docket usually consists mainly of cases in which the stakes are high, the case load is particularly high. Statistics are obtained from Yeazell 1994, p. 634. Between 2003 and 2007 the number of civil filings per judgeship varied between 372 and 414. Duff 2008, Table 3, p. 22.

400 Galanter 2004, Part V, p. 492.

judicial court employees was significantly enlarged between 1962 and 2002.[401] The spending on the Federal Justice System has increased since the early 1960s. Between 1962 and 2002 the percentage of the Federal Budget allocated to the courts went up from less than 0.5% to almost 2%.[402] Although magistrate judges and other paralegals can perform some judicial tasks, they cannot perform all judicial tasks and may not replace the judge at trial. A third reason why judges are no longer able to handle as many trials as before is related to the newly created middle phase of litigation which requires additional judicial time. Trial, once the centre of judicial attention, became 'one among many tasks'.[403] Courts have increasingly been forced to devote a large part of their civil work to issues like ruling on discovery disputes, deciding joinder issues, issuing scheduling orders, ordering pretrial conferences etc. Additional tasks for the judiciary leave less time to dispose of trials. The aforementioned reasons show that even with increased legal assistance a judge today cannot resolve as many trials as a judge in 1937. This explains why judges over the years were required to find mechanisms to avoid lengthy trials.

The decline in the number of trials in absolute numbers can partly be attributed to the rise of alternatives to the public justice system. Alternative forms of dispute resolution (ADR) have become increasingly popular over the last decades.[404] The use of arbitration clauses in contracts has become common.[405] The many alternatives to public justice, like mediation or arbitration, have often prevented parties from going to court at all.[406] 'Voting with their feet' has probably been among one of the many strategies of parties to avoid the public justice system in general and costly trials in particular. The American statistics on civil filings are quite remarkable. The number of civil filings in the U.S. District Courts has remained relatively constant between 1983 and 2002, despite the growth of the population and the Gross Domestic Product in the same time period.[407] In state courts it seems that the number of dispositions has even decreased over recent decades.[408] This is remarkable, as litigation rates are typically positively correlated with economic growth.[409]

Parties have been increasingly referred to ADR during court proceedings, unless they opt out on their own motion. The use of such alternatives to public justice (although not undisputed[410]) has generally been promoted by courts and

401 In 1962 there were 18.9 non judicial employees per U.S. District Judge. In 1992 there were 45.9 non judicial employees per U.S. District Judge. Galanter 2004, p. 502.

402 Galanter 2004, p. 505, Figure 31.

403 Yeazell 1994, p. 639.

404 For an overview of empirical data in this area see Stipanowich 2004.

405 See in general Murray 2006.

406 Stipanowich 2004.

407 Galanter 2004, Figures 16, 19 and 20.

408 Galanter 2004, p. 509, Table 5.

409 Clemenz & Gugler 1998; Leertouwer, van Tulder, Diephuis, Folkeringa & Eshuis 2005 p. 10-11 and Wollschläger 1998.

410 For a critical discussion see Murray 2008.

policymakers.[411] For judges, just like parties, alternative forms of dispute resolution have been one of the many strategies to avoid trials.

A second strategy to avoid trials is settlement. Settlement has become increasingly attractive for both parties and the courts. The creation of a new middle phase in litigation increased the willingness of parties to bring litigation to an end. The expensive and time consuming discovery process tends to make parties 'weary' of litigation. The median time from filing to disposition by trial increased from 16 to 20 months from 1963 to 2002.[412] The costs of discovery, which are largely symmetrical for both parties, have increased significantly since the introduction of the 1938 FRCP.[413] In addition, it is likely that more extensive discovery has increased mutual knowledge of the facts.[414] Both developments have contributed to willingness of parties to settle rather than proceed to trial.[415] Similarly, judges have increasingly made attempts to convince parties to settle.[416] As noted above, trials generate an increased workload for the court and often require that the judge makes tough decisions; both can be avoided if the parties settle the case. Judges often put a lot of pressure on the lawyers and parties to settle, especially if cases are complex.

The third and last strategy to avoid trials is by granting summary judgments. As set out in Section 3.4.2, the number of dismissals on the pleadings, summary judgments, and similar rulings that terminate a case has increased with the decline of trial.[417] As described above, judges are faced with many cases and can only resolve a small proportion of these cases by trials. Therefore, judges have increasingly been inclined to grant summary judgments. Summary judgments have been used increasingly as a means to 'clear' the court docket.

4.4. *Conclusion: the Privatization of Fact-Gathering*

A fairly popular theory that tries to explain the development of the law is based on the idea that legal changes are largely a result of the transplantation of rules of one legal system, into another legal system.[418] The history of the development of the United States' rules of procedure and evidence prior to 1938 partly supports this view. Changes in the American approach to fact-finding were often inspired by the rules of other legal systems. Until 1938, it seems that the civil procedural regimes of

411 In 1998, for example, Congress passed the Alternative Dispute Resolution Act. 28 U.S.C. Chapter 44, Section 651(b) states that '(...) Each United States district court shall authorize, by local rule adopted under Section 2071(a), the use of alternative dispute resolution processes in all civil actions, (...) Each United States district court shall devise and implement its own alternative dispute resolution program (...) to encourage and promote the use of alternative dispute resolution in its district'.

412 Galanter 2004, Figure 13.

413 There was little discovery prior to the Federal Rules, for relatively recent empirical data on the costs of discovery see Willging, Stienstra, Shaphard & Miletich 1998.

414 Priest & Klein 1984 argue that information symmetry will lead to settlement.

415 This point is also made by Yeazell 2004, p. 950-954.

416 See for a very critical account of this development: Resnik 2002, p. 162.

417 Yeazell 1994, p. 636 and Burbank 2004.

418 Ewald 1995.

the United States and those in Continental jurisdictions were converging. Millar, shortly before the introduction of the 1938 FRCP, wrote the following:

> 'A Continental jurist of today, observing the civil procedure of the Anglo-American jurisdictions, would find the contrast to his own system decidedly less pronounced than that which was encountered by his predecessor of a century ago. For in the amalgamation of law and equity, the broadened opportunity for inclusion of a plurality of a controversies in the same suit, the constantly expanding practice of dispensing with jury trial, the extension of pretrial disclosure to every class of proceeding, the welcome accorded to the declaratory action, and, slow as the process has been in the United States, the lessening of emphasis upon allegation as such, the development has been wholly in the direction of the procedural ideas commonly obtained on the Continent. So, too, the tendency exhibited in latter-day enactment to repose a higher measure of discretionary power in the court and to limit party control over both the content and progress of the cause is in keeping with the trend of modern Continental legislation as particularly exemplified in the Austrian Code of 1895'.[419]

Despite the growth of international commerce and transnational dispute resolution it seems that there has been no further convergence between American and Continental approaches to fact gathering and fact finding in civil litigation.[420] Although there are common developments in some areas, it seems that in general there has been a divergence between American and European systems since the 1930s. In the second half of the 20th century, the study of comparative civil procedure had little or no influence on the development of civil procedural rules in the United States.[421]

In the United States, the introduction of the FRCP in 1938 prepared the way for the privatization of the process of fact gathering in civil litigation. Trial, once the centre of the legal process, would no longer be a normal stage in the process of fact-finding. Discovery now dominates the process of fact-finding rather than being a method developed to prepare the way for trial. The centre of gravity in the fact-finding process has shifted from trial to discovery and thereby from the courtroom to the lawyer's office. Witnesses were once primarily heard in courtrooms. Now witnesses are generally deposed in lawyers' offices and such depositions are often not followed by a further examination at trial. Thereby the process of fact-gathering in civil litigation has been privatized. A new system has been designed and put into place that allows a thorough search for the facts with a minimum of court intervention and public expenses.[422]

The privatization of fact gathering in civil litigation has led to a power shift from appellate courts to trial courts, from trial courts to lawyers and from lawyers to clients.[423] As very few cases are terminated by means of a trial, appeal is often not

419 Millar 1936, p. 223.

420 Dubinsky 2008. Dubinsky argues that the rise in transnational litigation has not contributed to convergence.

421 Langbein 1995, p. 545: 'The study of comparative procedure in the United States has little following in academia, and virtually no audience in the courts or in legal policy circles'.

422 Yeazell 2004, p. 965.

423 Yeazell 1994, p. 667.

available. In the new middle phase of litigation, which generally escapes appellate control, trial courts have been granted considerable discretion. Fact-finding procedures are often not scrutinized by appellate courts. The privatization of the justice system in turn has taken the control over the process of fact-gathering away from the trial judge to lawyers. Lawyers generally operate outside the scrutiny of any court as judges are generally not inclined to get involved in discovery. As lawyers have increasingly come to dominate the process of fact-gathering the clients themselves, who can hire a partisan lawyer according to their own wishes, often have an increased influence over the process of fact-gathering and fact-finding.

Chapter 4

FACT-FINDING: A CONCISE GENERAL COMPARISON

This chapter builds upon the previous ones that provided a concise historic account of the fact-finding arrangements in the Netherlands, Austria and the United States. In Section 4.1, general conclusions will be drawn on the basis of these chapters. First, it will be concluded that rules are often 'transplanted' from one into another system. Nevertheless, there have hardly been any cross influences between American and Continental jurisdictions since the 1930s. It will be concluded that procedural systems have diverged: Continental and U.S. procedural systems grew further and further apart.

In Section 4.2 the main differences between the procedural systems of the Netherlands, Austria and the U.S. are briefly outlined. In Section 4.2.1 the different stages in the litigation process are discussed. It will be argued that these differences have an impact on the process of fact-finding. Next, the different roles of professionals in the process of litigation will be discussed. As set out above, changes on both sides of the Atlantic led to a shift in the roles of attorneys and judges. Judges have a prominent role in Continental fact-finding processes and much less so in the United States. Section 4.2.2 discusses data on the time to disposition in the Netherlands, Austria and the U.S. District Courts. In the previous chapters, empirical data in each of the three jurisdictions were discussed. These data are useful as a means to assess (one aspect of) the quality of fact-finding processes. Although the time to disposition can be measured relatively well, it will be argued that it is very difficult to make conclusive comparative judgments.

1. Legal Transplants and the Divergence of Laws

The Development of Law and Legal Transplants

Experienced computer programmers do not reinvent the wheel when they are asked to program a new major application. Of the many hundreds of pages of source code that will constitute a new application, only a small proportion will be truly new. For the larger part, programmers use classes, applets, modules and functions that have previously been developed by others. Computer programming largely seems to be about assembling the right building blocks. The theory of legal transplants observes that legislators are like computer programmers; legal reformers have a tendency to use rules and techniques that have been used, tried and tested elsewhere.[1]

Legal transplants may come in different sizes and shapes.[2] Sometimes only a single rule from abroad is used as a source of inspiration to draft a new single rule to address a specific legal problem.[3] At the other end of the spectrum, examples have been discussed in the previous chapters where whole codifications have been transplanted with little or no adaptations from one legal system into another. Not only rules may be subject to transplantation. Legal principles, legal methods, underlying philosophies and the central tenets of the system of legal education have frequently been transplanted from one jurisdiction to the other. The process of legal transplantation may be either voluntary or imposed by a colonizing or conquering nation. Once a rule is transplanted, it might begin a life of its own, adapting itself to the new environment and circumstances.[4]

On the basis of the developments sketched in Chapters 2 and 3, it can be concluded that there is plenty of support for the theory of legal transplants. During the drafting process of the 1895 Austrian Code of Civil Procedure, Franz Klein found useful building blocks in the English, French and German systems. Equally, American Codes like the Field Code and the Federal Rules of Civil Procedure were not drafted from scratch but were largely a result of 'cherry picking' from the available rules that had been tried and tested elsewhere. New and innovative codifications of procedural law have often been like new recipes: they use familiar ingredients to produce a novel blend. Successful 'innovative' procedural codifications, such as the Field Code, the French Code of 1806, the Austrian Code of 1895 and the 1938 Federal Rules of Civil Procedure have often been adopted entirely, without any significant modifications, in other jurisdictions. Even in modern times, it is a common strategy to try and improve existing legal systems by suggesting the adoption of rules that have produced satisfactory results elsewhere.[5]

There are stronger versions of the theory of legal transplants. Some have argued that the growth of a system of law should *primarily* be understood as a process whereby conservative legal elites, unmoved by pressure groups and changes in the social, economic, technical and institutional setting, transplant rules from one system into another system.[6] Others have tried to understand the

1 On the theory of legal transplants, see Ewald 1995.

2 Twining 2004.

3 The Dutch '*Wet Collectieve Afwikkeling Massaschade*' (Class Action Financial Settlement Act), for example, which entered into force in July 2005, added only a few provisions to the Dutch Civil Code. The Act was somewhat inspired by American class actions, yet portrays strong differences with American legislation.

4 On the feasibility of legal transplants see Kahn-Freud 1974; Lowenfeld 1997 and Damaska 1997b.

5 The recent Dutch recommendations to improve the procedural laws, for example, were clearly inspired by rules and regulations introduced elsewhere (Section 2.3.2).

6 Watson argued the law is created by a conservative legal elite that is primarily inclined to borrow rules from prestigious legal systems, Watson 1978. This theory of legal transplants hence opposes 'mirror theories' of the law. Mirror theories, in their strongest form, hold that →

development of the law as a combination of a weaker version of the theory of legal transplants and a 'Darwinian' perspective on rulemaking. This version holds that good rules will be more likely to be transplanted from one jurisdiction to another. Ultimately, this theory predicts that the best procedural rules will survive.[7] The historical descriptions in the preceding chapters do not provide support for these theories.[8]

The Divergence of Procedural Laws

Some have argued in favor of a strong version of the convergence theory, which holds that all national peculiarities in (procedural) law will ultimately be pulverized by the blender of globalization.[9] The theory basically holds that the diversity of legal cultures, rules and practices will not be able to withstand the unifying forces brought about by ever growing international trade and commerce. In effect, it claims that legal differences are a 'mere superstructure' that will automatically disappear once economic and social structures assimilate. There is reason to be skeptical towards such theories. They fail to account for the counterforce to harmonization such as the vested interests of professionals, the problem of path dependency and the existence of large scale commercial arbitration to resolve international disputes. Weaker versions of the convergence theory are more commonly defended in literature; such theories do not seem to extend much beyond the observation that procedural systems are converging.[10] At a global level, the weaker convergence theory has merit.[11]

This book can only partially shed light on the degree in which legal systems are converging. The methodology of this book is inadequate to confront the question of convergence directly, as I have primarily aimed to study national

the law is not in any way autonomous but is merely a mirror of society. See in this respect Watson 1993 and Ewald 1995.

7 See for a more sophisticated application of evolutionary theory in the area of law: Eckardt 2008 and Smits 2008b.

8 The former theory fails to provide an explanation of procedural innovations. In addition, it fails to recognize the ever growing importance of empirical research that predicts and evaluates the effects of changes in the procedural regime (see Rosenberg 1988a, p. 51). The latter theory is at odds with the observation that many rules of dubious quality are transplanted into other jurisdictions and have long remained influential (e.g. the hearsay rule). It ignores factors, such as the interests of pressure groups that cause bad rules to 'survive'. Moreover, legal ideas have often been transplanted because they have been imposed by new conquering powers or rulers, not because of their quality. Even if rules are voluntarily transplanted, the prestige and imperial power of the nation that first developed the rule rather than the inherent quality of the rule was often decisive (see Koschaker 1953, p. 136, on the reception of the 1804 French Civil Code elsewhere).

9 On the strong convergence thesis, see Merryman 1999a, p. 19-26.

10 Merkesinis for example claimed that common law and civil law systems have been converging, also in the area of procedure, see Markesinis 1994, p. 30. Also see Merryman 1999a.

11 Elsewhere, I have argued that some degree of convergence between procedural systems, particularly within Europe, can be perceived, Van Rhee & Verkerk 2006. Some authors even speak of the 'Europeanization' of civil procedural law, see Ervo, Gräns & Jokela 2009.

jurisdictions that portray strong differences. At a European level, it seems plausible to postulate a strong relationship between the rise and fall of the nation state and the convergence and divergence of law. The rise of the nation state between the 16th and 19th centuries has been linked to the rise of national courts, national legal education and national codifications.[12] These in turn have led to diversification of procedural laws and practices. The gradual downfall of the nation-state and the emergence of international and European organizations since the Second World War has been linked to the emergence of a new *ius commune*.[13] A study of the case law on Article 6 of the European Convention of Human Rights, the legislation enacted in the framework of the first pillar of the European Union, the success of the UNICITRAL Model Code of Arbitration and a study of the Woolf reforms in England would probably reveal an altogether different picture on the question of convergence than a comparative study that offsets Austrian and Dutch procedural law with U.S. federal law.

The historic overview in Chapters 2 and 3 reveals that in some areas there has been a convergence between legal systems. There have been common developments. In general, there was some degree of convergence between the Austrian system and the Dutch system. Similarly, American jurisdictions seem to have converged under the influence of the Field Code and the federal codifications. There have been many examples of cross-influences between common law and Continental procedural systems. The 1848 New York Field Code was influenced by Continental legislation (Section 3.2). Similarly, the Angelo-American rules that qualified parties to testify and the English rules on discovery had influenced the 1895 Austrian Code of Civil Procedure (Section 2.3). It is remarkable that European procedural rules have not been transplanted to the U.S. system since the 1930s. In the process of drafting or amending procedural legislation in the U.S., there have not been many instances of foreign borrowing (Chapter 3).[14]

Many new differences between Continental systems and U.S. systems have emerged since the 1930s. The emergence of a 'depositions culture' in the United States provides a clear example (see Chapter 6). Indeed, it is common in general comparative literature to speak of 'American exceptionalism' in the area of civil procedure.[15] Some of the exceptional features of the American system, such as the existence of the civil jury, have a fairly long history. Other exceptional features of the American system have only been developed during the last 70 years. The rules on discovery provide the best example (see Chapters 3 and 6). At the same time, in both the Netherlands and Austria, procedural novelties were introduced that

12 Having ones' own court structure is often a symbol of sovereignty, as is well illustrated by the creation of the Court of Appeal of Thorn in 1718. The Dutch town of Thorn is very insignificant in size. Its Court of Appeal dealt with an extraordinary small case load. The Court was nevertheless created as a symbol of Thorn's sovereign position until the downfall of the *Ancien Régime*. See Berkvens 2006.

13 Van Caenegem 2002, Chapter 2.

14 Stiefel & Maxeiner 1994, p. 150 and Langbein 1995. Equally, there were only very few instances of foreign borrowing when the new Swiss Code of Civil Procedure was drafted, see Baumgartner 2009.

15 Chase 2005, Chapter 4.

reshaped the process of litigation. Throughout the 20th century, many European jurisdictions, such as the Netherlands, had followed the Austrian example and had enhanced the role of the court in the process of fact-finding. It may be concluded that since the 1930s, Continental systems and U.S. systems of fact-finding have diverged. This diversion that took place since the 1930s poses a genuine challenge to both stronger and weaker forms of the convergence theory.

2. Fact-finding Processes: the Main Differences

2.1. *Concentrated and Dispersed Processes*

As indicated above, the general course of litigation in the Federal Courts of the United States differs greatly from the general structure of litigation on the Continent. These differences have largely come into existence since the 1930s. Figures 4.1, 4.2 and 4.3 provide simplified graphical representations of the different courses of an ordinary law suit in Austria, the Netherlands and the Federal Courts in the United States. A more detailed and accurate description of the ordinary course of litigation in each of these procedures was provided above. It must be noted that only a small proportion of all cases filed truly follow all stages indicated in Figures 4.1-4.3. In the previous chapter it was demonstrated that only a very small minority of all American cases make it to the trial stage. Most cases only go through the first stages before they are resolved by (unmediated) bilateral settlements or a summary judgment. In Austria and the Netherlands most cases are also terminated at an early point in time. In the Austrian County Courts (*Bezirksgerichte*), 508,958 orders for payment procedures (*Mahnsachen*) were initiated in 2007. In only 48,868 of these cases, the defendant opposed the order (*Einspruch*).[16] The case flow diagram in Figure 4.4 shows what happens to incoming cases at the Civil Law Section of Dutch District Courts. Roughly half of all cases are defended.[17] Of all defended cases, only a small proportion truly follows all steps depicted in Figure 4.2.

If we nevertheless compare Continental with American processes of fact gathering, it appears that Continental processes are more concentrated. Concentration in the early stages of litigation is even clearer in Austria than in the Netherlands. In most cases the process of fact gathering in Austria and the Netherlands consists of only one written pleading by each of the parties, followed by an oral preparatory hearing. In the United States, pretrial processes and modes of fact-gathering are dispersed. The process consists of a large number of possible steps: pleadings, motions for (and against) summary judgment, initial disclosure, discovery conferences, pretrial conferences, settlement conferences, requests for

16 This follows from an extract of the 'Betriebliches Informationssystem der Justiz' made available to me by an employee of the Austrian Ministry of Justice.

17 i.e. 2.9% is withdrawn, in 38.3% there is no reaction from the defendant and in 8.3% an attorney has contacted the court on behalf of the defendant but does not challenge the claim by means of an answer. Only in the remaining 50% of the cases the defendant files an answer.

discovery of documents, motions to compel discovery, separately filed interrogatories and depositions.

Two examples illustrate that the Continental modes of fact gathering are more concentrated than the American process of fact-gathering. First, the Dutch and the Austrian systems require the parties to identify in their pleadings the evidence they could adduce in support of their contentions of fact. Disclosure and the factual allegations of a party are thereby combined in a single document. In the Federal System in the United States, the parties first exchange the pleadings and only subsequently disclose the means of proof that will be used at trial in a separate document. Second, the pretrial interrogation of the opposing party on the Continent generally takes place at the oral preparatory hearing. During this hearing, the further course of the procedure will also be discussed and the judge will try to promote settlement. In the United States, these different activities are dealt with at different points in time. A scheduling order or a pretrial conference generally serves to schedule and plan the further course of the pretrial process. Often a separate settlement conference is scheduled in an attempt to settle the case. Depositions and interrogatories are often used alongside each other to put questions to the other party.

If we compare the presentation of evidence, a reverse pattern can be perceived. The American trial constitutes a single, continuous and uninterrupted event. Although 'bifurcation' of trial occasionally occurs in the United States, such is the rare exception rather than the rule. In Austria and the Netherlands, it is not uncommon for there to be a number of evidentiary hearings. Often there are several weeks or even months between these evidentiary hearings. Although a single evidentiary hearing is often prefered, it is common to schedule more than one hearing if that is more convenient.

A simple example, as given below, can clarify the difference between the American trial and the Continental 'sequence of evidentiary hearings'. Charlie, a promising 18 year old (American) football player gets injured as his vehicle collides with a truck driven by Mary. The injury prevents Charlie from pursuing his career as a professional football player. Charlie sues for damages, claiming that 1) Mary was driving at least twice the speed limit and 2) that without the injury he certainly would have made millions as a professional football player. Mary denies that she was speeding. In addition, she challenges the claim that Charlie really was a promising football player that would have made millions. Let us assume that both facts are genuinely disputed and decisive for the outcome of the case.

If this case made it to an American trial, evidence for both disputed facts would be presented during one single, uninterrupted trial. Although it is possible that trial takes a couple of days, the presentation of evidence would be concluded swiftly and without delay. If the jury finds that Mary is not liable, both parties prepared in vain for a discussion on the size of the damages.

If this case were filed in a Dutch court, and the judge determined that evidence for both facts was needed, the court would probably first order Charlie to prove that Mary was speeding. Probably, one hearing would be scheduled at which witnesses suggested by Charlie could testify to provide evidence for this first decisive matter of fact. If the witnesses did not testify that they saw Mary speeding, there would be no need for Mary to present counter evidence, and the court could deny the claim. If Charlie's witnesses did provide compelling testimony, Mary would be given an opportunity to present counter evidence. An evidentiary hearing would then be scheduled that would take place a couple of weeks later.

Only if the court came to the conclusion that Mary was speeding, would the second factual question be addressed: how much money would Charlie have made as a football player? To resolve the second factual issue, additional evidentiary hearings could be scheduled or the court could appoint an expert. If the court ultimately awarded Charlie his claim, the final judgment would probably be preceded by three or four evidentiary hearings, each several weeks apart from each other. The Dutch approach to the presentation of evidence does not lead to unnecessary preparation by lawyers; it may however have a negative impact on the total duration of the procedure.

Figure 4.1, Current Ordinary Course of Litigation before the U.S. District Courts, Compared to the Early Common Law Procedure. Simplified Graphical Representation.

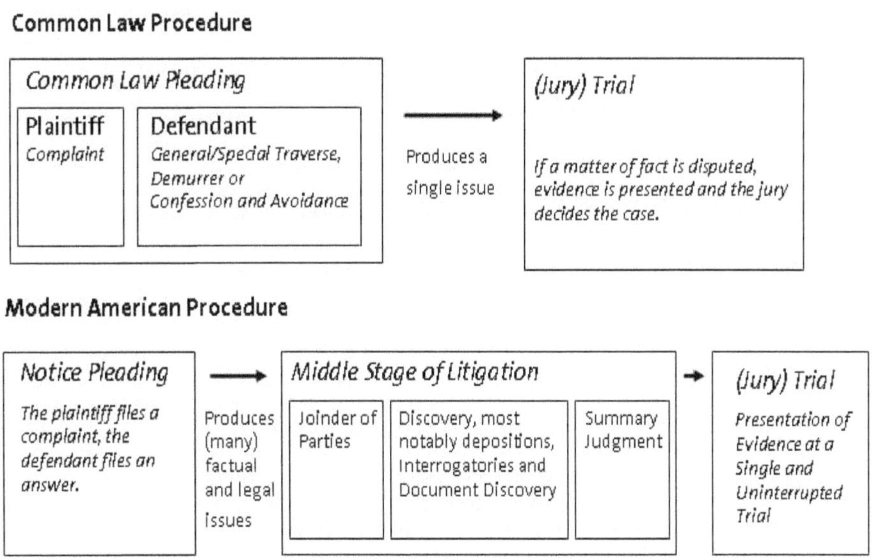

Figure 4.2, Current Dutch Structure of Litigation, Compared with Common Procedures in the 1990s. Simplified Graphical Representation.

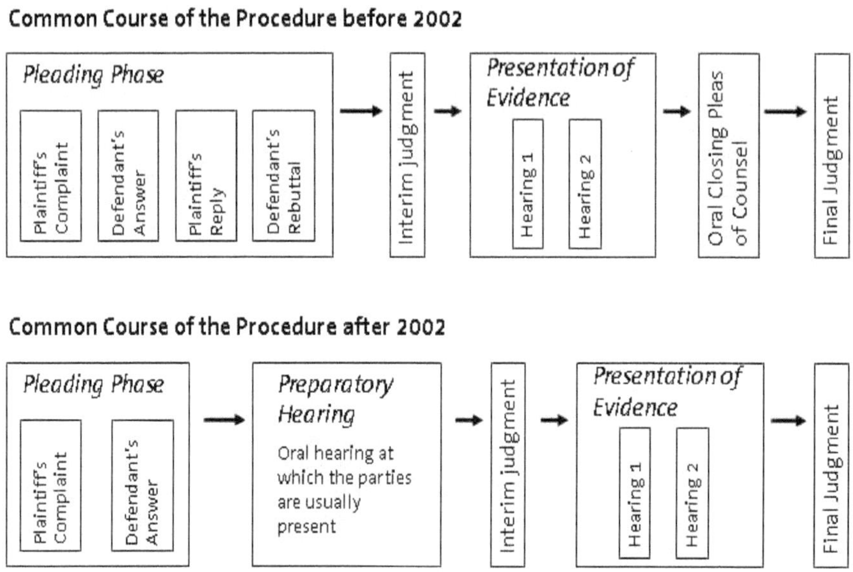

Figure 4.3, Current Austrian Ordinary Procedure Compared with the very Common Orders for Payment Procedure. Simplified Graphical Representation.

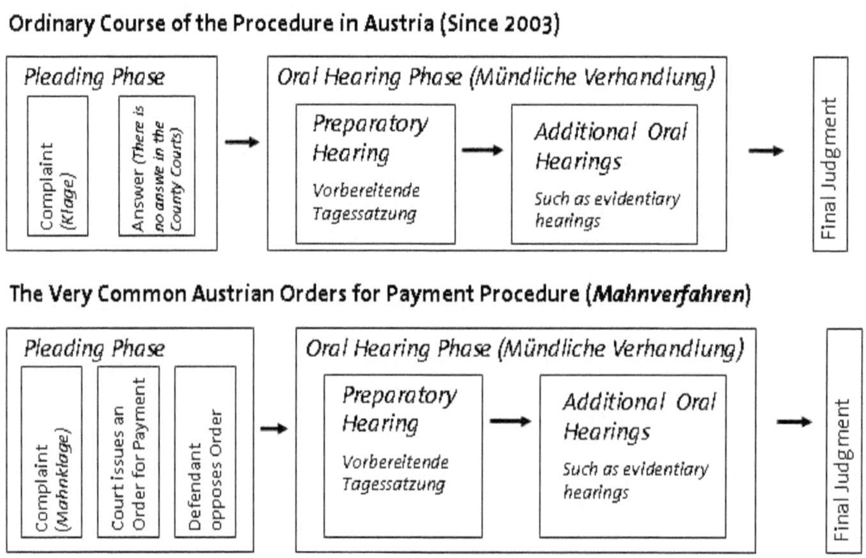

Figure 4.4, Flow Diagram, Civil Law Section of Dutch District Courts, 2003 Data.[18] *First Phases of the Procedure.*

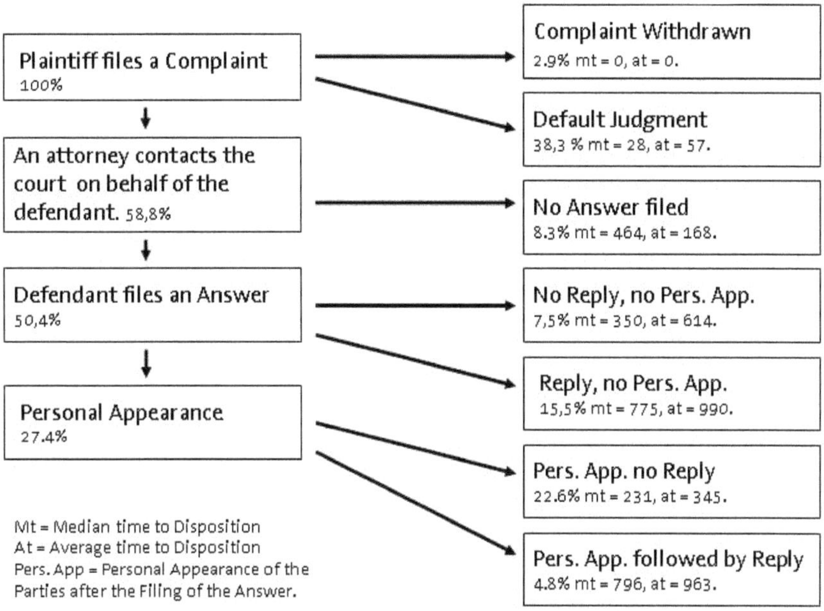

2.2. *Different Roles of the Actors in the Legal Process*

As set out in Chapters 2 and 3, both on the European Continent and in the United States there has been a shift in the respective roles of lawyers, judges and litigants in the legal process. Although this development was largely a matter of procedural practice, the changing roles of the actors in the legal process was accompanied by legislative change.

On the European Continent, the concept of managerial judging, as exemplified in the Austrian Code of 1895, spread throughout other parts of Europe during the 20th century. The abandonment of strict evidence rules, the increased emphasis on the pursuit of truth and the changes in the ordinary course of litigation have extended considerably the role of the court in the Continental legal process. The larger role of the court has led to a shift in power from the litigants and their lawyers to the court.

In the United States, the introduction of the Federal Rules of Civil Procedure (FRCP) in 1938 prepared the way for the privatization of the process of fact gathering in civil litigation. The centre of gravity of the legal process shifted from pleadings and trial to the newly introduced middle phase of the procedure.

18 Source: Eshuis 2007, Figure 32, p. 169. Eshuis based these findings on 708 Dutch cases pending before the Civil Law Section of the Dutch District Courts.

Discovery, largely conducted by lawyers, became the new centre stage in the process of fact-finding. The new system allowed a thorough search for the facts with only a minimum of government intervention. The privatization of the process of fact gathering has led to a power shift from appellate courts to trial courts and from trial courts to lawyers.

The fact that judges and attorneys fulfill different roles in Continental and American jurisdictions is related to the differences in the number of judges and attorneys. Although it is difficult to compare such figures, it is obvious that within American jurisdictions there are far more attorneys per judgeship than in the Netherlands and Austria (see Section 9.2).

The different roles of attorneys, judges and litigants in different legal systems are interrelated with the many rules that regulate the details of the process of fact-finding. As will be shown in Chapter 5, the different roles of attorneys, litigants and judges in the legal process has had a massive impact on the way in which expert evidence is gathered and presented in court. These different practices affect, and are affected by, the different rules on expert evidence in American and Continental jurisdictions. Moreover, as set out in Chapter 6, the interrogation of litigants through party driven discovery clearly differs from the interrogation of litigants by the judge during a Continental oral hearing. The use of different mechanisms of party interrogation is largely a result of different legal rules. Different practices have in turn created the need for new rules aimed to improve these practices.

Even if the rules of procedure are similar, the different roles of attorneys, litigants and judges may lead to diverging procedural practices in Continental and American jurisdictions. The 1895 Austrian rules on party driven discovery of documents, for example, were inspired by the English rules. Although the rules were not that different from rules in some common law jurisdictions, the Austrian rules were rarely used as there apparently was less need for party driven discovery rules in the Austrian system (see Sections 2.3.1 and 7.3). Case management provides another example. There has been plenty of focus on case management in American jurisdictions. If one compares Rule 16 FRCP with Continental rules on preparatory hearings, one finds striking similarities. In practice, FRCP Rule 16 is of less significance than similar rules on the Continent (see Section 6.1-6.2). Case Management in American practice seems to be largely concerned with setting deadlines and encouraging settlement and much less with discussing and narrowing down factual issues. During the pretrial stage of litigation, judges are generally not actively involved in eliciting the factual details of the dispute.

Pleading rules provide a last example of how similar rules operate differently when judges and attorneys fulfill different roles in the operation of the justice system. As was argued in Section 3.4.1, pleading rules are quite similar on both sides of the Atlantic. Differences in pleading rules do exist, but I think these are of minor importance. For example, Austrian and Dutch legislation requires litigants to identify the evidence they wish to use in their pleadings.[19] On the other hand,

19 Article 111 Dutch Code of Civil Procedure, Section 76 Austrian Code of Civil Procedure. Similar legislation exists elsewhere, Article 56(4) French Code of Civil Procedure requires the →

pleadings in the U.S. District Courts are usually more detailed on matters of jurisdiction.[20] Despite the apparent similarities in the rules on pleading, it has become a commonplace in comparative literature to state that Continental models often adhere to 'fact-pleading' whereas the Federal American system would adhere to 'notice pleading'.[21] This observation is correct in the sense that Dutch or Austrian pleadings are probably more detailed and thorough than American pleadings.[22] Differences between American and Continental practices do not flow from differences in the rules on pleading but are primarily a result of the different roles of judges and attorneys in both systems.

The main reason why pleadings provide more factual details on the Continent is that pleadings are of importance to the court. If they are important to the court, it is prudent for litigants to provide a comprehensive and sufficiently detailed account of the facts. On the European Continent, the judge almost always reads the pleadings in detail to prepare for the first oral hearing.[23] As a judge is inclined to stick to her preliminary theory of the facts, it is of strategic importance to convince her as soon as possible of the merits of one's case.[24] This tactical observation creates an incentive for attorneys to devote special attention to their pleadings. Furthermore, the pleadings are of importance as a Dutch or Austrian judge will ordinarily base her first interlocutory decision on the pleadings and matters discussed at the first oral hearing. Such decisions often are 'proof decisions' at which the court determines which facts require proof and which party has the burden of production.[25] As judges generally are inclined to narrow down the issues, parties have to be on guard that they provide sufficient factual details concerning genuine factual disputes. If the judge has the opinion that one party is withholding relevant information, it might well be the case that the judge establishes a fact to the detriment of that party without ordering the production of evidence.

In contrast, it seems that it is not uncommon for a judge in a U.S. District Court not to read the pleadings, unless the judge has a reason to do so.[26] It might very well

plaintiff to refer to the documents on which he bases his case. In the United States the Federal Rules require the parties to identify the evidence they intend to use as part of the disclosure requirements. See FRCP Rule 26.

20 FRCP Rule 8(a)(1).

21 E.g. American Law Institute & UNIDROIT 2006, p. 111 and Chase, Herschkoff, Silberman, Taniguchi & Varano 2007, Chapter 4, Part IV, p. 203.

22 The choice of terminology is confusing as it could wrongly leave behind the impression that Continental pleading should be associated with the formalistic practices under the Field Code.

23 I have failed to find hard empirical data in this respect. My observation is based on private conversations with mostly Dutch practitioners.

24 See my discussion of the so-called 'confirmation bias' in Section 8.2.

25 In the Netherlands it is common that the court will take a formal interlocutory decision in which it will determine which facts require evidence. In Austria the legislator indicated in 2002 that a formal decision (*Beweisbeschluss*) is no longer required, 962 BlgNr GP XXI, p. 36.

26 Due to large differences between courts it is hard to generalize or quantify my claim. I have not found sound empirical data on these issues. Clerks might – or might not – read the pleadings in more depth and very shortly brief the judge on the contents of the pleading. My →

be the case that the pleadings will not be thoroughly read at all. If one of the parties files a motion for summary judgment, the motion will often speak for itself and not require the court to read the underlying pleadings in detail. If the case is tried by a jury, the jury will certainly not read the pleadings. American pleadings, to conclude, are generally not a suitable means to influence the trier of fact.

Another reason why pleading is probably less extensive in the American Federal system is that a failure to comply with the rules on the substance of the pleadings will generally remain without consequences. The judge will not impose sanctions *ex officio,* and the opposing party will most likely not complain if the facts are not put forward in sufficient detail. The existence of discovery makes the enforcement of pleading rules of less importance. An example can clarify this point. In both American Federal and Dutch law a simple denial does generally not suffice to meet the legal pleading requirements. As the FRCP put it: 'a denial should meet the substance of the opposing party's allegation'. If the plaintiff, claiming for alimony, alleges: 'the defendant earns $6,000 a month' it does not seem to suffice if the defendant only writes in his answer 'denied'.[27] In the Netherlands, if the pleadings only state 'denied', it is likely - unless the issue is dealt with in more detail at an oral hearing - that the court will simply assume the defendant earns $6,000 each month. In the United States, a federal judge will not fulfill such an active role. In the example mentioned, an American plaintiff will probably not 'bug' the court by complaining about a violation of pleading rules. The problem will probably be solved in the discovery phase. The plaintiff could simply use an interrogatory to find out about the defendant's income.

2.3. *Comparing Fact-finding Processes: the Duration of Litigation*

It is interesting to assess the relative success of different jurisdictions in providing for an effective, fair, legitimate and efficient process of fact-finding. It is difficult to make conclusive judgments on the respective merits of different jurisdictions. Some recent large scale empirical studies in this area used defective methods.[28] Others

observations in this respect are based on private interviews with four attorneys that practiced law in different parts of the United States, a federal judge and two law clerks.

27 Dutch Court of Cassation, 13 November 1914, *NJ* 1915, 107.

28 A good example of a large scale empirical study that I find to be defective is Djankov, La Porta, Lopez-de-Silanes & Shleifer 2003. The authors, on the basis of questionnaires filled out by lawyers, measured and described the enforcement of two types of legal claims: recovering on a bounced cheque and evicting a tenant who owed rent. On the basis of the questionnaires a 'legal formalism index' was developed. The authors compared systems in the French legal family, the common law family, the German family and the socialist family. The authors found that formalism is greater in civil law systems than in common law systems and associated with higher expected duration of judicial proceedings, less consistency, less fairness etc. The design of this study is, in my view, problematic for various reasons. One obvious flaw seems to be in the choice of the two typical cases. Cheques are not equally used across jurisdictions, therefore recovering a bounced cheque may be a standard action in one jurisdiction and exceptional in another jurisdiction. The study also failed to account for the fact that the political will to protect tenants against eviction, rather than the deficiencies of the procedural apparatus, may explain the perceived differences in formalism.

have made use of theoretical models to predict the efficiency a procedural system. These studies often oversimplify reality to such an extent that I would be hesitant to attach too much value to these studies.[29]

In Chapter 6.2 some of the available empirical studies on the perceived fairness, costs and the effectiveness of court hearings and certain discovery devices will be discussed. On the basis of the available data, the conclusion will be drawn that the American approach of fact-gathering by means of discovery is probably more thorough, but at the same time more expensive, than Continental modes of fact gathering. In Chapter 5, Continental approaches to expert evidence will be contrasted with common law approaches to expert evidence. It will be concluded that it is difficult to judge which system is more effective. In Chapters 8 and 9, the democratic legitimacy of the legal process and the cost implications of democratic procedures will be addressed. It will be concluded that American jurisdictions are generally more democratic, although this does have negative implications for the costs of operating the justice system. In Chapter 10, to conclude, a theoretical framework will be presented that is useful in understanding how legal systems may create incentives for the parties to act in a way that is socially efficient.

In the remainder of this Section, I will make some more general remarks on the duration of civil litigation. Although litigants could feel court procedures to be 'rushed' and 'too short', complaints about undue delay are much more common.[30] Legislators have often remodeled the rules of procedure to make the legal process less time consuming, arguing that 'justice delayed is justice denied'. Beyond doubt, the process of fact-gathering and the preparation and presentation of evidence are by far the most time consuming stages in the litigation process.

There has been comparative literature that has shed some light on the duration of litigation in civil cases. A good example is the book 'Civil Justice in Crisis', edited by Zuckerman, which provides empirical data on the costs and duration of litigation in a number of jurisdictions, including the United States and the Netherlands.[31] Another good example is the statistical reports produced by the European Commission for the Efficiency of Justice in the framework of the Council of Europe.[32] In Austria, the Information System of the Ministry of Justice (*Betriebliches Informationssystem der Justiz*) is the best source of empirical information on the justice system. This system is however inaccessible to the general public. Data on the Dutch system and on the American Federal system are more widely and readily available.

The Austrian system resolves cases relatively quickly when compared to most other jurisdictions. Statistics in the 1960s already showed that the number of cases not concluded within a year is almost zero.[33] Data from 1996 show that of all civil cases filed at a court of first instance in 1996, 84.3% is concluded in the same year.

29 E.g. Froeb & Kobayashi 2001; Block, Parker, Vyborna & Dusek 2000 and Parker & Lewisch 1998.

30 See in general Van Rhee 2004.

31 Zuckerman 1999.

32 CEPEJ 2008.

33 Baur 1970.

The remaining 15.7% of cases includes cases filed in December 1996 and resolved three months later in February 1997. As shown in the Table 4.1, the differences between cases resolved by the District Courts (*Landesgerichte*) and County Courts (*Bezirksgerichte*) are large.

Table 4.1. Cases filed and resolved in 1996, cases pending on 31 December 1996[34]

Courts	Cases filed in 1996	Percentage of the cases concluded in 1996	Cases pending on 31/12/1996		
			% filed before 1/1/1996	% filed before 1/1/1995	% filed before 1/1/1994
County Court	774,208	87.6%	1.2%	0.4%	0.1%
District Court	90,433	56.5%	13.3%	5.3%	2.6%
Total	864,641	84.3%	2.4%	0,9%	0.4%

Recent data retrieved from the Ministry of Justice's Information System reveal that the figures today are comparable to those in 1996. In 2006, the average duration of contested civil cases before the County Courts (*Bezirksgerichte*) was 8.6 months (median 6.1 months). In uncontested cases the average duration was 2.8 months and the median duration 1.6 months.[35] The 2007 data on the cases filed and concluded in 2007 by the County Courts are listed in the Table 4.2.[36]

Table 4.2. Civil cases filed and resolved in 2007, Austrian County Courts

	Cases filed in 2007	Percentage of the cases concluded in 2007	Cases pending on 31/12/2007		
			% filed before 1/1/2007	% filed before 1/1/2006	% filed before 1/1/2005
County Court	604,761	83.4%	7.2%	2.1%	0.9%

In the Netherlands the average time to disposition has decreased over the last couple of years (see Table 4.3).[37] Especially contested cases handled by the Civil Law Division of the Dutch District Courts take relatively long. Table 4.3 indicates that defended cases take much longer to resolve than undefended cases that are resolved by default judgments. Table 4.3 and 4.4 also show that the value of the claim is positively correlated with the duration of the proceeding.

34 Clemenz & Gugler 1998, p. 16.

35 Oberhammer & Domej 2010, who quote an unpublished report of the Austrian Ministry of Justice. Also see the data of the Council of Europe, available at <www.coe.int/t/dghl/cooperation/cepej/evaluation/2008/austria_en.pdf>, question 93, last consulted in February 2010.

36 The jurisdiction of the *Bezirksgerichte* was slightly broadened after the introduction of the Euro (*Official State Journal* (BGBl) 2001/98). Before the introduction of the Euro, these courts were competent to hear all cases where the value of the claim did not exceed the 13,000 Schilling (roughly 9,450 Euro). Since the introduction of the Euro the amount was increased to 10,000 Euro.

37 Eshuis 2007, p. 157-160.

Table 4.3. Duration of litigation in commercial cases in days, the Netherlands, 2004-2008[38]

Court Division / Defended and Undefended Cases	2004 Mean	2005 Mean	2006 Mean	2008 Mean
Civil Law Division, Defended Cases	587	577	524	427
Civil Law Division, Default Judgments	34	33	35	42
County Court Div., Defended Cases	77	81	80	
County Court Div., Default Judgments	10	9	8	7

Table 4.4. Duration of litigation in defended cases in days, the Netherlands, Civil Law Division of the District Court, 2003[39]

Stakes (i.e. value of the claim)	Median	Mean	N
<10.000 Euro	253	481	1,097
10.000-25.000 Euro	308	533	1,303
>25.000 Euro	497	733	1,918
No specified amount claimed	580	745	1,529

In the U.S. District Courts in 1980, the median time for a case to move from filing to disposition was 8 months. For cases that were tried, the interval was 20 months.[40] More recent statistics show that the current time to disposition is comparable, albeit that the median time to disposition has slightly increased. Table 4.5 shows that the median time to disposition is considerably shorter in cases that require no court action than in cases that proceed to trial.

Table 4.5. U.S. District Courts, median time intervals from filing to disposition in months of civil cases, September 30, 2006-September 30, 2007[41]

Type of Cases		Number of Cases	Median Time to Disposition (Months)
All Cases		182,966	8.6
No Court Action		43,894	5.5
Court Action	Before Pretrial	106,752	7.9
	During or after Pretrial	22,849	13.8
	Trial	9,471	27.6

One of the reasons why it is extremely difficult to compare the time to disposition between cases in different legal systems is that the costs and duration of litigation are linked to case characteristics. As case characteristics of courts differ greatly, one cannot simply compare the average time to disposition of cases handled by U.S. District Courts with the average time of those handled by the Civil Law Section of a Dutch District Court.

38 *Jaarverslag 2006,* p. 32-35 and *Jaarverslag 2008,* Table 9a. The 2008 data were originally measured in weeks and did not provide one figure for all contested County Court cases.

39 Eshuis 2007, Table 13, p. 166.

40 Administrative Office of the U.S., 1980, Annual Report of Director, as discussed by Resnik 1984, p. 11.

41 Duff 2008, Table C5, p. 175. Note that the Table states that the median time interval for cases that went to trial is 127.6 months rather than 27.6 months. I assume this is an error.

As follows from Tables 4.3 and 4.5, uncontested cases, such as undefended orders for payment procedures and procedures that are disposed of by means of default judgments are quickly resolved. Therefore, differences in the percentage of uncontested cases will have a considerable effect on mean and average time to disposition. Of all 603,323 cases filed in the Austrian County Courts in 2007, 508,958 cases were orders for payment procedures (*Mahnsachen*). Out of these 508,958 cases, only 48,868 were contested (*Einspruch*). This implies that the bulk of all civil cases filed in the Austrian County Courts are uncontested orders for payment procedures. Austrian 1996 data indicated that more than 90% of all Austrian cases are uncontested.[42] This figure is relatively high.[43] It is therefore generally useful to compare data on the mean and average times to disposition in both defended and undefended cases.

Secondly, as is clear from Tables 4.1 and 4.4, the average time to disposition is generally larger if the stakes of a lawsuit are higher. In addition, it is generally known that courts handle many low value cases. In 61% of all cases filed in the Civil Law Section of the Dutch District Courts in 2003, the damages are below 20,000 Euro. In 83% of all cases the damages do not exceed 50,000 Euro.[44] Relevant in this respect is that the different rules on jurisdiction in Austria, the Netherlands and the United States lead to differences in the characteristics of cases handled by the respective courts. In the Netherlands, County Courts generally handle all cases where the value of the claim is lower than 5,000 Euro. In Austria, County Courts handle cases where the value of the claim is below 10,000 Euro. The diversity of citizenship jurisdiction of the U.S. District Courts is restricted to cases in which the value of the claim exceeds $75,000.[45] The fact that the median time to disposition of contested cases in the Dutch District Courts seems to be shorter than the median time to disposition of cases with court action in the United States is (partly) explained by the fact that Dutch courts handle relatively more low damages cases.[46]

There are many other factors which make it difficult to compare statistics on the duration of litigation in civil cases. One complicating factor is that there are different views on what is to be understood by a civil case. On the basis of the available data it is difficult to make conclusive comparative judgments.

42 Clemenz & Gugler 1998, p. 6.

43 In the Netherlands, in 2008, roughly 75% of all County Court cases were resolved by default judgments, see Diephuis, Eshuis & De Heer-De Lange 2010, p. 114.

44 Eshuis 2007, p. 165. For comparable 2008 data, see Diephuis, Eshuis & De Heer-De Lange 2010, p. 131.

45 See Section 49 Austrian JN, Article 93 Dutch Code of Civil Procedure and the Federal Courts Improvement Act of 1996, 28 U.S.C. Section 1332.

46 Trubek, Sarat, Felstiner, Kritzer and Grossman 1983 already concluded that the median stakes in Federal cases were $15,000. As the stakes in this study were considered to consist only out of the disputed part of the claim, the median claim must have been larger.

PART II

SPECIFIC CHAPTERS ON COMPARATIVE CIVIL PROCEDURE

INTRODUCTION

The following two Chapters discuss two specific areas of the law in greater detail: expert evidence and the interrogation of parties. The more detailed rules illustrate the general lines set out in Part I and Part III of this book.

As will be shown below, the Continental and American rules on expert evidence differ greatly. On the European continent, the testimony of experts is not primarily regarded as a means of proof. Experts are regarded as assistants of the court. They help the judge to interpret technical evidence. Therefore the judge, rather than the parties, is primarily responsible for the appointment of experts. Continental rules on expert evidence generally do provide parties opportunities to be involved in the production of expert evidence. In most American jurisdictions, judges seldom appoint experts. In the United States, expert witnesses are like other witnesses: they are selected, prepared and questioned by lawyers. Parties commonly each hire their own expert witness. Rules on disclosure and discovery are available to ensure an exchange of information and to avoid surprise at trial.

In Chapter 6, the different techniques to interrogate parties in civil cases will be discussed. This Chapter provides a historical introduction to the different procedural mechanisms to question the parties to a lawsuit. This historical introduction provides many examples of legal borrowing and shows that there have been areas of convergence. Presently, in the evidence stage of litigation, most modern jurisdictions enable the parties to give a testimony under oath. In the fact-gathering stage, new differences between legal systems have emerged. Depositions and interrogatories are available and used in the United States, whereas the personal appearance of the parties is the most significant means to question the parties on the Continent.

Chapter 5

EXPERT EVIDENCE[1]

Often judges and lawyers are faced with scientific questions which cannot be resolved without the help of specialists. Courts on the European Continent traditionally appoint experts themselves. In North American jurisdictions, both parties hire expert witnesses who inform the court or jury.[2] This Chapter contrasts Continental practices to those in common law jurisdictions to highlight the different structural and philosophical positions. This Chapter further examines 'mixed' procedural models that are replacing the court-centered and party-centered approaches to obtaining expert opinions.

1. The Continental Expert as an Auxiliary of the Court

1.1. *Expertise and its Relation to Judicial Case Management*

Procedural Codes on the European Continent have empowered judges to appoint experts. These Codes consider the expert to be a neutral and impartial auxiliary of the court. Although there are similarities between Continental jurisdictions, the court-centered approach to expertise is most rigorously applied in Austrian law.

In Austria, the relationship between the expert and the court should be understood in the light of the duty of the court to manage the process of fact-finding (*materielle Prozessleitung,* see Chapter 7).[3] The 1895 Code of Civil Procedure placed the judge under the duty to establish the facts truthfully. In order to fulfill this task, the Austrian judge was granted a wide range of managerial powers with regard to the production of evidence.[4] The judge could summon witnesses or order the parties to produce documents *ex officio*.[5] Additionally, the court could decide to ask an expert for assistance. The court-appointed expert serves the court and can be said

1 Large parts of this Chapter have been published before. See Verkerk 2009.

2 Jolowicz 2000, p. 226 discusses the differences between English law (before 1999) and French law. Langbein 1985, p. 835 discusses the distinction between US and German law.

3 Zechner 1986, p. 419.

4 On judicial powers in Austria, see Sections 2.3.1 and 7.2.2.

5 Section 183 Austrian Code of Civil Procedure.

to have a 'derived' legal duty to establish the facts truthfully.[6] The Explanatory Memorandum to the 1895 Austrian codification clearly states that it is the duty of the expert to support the court, regardless of whether the parties have suggested the taking of expert evidence or not.[7] Sperl has defined the Austrian expert as 'an auxiliary of the court', 'the judge's evidentiary instrument', 'a public law official' and 'a companion of the court'.[8] The Austrian Supreme Court (*Oberste Gerichtshof*) has affirmed this view, stating that the expert is 'a supporting body of public governmental institutions',[9] 'an assistant of the court'[10] and 'part of the public body'.[11]

As noted above, the expert is considered to be a 'public law official' in Austrian law.[12] The relationship between the parties, the judge and the expert is not a contractual one. In Austria, as well as in other civil law countries, the relationship between the expert and the court is defined in terms of public, not private, law.[13] The rights and duties of the expert are regulated by Acts of Parliament rather than private law instruments.[14]

The expert in Austria and in other Continental jurisdictions is not referred to as an 'expert witness' but simply called an 'expert' *(Sachverständige).* On the Continent, expert evidence is considered to be fundamentally different from witness testimony. The expert is appointed to draw conclusions on the basis of the available and relevant facts, something a witness cannot and may not do.[15] Although most modern Continental traditions list the findings of the expert amongst the means of proof,[16] it is technically disputed whether or not the expert's testimony is proof.[17]

6 Zechner 1986, p. 418: '(...) als Substitut des Richters im Dienste der objektiven Wahrheitsfindung als öffentliche und hoheitliche Aufgabe'.

7 Materialien 1897, p. 320: 'In einem Prozeßsystem mit freier Beweiswürdigung sind Sachverständige, (...) berufen, den Richter bei der Würdigung eines bestimmten Sachverhaltes zu unterstützen'.

8 Sperl 1925, p. 445: 'Der Sachverständige ist ein Gehilfe des Richters, sein Beweisorgan, ein Funktionär des öffentlichen Rechtes, ein Mitarbeiter des Gerichtes an der diesem obliegenden Aufgabe, streitige und wichtige Tatsachen zu erforschen und zu beurteilen'.

9 Austrian Supreme Court, 5 July 1934, SZ 16/134: 'ein Hilfsorgan einer öffentliche Behörde'.

10 Austrian Supreme Court, 13 May 1976, SZ 49/67, JBl 1976, 599; Austrian Supreme Court, 21 October 1999, Geschäftszahl 15Os112/99; Austrian Supreme Court, 20 October 2004, Geschäftszahl 7Ob247/04f: 'Hilfsperson des Gerichtes'.

11 Austrian Supreme Court, 20 October 2004, Geschäftszahl 7Ob247/04f: 'Teil der Hoheitsverwaltung'.

12 The expert is formally not considered to be 'in government service' as meant in the sense of Section 1(2) AHG. See in this respect Zechner 1986.

13 For Austrian law, see Zechner 1986; for Dutch law, see De Groot 2004, p. 79.

14 Austrian Code of Civil Procedure, Sections 353-354. See also the Austrian Law on Experts and Translators (*Bundesgesetz über die allgemein beeideten und gerichtlich zertifizierten Sachverständigen und Dolmetscher*, SDG) Official State Journal (BGBl) 1975/137, and, Article 199 Dutch Code of Civil Procedure.

15 Section 340(2) Austrian Code of Civil Procedure, Austrian Supreme Court, 27 March 1985, 3 Ob 503/85 and Article 163 Dutch Code of Civil Procedure.

16 Sections 351-367 Austrian Code of Civil Procedure. It also follows from the writings of Klein, see e.g. Klein 1900, p. 165. See also Articles 194-200 Dutch Code of Civil Procedure.

17 Zechner 1986, p. 417, for the Netherlands see Anema 1940, p. 48, p. 260.

Many Austrian authors have argued that the expert is primarily an 'assistant' of the court, although his findings may also constitute proof.[18] As a consequence, the differences between experts and witnesses in Austrian practice is wide. In Austria, as well as many other Continental systems, judges tend to appoint experts *ex officio* relatively often. Austrian judges, although they are generally empowered to do so, almost never decide to hear witnesses not suggested by the parties. In some Continental jurisdictions, such as the Netherlands, witness evidence is often 'polarized' and a witness in a civil case is often said to be 'my witness' or 'their witness'.[19] Experts in Continental systems, as auxiliaries of the court, are generally not subject to such polarization.

1.2. *Court-appointed Experts in Continental Jurisdictions*

An Austrian court has broad discretion to turn to experts in order to resolve difficult factual questions, but they may only appoint experts if evidence is needed.[20] Since 2002, the production of necessary evidence can be planned at a preparatory hearing.[21] Additionally, the formal requirements with respect to an interlocutory proof decision have been abolished.[22]

Although parties have a right to be heard, the judge makes the decision whether one or more experts will be appointed.[23] Usually, the court will decide to appoint an expert after this is suggested by one of the parties. In Austria, the court may appoint an expert against the will of both parties. Conversely, a court may also decide not to appoint an expert, even though both parties would like the court to do so.[24] Courts in other Continental systems, like France, Belgium, Germany and the Netherlands also have the power to decide whether an expert should be appointed.[25] The court should take into account all relevant factors when it uses its wide discretion. Amongst such factors are whether the court can obtain substitute

18 See e.g. Rechberger & Simotta 2009, No. 809, p. 430 and Fasching 1990, No. 996. For the Netherlands, see De Groot 2008, p. 137.

19 Differences between countries do exist. In the Netherlands parties are required to summon 'their' witnesses (Dutch Code of Civil Procedure, Article 170). For Austria, see Klein 1900, p. 167: 'Der Zeuge ist nicht Zeuge dieser oder der anderen Partei, *(...)* sondern er ist Prozesszeuge. Die Gerichtliche Ladung drückt diese öffentlich-rechtliche Function des Zeugen *(...)*'.

20 On the Austrian doctrine of Evidence, see in general Mayr 2004 and Bajons 2003.

21 Explanatory Memorandum, 962 BlgNr GP XXI, p. 36.

22 Klein 1900, p. 165: 'Mit der Befragung der Zeugen oder Sachverständigen darf erst nach Verkündung des Beweisbeschlusses begonnen werden'. The *Beweisbeschlussβ* was codified in former Section 277 Austrian Code of Civil Procedure.

23 Sections 183, 351(1) and 363(2) Austrian Code of Civil Procedure, Article 194(2) Dutch Code of Civil Procedure, Dutch Court of Cassation, 5 January 2001, *NJ* 2001, 77.

24 Klein 1900, p. 167, Dutch Court of Cassation, 6 December 2002, JOL 2002/667, *NJ* 2003, 63.

25 Article 232 French Code of Civil Procedure, Article 962 Belgian Judicial Code, Section 404 German Code of Civil Procedure and Article 194 Dutch Code of Civil Procedure.

evidence and whether the costs and duration of the expert's investigation are proportional to the value of the claim.[26]

The Austrian court also has discretion to determine how many experts should be appointed and who should be appointed.[27] The parties must be heard on these issues but contrary to codes in other Continental countries, the judge can decide not to hear the parties to avoid excessive costs or delay. In Germany, if the parties have agreed that 'Expert A' is the right man for the job, the judge is bound to appoint 'Expert A'.[28] Other small differences exist between Continental countries, but these have little practical impact.

Austrian law (like French law) prescribes that the courts keep and update a list of sworn experts.[29] Judges are not bound by these lists and the court may appoint experts not on the list. Nevertheless, these lists are the primary tool for the courts to find experts.[30] Courts in other civil law systems also tend to keep expert lists even if the law does not require so (e.g. in the Netherlands).[31]

Different Continental jurisdictions have adopted different policies on oath taking. Once the expert is appointed, some Continental jurisdictions require an oath before experts perform their duties or give testimony; other jurisdictions, such as the Netherlands, have no such requirement.[32] In Austria, the expert is sworn if either one of the parties or the court so requests.[33]

Continental codes generally have few provisions to specify how the expert must perform his task and have empowered the court to supervise the expert's investigations.[34] Since the 2002 Reform Act, the Austrian Code of Civil Procedure

26 See, e.g. with respect to Belgium, Article 875bis Belgian Judicial Code: 'De rechter beperkt de keuze van de onderzoeksmaatregel tot wat volstaat om het geschil op te lossen, waarbij de meest eenvoudige, snelle en goedkope maatregel de voorkeur geniet'. For the Netherlands, see Rutgers, Flach & Boon 1988, p. 327.

27 Section 352 Austrian Code of Civil Procedure. For the Netherlands, see Rutgers, Flach & Boon 1988, p. 331.

28 Section 404(4) German Code of Civil Procedure, former Article 964 Belgian Judicial Code and Taelman 2003, No. 17, p. 61-131.

29 Austrian Law on Experts and Translators (*SDG*), Section 3.

30 Krammer 1990, Section 3.1, p. 16. In France, the Courts of Appeal and the Court of Cassation keep track of lists; see the recently modified Law No. 71-498, 29 June 1971 and Dwyer 2008, p. 107.

31 In the Netherlands, such lists circulate in the courts. Judges can freely comment on those lists and share their experiences. The lists are full of comments such as 'the expert made a good and detailed report but took too much time to finish the report'. Similar lists exist in other countries such as Germany: Langbein 1985, p. 383. For Belgium, see Lysens 2008, p. 210.

32 In the Netherlands, the oath has been abolished: Rutgers, Flach & Boon 1988, p. 316. In Sweden, experts take an oath prior to being heard: Swedish Code, Chapter 40, Section 9. In Belgium, experts always take an oath before signing their report. Other countries like Germany take a middle way and an oath is not always needed, see German Code of Civil Procedure, Section 391; Rosenberg, Schwab & Gottwald 2004, §120, No. 51.

33 See Austrian Code of Civil Procedure, Section 357(2).

34 This is not explicitly codified in Austria, but follows from the more general '*materiele Prozessleitung*'. In other countries it is more explicitly codified, see Article 198(2) Dutch Code of Civil Procedure, Article 973(1) Belgian Judicial Code, and Article 241 French Code of Civil Procedure.

required the judge to actively manage the gathering of expert evidence and to see to it that the expert performs his task swiftly.[35]

The Austrian Code does not specify how to formulate questions the expert should address, for reasons of flexibility. The legislature has indicated that it favors an early exchange of information between the court and the expert regarding the issues that will be addressed as well as the further course of the research activities and the presentation of evidence.[36] In the Netherlands a more formalized procedure is in place. The parties are heard and generally asked to phrase draft questions.[37] In the formal judgment where the expert is appointed, the questions to be addressed by the expert are included.[38] A recent Belgian provision requires the court, the parties and the expert to meet and confer in order to discuss the questions put to the expert.[39]

Although the judge retains some form of supervision, an Austrian expert may to a large extent conduct his own independent investigation. The expert may require the parties to provide relevant information and may visit sites.[40] Experts may also require third parties to provide information.[41] Although it is generally believed that the expert may not delegate his responsibility for the investigation, the expert is entitled to consult other specialists that have expert knowledge in other areas.[42]

Austrian law requires the parties to be cooperative during the taking of expert evidence.[43] This implies that parties are required to provide the expert with all relevant documents and exhibits. The expert should be allowed to enter the premises of the parties or to conduct a physical or mental examination of the parties. Other Continental systems also require parties to cooperate with the court-appointed expert. Article 275(1) of the French Code of Civil Procedure states: 'The parties must give immediately to the expert all documents that the latter deems necessary for the implementation of his mission'. Both Article 198(3) Dutch Code of

35 962 BlgNr GP XXI, Beilagen, p. 36-37, Sections 357 and 359 Austrian Code of Civil Procedure. For a description of the 2002 reform of Austrian law, see Bajons 2005.

36 962 BlgNr GP XXI, Beilagen, p. 36-37.

37 Article 194(2) Dutch Code of Civil Procedure.

38 Article 194 Dutch Code of Civil Procedure.

39 Article 972 Belgian Judicial Code and Lysens 2008.

40 Section 359(2) Austrian Code of Civil Procedure and Article 198(3) Dutch Code of Civil Procedure.

41 Section 359(2) Austrian Code of Civil Procedure and Dutch Court of Cassation, 15 November 1972, *NJ* 1973, 153.

42 Article 278 French Code of Civil Procedure is more explicit: 'The expert may take the initiative of obtaining the opinion of another expert, but only in a specialised field different from his own'. See also Olivier 2000.

43 Since 2002 this implicitly follows from Section 359(2) Austrian Code of Civil Procedure. See 962 BlgNr GP XXI, p. 37. Before 2002 this followed from the general principle that parties have a duty to cooperate with the production of all evidence in general. See, e.g. Austrian Supreme Court, 11 May 2005, 9Ob12/05p.

Civil Procedure and Article 972bis Belgian Judicial Code state: 'Parties are obliged to cooperate with the investigations of the expert (...)'.[44]

The Austrian Code does not provide valid reasons for parties to refuse to cooperate with the taking of expert evidence. Nevertheless, privileges can be invoked to protect confidential information.[45] If a party claims that there is a valid reason to refuse cooperation, application of Section 305 of the Austrian Code seems appropriate. Section 305 of the Code regulates the justified refusal to hand over documents in order to protect confidential information. In case a party argues that there are valid reasons not to cooperate with the expert's investigation, the judge has to weigh the interests of the party against the general interest of finding the truth in the proceedings.[46]

The Austrian Code of Civil Procedure takes the oral testimony of the expert as a starting point.[47] The court may determine that a written report is sufficient on grounds of convenience and efficiency.[48] Due to the principle of immediacy it has been argued that hearing the expert in open court is preferable. If requested by either the court or the parties, the expert is required to clarify his written report orally.[49] If the expert is going to be heard, the judge normally questions the expert, allowing the parties and their attorneys to ask additional questions.[50]

Once the expert has reported, a Continental judge freely evaluates the findings of the expert.[51] The expert's findings do not bind the court and the court has a duty to weigh the conclusions of the expert against other available evidence.[52] In practice, it seems that the judge almost always takes a decision which is in line with the expert's findings.

The court decides who covers the expert's fees and expenses.[53] The Austrian judge also determines the compensation which the expert is to receive prior to the

44 Dutch Court of Cassation, 12 June 1953, *NJ* 1954, 61 and Dutch Court of Cassation 22 February 2008, *LJN* BB5626.

45 Rechberger in Fasching & Konecny 2002-2005, §359, No. 4 and Section 321 Austrian Code of Civil Procedure.

46 Rechberger in Fasching & Konecny 2002-2005, §359; Bienert-Nießl 2003, p. 361. For examples in the area of medical malpractice, see Austrian Supreme Court, 27 July 2006, 3Ob106/06v and Austrian Supreme Court27 July 2006, 3Ob106/06v.

47 This follows indirectly from Section 357 Austrian Code of Civil Procedure.

48 Section 357 Austrian Code of Civil Procedure, Rechberger in Rechberger 2000, §357, No. 1; Fasching 1990, No. 1011. Austrian law makes a distinction between two sorts of reports referred to as a *Befund* and a *Gutachten*. For more details, see Mayr 2004, p. 58. Judges often determine that a written report suffices: Krammer 1990, p. 27.

49 Section 357 Austrian Code of Civil Procedure.

50 Section 289 Austrian Code of Civil Procedure.

51 The Austrian Code of 1895 adheres to the free evaluation of evidence. See Rechberger & Simotta 2009, No. 753. Article 962 Belgian Judicial Code, Article 152(2) Dutch Code of Civil Procedure, Section 286 German Code of Civil Procedure and Article 246 French Code of Civil Procedure.

52 In Austria the judge is not bound by an agreement between the parties regarding the evidential value of the expert's findings: Austrian Supreme Court, 7 October 2003, 4 Ob 188/03f.

53 Sections 24-54 Austrian GebAG, Official State Journal (BGBl) 1975/136, Article 199 Dutch Code of Civil Procedure.

expert's investigations.[54] Other Continental traditions have similar rules.[55] In France the judge is to 'fix the payment of the expert in particular according to the steps taken, the respect of the given time limit and the quality of the work furnished'.[56] French law explicitly forbids the expert to accept any remuneration from the parties unless the court has ordered so.[57]

1.3. *Fair Trial and the Limits of Court-driven Expertise*

Although Continental courts may appoint experts at will and often even against the will of the parties, they do not embrace a model of an 'inquisitorial' and 'authoritarian' judiciary. Preferably, the gathering and presentation of expert evidence is jointly planned by the parties and the court at an early preparatory hearing. The parties' right to a fair trial inhibits excessive unilateral judicial activism and requires the court to involve the parties in the proceedings.

The judge has a duty to hear the parties. Article 6 of the European Convention on Human Rights requires that each party must in principle be enabled to have knowledge of and to comment on all relevant evidence with a view to influencing the court's decision.[58] In *Mantovanelli v. France* the parents of a deceased French patient had initiated a proceeding against the hospital as they believed the staff of the hospital had been negligent. The French administrative court subsequently appointed an expert who concluded that the staff had not been negligent. The plaintiffs demanded the appointment of a new expert as they had not been accurately informed about the expert's investigations, contrary to French law. Furthermore, the plaintiffs argued that the expert had referred to documents they could not access. The plaintiffs' claim was dismissed by the French courts, after which proceedings were initiated before the European Court of Human Rights (ECtHR). The Court concluded that the plaintiffs

> '(...) had thus been deprived of the opportunity to examine the persons who gave evidence to the expert, to submit comments to him on the documents examined and on the witness evidence taken and to ask him to carry out additional investigations. Admittedly, the expert report had later been communicated to the applicants, who could thus have challenged it in the administrative court. They had nevertheless been prevented from participating on an equal footing in the production of the report'.[59]

In the case *Cottin v. Belgium*[60] the ECtHR further extended this doctrine and determined that the possibilities for parties to comment on an expert's report after it

54 Section 39 Austrian GebAG, Official State Journal (BGBl) 1975/136.

55 Article 199 Dutch Code of Civil Procedure. Belgium seems to have an exceptional position, as the expert in principle determines the fee: Lysens 2008, Section 15.4.

56 Article 284 French Code of Civil Procedure.

57 Article 248 French Code of Civil Procedure.

58 See e.g. *Nideröst Huber* v. *Switzerland* (1998), 25 EHRR 709.

59 *Mantovanneli* v. *France*, Appl. No. 21497/93, 18 March 1997, ECHR 1997-II, No. 32, *NJ* 1998, 278, p. 425.

60 *Cottin* v. *Belgium*, Application No. 48386/99, 2 June 2005.

came into existence (possibly allowing the expert to react to such comments) is not a sufficient alternative to participation in the production of the report. This implies that if a party has not had the possibility of participating effectively in the production of the report this cannot be 'repaired' by hearing that party after the report has been drafted. The Court held that the Belgian judge should have appointed a new expert.[61]

The right to be heard as set out in Article 6 of the European Convention on Human Rights has influenced national jurisdictions. The Austrian Constitutional Court has held on the basis of Article 6 that parties must have an opportunity to discuss the factual issues with the expert and to oppose his or her views.[62] The right to be heard was also codified in national jurisdictions prior to the existence of the European Convention on Human Rights. In Austria, a general duty of the court to hear the parties and the parties' right to be present and ask questions during the presentation of evidence was guaranteed by the 1895 Code, along with more specific rights to be heard prior to the appointment of experts.[63]

Although Austria recognizes the right to be heard, it has been emphasized less than in other Continental jurisdictions.[64] The so-called *'principe de contradictoire'* (which includes the right to be heard) is considered to be the cornerstone of civil procedure in countries influenced by the French legal tradition.[65] The right to be heard in France (and Belgium)[66] includes that 1) the expert should communicate to each party the materials provided to the expert by the other party;[67] 2) the parties have a right to be present during the expert's investigation and 3) the parties have the right to ask questions or make comments with regard to the expert's investigations.[68] Similar rules exist in the Netherlands, where a judge may not make a decision to the detriment of a party if that decision is based on information or evidence on which that party could not properly comment.[69] The Dutch Court of Cassation has quashed various decisions in which lower courts did not properly allow parties to comment on expert evidence.[70]

As mentioned previously, the Austrian judge may decide not to hear the parties about 1) the number of experts that should be appointed and 2) the individuals that are suitable to be appointed as experts.[71] The judge may decline to hear the parties on these matters in order to avoid excessive costs or delay. If an

61 *Cottin* v. *Belgium*, Application No. 48386/99, 2 June 2005, para. 32.

62 Austrian Constitutional Court, 1 December 1986, Geschäftszahl B616/85, B448/86, JBl 1987, 511.

63 Sections 182a, 289(1) and 351(1) Austrian Code of Civil Procedure.

64 On the 'right to be heard' in general, see amongst others Sprung 1976 and Fasching 1990, No. 692-705.

65 Taylor 1996, p. 187.

66 See e.g. Article 973 of the Judicial Code and Taelman 2003, No. 40.

67 See e.g. Court of Cassation, 2e civ., 4 March 1998, *Juris-Data* No. 1998-001115.

68 In France this follows from general and specific regulations in the Code, see Articles 14-16 and 276 French Code of Civil Procedure and Taylor 1996, p. 203.

69 Article 19, 194(2) Dutch Code of Civil Procedure.

70 Verkerk 2007, Section 3.3.2 and the case law there mentioned.

71 Austrian Code of Civil Procedure, Section 352(2).

Austrian judge does not hear the parties, this might not have any legal consequences.[72] In other Continental countries the right to be heard prior to the appointment of experts is considered to be more important.

The Austrian system lacks formalized communication between the court, the expert and the parties. Austrian law requires the court to identify the facts that require evidence, but does not require the court to formulate questions which the expert should address.[73] There is no specific regulation that allows parties to put questions to the expert prior to or during the expert's investigations, but the parties may do so during a hearing with leave of the court.[74] This may create the danger that parties are insufficiently heard about the issues the expert will address.[75] In the Netherlands, parties are usually asked before the appointment of an expert to formulate questions.[76] The judge takes the suggestions of the parties and occasionally adds questions of his own. The judge subsequently formulates the questions that will be put to the expert, leaving out those questions suggested by the parties which the court considers inappropriate, irrelevant or leading. Austrian law also lacks a general formalized procedure which allows the parties to comment on the preliminary findings of the expert. Such procedures allow the parties to comment on the findings of the expert before the report is finalized and sent to the court. Procedures of this kind are commonly applied in the Netherlands and Belgium.[77]

It may be concluded that although the right to be heard is recognized in Austrian law, there are few specific regulations and procedures that truly manage to give substance to the right to be heard. As will be seen below, there have been complaints that the Austrian law and its application in practice could infringe Article 6 of the European Convention on Human Rights.[78]

Although the right to be heard forms the most significant limitation on the courts' powers to instruct experts, the right to a fair trial also implies that parties have a right to impartial experts. In several decisions, the European Court of Human Rights has recognized that the lack of neutrality on the part of a court-appointed expert may lead to a situation of inequality between the procedural positions of the parties. A lack of neutrality or impartiality can hence lead to a breach of the principle of 'equality of arms' which is inherent in the concept of fair trial as put down in Article 6(1) of the European Convention on Human Rights.[79]

72 Not hearing the parties in this respect is not considered a *Verfahrensmangel* in Austria: see Krammer 1990, p. 19.

73 This followed from former Section 277 Austrian Code of Civil Procedure.

74 Section 289 Austrian Code of Civil Procedure and Krammer 1990, Section 4.3.

75 Krammer 1990, Section 4.2.

76 Article 194(2) Dutch Code of Civil Procedure.

77 Article 976 Belgian Judicial Code, and Dutch Manual containing Guidelines for Experts, *Leidraad deskundige in civiele zaken*, para. 5.3.2., No. 25, available at <www.rechtspraak.nl>, last consulted in February 2010.

78 Krammer 1990, p. 19.

79 *Bönisch* v. *Austria*, Application No. 8658/79, 6 May 1985, Series A No. 92, *NJ* 1989, 385, Sections 30-35, ECtHR, *Sara Lind Eggertsdóttir v. Iceland*, Application No. 31930/04, 5 July 2007, Sections 47-55.0, ECtHR.

National codifications have often specified that court-appointed experts should be unbiased and impartial.[80] In Austria, the Code of Civil Procedure does not explicitly mention that the expert ought to be impartial. Nevertheless, the Austrian Code and many other Continental Codes provide for a procedural remedy against experts that are, or appear to be, partial or biased.[81] Parties may file an official request to challenge (i.e. recuse) the expert if it is feared that the expert is partial. Examples of valid grounds for challenging experts may include that the expert is a relative, a creditor or a good friend of one of the parties. If the expert is successfully challenged, the court will have to appoint another expert.

1.4. *The Danger of a too Influential Expert*

The Continental system that uses court-appointed experts has its merits. The system reduces incentives for experts to be partial or biased. There are also good reasons to assume that expert costs in Austrian courts are relatively low. Nevertheless, the Continental approach to evidence does have some serious drawbacks. In his book *Die Allmacht des Sachverstandigen* (which roughly translates as 'The Almighty Expert') Krammer states that the Austrian court-appointed expert is often too influential and it is almost impossible for the parties to convince the judge not to base his decision on the conclusions of the court-appointed expert.[82] The argument made by Krammer is often-heard in other Continental jurisdictions.

In theory, the Austrian judge must guard against possible mistakes by the expert.[83] Judges on the European Continent are faced with the very difficult task of determining all matters of fact, even if the subject-matter is highly technical. This task is extremely difficult and perhaps at times hardly possible; after all, a judge appoints an expert because the judge himself is not familiar with the technicalities of the subject-matter. There is reason to fear that the judge cannot properly identify and correct mistakes made by a court-appointed expert. Many judges hold that the judiciary is not sufficiently qualified to asses the expert's findings.[84] In legal practice the judge rarely deviates from the expert's conclusions, and often the court's

80 See e.g. Dutch Code of Civil Procedure, Article 198 or Swedish Judicial Code, Chapter 40, Article 2.

81 Sections 355–356 Austrian Code of Civil Procedure, Section 406 German Code of Civil Procedure, Article 234 French Code of Civil Procedure, and Article 966 Belgian Judicial Code. In the Netherlands the possibility to recuse an expert has been abolished by Act of 22 June 1923, Official State Journal (Stb.), 280.

82 Krammer 1990.

83 Judges must freely evaluate all evidence. Krammer 1990, Section 4.4.

84 In a 2008 survey by the weekly journal *Vrij Nederland* 651 members of the Dutch judiciary (489 of these were judges) were questioned. They were asked to respond to the statement 'The judge is competent enough to deal with cases in which one needs to depend on one or more experts' (*Vraag 32a, De rechter is deskundig genoeg in zaken waarbij men is aangewezen op de inschakeling van een of meer deskundigen*). Judges responded as follows: 1% strongly agree, 31% agree, 25% disagree, 4% strongly disagree, 39% no answer. The study did not distinguish between civil and criminal cases. See <www.vn.nl/extra/pdf/enqueterechters.PDF>, last consulted in February 2010.

judgment largely consists of quotations from the expert's report.[85] Although a judge could appoint another expert if she has doubts about the findings of the first expert, this option is often considered 'impractical'.[86] Often courts may not be inclined to critically assess the findings of the expert. If the court is already convinced that one reconstruction of facts is correct, experts are often appointed to provide the 'scientific base' for the court's decision.[87] If the expert then draws conclusions confirming the judge's preliminary theory, the court is probably not inclined to scrutinize the expert's findings.

Whereas the Continental judge is often not capable or inclined to identify and correct mistakes made by the expert, the parties might feel that they are not entitled to do so. De Groot argued that in the Netherlands the role of parties is too limited if experts are appointed by the court.[88] As discussed above, Austrian law provides the parties with some rights to participate. Austria must comply with Article 6 of the European Convention on Human Rights. Nevertheless, in many Continental countries, including Austria, lawyer's objections to the expert's methods or findings are often discarded on the ground that lawyers are not experts. As will be explored below, opposing the findings of a court-appointed expert by means of party appointed experts is not easy in many Continental systems.

The Austrian problem of the 'almighty' - yet not infallible - expert is troublesome as it can create a situation in which decision-making is effectively delegated to the expert. It follows from the constitutional framework that judges may not delegate their task as a fact-finder.[89] This problem may be exacerbated if the complaint that Austrian judges appoint experts too easily and too often is well-founded.[90] The fear that the court may delegate decision-making to the expert has also been a genuine concern in Vichy France. By the Law of 1944, recourse to experts was limited to those issues which were clearly beyond the competence of the court.[91] The legislature introduced this rule to avoid situations in which the judge would too easily delegate the decision-making to the expert.[92] Belgian law specifies that the expert can give a 'technical opinion' only, and the Belgian Court of

85 For example, a study of 20 French cases revealed that half the lines of the court's judgment on expert evidence consisted of arguments and quotations taken from the expert's report: Bourcier & De Bonis 1999, p. 25, n. 2.

86 Krammer 1990, p. 12.

87 This happens frequently. See Bourcier & De Bonis 1999, p. 52-55.

88 See e.g. De Groot 2008, p. 444-451.

89 The Austrian Federal Constitution is not very explicit (Section 86). More explicit is Article 11 of the Belgian Judicial Code.

90 Deixler-Hübner 1992, p. 251.

91 See former Article 302 French Code of Civil Procedure. Today the court is still limited as regards the degree to which it can make use of experts, see French Code of Civil Procedure, Article 263. It seems matters of law, for instance, may not always be delegated to an expert: French Code of Civil Procedure, Articles 232 and 238. Bourcier & De Bonis 1999, p. 21-24.

92 Taylor 1996, p. 191.

Cassation has quashed decisions in which a lower court had asked an expert whether or not the claim was justified.[93]

2. Party-Appointed Experts

2.1. *Austria*

Parties in Austria occasionally turn to privately funded experts, to see whether or not it would be wise to initiate court proceedings. The Austrian Code, like many other Continental Codes, does not mention experts appointed by the parties. Parties can try to use their experts' findings during litigation in order to influence the judge. First, party-appointed experts may be useful to comment effectively upon the findings of the court-appointed expert. This allows the parties to use their right to be heard to its full extent. Austrian case law however held that if the court appointed an expert, the judge has no duty to address and comment upon the differences of opinion between court-appointed and party-appointed experts. In these cases, the court may base its decision on the findings of the court-appointed expert without further motivation.[94] This view has rightly been criticized as it may infringe on the duty the court has to give reasons for its decision and impedes the right to be effectively heard.[95] Second, parties may seek to rely upon the findings of court-appointed experts as evidence. This is difficult in Austrian law, as is explained below.

The Austrian Code of Civil Procedure does not recognize party-appointed experts. If a party seeks to rely upon findings of a party-appointed expert the regulations on (court-appointed) expert evidence do not apply.[96] One may present expert evidence by 'disguising' it as either documentary evidence or as witness testimony. There have been doubts in Austria about the admissibility of the written report containing findings of the party-appointed expert. Written reports could infringe the principle of immediacy.[97] In Austrian literature, such reports are nevertheless considered to be acceptable as documentary evidence which the judge may freely evaluate (*Privatgutachten*).[98] Case law has further specified that such reports only provide evidence that the writer of the report holds a certain view.[99] In practice, courts have accepted reports of party-appointed experts as documentary evidence.[100] In evaluating the report, the court should take into account all relevant

93 This follows from Article 962 of the Belgian Judicial Code, Belgian Court of Cassation, 14 September 1992, Arr. Cass. 1991-92, 1099; Pas. 1992, I, 1021 and R.W. 1993-94, 45, discussed by Taelman 2003, No. 25-27.

94 See Rechberger in Fasching & Konecny 2002-2005, §351, No. 13 and the case law mentioned there.

95 Krammer 1990, Section 4.6.

96 Austrian Supreme Court, 29 October 1987, 7 Ob 629/87.

97 Lackner 1983, p. 518 and Fasching 1990, No. 1008.

98 Austrian Supreme Court 29, October 1987, 7 Ob 629/87 and Rechberger in Fasching & Konecny 2002-2005, §351, No. 12; Fasching 1990, No. 1008.

99 Rechberger in Fasching & Konecny 2002-2005, §351, No. 12 and the case law mentioned there.

100 Fasching 1990, No. 1008.

circumstances, such as how the expert was paid and whether both parties have been involved in the production of the report. Courts have been hesitant to subscribe significant evidential value to such reports.[101] The Court of Appeal of Vienna has quashed a decision by a lower court that based its decision solely on the report of a party-appointed expert.[102]

Austrian law provides no possibility for experts hired by the parties to give oral testimony. It has been argued that a party-appointed expert can be summoned as a witness.[103] Whether this is a viable option is questionable as the case law on witnesses with expert knowledge is very restrictive.[104] For example, a doctor who witnessed a car accident may testify employing medical terminology about the injury that resulted from the accident.[105] According to Austrian case law, such a witness may only testify about the facts which he or she observed and may not draw expert conclusions. The doctor may not give an expert opinion or answer general questions about professional practices.[106] Likewise, the testimony of such witnesses may not be used to challenge the conclusions of the court-appointed expert.[107] Therefore, in the light of such restrictive case law there are many barriers to a party-appointed expert acting as a witness in Austrian law.

Thus, party-appointed expert reports may have little evidential value themselves. They can be used to comment upon the findings of court appointed evidence. They may also be a useful means to plead a case with particularity. A party who adduces the findings of an expert can be confident that a judge cannot decide against the allegations of that party without first ordering the production of evidence.[108]

2.2. *Expert Witnesses in the United States*

Expert Witnesses and the Adversarial System

In Austria and other Continental jurisdictions, the judge plays a pivotal role providing expertise in litigation. The United States approach to experts is diametrically opposed to the Continental approach. Traditionally, the parties in common law jurisdictions have a central role in the gathering and presentation of expert evidence.[109] Today, the adversarial principle remains a leading principle of civil procedure in the United States (Chapter 8). In an adversarial system of adjudication, the decision-maker is neutral and passive and the proceedings are

101 Lackner 1983 and the case law mentioned there.

102 Rechberger in Fasching & Konecny 2002-2005, §351, No. 12.

103 Rechberger, in Fasching & Konecny 2002-2005, §351, No. 8 and the literature mentioned there.

104 Austrian Supreme Court, 2 July 2002, 8Ob110/02p.

105 Section 350 Austrian Code of Civil Procedure, example used by Fasching 1990, No. 969.

106 Austrian Supreme Court, 19 November 1975, 1Ob208/75.

107 Austrian Supreme Court, 2 July 2002, 8Ob110/02p.

108 Section 267 Austrian Code of Civil Procedure enables the court to determine when a matter of fact can be considered to be admitted. This provision can be used as a tool to narrow down the issues.

109 On the history of experts in England, see Learned Hand 1901 and Dwyer 2007b.

controlled by the parties and their lawyers. The adversarial principle holds that the parties are primarily responsible for the presentation of information and evidence.

In the United States, it is common that both parties each summon an expert witness to testify on the very same issues. Obviously, the expert witnesses of both parties almost always reach opposite conclusions. Empirical data published in 1991 indicate that in two-thirds of the trials in which an expert witness testified, the opposing party would also make use of one or more expert witnesses in the same area of expertise.[110]

In the United States, the parties (or rather their attorneys) will search for an expert if needed. The expert is typically hired and paid by the party's lawyer to provide services to the lawyer, with reimbursement of costs. Experts in the United States usually 'market' their services by advertising in bar association periodicals or by means of online witness directories.[111] Some bar associations publish lists of experts[112] and there are special organizations that certify and train expert witnesses and that can suggest a 'certified' expert.[113] Usually a party will try to find an expert who best supports that party's view and can provide compelling testimony. Sometimes lawyers engage in 'expert shopping': they ask experts to draft an expert opinion and subsequently choose not to use the opinion at trial if unfavorable.[114]

In order to avoid surprise at trial, parties are required to disclose the names of the expert witnesses whom they wish to examine at trial.[115] Since the 1993 Amendments of the Federal Rules of Civil Procedure (FRCP), parties are required to provide their opponent with a 'mandatory expert report'. This report should list the opinions that will be expressed by each expert witness who will testify, the grounds for that opinion, the data and exhibits considered by the expert witness, the qualifications of the expert witness including publications by the witness in the last 10 years, the remuneration received for the testimony and a list of cases in which the expert witness testified in the last four years.[116] Furthermore, the parties may use the traditional discovery devices to obtain materials beyond the mandatory report from the adversary's expert witness who will testify at trial.[117]

In the United States, expert witnesses are questioned like other witnesses. As trial in principle is a single continuous event, thorough preparation for trial is

110 Gross 1991, p. 1118-1120.

111 Gross 1991, p. 1131.

112 The Law Society in England publishes the *Law Society Gazette* Expert Witness Supplement. The *Law Society Gazette Guide to Expert Witnesses 2010* is available at <www.lawgazette.co.uk/supplements>, last consulted in February 2010. For a US directory, see <www.jurispro.com>, last consulted in February 2010.

113 A well-known example of such an organization in the United Kingdom is The Academy of Experts, see <www.academy-experts.org>, last consulted in February 2010. Such organizations also exist in the United States. For a critical approach to a similar organization, see Hansen 2000.

114 The work product rule subsequently prevents that the report will be discoverable. For a critical assessment of English law in this respect, see Dwyer 2007a, Part B3.

115 FRCP Rule 26(a)(2)(A).

116 FRCP Rule 26(a)(2).

117 Advisory Committee Note to Rule 26(a) as amended in 1993 and Joseph 2002, p. 22.

necessary. Thus it is common that attorneys are well prepared. It is also common that lawyers provide advice to the expert on the form and presentation of their testimony (see Section 6.2). Such preparation is considered inappropriate in England and Continental countries.[118] Although the court should exercise control over the mode and order of the interrogation of expert witnesses at trial,[119] the attorneys of both parties, by means of cross-examination, play the most significant role in the presentation of expert evidence.[120] Expert witnesses are usually 'repeat players'.[121] They often are experienced in facing a tough line of questioning from opposing counsel on their conclusions and credibility. The thoroughness in which expert witnesses are interrogated and challenged in the United States is unknown to Continental systems.

Expert Witnesses and the Role of the Court

Although the selection, preparation and questioning of experts is largely party driven, this does not imply that an American judge may remain passive. In this Section the duty of the court to act as a gatekeeper and the physical and mental examinations of persons will be discussed.

Expert evidence is not always admissible. The Federal Rules of Evidence (FRE) hold that all relevant evidence is admissible, except as otherwise provided by the Constitution, Acts of Congress, the FRE or other rules prescribed by the Supreme Court.[122] According to the FRE, expert evidence is inadmissible if it is not relevant, the expert is not qualified, or the evidence is not reliable. The parties may request the court to decide on the admissibility of expert evidence prior to trial.[123] If timely objections are raised, the court must act as a gatekeeper in order to exclude inadmissible expert evidence.[124] The court may schedule a hearing in which the admissibility is addressed in order to fulfill its obligation.[125]

The most widely discussed requirement is that the expert evidence must be reliable in order to be admissible. FRE Rule 702 currently requires that the testimony of the expert is based upon sufficient facts or data and that the expert testimony is the product of reliable principles and methods which have been

118 It usually follows from the Code of Conduct of lawyers that they should do everything not to give the impression that they would influence the content of the testimony of experts or witnesses. Austrian Code of Conduct for Lawyers (*Richtlinien für die Ausübung des Rechtsanwaltberufes und für die Überwachung der Pflichten des Rechtsanwalts*), 1977, Section 1 (8).

119 FRE Rule 611.

120 Cross-examination is often believed to be a powerful instrument in the pursuit of truth. Very famous in this respect is the often-quoted phrase of Wigmore: 'cross-examination is beyond any doubt the greatest legal engine ever invented for the discovery of truth'. The phrase has often been quoted by US courts, such as the United States Supreme Court in *Watkins* v. *Sowders* 449 US 341 (1981).

121 Gross 1991, p. 1120.

122 FRE Rule 402.

123 FRE Rule 104(a).

124 Patterson 2005, p. 171.

125 *Dodge v. Cotter Corp.*, 328 F.3d 1212, at 36. The court may however also perform its task in another way, see *Kirstein v. Parks Corp.*, 159 F.3d 1065 (1998), at 1067, *Jahn v. Equine Services*, 233 F.3d 382, (2000) at 393.

reliably applied to the facts of the case.[126] FRE Rule 702 has codified the earlier case law of the Supreme Court, most notably the case *Daubert v. Merell Dow Pharmaceuticals*.[127] In *Daubert*, the Supreme Court ordered federal trial judges to evaluate scientific expert witnesses to determine whether their testimony is both 'relevant' and 'reliable'. *Daubert* set forth a non-exclusive checklist for trial courts to determine whether expert witness evidence is reliable. The court may take into account: 1) whether the technique or theory of the expert can be tested; 2) whether the technique or theory has been subject to peer review and publication; 3) the rate of error of the technique or theory; 4) the existence and maintenance of standards and controls and 5) the degree in which the theory or technique has been generally accepted. In *Kumho Tire Co. v. Carmichael* the Supreme Court held that the test set out in *Daubert* is also applicable when nonscientific expert evidence needs to be evaluated.[128]

Since *Daubert*, expert evidence has been excluded significantly more often.[129] But the judge should not replace the role of the parties and their lawyers. As the Supreme Court stated in *Daubert*: 'Vigorous cross-examination, presentation of contrary evidence, and careful instruction of the burden of proof are the traditional and appropriate rules of attacking shaky but admissible evidence'.[130]

In the United States, special rules apply in case of a physical or mental examination of a party (Rule 35 FRCP). Since 1970, these rules have been extended to encompass other persons under the control or custody of a party.[131] Such an examination is firmly placed in the hands of the court. The court may determine when and where the examination takes place, who will be the examiner, who will be present during the examination, what the scope of the examination is, etc.[132] The general rules on discovery do not apply to these examinations. A party may request the court to order an examination of an opposing party by his expert witness. The Supreme Court has held that FRCP Rule 35 is 'free of constitutional difficulty as an invasion of privacy'.[133] Nevertheless, a request for an order for a physical or mental

126 Also see FRE Rule 703.

127 *Daubert v. Merrell Dow Pharmaceuticals*, 509 U.S. 579 (1993).

128 *Kumho Tire Co. v. Carmichael*, 526 U.S. 137 (1999).

129 Dixon & Gill 2002, a summary is available at <www.rand.org/pubs/research_briefs/RB9037/index1.html, last consulted in February 2010.

130 *Daubert v. Merrell Dow Pharmaceuticals*, 509 U.S. 579 (1993), at 595.

131 Advisory Committee Notes to the 1970 Amendments of Rule 35(a).

132 FRCP Rule 35(a). See for an example where the court prescribed how the examination should take place: *Ayat v. Societe Air Fr.*, 2007 U.S. Dist. LEXIS 31285; CCH Prod. Liab. Rep. P17, 730, at 24. The court - after a detailed discussion of the facts of the case and the possible medical tests- concluded: 'Air France's motion for Rule 35 examinations is GRANTED. (...) Air France may conduct the mental examination of Ayat as it proposes, using both a psychiatrist and a neuropsychologist. Neither a third party observer nor a recording device shall be permitted in the examining room. A neutral court appointed translator may be present. The Rorschach Test, the Wechsler Adult Intelligence Scale and the Wechsler Memory Scale are appropriate to assess Ayat's psychological condition'.

133 *Sibbach v. Wilson & Co.*, 312 U.S. 1; 61 S. Ct. 422; 85 L. Ed. 479; 1941 U.S. LEXIS 1032, *Schlagenhauf v. Holder*, 379 U.S. 104; 85 S. Ct. 234; 13 L. Ed. 2d 152; 1964 U.S. LEXIS 152. The Supreme Court specified that rule 35 'is within the scope of the Rules Enabling Act (28 U.S.C.
→

examination should be carefully considered due to the intrusive nature of medical examinations. Rule 35 specifies that the order may be made only if the subject matter is 'in controversy' and 'only on motion for good cause shown'.[134] This again requires the court to act as a gatekeeper. In this respect the Supreme Court in *Schlagenhauf v. Holder* held that:

> 'the "in controversy" and "good cause" requirements of [FRCP] Rule 35 (...) are not met by mere conclusory allegations of the pleadings - nor by mere relevance to the case - but require an affirmative showing by the movant that each condition as to which the examination is sought is really and genuinely in controversy and that good cause exists for ordering each particular examination. Obviously, what may be good cause for one type of examination may not be so for another. The ability of the movant to obtain the desired information by other means is also relevant.
> Rule 35, therefore, requires discriminating application by the trial judge, who must decide, as an initial matter in every case, whether the party requesting a mental or physical examination or examinations has adequately demonstrated the existence of the Rule's requirements of "in controversy" and "good cause," (...)'.[135]

Thus, the court may refuse to grant an order for a physical or mental examination of a party if the examination is dangerous or painful.[136] A request for examination has also been denied in cases where the requesting party has not tried less intrusive means to obtain the relevant information[137] or in cases where (all) relevant medical information had already been disclosed to the requesting party.[138]

We may conclude that a U.S. federal judge has an important role with respect to the physical and mental examinations of parties. One should not overrate the role of the court, as in practice most examinations take place without any court order pursuant to an agreement between the attorneys on both sides.[139]

Party Appointed Expert Witnesses: Costs and the Problem of Bias

The U.S. approach to expert evidence clearly has its merits. It is often argued that in an adversarial system the responsibility for the investigation is assigned to those who have an incentive to conduct the investigation thoroughly.[140] Thus, the system is likely to provide the trier of fact with the maximum amount of relevant evidence. This is especially important in areas in which there is no scientific consensus. For example, medical experts have been split on the question whether Myalgic

2072), which provides that the Rules "shall not abridge, enlarge or modify any substantive right"'.

134 An example of a case in which the court both granted and refused an examination on these grounds is *Eeoc v. Autozone*, 2007 U.S. Dist. LEXIS 53324.

135 *Schlagenhauf v. Holder*, 379 U.S. 104; 85 S. Ct. 234; 13 L. Ed. 2d 152; 1964 U.S. LEXIS 152 at 243.

136 Friedenthal, Kane & Miller 2005, p. 440.

137 *Marroni v. Matey*, 82 F.R.D. 371, 1979 U.S. Dist. LEXIS 13486, 'Plaintiffs have made no showing that the information they seek cannot be obtained by other discovery techniques. Until other methods are attempted, we believe that the "discriminating application" of Rule 35 demanded by the Court requires us to deny the motion'.

138 See e.g. *Briesacher v. AMG Res., Inc.*, 2005 U.S. Dist. LEXIS 37394.

139 Friedenthal, Kane & Miller 2005, p. 440, footnote 15.

140 Gross 1991 p. 1126.

Encephalomyelitis (ME) is to be considered a 'real, i.e. biological rather than behavioral or psychological, illness.[141] If a single expert were to give his opinion in court, it is likely that he would give an incomplete picture of the current knowledge of the syndrome. The U.S. adversarial model would provide a more complete account of the current debate in the scientific community. In addition, the U.S. model seems to be very fair in the sense that it provides both parties sufficient and equal legal opportunities to convince the trier of fact of the merits of their position.

The U.S. approach to expert evidence also has serious drawbacks. It has been much criticized because experts are not fully independent.[142] It is one of the parties who pays and selects the expert. Often that party's lawyer also thoroughly instructs the expert. Because the expert is not independent, there are reasons to believe that he or she will not be impartial. There are notorious examples of biased experts that adjust their expert opinion according to the wishes of the party who has hired them.[143] Partisan experts have been referred to as 'purchased commodities',[144] 'saxophones',[145] 'hired guns'[146] or even 'prostitutes'.[147] Some legal authorities like Judge Posner have indicated that bias is not an 'especially grave' problem as it seems there are incentives for the expert to be 'neutral' and 'honest'.[148] Empirical evidence suggests that the problem of bias in the United States is genuine. In a 1998-1999 survey, judges and attorneys were asked how frequently certain problems with expert evidence occurred on a scale from 1 (very infrequent) to 5 (very frequent). Both judges and attorneys claimed that the biggest problem was that 'Experts abandon objectivity and become advocates for the side that hired them' (average score: 3.7).[149] A 1992 survey of jurors showed that over 30% of the jurors believed that the experts were biased.[150]

Partisan experts who abandon objectivity and introduce 'junk science,'[151] rather than reliable knowledge, may mislead rather than help the trier of fact.[152] This

141 See a 2006 report on Myalgic Encephalomyelitis at <www.erythos.com/gibsonenquiry/Report.html>, last consulted February 2010.

142 See e.g. Mnookin 2007. Mnookin provides many examples. For an example of the experience of an expert himself, see Meier 1986.

143 Examples of US cases are mentioned by Gross 1991, Part II and Mnookin 2007. For an example of an English case, see *Vernon* v. *Bosley (No. 2)* [1997] 1 All ER 614.

144 Mnookin 2007, p. 111.

145 Langbein 1985, p. 835.

146 McEwan 1998, p. 158.

147 Michell & Mandhane 2005, p. 647, n. 69.

148 Posner 1999, p. 1537. Posner argues that expert witnesses have a financial interest in having a reputation as 'honest' as expert witnesses usually are repeat players. Furthermore, Posner argues that cross-examination, pretrial discovery and criteria set by *Daubert* serve as controls against bias.

149 Krafka, Dunn, Johnson, Cecil & Miletich 2002, Table 6. Available through the Federal Judicial Center at <www.fjc.gov>, last consulted in February 2010.

150 See the discussion and the study quoted by Harrison 2001, footnote 9.

151 The term 'Junk Science' has become popular following Peter Huber's work: *Galileo's Revenge, Junk Science in the Courtroom* (Basic Books: 1991).

152 These complaints are supported by surveys of judges and attorneys, see Krafka, Dunn, Johnson, Cecil & Miletich 2002.

can result in a 'battle of experts' in courts where such a battle is non-existent outside the courtroom. Partiality and opposing claims to scientific evidence may lead to distrust of expert scientific evidence in general, which subsequently leads to a devaluation of expert testimony. As Langbein put it: 'short of forbidding the use of experts altogether, we probably could not have designated a procedure better suited to minimize the influence of expertise'.[153]

Another drawback to the extensive use of party-appointed experts seems to be that it is more expensive than the use of a single court-appointed expert. The numerous opportunities to duplicate work seems to create cost inefficiencies in the United States.[154] Expert shopping might involve parties consulting a number of experts before deciding which expert will be used. When both parties appoint an expert to give an opinion on the same subject-matter, it is likely that much of the work done by one expert is also done by the other expert. Moreover, a thorough preparation for trial in the United States through the disclosure of mandatory expert reports, interrogatories, depositions and the discovery of documents leads to duplication. The U.S. system of adjudication requires that all evidence is presented during a single trial. The whole pretrial phase is designed to avoid any surprise at trial. Therefore, whatever happens at trial is often nothing but a skillfully presented duplication of (part of) the work already done. It is doubtful whether this duplication would improve the rectitude of the fact-finding process. To the extent that biased experts willingly provide an incomplete, inaccurate or even incorrect testimony, expertise may lead to error costs associated with wrong decisions.[155] On the basis of the reasons mentioned above, there have been complaints that common law jurisdictions are incapable of curbing the social costs of expertise.[156] Lord Woolf, argued that the use of expert witnesses and discovery had been the major generators of unnecessary costs in English civil litigation prior to 1999.[157] It should be noted, though, that I have not found empirical data that affirm or falsify these commonly held opinions.

2.3. *Party-appointed Experts in the Netherlands*

As in Austria, many other Continental jurisdictions are restrictive in allowing parties to adduce expert evidence. Although many codifications do not even mention party-appointed experts, exceptions do exist. Section 19 of Chapter 40 of the 1942 Swedish Code of Judicial Procedure, explicitly allows for the hearing of party-appointed experts.[158] Since 2001, the Spanish Code of Civil Procedure has also recognized experts retained by the litigants.[159]

153 Langbein 1985, p. 836.
154 See for a more detailed argument of the inefficiency of US litigation: Gross 1986.
155 Harrison 2001, Part I.
156 Harrison 2001, Part III and Jacob 2004, p. 402, p. 407.
157 Woolf 1996, Chapter 13, para. 1.
158 Section 19 states: 'As to experts not appointed by the court, but appointed by a party, the provisions in Sections 7 and 8 shall apply to the extent relevant. In other respects, when such →

In the Netherlands, party-appointed experts may be used to comment on the findings of court-appointed experts. If parties use their own experts' findings to challenge the conclusions of the court-appointed expert, the Dutch court's decision must provide 'sufficient insight into the court's reasoning to enable parties, third parties including the court of appeal, to verify and justify the decision'.[160]

Parties may also adduce the findings of their experts as evidence in three different ways. First, the party-appointed expert's written report can be adduced as documentary evidence.[161] The court is sometimes willing to attach significant value to such written reports, especially if both parties have participated in the construction of the expert's report. Second, since the early 20th century Dutch case law has determined that the party-appointed expert can be summoned and heard as a witness.[162] As in Austrian law, this raises the problem that witnesses may only testify about their direct perceptions of the facts of the case and not about their general expert knowledge.[163] At times, Dutch courts have been lenient in this respect.[164] The third way in which parties can use the findings of party-appointed experts is most innovative. Since 2002, the legislature has created a legal basis to hear party-appointed experts.[165] The newly introduced Article 200 Dutch Code of Civil Procedure states that the court may, on request of a party, hear experts that have not been appointed by the court.[166] The provision seems to be mainly inspired by regulations and practices in arbitration.[167]

It is very common in Dutch practice that parties adduce written expert reports. To my knowledge, there have not been any 'hard' empirical studies that show how often courts hear party-appointed experts. But there is reason to believe that Article 200 of the Dutch Code is largely neglected in legal practice.[168]

an expert is orally examined, the provisions concerning witnesses shall apply; however, if the court finds it suitable, all or part of a written opinion may be read aloud'.

159 Articles 336-338 Spanish Code of Civil Procedure as discussed by De Groot 2008, p. 104.

160 Dutch Court of Cassation, 5 December 2003, *NJ* 2004, 74, *Vredenburg/NHL.*

161 Rutgers, Flach & Boon 1988, p. 328.

162 Van den Berg 1999, Section. 3.5.2. and the case law mentioned there.

163 Dutch Code of Civil Procedure, Article 163 and De Hoop 1989, p. 718-719.

164 Van den Berg 1997, p. 53.

165 Jongbloed 2002, Section 9.2 and Asser 2002, p. 30. In 1988 the legislator was hesitant about party-appointed experts. The legislator feared that such experts would not be impartial, see Rutgers, Flach & Boon 1988, p. 328, p. 331.

166 The court hence has discretion in this area whereas the court may not refuse to hear witnesses: Snijders, Klaassen & Meijer 2007, Section 6.3.

167 Rutgers, Flach & Boon 1988, p. 374, the legislature referred to Article 1042(5) Dutch Code of Civil Procedure (provision on expertise in arbitration).

168 Searching the most comprehensive collection of case law at <www.rechtspraak.nl>, there were very few hits. I searched for *eigen deskundige* (i.e. party expert), which resulted in only 14 hits, amongst these not a single case in which the court decided to hear a party-appointed expert. Similarly searching for '200 Rv' (i.e. Article 200 Code of Civil Procedure) resulted in only six hits, in only one of these six cases the court had heard an expert according to Article 200. This search was conducted in October 2007. Similarly, a judge assured me that the District Court of Maastricht never made use of Article 200 Code of Civil Procedure between 2002 and October 2007.

3. Comparative Lessons and Mixed Models

3.1. *A Mixed Model: The Single Joint Expert in English Law*

In the 1996 Final Report on the Civil Justice System, Lord Woolf highlighted a major defect in the English system of civil litigation: it was too adversarial.[169] This report was the basis for the Civil Procedure Rules 1998 (CPR), with case management highlighted as one of the main pillars. The essence of case management is that the judicial system as a whole and the courts in particular regulate the content and progress of litigation. This is done by means of standard directions in small value or straightforward cases.[170] In more complicated cases, ad hoc decisions can be taken to determine how the case is to proceed.[171] The CPR have transferred procedural control from the parties and their lawyers to the court. Judges are expected to manage medium-sized or complex cases in order to prevent unnecessary delay, costs and unfairness. The rules ought to be interpreted in the light of the 'overriding objective' of 'enabling the court to deal with cases justly', as set out in CPR Rule 1.[172]

These general features of the new English procedural regime have been applied to the use of expertise as well. Lord Woolf had criticized the English practice concerning experts as it led to excessive costs and because experts sometimes took the role of partisan advocates rather than neutral fact-finders.[173] Lord Woolf believed that it was far from clear that a just result would be achieved if the judge was to choose between two conflicting expert opinions if evidence was highly technical.[174] The CPR require that the court grants permission to present expert evidence. The court cannot grant this permission too readily as it has a duty to restrict expert evidence to that which is reasonably required to resolve the dispute, in line with the overriding objective.[175] With respect to the way in which expert evidence is presented, the CPR clearly give preference to written reports.[176] The oral presentation of evidence is only allowed with leave of the court.

The CPR also stress the need for objectivity. The rules specify, in line with previous English case law, that the expert has an overriding duty to the court

169 Woolf 1996, Chapter I, Section 2.

170 See e.g. Appendix A to the Practice Direction accompanying CPR Part 27.

171 As defined by Andrews 2003a, p. 333.

172 CPR Rule 1.1: '(1) These Rules are a new procedural code with the overriding objective of enabling the court to deal with cases justly. (2) Dealing with a case justly includes, so far as is practicable - (a) ensuring that the parties are on an equal footing; (b) saving expense; (c) dealing with the case in ways which are proportionate - (i) to the amount of money involved; (ii) to the importance of the case; (iii) to the complexity of the issues; and (iv) to the financial position of each party; (d) ensuring that it is dealt with expeditiously and fairly; and (e) allotting to it an appropriate share of the court's resources, while taking into account the need to allot resources to other cases'.

173 Woolf 1996, Chapter 13, Sections 1 and 5.

174 The US case *Wells* v. *Ortho Pharmaceutical Corporation* 615 F Supp 262 (ND Ga 1985), as discussed by Gross 1991, p. 1121-1124 illustrates this point well.

175 CPR Rule 35.1.

176 CPR Rule 35.5.

irrespective of how the expert is paid.[177] The terminology has been adjusted accordingly; the CPR opted for the term 'expert' rather than the term 'expert witness'.[178]

The introduction of the 'single joint expert' has been the single biggest innovation in order to assure objectivity and limit the use of experts. The CPR specify that if both parties wish to present expert evidence on the same matter, the court may determine that evidence on that issue is given by one expert only.[179] Preferably, this single joint expert is chosen by the parties, although the court may impose an expert against the wishes of both parties. If the court allows each party to appoint an expert, opposing experts are required to meet as soon as possible in order to identify the controversial issues and to narrow down the factual dispute.[180]

The introduction of the CPR has had a large influence on English practice. There seems to be a consensus that the changes in English law with respect to expert evidence have successfully changed the English practice.[181] In 2000, only shortly after the introduction of the CPR, single joint experts were used in 46% of trials involving any experts.[182] It has been argued that the Woolf reforms have led to more objective expertise; it is unclear whether they have also successfully cut the costs of expert evidence.[183]

Recent amendments to English law have inspired changes in other common law countries. Since the changes to the New Zealand High Court Rules in 2002, experts have to agree to a 'Code of Conduct' which specifies that 'An expert witness has an overriding duty to assist the Court impartially on relevant matters within the expert's area of expertise'.[184] Similarly, recent changes in Australia have codified

177 *National Justice Compania Naviera SA v. Prudential Assurance Co. Ltd* [1993] 2 Lloyd's Rep 68. CPR Rule 35.3, Andrews 2003a, p. 754 and Dwyer 2007a, Part BII.

178 Earlier drafts of the CPR still used the older terminology. See in this respect Jolowicz 2000, p. 241.

179 CPR Rule 35.7.

180 CPR Rule 35.12.

181 Dwyer 2004, p. 5.

182 See the 2002 report, 'Further Findings: A Continuing Evaluation of the Civil Justice Reforms', available at <www.dca.gov.uk/civil/reform/ffreform.htm>, last consulted February 2010.

183 A March 2001 evaluation of the civil justice reforms by the Department for Constitutional Affairs concluded: 'The use of single joint experts appears to have worked well. It is likely that their use has contributed to a less adversarial culture, earlier settlement and may have cut costs': 'Emerging Findings: An Early Evaluation of the Civil Justice Reforms', available at <http://www.dca.gov.uk/civil/emerge/emerge.htm>, last consulted in February 2010. A later report indicated that there would however be reasons to assume that costs (in the pre-action phase) had increased: 'Further Findings: A Continuing Evaluation of the Civil Justice Reforms', August 2002, Section 7.7, available at <www.dca.gov.uk/civil/reform/ffreform.htm>, last consulted February 2010. Also see Goriely, Moorhead & Abrams 2002, Chapter 2.

184 High Court Amendment Rules 2002, Rule 25 and Sched. 2, effective 1 July 2002 (New Zealand).

that an expert has an 'overriding duty to assist the court' and have explicitly granted the court power to appoint an expert.[185]

3.2. *The Attractiveness of the Mixed Model*

The Austrian system almost exclusively turns to court-appointed experts, whereas the party-appointed expert witness dominates U.S. courtrooms. The approaches to expert evidence in Austria and the United States are posited at the 'extreme' ends of the spectrum. Both jurisdictions seem to apply a 'one-size-fits-all' approach to expert evidence. A mixed model, as implemented in England, is generally regarded as more promising.[186] It is obvious that advantages of the U.S. approach to expertise cure the ills of the Austrian approach, and vice-versa. If party-appointed experts could be used effectively on a larger scale in Austria, this would force courts to critically evaluate the findings of court-appointed experts and would increase the opportunities for parties to effectively comment on the findings of the expert. Similarly, the genuine threat of the appointment of neutral experts by U.S. judges could prevent biased testimony of party-appointed experts.[187]

Another attractive aspect of the mixed model is that it goes beyond the 'one-size-fits-all' approach to expertise. It is doubtful whether a single court-appointed expert is the best solution to all Austrian cases. It is equally doubtful whether the use of two party-appointed experts is the best solution to all U.S. cases. It seems that the use of a single (court-appointed) expert is the most suitable low-cost solution to simple, low value cases. Thus, in simple cases under English law the single joint expert is the rule, rather than the exception.[188]

If the issues at stake are larger, if parties had already retained experts prior to litigation or if the subject-matter of the case is more complex, it might well be worth the extra expense to involve more expertise in the proceedings. If expert evidence becomes very complex and the outcome is uncertain, then the need for a fair procedure which allows both parties to exercise a larger control over the proceedings seems to be more pressing. In such cases, it may be a fruitful to allow the use of party-appointed experts alongside, or instead of, court-appointed experts. Similarly, if parties have already consulted an expert prior to litigation, the extra costs of hearing such an expert would be relatively small. In short, there can be cases in which the 'marginal benefits' of involving party-appointed experts outweigh the 'marginal costs'. Accordingly, in England party-appointed experts are used more often in complex cases that have been assigned to the multi track.

185 Edmond 2003, p. 139–143.

186 See e.g. American Law Institute & Unidroit 2006, Principle 22. The Principles of Transnational Civil Procedure take the court-appointed expert as a starting point; the comments on Principle 22 acknowledge that party-appointed experts can provide valuable assistance in the analysis of difficult factual issues. See also Stürner 2005, p. 231–232 and Stürner 2007, p. 394.

187 Tomlin 2006, p. 24.

188 Zuckerman 2003, 20.30 and Andrews 2003a, p. 754.

3.3. *Comparative Lessons*

Over recent decades there has been a growing consensus that both the court and the parties should be actively involved in matters of expertise. Rule makers in common law jurisdictions have become convinced that judges should take an active stance at an early point in the procedure. The English Civil Procedure Rules require the involvement of the court, even in cases where parties each hire their own experts. Similarly, in the United States case management has been a central tenet of recent legislative reform. The 1990 Civil Justice Reform Act favored the 'early and ongoing control of the pretrial process through involvement of a judicial officer'.[189] Since 1993, the FRCP invite the court, at a pretrial conference, to limit the use of expert witnesses in order to avoid unnecessary proof or cumulative evidence.[190] At the same time, it has increasingly been recognized in Continental jurisdictions that the parties are entitled to a fair trial and should be involved in the gathering and presentation of expert evidence. In all systems, it seems that some form of cooperation between parties and the court is preferred over the non-cooperative 'pure adversarial' or 'pure inquisitorial' modes of gathering and presenting expert evidence.

In general, the different approaches to expert evidence presented above provide interesting rules and techniques that could serve as a source of inspiration to improve existing legal systems.[191] The common law rules that require the disclosure of information on the expertise of the expert witness would also be very useful in a Continental setting. If the Continental court-appointed expert would disclose information about his expertise, this would help the parties and the judge to assess the findings of the expert critically.[192] Similarly, it seems that the rules on the civil liability of experts in Continental jurisdictions could form a source of inspiration for Anglo-American jurisdictions. On the European Continent, experts can generally be held liable for damages.[193] In *Briscoe v. Lahue,* the U.S. Supreme Court held all witnesses immune from civil liability based on their testimony in judicial proceedings.[194] This case has frequently been cited to grant expert witnesses a similar immunity.[195] This implies that civil liability fails to function effectively as an incentive for U.S. (or English[196]) experts to give reliable testimony.

Whether or not central elements of a system of civil procedure can be taken separately from one system and implemented in another system is a more fundamental question. Despite its apparent benefits, it has proven to be very

189 28 U.S.C. §473.

190 FRCP Rule 26(c)(2)(D).

191 See, in general, on the methodology of 'legal transplants': Ewald 1995.

192 It has been argued in Dutch legal literature that it would make sense to introduce 'disclosure statements' like in England: see Van Dijk 2007, p. 434 and the literature quoted there.

193 See, for the Netherlands, Verkerk 2007, Section 3.1.3, Section 839 of the German Civil Code; for Austria, see Krammer 1990; for Belgium, see Cousy 2008.

194 *Briscoe v. LaHue* 460 US 325 (1983), 1983 US LEXIS 146.

195 There have also been cases in which courts have not applied *Briscoe* to expert witnesses. For more details, see Harrison 2001, p. 257, p. 287-290.

196 On case law in England similar to those in the U.S., see Dwyer 2008.

difficult to introduce court-appointed experts in the United States. In the first half of the 20th century, provisions were adopted in the federal courts and many states and territories that allow the court to appoint experts.[197] These changes have had little impact on practice in the U.S. District Courts.[198] A 1985 survey of all federal trial judges showed that 81% had never appointed an expert witness under FRE Rule 706.[199] Data about Californian courts published in 1991 show that 1,748 party experts were called to testify in 529 cases, but not a single expert had been appointed by the court.[200] These figures are surprising, as there have been several serious attempts to encourage the courts to exercise their powers under Rule 706.[201] Various tools have been developed that can help the court to find a suitable expert.[202] The most important reason that judges fail to appoint experts seems to be that the court-appointed expert does not 'fit' into the U.S. adversarial (procedural) culture.[203] In a survey of 81 judges, 39 judges cited 'respect for the adversarial system' as a reason for the infrequent appointment of experts by the court.[204] In an adversarial setting, the parties and their attorneys gather and present evidence. This model leads to a polarization of evidence in which evidence 'belongs' to either one of the parties.[205] In such a model, there is apparently no room for impartial court-appointed experts.

In the English system prior to 1999, the judge could appoint an 'assessor' or an 'independent expert'. In line with the adversarial principle the English courts were equally reluctant as U.S. District Courts, never appointing such experts on a large scale.[206] The small impact of Article 200 Dutch Code of Civil Procedure provides a Continental example that illustrates how difficult it is to change procedural practices by legislative reform and effectively implement a 'mixed model'.

Recent developments in England have shown that a mixed procedural model is feasible. Perhaps the fact that recent changes in England were part of a larger scheme, aimed at an overall change of procedural rules and culture, could provide an explanation for the impact of English reform in procedural practice.

Experiences in various legal systems may provide useful insights to implement a mixed model. The case law of the European Court of Human Rights could serve as an inspiration for U.S. judges that are faced with the question how to

197 Gross 1991, p. 1189.

198 In some areas the use of neutral court-appointed experts has been slightly more successful. In many jurisdictions 'medical review panels' have, for example, been formed that give neutral expert opinions in medical negligence cases during the pretrial phase. See Morill 1985, for a list of jurisdictions that have in one way or the other introduced the so-called 'medical review panels'.

199 Willging 1986.

200 Gross 1991, p. 1191.

201 Gross 1991, Part 4.

202 See e.g. the 'Court Appointed Scientific Experts' (CASE) at <www.aaas.org/spp/case/case.htm>, last consulted in February 2010.

203 On the relationship between culture and expertise in the U.S., see Chase 2005, p. 65 and Chapter 4.

204 Cecil & Willging 1994, p. 1018.

205 Damaska 1997a, p. 77-78.

206 Jolowicz 2000, p. 229 and the case law mentioned there.

combine aspects of adversarialism with court-appointed expertise. Conversely, the U.S. rule that requires that expert evidence should be 'reliable' seems a very reasonable standard that could be applied by a Dutch or Swedish court when determining whether to hear a party-appointed expert.

Chapter 6

DISCOVERY AND PARTY INTERROGATION

In civil litigation, information is seldom completely known to both parties. In addition, information is often unequally divided between the parties. In cases where a plaintiff initiates a lawsuit against a company for a violation of non-discrimination laws when hiring personnel, the defendant usually has more relevant information than the plaintiff.[1] If a patient is involved in a lawsuit against a hospital for medical negligence, the hospital usually has most of the relevant information.[2] In both examples mentioned, the plaintiff or the court would clearly be interested in putting questions to the defendant.

Parties are inclined to adduce favorable information out of their own motion. Often parties are inclined to withhold adverse information. It is generally believed to be of great importance that both parties have equal access to all available unprivileged information. Access to information held by the opponent is often vital for a litigant to make informed choices concerning settlement. Such information is also valuable to establish the facts correctly. For these reasons, legal systems have generally provided procedural devices to compel the parties to provide relevant information, regardless of whether that information is favorable. This Chapter provides a broad historic and comparative overview of the different mechanisms to question parties in the procedure.

1. History of Party Interrogation

1.1. *Written Interrogatories: A Shared Historic Background*

The Origins of fact-discovery in Roman Law: the Roman-Canonical Positiones

In the formulary period of Roman law, the *interrogatio in iure* provided the plaintiff with the possibility of interrogating a prospective party before the praetor regarding those facts needed to properly initiate an action.[3] A creditor, seeking to litigate

1 See e.g. European Court of Justice, 17 October 1989, 109/88.

2 See e.g. Dutch Court of Cassation, 20 November 1987, *NJ* 1988, 500.

3 Kaser & Hackl 1996, §34.

against the heir of his debtor, could by means of the interrogatories prior to the initiation of the action, find out whether the interrogated person was an heir and the portion of the estate to which he was entitled. The institution underwent a number of changes as the formulary proceedings were replaced by the *cognitio* procedure before a single trained judge in the post classical period of Roman Law. The Digest nevertheless retained the *interrogatio in iure* and devoted a title to it.[4] As in the classical law, the interrogation seemed to be limited to questioning prospective defendants in order to obtain information needed to properly constitute an action. Given the very restrictive use of the *interrogatio in iure,* it could be argued that it did not serve as a mechanism by which one party could question the opponent. The precise form of party interrogation under Roman law is not of relevance for present purposes. More important is the fact that the *interrogatio in iure* would at a later point in time be used as a mechanism of party interrogation.

The scope of the Roman *interrogatio in iure* was broadened in medieval times. The Romano-Canonical model allowed the use of interrogatories both before and after the definite constitution of the case.[5] Before the *litiscontestation,* as in Roman law, the plaintiff could put questions to the (prospective) defendant and possibly amend his claim accordingly. The interrogation of the opponent after the action had been initiated was more innovative. The plaintiff could, in his libel, request the judge to interrogate the defendant on a number of points of fact. The defendant was to answer upon his belief. The defendant had to answer either *credo* (I believe) or *non credo* (I do not believe).[6] If a party responded with *credo,* this was considered to be an 'admission of fact', making further evidence unnecessary. The fact that the defendant answered on belief and not upon his 'knowledge' implied he could answer *non credo* if he had insufficient knowledge to form a belief, thereby requiring the plaintiff to produce evidence. The defendant could also request the judge to interrogate the plaintiff in his pleading.[7]

The procedure as described above was used in ecclesiastical and secular courts until the early 13th century. In practice, the use of interrogatories after the *litiscontestation* was partially replaced by the procedure of *positiones.*[8] The form of the *positiones* was different in the sense that the *positiones* consisted of a number of facts that constituted the claim. Each position started with the word *Pono* which means 'I propound'. The *positiones* stated separately all the relevant facts already mentioned in the narrative part of the libel. The judge was to examine the *positiones* for admissibility. If these were admissible, they were put to the opposing party. The interrogating party was generally also required to confirm the *positiones.* An

4 D. 11.1. 'Concerning interrogatories which should be put in court and actions based on interrogatories'. D. 11.1.1 notes that interrogatories are not used frequently. Kaser & Hackl 1996, §90. p. 590.

5 Litewsky 1999, p. 321.

6 Litewsky 1999, p. 360. Some authors did allow the defendant to answer that he was in doubt (*dubito*) or had insufficient knowledge to form a belief (*nescio*).

7 Litewsky 1999, p. 357-359.

8 Litewsky 1999, p. 357. Litewski argues that interrogatories continued to be used.

example of *positiones* is provided by the *Speculum Iudiciale* of Durantis. In an action where the plaintiff claimed the transfer of land, the *positiones* could look as follows:

> 'I propound, in this case, the following matters under oath;
> that the parcel of land subject to litigation, was in use by Titius;
> I also propound that Titius sold me the aforementioned piece of land;
> also Titius has put me in the possession of the land;
> and also that I have paid Titius 10 gold coins as a price for the piece of land'.[9]

The *positiones* or interrogatories generally did not require the parties to take a separate oath. The parties were bound to be truthful under the general Calumnia oath (see Section 2.1.1). The aim of the interrogatories and the *positiones* was the same: to avoid the taking of unnecessary evidence.

The form in which the *positiones* were presented differed over time. In theory, the pleadings, the *positiones* and the written questions put to the witnesses (articles) could be three separate written documents. It obviously seemed more efficient to combine such documents. In certain localities, the libel would also contain the *positiones.* Sometimes the articles of proof were combined with the *positiones.* In other localities the libel would perform the triple role of combining the libel, the *positiones* and the articles.[10]

The Reception of the Positiones on the European Continent

The medieval system of interrogatories or *positiones* was used throughout Europe. The system continued to exist long after the 13th century, although its reception was different in different parts of the continent. In Austria, which was a part of the Holy Roman Empire, some elements of the system of *positiones* were adopted but their influence was limited. The procedure before the Imperial Chamber (*Reichskammergericht*) had required the insertion of *positiones* in the plaintiff's first pleading since the 16th century. The articles were submitted and the answers given under a special oath referred to as the *Glaubenseid.*[11] The system was reformed several times without much success. Before the Imperial Chamber, the use of *positiones* and articles fell in disfavor in the 18th century and was almost wholly set aside.[12] The General Judicial Ordinance of 1781, the first Code that unified procedural practices in Austria, no longer made use of *positiones* or articles to question the parties. The Code instead adhered to the simple principle that allegations that were not denied stood confessed.[13]

9 Durantis, *Speculum Judiciale,* Lib. II, Partic. II, Rubr. *De positionibus* as quoted by Millar 1937, p. 269: 'Pono ego talis in tali causa iuramento meo quod fundus de quo agitur fruit Titii. Item pono quod ipse Titius vendidit mihi dictum fundum. Item quod dictus Titius tradidit mihi possessionem dicti fundi. Item quod solvi eidem Titio decem libras pro pretio dicti fundi'.

10 Wedekind 1971, p. 98-99; Litewsky 1999, p. 361 and Millar 1937, p. 273-274.

11 Millar 1937, p. 424-426.

12 Oberhammer 1993, p. 70.

13 Section 11 General Judicial Ordinance: 'Würde ein Theil einige Umstände des Faktums, welche der Gegner für sich angeführet hat, in der darauf folgenden Rede nicht ausdrücklich, und zwar insbesondere widersprechen, so wären solche bey Erleidigung des Prozesses für wahr zu halten'.

Courts in the Low Countries had widely used the system of *positiones* in medieval and early modern times.[14] The High Court of Friesland made use of *positiones* until at least the late 18th century.[15] The answering of the *positiones* in Friesland was covered by the Calumnia oath. Similarly, before the Great Council of Malines in the 16th century, *positiones* were used. Each party would, under oath, affirm the facts he had alleged. Then one by one each party would, also under oath, say whether he believed (*credit*) or did not believe (*non credit*) whether the facts alleged by the opposing party were true.[16] Variations existed between the courts. Some courts would for instance require the parties to allege the *positiones* separately in writing whereas in other courts the *positiones* were included in the pleadings. At times, *positiones* were referred to as *articulen*, which shows that often no distinction was made between questions put to the parties and those put to the witnesses.[17] Parties were to respond to *artikelen* before the High Council of Holland, Zeeland and West Friesland.[18] In the Court of Holland in the 16th century, parties were first required to take an oath before they were to respond to the *articulen* of the opponent.[19] A system of party interrogation along French lines was implemented uniformly throughout the Low Countries with the introduction of the French codifications in the Netherlands in the beginning of the 19th century.

In France, elements of the Romano-Canonical system were gradually adopted in the 13th century.[20] The *positiones* were not adopted in their classical form but as articles of proof, containing assertions of fact that were used to interrogate both witnesses and parties. The examination of witnesses based on the articles of proof was usually done by special commissioners prior to examining the witnesses. The commissioners would report their findings to the judge after parties and witnesses had been examined. This practice continued until a 16th century Ordinance would separate the hearing of the parties from the hearing of witnesses.

From the 16th century onwards, a separate procedure existed to put questions to parties.[21] It would be known as the *interrogatoire sur faits et articles,* which translates as 'the interrogation on facts and articles'.[22] The method differed to some extent from the hearing on the basis of articles as described above. To avoid the possibility that parties would too easily deny facts alleged by the opponent, parties were no longer allowed to state whether or not they 'believed' or 'did not believe' the facts stated by the opponent were true (i.e. *credo* or *non credo*). Instead, they were to answer upon knowledge and their oath would be one of positive truth. The examination was before the judge and the interrogation of parties was no longer linked to the examination of witnesses. In some courts, the questions put to the

14 De Damhouder 1626, Chap. CLII, '*Van Positien*'.

15 Hempenius-Van Dijk 2004, p. 36-37, p. 60.

16 Van Rhee 1997, Chapter VII.

17 De Damhouder 1626, Chap. CLII, '*Van Positien*'.

18 Le Bailly & Verhas 2005, p. 46.

19 Wedekind 1971, p. 103.

20 Millar 1937, p. 278-279.

21 Its roots are commonly traced back to the royal Ordinance of Villers-Cotterets (1539). See Van Caenegem 1971, No. 28.

22 Wijffels 2005a.

other party had to be made known to that party in advance. If questions were known in advance, it gave the opponent ample time to compose his answers. Thus the possibilities for evasion were many and the utility of the interrogation was destroyed. Often the interrogating party was no longer required to affirm the facts and articles under oath himself. Instead, the interrogation became a procedural device each party could use to interrogate his adversary.

The 1667 Ordinance of Louis XIV used pre-existing law to comprehensively codify the interrogation on facts and articles.[23] The Ordinance required the interrogated party to be informed in advance about the 'facts and articles' that he would have to respond to.[24] This hampered the utility of the interrogation, but was partly offset by the fact that the judge could ask additional questions. The interrogation required the answering party to respond 'precise and pertinent' to each question. Therefore the answer was not restricted to the categorical 'yes' or 'no', allowing the interrogating party to phrase open-ended questions.[25] A failure to answer was considered to be an express admission; if a party 'denied the truth' he could be fined.[26] The interrogation itself took place in secrecy; the interrogating party could not be present.

The 1806 French Code of Civil Procedure copied the interrogation on facts and articles with little change from the 1667 Code Louis.[27] Perhaps the most important change was that the interrogation was now no longer under oath. The influence of the 1667 Code Louis and the 1806 Code of Civil Procedure caused the interrogation on facts and articles to be adopted in a large number of jurisdictions. The 1838 Dutch Code of Civil Procedure adopted the French provisions without any significant amendments.[28] The interrogation on facts and articles also found its way into the colonies of France and the Netherlands including Quebec[29] and Indonesia.[30]

The Louisiana Code of 1805 adopted interrogatories on facts and articles based on the French model.[31] The institution was retained in later Louisiana legislation. The Louisiana Code of 1870 allowed the parties to put questions to each other by filing interrogatories in writing. These interrogatories were to be annexed to the petition or the answer as was the case in equity proceedings. Thereby the opposing party was notified of the questions put to him or her prior to the interrogation.[32] With leave of the court, the interrogatories on facts and articles could be filed at a

23 Ordonnance Civile, 1667, as reprinted in 1996 by Dott. A. Giuffrè Editore, S.p.A. Milano, Titre X.

24 It was much critised for this reason. The 'Lecture faite de l'article I', printed along with the text of the legislation, mentions the criticism: 'L'on peut dire au contraire, que lorsque l'on communique les faits, c'est donner le moien de se preparer contre la vérité, (...)'.

25 Ordonnance Civile, 1667 Titre X, Article 7.

26 Ordonnance Civile, 1667 Titre X, Articles 4, 8.

27 Wijffels 2005a, Section 1.1 and Millar 1937, p. 282.

28 See former Articles 237-246 Dutch Code of Civil Procedure.

29 Millar 1937, footnote 351.

30 Former Articles 230-239 Wetboek van Burgerlijke Rechtsv. Ned. Indië, as quoted by Denijs 1936. On the Dutch influence in Indonesia, see Van Rhee 2008b.

31 Ralston 1940.

32 Article 347 La. Code of Practice of 1870.

later stage.[33] The interrogatories were either answered in writing or orally before the court.[34] If the interrogatories were answered orally, the interrogation would take place in open court. The interrogated party was bound to answer categorically and under oath. This implied that the interrogated party should either confess or deny the facts put to him.[35] A refusal or failure to answer was considered to be a confession of the facts alleged by the interrogating party.

The interrogatories on facts and articles gradually became less popular throughout the 19th century. In France between 1876 and 1880, the interrogation was used on average in 523 out of 164,186 cases annually before the Courts of First Instance. In the period 1900-1911, the interrogatories were used between 300 and 350 times per year.[36] In legal practice, the interrogatories on facts and articles would gradually be replaced by the more informal personal appearance of the parties. The interrogatories were eventually abolished by the Vichy Regime in 1942.[37]

In other jurisdictions, the interrogation on facts and articles also became less popular. Belgium abolished the interrogation in 1967, when the new Judicial Code (*Code Judiciaire, Gerechtelijk Wetboek*) was introduced. In Louisiana the use of interrogatories declined when parties became qualified to testify as witnesses in their own case in 1868.[38] They were eventually abolished and replaced by 'modern' interrogatories in the second half of the 20th century with the enactment of the new Louisiana Code of Civil Procedure.[39] In the Netherlands, the interrogation on facts and articles had long been criticized and ignored in legal practice.[40] According to Drabbe, it was used in only 42 out of 8,852 defended cases in 1961.[41] The 1988 Dutch Civil Evidence Act abolished the interrogation on facts and articles. The present relevance of interrogatories on the European continent is limited. A 'modernized' version of the *interrogatoire sur faits et articles* does however exist in Italy.[42]

33 Ralston 1940, p. 445-446.
34 Answering by commission was possible if the interrogated party resided outside the state.
35 Articles 347-353 La. Code of Practice of 1870.
36 These data are mentioned by Wijffels 2005a, footnote 8.
37 Herzog 1967, p. 52, §7.53 and Wijffels 2005a, Section 2.
38 Ralston 1940.
39 The new Code of Civil Procedure, presently still in force, contains provisions on interrogatories based on the FRCP (Articles 1457-1459).
40 Weve 1878, p. 230. The Lex Hartogh of 1896 had amended the hearing upon facts and articles. The most important changes were that the hearing was no longer inaccessible to lawyers and the party who had requested the hearing. For further criticism of the interrogation in the Netherlands see De Tombe-Grootenhuis 1993, p. 11, *HNJV* 1878 and 1915 and Funke 1986.
41 Drabbe 1965, p. 303.
42 '*Interrogatorio formale*', Article 228 of the Italian Code of Civil Procedure.

The Reception of the Positiones in Equity

It was through the ecclesiastical courts that the Romano-Canonical model affected the procedure before the English Court of Chancery.[43] The *positiones* and the plaintiff's opening pleading in English ecclesiastical courts were combined in a single procedural document. The document was referred to as an 'articulated libel'.[44] If needed, the *positiones* in the 'articulated libel' could later be used as articles of proof. The defendant was also able to list *positiones* in his first pleading.

The main features of pleading in the ecclesiastical courts influenced pleading in the Court of Chancery.[45] There, the opening pleading was referred to as the *bill of complaint*. It consisted of nine parts, of which three were devoted to factual issues. The *stating part* of the bill of complaint contained a narrative upon which the claim was based. The *charging part* contained charges of evidence on which the plaintiff sought a declaration from the defendant. The *interrogating part* contained specific questions put to the defendant. As the three distinctive parts of the bill generally dealt with the same matters, the bill was often repetitive. Of these three parts, the charging part of the bill had most in common with the Romano-Canonical *positiones*.

The defendant was required to respond to all three parts of the bill that dealt with the factual basis of the dispute in his answer. Although the plaintiff was generally not required to confirm parts of the bill under oath, the defendant was required to answer under oath. In the early chancery procedure, the defendant was examined *viva voce*. Soon however, the answer was in writing. In the written answer, the defendant 'blended' his responsive allegations with his answers to the charging and interrogating parts of the bill. If the defendant failed to answer, he stood in contempt of court and could be taken into custody until an answer was given. If custody did not suffice, the bill in its entirety could be taken as confessed to the detriment of the defendant. If the answer was not sufficient, the defendant could be ordered to provide further information.

A remarkable feature of the chancery procedure was that the defendant was not entitled to seek disclosure from the plaintiff. A defendant was required to file a *cross bill*, initiating a new procedure to question the plaintiff in the underlying case. The initiation of a new chancery procedure whose sole object was the discovery of information was also a popular instrument for parties involved in a common law procedure. The procedure was not without problems. Apart from increased technicalities, costs and delay this led to legal problems. If the procedure aimed to obtain discovery was separated from the procedure in which substantive relief was sought, it was not possible to draw adverse inferences (i.e. *poena confessi*) in the underlying procedure for a failure to comply with an order to provide information in the discovery procedure.

The system of fact discovery by means of the bill of chancery was - with minor adaptations - adopted in the American colonies and its fundamentals would only be subject to reform in the 19th and 20th centuries.

43 Langdell 1907.

44 Helmholz 2004, p. 323.

45 Millar 1937, p. 438.

1.2. *Diverging Modes of Fact-Discovery*

Limited effective Possibilities to Question the Parties in the early 19th Century
The different systems of written interrogatories as described above were often ineffective. At the same time, there were few other possibilities to question the parties. As explored in greater detail in Section 6.1.3, the parties generally could not be heard under oath as witnesses. To the extent that courts had powers to interrogate parties, judges were hesitant to use such powers under influence of the adversarial principle.

In England, the common law courts offered hardly any possibilities for questioning the parties. Blackstone's 'Commentaries on the Laws of England' (1768) had listed the lack of possibilities to interrogate the opposing party and to compel the inspection of documents in the possession of an opponent as two of the main drawbacks of the common law procedure.[46] According to Subrin, the adversarial system exemplified the 'each person for himself' mentality.[47] The idea that one party should aid the other was considered to be 'distasteful'. In general, discovery was traditionally very limited in the Anglo-American common law courts. At the same time the adversarial system had prevented judges from actively questioning the parties. At the Court of Chancery, slightly more liberal rules enabled the parties to address the problem of information inequality. In an action at the Court of Chancery, the plaintiff was entitled to put questions to the defendant. One could use the costly and lengthy equity procedure to obtain information that could subsequently be used in a common law court.

Likewise on the European continent, possibilities to question one's opponent were limited. The idea that one could compel the opponent to provide information adverse to his case was often rejected (*Nemo tenetur edere contra se principle,* Section 2.1). The 19th century Austrian system did not provide parties with any significant means to compel the opponent to provide adverse information or aid with the production of evidence.[48] Similarly, in Dutch legal practice in the second half of the 19th century, there were hardly any effective means to obtain adverse information held by the opponent. In countries like Austria and the Netherlands, the pleadings were not an effective vehicle to interrogate the opposing party. The interrogation on facts and articles, available in a number of jurisdictions, was generally believed to be ineffective. Judges who often had powers to interrogate the parties would strictly abide by the adversarial principle and seldom use their discretionary powers.[49] A

46 Blackstone 1768, Vol. 3, p. 382. Also see Millar 1952, p. 219 and Wigmore 1940, §1858 for a more detailed description of the limitations on the right to require the production of documents.

47 Subrin 1997, p. 695. '...the adversary system exemplified the "each person for himself" mentality. The idea that one should help opponents prepare their case was distasteful. There was a long-standing and widely-held belief that if either side could discover the factual position of the opponent, the discovering side would perjure testimony. Perhaps most importantly, at common law a party could neither take the stand nor force the opposing party to do so'.

48 Heimerl 1857, p. 44-45 and Klein 1891, p. 37 as quoted below.

49 See e.g. Van der S. 1857.

system of party oaths was in place to obtain a confession under oath from one's adversary. These oaths, discussed in greater detail in Section 6.1.3, were not useful as a discovery device.

The Pursuit of Truth and the Widening of Mechanisms to Interrogate the Litigants
Both on the continent and in Anglo-American jurisdictions, it was increasingly believed to be of importance that facts were established correctly. Well known proponents of these views include Jeremy Bentham and Franz Klein. In order to establish the facts truthfully, it was necessary that parties could be compelled to provide all relevant information. Both in the Anglo-American legal systems and on the Continent, different devices were implemented from the 19th century onwards to compel parties to produce adverse information.

Both on the European Continent and in the United States, parties were increasingly required to disclose information without awaiting a request. The American rules on disclosure *inter alia* require the parties to provide their opponent with a mandatory expert report (see Section 5.2.2) as well as the names of witnesses who will be used by that party at trial. Similar rules exist on the Continent. In addition, in Austria and the Netherlands, parties are required to provide a truthful and complete account of the facts (*Wahrheitspflicht, waarheidsplicht*).

In the following Sections, it will be shown that judges and parties were increasingly empowered to compel a litigant to answer questions. On the continent, mechanisms that allowed the court to question parties would become most prominent. In American jurisdictions, mechanisms that empowered parties to compel their adversaries to produce information would be used most widely.

1.2.1. The Continent: Personal Appearance of the Parties

A personal appearance of the parties is a court hearing in which the judge freely discusses the case with the parties and their lawyers. It has become increasingly more common in many Continental jurisdictions that a personal appearance is scheduled at an early point in the proceeding. Generally, the most important aims of the personal appearance are: 1) to clarify the issues that divide the parties; 2) to promote settlement; and 3) to discuss the further course of the proceedings.[50] Statements of the parties at a personal appearance are 'clarifying party statements'. The parties do not take an oath and their statements are not a means of proof.

The Increased Importance of the Personal Appearance of the Parties
On the European Continent the oral discussion of the case by the judge, parties and their lawyers has increasingly gained in importance. Many Continental jurisdictions now provide for oral hearings before the court. Provisions that allow the court to

50 For the Netherlands, see Bijlagen Handelingen Tweede Kamer, 19 574, No. 6, p. 2. Similar aims can be found in Section 258 Austrian Code of Civil Procedure and Sections 141, 278 and 279 German Code of Civil Procedure.

schedule informal hearings are not new.[51] Recent changes to Continental Codes do suggest that oral hearings have gained in importance. In Germany, for instance, Section 141(1) Code of Civil Procedure holds that 'the court shall order the parties to appear in person, if such seems necessary to clarify the facts'.[52] During the hearing, parties ought to 'speak freely' and are not supposed to read out written pleadings.[53] The court is required to discuss factual matters with the parties and to question them in order to clarify all relevant facts.[54] Section 756ter of the Belgian Judicial Code allows the judge - if the parties agree - to replace the traditional oral pleas of counsel by an 'interactive debate'. If a party opposes, the court can determine that such an 'interactive debate' takes place after the oral pleas.[55] The Swedish 1942 Code of Judicial Procedure, much like the Austrian Code, requires the court to actively 'investigate' the facts of the case. Chapter 43, Section 4 of the Code reads: '(...) The court shall also make certain that the case is investigated according to its nature and that irrelevant matters are not presented. Through questions and observations the court shall attempt to remedy any unclear and incomplete statement'.[56] In the Sections below, the use of a personal appearance to clarify matters of fact will be explored in greater detail by looking at the Austrian and Dutch systems.

The Questioning of Parties at Oral Hearings in Austrian Law

The idea that an active judge could question the parties on matters of fact was not a novelty introduced by the 1895 Code of Civil Procedure. The Prussian Code of 1781, had also favored an active judge who would question the parties on matters of fact. The 1781 Prussian General Judicial Ordinance (*Corpus Juris Fridericianum*) was based on the premise that it was the duty of the court to establish *ex officio* the veracity of facts in civil litigation. The judge would personally interrogate the parties, who

51 In post classical Roman Law, the court was relatively active in the process of fact-finding and would frequently interrogate the parties. Kaser & Hackl 1996, §91, II. §92 I: 'Die Parteiaussagen werden jetzt im allgemeinen nicht mehr durch wechselseitige Befragung der Streitteile gewonnen, sondern durch die Fragestellung des Richters'. The judge was entitled to interrogate the parties if such was necessary to examine the character of the matter in dispute, see C. 3.1.9.

52 Section 141(1) German Code of Civil Procedure: 'Das Gericht soll das persönliche Erscheinen beider Parteien anordnen, wenn dies zur Aufklärung des Sachverhalts geboten erscheint (...)'.

53 See Section 137 of the German Code of Civil Procedure.

54 See Section 139 of the German Code of Civil Procedure.

55 Article 756ter: 'Tijdens dan wel vóór de pleitzitting kan de rechter voorstellen om de pleidooien te vervangen door een interactief debat. Indien de partijen daarmee instemmen, leidt de rechter het debat, waarbij hij de mogelijkheid heeft de partijen te oriënteren naar aangelegenheden die hij relevant vindt en die van aard zijn hem opheldering te verschaffen. Tijdens dat debat mogen de partijen vragen stellen die niet door de rechter zijn opgeworpen, op voorwaarde dat deze hetzij in hun geschriften werden aangevoerd, hetzij gekoppeld zijn aan de toepassing van artikel 735 hetzij betrekking hebben op een onregelmatigheid die de procedure van instaatstelling aantast. Indien een partij er zich tegen verzet dat de pleidooien door een interactief debat worden vervangen, kan het debat desondanks na de pleidooien plaatsvinden'.

56 The provision was amended in 1987. The Swedish Code in English is available at www.sweden.gov.se/content/1/c6/02/77/78/30607300.pdf, also see, <www.riksdagen.se/webbnav/index.aspx?nid=3911&bet=1942:740>, last consulted in February 2010.

were obliged to appear personally before the court and inform the court truthfully about matters of fact. Sections 10 and 13 of the Ordinance stated: 'Section 10. In the investigation of a cause, therefore, the duties of the judge rest upon the essential principle that he must strive, in the surest and directest way, to ascertain and establish the truth of the underlying facts. (...) Section 13 (...) The parties are thus bound to lay before the judge truly and to the best of their knowledge the facts pertinent to the decision of their cause'.[57]

Section 20 of the Austrian 1873 Law on the Proceedings in Petty Causes specified that hearing the parties in court was one of the stages in the proceeding. At this hearing, the judge was expected to put appropriate questions to the parties in order to 'clarify obscure claims, complete the facts if parties had alleged insufficient facts, identify the means of proof that could be used, and ensure in general that all issues would be addressed that are needed to establish the facts'.[58] Franz Klein, who drafted the Austrian Code of 1895, was inspired by these earlier developments in Germany and Austria.[59]

In some significant respects, the 1895 Code of Civil Procedure deviated from its predecessors: the General Judicial Ordinance and the West Galician Ordinance. As set out in Section 2.3.1.2, a leading principle of the Code was that the concentrated oral hearing was the most important phase in litigation. In 2002, the first steps in the course of the proceedings were altered in an attempt to 'speed up' the process of litigation. The first hearing (*erste Tagsatzung*), which did not function to discuss the subject matter of the dispute, was abolished.[60] Instead a 'preparatory hearing' (*vorbereitende Tagsatzung*) is scheduled after the statement of defense. The preparatory hearing serves to promote settlement, to discuss factual and legal maters and to discuss the further course of the proceedings, for instance by setting a time-table.[61] Currently, Section 258 of the Civil Procedural Code reads:

> 'Section 258 (1) The preparatory hearing, which forms a part of the oral phase of the procedure, serves to 1. decide upon preliminary defenses (...), 2. to hear the parties (Sections 177-179), 3. to discuss legal and factual matters (...), 4. to attempt settlement and - if settlement fails - discuss the further coarse of litigation and to announce the procedural steps that will follow 5. - if such is effective - present and discuss evidence and conduct a formal interrogation of the parties.
> (2) Parties and their attorneys have a duty to ascertain that during the preparatory hearing factual matters and settlement can be discussed adequately. Thereto a party or,

57 Translation by Engelmann 1927, p. 591.

58 Section 20 Law on the Proceedings in Petty Causes: 'Der Richter hat zunächts die Parteien mit ihrem Begehren, thatsächlichen Erklärungen und Beweisanbietungen zu hören. Er hat durch geeignete Fragen darauf hinzuwirken, das unklare Begehren erläutert, ungenügende Angaben geltend gemachter Thatsachen ergänzt, die Beweismittel bezeignet und überhaupt alle zur Feststellung des Sachverhaltes nöthigen Erklärungen abgegeben werden. Der Rechte unkundige Parteien sind über die im Unterlassungsfalle eintretenden Rechtsfolgen zu belehren'.

59 Klein 1891, p. 33, footnote 33.

60 962 BlgNr GP XXI, p. 17.

61 Sections 257, 258 Code of Civil Procedure and 962 BlgNr GP XXI, p. 18, 33.

if the party cannot clarify matters of fact, an informed person has to be available to assist the attorney during the hearing'.[62]

Franz Klein had considered the pursuit of truth as one of the central ends of civil litigation. He believed that the early judicial examination of the parties in open court would be amongst the most suitable instruments to establish the facts truthfully.[63] Preferably, the parties would be heard orally by the judge who would later decide the case (principle of immediacy). Klein envisaged oral hearings that were relatively informal and allowed the judge and the parties to cooperate and freely discuss matters of fact. The judge and the parties could then jointly set aside those issues that were not relevant or not genuinely disputed and identify those factual issues that would be decisive for the resolution of the case.

Klein seems to have distrusted the parties, and as early as 1885 complained about the lack of truthfulness before the courts.[64] He stressed the importance of truthfulness by the parties as vital to the process of fact-finding.[65] Klein believed that a judge who actively puts questions to the parties could clarify matters of fact, and simultaneously diminish the possibilities of the parties to be untruthful. He argued that the parties had a duty to be truthful if they were interrogated. At the same time, he was of the opinion that the judge had to formulate questions to establish the facts correctly.[66]

In his *Pro Futuro* (1891), Klein argued that the legislature should empower judges to actively question the litigants and order them to personally appear before the court.[67] An active judge would not remain passive if the statements of parties in

62 Section 258 Code of Civil Procedure: '(1) Die vorbereitende Tagsatzung als Teil der mündlichen Streitverhandlung dient 1. der Entscheidung über die Prozesseinreden, soweit darüber nicht schon nach § 189 Abs. 2 abgesondert verhandelt und entschieden wurde, 2. dem Vortrag der Parteien (§§ 177 bis 179), 3. der Erörterung des Sach- und Rechtsvorbringens auch in rechtlicher Hinsicht, 4. der Vornahme eines Vergleichsversuchs sowie bei dessen Scheitern der Erörterung des weiteren Fortgangs des Prozesses und der Bekanntgabe des Prozessprogramms und 5. - soweit zweckmäßig - auch der Einvernahme der Parteien und Durchführung des weiteren Beweisverfahrens. (2) Die Parteien und ihre Vertreter haben dafür zu sorgen, dass in der vorbereitenden Tagsatzung der Sachverhalt und allfällige Vergleichsmöglichkeiten umfassend erörtert werden können. Zu diesem Zweck ist die Partei oder, soweit diese zur Aufklärung des Sachverhalts nicht beitragen kann, eine informierte Person zur Unterstützung des Vertreters stellig zu machen'.

63 Baur 1970, p. 446.

64 Klein 1885, p. 127-129.

65 Klein 1885, p. 133: 'im mündlichen Verfahren auf das Gebot der Wahrhaftigkeit der grösste Wert gelegt werden muss'.

66 See Klein 1885, p. 133 and Klein 1891, p. 32.

67 Klein 1891, p. 32: 'Die von der Gesetzgebung klar anzuerkennenden Befugnisse des Richters in Sachen der Proceßinstruction wären demnach: Daß Gericht darf von den Parteien alle zur Erläuterung unklarer Anträge und zur Feststellung des Thatbestandes der geltend gemachten Rechte und Anspruche (Sachbegehren) nothwendigen Mittheilungen und Aufschlüsse, u. zw. Mittels Befragung der Parteien oder in anderer Form (directe Auffordering unter genauer Bezeignung des aufzuklärenden Verhältnisses) begehren. Um Solche Aufklärung zu erhalten, muß dem Richter gestattet sein, erforderlichen Falles das persönliche Erscheinen der Partei zu verlangen (...)'.

the pleadings were unclear, incomplete or contradictory. She would question the parties to determine what is true and what is truthful. At such a hearing, the judge would freely discuss the factual issues with cooperative parties, such that factual matters could be dealt with truthfully and efficiently.[68] In accordance with Klein's writings, the role of the court during the oral hearings was emphasized in the 1895 Code of Civil Procedure. Section 182 of the Civil Procedural Code reads as follows:

> 'Section 182 The presiding judge should, during the oral hearing, by means of questioning the parties, or in any other way, make sure that those facts relevant for the final decision are adduced; the judge should also make sure that parties supplement insufficient factual allegations with those facts needed to support a claim or defense; the judge should further make sure that all evidence is properly identified and that factual matters are clarified in correspondence with the truth, if this is necessary to establish the facts needed to support a claim or defense'.[69]

Section 182 should be read in conjunction with other provisions in the Code of Civil Procedure that require the judge to discuss the factual basis of the dispute with the parties.[70] The duty of the judge to clarify the facts of the case implies that the court may not assume that written pleadings provide a full and sufficient basis for the resolution of the case. The court should determine which facts are relevant and which facts are irrelevant and may not simply deny the plaintiff his claim because a fact needed for the application of the relevant legal rule is not mentioned in the complaint.[71] In such cases a judge should ask the plaintiff to amend his pleading.[72] He is required to determine which facts are truly disputed. Factual allegations of both parties might seem to constitute genuine disputes of fact if one merely reads

68 Klein 1901, p. 136, 'Für die Gründlichkeit ist aufs beste gesorgt durch eine wahrhaft mündlich-unmittelbare Verhandlung, die meist in einem Zuge ohne stockende Unterbrechung abläuft, durch das persönliche Erscheinen der Parteien, die sich von ihrem Vertreter unterstützt, mit dem Gerichte frei und ungezwungen über den Streitfall aussprechen, und durch die intensive richterliche Prozessleitung, der es nicht selten gelingt, binnen kurzem den maßgebenden Sachverhalt aus dem Wuste des Vorbringens herauszuschälen, so dass sich nun die ganze Aufmerksamkeit aller Beteiligten auf diese wenigen entscheidenden Punkte konzentrieren kann. Ferner wird die Gründlichkeit wesentlich gefördert durch die regelmäßig vor dem erkennenden Gerichte stattfindende Beweisaugnahme, durch die an Stelle des formalen Eides eingeführte Einvernehmung der Parteien, durch eine gleichfalls wahrhaft mündliche Berufungsverhandlung usw'.

69 'Der Vorsitzende hat bei der mündlichen Verhandlung durch Fragestellung oder in anderer Weise darauf hinzuwirken, dass die für die Entscheidung erheblichen tatsächlichen Angaben gemacht oder ungenügende Angaben über die zur Begründung oder Bekämpfung des Anspruches geltend gemachten Umstände vervollständigt, die Beweismittel für diese Angaben bezeichnet oder die angebotenen Beweise ergänzt und überhaupt alle Aufschlüsse gegeben werden, welche zur wahrheitsmäßigen Feststellung des Tatbestandes der von den Parteien behaupteten Rechte und Ansprüche notwendig erscheinen'.

70 Sections 258 and 259 Code of Civil Procedure currently in force, see Schragel in Fasching & Konecny 2002-2005, §182, No. 1: 'Die Bestimmung des §182 Abs 1 Z 3 ZPO steht in untrennbarem Zusammenhang mit der Regelung des §258 Abs 1 Z3 ZPO, (...)'.

71 See also Section 182(2) Code of Civil Procedure, Fasching 1990, No. 656 and Fucik in Rechberger 2000, §182, No. 1.

72 Section 84 Code of Civil Procedure.

the written pleadings. At an oral hearing, it often becomes clear that these facts are not truly disputed. By setting aside facts as acknowledged (Sections 266-267 Code of Civil Procedure), the court can avoid the unnecessary taking of evidence. If certain factual issues are truly disputed, a judge ought to discuss with the parties what evidence should be examined.[73]

The Personal Appearance of the Parties in the Netherlands

The 1667 French Royal Ordinance recognized a new form of party interrogation. Before the mercantile tribunal, parties could be heard by the court orally and informally.[74] The hearing was termed the *comparution personelle* which roughly translates as 'the personal appearance of the parties'. The personal appearance was much more flexible than the formal interrogation on facts and articles. The personal appearance became increasingly popular and its use was extended to courts other then the mercantile tribunal. The hearing was before the judge who decided the case rather than a commissioner. It took place in open court and the questions were not known to the parties in advance. Unlike the interrogation on facts and articles, the hearing could be ordered by the court *ex officio*.[75] The personal appearance of the parties gradually replaced the formal interrogation as it was cheaper, simpler and a more effective way to learn about the facts of the case.

Article 119 of the 1806 French Code of Civil Procedure stated that 'if the judgment orders the appearance of the parties, it has to state the date of the hearing'. This provision, which was somewhat unclear, was considered to be a legal basis for the judge to order a personal appearance of the parties.[76] Draft proposals for a new revised Code of Civil Procedure in the last decade of the 19th century had proposed replacing the interrogation on facts and articles by a more explicitly regulated personal appearance.[77] It was not until 1942 that a statute abolished the interrogation on facts and articles and implemented a more extensive regulation on the personal appearance of the parties.[78] Article 184 of the French Code of Civil Procedure currently states that 'A judge may, in any matter, order the parties, or one of them, to appear in person', allowing the court to examine one or both parties.[79]

The 1838 Dutch Code of Civil Procedure allowed the judge to request the parties to appear before him. The judge could order the parties to appear in an attempt to promote a settlement (*schikkingscomparitie*) on the basis of Article 19 Code of Civil Procedure.[80] Article 49 Code of Civil Procedure offered a second possibility for the judge to hear the parties. The provision, a translation of Article 119 of the

73 Detailed in this respect is Schragel in Fasching & Konecny 2002-2005, §182, No. 6.
74 Ordonnance Civile, 1667, Titre XVI.
75 Millar 1937, p. 281.
76 See for instance some of the case law discussed in Bourdeaux 1937, p. 73. The text of the provision in French: 'Si le jugement ordonne la comparution de parties, il indiquera le jour de la comparution'.
77 See in general Wijffels 2005a.
78 Wijffels 2005a, p. 240.
79 Translation: <www.Legifrance.gouv.fr>, last consulted in February 2010.
80 Former Article 19 Code of Civil Procedure and Van Boneval Faure 1893, Section 88.

1806 French Code of Civil Procedure, was adopted by the legislator to provide the judge with powers to hear the parties.[81] If parties refused to answer or failed to appear, the judge could make use of presumptive evidence to that parties' detriment.[82] Article 49 was, however, neglected in legal practice.[83]

Near the end of the 19th century and throughout the 20th century, many stressed the need for effective mechanisms of party interrogation.[84] Although it seems that a majority of Dutch jurists favored the wider use of oral hearings at which parties could be questioned,[85] reform was very modest and oral hearings were seldom scheduled.[86] A 1920 draft for a new Code of Civil Procedure, strongly influenced by the Austrian Code, favored wider possibilities for the judge to question the parties. The draft was never enacted. In 1923 however, a new provision was introduced that allowed the judge to compel parties *ex officio* to appear before him and to provide information (*inlichtingencomparitie, Article 19a*). Parties could also question each other through their lawyers. If parties did not appear or refused to answer, the judge could draw adverse inferences or make use of presumptions.[87] In theory, a clear distinction between an appearance in court aimed at encouraging a settlement and appearances aimed at the clarification of facts existed.[88] In the latter

81 Wijffels 2005a.

82 Star Busmann 1938, p. 618.

83 Van der S. 1857, p. 189-191.

84 Caroli and Hartzfeld for instance argued in 1907 that the judge should be empowered to question parties and use their testimonies as evidence. Both Caroli and Hartzfeld pointed to the English (and Austrian) system where a party testimony could be used to support or weaken a party's case. Hartzfeld 1907, p. 153-154; Caroli 1907, p. 52-54.

85 In 1878 the members of the Dutch Association of Jurists (NJV) voted in favour of a rule that would permit the judge (46 out of 57 votes) and the parties (52 out of 60 votes) to put questions to each other at a personal appearance. Similarly, those present at the meeting thought it would be salutary if the judge would draw adverse inferences in case parties would refuse to answer or would remain absent at the personal appearance. Questions 3 and 4, 'Behoort dan, op verzoek van een van beiden te worden toegelaten het wederkeerig ondervragen van partijen door elkander, voor den rechter die van de zaak kennis neemt? Antw. Ja (52 Ja, 8 Neen)', 'Moet in elk geval de rechter de bevoegdheid hebben ambtshalve partijen voor zich te doen verschijnen, ten einde over en weder te worden gehoord? Antw. Ja (46 ja, 11 Neen)'. Question 3e, 'Moet aan het wegblijven van eene der partijen of hare weigering om te antwoorden het rechtsgevolg verbonden worden, dat de feiten, door de tegenpartij in hare conclusie vermeld, voor erkend kunnen worden gehouden? Antw: Ja'. In 1915 A large majority of the members of the Dutch Association of Jurists favored also a more active role for the court with respect to the interrogation of parties, *HNJV* 1915, p. 92.

86 In 1915, the annual conference of the Dutch Association of Jurists discussed whether the judge should be allowed to order the parties to appear personally before the court to clarify the facts. During the hearing A lawyer with 55 years of experience claimed he had never experienced a judge asking parties or lawyers to clarify the facts stated in the written pleadings. *HNJV* 1915, p. 16. Others claimed they had had such experiences. *HNJV* 1915, p. 80. Nolst Trenité explained that the District Court of Utrecht made use 'quite frequently' of personal appearances before the court. He noted it had been used 6 times in 1913 and 1914, *HNJV* 1915, p. 72.

87 District Court Assen, 27 June 1950, *NJ* 1951, 194.

88 Current Articles 87 and 88 Code of Civil Procedure, former Articles 19 and 19a Code of Civil Procedure.

case, the judge would compel parties to clarify some of their statements or to provide additional information. In the former case, a judge would urge the parties to reach an agreement and settle their dispute.[89] In practice, personal appearances before the court usually served both purposes simultaneously.

Only gradually were judges inclined to use their powers under Article 19a. It was not until the second half of the 20th century that the personal appearance of the parties became widely used. From 1965 onwards, experiments were conducted in the Rotterdam District Court with what was later referred to as the model of 'a personal appearance after the submission of the answer' (*comparitie na antwoord*). In these experiments, after the complaint and the answer had been filed, the court would schedule a personal appearance. The hearing served to clarify matters of fact, encourage settlement and to discuss the further course of the action if the case had not been settled.

By Act of Parliament on the 1st of December 1989, former Article 141a Code of Civil Procedure codified the practice in which a personal appearance was scheduled after the filing of the defendant's answer. The provision required the judge to decide, after the statement of defense had been filed, whether or not the case was fit for a personal appearance of the parties.[90] Since the 2002 Reform Act a personal appearance should be ordered by the judge unless there are reasons not to do so. At present, a personal appearance is ordered after the statement of defense in a large majority of cases (see Section 2.4.1).

The personal appearance primarily allows the judge to question parties, but also enables the parties to question each other. At first, parties could only question each other through their counsel.[91] Since the revision of the Code of Civil Procedure in 2002, parties may question each other directly.[92] Similarly, a series of amendments has gradually empowered the court to question the parties on any occasion. In 1896, the Code of Civil Procedure was revised and a second paragraph was added to former Article 144 Code of Civil Procedure. Since 1896 the judge could, during the oral closing arguments of counsel, ask questions of the parties and their lawyers concerning the content of their written and oral statements. In 1988, a provision was introduced that allowed the judge and the opposing party to put questions to a party after the examination of witnesses.[93] In 2002, the court was empowered to hear parties and request them to clarify their statements of fact on any occasion.[94] The judge may, for instance, put questions to the parties during a local visit or after experts have been heard. Currently Articles 131, 87 and 88 read as follows:

89 Marx 1926.

90 For a discussion of the proposal see Stein 1987.

91 Former Article 19a(2) Code of Civil Procedure.

92 Article 88 Code of Civil Procedure.

93 Former Article 205(3) Code of Civil Procedure, Article 179(3) Code of Civil Procedure.

94 See the provisions below and the more general Article 22 Code of Civil Procedure.

'*Article 131* After the defendant has submitted his answer, the judge will order a personal appearance of the parties as set out in Article 87 or Article 88, unless he decides that the case is not suitable for a personal appearance of the parties (...)'.

'*Article 87* (1) The judge may, on request of both or one of the parties or *ex officio*, in all situations and in each stage of the proceeding, order a personal appearance of the parties before the court in order to promote settlement. (2) Parties should appear before the court in person or by means of representation. (...) The court may order that the parties appear in person (...)'.

'*Article 88* (1) A personal appearance of the parties before the court may also be ordered to provide information to the judge. Article 87, second paragraph is applicable. (2) The judge interrogates the parties. Parties may put questions to each other, although the court may determine that a question need not be answered (3) (...)'.[95]

The Dutch Code does not require the judge to actively ensure that facts relevant to a claim or defense are established in accordance with the truth. The Dutch legal system has no equivalent of Section 182 of the Austrian Code. It follows from Article 24 of the Dutch Code that the judge investigates and decides upon a case on the basis of the facts alleged by the parties.[96] This implies that the judge may ask parties to clarify their allegations. The judge may, however, not put questions to a party unrelated to the issues alleged by either of the parties. Likewise, the judge is in principle not supposed to raise questions about undisputed facts. In practice, it is not always easy to draw a line between clarifying questions and questions that go beyond the (disputed) allegations of the parties.

1.2.2. Pretrial Conferences in American Law

Pretrial conferences in the Federal system of the United States are somewhat akin to preparatory oral hearings on the European continent. Fragments of FRCP Rule 16 are quoted below.

'*Rule 16. Pretrial conferences; scheduling; management*
(a) Purposes of a pretrial conference. In any action, the court may order the attorneys and any unrepresented parties to appear for one or more pretrial conferences for such purposes as: (1) expediting disposition of the action; (2) establishing early and

95 'Artikel 131 Nadat gedaagde voor antwoord heeft geconcludeerd, beveelt de rechter een verschijning van partijen ter terechtzitting als bedoeld in artikel 87 of 88, tenzij hij oordeelt dat de zaak daarvoor niet geschikt is. (...)', 'Artikel 87 (1) De rechter kan, op verzoek van partijen of van een van hen dan wel ambtshalve, in alle gevallen en in elke stand van het geding een verschijning van partijen ter terechtzitting bevelen te einde een schikking te beproeven. (2) Partijen verschijnen ter terechtzitting in persoon of bij gemachtigde. (...) De rechter kan verschijning in persoon bevelen (...)', and 'Artikel 88 (1) Een verschijning van partijen ter terechtzitting kan ook worden bevolen tot het geven van inlichtingen aan de rechter. Artikel 87, tweede lid, is van toepassing. (2) De rechter ondervraagt partijen. Partijen kunnen elkaar vragen stellen, behoudens de bevoegdheid van de rechter om te beletten dat aan een bepaalde vraag gevolg wordt gegeven. (3) (...)'.

96 See Section 2.3.2.

continuing control (...); (3) discouraging wasteful pretrial activities; (4) improving the quality of the trial through more thorough preparation; and (5) facilitating settlement. *(b) Scheduling.* (1) Scheduling order. Except in categories of actions exempted by local rule, the (...) judge (...) must issue a scheduling order (...)
(c) Attendance and matters for consideration at a pretrial conference. (1) Attendance. A represented party must authorize at least one of its attorneys to make stipulations and admissions about all matters that can reasonably be anticipated for discussion at a pretrial conference. If appropriate, the court may require that a party or its representative be present or reasonably available by other means to consider possible settlement. (2) Matters for consideration. At any pretrial conference, the court may consider and take appropriate action on the following matters: (a) formulating and simplifying the issues, and eliminating frivolous claims or defenses; (b) amending the pleadings if necessary or desirable; (c) obtaining admissions and stipulations about facts and documents to avoid unnecessary proof, and ruling in advance on the admissibility of evidence; (d) avoiding unnecessary proof and cumulative evidence, and limiting the use of testimony under federal rule of evidence 702; (e) determining the appropriateness and timing of summary adjudication under rule 56; (f) controlling and scheduling discovery, including orders affecting disclosures and discovery under rule 26 and rules 29 through 37; (g) identifying witnesses and documents, scheduling the filing and exchange of any pretrial briefs, and setting dates for further conferences and for trial; (h) referring matters to a magistrate judge or a master; (i) settling the case and using special procedures to assist in resolving the dispute when authorized by statute or local rule; (...)'

Upon a first reading of FRCP Rule 16, one has to conclude that from a legal perspective the pretrial conference is more or less similar to the preparatory hearings in Continental legal systems. Rule 16 is construed broadly, allowing the court to use the conference for the 'the formulation and simplification of the issues' and to obtain 'admissions of fact and of documents which will avoid unnecessary proof'. The court may require the parties to be present. Although Rule 16 may be similar to rules in Continental jurisdictions, federal judges are very reluctant to use their discretion to the fullest extent.[97] Two differences are most striking. First, parties are seldom present at a Rule 16 conference, whereas the presence of the parties at a preparatory hearing on the Continent is the general rule. Although more accurate empirical research is needed, I understood from a number of practitioners from different parts of the United States that parties seldom or never attend Rule 16 conferences. An experienced practitioner, who intended to bring his client to a Rule 16 conference, told the anecdote that a judge had kindly requested the party to wait outside the judge's chambers as the judge and the attorneys held the conference. In the U.S. District Courts, it seems that Rule 16 conferences normally take place in the judge's chambers with only the attorneys present.[98]

A second difference is that Rule 16 conferences are generally not used as a device to discuss and simplify factual issues at an early point in the procedure.

97 Such as Articles 87, 88 and 131 Dutch Code of Civil Procedure and Section 258 Austrian Code of Civil Procedure.

98 Unfortunately, I have not found empirical data on the matter. These observations are based on conversations with several people working in the U.S. District Court in Detroit and several attorneys that practiced law in New York and Michigan. The anecdote was told to me by an experienced Maine litigator.

Although differences between the courts are very large, it seems that pretrial hearings in the United States focus mainly on setting a number of deadlines (i.e. making or adjusting a scheduling order) and exploring whether parties would be willing to settle. In a Continental setting, the first hearing often serves to identify the issues that require evidence. It seems that the broad availability of discovery, the adversarial ideal and the larger caseloads per judge prevent American judges from using conferences to clarify factual matters and narrow down the issues.[99] These differences affect the importance and duration of such hearings. Continental preparatory hearings held early in the case and with the parties present are often crucial for the further course of the proceedings. These hearings generally take some time (90-120 minutes, see Section 6.2.1 and 2.4.1). Rule 16 conferences are generally shorter and a less vital part of the legal process. Although there are large differences between the different U.S. District Courts, it seems that courts commonly schedule approximately 30 minutes for a Rule 16 hearing.[100]

1.2.3. Anglo-American Law: Fact Discovery

In Anglo-American jurisdictions, the introduction of rules on discovery has led to wider possibilities for interrogating the parties. The discovery mechanisms that may be used to question the parties are interrogatories, requests for admission and depositions. These three mechanisms are party-directed means of interrogation. They operate largely extra-judicially. Only if there is a disagreement between the parties or an alleged noncompliance with the rules, will the judge be involved. A party may demand that the court grant an order to compel discovery, a protective order, or impose sanctions.[101] As has been argued in Section 3.4.2, discovery has become increasingly important since the introduction of the Federal Rules of Civil Procedure (FRCP). Currently interrogatories and depositions serve as the most significant forms of party interrogation in the U.S. federal civil procedural system.

Discovery before the 1938 Federal Rules

America, rather than England, took the initiative in allowing common law courts to compel the discovery of information.[102] Discovery was probably first introduced in the general common law procedure in 1828 in Mississippi.[103] The Mississippi legislation enabled the parties to file an equitable petition for discovery that would be a part of the common law procedure. Similar legislation, that expressly provided for the incorporation of interrogatories, was passed in Missouri in 1835 and in

99 See in general the discussion in Chapter 3 and 5.3. Clark had resisted the idea that the pretrial conference would be used to deprive lawyers and clients of their freedom to make use of the broadly available discovery devices, Subrin 1986 p. 982.

100 Unfortunately, I have not found empirical data on this matter. My estimate is based on a number of pretrial conferences that I attended in one U.S. District Court and a number of conversations with attorneys that practiced throughout the United States. In literature, I have found similar figures. E.g. Lynch 1963, p. 179.

101 FRCP Rules 26, 35, 37.

102 Millar 1937, p. 446-448.

103 Act of 16 February 1828, as quoted by Millar 1937, p. 446.

Arkansas in 1837.[104] As civil procedural law increasingly became subject to codification, new rules on discovery were introduced.

Under the old rules of equity, the defendant was to answer only the interrogatories that were clearly specified as such in an interrogatory part of the Bill of Complaint. In the 19th century some state jurisdictions introduced interrogatories in common law courts.[105] An 1831 Virginia statute is an early example of legislation that allowed both parties in a common law action to make use of interrogatories. The interrogatories were to be answered if these were 'material, pertinent and such as the interrogated party would have to answer in chancery'. The statute was copied by Alabama in 1837 and by Georgia in 1847.[106] At the Federal level, the Equity Rules of 1912 allowing both parties to file interrogatories detached from the Bill of Complaint without leave of the court.[107] Only if parties wished to file a second set of interrogatories, was leave of the court required.

Although the use of interrogatories in American jurisdictions became more popular, they were vulnerable to abuse, if filed without prior leave of the court. In Massachusetts, problems with interrogatories were reported. Parties allegedly filed too many interrogatories.[108] In 1929, the problems in Massachusetts were partly tackled by limiting parties to no more than 30 interrogatories. In England, the Common Law Procedure Act of 1854 introduced interrogatories in the courts at law.[109] Interrogatories could only be used with permission of the court. The Judicature Acts (1873-1875) widened the use of discovery and allowed interrogatories to be used freely without consent of the court. The free use of interrogatories was found wasteful and expensive.[110] After 1893, leave of the court was again needed.[111]

Since the early 19th century, rules have been adopted that allowed a party to request the other to admit that a document was genuine.[112] The rule was codified in Section 342 of the 1848 New York Field Code and Rule 58 of the Federal Rules of Equity. As requests for admission were generally limited to issues like the authenticity of documents, the usefulness of requests for admission was also limited.

104 Acts of 17 March 1835, Sections 10-14: Rev. Stat. of Missouri (1835) p. 462-463 and Act of 18 December 1837, Sections 93-97: Rev. Stat. of Arkansas (1837) c. 116, p. 632, as quoted by Millar 1937, p. 446.

105 Millar 1952, p. 205.

106 Act of 16 April 1831, c. 11, Section 68: Virginia Laws, 1830-31, p. 65 as quoted by Millar 1937, p. 447.

107 Federal Equity Rules, Rule 58, also see Millar 1952, p. 212.

108 Subrin 1997, p. 707. Subrin quotes and discusses the work of Ragland.

109 17, 18 Vict. C. 125, §51 as quoted by Millar 1936, p. 207.

110 Jolowicz 2000, p. 42-43.

111 Throughout the 20th century, leave was rarely granted as courts only allowed interrogatories if they were believed to be necessary for a fair disposal of the action (Jacob 1982, p. 76). Interrogatories nearly disappeared from the English system, until they became available again without prior leave in 1990. Since 1999, the court is entitled to restrict the use of interrogatories (now referred to as requests for 'further information' or 'notices to admit facts' see CPR 18.1 and 32.18).

112 Millar 1952, p. 216.

Traditionally, common law had not provided for the oral examination of parties before or during trial. An oral examination of witnesses by means of a deposition was also exceptional. The Judiciary Act of 1789 had authorized the deposition *de bene esse* to record the testimony of a witness who would most likely not be available at the trial.[113] Section 30 of the Judiciary Act read as follows:

> '(...) And when the testimony of any person shall be necessary in any civil cause depending in any district in any court of the United States, who shall live at a greater distance from the place of trial than one hundred miles, or is bound on a voyage to sea, or is about to go out of the United States, or out of such district, and to a greater distance from the place of trial than as aforesaid, before the time of trial, or is ancient or very infirm, the deposition of such person may be taken *de bene esse* before any justice or judge (...). *Provided*, That nothing herein shall be construed to prevent any court of the United States from granting a *dedimus potestatem* to take depositions according to common usage, when it may be necessary to prevent a failure or delay of justice, which power they shall severally possess, nor to extend to depositions taken in *perpetuam rei memoriam*, which if they relate to matters that may be cognizable in any court of the United States, a circuit court on application thereto made as a court of equity, may, according to the usages in chancery direct to be taken'.

In practice, the rules on granting a *dedimus potestatem* as mentioned in Section 30 of the Judiciary Act were construed narrowly; the taking of depositions was generally limited to those situations where such was needed to 'preserve' testimony of witnesses.[114]

In many American legal systems, depositions would continue to be used only in exceptional cases. Rule 47 of the Federal Equity Rules of 1912 allowed the taking of depositions with leave of the court when statutes specified so or in exceptional circumstances.[115] Other than the quoted passage from the Judiciary Act, there were very few or no federal statutes that allowed the taking of depositions.[116] The main purpose of these rules was to preserve evidence and obtain proof, not to allow for the discovery of information.[117]

An 1847 New York statute had allowed the parties to examine each other in both legal and equitable proceedings at trial.[118] The subsequent Field Code of 1848, expanded the oral examination of parties by specifying that the examination could also take place before trial. The examination of the parties before trial by means of a deposition took place before the judge.[119] The Field Code did not provide for written interrogatories. As a consequence, depositions were the most important

113 Judiciary Act, 1 Stat 73, 24 September 1789.

114 Note 1961, p. 949.

115 Rule 47 of the 1912 Federal Equity Rules.

116 Subrin 1997, p. 698 and Sunderland 1938, p. 19.

117 Sunderland 1938, p. 20.

118 A statute of 1947 had authorized the parties in proceedings in both common law and equitable jurisdictions to question each other before or at trial. New York Laws 1847, c. 462, p. 630-631 as discussed by Millar 1952, p. 206 and Millar 1937, p. 447.

119 Subrin 1988, p. 333.

means of discovery available to the parties. As parties were not (yet) qualified to testify as witnesses, the introduction of depositions was rather innovative.

Pursuant to the introduction of the Field Code elsewhere, the questioning of the opponent by means of depositions became the prevailing method of fact-discovery in most states and met an even wider acceptance in Canada.[120] By the end of the 19th century, the oral examination before trial thereby had replaced the written chancery method by means of bill and answer in a majority of jurisdictions. It is generally believed that the oral examination of the opposing party was far more effective to elicit the facts of the case.[121]

In the beginning of the 20th century most states adopted a more liberal approach to discovery.[122] In the early 1930s, only very few states, like Illinois, still used the interrogating part of the equity bill as a discovery device. Separately filed interrogatories were the exclusive form of discovery in about half a dozen states, like Connecticut. Much more popular was the oral examination of the opposing parties by means of depositions. In line with the Field Code, depositions were the only method of discovery in the majority of states. In other states, like Alabama and Arkansas, both interrogatories and depositions were accepted as a means of discovery. Other states had provisions that allowed to a limited degree the pretrial inspection of property. Notices to admit had also been recognized in several states and common law jurisdictions outside the United States.[123] Ragland, who wrote a leading handbook on discovery before trial in the early 1930s, concluded that many states provided that opposing parties could be examined and interrogated for discovery.[124] Ragland believed that discovery had made 'a vital contribution to the general administration of justice'.[125]

Although the scope of pretrial discovery was slightly broadened in the 19th and early 20th century, discovery was often still very limited. In Federal Courts, the Conformity Act was often construed narrowly, such that broader state rules on discovery could generally not be applied in the 'law side' of the federal courts.[126] Similarly, at the 'equity side' of the Federal Courts discovery was limited. Sunderland lamented that Federal Equity Rule 58 was the 'only provision in the entire federal system intended for discovery'.[127] Rule 58 according to Sunderland was not very useful because written interrogatories were less effective than oral examinations and limited to facts that support one's own case.[128] It was not until the introduction of the new 1938 FRCP that discovery would become a true cornerstone of the American civil procedural system.

120 Millar 1936, p. 206 and Millar 1937, footnote 351.
121 See e.g. Sunderland 1932, p. 875.
122 See in general: Subrin 1997, p. 703-705 and Sunderland 1932, p. 869-875.
123 Subrin 1997, p. 706.
124 Ragland, Discovery before Trial, p. 37, as quoted by Subrin 1997, p. 710.
125 Ragland, Discovery before Trial, p. 266, as quoted by Subrin 1997, p. 710.
126 Note 1961, p. 950.
127 Sunderland 1938, p. 20.
128 Sunderland 1938, p. 21.

Discovery under the Federal Rules of Civil Procedure
The drafters of the FRCP had adopted broad and liberal rules on discovery to prevent the withholding of information and surprises at trial (Section 3.2.2.2). FRCP Rule 26 currently holds that 'parties may obtain discovery regarding any non-privileged matter that is relevant to any party's claim or defense'. Relevant information need not be admissible if the discovery 'appears to be reasonably calculated to lead to the discovery of admissible evidence'. The content of the 1938 FRCP was revolutionary and implied a break with the historic means of fact discovery. Striking features were that discovery was accorded a broad and liberal treatment and that the system operated without any significant court intervention (Section 3.2.2.2). The FRCP discovery rules influenced the rules in most state jurisdictions.[129]

The FRCP on written interrogatories were inspired by Federal Equity Rule 58.[130] Once the court granted leave to serve interrogatories, questions could be sent directly to the opposing party. Partly because questions did not require any advance court approval, interrogatories proved to be a quick and popular instrument of discovery in the hands of the interrogating party.[131]

FRCP Rule 33 was amended in 1946 to provide that the number of interrogatories could be limited to protect the opposing party from annoyance, expense, embarrassment or oppression. To protect the court from a large number of motions raised by the parties, the 'mechanics' of interrogatories were changed in 1970.[132] Leave of the court for service is no longer necessary, time for response was extended to 30 days, and the burden to object was shifted to the interrogating party. The procedure since has been simplified and operates without court involvement.[133] Questions are normally sent to the opposing party by mail. The opposing party answers these questions on the basis of personal knowledge or knowledge that can reasonably be obtained. The written answers are subsequently sent to the interrogating party by mail. The court is only involved if a dispute arises. For instance, if the interrogated party believes a question is improper, that party may state the grounds for refusing to answer the question instead of giving an answer. The interrogating party may then seek a court order requiring an answer. Since 1993, each party is in principle limited to filing no more than 25 interrogatories.[134]

The 1912 Federal Equity Rules had limited the scope of requests for admissions to the execution and authenticity of documents. FRCP Rule 36 extended the use of admissions to cover all material facts. The 1970 FRCP amendments further extended the use of admissions to include opinions on facts and the

129 The FRCP rules on discovery were implemented in state jurisdictions such as Arizona (1939), Colorado (1941), New Mexico (1942), Delaware (1947), New Jersey (1948) and Utah (1949).
130 Sunderland 1938, p. 24. Sunderland claimed that the New Federal Rules are substantially the same as the Rules on Equity with regard to interrogatories. Also see the Advisory Committee Notes to Rule 33.
131 Note 1961, p. 960.
132 See Note 1961, p. 963 on the burden on the courts due to the practice of interrogatories.
133 FRCP Rule 33.
134 FRCP Rule 33(a).

application of law to the facts.[135] Rule 36 allows each party to serve another party a written request to admit the truth of 'matters' separately set forth. The other party must either admit or deny the matter or put forward the reasons why the matter cannot be truthfully denied or admitted. Any matter admitted by the interrogated party is conclusively established unless the court on motion permits a withdrawal or amendment of the admission. The main purpose of requests for admissions is to narrow down the issue by eliminating facts not disputed.[136] To summarize, requests for admissions have many similarities to the *positiones* in Romano-Canonical procedure.

As is the case with the exchange of interrogatories, requests for admission work extra-judicially. Only if there is a dispute can the court be called upon to order a party to respond to the admissions or to grant protection.

Requests to admit the authenticity of documents have proven to be useful. In other instances requests for admissions are much less effective than interrogatories which allow a party to phrase open ended questions. In practice, parties faced with requests for admissions tend to deny most facts put to them. The reluctance of courts and legislators to provide sanctions to ensure compliance with the rules has further undermined the effectiveness of requests for admissions.[137] It seems that, due to their ineffectiveness, admissions have not been used much in legal practice.[138]

In the early 1930s, there were only seven states that permitted the parties to take oral depositions from both parties and witnesses as a matter of right.[139] In four of those states, the deposition took place before an officer empowered to compel answers and to decide objections.[140] In the remaining three states (Indiana, Kentucky and Texas), the questioning of witnesses took place in the absence of a judicial officer. In these states, the deposition was adjourned if a ruling of the court was obtained.[141]

The rules on depositions would prove to be the most revolutionary change introduced by the FRCP. As in Indiana, Texas and Kentucky, the Federal Rules allowed the parties to take oral depositions of both parties and witnesses as a matter of right and in the absence of a judicial officer ruling on objections or deciding at the time on the scope of the questioning.[142] The taking of a deposition initially required leave of the court. The 1946 amendments to FRCP Rule 26 abolished this

135 The Amendments wished to avoid conflicts as to whether a request for admission on matters of opinion or 'mixed law and fact' would be covered by the rule. See the Advisory Committee Note to the 1970 Amendment of Rule 36. Also see Finman 1962.

136 Advisory Committee Notes to the 1970 Amendment of Rule 36.

137 Friedenthal, Kane & Miller 2005, §7.10, p. 433.

138 Requests for admissions are not used frequently. See Note 1961, p. 968-970: 'It seems that rule 36 has been more abused than used'. Also see Striegel 1965, p. 47-48 and Frank 2004, p. 258.

139 These states were: Ohio, Kentucky, New Hampshire, Missouri, Nebraska, Indiana and Texas, see Ragland at 51, as quoted by Subrin 1997, p. 703.

140 Ragland at 104, as quoted by Subrin 1997, p. 703.

141 Ragland at 97, as quoted by Subrin 1997, p. 703.

142 Subrin 1997, p. 703-704.

requirement except if notice of the taking of deposition is served within 20 days after the commencement of the proceedings.[143]

The new rules deliberately broadened the scope and purpose of discovery. Before 1938, depositions were mainly used to preserve evidence that would otherwise be unavailable at trial. Under the FRCP, parties can use depositions either for discovery or for use as evidence, or both.[144] The wide use of depositions in the United States as a means of discovery is very exceptional. In England, depositions have never been introduced as a discovery device and - similar to federal American law before 1938 - only serve as a means to preserve evidence that would otherwise not be available at trial.[145]

Although the mechanics of the rules have changed, the fundamentals of the rules on depositions have remained largely unchanged. Most changes to the rules aimed to avoid abuse. The 1993 and 2000 Amendments to the FRCP introduced limits to the use of discovery in order to reduce costs and delay. Without leave of the court, parties may not take more than 10 depositions which may each last no longer than one day or seven hours.[146]

Under modern discovery rules, an attorney schedules a deposition merely by notifying opposing counsel where and when the deposition will be taken.[147] In practice, depositions are usually jointly planned by the attorneys, parties and witnesses, often pursuant to a 'discovery plan'.[148] Typically, a deposition is taken in a lawyers' office.

Witnesses or parties are generally prepared by their attorneys before they are deposed.[149] Witness preparation is a process whereby a witness and an attorney meet and discuss the future testimony of the witness. American attorneys generally prepare the testimony of the witness to improve the credibility and persuasiveness of witnesses, alleviate their natural fear and permit witnesses to present their testimony in the clearest, most accurate, and persuasive manner.[150] The witness preparation generally consists of three components, 1) informing the witness about giving testimony and about his previous statements, 2) informing the attorney about the knowledge of the witness, and 3) advising the witness about how to deliver his testimony.[151]

The judge is not present at a deposition. A deposition is taken before 'an officer authorized to administer oaths' or by any other person the parties agree upon.[152] Usually this 'officer' is a court reporter, who makes a record of the deposition either by audio, audiovisual or stenographic means.

143 FRCP Rule 30(a)(2).
144 Sunderland 1938, p. 22. The Advisory Committee Notes to FRCP Rule 26 also state that depositions may be used for the purpose of discovery, obtaining evidence or both.
145 Jolowicz 2000, p. 43.
146 FRCP Rule 30(a) and Rule 30(d).
147 FRCP Rule 30(b).
148 FRCP Rule 26(f).
149 See for a practical handbook on 'how to prepare parties and witnesses': Israel 2004, Part 3.
150 Israel 2004, p. 103-104.
151 Boccaccini 2002, p. 164.
152 FRCP Rules 28(a) and 29.

The cross-examination of a party or witness will 'proceed as they would at trial under the Federal Rules of Evidence'.[153] The examination may address any matter not privileged that is relevant to a claim or defense.[154] Objections to questions can be made by an attorney. However, the rules have been revised in 1993 to ensure that objections do not interrupt the examination and cannot be abused by lawyers to make suggestions or instruct the witness or party.[155] Parties themselves generally do not object to questions.

The FRCP also provide for 'written depositions'.[156] The procedure deviates from oral depositions as the attorneys of both parties are usually not present. Questions that should be put to a party or witness are filed by counsel of both sides, after which an officer reads the questions to the witness who responds orally. The answers are recorded. Written depositions - which have some resemblance with the French interrogation on facts and articles - are used infrequently.[157]

1.2.4. Party-driven Fact-Discovery on the Continent

Continental jurisdictions generally provide for rules that enable the parties to interrogate their adversary. One example is the Dutch rule that allows depositions before or during the course of an action, as set out in Section 6.1.3. Another clear example of party-driven interrogation of the opposing party in the 'pretrial' stage of the proceedings is discussed below.

Franz Klein, who was inspired by the English regulations on discovery, was of the opinion that the parties had to be empowered to question their opponent on all relevant matters of fact.[158] The Austrian Code of 1895 accordingly codified the possibility for parties to put questions to their opponents during the oral phase of the procedure. Section 184 Code of Civil Procedure - which has remained unchanged ever since - reads as follows:

> 'Section 184(1) Each party may in order to clarify the facts, on all issues related to subject matter of the case or the oral hearing, request the court to put questions to the opposing party or his lawyer, or may, with permission of the court, personally put questions to the opposing party or his lawyer concerning facts relevant to the dispute, in particular also about the existence and the availability of relevant documents, exhibits and other useful means of proof.

153 FRCP Rule 30(c), an exception is made for FRE 103 and 615.

154 FRCP Rule 26 (b)(1).

155 The 1993 Amendments to the FRCP had amended Rule 30(d) to address deposition conduct. Surveys show that undesirable conduct, such as attorney's coaching witnesses or instructing witnesses not to answer, was however not entirely eliminated: Willging, Stienstra, Shaphard & Miletich 1998, p. 539.

156 FRCP Rule 31.

157 Friedenthal, Kane & Miller 2005, §7.8, p. 426 and Note 1961, p. 958.

158 Klein 1891, p. 47: 'Es ist den Parteien die Befugniß gegenseitiger Befragung über alle den Gegenstand des Rechtsstreites betreffenden, für die gegenwärtige Procesführung des Fragenden erheblichen Umstände (Sachverhalt, Legitimationspunkt, Beweismittel) zuzuerkennen'.

(2) If the presiding judge sets aside a question as inappropriate, or if the opponent contests the admissibility of a question, a party can request a decision on the issue of the full panel of judges'.[159]

Section 184 should be read in conjunction with other provisions of the Code of Civil Procedure related to the oral hearing. Section 184 provides that questions can be put to the opposing party by the judge or directly by the interrogating party. As the oral hearings are generally informal and the court and the parties are to discuss matters of fact in a cooperative manner, it is generally most appropriate if questions are put directly to the opposing party.[160] As the interrogation of a party takes place during an oral hearing, the judge is always present. The judge may decide that inappropriate questions need not be answered. The Code leaves it to the court to determine whether a question is inappropriate. Questions may be held inappropriate if they are offensive, harassing or not related to the subject matter of the case.[161]

Section 184 was clearly meant as a means to allow the parties to discover information held by their adversary.[162] Klein himself believed that parties had a duty to support each other and could be compelled to produce adverse information.[163] In academic literature, it is generally believed that Section 184 may serve as a discovery device and even as a means to 'fish' for information.[164] Nevertheless, some judges have not been willing to order parties to provide their opponents with adverse information. Schragel wrote in a leading Austrian commentary to the Austrian Code that the duty of parties to cooperate should not imply that a party should be compelled to provide support to the opposing party. According to Schragel a refusal of a party to aid one's opponent by identifying relevant evidence should by itself not be a sufficient reason for a judge to draw adverse inferences.[165] Schragel's opinion is inconsistent with Klein's intention and the general principles of the 1895 Austrian Code.

159 '1) Jede Partei kann zur Aufklärung des Sachverhaltes über alle den Gegenstand des Rechtsstreites oder der mündlichen Verhandlung betreffenden, für die Prozessführung erheblichen Umstände und insbesondere auch über das Vorhandensein und die Beschaffenheit der zur Prozessführung dienlichen Urkunden, Auskunftssachen und Augenscheinsgegenstände an die anwesende Gegenpartei oder deren Vertreter Fragen durch den Vorsitzenden stellen lassen oder mit dessen Zustimmung unmittelbar selbst stellen. (2) Wird eine Frage vom Vorsitzenden als unangemessen zurückgewiesen oder die Zulässigkeit einer Frage vom Gegner bestritten, so kann die Partei darüber die Entscheidung des Senates begehren'.

160 Schragel in Fasching & Konecny 2002-2005, §184, No. 1.

161 Schragel in Fasching & Konecny 2002-2005, §184, No. 2.

162 Oberhammer 1999, p. 59 *et seq.*

163 Klein 1891, p. 47, uses the notion 'Gegenseitige Unterstützung'.

164 Klicka 1992, p. 184: 'In diesem Rahmen ist die Partei kraft ausdrücklicher gesetzlicher Vorschrift (§184 Abs 1 ZPO) verpflichtet, nicht nur unmittelbar Angaben zum Sachverhalt zu machen (was ist geschehen) sondern auf entsprechende Fragen des Richters bzw der Gegenpartei auch Angaben über allfällige weitere beweismittel zu machen'. Also see Kralik 1988, p. 92.

165 Schragel in Fasching & Konecny 2002-2005, §184, No. 3: 'Die Mitwirkungspflicht der Parteien hat keineswegs so weit zu gehen, die Gegenseite zu unterstützen. Insb die Weigerung, der →

In Austrian practice, it is not uncommon for parties (or rather their lawyers), to put questions to each other during the discussion of the factual matters of the case. Generally, the judge starts interrogating the parties, after which the attorneys on both sides ask a number of short questions to opposing counsel or the opposing party. There are a couple of other provisions that provide a legal basis for putting questions to one's adversary.[166] The importance of Section 184 seems limited; the provision is seldom explicitly referred to and has not been the subject of academic or political debates.[167]

1.3. *Interrogation of Parties as Evidence*

1.3.1. Formal Party Oaths

An oath is essentially the calling upon a holy and higher authority, mostly God.[168] Oaths are commonly used in civil proceedings; it is assumed that one is more eager to tell the truth if one fears to offend God.[169] In case neither conscience nor fear of God sufficed, criminal sanctions against perjury have always existed to deter litigants and witnesses from giving false testimonies under oath.[170] It has been a common practice to provide for procedural rules that allow the parties in a lawsuit to affirm their allegations under oath. This Section discusses a number of mechanisms to decide the case or matters of fact by a formalized oath taking.

Formal Oaths in Roman Law

In Roman law, there were possibilities for the parties to resolve (part of) the dispute by oath taking. Such oaths were not considered to be a means of proof.[171] The Justinian Digests indicate that the (decisory) oath is to be seen as a settlement between the parties to resolve the dispute or part of it.[172] It might be that parties had agreed to resolve their dispute by means of oath taking (*jusjurandum voluntarium*) or it was possible that one of the parties would request the other party to take the oath during the proceedings (*jusjurandum necessarium*). In both cases the oath was about

Gegenseite dabei behilflich zu sein, Zeugen oder andere Beweismittel ausfindig zu machen, darf für sich allein bei der Beweiswürdigung nicht zur Annahme führen, das verweigerte Beweismittel hätte für die befragte Partei Nachteile zutage gebracht. Inwieweit vertragliche, vorvertragliche oder sonstige Aufklärungspflichten anderen gegenüber stehen, ist nach materiellem Recht zu beurteilen; eine prozessuale Aufklärungspflicht ist aus §184 ZPO nicht abzuleiten'.

166 See for instance Sections 258(2), 289, 341 and 375 Code of Civil Procedure.

167 Fasching 1990, a 1200 page handbook on Civil Procedure, only makes two very short references to the provision.

168 Opzoomer & Levy 1906, p. 85.

169 Pitlo & Hidma 1981, p. 136-137.

170 See e.g. Article 207 Dutch Penal Code and Section 288 paragraph 1 Austrian Penal Code. The number of convictions for perjury is low, see: Nagel 1951, p. 7-14.

171 Kaser & Hackl 1996, §36.

172 D. 12.2.3.1, D. 12.2.3.2 and D. 12.2.3.7. Also see Silving 1959, p. 1339.

a legal or factual issue that was decisive for the controversy in question.[173] Roman law also allowed the judge to order one of the parties to take an oath to supplement incomplete proof (*jusjurandum judiciale*). Such an oath could properly be referred to as 'evidence' of the facts of the case.[174] The different ways of oath taking in Roman law were implemented - with some modifications - in the Romano-Canonical system of proof. Formal party oaths based on Roman law were important in medieval and modern European Continental procedures.

Formal Oaths in English Law

Formal oaths similar to those on the Continent were used in England in early medieval times in ecclesiastical and Admiralty cases.[175] However, formal oaths based on Roman law failed to have a lasting influence in Angelo-American law. Nevertheless, formal oaths were used in English civil litigation to resolve disputes. In medieval England, as in Germanic customary law, disputes were commonly disposed of by means of oath helpers, also known as compurgators.[176] A party was required to take an oath together with a number of compurgators to decide the case in his favor. These compurgators were generally not witnesses and did not testify under oath regarding matters of fact they had personally witnessed. Compurgators swore on the truthfulness of another person's oath. This mode of trial, referred to as 'wager of law', was a favored mode of trial until it steadily became less common and eventually exceptional in the 15th and 16th century. Throughout the 17th and 18th centuries, trial by wager of law was very rare. Parliament finally abolished it in 1833.[177]

Formal Party Oaths on the European Continent

The formal oaths of the Roman legal system served as a basis for the party oaths under the Romano-Canonical procedure.[178] Eventually, the formal oaths recognized in the Roman-Canonical procedural model were implemented in a number of national procedural systems, including Spain, France, Italy, Germany, the Scandinavian countries and Scotland.[179] In this Section, I will focus on the formal party oaths in Austria and the Netherlands.

In Austria and the Netherlands, the influence of Romano-Canonical procedure was decisive and explains the many similarities between the formal oaths.[180] The influence of customary law on the development of formal party oaths was limited.[181] Many German codifications adopted formal party oaths.[182] The Austrian

173 Millar 1923, p. 95.
174 Millar 1923, p. 96.
175 Helmholz 2004, p. 335-336 and Millar 1937, p. 454. In equity parties were examined, yet there was no clear equivalent of the Continental formal oaths, Macnair 1999, p. 219.
176 For the use of compurgators in Germanic law see Engelmann 1927, Book 1, §57.
177 This paragraph is based on Thayer 1898, p. 25-35 and Silving 1959, p. 1363-1370.
178 Litewsky 1999, p. 428 *et seq.*
179 Millar 1923, p. 102 and Oberhammer & Domej 2005.
180 D. 12.2-12.3. For the Netherlands, see: Anema 1940, Chapter VII; for Austria, see: Maelzer 1931, Chapters 1 and 2.
181 Anema 1940, Chapter VII, on Roman law, see Kaser & Hackl 1996, §36.

General Judicial Ordinance of 1781 had codified the formal oaths in Chapters 18-22 (Sections 203-237). The West Galician Ordinance contained similar provisions (Sections 275-289). Although there were some differences between both codifications, both recognized three sorts of oaths: the decisory oath, the supplementary oath and the estimatory oath.[183] Former Articles 1902-1982 of the Dutch Civil Code of 1838 contained various provisions on evidence, including provisions on the formal party oaths.[184] The Civil Code made a distinction between two types of oaths:[185] an oath directed by one party to the other, the decisory oath[186] and an oath directed by the court. The judge could *ex officio* order a party to take the supplementary oath or the estimatory oath.[187] For this discussion, the decisory oath and the supplementary oath are most relevant.

The decisory oath could be used as a means to resolve a dispute about facts. A party could direct the other party to take the oath with respect to a specific fact. If the other party agreed to do so, his statement was binding. If a party refused to take the oath, such a refusal would be construed against him.[188] Directing a decisory oath was something like an offer made by the party requesting such an oath to be rendered: If you, opposing party, are willing (or daring) to confirm under oath a certain matter of fact that I deny, then I will stick to your statement and it will be established as such. If not, the facts will be established in my advantage.[189] The fact that the decisory oath was binding implied that no rebuttal could be used against the oath. In the Netherlands - but not in Austria - a revision of the verdict was not even possible if it was later proven that perjury was committed.[190]

The decisory oath was generally taken only by a party with first hand knowledge of the facts.[191] The decisory oath was mostly used in cases where the party who requested the oath had little or no evidence and trusted his opponent's honesty. The decisory oath was useless if one's opponent was dishonest and did not fear God. A small example clarifies the working of the decisory oath: Person A requests person B to return 1,000,- guilders, which B borrowed from A. A gave the money to B but A cannot prove that B received the money. She orders B to take the

182 Maelzer 1931, Chapter 2.

183 See for a detailed description: Füger Von Rechtborn 1865. German and Latin terminology: Decisory oath: *Haupteid/Juramentum litis decisivum*. The supplementary oath: *Erfüllungseid/Juramentum suppletorium & purgatorium*. Estimatory oath: *Schätzungseid/Juramentum in litem*.

184 *Gerechtelijke eed*, Articles 1966-1982 of the Civil Code. The Dutch provisions were based on Articles 1357-1369 of the 1804 French Civil Code.

185 Former Article 1966 Dutch Civil Code.

186 Former Article 1967 Dutch Civil Code, *de beslissende/decisoire eed*.

187 Dutch terminology: *aanvullende eed* and the *schattingseed*.

188 A party could take the oath or refuse to take the oath, sometimes he could also 'redirect' the decisory oath (Section 1971 Dutch Civil Code, Section 205 Austrian General Judicial Ordinance).

189 Feith 1892, p. 14.

190 Compare former Article 382 Code of Civil Procedure and De Vrieze 1943 with Section 234 Austrian General Judicial Ordinance.

191 Former Article 1968 Dutch Civil Code and Anema 1940, p. 474. For Austria see Section 206 of the General Judicial Ordinance, Section 279 of the West Galician Ordinance and Füger Von Rechtborn 1865, p. 43-59.

decisory oath, hoping that B will respect the oath and speak the truth. B can choose between 4 options: 1) take the oath and honestly admit that A gave money to B (the fact that A gave money to B will be established accordingly and other evidence will not be needed); 2) take the oath, but falsely deny that he received money from A (the judge will hold that A has not given B any money, A will not be allowed to present counter evidence); 3) refuse to take the oath (the court will determine that A gave money to B without allowing counter evidence and without requiring further evidence) or 4) redirect the oath (the outcome of the case then depends on the oath taken by A).

The exact legal status of formal party oaths has been much disputed over time.[192] In line with Roman law, some regarded the decisory oath as a contract, others did not.[193] Similar to Roman law, the decisory oath was regarded as a means to resolve the dispute between the parties.[194] In Austria during the 17th century, formal party oaths functioned as a means to dispose of a claim or a defense.[195] Others regarded the judicial oath as a means of proof.[196] The Austrian codification of 1781 and the 1838 Dutch Code of Civil Procedure listed the decisory oath amongst the means of proof.[197]

The supplementary oath could also be used to provide evidence for a matter of fact. The older Austrian codifications held that the judge could only order the taking of the supplementary oath if such was suggested by the party who would take the oath.[198] If a party was unwilling to take an oath, this could be construed against him or her.[199] In the Netherlands, the judge could *ex officio* order one of the parties to take a supplementary oath in order to obtain evidence for a matter of fact.[200] The taking of the oath could only be ordered if other evidence was available but did not provide full proof.[201] The former Austrian codifications had specified that at least half evidence was needed (half proof).[202] Courts in the Netherlands and Austria could for instance order the supplementary oath if there was only a single reliable witness to prove a matter of fact.[203]

The judge could only order parties to take the supplementary oath. This could be very troublesome as many potential witnesses, such as family members of the parties, could not testify as witnesses due to exclusionary rules of evidence.[204]

192 Litewsky 1999, p. 430. This discussion already took place in medieval times.
193 On different theories about the legal status of the oath see Anema 1940, p. 457-464.
194 See e.g. Gratama Committee 1921b, p. 184.
195 Oberhammer 1999, footnote 10.
196 Feith 1892, p. 26, p. 30 and Pitlo & Hidma 1981, p. 139-142.
197 Endemann 1891, p. 282 and Münks 1992, §5.4, p. 62. Dutch courts have refused the taking of the decisory oath with respect to matters of law, Anema 1940, p. 472.
198 Section 212 General Judicial Ordinance and Section 286 West Galician Ordinance.
199 Section 213 General Judicial Ordinance and Section 287 West Galician Ordinance.
200 Former Article 1977 of the Civil Code.
201 Former Article 1979 of the Civil Code.
202 Section 212 General Judicial Ordinance and Section 286 West Galician Ordinance.
203 Dutch Court of Cassation, 3 April 1890, *W.* 5856 and Dutch Court of Cassation, 23 March 1956, *NJ* 1956, 253. See Section 137 *et seq.* Austrian General Judicial Ordinance.
204 See e.g. Section 141 Austrian General Judicial Ordinance.

Parties could only take the oath with respect to facts they personally experienced. The following example clarifies the problems parties could encounter:[205] Two vehicles collide and the plaintiff needs proof of the defendant's fault in order to obtain damages. The plaintiff's son drove the vehicle in question; the plaintiff himself was not present. Only one other witness saw the accident. His statement alone does not suffice. Neither the father nor the son could take the supplementary oath nor could either one of them be heard as a witness.[206]

The formal party oaths were not undisputed means of proof.[207] Most importantly, the formal party oaths were often seen as unsatisfactory means to decide matters of fact correctly.[208] Franz Klein regarded the formal oath - like ordeals and duels - as remnants of the irrational early medieval procedure.[209] The 1895 Austrian Code of Civil Procedure accordingly replaced the formal party oaths by a new system of party interrogation under oath. In the Netherlands, the formal party oaths were also criticized in the early 20th century. An unsuccessful 1920 draft Code of Civil Procedure suggested the abolition of the decisory oath.[210] Nonetheless, many continued to support the formal oaths. In 1951, a great majority of the members of the Dutch Association of Jurists (*NJV*, 1951) answered 'yes' when asked whether the decisory oath should be maintained as a means of proof.[211] Eventually, the formal party oaths would be abolished in the Netherlands by the Civil Evidence Act of 1988.

Although the formal oaths have been abolished in Austria and the Netherlands, there are at least two reasons why it is relevant to consider them. First, the formal oaths are still used in a number of European jurisdictions. A system of party oaths is still in force in many countries today, including France, Italy, Turkey and Belgium.[212] Nonetheless, it seems that in these countries the formal party oaths are not frequently used.[213] Second, the formal party oaths have thoroughly shaped much of the later regulations on the interrogation of parties, such as the present German and Dutch regulations. Many countries have been hesitant to enable the parties to testify as witnesses and have implemented 'half way' solutions. German,

205 Van Creveld 1940.

206 Later, a supplementary oath could be ordered if a party had not witnessed the facts, Dutch Court of Cassation, 3 January 1924, *NJ* 1924, 252.

207 For a summary of the critique see Star Busmann 1938, p. 619.

208 Feith 1892, p. 39.

209 Klein 1901, p. 123.

210 Gratama Committee 1921b, p. 183.

211 *HNJV* 1951, p. 79-81.

212 See Articles 1357-1369 French Civil Code; Article 2736 *et seq.* of the Italian Civil Code; Article 233 of the Italian Civil Code of Civil Procedure and Articles 1357-1369 of the Belgian Civil Code. The Turkish Code of Civil Procedure of 1927 had adopted both the supplementary oath and the decisory oath (*Hukuk Usulu Muhakemeleri Kanunu*, Articles 344-362). A new Code of Civil Procedure drafted in 2006 that will probably enter into force in the near future abolishes the supplementary oath but retains the decisory oath (*Hukuk Muhakemeleri Kanunu Tasarisi*, Articles 228-242).

213 I have failed to find reliable empirical data. Herzog 1967, §7.56 claims the oath is not used frequently in France. In private conversations, attorneys assured me the formal oaths were not used frequently in Italy and Belgium.

Dutch and Austrian law provide examples of jurisdictions in which the new rules on the testimony of parties have been influenced by the older rules on the taking of the oath. Current Section 445 of the German Code of Civil Procedure has striking similarities with the decisory oath. Similarly, Sections 447 and 448 of the German Code of Civil Procedure are modeled after the supplementary oath. Two provisions of the Austrian Code of 1895 also contain remnants of the old party oaths.[214] If parties wished to settle their case, Section 205 of the 1895 Code of Civil Procedure explicitly allowed the parties to decide that the outcome of the settlement would depend on the taking of an oath. This provision was abolished in 2002 as it was seldom used, but it had a clear resemblance with the decisory oath as understood in Roman law.[215] According to Section 273 Code of Civil Procedure, the judge may decide that the value of the claim would depend on the interrogation of a party under oath. Still in force today, this provision is clearly derived from the estimatory oath.

1.3.2. Hearing the Parties as Witnesses

The Incompetence of Parties to Testify

Many legal systems have made parties incompetent to testify as witnesses under oath. The Digest for instance had specified that no one is a satisfactory witness in his own case.[216] The Romano-Canonical model of procedure, as well as the English common law, did not allow parties to take the stand. Today, many legal systems do not allow parties to testify as witnesses in their own cases.[217] Fear of perjury has frequently been mentioned as an argument to refuse parties the right to testify.[218] Another argument is that parties have an interest in the outcome and may be inclined to give a dishonest testimony. Even if parties are not dishonest, psychological studies have demonstrated that our minds are 'inherently biased'. We tend to be more able to recall information that is favorable to us than information that is unfavorable.[219] Therefore, it has been argued that the testimony of parties is so unreliable that it is better not to consider it at all.

Rules that made parties incompetent to testify were generally part of a larger body of rules that banned certain categories of people from testifying as witnesses under oath. Those previously convicted for crimes, particularly perjury, were

214 More examples exist, see Section 60 and 307 Code of Civil Procedure.

215 962 BlgNr GP XXI, p. 27: 'Diese Form des Vergleichs ist heute völlig bedeutungslos geworden. (...) Die Regelungen sollen daher im Sinne einer Rechtsbereinigung aufgehoben werden'.

216 D. 22.5.10, Pomponius, Sabianus, Book 1.

217 Such as Italy, Belgium and France, see Van Rhee 2005b, Part 2B and M. Tarufo, as quoted in Chase, Herschkoff, Silberman, Taniguchi & Varano 2007, p. 262.

218 Perjury was considered a 'mortal sin'. See St. Thomas Aquinas, *Summa Theologica*, Second Part of the Second Part, Quest. 69, Article 1. It had to be avoided. Also see Litewsky 1999, p. 429 and Bodanksy 1981, p. 130.

219 See Bahrick, Hall & Berger 1996. This study measured whether students could recall their high school grades. Students could with great accuracy recall their A's but had more difficulties to recall their D's.

generally believed to be unfit to testify. The Romano-Canonical system held that various categories of witnesses, like close relatives of the parties, were unqualified to testify.[220] Similarly in England the rule that excluded parties as witnesses was intrinsically linked to a more general rule that made all those that had an interest in the case unqualified to testify.[221] According to Wigmore, the rule that banned parties from testifying in their own cases was established in the 16th century and was linked to the emergence of the 'jury trial' and the 'modern witness'.[222] In the mid 17th century, the rule that disqualified all parties-in-interest was established as a general expansion of the rule that disqualified parties.[223] Throughout the 18th and in the beginning of the 19th century, the rule that excluded parties from testifying continued to exist without much resistance.

The English legal system was the first European jurisdiction that made parties competent to testify as witnesses in their own case (1851). The Austrian legal system was - to my knowledge - the first modern jurisdiction on the European continent that abolished formal party oaths and allowed the testimony of parties to function as a means of proof (1895). The developments in England, the United States, Austria and the Netherlands, reveal that parties were increasingly questioned in a way similar to the examination of witnesses.[224]

Anglo-American Developments: Granting Parties the Right to Testify

Common law jurisdictions had traditionally disqualified those that had an interest in the case from testifying as witnesses. The system of exclusionary rules was increasingly criticized as truth distorting. Bentham argued that exclusionary rules were 'manifestly an extreme and a most disastrous remedy'.[225] Anglo-American jurisdictions were the first to remove rules that banned party witnesses.[226]

England took the first steps to remove exclusionary rules by the Lord Denman Act of 1843. Lord Denman had argued that incapacities to testify had obstructed the 'inquiry after truth', and that it was desirable that 'full information as to the facts in issue' should be laid before the trier of fact.[227] The Lord Denman Act abolished the rule that made convicts of serious criminal offences unqualified to testify. Similarly, those who had an interest in the case were no longer banned from giving testimony.

220 Alse see Section 141 of the 1781 Austrian General Judicial Ordinance and Articles 1933-1938 of the 1838 Dutch Civil Code.

221 Parties were generally excluded to testify; the rule could be evaded. Lord Mansfield referred cases to arbitration specifying that the parties would there be heard under oath, Langbein 1996, p. 1185.

222 For a more detailed account, critical of Wigmore's analysis, see Macnair 1999, p. 204.

223 Wigmore 1940, §575-576 and Bodanksy 1981 p. 92. On party disqualification in equity see Macnair 1999, p. 210.

224 Münks 1992 and Maelzer 1931.

225 See Benthams views as quoted and described by Allen 1997, p. 99. See Wigmore 1940, Vol. 2, §576-577. Bodanksy 1981, p. 99 concluded: 'Thus, the attack on the disqualification of parties was based primarily on the unsoundness of the common law exclusion in principle and the necessity of reform in the interest of discovering the truth and ensuring justice'.

226 For a history on these rules, see Wigmore 1940, Vol. 2, §575 and the opinion of Justice Brennan in *Ferguson v. Georgia*, 365 U.S. 570 (1961) at 573.

227 Lord Denman, preamble to the bill, as quoted by Allen 1997, p. 100-101.

The Lord Denman Act provided that any defendant in a chancery procedure might be examined on behalf of a plaintiff or co-defendant.[228] However, parties to a case remained unqualified to testify in the common law courts.

In order to enable parties to testify in the Common Law Courts, a 'Bill to enable Parties to be examined on the Trial of Civil Actions' was presented without success in 1845. More successful were the English County Court Acts of 1846; these Acts allowed parties to testify as witnesses in cases pending before these inferior courts.[229] An opinion poll conducted a couple of years later by the 'Law Amendment Society', showed that a great majority of the County Court judges was in favor of admitting the testimony of the parties as evidence. A new bill to allow parties to give evidence in the superior Courts of Common Law in England was prepared 1851. On the 1st of November 1851, the Act that enabled the parties to testify entered into force.[230]

Connecticut had been the first common law jurisdiction to remove all rules banning parties from taking the stand in 1849. It was, however, mostly the English example that invoked changes throughout the United States.[231] Within a number of years, the example set in Connecticut and England was followed in other jurisdictions.[232] The New York Field Code of 1848 had abolished the incompetence from interest, but parties were still left incompetent to testify in their own cases. The 1850 amended version of the Field Code made the parties competent to testify as witnesses as well. The Commissioners that drafted the 1850 Field Code made explicit reference to the developments in Connecticut and the works of Bentham as well as English reports of the 'Law Amendment Society'.[233] Section 1708 of the 1850 Code of Procedure read as follows:

> 'All persons, without exception, otherwise than as specified in the next two sections, who, having organs of sense, can perceive, and perceiving can make known their perceptions to others, may be witnesses. Therefore neither parties, nor persons who have an interest in the event of an action or proceeding, are excluded; nor those who have been convicted of crime; nor persons on account of their opinions on matters of religious belief: although in every case the credibility of the witness may be drawn in question, as provided in section 1680'.

Within a couple of decades, all American jurisdictions had followed the English example. Michigan abolished the rule that banned non-party witnesses with an interest in the outcome of the case as early as 1846.[234] In the Federal Courts, an 1864 Act of Congress rendered parties competent to testify in civil cases. By 1900, civil parties were competent to testify in their own case in all American jurisdictions.[235]

228 6 & 7 Vict. C. 85, §1 as quoted by Millar 1937, p. 442.
229 Section 83, 9 & 10 Vict. c 95 as quoted by Allen 1997, p. 102. Millar 1937, p. 448.
230 Allen 1997, Chapter 4, p. 110-122 discusses the Act in detail.
231 Bodanksy 1981, p. 105.
232 Field Code 1850, p. 715, comments after Section 1708.
233 Field Code 1850, p. 715-725.
234 Wigmore 1940, §576 p. 693.
235 Bodanksy 1981, p. 93.

Although the testimony of parties was no longer excluded, most American jurisdictions enacted new rules that excluded a survivor's testimony of a transaction with a decedent, when offered against the decedent's estate.[236] The rule is generally referred to as the 'Dead Man's Statute'. This rule can still bar a party in a suit from testifying in exceptional cases when the party litigates against the heirs of a deceased concerning the latter's estate. Dead Man's Statutes were enacted in most American jurisdictions at roughly the same time, often as part of the same statute that granted parties competency to testify.[237] Modern codifications, like the FRE, have not preserved the 'Dead Man's Statute'. However, the statute is still in force in a number of American jurisdictions.[238]

Party Interrogation as Evidence in Austria

Austria was, to my knowledge, the first Continental jurisdiction to abolish the rule that made parties incompetent to testify under oath. Austrian advancements in turn influenced other countries on the European Continent. Changes to the Continental codes generally involved many compromises. This led to the creation of two sets of rules: rules that applied to the examination of witnesses and slightly different rules that applied to the examination of parties. The latter set of rules often had some resemblance to the formal party oaths.

In Austria, the academic Glaser was the first to propose the abolition of the formal party oaths.[239] Glaser was inspired by American law and the English Civil Evidence Act of 1851.[240] Glaser became the Austrian minister of Justice in 1871 and implemented his ideas in the 1873 Law on the Proceedings in Petty Causes (*Bagatellverfahren*). The 1873 Act declared that the formal party oaths were not applicable.[241] The judge could order the hearing of parties as witnesses on request of a party or *ex officio* if insufficient evidence was presented by the parties.[242] The testimony of parties was under oath and aimed to provide evidence. Criminal law penalties which applied in case of perjury did not apply to parties who testified under oath.[243] There were mixed feelings about the success of the novelties introduced by the 1873 Act.[244] Nevertheless, the 1876, 1881 and 1893 Drafts for a new Austrian Code of Civil Procedure had proposed preserving and extending the possibilities for the parties testify.[245] The early legislation and drafts paved the way for the abolition of the formal party oaths by the 1895 Code of Civil Procedure.[246]

236 Wigmore 1940, §578.

237 Bodanksy 1981, p. 105 and Wigmore 1940 § 488 and 578.

238 Best 2004, §578. It has been abolished by other states, sometimes already in the 19th century, see Sunderland 1932, p. 868 and the references to state law there mentioned.

239 See Oberhammer 1999 for a discussion of the works of Glaser.

240 Oberhammer 1999, p. 298-299 and Maelzer 1931, §6, p. 36.

241 Section 65, Law on the Proceedings in Petty Causes.

242 Section 53, Law on the Proceedings in Petty Causes.

243 Section 58, Law on the Proceedings in Petty Causes.

244 Materialien 1897, p. 324-325.

245 Klein & Engel 1927, p. 364 and Maelzer 1931, §6, p. 37.

246 The Explanatory Memorandum of the 1895 Code explicitly referred to experiences with the Law on the Proceedings in Petty Causes, Materialien 1897, p. 323-325.

Klein rejected formal party oaths because they would be a product of religious ideology rather than reason.[247] Furthermore, he believed that these oaths did not fit into a legal system that proclaimed a free evaluation of evidence.[248] Klein had a positive attitude towards the English law with respect to the interrogation of parties and the interrogation of parties under the 1873 law on the proceedings on petty causes (*Bagatellverfahren*).[249] The 1895 Code of Civil Procedure abolished the formal party oaths. The final wording of the rules was a carefully formulated compromise between the party oaths on the one hand and free interrogation of parties as witnesses on the other hand.[250] Unlike English law and the Law on the Proceedings in Petty Causes, the 1895 Code did not allow parties to be heard as witnesses. Instead the 'party interrogation' (*Parteivernehmung*) was introduced as a separate means of proof.[251]

Most provisions that apply to the hearing of witnesses also apply to the hearing of parties.[252] In many respects 'party interrogation' differed from 'examination of witnesses'. The most important distinctive features of party interrogation will be discussed below.[253] First, the interrogation of parties consisted of two stages. In the first obligatory stage parties would be freely interrogated without being under oath.[254] If the judge believed the free interrogation did not suffice to determine the truth of a statement of fact, the judge could proceed to the second (optional) stage and order the interrogation of a party under oath.[255]

Second, party interrogation was a 'subsidiary' means of proof. The interrogation by itself could not provide full proof for a matter of fact.[256] This rule is a remnant of the medieval practice, in which the supplementary oath would provide 'half proof'. Furthermore, 'party interrogation' was considered to be a means of proof that would only be needed if other evidence was inconclusive.[257] The interrogation of parties could be ordered only if the judge was still undecided on a matter of fact after all other evidence had been presented.

The third remarkable feature of party interrogation is that only one of the parties could be interrogated under oath. Although both parties should in principle

247 Klein 1901, p. 123.

248 Klein & Engel 1927, p. 264-266.

249 Klein 1891, p. 41 and Klein & Engel 1927, p. 364: 'Diese Erfahrungen waren solche, dass keine Notwendigkeit vorlag, dieses Vorhaben aufzugeben'.

250 Klein 1900, p. 171.

251 Klein 1900, p. 172.

252 Sections 375(1), 377 and 380(1) Austrian Code of Civil Procedure. On criminal law sanctions, also see Chapter 21 Austrian Criminal Code (*Strafgesetzbuch*, StGB) and Section 377(3) Code of Civil Procedure. Spenling in Fasching & Konecny 2002-2005, Section 371, No. 5 and Klein 1900, Chapter 8.

254 Section 367 Code of Civil Procedure.

255 Section 377(1) Code of Civil Procedure.

256 Section 371(2) Code of Civil Procedure.

257 Materialien 1897, II. p. 325.

be interrogated in the 'first stage' of party interrogation,[258] only one of them could testify under oath.[259]

The last distinctive feature of the interrogation of parties is that parties could not be physically compelled to appear in court in order to testify.[260] This rule presently still exists. If a party, without a valid justification,[261] refuses to appear in court or refuses to give a (truthful) answer to questions, the judge will take this into account when freely evaluating all evidence.[262]

Statistical material is available on the use of the party interrogation under oath in 1900 and 1910.[263] In 1900, a party interrogation under oath was ordered in 17% of all defended cases before the courts of first instance. In 1910, an interrogation of parties was ordered in approximately 10% of all defended cases. The total number of party interrogations must have been (much) larger, as the hearing under oath is only the optional second stage of the party interrogation. An explanation for the fact that the interrogation of parties under oath gradually became less popular is that judges increasingly felt they were not impartial if they only heard one party under oath.[264] It seems that the first stage of the party interrogation continued to be used frequently in legal practice throughout the 20th century.

The 1983 Austrian Reform Act made two significant amendments to the rules on the interrogation of parties. First, the 1983 reform abolished the subsidiary character of party interrogation. This change has generally been received well in literature.[265] The main argument in favor of the procedural reform in this respect is that the subsidiary party interrogation does not fit into a system in which evidence is freely evaluated by the judge. Secondly, the 1983 reform made it possible to interrogate both parties under oath. The Reform Act removed the features of party interrogation which were most clearly influenced by the supplementary oath. The Act demonstrated a true break with the Romano-Canonical heritage in the area of party interrogation.[266]

In present day Austrian practice, the interrogation of parties plays an important role. The judge determines the order in which parties will be heard. The judge may order the interrogation of the parties *ex officio*, but usually the court does so after one of the parties has suggested it as a means of proof in their written

258 Section 376(2) Code of Civil Procedure. The judge was not obliged to hear both parties and neither party had a right to be interrogated, Materialien 1897, p. 325.

259 Section 377(2) Code of Civil Procedure. Even on appeal, the other party could not be heard under oath, Section 489(1) Code of Civil Procedure.

260 Sections 333(1) and 380(3) Code of Civil Procedure.

261 No sanctions are imposed if there are good reasons not to attend a hearing, e.g. being in hospital. Austrian Supreme Court, 30 October 1989, Geschäftszahl 6 Ob 688/89 and Supreme Court, 26 May 1961, Geschäftszahl 2 Ob 212/61, EvBl 1961/437 S 554 = RZ 1961,183: 'Nur wenn die Partei zur Vernehmung nicht erscheinen wollte, tritt Beweiswürdigung nach § 381 ZPO ein'.

262 Section 381 Code of Civil Procedure.

263 Klein & Engel 1927, Table 11, p. 373.

264 Klang 1948.

265 Oberhammer 1999, p. 300.

266 Nevertheless, Sections 60, 307, 273 and 274 of the current Code of Civil Procedure are remnants of the party oaths.

pleadings.[267] Generally, the interrogation of the parties takes place at the beginning of the proceedings before the taking of other evidence. Since the 2002 reform, the Code explicitly mentions that parties may be interrogated at the first preparatory hearing (*vorbereitende Tagessatzung*).[268] It is not uncommon for the court, when inviting the parties to attend the preparatory hearing, to indicate that the court has the intention of interrogating them.[269] Usually both parties will be heard during the proceeding.[270] The judge may choose not to hear one party, for instance if that party has no relevant information about the facts that require evidence.[271] The judge will start the interrogation by instructing the parties that they have a duty to be truthful and that they may be heard on the matter under oath.[272] In the present Austrian practice, the taking of the oath after a free interrogation of the parties seldom occurs.[273] Although the judge will generally first put questions to a party, each party has the right to formulate questions which the judge can subsequently put to the opposing party. With leave of the court, a party is also allowed to directly question his opponent.[274] The judge may set aside inappropriate questions.[275] Usually an attorney will put questions directly to the opposing party. In legal practice the interrogation of parties offers a very good opportunity for both the judge and attorneys to question a party in the proceeding.

The Influence of the Austrian Regulations on Party Interrogation

The English changes were generally viewed with interest in Continental jurisdictions, yet were often considered to be too radical. Legislators have been hesitant to allow parties to take the stand as witnesses and testify under oath. Even in Europe today, one finds many regulations on party interrogation that do not allow parties to testify under oath.[276] The 1895 Austrian provisions on party interrogation were often considered to be a reasonable alternative and have been transplanted to other European countries.

267 Spenling in Fasching & Konecny 2002-2005, §371, No. 14-16. Usually, the interrogation of parties is shortly abbreviated to PV. Parties generally have the right to be heard, Sections 372 and 275 Austrian Code of Civil Procedure.

268 See Section 258(1)(5) Code of Civil Procedure.

269 Rechberger & Simotta 2009, No. 819, p. 438: 'Heute werden die Parteien regelmäßig gleich zu Beginn des Beweisverfahrens vernommen (...)'.

270 Section 376(2) Code of Civil Procedure. Oberhammer 1999, p. 300: '(...) Es wird (...) als Wohltat empfunden, dass heute in praktisch jedem Prozeß am Anfang des Beweisverfahrens (...) beide Parteien vernommen werden'.

271 Section 374 Code of Civil Procedure.

272 Sections 376(2), 340(1) Code of Civil Procedure and Rechberger & Simotta 2009, No. 822, p. 439.

273 Rechberger & Simotta 2009, No. 822, p. 439: 'die Beeidigung der Partei ist heute selten geworden'. Spenling mentions that the taking of an oath is the exception rather than the rule. Spenling in Fasching & Konecny 2002-2005, §376, No. 1.

274 Sections 289, 341 and 375 Code of Civil Procedure.

275 Section 289(1) Code of Civil Procedure.

276 See e.g. Article 992 of the Belgian Judicial Code and Chapter 37 of the Swedish Code of Judicial Procedure.

In Norway, the 1915 Code of Civil Procedure adapted rules on the interrogation of parties that closely mirrored those in Austria. As in Austria, the regulation enabled the interrogation of parties upon motion by the other party or pursuant to a court order. The rules on witnesses applied, but direct sanctions could not be imposed on the parties. The Norwegian Code of 1915 did not adopt a rule that exempted the testimony of parties from the free evaluation of evidence.[277] A new Norwegian Code that has been recently introduced still provides that rules on the examination of witnesses apply to the interrogation of parties. The interrogation of parties is still regulated in a separate Chapter of the Code.[278]

The 1916 Danish Code of Civil Procedure also adopted rules inspired by the Austrian rules on party interrogation.[279] The Danish rules were more party driven; the interrogation of parties was only available upon a motion raised by the other party and the parties and their lawyers were more active when examining both parties and witnesses. Furthermore, the Danish examination of parties was not regarded as a subsidiary means of proof and could be ordered before the examination of other evidence. The rules on formal party oaths were, however, not abolished in 1916.

In Germany, the formal party oaths were abolished in 1933 and replaced by rules on party interrogation that were clearly inspired by the Austrian Code of Civil Procedure.[280] The German provisions that recognize party interrogation as a separate and subsidiary means of proof have remained in force.[281]

Croatia, formerly part of Yugoslavia, thoroughly revised its procedural rules in 2003.[282] Presently, the hearing of parties in Croatia is considered to be a subsidiary means of proof that may only be used if there is no other evidence or if other evidence is not conclusive.[283] The rules on the interrogation of witnesses also apply to the interrogation of parties. Parties do not testify under oath and direct coercive sanctions may not be applied against parties who are unwilling to appear in court or answer questions.[284]

In Poland, Austrian influence was very strong in the first half of the 20th century. Presently, Article 299 of the Polish Code of Civil Procedure states that: 'after all evidence has been examined and the judge has insufficient knowledge to rule on relevant facts, the judge may decide to hear the parties in order to clarify

277 Wrede 1923.

278 Chapter 23 Norwegian Code of Civil Procedure. A translation of the Code is available at <www.ub.uio.no/ujur/ulovdata/lov-20050617-090-eng.pdf>, last consulted in February 2010.

279 Wrede 1923.

280 See Maelzer 1931 and Oberhammer 1999, p. 301, for a general discussion of the 1933 reform.

281 Sections 445-448 of the German Code of Civil Procedure.

282 Although the Croatian Code was amended since 2003, its provisions on party interrogation have remained unchanged.

283 Article 264, Croatian Code of Civil Procedure: '(...) The court may decide to provide evidence by hearing the parties when there is no other evidence or when despite the presentation of other evidence it establishes that this is necessary to ascertain important facts'.

284 Articles 269-271 Croatian Code of Civil Procedure.

these facts'.[285] The Polish Code specifies that provisions that apply to the examination of witnesses also apply to the examination of parties. Direct compulsory sanctions, such as imprisonment, may not be imposed on the parties.[286]

The Netherlands: Parties Testifying as Witnesses

The Dutch Code of 1838 did not explicitly prohibit the parties from testifying as witnesses. It was considered to be self evident that parties were not fit to testify as witnesses.[287] Courts were often faced with difficult practical questions such as: who exactly is a party in the proceedings? In 1916, the Court of Cassation decided that the manager of a firm, who acts on behalf of the firm in the proceedings, had to be identified with the firm such that he could be regarded as a party in the proceedings. This implied that the testimony of a manager was inadmissible, although the manager was not a party in the proceeding.[288] Similarly, a mayor could not testify in a case in which the municipality formally was a party to the law suit.[289] Conversely, other case law specified that if a creditor had gone bankrupt, he could testify in a case in which the 'curator' was the formal party.[290] It seemed one could testify if one had transferred an obligation to someone else. Some argued that flexibility was needed to prevent parties from dodging the rules by transferring one's claim.[291]

Both English and Austrian regulations that allowed parties to testify under oath were widely discussed. In a contribution to the law journal *Themis* in 1898, an anonymous author drew attention to the English rules that enabled parties to testify. The author was positive towards these English developments and regarded them as a good example for the Netherlands.[292] Some of the unsuccessful drafts for a new Code of Civil Procedure in the early 20th century showed a strong influence of the Austrian Code of Civil Procedure. A 1911 Draft proposed allowing the judge to use the statements of parties, their absence, their refusal to answer or the fact that they dodge questions, as evidence.[293] A 1912 Draft allowed parties to take an oath with respect to their statements after they had been informally heard.[294] A 1920 Draft proposed abolishing the judicial oath and amending the 'supplementary

285 Article 299 Polish Code of Civil Procedure: 'Jeżeli po wyczerpaniu środków dowodowych lub w ich braku pozostały nie wyjaśnione fakty istotne dla rozstrzygnięcia sprawy, sąd dla wyjaśnienia tych faktów zarządzi dowód z przesłuchania stron'.

286 Article 304(2) Polish Code of Civil Procedure.

287 Veegens & Oppenheim 1921, p. 429. Also see Van Bell 1866, p. 89, discussing witness disqualifications but not even noting that parties could not take the stand.

288 Court of Cassation, 28 April 1916, W. 9977: 'De directeur eener N.V.(...) te beschouwen als partij in het geding'.

289 Court of Cassation, 26 January 1928, W. 11786, *NJ* 1928, 671 and Court of Cassation, 9 January 1942, *NJ* 1942, 302.

290 *HNJV* 1951, p. 30.

291 Van Creveld 1959.

292 Anonymous 1898, p. 368-369.

293 Article 127 of the 1911 Draft Code of Civil Procedure of the Dutch Association of Jurists (*NJV*).

294 Article 65 of the Draft Code of Civil Procedure of the Liberal Democratic Union (*VDB*).

oath'.[295] According to this draft, the judge was required to freely interrogate both parties before the judge would decide whether or not to require one party to take an oath.[296]

There seemed to be little support amongst jurists for granting parties the right to testify.[297] Often, it was not even considered an issue. A 1901 proposal to change the law of evidence simply noted that the roles of parties and witnesses exclude each other; no further argumentation was needed.[298] Between 1878 and 1951 the Dutch Association of Jurists thrice discussed the hearing of parties in civil cases at its annual conference. On each occasion, members of the association were asked whether parties should be qualified to take the stand as a witness. On each occasion, a large majority of the members present voted against hearing parties as witnesses.[299]

Legislative proposals to review the rules of evidence in 1959 and 1969 refused parties the right to testify as witnesses.[300] In 1970, a report of a joint Committee of the Judiciary and the Dutch Bar Association advised the Government that parties should be allowed to act as witnesses. Arguments that the parties would give biased testimony were not viable according to the Committee. After all, other witnesses might not be fully impartial either. The Committee stressed the importance of the pursuit of truth as its main justification for its controversial proposal.[301] The discussion that followed would delay the introduction of the Civil Evidence Act for almost two more decades.[302]

According to many, the most important argument for allowing parties to take the stand was that it would remove potential inequality between them.[303] Suppose that two individuals (a natural person and an employee of a corporation) had a conversation which would later prove to be decisive in a legal dispute. In the civil case, the natural person would not be competent to testify whereas the employee, not formally a party, could testify. Therefore, one party would have evidence available, whereas the other party would not. Such a case was brought before the European Court of Human Rights in 1993. In the so-called 'Dombo case', the ECtHR

295 Gratama, who chaired the commission that drafted the Code, had at an earlier occasion fiercely argued against granting parties the right to testify, *HNJV*, 1915, p. 31-32.

296 Gratama Committee 1921b, p. 186.

297 De Tombe-Grootenhuis 1993, p. 22.

298 Feith Committee 1901, p. 131.

299 In 1878, 55 out of 61 members of the Dutch Association of Jurists voted against hearing parties as witnesses. *HNJV* 1878, vraag 2. Further see *HNJV*, 1915, p. 30-31. In 1951 a large majority of the members of the association voted that the decisory oath should be maintained as a means of proof. Furthermore, members also voted to preserve the supplementary oath, see *HNJV*, 1951, p. 79-81.

300 See in general Section 2.3.2.2.

301 'Commissie van advies van de Nederlandse Vereniging voor de Rechtspraak en de Nederlandse Orde van Advocaten'. Appendix of *Advocatenblad*, 15 June 1970, p. 5, p. 7.

302 See *inter alia:* Pos 1971; Gras & Wiersema 1986; Crèvecouer 1975; Rutgers, Flach & Boon 1988, p. 174; Hartogh 1965 and Drabbe 1965.

303 Rutgers, Flach & Boon 1988, p. 175. Similar conclusions have been drawn in other jurisdictions. See for instance *Ferguson v. Georgia*, 365 U.S. 570 (1961) at 570-571, 577-578, Bodanksy 1981, p. 93.

concluded that there was a violation of the principle of 'equality of arms' as laid down in Article 6 of the European Convention of Human Rights.[304] 'Equality of arms', the Court rephrased, implied that 'each party must be afforded a reasonable opportunity to present his case - including his evidence - under conditions that do not place him at a substantial disadvantage vis-à-vis his opponent'.[305] The court continued:

> '34. In the instant case, it was incumbent upon the applicant company to prove that there was an oral agreement between it and the Bank to extend certain credit facilities. Only two persons had been present at the meeting at which this agreement had allegedly been reached, namely Mr van Reijendam representing the applicant company and Mr van W. representing the Bank. Yet only one of these two key persons was permitted to be heard, namely the person who had represented the Bank. The applicant company was denied the possibility of calling the person who had represented it, because the Court of Appeal identified him with the applicant company itself.
> 35. During the relevant negotiations Mr van Reijendam and Mr van W. acted on an equal footing, both being empowered to negotiate on behalf of their respective parties. It is therefore difficult to see why they should not both have been allowed to give evidence. The applicant company was thus placed at a substantial disadvantage vis-à-vis the Bank and there has accordingly been a violation of Article 6 §1'.

Similar situations could occur if an employee litigated against his or her employer, or if one litigated against someone (i.e. an insurance company) who had obtained an obligation by transfer. A possible inequality of arms seems to be inherent to a system which does not allow parties to testify. De Tombe-Grootenhuis had studied 211 Dutch cases resolved in 1990 in which a party was heard as a witness.[306] In 109 of these, a natural person litigated against a legal person. According to De Tombe-Grootenhuis, if natural persons were not qualified to testify, an inequality could have arisen in 107 of these 109 cases.[307]

The 1988 Civil Evidence Act abolished the formal party oaths and made parties competent to testify as witnesses. Contrary to the Austrian Code of Civil Procedure, the Dutch Code did not consider the interrogation of parties to be a separate means of proof. Nevertheless, the rules on witnesses contained some exceptions and provisions that applied to parties only. Like in the Austrian Code of 1895, traces of the formal party oaths influenced the new legislation. Article 164(2) Code of Civil Procedure currently specifies that parties are qualified to testify but also contains an additional rule that applies to parties only:[308]

304 European Court of Human Rights, 27 October 1993, Publ. CEDH, série A, Vol. 274, *NJ* 1994, 534.

305 European Court of Human Rights, 27 October 1993, *NJ* 1994, 534, 33.

306 De Tombe-Grootenhuis 1993, Chapter 5.

307 De Tombe-Grootenhuis 1993, Section 7.1.

308 Translation based on Hebly 1992. Former Article 213 Code of Civil Procedure: 'Artikel 164 (1) Ook partijen kunnen als getuigen optreden. (2) Indien een partij als getuige is gehoord kan haar verklaring omtrent door haar te bewijzen feiten geen bewijs in haar voordeel opleveren, tenzij de verklaring strekt ter aanvulling van onvolledig bewijs. (3)…'.

> 'Article 164 (1) Parties are also qualified to testify as witnesses. (2) If a party has been examined as a witness, his or her testimony cannot serve to provide full proof for the allegations that party is required to prove, unless the examination serves to supplement other incomplete evidence. (3) (...)'

Thus, the witness statement of a party has a limited probative value. Article 164(2) of the Code seems to be a remnant of the supplementary oath which only provided 'half proof'. The Court of Cassation has further explained the meaning of the provision. First, it should be noted that the restriction does not apply to rebuttal evidence. A sole witness statement of a party can be sufficient to rebut evidence presented by the other party.[309] Furthermore, the rule also applies if there are two or more plaintiffs or defendants all of whom testify in favor of a certain fact.[310] There are a variety of 'tricks' that can be applied to dodge Article 164(2). One may put a party's statement down in writing and submit it as documentary evidence which can be freely evaluated by the court.[311] Likewise, it is possible to transfer one's claim prior to litigation and subsequently be summoned as a 'normal' witness in the proceedings.[312] However, it seems Article 164(2) Code of Civil Procedure has little practical impact. Without it, judges probably would not often base their decision on the testimony of a single party witness either.

There have been (and there still are) objections against the limited evidentiary value of the witness statements of parties. The main objection deals with the fact that the rule could infringe upon the principle of equality of arms. For this reason, it was unsuccessfully suggested that Article 164(2) of the Code be abolished in 2002.[313] The Dutch Court of Cassation has held that Article 164(2) does not violate Article 6 of the European Convention of Human Rights, yet recognizes that there can be circumstances in which the application of the provision can lead to a violation of Article 6.[314] Similar discussions exist in Germany; the German party interrogation is also a subsidiary means of proof and it has been argued that this could violate Article 6 of the Convention.[315]

As in Austria, the Dutch legislature did not wish to impose direct compulsory sanctions on the parties. Parties have a duty to testify if they are summoned, yet they cannot be forced to do so.[316] Unlike other witnesses, parties, cannot be detained

309 Court of Cassation, 7 April 2000, *NJ* 2001, 32.

310 Fernhout 2005.

311 Court of Cassation, 24 January 2003, *NJ* 2003, 166 and Court of Cassation, 2 May 2003, *NJ* 2003, 468.

312 Court of Cassation, 24 June 2005, *LJN* AT2449.

313 Van Mierlo & Bart 2002, p. 34, 362.

314 Court of Cassation, 13 April 2001, *NJ* 2002, 391, r.o. 3.4 . Also see the opinion of the Advocate General, r.o. 3.16 of Court of Cassation, 15 April 2005, *NJ* 2005, 272. 'dat er omstandigheden kunnen zijn waarin de toepassing van de bepaling wel in strijd kan zijn met art. 6 EVRM'. See Court of Cassation, 11 February 2000, *NJ* 2001, 526 and Court of Cassation, 10 August 2001, *NJ* 2001, 526.

315 See Oberhammer 1999, p. 308-311 and the literature there mentioned. German Code of Civil Procedure Sections 445 *et seq.* Oberhammer & Domej 2005; Rosenberg, Schwab & Gottwald 2004, §122.

316 Explanatory Memorandum, Rutgers, Flach & Boon 1988, p. 176.

in prison if they refuse to testify.[317] If parties refuse to testify, indirect sanctions will be applied; normally this means that the judge will draw adverse inferences.[318]

Depositions in Dutch Law

Depositions to perpetuate testimony before the commencement of the action under FRCP Rule 27 will be granted if the court is satisfied 'that the testimony may prevent a failure or delay of justice'. Similar rules exist in the Netherlands; providing for the 'preliminary hearing of witnesses'. The Dutch rules are interesting as they effectively allow for a broad discovery of information prior to the commencement of the action. The Dutch rules on depositions before the initiation of the action are in fact more liberal than their U.S. counterparts.

In the Netherlands, it has been possible for a long time to hear witnesses before litigation commences or before the court orders the production of evidence.[319] Traditionally, depositions in the Netherlands were not widely available and only aimed to avoid loss of information that would otherwise be unavailable. Article 876 of the 1838 Code of Civil Procedure allowed prospective parties to hear witnesses of fact prior to litigation. A party could request the judge to hear a witness prior to the initiation of the action if the witness was very old, seriously ill, about to leave the country, or because of other reasons the judge believed to be valid. The courts generally restricted the application of Article 876 of the Code.[320]

In legal literature, it was argued that a wider use of depositions could help parties to be better informed about their respective positions.[321] Accordingly, the possibilities of hearing witnesses prior to litigation have been widened by law in 1951.[322] From 1951 onwards, witnesses could be heard prior to litigation. The rule aimed at enabling parties to make informed decisions about settlement or filing a case. The Explanatory Memorandum explains:

> 'In order to avoid proceedings based on incorrect knowledge of facts and to avoid unnecessary factual debates, it is desirable to allow the parties before the commencement of the action, by means of depositions, to verify the factual basis of the dispute: apart from reducing unnecessary delay, this offers the advantage that the clarification of the facts will perhaps allow parties to make a more accurate estimate of their odds of winning a case and will hence make parties more willing to settle the dispute'.[323]

317 Former Article 199 Code of Civil Procedure, Article 173(2) Code of Civil Procedure.

318 Former Articles 205(4) and 213(2) Code of Civil Procedure, Article 164 Code of Civil Procedure.

319 I have chosen to refer to the Dutch 'voorlopig getuigenverhoor', which literally means 'preliminary hearing of witnesses', as 'depositions'. These depositions strongly differ from depositions in U.S. federal law. A judge is always present at a Dutch 'deposition'.

320 Court of Cassation, 16 January 1928, W. 11786, *NJ* 1928, 329. Star Busmann 1955, No. 283.

321 Bloemers 1948.

322 Act of 18 July 1951, *Official State Journal* (Stb.), 302.

323 Tweede Kamer, Zitting 1949-1950, 1585, No. 3, p. 3: 'Ten einde op een onjuiste grondslag gebaseerde procedures en onnodige debatten (...) te vermijden, is het wenselijk procespartijen in staat te stellen voor de aanvang van het geding door voorlopige getuigenverhoren de →

The 1951 Act marked a shift in the objectives and availability of depositions. Although there have been some minor changes since 1951, the provisions it introduced are still in place today.[324] Since 1951, the Court of Cassation has confirmed that the hearing of witnesses prior to litigation aims not only to preserve evidence but also 1) to give possible future litigants an opportunity to clarify factual issues before litigation in order to make informed choices or 2) to know against whom a claim could be addressed.[325] It must be noted that depositions in the Netherlands always take place before a judge.

The regulations that apply to the hearing of witnesses also apply to the taking of depositions.[326] Depositions are usually taken before the commencement of the action, but the court may also, on a party's motion, order the taking of a deposition during the proceeding.[327] Although the law states that the judge 'may' order a deposition, case law has held that the judge 'must' order a deposition if the request is not abusive[328] and certain conditions have been met.[329] If one requests the court to order a deposition, one should specify with sufficient detail: 1) the prospective claim; 2) the issues on which the witness should be questioned and 3) that the deposition is relevant to a prospective claim.[330] The requirements for detail and identification of issues in the request aim to avoid 'abuse' and 'fishing expeditions'.[331] Nevertheless, it is claimed that depositions serve to engage in fishing expedition in Dutch legal practice.[332]

Once parties could testify as witnesses, prospective parties could be summoned as witnesses before the commencement of the proceedings.[333] The availability of depositions as a matter of right has empowered parties to question their prospective opponents in a lawsuit before the commencement of an action. Although the judge will normally put questions to the interrogated party, the party

feitelijke grondslag van het geschil te doen vaststellen: dat biedt, behalve de vermijding van onnodige vertraging, het voordeel dat opheldering omtrent de feiten allicht procespartijen tot een juistere waardering van hun proceskansen en daardoor gemakkelijker tot schikking zal leiden'.

324 In 1988 the provision was codified in Article 214. Since the 2002 reform the provision is codified in Article 186 Code of Civil Procedure. There were only minor changes to the content.

325 Court of Cassation, 24 March 1995, *NJ* 1998, 414 r.o. 3.4.4.

326 Article 189 Code of Civil Procedure, Former Article 217 Code of Civil Procedure.

327 Article 186 (2) Code of Civil Procedure.

328 Court of Cassation, 11 February 2005, *NJ* 2005, 442 and Court of Cassation, 21 November 2008, *LJN* BF 3938.

329 Court of Cassation, 19 February 1993, *NJ* 1994, 345 and Court of Cassation, 6 June 2008, *LJN*: BC3354.

330 Article 187(3) Code of Civil Procedure, Court of Cassation, 24 June 1988, *NJ* 1989, 121, Court of Cassation, 13 September 2002, *RvdW* 2002, 135, Paragraph 3.1.3 and Court of Cassation 19 March 2010, *LJN*: BK8146. Also see the opinion of E.M. Wesseling-van Gent, Court of Cassation, 6 June 2008, *LJN*: BC3354, R07/117HR at 2.3.

331 Dutch Court of Cassation, 29 October 2004, *LJN*: AR4980, *JOL* 2004, 713.

332 Klaassen 2009, p. 61.

333 Former Article 220, current Article 193 Code of Civil Procedure. Before 1988 one could not hear parties before the commencement of the action. For an early plea to create regulations that would allow the questioning of a prospective opponent party, see Drabbe 1962.

who requested the deposition determines the issues that will be addressed, and may as a matter of right question the (prospective) opponent.[334]

2. Principles and Comparative Analysis

2.1. *The Practice of Party Interrogation*

This Section provides empirical data on the most frequently used mechanisms of party interrogation. A concise overview of the available empirical data is restricted to the personal appearance of the parties in the Netherlands and discovery in U.S. District Courts. Both mechanisms are used on a much broader scale than the examination of the parties as witnesses at an evidentiary hearing. After all, the presentation of evidence takes place in only a small minority of cases. A brief discussion of the available empirical data is useful to enhance our understanding of the operation and effectiveness of legal rules in practice. In addition, these data support the claim that both jurisdictions have adopted fundamentally different mechanisms of pretrial party interrogation.

2.1.1. The Frequency, Length and Duration of Party Interrogation

Use of United States' Discovery Provisions

Several studies have shed light on the degree in which discovery is used in American legal practice. A 1978 study of the Federal Judicial Center, involving more than 3,000 federal cases, revealed that no formal discovery was conducted in 52% of all cases and 72% of all cases had no more than two discovery events. Fewer than 5% of the cases studied involved more than ten discovery requests.[335] Similarly, the Civil Litigation Research Project reviewed 1,649 cases that were concluded by five different U.S. District Courts in 1978. This study showed that discovery events took place in less than half of the cases.[336] A study by the NCSC on the basis of data from five state courts between 1990 and 1993 revealed that discovery took place in 58% of all cases.[337] The study showed that in 14% of the cases involving discovery, the number of discovery requests was eleven or more.[338] A 1996 RAND report - based on 1992 and 1993 data - aimed to evaluate the 1990 Civil Justice Reform Act by comparing data from 20 different District Courts. The study showed that 80% of the time spent by lawyers on discovery was spent in cases that lasted longer than 270 days.[339] In cases that were terminated within 270 days, little or no discovery took place.[340]

334 Article 179(2) Code of Civil Procedure.

335 See a study by Connolly *et al.* as discussed by McKenna & Wiggins 1998, p. 790 and Mullenix 1993. p. 1434-1435.

336 Trubek, Sarat, Felstiner, Kritzer and Grossman 1983, p. 89-90.

337 See the study by Keilitz *et al.*, as discussed by Mullenix 1993, p. 1441.

338 See the study by Keilitz *et al.*, as discussed by Mullenix 1993, p. 1440.

339 Kakalik, Hensler, McCaffrey, Oshiro, Pace & Vaiana 1996, Table 2.1.

340 McKenna & Wiggins 1998, p. 970.

The Columbia Survey, based on data in the early 1960s, concluded that oral depositions and interrogatories were the most frequently used discovery devices.[341] A study by the Federal Judiciary Center in 1978 confirmed this finding and showed that depositions and interrogatories were most often used, followed by document requests. Other discovery devices together accounted for only 14% of all discovery requests.[342] A 1997 national survey, conducted by Willging *et al.*, made use of a questionnaire sent to 2,000 lawyers who had worked on 1,000 cases that were likely to have discovery.[343] The questionnaire was filled out by 1,178 lawyers. The percentage of cases in which a specified discovery activity did take place is shown below.

Table 6.1. Use of discovery devices[344]

Document production	84% of all cases with discovery
Interrogatories	81% of all cases with discovery
Depositions	67% of all cases with discovery
Initial Disclosure	58% of all cases with discovery
Expert Disclosure	29% of all cases with discovery
Expert Discovery	20% of all cases with discovery

Since 1993, the maximum number of interrogatories has been 25 unless the court determines otherwise. It seems this new rule is restrictive. The 1996 RAND survey showed that a numerical limit on the interrogatories typically cuts 16 lawyer work hours.[345] In practice, it seems common that lawyers file the maximum number of interrogatories.

Since 1993, the default maximum number of depositions is 10. The 2000 Amendments to the FRCP introduced a presumptive limit on the length of depositions of one day or seven hours. The 1997 study by Willging *et al.*, that evaluated the 1993 Amendments, showed that 75% of the attorneys who reported that depositions were used in their case said that seven or fewer individuals were deposed. This shows that the limit of ten depositions is often not a true restriction.[346] The study revealed that a time limit on the depositions could prove useful. The study showed that 25% of attorneys that had used depositions reported problems with this discovery device. The most frequent complaint (12% of those who used depositions) was that depositions took too much time. The median length of the longest deposition was four hours. In 25% of all cases with depositions, the longest deposition took seven hours or more.[347] If a six hour time limit for depositions had been implemented, this would have affected 30% of the cases in the sample.[348]

341 Rosenberg 1969, p. 489.
342 The findings of the FJC Discovery Study as discussed by Mullenix 1993, p. 1435.
343 Willging, Stienstra, Shaphard & Miletich 1998.
344 Willging, Stienstra, Shaphard & Miletich 1998, p. 530.
345 Kakalik, Hensler, McCaffrey, Oshiro, Pace & Vaiana 1996, p. 56.
346 Willging, Stienstra, Shaphard & Miletich 1998, p. 538.
347 Willging, Stienstra, Shaphard & Miletich 1998, p. 538.
348 Willging, Stienstra, Shaphard & Miletich 1998, p. 539.

The Use of the Personal Appearance of the Parties in the Netherlands

At the Civil Law Sections of the Dutch District Court, the defendant files an answer in roughly 50% of all cases. A personal appearance is scheduled in a large majority of all defended cases (see Section 2.4.1). There are large differences between courts regarding the average duration of the hearing. It is common that courts schedule either 90 minutes or 120 minutes for a personal appearance of the parties (see Section 2.4.1).

Van der Linden's study provides the most detailed data on the personal appearance of the parties.[349] The findings of this study were based on observations, interviews and surveys related to 150 personal appearances before the court, 75 in the District Court of 's-Hertogenbosch and 75 in the District Court of Utrecht. Each of the 150 cases was pending before the Civil Law Section of the District Court in 2006 or 2007. At least one of the parties in each case was a natural person. The courts of Utrecht and 's-Hertogenbosch generally schedule respectively two and three hours for a personal appearance. Table 6.2 shows how much time is on average used for clarifying the subject matter of the dispute (i.e. largely matters of fact), probing a settlement and drafting either a settlement agreement or a concise summary of the issues discussed.

Table 6.2. Average use of time at a personal appearance[350]

	Court of 's-Hertogenbosch	Court of Utrecht
Clarification of the subject matter of the dispute	56 minutes	48 minutes
Probing a Settlement (largely in the absence of the judge)	55 minutes	42 minutes
Time needed to draft and sign either the settlement agreement or the minutes of the issues discussed.	20/28 minutes	17/22 minutes
Average time needed for the personal appearance	145 minutes	116 minutes

The average time spent at a personal appearance to clarify the subject matter of the dispute is less than an hour. The time spent to interrogate both parties is even less, as lawyers are also involved in discussing the subject matter of the dispute on behalf of the parties. The average speaking time of each party on the subject matter of the dispute is about seven or eight minutes (see Table 6.3). Judges generally put questions to parties; it seems parties and lawyers seldom put questions to the opposing party during a hearing.[351]

349 Van der Linden 2008 and Van der Linden, Klijn & Van Tulder 2009 and Van der Linden 2010.

350 Van der Linden 2008, paragraph 3.3, Table 17.

351 I have found no hard empirical evidence to support this statement. Nevertheless, I have learned from private conversations with several practitioners and experts that it is not common that parties question each other. If they do so, they often do not address the opponent party directly, but address the judge, e.g. 'Your honour, I would be very pleased to hear from the opponent party why she phoned my client the 3rd of March 2009(...)'.

Table 6.3. Average speaking time[352]

	Average Speaking time
Plaintiff	7 m 42 sec
Defendant	7 min 10 sec
Plaintiffs Lawyer	8 min 1 sec
Defendant's Lawyer	7 min 5 sec.

The study further showed that judges on average would interrupt each speaker less than once during the personal appearance. Judges do often summarize the issues brought forward by the litigants or their lawyers.[353]

2.1.2. The Costs, Effectiveness and Fairness of Party Interrogation

There are a number of interrelated standards that can be useful to appraise specific mechanisms of party interrogation: the effectiveness, costs, and fairness of party interrogation will be discussed below.[354] An overview of some of the available empirical studies in this area will be provided to appraise the American rules on discovery and the Dutch personal appearance of the parties.

Effectiveness of Discovery and the Personal Appearance
Modes of party interrogation are effective if they are suitable means to clarify matters of fact and discover relevant information. The American discovery system seems to be more thorough than the Dutch personal appearance of the parties. Written interrogatories, frequently used in the United States, are not available in the Netherlands. Also as mentioned in the previous Section, there is more time for a thorough and critical interrogation of parties at an American deposition than at a Continental preparatory hearing. As the American system is more thorough, one would expect that the American system is also more effective, especially if parties are deposed. It seems to be more difficult for parties in an American lawsuit to withhold adverse information. It is, however, difficult to draw firm conclusions in this respect on the basis of the available data.

On the basis of surveys conducted of American lawyers, one may conclude that discovery in the United States generally functions well to enhance the mutual knowledge of facts and to avoid surprise at trial.[355] The most important finding of the Columbia Survey was that discovery did what it was designed for. Discovery enhanced the mutual knowledge of relevant facts.[356] Discovery took place in all but 17% of civil cases. At trial, parties made use of materials obtained by discovery in 77% of all cases. In three fourths of the cases where lawyers used discovered materials at trial, lawyers claimed that without discovery they would not have

352 Van der Linden 2008, paragraph 3.5, Table 20.
353 Van der Linden 2008, paragraph 3.5, Tables 22a and 22b.
354 Van der Linden 2008, Chapter 6 for instance shows that the perceived effectiveness of the Dutch personal appearance is positively correlated with the perceived fairness of the hearing.
355 Also see McKenna & Wiggins 1998, p. 794-795.
356 Rosenberg 1969, p. 488-490.

obtained the evidence. The 1979 survey by Brazil requested lawyers to indicate in what percentage of settled cases they believed that their adversary had not discovered all relevant information. On average, lawyers believed that in 30% of all settled cases, their adversary did not have access to all significant information. In larger and more complex cases it occurred more often that the opposing party had not obtained knowledge of all relevant information by means of discovery.[357] It seems that discovery managed relatively well to avoid surprise at trial. In 20% of all trials, lawyers were surprised by new evidence and information.[358]

In the Netherlands, surveys indicate that a majority of parties, attorneys and judges agree that matters of fact have been adequately disclosed after the personal appearance was concluded. In cases in which no settlement was reached, Van der Linden asked parties and attorneys to indicate whether 'All information relevant to the case has been brought forward'.[359] Judges were asked to respond to the statement: 'All information needed to make a good decision in this case was brought forward'.[360] Parties, attorneys and lawyers were asked to respond to these questions on a five point scale. The findings are listed in the Table below.

Table 6.4. All information relevant to the case has been brought forward[361]

	Parties (n=170)	Lawyers (n=184)	Judges (n=102)
Strongly disagree[362]	7.1%	4.3%	2.0%
Disagree	17.1%	12.0%	10.8%
Partly Agree, Partly Disagree	18.2%	17.4%	11.8%
Agree	48.2%	53.3%	46.1%
Strongly Agree	9.4%	13.0%	29.4%
Total	100%	100%	100%

The study shows that not all information was discussed at the hearing for different reasons. These include: the refusal of a judge to take documents into consideration that had been filed belatedly; insufficient time to deal with all factual details; situations in which parties deliberately withheld information; inadequate preparation by the judge or one of the parties; and the choice of a judge to narrow down the dispute.[363]

357 Brazil 1980, p. 812.
358 Brazil 1980, p. 818.
359 'Alle informatie die van belang is in deze zaak is op tafel gekomen'.
360 'Alle informatie die van belang is voor het nemen van een goede beslissing is op tafel gekomen'.
361 Van der Linden 2008, Table 41.
362 In Dutch: 'zeer oneens, oneens, beetje oneens/beetje eens, eens, zeer eens'.
363 16 out of 170 parties indicated that information had (deliberately) been withheld. In six of these instances a party indicated both parties had withheld information. In six cases a party indicated the opponent party had withheld information; in four cases parties admitted that they had withheld relevant information.

Costs and Time needed to Complete Discovery
It is not easy to compare the costs of American discovery with those of Dutch court hearings. Court fees are relatively low in U.S. District Courts. Parties are generally required to pay a fixed fee of $350.[364] In the Netherlands, court fees of the Civil Law Section of the District Courts generally equal 2.2% of the value of the claim with a minimum of €240 and maximum of €4,941.[365] Lawyers fees constitute the largest part of the costs of litigation. Dutch personal appearances before the court serve a number of purposes, and less than an hour is spent discussing factual matters. The lawyers' fees associated with the interrogation of the parties at a personal appearance therefore seem to be limited. Lawyers' fees related to discovery in the United States are probably larger. As American discovery practices are often believed to be expensive, my discussion of empirical data is restricted to the costs of discovery.

In the United States, lawyers devote a significant amount of their working hours to discovery. A 1977 study by the Federal Judicial Center showed that discovery could be relatively time consuming. The study showed that in six districts the median time needed for completion of discovery varied between 113 and 302 days.[366] Data from five different District Courts, based on 1,812 interviews concerning 1,649 'middle range disputes'[367] that were resolved in 1978, showed that the median time spent on a case was 30.4 hours (mean time: 72.9 hours). Discovery was the activity that consumed the biggest proportion of the time lawyers devoted to a case: 16.7%. The proportion of time spent on discovery was slightly larger than time spent on conferring with the client (16%) and settlement discussions (15.1%).[368] The aforementioned 1996 RAND report showed that, in cases that lasted longer than 270 days, the average total lawyer work hours per litigant equaled 232, of which most hours were spent on discovery (83 hours, i.e. 36% of all work done).[369]

Discovery is generally costly. Nevertheless, it seems that the costs of discovery are not disproportional to the stakes of the case in a majority of cases.[370] The 1979 Brazil study concluded that '(d)iscovery is not a pervasive litigation cost problem for the majority of cases'. The costs are, however, very high in a minority of the cases.[371] The aforementioned study of Willging *et al.*, based on 1997 data, showed that the median total costs of litigation reported by attorneys were $13,000 per client. About half of these costs were related to disclosure and discovery.[372] The median discovery expenses were about 3% of the value of the claim.[373] The study also revealed that depositions were particularly expensive. If more money was

364 Title 28, U.S. Code, Section 1914.
365 'Handleiding tarieven in burgerlijke zaken, Hoofdstuk 1, Artikel 2, lid 2 sub 2'.
366 Flanders 1978, Tables 2, 3 and 4.
367 Cases in which the claim was smaller than $1,000 and 'mega cases' were excluded.
368 Trubek, Sarat, Felstiner, Kritzer and Grossman 1983, p. 90-91.
369 Kakalik, Hensler, McCaffrey, Oshiro, Pace & Vaiana 1996, Table 2.3.
370 Data on the costs of discovery before the 1960s seem to be lacking, Rosenberg 1988a, p. 30.
371 Kakalik, Hensler, McCaffrey, Oshiro, Pace & Vaiana 1996, p. xxvii.
372 Willging, Stienstra, Shaphard & Miletich 1998, p. 548, Table IV.
373 Willging, Stienstra, Shaphard & Miletich 1998, p. 531.

spent on depositions, the time to resolve the dispute was longer.[374] The median expenses of specific discovery activities per client are listed in the Table below.[375]

Table 6.5. Costs of discovery

Document production	$1,100
Interrogatories	$1,000
Depositions	$3,500
Initial Disclosure	$750
Expert Disclosure and Expert Discovery	$1,375
Meet and confer/discovery planning	$600

Fairness of the Personal Appearance of the Parties

The American adversarial system is often justified on the grounds that it is superior in terms of fairness. It is feared that if judges actively question the parties, this will negatively affect the perceived fairness of the procedure. The argument has some merit, but it must be admitted that there are many other factors that affect litigants' perception of fairness (see Chapter 8). It is very difficult to compare perceived fairness of discovery in the United States with perceived fairness of Dutch court hearings, because the precise methodologies used to measure fairness differ greatly. It is, however, clear that surveys do not reveal that litigants believe that the procedure at a Dutch personal appearance is unjust or unfair. On the contrary, litigants seem to prefer a procedure in which a personal appearance of the parties is scheduled.

To my knowledge there are no American studies that aimed to measure the perceived fairness of interrogatories and depositions of parties. There have been studies that aimed to measure the litigants' perceived fairness of American court hearings, such as trials or settlement conferences. Lind *et al.* (1990) asked litigants who were involved in tort cases and had attended either trials or settlement conferences whether they perceived the procedure used for resolving their dispute as fair. Litigants answered on a four point scale (i.e. 'very unfair', 'somewhat unfair', 'somewhat fair', 'very fair', scale values 1-4). The mean score obtained for litigants who attended trials equaled 2.70 (n=97) and the mean score of litigants who attended a settlement conference was 2.76 (n=52).[376]

In general, Dutch surveys indicate that most litigants are satisfied with the way in which the judge conducts oral hearings.[377] A survey of litigants who attended a civil hearing in the District Courts of Utrecht and Breda in 2007, as indicated in Table 6.6, showed that litigants generally believed the judge took sufficient time and that they had been treated fairly.

374 Willging, Stienstra, Shaphard & Miletich 1998, p. 540.

375 Willging, Stienstra, Shaphard & Miletich 1998, p. 540, 577. No significant difference was found between the costs of plaintiffs and defendants.

376 Lind, Maccoun, Ebener, Felstiner, Hensler, Resnik & Tyler 1990, p. 992. Note that the data were obtained in different courts, which makes it difficult to compare the figures.

377 See Van Erp, Niemijer, Ter Voert & Meijer 2007, Chapter 5 on surveys conducted under litigants and professionals between 2001 and 2004.

Table 6.6. Fairness: responses of litigants in civil cases[378]

	Civil Section of the Court (n=20)			County Court Section (n=30)		
	yes	no	do not know	yes	no	do not know
I could tell my story	90%	5%	5%	60%	37%	3%
The judge knew the case well	70%	10%	20%	50%	43%	7%
The judge took sufficient time	100%	0%	0%	87%	13%	0%
I was treated fairly	95%	0%	5%	97%	3%	0%

Van der Linden's study measured the fairness of the procedure by using an adapted version of a questionnaire developed by Colquit.[379] The questionnaire aimed to measure procedural justice (i.e. whether the judge was biased and treated the parties equally), interpersonal justice (i.e. whether the judge treated the parties respectfully), and informational justice (i.e. whether the judge provided information about the procedure) as distinct dimensions of justice.[380] The questionnaire used by Van der Linden consisted of 14 statements, each linked to one of the dimensions of justice. Litigants and attorneys were asked to respond to these statements on a five point scale, where the anchors 1 and 5 respectively corresponded to a very unfair procedure and a very fair procedure. The study revealed that a large majority of the parties and attorneys believed that the procedure during the court hearing had been just. No significant differences in the perception of fairness were found between plaintiffs and defendants, lawyers for plaintiffs and lawyers for defendants or between the courts of 's Hertogenbosch and Utrecht. The averages of the answers given to the categories of questions by litigants and their lawyers are shown in Table 6.7.[381]

Table 6.7. Perceived fairness of the personal appearance, average scores per category

	Parties	Lawyers
Procedural Justice (5 questions)	3.98	4.14
Treatment by the Judge (3 questions)	4.23	4.32
Information given about the hearing (6 questions)	3.78	3.88

A study by Eshuis, published in 2009, revealed that parties perceive proceedings with a personal appearance of the parties as fairer than proceedings without such a hearing. The total sample in this study consisted of 1,500 civil cases that were concluded in 2004 by two medium-sized Dutch District Courts. The case files of these cases have been studied and a questionnaire was sent to all parties involved.

378 Mein, Verberk & Vos 2008, p. 105-106. Questions in Dutch: '1) ik kan/kon verhaal kwijt, 2) rechter kent/kende mijn zaak goed, 3) rechter neemt/nam genoeg tijd 4) krijg/kreeg rechtvaardige behandeling'.

379 Colquit 2001.

380 Van der Linden 2008, Table 4. The questions follow the general pattern of the questionnaire developed by Colquit 2001, Table 1.

381 Based on Van der Linden 2008, Chapter 5, Table 45.

Surveys of 381 cases were returned. Litigants were interviewed about 174 cases. Three dimensions of procedural justice were measured three years after the cases were concluded: 1) relational justice (which included questions on the impartiality and neutrality of the court), 2) informational justice (whether the course of the proceedings had been clarified) and 3) voice (whether the parties felt they were heard). Litigants were asked to answer a number of questions on the fairness of the procedure, on the basis of which a score between -1 (very unfair) and 1 (very fair) was calculated. The table below lists the average scores of litigants who had been interviewed.[382]

Table 6.8. Perceived fairness of the procedure, average scores

	Procedures with a Personal Appearance of the Parties	Procedures without a Personal Appearance of the Parties
Informational Justice	0.43	0.39
Relational Justice	0.72	0.60
Voice	0.46	0.41

2.2. *Principles of Party Interrogation*

Summarizing the issues discussed above, it may be concluded that there are many different techniques to question the parties in the litigation process. Below, a number of areas in which these modes of party-interrogation differ will be addressed.

2.2.1. Evidence and Party Allegation

The decisory oath in Roman law served to resolve the dispute altogether by oath taking. Similarly, many legal systems have provided rules that allow parties to be questioned before the proceedings in order to: 1) allow parties to make informed choices about settlement or the initiation of litigation; 2) to avoid the loss of information; or 3) to obtain information needed to initiate litigation. The Dutch regulations on the taking of depositions before trial, as well as some of the English pre-action protocols, provide examples of such rules. Most of the time, the interrogation of parties serves the process of fact-finding. Parties are interrogated in order to determine matters of fact relevant to a claim or defense.

Central to the process of fact-finding is a distinction between the allegations of the parties on the one hand, and evidence that supports or weakens these allegations on the other. Usually this distinction mirrors an ordinary structure of the proceedings. First, both parties each provide - usually in their pleadings - what they believe to be the underlying facts of the case. Subsequently, parties are questioned on matters of fact related to their claims, defenses and pleadings. These statements are what I refer to as 'party allegations'. They serve primarily to identify the issues that divide the parties. After these have been identified, it might be the case that there is a genuine dispute on one or more matters of fact. In that case,

382 Eshuis 2009, Section 7.1, Table 20, p. 84, p. 88.

parties provide evidence in order to convince the judge that their version of the facts is correct, or at least more plausible than that of the opponent. Parties may testify in order to provide evidence. If an American plaintiff takes the witness stand at trial, her statement does not aim to frame the issues but serves to provide evidence.

Present day American jurisdictions make a clear distinction between the two different kinds of party declarations. The testimony of a party when interrogated as a witness at trial is 'evidence'. The statements of the parties in response to interrogatories or at a deposition are 'party allegations'. Although the pretrial statements of the parties can be used at trial, the distinction is relatively clear and coincides with the divide between pretrial and trial.

On the European continent, legal systems have not always made this clear distinction. As there is no jury, there is no clear divide between pretrial and trial (See Chapter 8). The Continental judge must take into account the statements of the parties and lawyers during all stages of the proceeding when freely evaluating all evidence.[383] The American jury only takes into account evidence presented at trial. Unless pretrial declarations are used at trial, the jury has no knowledge of the declarations in the pretrial stage of litigation.

The use of depositions in the Netherlands prior to the initiation of the action provides one example that illustrates that a distinction between 'party allegation' and 'evidence' is not always consistently applied. These rules on depositions allow the taking of 'evidence' in order to 'identify the issues' prior to the commencement of an action.

In Austria, an abundance of legal sources indicates that a theoretical distinction between the allegations of the parties and the party interrogation as evidence exists in Austrian law.[384] Case law has held that the testimony of parties (*Parteivernehmung*) does not replace the allegations and positions of parties set out in the written pleadings.[385] Although the Austrian system makes a distinction in theory between 'party allegation' and 'evidence', this is not always done consistently. The allegations made at an interrogation of parties (*Parteivernehmung*) should be identified as evidence. Presently, this party interrogation often takes place at a preparatory hearing. This practice in many Austrian courts is at odds with a strict divide between 'party allegation' and 'evidence'.

383 Article 149 Dutch Code of Civil Procedure and Section 272 Austrian Code of Civil Procedure.

384 Rechberger & Simotta 2009, No. 819, p. 438: 'Die Parteivernehmung ist als Beweismittel von der "informativen Befragung" und von der Anhörung der Partei zu unterschieden (...)'. Klein 1900, p. 175: 'Die Parteivernehmung als Beweismittel ist grundverschieden von den thatsächlichen Anführungen in den Parteivorträgen (§. 177, Abs. 1), von der Befragung oder Anhörung der Parteien bei der contradictorischen Sachsverhalterörterung und insbesondere auch von der Parteierklärung über thatsächliche Umstände infolge Befragung durch den Vorsitzenden oder durch den Gegner (§§. 182 und 184)'. König 1982, p. 413.

385 Supreme Court 20061018, Geschäftszahl 9Ob104/06v and Austrian Supreme Court 1 December 1954 Ob 777/54: 'Angaben in der Parteiaussage können Prozessbehauptungen nicht ersetzen'. Also see Spenling in Fasching & Konecny 2002-2005, §271, Nos. 11-12. This implies that if a party acknowledges facts alleged by the opponent party while giving a testimony, such is to be understood as evidence in favor of the opponent party and not as an acknowledgement of fact according to Section 266 Austrian Code of Civil Procedure.

2.2.2. Rigidity and Flexibility

Categorical Answers and Open-ended Questions

Some methods of party interrogation require a party to provide a simple 'yes' or 'no' answer. Most legal systems have a rule that states that anything not denied stands admitted. Thereby pleadings are effectively a means to ask an opponent to admit or deny factual allegations. The charging part of the Bill of complaint in Equity proceedings provides a very clear example of a request to the opponent to admit or deny (or explain why one cannot admit or deny) statements of fact. In the previous Sections, a wide variety of procedural mechanisms were discussed that more explicitly offered parties the possibility to request their opponent to admit or deny a statement of fact. These include the Romano-Canonical system of *positiones* and the present FRCP provisions on 'requests for admission'. The system of party oaths provides another example of regulations that require parties to admit or deny a single fact.

Questions that require parties to either 'admit' or 'deny' a statement of fact are relatively simple, require little time to answer and are therefore often cheap. Nevertheless, such procedural tools have proven to be fairly rigid as well and are often useless to obtain information held by the opponent. Questions of the form: 'Will you admit that 'such and such' is true?' require the interrogating party to know what 'such and such' is.[386] Questions of that form are useless if one would like to find out 'who the eyewitnesses were that saw the traffic accident' or 'what the annual turnover is of firm X'. It is much more useful if parties are required to provide answers to open-ended questions. Interrogatories can be used to require the defendant to identify 'the doctors that treated the defendant between October 2005 and January 2006'. Interrogatories are more flexible and therefore more popular as a discovery device than requests for admission in U.S. practice.

Written versus Oral Examination of Parties[387]

Written interrogatories are often considered to be a more practical means to obtain information from the opponent. It can be convenient to make use of written questions especially if the questions one would like to put to the opponent are specific, not open-ended, few in number and unrelated. If a number of such questions are swiftly exchanged between the parties, written interrogatories allow for a relatively simple and efficient interrogation.

Although written questions can be cheap and useful, the oral examination of parties is usually preferred.[388] Oral examinations of parties are believed to be superior in eliciting the facts of the case.[389] If the questions are put to the opposing party in writing, this allows the party to read all questions carefully in advance and to take the time needed to frame protective, evasive and favorable answers. If the

386 See Finman 1962.

387 See in general Carpi & Cartells 2008.

388 See e.g. Millar 1936: 'The conviction is more and more coming to prevail that the value of the oral examination as a means of discovery far surpasses that of the written interrogatory'.

389 See e.g. Sunderland 1932, p. 875 and Klein 1885, p. 127-129.

examination takes place in open court, non verbal communication is not concealed. Paper does not blush. If the questions are to be presented in writing, all questions usually should be presented at once. This implies that the interrogating party cannot use previously given answers to frame new questions. In case of an oral examination, the interrogating party is able to ask successive questions that elaborate on the answers given. This is especially useful if an answer to a question is unexpected.

Many traditional discovery devices required the parties to provide answers in writing. Some of these combined written and oral elements. The interrogation on facts and articles, much like the modern American depositions by written questions, was an oral examination with written questions. These were previously communicated to the interrogated party and would be read to the party at an oral hearing. Legal systems increasingly question the parties orally. On the European continent, personal appearances of the parties have become popular. The oral examination of parties by means of depositions is very common in the United States. Similarly, many legal systems have allowed parties to give an oral testimony in court. The increased use of oral mechanisms of party interrogation has not made the use of written mechanisms of fact-discovery obsolete. In the United States, it is common to use both devices alongside each other. Similarly, written mechanisms may be useful in cases where an oral hearing is too expensive.[390]

2.2.3. The Preparation of Testimony

Whether parties have prepared their answers in cooperation with their lawyer can influence the form and content of the answers given. It is common for an attorney and a party to jointly prepare and respond to the allegations of the opposing party in the pleadings. Similarly, it is common for a lawyer to help his client to respond to written interrogatories. It is well known in legal practice that pleadings or answers to written interrogatories drafted by lawyers differ from answers that parties would have given without legal assistance.

It is also common to prepare a party for an oral examination. On the European continent, lawyers usually speak to their clients prior to an examination. Lawyers can provide their clients with advice concerning their testimony. However, there is no 'culture' of thorough 'preparation' on the European continent.[391] In some Continental jurisdictions it was traditionally considered to be inappropriate to speak to witnesses before the proceedings. The 1957 German 'Guidelines to Practice Law' directed attorneys not to question witnesses outside the courtroom unless such was 'justified by extraordinary circumstances'.[392] Presently, the ethical Codes

390 The European Small Claims procedure (Regulation (EC) No. 861/2007) takes the written procedure as a starting point. The procedure deals with cases where the stakes are low and potential costs of an oral hearing are high due to the transnational nature of the dispute.

391 See Langbein 1985, p. 834.

392 *Richtlinien für die Ausübung des Anwaltsberuf*, 11. Mai 1957, §4(2): 'Unbeschadet de Bestimmungen in §58 der Richtlinien empfiehlt sich eine aussergerichtliche Befragung von →

of most Continental countries do allow lawyers to contact witnesses, yet lawyers are careful not to convey the impression that they tried to influence the witness.[393] Thorough preparation of witnesses does not seem to be common.

In the United States it is normal for an attorney to prepare witnesses - including party witnesses - prior to giving testimony at a deposition or at trial. It seems that the preparation of parties for an examination is done more frequently and thoroughly in the United States. It is considered appropriate and essential for a lawyer to prepare witnesses.[394] The Restatement (3rd) of the Law Governing Lawyers states in Section 116 that 'A lawyer may interview a witness for the purpose of preparing the witness to testify'.

Preparation is not uncontroversial. It is possible that instruction and rehearsal concerning the form of the testimony will affect the content of the testimony. Research has shown that witness preparation can distort the memory of a witness. Suggestive questions can cause witnesses to recall facts incorrectly and repeated questioning can cause uncertain witnesses to become more certain and confident than they were before.[395] Witnesses could be prepared to unknowingly provide a false or misleading testimony.

In a study conducted by Sheppard and Vidmar, in which students simulated adversarial (i.e. preparation and attorney led interrogation) and inquisitorial modes of witness interrogation, the authors concluded that 'adversary procedures may result in biased testimony and subsequently influence the decisions of adjudicators'.[396]

In a study by Wells *et al* (1981) using undergraduate students, half of the participants that had witnessed a theft were prepared before giving testimony, and the other half of the witnesses were not prepared. All witnesses were cross-examined by means of the same set of questions and the cross-examination was videotaped. The videotapes were watched by different groups of mock jurors. The mock jurors were asked whether they believed the witness was confident, whether the witness was correct, whether the defendant was guilty and whether they felt the witness had been coached. The study revealed that prepared witnesses felt more confident and were perceived to be more confident by mock jurors; mock jurors

Zeugen nur, wenn sie durch besondere Umstände gerechtfertigt ist'. In 1973 less cautious rules were adopted. See BRAK Richtlinien von 21. Juni 1973, §6(1).

393 For Austria, see *Richtlinien für die Ausübung des Rechtsanwaltberufes und für die Überwachung der Pflichten des Rechtsanwalts, 1977, Artikel 1, §8*: 'Der Kontakt mit Zeugen vor und auch während eines anhängiges Verfahrens ist zulässig; jedoch muss jede Form der unzulässigen Beeinflussung vermieden werden'. For the Netherlands, see *Gedragsregels voor Advocaten, 1992, Regel 16 (regel 25 oud)*: '1. Personen die door de wederpartij als getuige zijn aangezegd of kennelijk zullen worden aangezegd, zal de advocaat vóór het verhoor niet mogen horen. 2. (...) 3. Deze bepalingen gelden niet ten aanzien van de eigen cliënt en personen in dienst van of in een bijzondere relatie staande tot de eigen cliënt'.

394 See e.g. Israel 2004, Section 7.05.

395 Boccaccini 2002, p. 166.

396 Sheppard & Vidmar 1980.

were more likely to believe the defendant was guilty when the witness was prepared and they could not tell which witness was prepared.[397]

A study by Spanos (1991), showed that witnesses who were not prepared gave shorter answers on direct examination and were perceived to be less certain on cross-examination than prepared witnesses.[398]

Other studies have shown that there is a relationship between the form of testimony and the perceived credibility and persuasiveness of the testimony. Witnesses who speak with confidence and assertiveness are perceived to be more trustworthy, truthful and convincing than those who speak with hesitance and uncertainty. Similarly, witnesses who give long narrative answers are perceived to be more competent than those who give short answers. Non-verbal communication also influences how the speaker is perceived by others. Witnesses who look at jurors, make gestures that are interpreted positively and use a variations of pitch and loudness are perceived to be more credible than those who look away, do not make gestures and speak with a flat voice.[399]

Landsman, on the basis of the aforementioned studies and insights, argues that the best way to avoid memory distortion of a potential witness is to shield the witness from suggestion. Therefore Landsman proposed restricting pretrial contact between attorneys and disinterested witnesses in civil cases in order to reduce attorney induced distortion.[400] As parties are involved in the lawsuit and contact their lawyers, it seems impossible to shield them from all suggestions.

2.2.4. Direct and Indirect Sanctions

A Refusal to Answer: Direct or Indirect Sanctions

If parties refuse to appear at a hearing or refuse to respond to a question without a valid justification, sanctions can be imposed. Complaints amongst lawyers about the lack of sanctions seem to be common in the United States as well as on the European Continent. Common sanctions in all legal systems are cost orders and the drawing of adverse inferences. Most legal systems recognize a much wider range of possible sanctions. FRCP Rule 37 allows the court to strike (all or parts of the) pleadings, dismiss (all or parts of) the action, render a default judgment against the disobedient party or hold the disobedient party in contempt of court. The main difference with regard to sanctions is that on the continent, direct sanctions are generally not available against parties.[401] In Austria and the Netherlands, parties have a duty to testify if they are summoned, yet they cannot be compelled to do so.

397 Boccaccini 2002, p. 167.
398 *Ibidem.*
399 Boccaccini 2002, p. 174-181.
400 Landsman 1983, p. 564-565.
401 Also see in this respect American Law Institute & UNIDROIT 2006, Principle 17.

Unlike normal witnesses, parties cannot be detained in prison or physically forced to appear in court.[402]

False Testimony and the Use of Oaths
If parties willingly provide false answers to questions, judges can usually apply a wide range of sanctions. Austrian judges may for instance impose fines; American judges can hold the party in contempt of court.[403] More severe sanctions apply if parties willingly give a false testimony under oath. If one commits perjury, one does not only offend God but one also violates penal laws. American jurisdictions have frequently resorted to the use of oaths to ensure candor.

Many mechanisms of party interrogation require the parties to take an oath. Oaths are presently used to a limited extent in the Netherlands. Only the testimony of a party as a witness is under oath.[404] In Austria, oath taking is not mandatory prior to the hearing of a witness or a party at an evidentiary hearing.[405] In Austrian legal practice, the taking of oaths by witnesses or parties is uncommon.[406]

American jurisdictions have resorted to oaths extensively. Inspired by the Field Code, many state jurisdictions have even resorted to sworn pleadings to ensure candor. The rule was often criticized because it offered an obstacle to the presentation of inconsistent defenses.[407] Under the FRCP, pleadings are no longer under oath although Rule 11 requires attorneys to sign pleadings to deter abuse. Nonetheless, interrogatories, depositions and the testimony of parties at trial are all under oath.[408]

2.2.5. The Scope and Admissibility of Party Interrogation

The Existence of Mechanisms to Interrogate Parties
The historical overview of the different mechanisms that exist to question the parties shows that throughout the 19th and the 20th centuries there has been an increase in the available mechanisms to interrogate parties. The English, Dutch and Austrian systems in the early 19th century provided only limited and ineffective means to question parties. Written pleadings and written interrogatories that often only required a party to give a categorical answer made it difficult to discover adverse information. Both on the Continent and in the U.S., more effective mechanisms were introduced. The Austrian Code of 1895 provided extensive possibilities to interrogate the parties. The FRCP provides the most extensive set of procedural mechanisms.

402 Sections 333(1) and 380(3) Austrian Code of Civil Procedure; Article 173(2) Dutch Code of Civil Procedure and Rutgers, Flach & Boon 1988, p. 176.
403 Section 220 Austrian Code of Civil Procedure and FRCP Rule 37.
404 For an historical account see Hidma 1981.
405 Section 336(2) Code of Civil Procedure.
406 See Rechberger in Rechberger 2000, §336, No. 1.
407 Millar 1936, p. 199.
408 See FRCP Rules 30(b)(5)(A)(iv) and 33(b)(3), and FRE Rule 603.

The Admissibility and Evidentiary Value of the Statements of Parties

In the early 19th century, parties were not qualified to testify as witnesses under oath and the older systems of oath taking to resolve claims or factual disputes were fairly ineffective. The possibilities for parties to give testimony have been substantially expanded in many countries. Anglo-American systems have led the way and have made the parties competent to testify in the second half of the 19th century. Save for the enactment of the 'Dead Man's Statute' in a number of American jurisdictions, parties can be interrogated at trial without any restrictions. On the European continent, many systems today still do not allow the parties to be freely interrogated as witnesses in their own case. The Austrian system was the first Continental jurisdiction to make parties competent to provide a testimony under oath. However, the Austrian system was still largely modeled after the old system of party oaths. Until 1983, the Austrian rules limited the evidentiary value of a party's testimony and only allowed one party to be heard under oath. In Germany and the Netherlands, the testimony of a party is still insufficient to provide full proof.

The Scope of Interrogation

Traditionally, in many European Continental countries, it was believed to be improper to require a party to provide adverse information (see Section 2.4.2). Presently, it is generally accepted that parties may not refuse to answer questions on the ground that the answer could be detrimental to their case.[409] Nevertheless, there are limits to the questions that parties can be required to answer. An obvious restriction is that questions put to a party must be relevant to the subject matter of the case. Another common restriction is that the law recognizes privileges that grant parties the right to withhold information.

The scope of discovery in the Federal courts of the United States seems to go far beyond the mere prevention of surprise at trial. Discovery allows the parties to conduct a 'broad search for facts' (see Section 3.2). The rules are liberal in the sense that all non-privileged information relevant to any party's claim or defense is discoverable. It is not required that information sought is admissible as long as discovery 'appears to be reasonably calculated to lead to the discovery of admissible evidence'.[410] For several reasons, the scope of discovery in American practice is much broader than the scope of discovery on the continent. First, Continental judges are present during the oral examinations of parties and will seldom allow parties leeway to interrogate the adversary party for hours. Judges that do not wish to spend too much time on discussing matters of fact will immediately cut off lines of questioning that are not directly relevant to the case. During an American deposition a sequence of irrelevant questions must be answered by the interrogated party even if that party's lawyer objects. Second, Continental judges seem to be much more on guard to prevent parties from 'fishing' for information. The idea that court procedures should allow a 'broad search for facts' has never been widely accepted on the continent. Austrian judges often apply a very restrictive

409 See e.g. Section 321(1)(2) Austrian Code of Civil Procedure. See in general Sections 2.4.2 and 7.3.

410 FRCP, Rule 26(b)(1).

interpretation of the Code of Civil Procedure. They have at times categorically refused to order the taking of evidence aimed at discovering new facts (*Ausforschungsbeweis*).[411] A third point closely related to the first two is that on the continent the party seeking discovery has to convince the court that there is a good reason to order the discovery. In the United States, the burden is upon the party who asserts a protection against unreasonable requests for the disclosure of information. A comparison between the (previously existing) Continental interrogation on facts and articles with modern American interrogatories provides a good example. The Continental interrogatories were examined by the court. Only if the questions were appropriate would these be put to the opposing party. In the United States, interrogatories are not evaluated by the court. It is for the responding party to state the grounds for objecting to an interrogatory 'with specificity' or to file a motion for a protective order.

2.2.6. Court-Directed and Party-Directed Modes of Examination

Some procedural devices primarily aim to enable the court to examine the parties. Other mechanisms are designed to allow parties to examine their opponents, such as interrogatories. Continental systems have gradually moved towards forms of party interrogation that allow the court to question the parties. The demise of the interrogation on facts and articles in France and the Netherlands and its replacement by the personal appearance of the parties provides a clear example of a trend from party-directed forms of party interrogation towards judge-directed forms of party interrogation. Today in the Netherlands, Germany and Austria, it is primarily the judge who questions parties at a preparatory hearing. Nevertheless, parties are allowed to put (additional) questions to each other.

In the United States, rules have been designed and amended to make discovery an extrajudicial process. Interrogatories and depositions, the two most common devices for questioning parties, operate without court involvement. Judges normally have no clue as to what precisely goes on during the process of discovery. Only when the judge is asked to rule on a motion will the parties provide the judge with some information obtained during discovery. In a motion for summary judgment, a lawyer could quote a number of relevant fragments of a deposition transcript.

When parties are interrogated to provide evidence, Continental and American Codes both allow the court to question parties and allow parties to question each other.[412] Practices on the European continent differ from American practices however. On the continent, the examination is largely court-driven. The judge will primarily put questions to parties. American practice is party-driven; attorneys cross-examine the parties. American judges do not often make use of their powers to interrogate witnesses.

411 Kralik 1988, p. 93 and Rechberger in Fasching & Konecny 2002-2005, Section 266, No. 82.

412 E.g. Sections 340, 341 and 289 Austrian Code of Civil Procedure and FRE 611 and 614.

The diverging modes of party interrogation in the U.S. federal system and the Continental legal systems since the 1930s provide an excellent example of the much broader divide between 'adversarial' and 'less adversarial' systems.

Mediacy and Immediacy

Whether the judge who ultimately decides the case will be present at the oral interrogation of the parties (*immediacy*), or will only be presented with a transcript of the interrogation (*mediacy*), is closely related to the difference between party-directed and court-directed modes of interrogation.[413]

Traditionally on the Continent, the principle of immediacy carried little weight and judges who operated under the Romano-Canonical rules of procedure often delegated the interrogation of parties and witnesses to special commissioners.[414] Many Continental systems of party interrogation, such as the French interrogation on facts and articles did not take place in the presence of the judge who would render the judgment. The English common law traditionally adhered to the principle of immediacy in its normal mode of trial by jury.

Currently, on the European continent the interrogation of parties generally takes place in the presence of the judge who will ultimately decide the case. The Austrian Code of 1895 adheres to the principle of immediacy (Section 2.3). The judge who will decide the case is usually present when parties are interrogated, both in the preparatory and evidentiary phase of the proceeding.[415] Presently, in the United States the interrogation of parties as witnesses at trial generally takes place in the presence of the judge. Few cases however make it to trial. If cases do not make it to trial, judges often do not meet the parties. Lawyers frequently quote the transcripts of a deposition in a motion for summary judgment. Judges will be asked in such cases to base their judgment solely on fragments of the transcript of an extrajudicial hearing of parties at a deposition.

2.2.7. Recording the Interrogation

The written report of the interrogation of parties is extremely relevant for practitioners. Records of personal appearances before the court, depositions and the testimony of parties as witnesses can be decisive when drafting a motion or a judgment.

Records of a hearing on the European continent are generally concise and provide only a short summary of the most important factual, legal and procedural issues discussed. Usually judges dictate a summary, providing the parties the possibility of adding their comments. In Austria, the report of the oral hearings should contain 'a concise summary of the factual issues discussed'.[416] The judge

413 Millar 1923, §8.
414 Millar 1923, p. 152.
415 Exceptions do exist, see for instance Section 282 Austrian Code of Civil Procedure.
416 *Verhandlungsprotokolle.* Section 209 Code of Civil Procedure: 'In jedes Protokoll (...) ist (...) der Inhalt des auf den Sachverhalt sich beziehenden beiderseitigen Vorbringens in gedrängt zusammenfassender Darstellung aufzunehmen'.

usually summarizes the factual issues in the report but gives the parties the possibility of commenting. If the parties believe the summary is inadequate, the report can be amended or the objections of that party will be mentioned in the report.[417] Parties will read the report and will be asked to sign it. Similar recording practices exist in other countries, such as the Netherlands.[418] I personally observed that it is common for a report of a Dutch hearing to be one or two pages in length.

In the United States, stenography was introduced in the courts in the second half of the 19th century.[419] It would become a powerful instrument to ensure that every word uttered during a deposition or trial would be recorded. In response to newly developed technologies, the 1993 Amendments to the FRCP also allowed the parties to record depositions by means of audio or audiovisual recording.[420]

Regardless of the way in which the deposition is recorded, it is common in the United States that a verbatim transcript of the record is prepared. The transcripts of depositions are of great importance in a large proportion of lawsuits and often serve as the prime source of information.[421] As it is very common for depositions to take 2-4 hours, the transcripts which mention every word uttered can be very extensive. The transcripts of depositions in a single large case can easily fill a couple of shelves.

The extensive practice of recording and making verbatim transcripts in the United States is very thorough and precise. The large amount of paperwork involved in working with verbatim transcripts also generates a lot of work. As court reporters are generally paid by the page and lawyers by the hour, the use of such extensive transcripts is very costly.

2.3. *Diverging Principles in a Comparative Perspective*

If we observe the historical analysis above, a number of common developments can be identified. Both in European Continental jurisdictions and in the United States, the number of effective mechanisms for party interrogation in the pretrial phase of litigation increased. Similarly, the rule that banned parties from testifying under oath was abolished in Anglo-American and a number of Continental jurisdictions.

The differences between modern jurisdictions are largest in the fact-gathering stage of litigation. Depositions and interrogatories are the most common pretrial mechanisms for party interrogation in the U.S. In the Netherlands, Austria and many other Continental jurisdictions, parties are often heard at a preparatory court hearing. It seems that the American discovery practices, especially if parties are deposed, are more thorough and at the same time more costly than the Austrian and Dutch mechanisms of party interrogation.

417 Section 212 Code of Civil Procedure.

418 Article 88(3) Dutch Code of Civil Procedure. Also see Articles 194-195 French Code of Civil Procedure.

419 Lettow Lerner 2000.

420 FRCP, Rule 30(B)(3).

421 See e.g. Israel 2004, Israel repeatedly argues: 'the transcript is everything'.

The many differences between European Continental and American modes of party interrogation are correlative. These differences flow from two philosophical differences between American and Continental systems: the adversarial system and the use of a civil jury (also see Chapter 8).

The civil jury creates the need for an uninterrupted trial (see Section 8.3). This affects the way in which parties are interrogated. At trial, the statements of parties in the pretrial phase largely remain unknown to the jury. This implies that the jury cannot take into account pretrial statements of the parties when giving its verdict, unless these pretrial statements are presented at trial. The use of the civil jury in the United States thus creates the need for a sharp distinction between the interrogation of parties during the pretrial stage of litigation and the presentation of party testimony as evidence at trial. Such a sharp distinction is not made on the European continent. A European judge who reads the pleadings and attends the preparatory oral hearing before the court generally also renders the final judgment. The doctrine of the free evaluation of evidence holds that the judge may, *inter alia,* take into account every bit of information discussed at a preparatory hearing when evaluating all evidence. This implies that the inability of parties to testify under oath in an Anglo-American setting was more problematic than in a Continental setting.

The existence of a clear divide between the interrogation of parties in the pretrial stage and the interrogation at trial prevents the smooth application of indirect sanctions in the United States. If the parties are uncooperative in the pretrial stage, a (magistrate) judge decides discovery motions whereas the jury renders the final verdict. The jury did not attend the discovery motion. It is complicated and time-consuming to explain the jury that a party was not sufficiently forthcoming. It is also difficult to request the jury to draw adverse inferences if parties are uncooperative. Direct sanctions are hence more appropriate in an American setting.

The degree to which the court is involved in the interrogation of parties explains some of the differences between American and Continental approaches to party interrogation. First, the absence of the judge at American depositions contributed to the broadening of the scope of discovery. If irrelevant questions are put to the parties, these have to be answered despite objections of counsel. Objections only become relevant at a later point in time. At a deposition, parties can freely search for further information and learn about all facts known by the opponent. Although financial constraints may set limitations, attorneys have quite some time and leeway to engage in 'a broad search for facts'. On the continent, the presence of the judge sets limits on the time available to interrogate the parties. Judges will generally not allow a hearing to take more than two or three hours. Attorneys are generally hesitant to put too many questions to the opposing party: the judge might think that attorney believes the judge did a bad job questioning that party in the first place. Similarly, counsel is careful with formulating questions that 'fish' for information or questions of which the relevance is not immediately clear: if the answers to such questions do not lead to anything related to the case, the attorney could leave a bad impression with the court.

Second, the presence of the judge at an interrogation of parties in the pretrial stage of litigation makes it relatively easy to make a brief report that summarizes the main issues discussed at the hearing. The judge generally dictates a summary; the parties may make some suggestions. In the presence of the judge who will ultimately decide the case, the parties are not likely to get involved in a fierce debate concerning the precise content of the report. To the extent that debates on these matters do take place, these can be resolved quickly by the judge. In the United States, where depositions typically take place in a lawyers' office, the absence of the judge could create difficulties when drafting such a summary. As lawyers generally have opposing interests, it is probable that a disagreement could arise as to what would constitute a good summary. If a dispute arises concerning the summary, there is no one available to decide upon the matter. To avoid such inconveniences: it is best to simply record every single word uttered.

Third, the preparation of witnesses fits better into a strict adversarial model in which parties present their evidence than in a model in which every witness is considered to provide a public duty towards the court. In an adversarial model, evidence is 'polarized' and belongs to either of the parties. Each party tries to present 'his witnesses' as favorably as possible. In the Austrian procedural model, witnesses should not be either the plaintiffs or the defendant's witness: all witnesses fulfill a public duty to the court. The judge who will lead the interrogation is not interested in questioning a witness in such a way that the testimony is favorable to either of the parties. Thus, this model is inconsistent with the practice of witness preparation.

Fourth, the degree to which the court is involved in the interrogation of witnesses clearly has an impact on the mode of the interrogation. In the United States, cross-examination is the rule, examination by the court is the exception. In Austria and the Netherlands, judges generally question the parties; cross-examination is an exception. This obviously has a large impact on the questions put to the parties. Judges generally ask general questions that allow the parties to tell their versions of the facts in their own words. Judges seldom interrupt and parties generally volunteer to provide a long narrative account, even if a short answer would have sufficed. In the United States, the parties are prepared not to volunteer and to give precise answers to the questions.[422] At a deposition, attorneys search for facts beyond the version of the facts that a party presents. Every detail that could be relevant is explored. At trial however, attorneys seldom ask a question to which they do not know the answer.

422 A party volunteers if he or she provides information that goes beyond the scope of the question. American witnesses and parties are prepared not to volunteer. See Israel 2004, Section 14.09, p. 138.

PART III

COMPARATIVE CIVIL LITIGATION: IDEOLOGY, THEORY AND PSYCHOLOGY

INTRODUCTION

At a first glance, procedural rules that regulate the process of fact-finding often seem inconsistent, unrelated and incoherent. However, in most jurisdictions procedural regulations are not merely 'a bunch of rules'. These regulations often constitute a carefully designed system. Generally, a number of underlying principles, guidelines, theories and objectives can be identified that clarify and justify more specific rules of procedure. The Chapters below should be understood as a search for these basic principles within the Austrian and U.S. systems of civil procedure.

In Chapter 7, it will be argued that the 1895 Austrian Code of Civil Procedure is based on a utilitarian model. Franz Klein, who drafted the Austrian Code, argued that the central aims of the legal process are to enforce substantive law, swiftly and at low cost. As a means to these ends, Klein had proposed to strengthen the role of the judge and to place a greater emphasis on the pursuit of truth in litigation. These objectives and principles of the Austrian Code provided the framework for specific Austrian rules on the process of fact gathering and evidence.

In Chapter 8, I will aim to make a rational reconstruction of the U.S. federal rules on fact-finding. It will be argued that the existence of the civil jury and the strong adherence to the adversarial system are the pivotal and distinctive features of the American rules on fact-finding. The civil jury and the adversarial system explain many specific American fact-finding arrangements.

The main aim of Chapter 7 and Chapter 8 is not to give accurate descriptions of the Austrian and American legal systems, but to enhance the understanding of the underlying principles of these systems. Each of these systems will be represented as a single and structured whole. An attempt will be made to provide the most persuasive rationales behind the distinctive characteristics of these systems. Only to a very limited extent will I criticize either one of these systems.

Chapter 9, which builds on Chapter 7 and Chapter 8, aims to provide a partial explanation for the differences between systems. It will be argued that the main differences between the legal systems flow from different political and theoretical views of those that determine and shape the form of the legal process. Essential to understanding the different fact-finding arrangements are: 1) the different views on the role of the state in society and 2) the way in which democratic ideals have affected the rules and institutions that shape the litigation process.

Chapter 7

THE AUSTRIAN MODEL: A UTILITARIAN APPROACH TO CIVIL LITIGATION

1. The Social Model of Civil Procedure

Franz Klein was the intellectual father of the Austrian Code of Civil Procedure of 1895. The Austrian Code has been influential in a number of Continental jurisdictions. Its provisions on fact-gathering and evidence have remained largely untouched since 1895 (see Section 2.3.1). This Chapter provides a rational reconstruction of the Austrian procedural model. It is a relatively simple task as Franz Klein was very explicit about the ideas, objectives and assumptions underlying the Austrian procedural legislation.

It is said that Franz Klein proposed a 'social model' of civil procedure. That does not mean that Klein was primarily concerned about the weaker members of society. Nor does the social model imply that there would be no role for private practitioners in the legal process.[1] Rather, Klein's model addressed civil procedural issues from a grand sociological perspective. Three main tenets seem to be central to Klein's 'social model' of civil litigation:

1. The social model takes society as a whole as a starting point;
2. The social model assumes that the final end of government policy is the maximization of the total welfare;
3. The social model holds that society is best served if substantive law is enforced swiftly and at low costs.

1.1. *A Collectivistic Point of Departure*

The departure point of classical liberalism is that individuals are free and have certain natural rights.[2] Society is seen as a collection of individuals. The state and courts are institutions that aim to protect the freedom and the rights of individuals.

1 Klein & Engel 1927, p. 203.
2 See e.g. Locke 1690.

Liberalism is in essence individualistic. Liberal political theories have often been used to argue in favor of a procedural system that respects the autonomy of parties. In the realm of private law parties are free to resolve their disputes according to their own preferences. In the late 19th century classical liberalism was no longer the only dominant political ideology. The role of the nation state in society was rapidly increasing.[3] Klein's views fit well in the political timeframe of late 19th century Austria.[4]

Klein's perspective on society differs from the liberal perspective.[5] In describing society, he often made use of Plato's popular metaphor of the human body.[6] The metaphor shows the more collectivist and corporatist approach of Klein. Not the individual, but society as a whole, is the starting point for the Austrian codification. Klein himself is very explicit in this respect:

> 'Civil Procedure is a public service, a part of the legal order and it serves the state. (…) it is rooted in the existence of conflicts of interests, in both the area of private law and all other public domains, that create the need for institutions to resolve these conflicts. There are three fundamental starting points to address all matters of the state: the approach of the ruling Government, the approach of individuals that form the state and the approach that takes the community of the people as a starting point. These differing perspectives are at the same time principles of design. (…) the history of civil procedure provides examples of court procedures that are based on the first perspective: the late Roman and Justinian procedure; the second perspective: the later procedure of the *gemeine Recht* and the French and German procedure; and the last approach: the Germanic court procedures, the Prussian *Corpus Juris Fridericianum* and - although its predecessor belonged to the second category - the present Austrian procedure'.[7]

3 Klein & Engel 1927, p. 187: 'Er gibt sich, wie es mehr oder weniger alle historischen Prozesse getan haben, als ein Kind seiner Zeit, der Wende des 19. Jahrhunderts, für welche der Gedanke einer Einordnung der persönlichen Interessen in die Interessen des Gemeinwohles und die Erklärung individuellen Vorgänge aus dem gesellschaftlichen Untergrunde kennzeichnend ist'.

4 Stampfer 1998, Chapters 2 and 3.

5 Klein's political views were moderately left winged. Klein was also politically active, see Sprung 1988. Klein has in this respect been inspired by his teacher Anton Menger, see Stampfer 1998, p. 85.

6 Plato, the Republic, Book IV and Klein 1901, p. 118: 'Der Prozeß (...) Daher ist er durch eine Verletzung der Rechtsordnung bedingt und wirkt ihr gegenüber ähnlich wie etwa die ärztliche Heilkunst bei Gesundheitsstörungen: beide wollen Wiedergerstellung, nicht Neuschöpfung'.

7 Klein & Engel 1927, p. 187: 'Der Zivilprozeß ist eine Staatsanstalt, ein Bestandteil der Rechtsordnung und hat, (…), staatliche Bestimmung. (…) seine Wurzeln sind Interessenkonflikte, die es sowohl im Gebiete des Privatrechtes wie in allen übrigen Bereichen des Gemeinlebes gibt und die daher auch überall Anstalten zu ihrer Schlichtung notwendig machen. Für alles Staatliche gibt es drei Betrachtungsweisen: die der herrschenden Gewalt, die der einzelnen dem Staate angehörigen Personen und dann die der Gesamtheit, der Gesellschaft. Diese Betrachtungsweisen sind zugleich Konstruktionsprinzipien. (…) aus der Geschichte des Prozessrechtes sind Beispiele für die erste Anschauungsweise der spätrömische und justinianeische Prozeß, für die zweite der spätere gemeinrechtliche Prozeß und der heutige Prozeß in Frankreich und im Deutschen Reiche, für die letzte endlich das →

In his collectivistic approach towards society and the state, Klein seems to be influenced by the works of Rousseau.[8] Klein argued - as did Rousseau - that society was not merely a collection of individuals but that the individual was a creation of society:[9]

> 'In our era, human beings solely live in larger groups; a single person, an individual and his potential to influence his surroundings are not destroyed by the flourishing of culture; but are created by the flourishing of culture'.[10]

From this grand political perspective we can descend to the proceedings before a court of justice. Proceedings serve to resolve conflicts. According to the social model, judicial conflict is clearly not something that only concerns the private interests of the parties. Private interests need to be protected because society as a whole has expressed this desire. The individual interests should only be protected because they form a part of interest of the community.[11] Conflicts, according to the Austrian model, are primarily a public evil.[12] Klein used the metaphor of the human body to clarify his views: every conflict between two litigants is regarded as a bodily wound of society. The wound harms the parts of 'the body' that are damaged, yet the body as a whole suffers if the wound is not adequately healed. Klein essentially argued that the interests at stake in each civil case go far beyond the interests of the parties involved. Individual conflicts lead to a waste of time and money and an inefficient allocation of resources in society. It leads to anger and hatred between the litigants, which are fatal passions to society as a whole.[13] To resolve conflicts, the judge (i.e. a representative of the state) should not only take into account the interests of the litigants but also the interests of society at large.[14] Although the public interests are clearest in family law matters, other parts of private law are not to be excluded. Every single procedure creates positive (or

Germanische Gerichtsverfahren, der Friedericianische Prozeß in Preußen, und während sein Vorläufer zur zweiten Gruppe zählte, der gegenwärtige österreichischen Prozeß'.

8 Klein 1901, p. 118-119. Klein refers to a 'contrat sociale' as a base for government resolution of disputes as opposed to self help. His use of French indicates that he refers to the works of Rousseau.

9 See for instance Gourevitch 2004, The Social Contract, Book 1, Chapter 8 and Book 2, Chapter 5.

10 Klein 1901, p. 119: 'Der Mensch lebt in dieser Epoche ausschließlich in Gesellschaftsgruppen; der Einzelne, das Individuum und sein Herrschaftskreis ist durch das Aufblühen der Kultur nicht vernichtet sondern erst geschaffen worden'.

11 Klein & Engel 1927, p. 188: 'Die einzelnen Rechtsverhältnisse und Rechte genießen den Schutz nur als Teile, als Zellen dieses Ganzen'.

12 Lewisch 1998a.

13 Sprung 1977, p. 393.

14 Klein & Engel 1927, p. 187: 'Als geistiger Ausgangspunkt des gegenwärtigen österreichischen Prozesses kann demnach die Auffassung hingestellt werden, dass diejenigen Interessenkonflikte, die als Recht geltende Regeln das Gesellschaftslebens berühren, eben dadurch gesellschaftliche Bedeutung erlangen und deshalb nicht bloß materiell nach den im Gesetze verkörperten publizistischen, staatlichen und gesellschaftlichen Abmessungen geschlichtet werden müssen, sondern dass aus demselben Grund auch in den Formen der Austragung solcher Konflikte auf die Interessen von Staat und Gesellschaft Rücksicht zu nehmen ist'.

negative) externalities, as economists would call it today.[15] Court decisions also influence the behavior of citizens that do not resolve their disputes in court.[16] If a court rightly holds that a party has breached his contract and is required to pay damages, this has an effect on society at large. Such a decision could deter others from breaching their contracts. Hence, civil procedure fulfills the role of the doctor. Civil procedure should heal the wound in the body of society before it does further damage. The question that remains so far unanswered is: what makes a good doctor and when is the body of society considered healthy?

1.2. *A Utilitarian Perspective*

The precise details of a model which takes the community as a starting point depend on the ends the state pursues. Generally accepted ends of the state are protection of individual rights and the preservation of the legal order. Klein however, does not regard the protection of individual rights as a final end for the state, but as a means to strive for a more remote and central objective.[17] It appears that Klein's writings are, in essence, utilitarian.[18] He argued that although the state could not guarantee the well-being of individuals, it should try to maximize the welfare of society.[19] Klein argued that such a utilitarian approach does not necessarily threaten the freedom of individuals.[20] He believed that the protection of the rights and freedom of individuals are an important means to safeguard the welfare of society.[21]

Klein unfortunately did not explicitly define what he meant by 'maximizing the welfare of society as a whole'. It seems to me that his views are in line with the

15 Lewisch 1998a, p. 106-107.

16 Only a small proportion of all conflicts is resolved through the legal process. See in general: Genn 1999; Velthoven & Ter Voert 2004 and Velthoven & Klein Haarhuis 2010.

17 Klein & Engel 1927, p. 188.

18 Stampfer 1998, p. 90: 'Die ZPO ist Teil einer breit zu verstehenden, utilitaristisch geprägten Sozialpolitik von oben'.

19 Klein & Engel 1927, p. 191: 'Vorkehrungen treffen, um Nachteile von der Gesellschaft abzuwehren und zu ihrer Konsistenz, zu ihrem Gedeihen beizutragen, heißt für die Wohlfahrt der Gesellschaft sorgen. (...) Der Wohlfahrtszweck als Staatsaufgabe hat unter den Staatsrechtslehrern einen schlechten Klang und für einzelne politische Parteien ist er mit dem Polizeistaat oder überhaupt dem absoluten Staate identisch und damit auch verurteilt. Mit diesen Uebertreibungen wird man ebenso wenig operieren dürfen (...). Die einzelnen Menschen nach ihren Bedürfnissen und Wünschen glücklich machen, das kann der Staat nicht, aber die Wohlfahrt des Ganzen kann und darf er gleichfalls nicht aus dem Programme seiner Aufgaben streichen'.

20 Klein & Engel 1927, p. 192: 'Die moderne Entwicklung beweist aber doch auch wieder, dass der Wohlfahrtszweck verfolgt werden kann, ohne dass die freie Sphäre des Individuums aufgehoben würde'.

21 Klein & Engel 1927, p. 188: 'Das objektive Recht selbst liegt natürlich dem Staate auch nicht um seiner selbst willen am Herzen, vielmehr berührt sich der staatliche Rechtsschutz vermöge seiner Funktion mit der sonstigen dem Schutze und der Förderung der Gesellschaft gewidmeten staatlichen Tätigkeit; diese zielt auch als Rechtsschutz auf das Wohl der Gesellschaft ab. Rechtszweck und das Wohl der Gesellschaft betreffende Zwecke können deshalb nicht in einem prinzipiellen Gegensatze stehen, (...)'.

general principles of utilitarianism as set out by Jeremy Bentham.[22] This resemblance seems to be accidental, as there are no traces of a direct influence of Bentham on Klein.[23] Klein's views on procedure and evidence were also remarkably similar to those of Bentham. Bentham considered it the main objective of procedural law to 'give execution and effect throughout' to the substantive branch of the law. Apart from this main objective Bentham recognized three collateral ends of justice: the avoidance of unnecessary delay, vexation, and expenses.[24] If the legislator faced conflicts between the main and collateral ends, the issue was to be determined by the application of the 'principle of utility'. More particularly, Bentham stressed the importance of pursuit of truth and believed that the legislator had to ensure that all evidence was forthcoming. He favored the free evaluation of all evidence and believed that the court should be empowered to guard against vexation, costs and delay.[25] As will be shown in the Sections below, these principles are in accordance with Klein's social model.[26]

Departing from the grand perspective of maximizing welfare in society at large, Klein subsequently addressed civil procedural issues from a macro-economic perspective.[27] According to him, a procedural Code is nothing but a document that describes the way in which certain tasks are performed. The judge, parties and lawyers cooperate in order to reach a final decision. Klein argued that civil proceedings do not generate revenue or produce tradable goods. At best, civil proceedings resolve the question how the goods produced in society should be distributed.[28] Every conflict should be seen as a technical failure in the smooth operation of society. As we saw in the previous Section, the primary role of legal proceedings is the resolution of disputes as 'wounds in the body of society'. Just as modern law and economics scholars argue that civil litigation aims to minimize direct and error costs, Klein argued that a procedural system aims to reduce the operational costs of society.[29] The litigation process aims to limit the negative effects that conflicts have on the total welfare in society.

Klein believed that the application of utilitarian ideas should certainly be implemented in the civil justice system. Procedural rules should be designed such that these contribute to the maximization of welfare.[30] The free market economy

22 See in general Bentham 1781.

23 I have not found references to the works of Bentham in the works of Klein. It seems Klein was more influenced by Austrian intellectuals of his time and his teacher Menger than by English jurisprudence, see Sprung 1988 and Stampfer 1998.

24 Bentham 1827, Vol. 1, p. 24-25, p. 33-34 and Twining 2006, p. 42.

25 Bentham 1827, p. 27-32 and Twining 2006, p. 43-44.

26 In some area's Kleins views differed from those of Bentham. Bentham for instance had much less confidence in judicial interrogation of witnesses and parties than Klein. See Landsman 1990, p. 1180.

27 Rechberger 1998 and Sprung 1977, p. 393.

28 Lewisch 1998a.

29 See e.g. Posner 1973.

30 Klein & Engel 1927, p 192: 'Die Anwendung de Wohlfahrtsgedankens auf den Prozess wird am wenigsten angefochten werden können. (...) Die Wohlfahrtsförderung besteht hier nur darin, dass der Gesellschaftsschutz verbessert und verfeinert wird (...) Daß der Wohlfahrtszweck des Staates in einer staatlich und gesellschaftlich so wichtigen Einrichtung →

forces most firms to organize themselves according to leading economic principles. According to Klein these economic principles should also thoroughly influence proceedings before the courts of justice. All activities performed during the proceedings should be efficient. Activities should not be performed if these ultimately do not have a positive impact on the welfare of society. The next - and most practical - question that rises is: how to design court procedures that limit the negative welfare effects of conflicts?

1.3. *The Ends of Civil Litigation*

According to Klein, the final end of civil litigation is to increase the welfare of society by limiting the negative welfare effects of conflicts. The metaphor of the 'wound' in the 'body' of society was used to clarify the effects of conflicts. According to Klein, good court procedures efficiently and correctly establish the facts (diagnosis) and apply substantive law to these facts (medicine). It must be noted that Klein assumed that substantive private law was designed to maximize welfare. Procedural law could be seen as a 'handmaid' to substantive law. Klein identified three core aims of civil litigation: 1) the enforcement of substantive law, 2) the swift resolution of disputes and 3) cost efficiency.[31] This 'trinity of procedural aims' is still frequently defended in modern procedural literature.[32] Modern law and economics literature which could also be called 'utilitarian', seems to identify similar ends of civil litigation.[33] The three ends of the litigation process are discussed below.

Rectitude of the Final Decision

In order to enforce substantive law, Klein argued that the underlying relevant facts should be established truthfully and the appropriate substantive rules should be applied correctly to these facts.[34] Klein believed that in order to resolve the conflict, it was required that the relevant and underlying facts be correctly established.[35] If the final decision is based on only a small and distorted selection of relevant facts, the chances that the final decision would be correct are small.

wie es der Zivilprozeß ist, einen Widerschein hat, kann sonach um so weniger fehlerhaft sein, wenn dieser Widerschein ebenso in wichtigeren Partien des Privatrechts wahrnehmbar ist und sich dort unleugbar ausdehnt'.

31 Klein works out this 'trinity of procedural ends' in various texts. See Klein 1901, p. 130 *et seq.* and Klein & Engel 1927, p. 199 *et seq.*

32 See for example: Zuckerman 1999, Chapter 1.

33 See e.g. Posner 1973, p. 399 and Chapter 10.

34 Klein & Engel 1927,p. 200: 'Wenn der Rechtskonflikt eine leichtere oder schwerere Wunde am Gesellschaftskörper ist, hat das Urteil eben diese Wunde zu heilen. Es muss, wie früher gesagt wurde, das gerade für diese Wunde notwendige Heilmittel gefunden werden, und es ergibt sich daraus, dass - die Wunde für den Sachverhalt der Komplikation und das materielle Recht als Medizin genommen - die Heilung de Wunde und die Gesundung des Gesellschaftskörpers von der an diesem Sachverhalte gemessenen Richtigkeit des Urteiles, (...)'.

35 Klein & Engel 1927, p. 199.

Klein explicitly mentioned that civil litigation should provide all with adequate protection of civil rights.[36] From the collectivist and corporatist approach of Klein's model we already derived that the protection of individual rights is not an end in itself, but needed to secure the legal order as a whole. Klein briefly summarized his views in this respect as follows:

> '(...) it is certainly not unimportant how a final decision on the plaintiff's claim is reached, whether the law has been correctly applied, and whether justice is done. This sheds a new light on the social importance (...) of rules on the relation between the court and the parties in the process of fact-gathering, as the efforts of both the parties and the court to gather complete and consistent factual materials will ensure that the final decision more often correctly establishes the legal relationship between the parties'.[37]

Efficiency and the Bureaucratization of Adjudication

Klein argued that procedural forms and requirements should not erode the utility of the court system from an individual and public perspective.[38] In order to maximize the total welfare of society, resources should be allocated efficiently and litigation should be conducted swiftly and at low cost. Every allocation of labor, money or time is a loss if it does not contribute to the ends of civil procedure.[39]

First, Klein argued proceedings should be concluded swiftly. Conflicts disturb the mutual cooperation between people. Conflicts lead to hatred and frustration that could spread and deepen if not swiftly tackled. During litigation, the money or objects that are subject to the conflict can often not be allocated efficiently while the case is pending. The efficient allocation of resources should be hampered as little and as briefly as possible in order to increase the overall welfare. For these and other reasons, Klein argued that proceedings should be designed in such a way that delay would be avoided.[40] Second, expensive litigation in low-value cases can often be regarded as a social loss.[41] Expensive trials are especially troublesome if both parties litigate in good faith. If it costs society more to resolve a conflict than to leave it unresolved, litigation will not increase the overall welfare.

In order to save money and time, Klein believed that it was relevant to allocate labor in an efficient way.[42] He argued that the history of labor showed an increasing efficiency in the way in which labor had been allocated. Throughout history, a

36 Klein & Engel 1927, p. 193.

37 Klein 1901, p. 131: '(...) ist es, (...), gewiß nicht nebensächlich, wie im Prozeß über die Klage entscheiden wird, ob das Gesetz richtig angewendet und ob so geurteilt wird, das Recht Recht bleibt. Einerseits fällt von hier ein neues Licht auf die sociale Wichtigkeit der (...) Vorschriften über das Verhaltnis zwischen Gericht und Partei bei der Stoffsammlung, den bei gemeinsamen Bemühungen beider um die Vollständigkeit und Schlüssigkeit des Prozessmateriales dürfte das Urteil viel häufiger den Rechtsgehalt des streitigen Verhältnisses richtig feststellen'.

38 Klein & Engel 1927, p. 194 *et seq.*

39 On the view of Klein on 'economic' procedures, see Rechberger 1998.

40 Klein & Engel 1927, p. 196.

41 Klein & Engel 1927, p. 194.

42 Klein & Engel 1927, p. 198.

system of self-help has been replaced by a system in which specialized judges and lawyers cooperate to resolve disputes. Klein favored such specialization, as it allowed more work to be done with less labor. He proposed what Weber referred to as bureaucratization, a process which could offer 'the optimal possibility for the realization of the principle of division of labor in administration according to purely technical considerations'.[43] The bureaucratic approach to litigation allocated individual tasks to 'functionaries who are trained as specialists and who continuously add to their experience by constant practice'.[44] Bureaucratization promotes efficiency; to quote Weber: 'A fully developed bureaucratic administration stands in the same relationship to non-bureaucratic forms as machinery to non-mechanical modes of production'.[45]

2. Refutation of the Adversarial System

Klein emphasized the role of the court in implementing the social model of civil litigation. A managerial judge was believed to be most capable of safeguarding the swift enforcement of substantive law. Parties tend to promote their private interests whereas the judge has no interest in the outcome of a particular case. As noted above, each case is important to society at large. Klein believed that the judge could represent the state and pursue the common good in litigation.[46] Thereto, Klein proposed to enhance judicial powers.

2.1. *The Principles of Party-Disposition and Party-Presentation*

In the 19th century, Von Gönner identified a number of principles to describe the relation between the court and the litigants.[47] These principles will be briefly discussed in the next Sections.[48]

The *Dispositionsmaxime* (which I will translate as 'the principle of party-disposition') defines a first division of tasks between the parties and the judge. This principle states that parties determine the subject matter of litigation. One can make a distinction between the formal and the substantive principle of party-disposition. The formal principle of party-disposition entails that the initiation of the proceedings is an action that can solely be performed by the person who claims to have a certain right and is able to initiate an action.[49] This implies that the judge is bound to the initiative of parties. Only a party may decide to file a claim or to invoke a remedy. Equally, the parties decide to withdraw their complaint or to acknowledge or oppose a claim or defense of the opponent. The substantive principle of party-disposition holds that the parties determine the scope of the

43 Weber 1954, p. 350.
44 Weber 1954, p. 350.
45 Weber 1954, p. 349, Chapter XIV.
46 Klein & Engel 1927, p. 204.
47 Von Gönner 1801; Böhm 1978 and Bosch-Boesjes 1991, Chapter 1.
48 A discussion of these principles in English is provided by Millar 1923.
49 Von Gönner 1801, p. 303: 'nemo iudex sine actore', 'Wo kein Klager ist, da ist kein Richter'.

dispute. They set the boundaries of their controversy.[50] The judge may not decide upon matters not asked for by the parties. It also implies that the plaintiff decides against whom the case is brought. A judge may not *sua sponte* introduce third parties to the proceedings.

The principle of party-disposition is contrasted with the inquisitorial principle (*Inquisitionsmaxime*). According to the latter principle, the state may initiate a case on behalf of a citizen and the judge is entitled to award the plaintiff something he has not asked for.

The second division of tasks between the parties and the judge concerns the responsibility for the gathering of facts and the presentation of evidence. According to the *Verhandlungsmaxime* (principle of party-presentation), the parties are fully responsible for the process of fact-finding.[51] This principle holds that a judge may only take into consideration facts alleged by parties. In order to reach a verdict, she may not conduct her own research to gather additional facts. Furthermore, the selection and presentation of evidence is to be done by the parties and not by the judge.[52] Klein provided the following summary definition of the principle of party-presentation: 'the factual grounds of the dispute belong to the parties'.[53]

The *Untersuchungsmaxime* (principle of judicial investigation) is the opposite of the principle of party-presentation. It teaches that once an issue is raised before a judge, the judge may search for facts on his own initiative. Modern jurisdictions can generally be placed on a continuum between the theoretical extremes of 'pure judicial investigation' and 'pure party-presentation'.

The Acceptance of the Principle of Party Disposition in Austrian Law

The Austrian General Judicial Ordinance (*Allgemeine Gerichtsordnung*) strictly adhered to the principle of party-disposition. The principle of party-disposition has also been respected in Austrian law since the introduction of the 1895 Code of Civil Procedure.[54] Presently, parties initiate the proceedings with their statement of claim (*Klage*).[55] Only the parties may amend or withdraw their claim,[56] and ultimately the parties themselves decide whether or not they wish to settle.[57] An Austrian judge may not grant the plaintiff something he or she has not claimed.[58] A Court of Appeal may not overturn a decision of a lower court on grounds not raised by the parties.[59] However, the principle of party-disposition does not imply that the court remains passive in the process of litigation.[60]

50 Von Gönner 1801, p. 303: 'Ohne Voraussetzungen zweier streitende Theile kein Rechtstreit'.
51 Translation used by Millar 1923, p. 11.
52 Millar 1923, §3.
53 Klein 1891, p. 10: 'Der Prozessstoff ist Eigenthum der Parteien!'.
54 Rechberger & Simotta 2009, Nos. 401-402, p. 203-204.
55 Sections 226 and 228 Code of Civil Procedure.
56 Sections 235 and 237 Code of Civil Procedure.
57 Section 204 Code of Civil Procedure.
58 Section 405 Code of Civil Procedure.
59 Sections 462, 540 Code of Civil Procedure.
60 Klein 1901, p. 128.

Klein's Critique on the Principle of Party-Presentation

In his book *Pro Futuro* (1891), Klein discussed the principle of party-presentation as it applied in Austria.[61] Klein argued that it gave rise to excessive costs and delays and led to a situation where the civil justice system was inaccessible to the larger part of society and too easily abused by others.[62] According to Klein, parties in the 19th century Austrian system were sovereign, free to command the judge who could not do anything against the will of the parties.[63] Furthermore, a party was sovereign in its relation to the other party in the proceedings. There were no possibilities for one party in the proceedings to compel the other party to cooperate in the process of fact-finding. Klein admired English law because parties in an English lawsuit could resort to discovery to force their opponents to reveal relevant facts and evidence.[64] Also in comparison with other civil law jurisdictions, Klein argued that the Austrian system granted parties an unlimited freedom to refuse to cooperate in the proceedings.[65]

According to Klein, the sovereignty and autonomy of parties under the regime of the General Judicial Ordinance was often justified by arguing that proceedings were an organized battle before the court. In explaining the practice of civil proceedings in Austria, Klein compared court procedures with 'a war without a Red Cross'.[66] He disapproved of the Austrian practices.

Klein's critique on 19th century Austrian adjudication is similar to criticism of adversarialism in other jurisdictions. In 1906, Roscoe Pound wrote of the 'sporting theory of justice' which he believed prevailed in the United States.[67] Similarly,

61 Klein 1891 and Oberhammer 1993, p. 33-42.

62 Klein 1891, p. 21, p. 22: 'Für den einen, grösseren Theil der Bevölkerung und der Rechtssuchenden unbrauchbar, für den anderen allzuleicht missbrauchbar (...)'.

63 Klein 1891, p. 36: 'In der Souveränetät liegt ein Doppeltes: Andere seinem Willen beugen und selbst keinen bestimmenden Willen über sich haben. Unser geltendes Proceßrecht gewährt der Partei die Souveränetät nach beiden Seiten: Herrschaft über den Richter - unbeschränkte Selbstständigkeit gegenüber der anderen Partei, keine gegenseitige Handlungs-, Leistungspflicht der Parteien im Processe'.

64 Klein 1891, p. 41: 'Einen stärkeren Contrast zum Rechte unserer Gerichtsordnungen als den heutigen englischen Proceß kann Mann sich kaum denken. Die Parteien können da über alle sie interessierenden Gegenstande des Processes, oder genauer gesagt, über alle das Recht des Fragenden betreffende Umstände an einander Fragen stellen (interrogatories, discovery by interrogatories). (...) Die englischen Rechtsanschauung nimmt es mit dieser Mittheilungspflicht so streng als möglich, das zeigen deren Sanctionen'.

65 Klein 1891, p. 42-44.

66 Klein 1891, p. 39: 'Es ist dies die Idee des Kampfes, die Auffassung des Processes als ein der Rechtseroberung dienendes sich gegenseitig Bekämpfen der Parteien. Der Jugend wird der Moralgrundsatz eingeprägt, man müsse auch dem Feinde in der Noth helfen, aber im Prozesse ist das etwas ganz Anderes! Der Proceß ist ein Krieg, in dem sich die Parteien als ingrimmig hassende, auf gegenseitige Vernichtung bedachte Feinde mit alle Mitteln niederzuringen bemühen - und dazu das Recht haben. (...) und in dem man namentlich auch den Gegner ruhig sich verbluten sehen kann, ohne juristische oder ethische Hilfeleitungspflicht; sozusagen ein Krieg ohne rothes Kreuz. In dieser Idee des Kampfes liegt den Meisten die "moralische" Rechtfertigung für die aus dem Souveränetätsgedanken herrührende Verunstaltung der Parteibeziehungen'.

67 Pound 1906, p. 447.

Frankel wrote: 'We set the parties fighting. We expect that they will equip themselves with professional fighters - lawyers - to wield the special weapons, gather the added ammunition, and marshal the forces for what will be, if it goes all the way, an all-or-nothing contest'.[68]

2.2. *The Introduction of the Managerial Judge*

In accordance with Klein's ideas, the 1895 Austrian Code of Civil Procedure granted the court a number of managerial powers.[69] In Austrian literature, a distinction is made between two sorts of case management. On the one hand, the Austrian judge may make timetables, serve documents and set dates for court hearings.[70] Such management focuses on the form and structure of litigation and is referred to as 'procedural case management' (*die formelle Prozessleitung*).[71] On the other hand, the judge should actively manage the 'substance' of the process of fact-finding. The judge should ascertain that relevant facts are presented; the court must identify facts that require evidence and should also ensure that relevant evidence is examined. This is referred to as 'substantive case management' (*die materielle Prozessleitung*).[72]

Procedural Case Management

The 1895 Civil Procedural Code granted the court powers to monitor and manage the progress of the proceeding. The Austrian courts are responsible for serving almost all procedural documents.[73] According to the Code, the court schedules the first oral hearing. If more oral hearings were needed, the court also determines when these take place.[74] During the first hearing, the court could try to stimulate early settlement of the case. If settlement failed, the court is required to discuss the further course of litigation with the parties.[75] The Austrian judge is empowered to structure and lead oral hearings such that the case can be disposed of quickly, and if possible, without any interruptions.[76] The judge may for example determine the order in which legal and factual issues will be addressed.[77]

68 Frankel 1980, p. 54.
69 Oberhammer & Domej 2005.
70 Sections 138, 180, 181 and 185 Code of Civil Procedure.
71 See for instance Rechberger & Simotta 2009, No. 605, p. 308: ‚Sie umfasst alle den Prozessbetrieb (...), also alle den äußeren Gang des Verfahrens betreffenden Gerichtshandlungen, wie Anberaumung von Tagsatzungen, Ladungen, Zustellungen, Fristerstreckungen'. Also see Fasching 1990, Nos. 779-789.
72 Ballon 2004, No. 141 and Rechberger & Simotta 2009, No. 605, p. 308: 'Sie ist die auf die Sammlung, Gliederung und Aufbereitung des Prozess-stoffes (Tatsachenvorbringen und Beweisanbote) gerichtete Tätigkeit des Gerichtes, wie zB die Befragung der Zeugen und Parteien...'.
73 E.g. Section 87 Code of Civil Procedure.
74 Sections 257 and 181 Code of Civil Procedure.
75 Section 258 Code of Civil Procedure, newly introduced in 2002.
76 Section 180 Code of Civil Procedure.
77 Section 189 Code of Civil Procedure.

Substantive Case Management and the Principle of Judicial Investigation
The 1895 Civil Procedural Code granted the court a number of powers to actively participate in and manage the process of fact-finding (*materielle Prozessleitung*).[78] In Austria, substantive case management implies that the judge has a duty to establish the facts truthfully (see Chapter 6.1.2.1). The court can *inter alia* do so by interrogating the parties thoroughly. The court's powers are also preeminent when it comes to the production of evidence. The court may *ex officio* order the hearing of parties, witnesses or experts and require that documents and exhibits are produced (Section 7.3).[79]

The 1895 Code of Civil Procedure enhanced the powers of the court. It clearly departed from the principle of party-presentation. Since the enactment of the 1895 Code, it could be argued that the Austrian system has adhered to a weaker version of the principle of judicial investigation (*Untersuchungsgrundsatz*).[80] Only a few elements of the principle of party-presentation still prevail in Austrian law.[81] Parties have the duty to allege all relevant factual information truthfully and should present evidence or suggest the taking of evidence.[82] The Austrian system has continued to recognize that facts alleged by one party and acknowledged by the opposing party require no evidence.[83] If a party explicitly acknowledges facts alleged by the opposing party, the judge should, according to the prevailing case law, establish these facts without examining them.[84] In my opinion, this rule should not be seen as recognition of the principle of party-presentation.[85] Rather, this rule serves to avoid costs and delay. If parties have opposed interests, there is no reason to assume that explicitly acknowledged facts are incorrect. If however, the judge has reasons to doubt whether such explicitly acknowledged statements are true, Austrian case law has held that the judge may demand evidence for undisputed facts.[86] According to the Austrian Code, it is not required that parties explicitly adduce or plead facts before the judge can base her decision on these facts.[87]

78 Klein & Engel 1927, Chapter 11 B.

79 Sections 183 and 371 Code of Civil Procedure.

80 Rechberger & Simotta 2009, No. 403, p. 204: 'Der abgeschwächte Untersuchungsgrundsatz'. Klicka 1992, p. 233 stated the Austrian system is a mix (*Mischform*) of adversarial and inquisitorial elements.

81 A good example is Section 183(2) according to which both parties may oppose the *ex officio* hearing of a witness or order for the production of a document.

82 Sections 226 and 239 Code of Civil Procedure. On the duty to allege facts truthfully see Section 178 Code of Civil Procedure as discussed by Oberhammer 1993, p. 59 *et seq.*

83 Sections 266, 395 and 396(1) Code of Civil Procedure.

84 Rechberger & Simotta 2009, No. 775, p. 404 and the case law there cited.

85 Also see Klein 1900, p. 152.

86 Rechberger & Simotta 2009, No. 775, p. 404.

87 Many scholars have come to the conclusion that the judge may base his decision on facts not alleged or pleaded by either of the parties, for instance if new facts are discovered during the taking of evidence See the literature mentioned by Bajons 2003, No. 18, p. 440 and the discussion below.

3. The Pursuit of Truth

As mentioned above, the process of fact-finding is of great significance within the social model of Klein.[88] In order to enforce substantive law, it is required that facts be established in accordance with the truth. Legal rules to establish the facts correctly will be discussed below.

3.1. *Formal and Substantive Truth*

In a speech on the ideological influences on civil proceedings, Klein sketched the development of the importance of truth in civil proceedings from the Roman times onwards. According to Klein, all was well in the classical Roman times when lay judges used their common sense to determine the facts. But from the 5th century onwards, irrational methods of proof were widely used throughout Europe, like formal oaths, duels and trials by fire and water. Klein refutes these procedures whereby the outcome was the result of luck or dueling skills rather than the facts of the case.[89] He argued that humanism led us out of the darkness and into the light by reintroducing the concepts of Roman law. The Romano-Canonical procedure had rationalized the process of fact-finding and the law of evidence. However, humanism had only partly succeeded.[90] The detailed rules of the Romano-Canonical procedure had created a distinction between what one normally conceives as truth and 'legal truth'.[91] Klein rejected the Romano-Canonical rules of proof, its written procedures, secrecy, and lack of immediacy which had contributed to the existence of two notions of truth. Instead, he favored the free evaluation of evidence, the focus on oral and public proceedings, and the principle of immediacy. Klein hoped to abolish a judicial practice in which the process of fact-finding before the court differed from the way in which a rational man would determine the truth of a factual statement in his everyday life.

In modern jurisdictions, it is sometimes also claimed that a dichotomy between fact-finding in the courtroom and fact-finding in every day life exists.[92]

88 Parker & Lewisch 1998, p. 203-210.

89 Klein 1901, p. 123.

90 Note that Klein identifies humanism with the making of the Roman-Canonical procedure from the 12th century onwards. Now it is common to situate legal humanism in the 16th and 17th century.

91 Klein 1901, p. 123: 'Diese Regeln stellen die Deklination der richterlichen Beurteilung vom Wahrheitsziele dar; mit ihnen dehnt sich der falsche Satz von der zweifachen Wahrheit aus der philosophisch-theologischen Lehre auf das Rechtsleben aus und schafft da einen - leider auch heute noch nicht ganz überwundenen - Zweispalt zwischen gemeiner und juridischer Wahrheit, der für natürliches Denken unverständlich ist und den Rechtschutz bisweilen unsicher und riskant macht. Musste doch das erworbene Recht gegebenenfalls aberkannt werden, weil zufällig für die entscheidende Tatsache nicht zwei unverdächtige Zeugen dem Richter vorgeführt werden können!'.

92 The point is often made in American literature. See e.g. Frankel 1980, p. 54: 'We are not so much as slightly rocked in this assumption by the fact that other seekers after truth have not emulated us. Ours is, after all, a special world of special cases. Even we who made and run →

Langbein claimed that this dichotomy exists in American courts today. His example is edifying:

> 'My favorite example. I'll tell you a really important decision in your personal life - getting married. How dare you do this without lawyers. I mean -I've come to take a shine to Ermaline and I'm thinking about marrying Ermaline. Ermaline, Ermaline, run away with me. But before I do, isn't it obvious that the way to make this decision is to hire some lawyers and to conduct discovery - for and against her - and partisan experts to talk about marriage and demarriage. Once again, guess what, we don't do it folks, we don't do it. The only place that we in the Anglo-American world reserve for the use of these stupid procedures is our law courts'.[93]

Although Klein avoided the use of the terminology in his doctrinal writings, it is not uncommon in legal doctrine to make a distinction between 'substantive truth' and 'formal truth'.[94] The facts as they actually occurred, the true facts, are referred to as 'substantive truth'. The judge establishes the facts of the case. Whatever the judge or jury establishes as facts is usually referred to as 'formal truth' or 'legal truth'. The government's explanatory memorandum to the 1895 Code of Civil Procedure explicitly stressed the importance of 'substantive truth' (*materielle Wahrheit*).[95] Klein mostly avoided using the wording 'substantive truth'. I assume he wanted to avoid some of the philosophical difficulties involved with the notion of 'substantive truth'. Klein was well aware that what is perceived to be the truth today may very well be superseded a decade later. As history proceeds, each truth becomes an error.[96]

As Klein favored the pursuit of substantive truth, he believed that the final decision of the judge should not merely reflect the statement of the parties. The judge has a duty to search for the truth, and must reconstruct the correct factual basis as the main ingredient for a just decision.[97] The following quote summarizes his view on the matter:

> The Austrian system 'holds that the rectitude of the judgment also depends on a possibly perfect correspondence between the facts on which the judgment is based and that which has truly happened. It is not satisfied if the decision repeats the facts that have been adduced but requires that the decision reflects the factual social events and relations; instead of legal reality, it focuses on the pragmatic social reality and aims to

that world would fear for our lives if physicians, disagreeing about the cause of our chest pains, sought to resolve the issue by our forms of interrogation, badgering and other forensics'.

93 Langbein 1993, p. 161.

94 This distinction is often encountered in literature, see for instance Summers 2000, p. 286.

95 Materialien 1897, p. 260.

96 Klein 1901, p. 122: 'Was der einen Periode als das letztmögliche Ziel des geistigen Erkennens und als die allein richtige Denkweise, als die untrüglichste, sicherste Wahrheit erscheint, ist in der nächsten Periode überholt, wird als Torheit und Verirrung mitleidig verlacht. (...) im Flusse der Geschichte besehen, ist die Wahrheit nur eine Irrtumsphase'.

97 Klein 1901, p. 122: 'Aufgabe des Richters ist es, nach Wahrheit zu forschen, Wahrheit zu verkünden, denn ein wahres, richtiges Bild der Tatsachen ist die Hauptbedingung eines gerechten Spruches'.

get as close to this reality as possible, without infringing upon protected private information'.[98]

Limits to the Pursuit of Substantive Truth

Although the social model of civil procedure stresses the importance of truth, it does recognize that 'truth' is not an end in itself. Truth is important because it is important that the final judicial decision is correct.[99] The rectitude of the final decision in turn is ultimately of importance as a means to secure the overall welfare of society. It hence follows directly from Klein's approach that 'truth' should not be pursued at all costs. For example, the Austrian Code provides only limited possibility to challenge factual decisions of the court at first instance on appeal.[100] The system also provides for use of adverse inferences as a sanctioning mechanism. If parties violate procedural rules or refuse to cooperate, an Austrian judge will often establish facts contrary to that party's interest.[101] Such a sanction fits well into Klein's social model, even though it is not in the interest of the pursuit of truth. Furthermore, Klein acknowledges the existence of other interests than resolving a dispute efficiently and correctly. Like other jurisdictions Austria recognizes privileges and provides for rules that protect parties against the disclosure of confidential information, such as trade secrets.[102]

3.2. *The Pursuit of Truth: Practical Implementation*

Many innovations of the 1895 Austrian Code of Civil Procedure aimed at enhancing the possibilities of effectively establishing the facts correctly.[103] To implement a procedure in which information was forthcoming, the 1895 codification 1) required the judge to investigate the facts of the case; 2) required the parties to be truthful; 3) made fact-discovery widely available and 4) removed technical regulations that hampered the pursuit of truth. Each of these issues will be discussed below.

98 Klein & Engel 1927, p. 199: 'Er hält die Richtigkeit des Urteils auch bedingt durch eine möglichst vollständige Kongruenz des Sachverhaltes, auf Grund dessen geurteilt wird, mit dem was sich wirklich zugetragen hat. Er ist nicht damit zufrieden, dass die Entscheidung dem entspricht, was gerade angeführt wird, sondern will, dass sie den tatsächlichen gesellschaftlichen Vorfällen und Verhältnissen entspricht, hat also statt bloß relativer juristischer Richtigkeit sozusagen die pragmatische soziale Richtigkeit im Auge, will sich ihr wenigstens soweit nähern, als es sein kann, ohne geschützte Individualsphären anzutasten'.

99 It is generally accepted that there is a difference between procedures aimed at establishing facts truthfully and procedures aimed at 'doing justice', see for instance Thibaut & Walker 1978, p. 543.

100 The 1895 Code introduced a *Neuerungsverbot* that forbids the parties to allege new claims or facts on appeal. Section 482 Code of Civil Procedure and Rechberger & Simotta 2009, Nos. 750 and 984.

101 Section 272(2) Code of Civil Procedure.

102 Sections 305 and 321 Code of Civil Procedure and Klein 1891, p. 47.

103 Klein 1901, p. 136, quoted at length below.

In his early writings, Klein argued that the lack of truthfulness by a party was harmful to the opposing party and the community at large.[104] Klein believed that two instruments were needed to ban untruthfulness by the parties during the proceedings. First, it was necessary to punish parties if they were untruthful. Klein argued that the judge should have powers to impose sanctions if parties violated their duty to be truthful.[105] Second, Klein proposed to increase the managerial role of the court in the proceedings *(Prozessleitung)*.[106] In accordance with Klein's writings, the role of the court during oral hearings was emphasized in the 1895 Code of Civil Procedure. Section 182 of the Civil Procedural Code encouraged the judge to question the parties. The provision required the judge to 'make sure that all evidence is properly identified and that factual matters are clarified in correspondence with the truth' (see Chapter 6).

The 1895 Code empowered the court to order the production of evidence. Section 183 of the Code allows the judge to order the parties to appear before the court in person or to produce documents that either party had referred to, drawings and other exhibits. The provision also allows the court to order a local visit to a scene of the dispute, to appoint an expert or to hear witnesses *ex officio*. However, if both parties oppose it, the judge may not hear a witness or order the production of documents.[107] Equally, the judge should take a pro-active role in the presentation of evidence. The judge is required to put appropriate questions to witnesses; subsequently the parties and their attorneys may - with leave of the court - ask additional questions.[108]

104 Klein 1885, p. 127: 'Denn die Anstellung einer mit falschen Behauptungen begründeten Klage, das lügenhafte Bestreiten der wahren Klagsangaben ist Verkümmerung des ruhigen Rechtsgenusses und damit selbst Rechtsverletzung. Die vorsätzliche Erschwerung des Rechtsschutzes und der Rechtsverfolgung durch falsches Behaupten verletzt nicht nur das Interesse der Gemeinschaft, (…), sondern wesentlich auch das des Gegners'.

105 Klein 1885, p. 129: 'Es sollte jedoch dem Richter - schon aus sozusagen process-erzehlichen Gründen - die Möglichkeit nicht benommen sein, aufgedeckte bewusste Wahrheits-verletzungen ausserdem mit einem Strafnachteile zu belegen'. p. 132: 'Keinesfalls aber sollte bei einer künstigen Reform des österr. Prozessrechts, (...), das Institut der Lügenstrafen (vermögensstrafen) aufgegeben werden, (...)'.

106 Klein 1885, p. 129: 'Für die Realisierung dieser Wahrhaftigkeits-Pflicht stehen nun zwei Wege offen: die Aufnahme einer intensiven richterlichen (materiellen) Prozessleitung und die Bedrohung der Kontravention des Lügenverbots mit Strafen. Ein solche Prozessleitung -mag sie auch wie im R.C.P. in erster Linie dem Wahrheitszwecke als Prozesszweck dienen) - ist nebenbei immer staatliche gerichtseitige directe Realisirung der Pflicht zur Wahrhaftigkeit. (...) Nur der ihr obliegenden Wahrhaftigkeits-Pflicht wegen hat die Partei keinen Anspruch darauf, dass sich der Richter mit ihrer vielleicht künstlich vieldeutigen Behauptung begnüge, sondern muss es zulassen, dass das Gericht auch wider ihren Willen zergliedere, aufkläre, undeutliche Punkte frageweise hervorhebe und die Wahrheit durch selbständige Heranziehung von Beweisen ausfindig mache'.

107 Section 183 Code of Civil Procedure.

108 Sections 288 and 340 Code of Civil Procedure.

These judicial powers to manage the proceedings aim to establish the facts correctly and efficiently.[109] This implies that the judge should use his powers only if necessary to establish the facts correctly.[110] It is perfectly fine if Austrian judges rarely make use of their powers to order the production of evidence not suggested by the parties. Klein believed that oral examination and immediacy would allow an active judge to freely discuss the factual issues with cooperative parties such that facts could be established correctly and efficiently.[111]

It depends on the qualities and skills of the individual judge whether the judicial discretion is used successfully and effectively.[112] If the judge remains too passive, it could hamper the swift resolution of disputes and the pursuit of truth. If the judge becomes too active in the process of fact-finding, she may infringe upon the principle of impartiality. The judge may only exercise her duties as long as she remains impartial.[113] In performing her managerial tasks the judge should not become 'a legal friend of either one of the parties'.[114] The judge may for instance not help one party by formulating specific facts needed to acquire a legal result.[115]

The 19th century Austrian system did not provide parties with any significant means to compel an opponent to provide information or produce evidence.[116] In his

109 Baur 1970, p. 446: 'Die richterliche Prozeßleitung hat sicher den Zweck, die Verhandlung so sachgemäß zu führen, dass ein der Wahrheit möglichst nahe kommendes Urteil in angemessener Zeit erreicht werden kann'.

110 Sprung 1977, p. 383 and Kralik 1988, p. 92.

111 Klein 1901, p. 136: 'Für die Gründlichkeit ist aufs beste gesorgt durch eine wahrhaft mündlich-unmittelbare Verhandlung, die meist in einem Zuge ohne stockende Unterbrechung abläuft, durch das persönliche Erscheinen der Parteien, die sich von ihrem Vertreter unterstützt, mit dem Gerichte frei und ungezwungen über den Streitfall aussprechen, und durch die intensive richterliche Prozessleitung , der es nicht selten gelingt, binnen kurzem den maßgebenden Sachverhalt aus dem Wuste des Vorbringens herauszuschälen, so dass sich nun die ganze Aufmerksamkeit aller Beteiligten auf diese wenigen entscheidenden Punkte konzentrieren kann. Ferner wird die Gründlichkeit wesentlich gefördert durch die regelmäßig vor dem erkennenden Gerichte stattfindende Beweisaugnahme, durch die an Stelle des formalen Eides eingeführte Einvernehmung der Parteien, durch eine gleichfalls wahrhaft mündliche Berufungsverhandlung usw'.

112 Kralik 1988, p. 92.

113 Austrian law has always held that the judge should remain impartial. See §19 Jurisdiktionsnorm, Austrian Supreme Court 21.12.2004, 4 Ob 253/04s and Article 6 of the European Convention of Human Rights.

114 Also see Rechberger & Simotta 2009, No. 606 p. 308: 'Die Anleitungspflicht nach §§ 182 und 432 ZPO findet jedenfalls immer dort ihre Grenze, wo sie den Anschein der Parteilichkeit des Richters erregen könnte. Der Richter darf nicht zum Ratgeber oder Rechtsfreund einer Partei werden'.

115 Rechberger & Simotta 2009, No. 606-607, p. 308-309.

116 Heimerl 1857, p. 44-45: 'Ihr Dispositionsrecht und der darauf ruhende Verzicht ist von bedeutenden Einflusse, reicht aber nur so weit, als der Gegentheil nicht verletzt wird. Bei der Verfolgung ihres Zweckes sind sie zwar nicht verpflichtet, sich wechselweise in der Erreichung ihres regelmäßig collidirenden Zieles zu unterstützen und sich im Prozesse die Beweisführung zu erleichtern; sie sollen aber -obgleich sie sich als Streitende gegenüberstellen, doch auch nicht das Gegentheil thun'. Klein 1891, p. 37: 'keine Partei ist aus dem Procesverhältnisse dem Gegner zur Gewährung irgend einer Unterstütßung in der Proceßführung verpflichtet'.

work *Pro Futuro* (1891), Klein had already argued in favor of more duties for parties to provide their opponents with information.[117] Klein took the English regulations on discovery as an example and argued that parties should be allowed to: 1) question the opposing party with respect to all relevant facts; 2) question the opposing party with respect to the existence and availability of evidence; and 3) to request the production of documents and exhibits under control of an opponent.[118] The 1895 Code of Civil Procedure implemented each of these suggestions. Parties may question their opponents during the oral hearing about all relevant factual issues including the availability and existence of evidence (see Section 6.1.2.4). Parties may also demand inspection of documents and other means of proof under control of their opponent.[119] Sections 303-309 Code of Civil Procedure empower the parties to compel each other to produce documents or exhibits.[120] Section 303 is cited below.

> 'Section 303, Production of Documents by the Opponent
> (1) If one party claims that a document that he would need to prove his statements of fact is in the hands of the opponent, the judge may upon a motion by that party compel (...) the opponent to produce the document. (2) The party who demands production should provide a copy of the document or, if such is not possible, provide a description, as detailed as possible, of the content of the document, and also specify the facts the document provides evidence for. It should be indicated why it is likely that the opposing party has the document in its possession. (3) If the decision on the motion to produce a document is not taken during the oral hearing, the opposing party should be heard either in writing or orally'.[121]

117 *Wechselweise Unterstützingspflicht*, Klein 1891, p. 47 *et seq.* Also see Kralik 1988, p. 92-93.

118 Klein 1891, p. 47, p. 50: 'Es ist den Parteien die Befugniß gegenseitiger Befragung über alle den Gegenstand des Rechtsstreites betreffenden, für die gegenwärtige Procesführung des Fragenden erheblichen Umstände (Sachverhalt, Legitimationspunkt, Beweismittel) zuzuerkennen. (...) Die Motive zum Entwurfe des Gesetzes über das Bagatellverfahren erklärten sie damit, dass jedem Bestreben entgegenzutreten sei, "das darauf abzielt, der Gegenpartei die Beweismittel vorzuenthalten". Das ist an herrlicher Gedanke (...) Endlich Fragerecht betreffs Vorhandenseins Beschaffenheit Auskunfstsachen, Augenscheinsgegenständen oder anderen Sachen, deren Bezichtigung wie z.B. bei Proben und Mustern auch außer dem Falle eines Augenscheines zur Informierung einer Partei von Wichtigkeit sein kann, und Pflicht diese Dinge nach Analogie des ad. 2. Gesagten zum Zwecke der Beweisführung, des Augenscheins und der Besichtigung vorzuweisen'.

119 Section 228 Code of Civil Procedure.

120 Sections 303-305, 318 Code of Civil Procedure.

121 'Vorlegung der Urkunde durch den Gegner. §303. (1) Wenn eine Partei behauptet, dass sich eine für ihre Beweisführung erhebliche Urkunde in den Händen des Gegners befindet, so kann auf ihren Antrag das Gericht dem Gegner die Vorlage der Urkunde durch Beschluss auftragen. (2) Die antragstellende Partei hat eine Abschrift der vom Gegner vorzulegenden Urkunde beizubringen oder, wenn sie dies nicht vermag, den Inhalt der Urkunde möglichst genau und vollständig anzugeben, sowie die Thatsachen anzuführen, welche durch die vorzulegende Urkunde bewiesen werden sollen. Desgleichen sind die Umstände darzulegen, welche den Besitz der Urkunde seitens des Gegners wahrscheinlich machen. (3) Der Entscheidung über den Antrag hat, wenn derselbe außerhalb der mündlichen Verhandlung gestellt wird, eine mündliche oder schriftliche Einvernehmung des Gegners vorauszugehen'.

The court may only refuse to order the production of documents if there are weighty reasons to do so.[122] Sections 318 and 329 Austrian Code of Civil Procedure provide that the rules on document discovery also apply to exhibits and a local visit to a scene of the dispute. Thus, the 1895 Austrian Code of Civil Procedure created a system of rules that allow parties to obtain information and evidence in control or possession of their adversary.[123] The rationale behind these rules is to assure that the facts of the case are ultimately determined correctly.[124] In Austria the role of the judge is much more prominent than in Anglo-American jurisdictions and leave of the court is needed before a party is obliged to produce a document. In addition, it is required that parties identify precisely what document or object they would like their adversary to produce. A request to produce 'all documents related to the purchase of real estate in 2009' would certainly not meet this requirement.

In Austria, parties are not free to withhold relevant facts. Section 178(1) of the Civil Procedural Code prescribes the parties to provide an accurate, complete and truthful account of relevant facts and circumstances during the oral phase of the proceeding (also see Section 2.4.2.2). The provision implies that parties have a general duty to be cooperative in the process of fact-finding.[125] Section 178(1) is meant to ensure that the facts are ultimately correctly established.[126]

The 1895 Code of Civil Procedure removed procedural rules that hampered the process of fact-finding. The Austrian Code replaced the formal party oath by the informal party interrogation (*Parteivernehmung*, see Section 6.1.3). Many other restrictions on the admissibility of evidence were removed. The old rule that held that certain commercial administrative documents were not admissible as evidence if these documents were drafted longer than one year and 6 weeks ago was not

122 Section 305 Code of Civil Procedure, the court may for instance refuse to order the production of a document is such would reveal trade secrets or if such would lead to violation of a professional duty to treat certain information with confidentiality.

123 Klicka 1992, p. 234: 'Zusammenfassen kann man daher sagen, dass die ZPO ein beinahe komplettes System an Rechtsvorschriften besitzt, um die Beweismittel zur Sachverhaltsermittlung weitestgehend zu nutzen, wenn die beweisbelastete Partei einen konkreten und klar substantiierten Tatsachenvortrag erstattet hat. Dann hat die nicht beweisbelastete Partei, sofern es ihr möglich und zumutbar ist, bei der Ausnützung der Beweismittel weitgehend mitzuwirken'.

124 Klicka 1992, p. 231: 'In diesem Sinn hat die prozessuale Aufklärungspflicht auch die richterliche Wahrheitsfindung und damit letztlich die Gerechtigkeit des Richterspruchs zum Ziel'.

125 Austrian Supreme Court, 11 May 2005, 9Ob12/05p: 'Wie bereits in SZ 74/191 dargelegt wurde, handelt es sich bei der Obliegenheit der nicht beweisbelasteten Partei, über dem Prozessgegner unbekannte Vorgänge in ihrer Sphäre Auskunft zu geben, um eine aus allgemeinen Bestimmungen der ZPO abgeleitete prozessuale Mitwirkungspflicht zur Erforschung der Wahrheit. In diesem Zusammenhang wurde besonders auf die gesetzlich normierte Wahrheits- und Vollständigkeitspflicht (§§178, 377 ZPO) hingewiesen. Darüber hinaus kennt die ZPO eine Reihe weiterer prozessualer Mitwirkungspflichten der Parteien, (...)'. Also see Bienert-Nießl 2003 and the related arguments by Stürner on the German provision, Stürner 1976.

126 Klein & Engel 1927, p. 318: 'dass auch hier die wahrheitsmaßige Feststellung des Tatbestandes der Rechte und Ansprüche als Ziel hingestellt wird'.

retained under the 1895 Code of Civil Procedure.[127] Similarly, those who were convicted of certain crimes were no longer incompetent testify as witnesses.[128] Another important change was the introduction of free evaluation of evidence (See Section 2.3.1.2).

4. Critical Observations

In the previous Sections, I have tried to provide a clear and convincing account of the procedural model developed by Franz Klein. In many ways, Klein's model could still be considered 'modern'. After all, many aspects of the social model remain influential in numerous Continental jurisdictions. Nevertheless, I believe it is fair to add some critical comments. In general, Klein's views are lopsided for at least two reasons.

First, it is remarkable to see that the writings of Klein attach little value to the fairness of the judicial process and the satisfaction of litigants (also see Chapter 5). Klein primarily seemed to focus on the rectitude of the decision and the efficiency of litigation. Klein's view on civil litigation appears to be akin to 'a guy's perspective on shopping': its all about getting a good pair of jeans as quickly and cheaply as possible. Just like women are quick to point out the value of spending an enjoyable day strolling through a shopping mall, it is important to point out the value of procedural fairness (see Section 8.2).

Second, one senses if one reads through Klein's texts, that the Austrian model distrusts both the parties and their lawyers. His *Habilitation* thesis discussed vexatious litigation and the evils of adversarialism in depth. In his texts, one finds numerous phrases in which he argues that parties abuse procedural rules and frustrate the litigation process.[129] One does not find lengthy passages in which he describes the ways in which lawyers or parties could provide a solution to pressing procedural problems. It seems that Franz Klein was of the opinion that legislation and judicial intervention were to be regarded as a means to remedy problems created by the parties and their lawyers. Klein primarily provides top down solutions to procedural problems.[130] His views could be labeled 'authoritarian'.

It must be noted that later Austrian doctrinal works, as well as later reforms of the Austrian Code of Civil Procedure (see Sections 2.3.1), have placed more emphasis on issues of fairness. It is also increasingly stressed that litigation is above

127 Section 120 General Judicial Ordinance.

128 Section 140 General Judicial Ordinance.

129 See for instance Klein 1891, p. 72-73: 'Es ist alle Tage wahrzunehmen und wiederholt sich allerorten: die Parteien benützen die bestehenden Prozesseinrichtungen und Formen oft im vollen Bewusstsein, dass es an einem legitimen Zweck fehlt, lediglich als Mittel zur Erreichung unehrlicher, verwerflicher, schlimmer Absichten, insbesondere zur Verhinderung, Erschwerung oder Trübung der Entscheidung, zur Verzögerung derselben oder zum Verschleife und zur unnötigen Komplizierung des Verfahrens, zur Verkürzung und Gefährdung der prozessualen Stellung des Gegners u.s.w. Man kann dies kurz Missbrauch der Prozesseinrichtungen nennen'.

130 Oberhammer & Domej 2010.

all a matter of cooperation between the judge and the parties.[131] Some of the problematic aspects of Klein's model may therefore not necessarily constitute just criticism of the present Austrian system.

131 It is not uncommon in Austrian literature to refer to the 'Arbeitsgemeinschaft Zivilprozess', as was done in the 1927 book (published after Klein's death) on Austrian Civil Procedure that was written by both Klein and Engel. See for instance Rechberger & Simotta 2009, No. 399, p. 202. I have not come across this notion in earlier works of Klein.

Chapter 8

A RECONSTRUCTION OF THE U.S. MODEL: DEMOCRACY AND ADVERSARIALISM

1. Introduction

The United States' fact-finding arrangements have never been 'designed'. There was no academic work or political pamphlet that served as a blueprint for the present day United States civil procedural system. Rather, the present day approach to fact-finding is the result of the historical process set out in Chapter 3. U.S. fact-finding arrangements have their origins in the English common law. Over the past centuries these gradually developed into a unified body of rules. The Federal Rules of Civil Procedure and the Federal Rules of Evidence (FRE) provide a coherent, well structured and easily accessible set of rules. These rules are in part the result of an evolutionary process, not of revolutionary design.

The Federal Rules of Civil Procedure (FRCP) specify that disputes should be resolved in a just, speedy and inexpensive way.[1] Although these aims seem similar to those of the Austrian Code, I will argue that the U.S. approach to fact-finding has a multitude of distinctive features. In this Chapter, I will offer a 'rational reconstruction' of the United States Federal litigation system. I believe that two distinctive features of the U.S. system are most prominent: the adversarial system and the civil jury. These are the cornerstones of the system. Once the choice for the adversarial system and the civil jury is made, the procedural landscape is no longer an infinite universe.

2. The Adversarial System

2.1. *Defining the Adversarial System*

In a nutshell, the adversarial system is a system of adjudication in which: 1) the decision maker is neutral and passive; 2) the proceedings are controlled by the

1 FRCP, Rule 1: 'These rules (...) shall be construed and administered to secure the just, speedy and inexpensive determination of every action'.

parties, who are primarily responsible for the presentation of information and evidence and 3) lawyers represent their clients as 'zealous advocates'.[2]

From the 17th century onwards, more and more adversarial mechanisms found their way into the English and American legal systems. According to Landsman, the adversarial system had become firmly established by the end of the 1700s in both England and the United States.[3] Today, adversarialism is generally considered to be a defining characteristic of the legal system of the United States.[4] In civil cases, the right to an adversary process falls under the rubric of 'procedural Due Process' as guaranteed under the 14th Amendment to the United States Constitution.[5]

Adversarial and Inquisitorial Models of Litigation

The adversarial principle is generally contrasted with the 'inquisitorial' approach to litigation.[6] The adversarial system insists upon strictly separating the active factual investigation from the more passive functions of evaluating evidence and rendering a decision.[7] The adjudicator in an adversarial setting will be rather passive during the fact-gathering process and the presentation of evidence. In a pure inquisitorial system, the adjudicator actively intervenes in the process of fact-finding and the parties play a minor role in presenting and gathering the facts. As discussed in Section 7.2, a slightly more refined terminology is used in German literature to describe the respective roles of the parties, their lawyers, and the judge in the process of fact finding.

Pure adversarial and pure inquisitorial procedures are only theoretical constructs. In practice, procedural models combine both inquisitorial and adversarial elements. The Austrian system has many inquisitorial elements. It would however be inaccurate to label Continental civil procedural systems as inquisitorial.[8] In the Netherlands and Germany, the judicial quest for truth may not go beyond the facts pleaded by the parties.[9] Continental civil law systems are less adversarial than the American procedure when it comes to the presentation of evidence. Once facts are alleged, the court has a reasonable control over the production and presentation of evidence.[10] Criminal proceedings on the European continent could be labeled as non-adversarial or perhaps even 'moderately inquisitorial'. In criminal cases a Continental judge may disregard a defendant's guilty plea or an admission of fact. Additionally, the judge may try to search for facts beyond the facts alleged by the public prosecutor and the defendant. American jury trials provide an example of proceedings in which adversarial elements are

2 Belliotti 1988.
3 Landsman 1988, p. 15.
4 E.g. Langbein 1993 and Friedenthal, Kane & Miller 2005 p. 2-3. Some have even referred to it as a 'gospel', e.g. Kaufman, as quoted by Cappelletti 1970, p. 880.
5 Landsman 1988, p. 1, p. 36-37.
6 Jolowicz 2003 and Van Koppen & Penrod 2003.
7 For a very accessible introduction, see Burnham 2006, Chapter 3.
8 See Bernstein 1987, Part I. Landsman 1988, p. 38-39 provides such an 'inaccurate' description.
9 Bernstein 1987, p. 592.
10 See the discussion of Dutch law in Section 2.3, also see Kötz 2003, p. 69.

predominant. The jurors are 'cast in the role of potted courtroom plants', they have no proof initiative and are often not allowed to question the witnesses.[11]

From a comparative and historical perspective, the rise and fall of adversarial litigation appears to have gone hand in hand with the rise and fall of 'laissez faire' liberalism. In recent history we seem to have witnessed the 'fall' of adversarialism in a number of jurisdictions. The introduction of the 1895 Code of Civil Procedure in Austria and incremental reforms in the Netherlands over the last century well illustrate this change (see Chapter 2.4.4). The same trend can be perceived in common law jurisdictions. The Woolf reform in England provides a good example in this respect.[12]

2.2. *The Rationale behind the Adversarial System*

Apart from the fact that people from all over the world admire the American adversary trial as a great setting for movies and novels, there have been other more compelling reasons in favor of an adversarial procedure. It has been argued that the adversarial system is more effective in getting at the truth as the adversary system rightly aligns incentives.[13] On the other hand, parties in an adversarial system also have an incentive to distort facts or shift attention away from relevant matters (see Chapter 10). In this Section, I will discuss the two most compelling reasons for the adversarial system: 1) it safeguards against premature decision-making and 2) it has a positive impact on litigant's perception of fairness.

2.2.1. Adversarialism and Premature Decisions

Preliminary Theories, Belief Persistence and Confirmation Bias

All people are inclined to start theorizing about the meaning of certain facts, even if only a small proportion of relevant information has been provided. After the evaluation of other relevant information preliminary theories may be revised. However, psychological research has shown that people tend to hold on to their initial beliefs even if it is later shown that there is no compelling evidence supporting these beliefs. This phenomenon is generally referred to as 'belief perseverance' or 'belief persistence'.[14] People tend to overestimate the probability that their preliminary theory is correct.[15] Closely related to 'belief perseverance' is the phenomenon to which psychologists refer as 'confirmation bias'. Confirmation bias connotes 'the seeking or interpreting of evidence in ways that are partial to existing beliefs, expectations, or a hypothesis in hand'.[16] Although people

11 This metaphor is used by Damaska 1997a, p. 90.

12 Andrews 1995 and Verkerk 2005b.

13 See e.g. Schwarzer 1989, Part IIB, p. 709. The United States' Supreme Court in *Watkins v. Sowders*, 449 U.S. 341 (1981) held that 'under our adversary system of justice, cross-examination has always been considered a most effective way to ascertain truth'.

14 Crombag 2006.

15 Koriat & Fiedler 2006.

16 Definition by Nickerson 1998.

sometimes deliberately seek or evaluate evidence in order to find support for their beliefs and hold on to them, the phenomena 'confirmation bias' and 'belief persistence' refer to less conscious processes. A great amount of evidence shows that 'confirmation bias' and 'belief perseverance' are strong and influential psychological phenomena.[17] As a result, the prior experience with other comparable cases will carry a more than proportional weight in the final findings about facts (expectancy bias). Similarly, the materials first evaluated will tend to be overvalued (primacy effect).

In the judicial process an adjudicator can construct a preliminary theory on the basis of 1) prior experience with comparable cases and 2) part of the information (e.g. the pleadings) that has already been evaluated.

Judges - like all other people - are inclined to attach too much value to the information on which the preliminary theory is based. Empirical research has shown that the order in which information is offered to the judge clearly influences his or her decision. In a study by Schünemann and Bandilla, 35 professional German criminal judges were asked to give a judgment on the same case. The case was considered to be a 'hard case' in the sense that reasonable men could decide the case differently. Half of the judges were given investigative records incriminating the suspect prior to the hearing; the others received no information in advance. In the end, all judges received the same information. Those that had received the investigating records in advance all found that the suspect was guilty. Approximately half of the judges that did not receive the investigative records in advance convicted the suspect.[18] This study confirms that judges 1) create preliminary theories and 2) are inclined to stick to these theories.

Similarly, laboratory studies have shown that the cases previously adjudicated by the trier of fact are likely to contribute to the formation of a preliminary theory. Thibaut and Walker conducted a study with undergraduate students by having them first decide six cases similar to the test case. In five out of these six cases, the defendant had clearly acted unlawfully. In the test case, those that had decided the other six cases more often judged that the defendant acted unlawfully. Thibaut and Walker tested whether this (undesirable) effect of the bias was larger if the same evidence was presented by one attorney (i.e. inquisitorial presentation) or two attorneys (i.e. adversary presentation). The findings of this study were that the adversary presentation of evidence was more effective in combating the expectancy bias.[19] These findings are interesting, even though one should be careful to interpret the findings of laboratory studies.

17 Nickerson 1998, p. 177.

18 Schünemann & Bandilla 1989. Earlier laboratory studies had already shown that the order in which evidence is presented influences the final outcome of the case, Thibaut & Walker 1975, Chapter 7.

19 Thibaut & Walker 1975, Chapter 6.

Adversarialism as a Means to avoid Premature Decisions

In a legal setting it is considered undesirable if the trier of fact persists too much in his or her initial beliefs or primarily seeks information that confirms his or her theory. Often we believe that it is much more desirable to search for information that could falsify a theory about the facts. If the trier of fact is affected by a 'confirmation bias' and by 'belief perseverance', this can have a negative impact on both the accuracy and the fairness of the process of fact-finding.

The strongest argument in favor of the adversarial system is that decision-makers who actively investigate the facts and collect the evidence themselves tend to make a preliminary decision prior to the evaluation of all relevant facts. It has been argued that preliminary theorizing is more troublesome if a decision-maker actively investigates and manages the process of fact-finding.[20] The decision maker will: 1) be forced to construct a preliminary theory on the basis of a small selection of all relevant information in order to determine the further course of the action and 2) when evidence is taken, focus on evaluating evidence that supports this theory (confirmation bias). As an ABA Committee Report put it: 'what starts as a preliminary diagnosis designed to direct the inquiry tends, quickly and imperceptibly, to become a fixed conclusion, as all that confirms the diagnosis makes a strong imprint on the mind, while all that runs counter to it is received with diverted attention'.[21]

The adversarial system is considered to be an effective remedy against premature decision-making. By holding the parties responsible for the process of fact-finding, the need for preliminary theorizing by the decision-maker disappears. Thereby the danger of hasty conclusions, based on a small part of all relevant information, is reduced. Rather, both parties can present all the details and evidence of the case leaving the judge in 'suspension' until the last bits of material have been alleged.[22] The extent to which procedural regimes encourage a trier of fact to resort to premature decision making will be discussed below.

It is relevant to see that in some procedural settings the 'primacy effect' can lead to a bias whereas in other procedural settings the negative effects of the 'primacy effect' could be diminished. In ordinary proceedings before the Austrian County Courts, the defendant is not required to file a statement of defense prior to the first oral hearing.[23] This is understandable from the perspective of 'efficiency', but it leads to a structural bias in favor of the plaintiff as shown by the aforementioned study by Schünemann and Bandilla.

A jury trial in the United States is designed in a way that limits the primacy effect. Jurors are expected to enter the court room as a 'tabula rasa'.[24] The danger of

20 Landsman 1988, p. 2-3.

21 *Professional Responsibility: Report of the Joint Conference*, 44 A.B.A.J. 1159 (1958), quoted by Fuller 1961, p. 39-40.

22 Fuller 1978, p. 382.

23 Section 440(2) Austrian Code of Civil Procedure.

24 Such is of course difficult if jurors have heard 'pretrial publicity' in bigger cases. Research indicates that such publicity can bias jury decision-making, Ruva, McEvoy & Becker Bryant 2007.

bias due to the primacy effect is smaller as all information is presented to the jurors during one uninterrupted event in which attorneys can provide the jurors with information in turns. The jury will probably also be less subject to an expectancy bias than a judge, as a juror is less likely to have had prior experiences with similar cases.

A second relevant issue is the effect of the preliminary theory on the processing of new materials. If the trier of fact is active in the process of fact-finding, he is inclined to only consider evidence that supports his preliminary theory (confirmation bias). Again the procedural regime is to some extent capable of avoiding such effects. An Austrian or Dutch judge may either appoint an expert or not appoint one. Due to the 'confirmation bias' the judge is inclined to do that which is more likely to support his preliminary theory.[25] The American jury, on the other hand, has no discretion to appoint experts. The jury cannot decide whether or not an expert will be heard. Therefore it is not possible that the 'confirmation bias' of a juror will affect the evidence which will be evaluated.

The confirmation bias may also affect the way in which evidence will be presented. An Austrian or Dutch judge might be inclined to ask clarifying questions to witnesses who support his preliminary theory and critical questions to witnesses who challenge their theory. Again, by contrast, the juror in the United States is traditionally not entitled to question witnesses (see Sections 3.1-3.2).

Another way in which procedural settings can avoid belief persistence is to form a panel of adjudicators. Different persons might each have a different preliminary theory about the facts of the case. If different persons are bound to reach consensus on the factual issues, each is encouraged to be critical of his or her preliminary theory. In a panel of three judges, it is possible that judges assign a different weight to each of the means of proof because they have differing preliminary theories. If they can reach consensus, it is likely that their final decision is less affected by belief persistence. Again, the jury in the United States would provide a good example of a trier of fact that is least likely to be influenced by belief persistence.[26]

We may conclude that in the American adversarial system - especially in case of jury trials - there are many safeguards against premature decision-making and early bias. In this respect, the American adversarial system has an edge over other procedural systems.

25 Crombag 2006.

26 Jurors tend to construct different theories, Kuhn, Weinstock & Flaton 1994, p. 295. Social exchange between the jurors may correct for individual bias. Empirical findings have frequently shown that the verdict preferred by the majority of jurors on the first ballot was the jury's final verdict over 90% of the time, Devine, Clayton, Dunford, Seying & Pryce 2001, p. 623.

2.2.2. The Adversarial System and Perceived Procedural Fairness

Procedural Justice: What constitutes a fair Procedure?

Different studies, in distinct settings and in different countries have produced a consistent set of criteria that determine whether or not people will rate a procedure as fair.[27] Differently put, individuals use a number of dimensions in their assessment of procedural justice.[28] It seems that three issues are most relevant to citizens in their assessment of the fairness of a procedure. First, procedures are considered to be fairer if parties have had a possibility to voice their opinion. It is one of the most frequently replicated effects in general psychological research on procedural justice that people respond positively to procedures that give them an opportunity to be heard. Many studies have shown that people that have an opportunity to voice their opinion tend to rate the procedure as more fair.[29] Moreover, people tend to evaluate a procedure as unfair if they did not have a possibility to express their opinion. Second, procedures are rated as fair if the decision maker was impartial. An impartial decision maker is neutral, unbiased, and treats all parties equally and fairly. A third factor that impacts the degree in which citizens rate a procedure as fair is whether or not they have been treated with dignity, honesty and trust. People care about whether or not they receive assurance that the decision maker listened to them and cared about their case and rights.[30]

Perhaps surprisingly, studies have shown that the outcome as well as the (perceived) costs and duration of the legal process have only a limited impact on citizen's perceptions of the fairness of the procedure.[31]

The Adversarial System as a Means to ensure Fair Procedures

According to Fuller, the 'essence of the adversarial system is that each side is accorded a participation in the decision that is reached, a participation that takes the form of presenting proofs and arguments'.[32] Litigants feel that the best arguments in favor of their case have been adequately expressed and presented to the adjudicator when they receive ample opportunities to present and plan their case according to their own wishes. The adversarial system thereby creates the possibility for the litigants to voice their opinion.

27 See in general: Welsch 2003; Tyler 2001; Lind 1998 and Shestowsky 2004.

28 See Colquit 2001.

29 See Lind, Kanfer & Earley 1990 and Van Prooijen, Van den Bos, Lind & Wilke 2006, p. 632 and the literature there quoted.

30 A study by Tyler, for example, showed that the most important factors that shaped citizens to regard procedures as fair were whether authorities were impartial (i.e. honest and trying to be fair) and ethical (i.e. whether authorities were polite and showed concern for citizens rights), Tyler 1990, Table 11.1, p. 137, Figure 10.1, p. 129.

31 See for instance Lind, Maccoun, Ebener, Felstiner, Hensler, Resnik & Tyler 1990, p. 969-970, p. 973-976. This study shows there is a weak (often not significant) relationship between (perceived) costs and duration of the procedure and the perceived fairness and satisfaction with the outcome.

32 Fuller 1961, p. 40.

By curbing the involvement of the trier of fact, the adversarial system eliminates the possibility that the judge creates the appearance that he is partial, not neutral or biased. Suppose for instance, that a witness's testimony contradicts an earlier statement given by that witness. There can be several reasons for this contradiction, ranging from a simple misunderstanding to a deliberate lie. If the judge confronts the witness with the contradiction, pressing him for an explanation, he could convey the impression that he believes the witness is not reliable. The party who suggested the witness might feel that the judge is biased. If the witness is not confronted with the contradiction, the other party will have the impression that the judge believes the contradiction is unimportant. Either way, the judge might create the appearance that he is not fully neutral and unbiased.[33]

In an adversarial system, to conclude, parties have a possibility to voice their opinion and it is easier for the judge to appear impartial and neutral. As discussed above, this positively affects the perceived fairness of the legal process.

The Importance of Procedural Justice

It is important that parties believe that the procedure is fair. Fairness is often considered as a desired quality in itself, but is also of great importance for other reasons.[34]

Litigants more often believe the outcome is acceptable if the procedure is perceived as fair. There have been a number of studies that reveal a strong correlation between the litigants' perception of procedural justice (i.e. fairness) and their perception of the degree in which the outcome was fair.[35] This correlation is strongest if the outcome of the legal process is to the detriment of a litigant.[36]

Empirical studies have consistently shown that a high litigant's perception of fairness will lead to a greater support for legal institutions and authorities.[37] A survey by Tyler in the 1980s of defendants in traffic and misdemeanor courts showed that positive attitudes about the judge and the courts were positively correlated with the perceived fairness of the proceedings.[38] A survey by Mein *et al* (2006) showed that 96% of the litigants in Dutch District Court believed that the court hearing they had attended was fair. The same survey showed that the trust that litigants had in the judiciary, was greater after the hearing than before the hearing.[39] Similarly, a study by Benesh (2006), revealed a very significant correlation between perceived fairness and the level of confidence citizens had in the courts in their community.[40] To what extent the perceived legitimacy of institutions is truly caused by the perceptions of fairness is a different question. It is very questionable

33 The example is taken from Burnham 2006, p. 82.

34 Lind & Tyler 1988, p. 64.

35 Van den Bos, Wilke, Lind, & Vermunt 1998; Lind, Walker, Kurtz, Musante & Thibaut 1980 and Tyler 2001 p. 65-66.

36 Lind & Tyler 1988, p. 66-70.

37 Benesh 2006, p. 699 and Tyler 2001, p. 66.

38 Lind & Tyler 1988, p. 65-66.

39 Mein, Verberk & Vos 2008, p. 69, Tables 15 and 17.

40 Benesh 2006, p. 703. Benesh concluded that the citizen's perceptions of fairness are 'mightily influential on confidence in the state courts'.

whether or not the perceived fairness of the procedures used by the U.S. Supreme Court causes citizens to believe that the Supreme Court is legitimate. It seems more plausible that perceived legitimacy of the U.S. Supreme Court affects the perceptions of fairness of the procedures used by the Supreme Court.[41] With regard to the perceptions of litigants who had experiences with general jurisdiction courts, it seems much more likely that perceptions of fairness cause changes in the perceived legitimacy of the courts.[42]

There is also evidence that suggests that litigants' positive appraisal of the fairness of a procedure helps to reduce post-litigation friction and thereby facilitates compliance with the final decision. A judgment often does not end a conflict as is well illustrated by the fact that a large proportion of judgments is not complied with.[43] Since the 1980s, researchers have consistently found that if authorities treat people with fairness, respect and neutrality, people are more willing to cooperate with these authorities and are more likely to comply with their decisions.[44] Empirical studies have also indicated that the perceived legitimacy of legal authorities is also positively correlated with compliance with the law.[45]

Fairness of the Legal Process: Comparative Remarks

All modern procedural systems are at least in part adversarial. In all modern systems there are devices to ensure that parties can voice their opinion. There seems to be no empirical evidence that reveals that litigants experience the procedure in the United States as 'more fair' than the procedure in less adversarial jurisdictions like Austria or the Netherlands. As discussed in Chapter 6, Dutch litigants are generally of the opinion that the Dutch legal process and court hearings are conducted fairly. It is difficult to make conclusive judgments in this respect.[46]

Some laboratory studies have tried to measure the perceived fairness of adversarial, inquisitorial and mixed systems. An early and simple laboratory study by Thibaut and Walker indicated that litigant satisfaction is greater in an adversarial setting in which parties can choose their own lawyer than in a setting in which a single lawyer would be assigned to represent the facts of the case for both parties. Their studies also indicated that litigant satisfaction is higher if the attorney is given a conditional fee.[47] One should, however, be careful to interpret these findings. Given the setting provided in these experiments, the Dutch, Austrian and U.S. civil procedural systems all qualify as adversarial systems. In another laboratory study,

41 For a debate on this question see Mondak 1993.
42 Mondak 1993, p. 608.
43 For Dutch empirical data, see Van Koppen & Malsch 1992 and Eshuis 2009.
44 For an overview of literature, see Murphy & Tyler 2008, p. 653 and Verkerk 2010.
45 See Tyler 1990, Table 3.1, Chapter 12. This is however not always the case. In the Netherlands for example, proceedings in which a personal appearance is scheduled are rated as more fair but have lower compliance rates, see Eshuis 2009, p. 81.
46 Empirical data are often inadequate to compare between jurisdictions. Interesting, but certainly not adequate to address the questions here discussed, is a comparative classroom experiment in which it was concluded that 'perceived fairness' of Continental and common law procedures 'was comparable', Murray 1997, p. 254.
47 Thibaut & Walker 1975, Chapters 8 and 9.

Thibaut and Walker tried to measure whether the degree in which the judge was active during trial (by asking questions) affected the degree in which the parties felt they had control over the proceedings. The results of the study failed to confirm their expectation that parties would experience more control over the proceedings if the judge did not actively ask questions.[48] More recent laboratory studies have indicated that litigants prefer hybrid models (that combine adversarial and inquisitorial elements) over a strict adversarial model.[49]

2.3. *The Influence of the Adversarial System on Fact-finding*

The adversarial system has shaped the civil justice system of the United States in many ways. The 'work product rule', which limits the scope of discovery, can be understood against the background of the adversarial system. If the work-product of lawyers were subject to discovery, this would seriously hamper the ability of lawyers to perform their work as persuasive and zealous advocates.[50] In several other areas, the strict application of the adversarial system has led to rules and practices that deviate from rules and practices on the European continent. American pretrial discovery, the presentation of evidence and exclusionary rules of evidence provide the clearest examples of how the adversarial system has influenced the process of fact-finding in the United States.

The Adversarial System and Pretrial Discovery

In order to give both parties a fair opportunity to present their case at trial, it is broadly recognized that there should be equal access to relevant information and evidence. There is a need for rules that prevent litigation from devolving 'into a game of hide the ball' (see Section 3.2.2.2).[51] This implies that it must be possible to obligate the parties to exchange available information and evidence. In an adversarial system, the judge does not actively participate in the gathering of information and the presentation of evidence. In such a system, the judge should refrain from actively enforcing the full exchange of information prior to the presentation of evidence at trial. The adversary procedure, together with a basic notion of procedural fairness, creates the need for rules that empower the parties to enforce their opponents to provide information and produce evidence. This is the main reason why the United States favors a party-driven discovery procedure to enforce a fair access to information and evidence.[52] In Austria on the other hand, the

48 Thibaut & Walker 1975, Chapter 10 and Shestowsky 2004.

49 Poythress 1994.

50 Without the work product rule lawyers would for instance be encouraged not to put anything down in writing in order to avoid the possible future disclosure of documents. This would clearly be a burden to a proper preparation, see Kane 1964.

51 This metaphor is frequently used. See for instance *Roden-Kaczmarek v. Village of Lyons*, 2006 U.S. Dist. LEXIS 85226. 'Discovery in a civil case, and the preparation of a final pretrial order, is not a game of hide-the-ball in which the opposing party has to guess at what evidence may be offered at trial'.

52 Landsman 1988, p. 4.

court should actively try to gather all relevant facts in order to discover the 'truth'. Instead of using pretrial discovery devices to obtain relevant information, the Austrian judge will question the parties about the factual basis of the dispute during oral hearings.

The Adversarial System and the Presentation of Evidence

In the United States, the adversarial system has deeply influenced the way in which evidence is presented to the trier of fact. Attorneys on both sides will determine what evidence will be presented and in what order. The judge remains passive as long as the parties abide by the procedural rules. It has long been held improper for the judge to intervene and to extensively question the witnesses.[53] Over the years, there have been attempts to limit the adversarial approach and courts have been empowered to call and question witnesses.[54] Courts do not tend to use these powers and prefer to leave the selection, questioning and cross-examination of witnesses to the lawyers. Similarly, it is lawyers who will try to question the credibility of the witness (impeachment of witnesses). In contrast, on the European continent, it is usually the judge who will primarily question the witness. Generally, the witness is given an opportunity to tell his story without being interrupted. The judge will then ask some clarifying questions after which counsel of each side will be given an opportunity to question the witness.

The adversarial system has led to a polarization of evidence in American courts. Evidence is considered to 'belong' to the party that offered it. The classic ban on impeaching one's own witness and the careful preparation of (expert) witnesses by counsel illustrate this polarization.[55] Evidence itself is not considered to be neutral. Rather the means of proof are considered to be partisan tools to construct one's own arguments or missiles to attack the arguments of the opposing party. A witness who testifies to the detriment of the party that called him to take the stand is considered to be a Benedict Arnold (i.e. turncoat). Such a polarization of evidence is perhaps best demonstrated by comparing the diverging approaches to expert evidence in Austria and the United States (see Chapter 5). In Austria witnesses and experts are considered to be performing a duty towards the court. In Austria it would be improper to use terminology as 'the opposing party's witness' or 'my expert'.[56]

53 Friedenthal, Kane & Miller 2005, §10.1, p. 494.

54 FRE, Rule 614 (a), 614(b) and 706. For an early attempt to limit adversarialism, see American Law Institute 1942.

55 See Damaska 1997a, p. 77-78. The ban on impeaching ones' own witness no longer exists in most American jurisdictions.

56 See Klein 1900, p. 167: 'Der Zeuge ist nicht Zeuge dieser oder der anderen Partei, die "ihre" Zeugen mitbringt, wie sie früher "ihren" Sachverständigen nominiert hat, sondern er ist Prozesszeuge. Die gerichtliche Ladung drückt diese öffentlich-rechtliche Funktion des Zeugen, dass er der Justiz dient und nicht einer bestimmten Partei, besser aus und ist auch aus diesem Gesichtspunkte jenem formlosen Vorgange vorzuziehen'.

The Adversary System and the Exclusionary Rules of Evidence
Exclusionary rules of evidence declare that a piece of evidence should not be considered at all by the trier of fact. It has frequently been argued that the adversarial scheme of fact-finding provides compelling reasons for exclusionary rules of evidence.[57] The link between the adversarial system and the exclusion of hearsay evidence is clearest.[58] If the testimony of a declarant that did not testify in court were admissible, this would effectively lead to an evisceration of the right to cross-examination. The adversarial system, generally believed to imply that counsel has a right to cross-examine witnesses, therefore provides a foundation for the exclusion of hearsay evidence.

There has been a discussion amongst historians about whether or not exclusionary rules of evidence find their origin in the civil jury or in the adversarial system.[59] Both the civil jury and the adversarial system may however provide a justification for exclusionary rules of evidence (see Section 8.3.3).

3. The Civil Jury

The second distinguishing feature of the American approach to civil litigation is that it uses the civil jury at a large scale to decide on matters of fact. The adversarial system prefers a neutral and passive decision maker. A panel of laymen is the ultimate example of such a neutral and passive decision maker.[60] The institution of the jury therefore fits well in the American adversarial system.

3.1. *Introduction*

The Wide Use of the American Jury
Most colonies of the British Empire adopted a judicial system similar to that of England and also retained the institution of the civil jury.[61] However, in most common law jurisdictions the jury in civil cases has gradually disappeared. Throughout the last few centuries, trials by judge alone have gradually replaced the trial by jury as the normal mode to decide on factual issues. In England, the civil jury effectively disappeared in the second half of the 19th century. The 1846 County Court Acts had made the jury trial optional. By 1850 jury trials in the County Courts were exceptional.[62] The English Common Law Procedure Act made trial by judge available in the common law courts if the parties agreed and the court gave consent.

57 E.g. Damaska 1997a, p. 80, p. 84 and American Law Institute 1942, Introductory Note to Chapter 6.
58 Landsman 1990, p. 1156-1157.
59 Friedman 2002 and Langbein 1996, p. 1169.
60 Landsman 1988, p. 3.
61 Landsman 1992, p. 582-592.
62 In 1850, 769 out of 217,173 trials in the County Courts were tried by jury, *The Times*, 22 January 1852, discussed by Hanly 2005, p. 273. For extensive statistics between 1837 and 1914, see Lobban 2002.

The rate of jury trials declined slowly pursuant to the Act.[63] The commissioners' report leading to the Judicature Acts of 1873-1875 questioned the use of civil juries as an appropriate means to establish the facts.[64] In 1883, it became the general rule that trial would be by judge alone unless the parties wished otherwise. In 1933, it was determined that the court could decide upon the mode of trial. In 1965, the Court of Appeal held that the court could only make use of this discretion in exceptional circumstances.[65] Today only a very small proportion of trials in England take place before a civil jury.

In the United States, the right to a jury trial is guaranteed by the U.S. Constitution.[66] Trial by civil jury is considered a common mode of resolving disputes.[67] The jury enjoys significant support amongst legal scholars.[68] In addition, empirical studies have shown that citizens have a solid belief that the jury is a sound institution.[69] The United States currently seems to be the only modern nation in the world that uses civil juries at a large scale. Data show that jury trials take place frequently in U.S. District Courts. The proportion of cases that reach the trial stage is however very small (See Chapter 3). The relative proportion of trials by jury as opposed to bench trials increased. In 2000, jury trials accounted for more than 60% of all trials.[70] On the basis of data between 1959 and 1979 from Cook County, Illinois, voters faced an annual probability of 0.38% to fulfill jury service in a civil case. This is equal to serving once every 186.7 years.[71]

The Role of the Civil Jury in the United States

If a party entitled to a trial by jury requests a jury trial, a jury is formed once the case reaches the trial phase.[72] Potential jurors are randomly selected from the population by making use of lists on which voters are registered.[73] A panel of jurors is called for jury service, and from this panel a number of jurors will be selected to

63 Hanly 2005, p. 277-278.

64 Jenks 1949, p. 377. The judge was believed to be better able to find facts. See for the proposition of the Judicature Commissioners: Parliamentary Papers 1868-1869, Vol. XXV, p. 12-13.

65 *Ward* v. *James* [1966] 1 Q.B. 273, [1965] 1 All ER 563, discussed by Jolowicz 2000, p. 29.

66 See the discussion of the 7th amendment of the U.S. Constitution below. See Friedenthal, Kane & Miller 2005, §11.4 and §11.5 on the scope of the right to a jury trial.

67 See Hans & Albertson 2003, p. 1503-1506 and the studies there mentioned

68 Priest refers to it as an 'extraordinary national consensus on the merits of the civil jury'. Priest 1990, p. 162. Many scholars and practitioners support the institution of the jury, see e.g. Kalven 1964.

69 See for instance the literature discussed in Roberts & Hough 2009, p. 31.

70 Higginbotham 2002, Charts 7 and 8.

71 Priest 1990, p. 188.

72 Parties will have to indicate early in the proceedings that they want a jury trial. If they do not do so in due time the trial will be by judge alone. See FRCP, Rule 38(b) and 38(d).

73 28 U.S.C. §1861; Friedenthal, Kane & Miller 2005, §11.10.

form the jury. By the U.S. Constitution, the jury may contain no less than 6 and no more than 12 members.[74]

During jury selection (*voir dire*), all potential jurors in the panel will be screened by means of questioning in order to determine whether the juror lacks qualification or is biased. The screening of the jurors was traditionally done by lawyers, but presently this is mostly done by the court.[75] The judge may challenge jurors for cause; for instance, if the *voir dire* inquiry reveals that a juror is biased or related to either of the parties.[76] Each party may challenge up to three jurors, even if no cause has been established against these jurors (peremptory challenges).[77]

Although it is hard to draw the line between fact and law, it is generally argued that the jury is responsible for the determinations of fact and that the judge is responsible for matters of law.[78] Judges are to instruct the jury on matters of law either during trial or after the closing pleas of counsel.[79] During trial, the jury was traditionally the ultimate example of a neutral and passive fact-finder. Since the 19th century, it is considered inappropriate for the jury to ask questions, take notes or to discuss the case prior to the evaluation of all evidence.[80] Courts in the United States have recently become more lenient in this respect and many courts allow jurors to take notes or provide for ways in which jurors may ask questions.[81]

The trial judge decides on one of the three forms of the verdict.[82] The traditional and still very common verdict form is the 'general verdict' in which the jury decides in favor of either of the parties without disclosing the grounds for its verdict.[83] The court may also require the jury to answer additional questions on matters of fact (General Verdict Accompanied by Answer to Interrogatories) or require the jury to give a verdict on issues of fact only (Special Verdict).[84] Although

74 FRCP Rule 48. Traditionally the civil jury has 12 members. In *Colgrove v. Battin*, 413 U.S. 149,157, (1973), the Supreme Court held that a jury of 6 members does not violate the Constitution; Friedenthal, Kane & Miller 2005, §11.11.

75 FRCP Rule 47(a); Landsman 1999, p. 292.

76 28 U.S.C. §1870.

77 28 U.S.C. §1870. Although attorneys are free to strike out jurors without explanation or justification, there are limits. Striking out jurors on the basis of gender or race can be unacceptable. See *Batson v. Kentucky*, 476 U.S. 79 (1986) and *J.E.B. v. Alabama ex rel. T.B.*, 511 U.S. 127 (1994).

78 Friedenthal, Kane & Miller 2005, §11.2.

79 Parties do have a possibility to influence the judge's instructions, FRCP Rule 51. In practice there are complaints about the complexity and technicality of instructions, Landsman 1999, Part VII.

80 Note 1964.

81 Cowan 2003; Heuer & Penrod 1996 and Landsman 1999, p. 298.

82 Friedenthal, Kane & Miller 2005, Chapter 11.

83 Vidmar 2003, p. 109 *et seq.*

84 FRCP Rule 49.

there are exceptions to the rule, the jury should normally reach a unanimous verdict.[85]

3.2. *The Rationale behind the Civil Jury*

The Jury as a Legal Institution

In 1973, the U.S. Supreme Court held that it is the purpose of jury trial in civil cases to assure a 'fair and equitable resolution of factual issues'.[86] The Supreme Court seems to justify the civil jury on grounds of its role as a fact-finder. Although such cases do not arise frequently, it is argued that the jury would be especially competent to resolve disputes involving complex societal values or cases in which the government is a party to the proceeding.[87]

Some have argued that the jury is incompetent to decide on complex factual matters.[88] Empirical studies do not support this claim.[89] Studies have shown that judges generally agree with the findings of the jury regardless of the complexity of the case.[90] A survey in 2000 showed that 77% of the federal judges believed that juries did very well in reaching a just and fair verdict.[91] Other studies showed that the findings of the jury in medical malpractice cases correspond with the (protected) opinions of physicians summoned by the insurance company prior to trial.[92] Similarly, detailed studies of complex cases and interviews with jurors show that the jury is capable of intellectually grasping the main factual debates in complex cases.[93]

Others have criticized the civil jury on grounds of efficiency. In the United States there have been frequent complaints about the fact that the jury is too expensive and causes too much delay.[94] These complaints are by no means new.[95] In 1901, Coxe argued:

85 FRCP Rule 48 holds that the verdict shall be unanimous unless the parties stipulate otherwise. Many states provide for a non-unanimous verdict in civil actions, see Friedenthal, Kane & Miller 2005, §11.11.

86 *Colgrove v. Battin*, 413 U.S. 149,157,(1973). The full quote is: 'The purpose of the jury trial in criminal cases is to prevent government oppression and, in criminal and civil cases, to assure a fair and equitable resolution of factual issues'.

87 Priest 1990.

88 See for instance *In Re Japanese Electronics Products Antitrust Litigation*, 631 F.2d 1069 (3rd Cir. 1980) and Langbein 1993, p. 167. Langbein argues that the jury selection excludes the able ones.

89 For an overview, see Vidmar 2003, Part II; Hans & Albertson 2003, p. 1509 and Note 1997, p. 1425-1427.

90 According to Kalven & Zeisel 1971, Chapter 5, the professional judge and the jury agreed in approximately 4 out of 5 (criminal and civil) cases on the outcome. These findings have been confirmed by later studies, such as Heuer & Penrod 1994. This study also shows that the complexity as perceived by the judge did not influence the level of judge-jury agreement.

91 Pusey 2000.

92 Vidmar 2003, Part 2 and the studies quoted there.

93 Vidmar 2003, Part 2 and Kalven & Zeisel 1971, Chapter 11.

94 Landsman 1992, Part IV and Sunderland 1914.

> 'In trials of wide public interests the delay in procuring a jury often extends to weeks and months. Hundreds of busy men are inconvenienced, an enormous expense is incurred and the time of bench and bar is frittered away. As a simple and efficient means of arriving at the truth, trial by jury, when so impeded, becomes not only an intolerable burden, but a reproach to our jurisprudence'.[96]

Empirical research supports much of this criticism and indicates that the direct costs of jury trials are considerably higher than those of bench trials and that jury trials are also more time-consuming.[97] In addition, the considerable set of rules created to accommodate the jury seem to be the cause of indirect costs.

It would be wrong to address the civil jury merely from an instrumental perspective. If the sole purpose of the jury was to resolve factual issues correctly and efficiently, there would be few reasons not to thoroughly revise the institution or replace the jury by a professional judge altogether. The role of the jury is not limited to its procedural function as a trier of fact. The civil jury is also a political institution, inseparable from the government and administration of the United States.

The Civil Jury as a Political Institution

Although the American jury springs from its English parent, it has gone through a host of changes since. Prior to the American Revolution, colonists regarded the jury in both civil and criminal cases as a means to ensure their independence of judges appointed by the colonial government.[98] Struggles between the colonists and the British authorities over jury rights became an aspect in the fight for independence. After independence, several states included the right to a jury trial (in civil cases) in their Constitutions.[99]

The Federal Constitution drafted in 1787 did not include the right to a jury trial in civil cases. Hamilton defended the omission by pointing out that there was no 'inseparable connection between the existence of liberty, and the trial by jury in civil cases'.[100] The Antifederalists fiercely and successfully opposed this position. They regarded the jury as a 'symbol of democracy' which was needed to constrain the judiciary.[101] In addition, the jury was seen as a means to prevent the government from violating the Constitution. The natural rights theory which prevailed at the time held that natural law was accessible to the ordinary man. As the constitution was regarded to be a codification of natural law, lay men were believed to be capable to understand and protect the Constitution.[102]

95 Note 1964.
96 Coxe 1901.
97 Note 1997, p. 1424 and Landsman 1992, Part IV.
98 Landsman 1992, p. 596 and Carrington 2003, Part II. For a concise historic overview see Justice White's decision in *Duncan v. Louisiana*, 391 U.S. 145; 88 S. Ct. 1444; 20 L. Ed. 2d 491; 1968 U.S. LEXIS 1631; 45 Ohio Op. 2d 198.
99 Landsman 1992, p. 596.
100 Hamilton, Madison & Jay 1788, Paper No. 83.
101 Landsman 1992, p. 599 and Carrington 2003, p. 83.
102 Note 1964, p. 170-172.

Since 1791, the 'right to a jury trial' has been firmly embedded in the United States Constitution. The seventh amendment to the Constitution has provided that 'in suits at common law, where the value in controversy shall exceed twenty dollars, the right of trial by jury shall be preserved, and no fact tried by a jury, shall be otherwise re-examined in any court of the United States, than according to the rules of the common law'. In 1935, the Supreme Court interpreted the seventh amendment by holding that:

> 'With, perhaps, some exceptions, trial by jury has always been, and still is, generally regarded as the normal and preferable mode of disposing of issues of fact in civil cases at law as well as in criminal cases. Maintenance of the jury as a fact-finding body is of such importance and occupies so firm a place in our history and jurisprudence that any seeming curtailment of the right to a jury trial should be scrutinized with the utmost care'.[103]

The history of the civil jury in the United States shows that the institution is a political one.[104] The jury allows for the direct participation of the citizens in matters of government as heralded by the Antifederalists.[105] De Tocqueville concluded in the 1830s that the civil jury in essence is a political institution and an extreme consequence of the 'sovereignty of the people'.[106] As a democratic institution, the jury is a forum for deliberative democracy.

Moreover, the jury - as well as the adversarial system[107] - has an important function to constrain the judiciary. To be judged by ones' peers is a bulwark against an oppressive, ignorant, cruel or biased judiciary.[108] Federalists like Hamilton admitted that the jury would function as a security against corrupted judges.[109] Jeremy Bentham even regarded it as the primary task of the jury to control the judiciary.[110]

The jury is also said to bind the citizens to the government and the laws of the state. The jury educates the people about the importance of the rule of law. Data about the reaction of jurors on their experiences reveal that jury service was 'very often a major and moving experience in the life of the citizen-juror'.[111] Citizens that

103 *Dimick v. Schiedt*, 293 U.S. 474; 55 S. Ct. 296; 79 L. Ed. 603; 1935 U.S. LEXIS 5 at 301.

104 See e.g. the debate concerning the question whether or not the judge would be allowed to provide the jury with comments on the evidence presented at trial, Lettow Lerner 2000, p. 219.

105 Note 1997, p. 1437.

106 De Tocqueville 1899, Book 1, Chapter 16.

107 E.g. Landsman 1988, p. 33.

108 The Declaration of Rights of 1774 that resulted from the first Continental Congress had regarded the right to be 'tried by ones peers' in this context (Right No. 5). Also see Note 1997, p. 1429.

109 Hamilton, Madison & Jay 1788, Paper No. 83.

110 Bentham 1838, Chapter XXIII: 'Taken in its most extensive sense, a jury may be defined an occasional body of non-professional and non-official judges, employed to constitute and apply a check to the power of a professional or official judge, or body of judges'.

111 Kalven 1964, p. 1062.

have served as a juror in a state court on average have more confidence in these courts than citizens that have not served as jurors.[112] As De Tocqueville put it:

> 'It teaches men to practice equity; every man learns to judge his neighbor as he would himself be judged. And this is especially true of the jury in civil causes, for while the number of persons who have reason to apprehend a criminal prosecution is small, everyone is liable to have a lawsuit. The jury teaches every man not to recoil before the responsibility of his own actions and impresses him with that manly confidence without which no political virtue can exist. It invests each citizen with a kind of magistracy; it makes them all feel the duties which they are bound to discharge towards society and the part which they take in its government. By obliging men to turn their attention to other affairs than their own, it rubs off that private selfishness which is the rust of society'.[113]

It must be noted that the exact role of the American jury has not been the same over the years. The jury now responds to different needs than those proclaimed by the Antifederalists in the 18th century.[114] The fact that Senators and the President are presently directly elected limits to some extent the need for direct citizen participation. On the other hand, one could argue that the rise of individualism increases the need to bind citizens to the government and the laws of the state.[115]

3.3. *The Influence of the Jury on the Process of Fact-Finding*

It has been argued that common law's fact-finding agreements are first and foremost 'the child of the jury system'.[116] Although not many cases eventually culminate in a jury trial, the influence of the jury extends to the pretrial stage of litigation and bench trials. Many rules in common law procedural systems have arranged themselves around the jury like 'iron filings around a magnet'.[117] Amongst the distinctive features of the U.S. model of fact-finding rooted in the jury system are: 1) a single, continuous and concentrated presentation of evidence at trial; 2) far-reaching rules that allow an effective preparation for trial (pretrial discovery); 3) the preference of oral over written evidence; 4) exclusionary rules of evidence and 5) the use of direct compulsory sanctions towards the parties.

The Jury and the Structure of American Litigation

The jury system has thoroughly influenced the structure of litigation in common law countries. The presentation of evidence on the European continent takes place at different hearings, often scheduled weeks or even months apart from each other. Such a model cannot properly function in common law courts. It would be extremely cumbersome and inefficient for the usually twelve members of the jury to

112 Benesh 2006, p. 703.
113 De Tocqueville 1899, Book 1, Chapter 16. The quote is still relevant today for both men and women.
114 Note 1964.
115 Carrington 2003, p. 93.
116 Thayer 1898, p. 266 as quoted by Damaska 1997a, p. 2.
117 This illustrative metaphor is used by Kaplan 1961.

be dismissed and reconvened weeks later a couple of times in succession. A U.S. trial is a single uninterrupted event. It often happens that trials take longer than a single day, meaning that jurors are dismissed in the afternoon to be reconvened the next morning. Trial hearings are, however, not weeks apart. If the jury had to reconvene every couple of months, it would become more and more difficult for the jury to not talk or read about issues related to the case. There would be reasons to fear that the jurors would fail to recollect factual matters discussed a long time ago. Moreover, the odds would increase that a juror would cease to be available before all the evidence is presented. In short, the jury has created the need for a single, concentrated and possibly uninterrupted trial in which all evidence will be presented to the trier of fact.[118] The jury has thereby created the need for a 'two stage procedure'.[119] The institution of the jury explains the well known divide in American law between the 'pretrial stage' and the 'trial stage' of litigation.

The Jury and the Need for Broad Discovery Devices

As argued above, evidence is to be presented to the jury during a single, concentrated and uninterrupted event. At the same time, the pursuit of truth and equal access to relevant information are believed to be of importance in litigation. These different aims require that both sides must be fully prepared for trial. Trial does not allow the parties a couple of days leave in order to formulate a response to the allegations of the opposing party. It is therefore important that all relevant information that will be presented at trial is known in advance by both parties. A party must be informed about the evidence his adversary will use at trial. During the 19th century much emphasis was on the pleadings in order to allow a full exchange of information.[120] Throughout the 20th century, the full preparation for trial was the single biggest argument for liberal rules on discovery.[121] Broad American discovery is thereby an indirect consequence of the right to a jury trial.[122]

The Jury and the Preference for Oral Evidence

Common law jurisdictions seem to favor oral evidence over written evidence, which is a direct consequence of the civil jury. First of all it must be noted that a large proportion of the population in the United States - past and present - is not sufficiently literate to read case files.[123] Second, by assuring that the jurors obtain information in the court room, it can be guaranteed that all jurors are (equally) informed about the case. In contrast, on the European continent written evidence was traditionally preferred over oral testimony. Continental judges often based

118 Carrington 2003, p. 91; Kaplan 1961, p. 54; Kötz 2003, p. 72 and Von Mehren 1982, p. 364-365.

119 The average length of trial is more than a day, see Chapter 3 for empirical data.

120 Carrington 2003, p. 91. The specifics of common law pleading - as argued by Millar - could also be explained by referring to the role of the civil jury, Millar 1926, p. 401.

121 Sunderland 1932; Von Mehren 1982, Section II. Also see *Hickman v. Taylor*, 329 U.S. 495 (1947) at 507: 'The deposition-discovery procedure simply advances the stage at which disclosure can be compelled from the time of trial to the period preceding it, thus reducing the possibility of surprise'.

122 Kötz 2003, p. 73.

123 See e.g. NCES 2006.

their decision on the basis of written summaries of the witnesses testimony (see Chapter 2.2). Early Continental codifications limited the evidential value of the testimony of witnesses and generally awarded much more value to documentary evidence.

The Jury and the Rules on Admissibility of Evidence

It has been argued that the law of evidence is 'a gloss on trial by jury' and 'a tribute to the jury as an institution' without whom 'nobody would need most of these rules'.[124] This is especially true for the rules on the admissibility of evidence. The law on evidence is said to compensate for the easily influenced and often irrational adjudication by laymen.[125] Detailed rules on the admissibility of evidence try to keep relevant but less reliable evidence outside the courtroom. These rules are designed to prevent a sly and cunning attorney to mislead the jury. Rule 403 FRE is most explicit: 'Although relevant, evidence may be excluded if its probative value is substantially outweighed by the danger of unfair prejudice, confusion of the issues, or misleading the jury (...)' Other rules, like the hearsay rule or the best evidence rule have also been justified on these grounds.[126] These exclusionary rules rest on the paradoxical assumption that elimination of relevant evidence can improve the accuracy of the fact-finding process. [127]

Rules that declare evidence inadmissible are stringent species of rules that limit the weight of evidence.[128] Continental legal systems traditionally also excluded certain means of proof, but resorted to a much greater degree to rules that limit the probative value of unreliable evidence (Chapter 2). An example is the Continental rule that attributes a limited evidential value (e.g. half proof) to the testimony of a party.[129] Rules that declare evidence inadmissible would not fit very well in a Continental setting.[130] It is difficult for a judge to decide that evidence is inadmissible and subsequently disregard the evidence altogether when freely evaluating the remaining evidence. It would be impractical to involve another judge to rule on admissibility as judges generally handle a case from the beginning to the end. Rules that restrict the weight of evidence without reducing it to zero would not fit in the American system. One cannot require lay adjudicators to apply complex rules on the probative value of evidence. Contrary to civil law jurisdictions, this leads to a system in which there are only two options: either the evidence is

124 Friedman 1985, p. 402 and Friedman 1998, p. 204.

125 Damaska 1997a, p. 28: 'It is therefore no wonder that the oldest and most widely accepted justification for distinctive Anglo-American evidence rules is the need to compensate for the alleged intellectual and emotional frailties of amateurs cast in the role of occasional judges'. Also see Sunderland 1914, p. 311-312; Landsman 1988, p. 30, and Murray & Sheldon 2003.

126 The idea that the hearsay rule is justified by the institution of the jury has a long history. See Langbein 1996, p. 1169, quoting case law of the early 19th century, around the time the hearsay rule developed.

127 Damaska 1997a, p. 14.

128 Damaska 1997a, p. 18.

129 See Section 6.1.3.

130 Damaska 1991, p. 427.

admissible (and may provide full evidence), or it is not admissible (and hence has a probative weight of zero).

The American rules against unreliable evidence are much more restrictive than those in present day civil law jurisdictions. To the extent that rules on weight still exist in civil law jurisdictions, these are less restrictive than the exclusion of evidence altogether. Moreover, one will search in vain in the Dutch or Austrian Code of Civil Procedure to find an equivalent for rules that exclude hearsay or character evidence.[131]

The Civil Jury and the Nature of Sanctions

Lay adjudicators are not only incapable of applying detailed rules on the weight of evidence, it is also difficult to require lay adjudicators to apply indirect sanctions. On the European continent, it is very common for judges to draw adverse inferences if a party is uncooperative during the process of fact-finding. In the United States it is difficult to require untrained adjudicators to apply indirect sanctions and one will therefore sooner enforce cooperative behavior.[132] The sanctions that apply if parties refuse to give testimony, provide a good example of these different approaches (see Chapter 6).

4. Critical Observations

I have tried to provide a persuasive and coherent description of the (federal) American fact-finding arrangements. The picture emerging from the analysis above might be too rosy. At times, I have found it quite difficult to provide a rationale for specific American fact-finding arrangements. The hearsay rule, for example, seems hard to justify. The hearsay rule is overly complex, thereby creating the need for litigants to hire expensive legal advisors and thus adding to the costs of litigation. In addition, the rule may lead to the exclusion of relevant evidence and thereby distort the accuracy of the process of fact-finding. Three more general critical observations are listed below.

It was argued that many American regulations exist to accommodate the civil jury. There is often no justification to apply these rules in cases that will never be tried by a jury. The exclusionary rules of evidence apply to both jury and non-jury cases. Such rules have manifest disadvantages. According to Sheldon and Murray these rules of evidence that state as an objective to 'secure fairness (...) to the end that truth may be ascertained and proceedings justly determined' often do exactly the opposite as they provide parties with legal assistance with an advantage unrelated to the merits of the case.[133] Sheldon and Murray argued that exclusionary

131 Often hearsay evidence is accorded less weight in the evaluation of evidence by Continental courts, e.g. Dutch Court of Cassation, 23 May 2008, BC8689, C06/094HR.

132 Stürner 2001, p. 881: 'The preparation of a trial before lay jurors is not sufficiently effective if it takes place on the basis of fictions; to be properly presented full knowledge of all real facts is essential. The Anglo-American preference for direct compulsory sanctions is the understandable consequence of this need to know all the real facts and the full truth'.

133 Murray & Sheldon 2003, p. 230.

rules of evidence should not be applied in non-jury cases.[134] Equally, there is no need for a single uninterrupted trial at which all evidence is presented in non jury cases. It is probably often not necessary to summon a witness at trial if the witness has already been deposed for 5 hours and the transcript of the deposition is available. One could also doubt whether broad rules of discovery are needed in cases that will never be tried by a jury. It seems that much can be gained if a separate procedure, more akin to the Continental procedure, is designed for those American cases that may ultimately be tried by the judge.

Furthermore, the American system downplays disadvantages associated with the adversarial system (see Chapters 7 and 10). The adversarial system creates incentives to distort the process of fact-finding and may provide rich litigants an unfair advantage over poorer litigants. The system tends to encourage an over expenditure on fact-finding and therefore seems to be relatively inefficient. It has been argued that the American system is incapable of handling a claim worth the annual income of the median U.S. household.[135]

A last point that deserves to be noted is that over the last decades, there has been a striking divergence between the reality of litigation and the premises and fundamentals of procedural regulations. I have argued that the American fact-finding arrangements are designed and arranged for the adversarial resolution of disputes by jury trial. There is no need for broad discovery rules aimed to avoid surprise at trial, if there is no trial. There is no need to argue whether or not evidence may be presented to the jury, in cases where no jury will ever be assembled.[136] In Chapter 3 it was explained that trials have gradually vanished. With the decline of (jury) trial, the justification for many procedural arrangements is waning.

134 Murray & Sheldon 2003.
135 Yeazell 2004, p. 966.
136 Schwarzer 1989, p. 714.

Chapter 9

POLITICAL IDEOLOGY, DEMOCRACY AND THE DIVERSE FORMS OF PROCEDURE

1. Introduction

Making an important decision generally requires a decision maker to gather information and to make a rational judgment on matters of fact. Business decisions require that the management of a firm is enabled to make a cost-benefit analysis based on reliable data and good predictions about future markets. Doctors perform a number of tests to gather relevant information before making a diagnosis of an illness. In such situations, hypotheses are formulated, opposing views are articulated and professional men and women try to use their common sense and reason to decide on matters of fact. The tests run by doctors are generally the same, regardless of whether one visits an English, Dutch or an American hospital. Students that are taught corporate decision-making at a Dutch university, generally use a textbook that is also used at American or German universities. By and large, the procedures and good practices for determining matters of fact in an economic or medical setting are the same across borders. Not so in the realm of civil litigation. The procedures for decision-making before the courts of modern democratic societies differ greatly. Differences between jurisdictions are especially large with regard to the procedures that regulate fact-gathering and fact-finding. Such procedures are often highly complex and sometimes archaic. Despite cultural and language barriers it is possible and common for medical, technical and economic professionals to do their work abroad. In contrast, procedural systems abroad can be so fundamentally different that lawyers are generally utterly incompetent to practice law in another country. This is well illustrated by the little use that has been made of legislation that enables the 'free movement of lawyers' in the European Union.[1] Such differences between countries require an explanation; this Chapter aims to provide it.

The judicial process and its methods of fact-gathering and fact-finding differ in at least three important respects from the methods applied in other settings. First,

1 Claessens 2008, p. 6.

courts have a duty to make a decision regardless of how difficult the subject matter is. Courts, unlike scientists, cannot remain undecided and postpone their decision for a decade or two until further research is conducted. Second, the parties in a lawsuit often have opposing interests. Parties almost always pursue different ends. Doctors and patients, when making a diagnosis, usually pursue the same ends: the well-being of the patient. The fact that parties have opposing interests makes the process of fact gathering and fact finding more difficult as parties may not be inclined to cooperate (see Chapter 10). A third way in which decision-making in the courtroom differs from decision-making in the boardroom is that courts are a branch of government. The third difference will be considered in greater detail in this Chapter.

There are many possible explanations for the different modes of fact-gathering and fact-finding applied before the courts in different countries. One particularly interesting explanation is provided by public choice theory. This theory explains legal systems by focusing on the interests of the well-organized players involved in the legal process. Lawyers are well organized, often overrepresented in political organs and shape the customs that give body to the procedural rules. Lawyers profit from excessive complexity and overly formalistic procedures that will enhance the market for their services. Lawyers often strive to make the procedures more formalistic, more complex and more technical than socially optimal.[2] The American hearsay rule provides a good example of a much too complex rule that creates the need for lawyers. The U.S. Supreme Court observed in *Faretta v. California* (1975) that 'even the intelligent and educated layman (...) is unfamiliar with the rules of evidence' and will without proper legal assistance 'in all but an extraordinarily small number of cases' lose his case.[3] Lawyers are not the only groups of legal professionals that have an interest in overly complex procedural systems. Bailiffs, court reporters and judges all have an interest in maintaining certain overly complex rules. Academics are no different in this respect: the more complex the rules are, the greater the need for specialists that teach law, write treatises or measure the effects of the law. One need not search long to find a list of rules that are excessively complex and at the same time serve the interests of legal professionals.[4]

An explanatory framework that focuses on the interests of professionals in a legal system may provide a very powerful framework to explain why procedural systems are needlessly complex. This approach may explain why differences between countries exist: complex procedural rules are more rewarding for a nationally organized group of legal professionals if they differ from the complex rules abroad. Differences between national jurisdictions may serve to fend off competition from foreign professionals. Nevertheless, these explanations fail to explain why some rules of procedure develop in one country while other rules

2 Ogus 2002.

3 *Faretta v. California* 422 U.S. 806; 95 S. Ct. 2525; 45 L. Ed. 2d 562; 1975 U.S. LEXIS 83 at 838.

4 Dutch examples include the duty to be represented by an attorney and rules that require that the complaint is served by a bailiff on the defendant (at a price of roughly 90 Euro's). E.g. Articles 45, 121 Code of Civil Procedure.

develop in another country. The interests of legal professionals explain *why* differences exist, yet cannot explain *which* differences exist. Public choice explanations provide only a partial explanation. I argue that differences between procedural regimes are linked to different conceptions of the state, its institutions and democracy.

2. Procedure and the Role of the State

The Reactive and the Activist State

In his 'The Faces of Justice and State Authority: a Comparative Approach to the Legal Process', Damaska posits two dimensions to describe systems of procedure.[5] One of these dimensions contrasts the reactive state with the activist state. The reactive state, much in line with classical liberal theory, leaves it to the citizens to pursue their own ends. A 'laissez faire' reactive state generally confines itself to a small number of policy areas and fulfills a relatively modest role in civil society. The activist state, on the contrary, embraces a model of a good society. Here, the state, ultimately determines what ought to be done. The state implements policies that aim to improve society in accordance with its model of a good society. The policies of the activist state are of a greater importance than the desires of individual citizens. An activist state designed along utilitarian lines could create a wide range of policies to increase welfare in society. An activist state that is concerned with the fair distribution of welfare could enact legislation to redistribute wealth. Within an activist state, all spheres of life can potentially be shaped by the policy of the state. The point made by Damaska is that these different views on the role of the state in society have an impact on the forms of procedure. Similar arguments have been made by others.[6] As explained in Chapter 7, Klein also argued that political views on the role of the state in society affect the objectives of court procedures.

It must be noted that a distinction between pure activist states and pure reactive states can only be made in the abstract. All jurisdictions discussed tend to provide solutions between these two extremes. Nevertheless, some procedural regimes are posited closer to that of a pure activist state whereas other systems are posited closer to the pure reactive state. On the continuum between the two extremes of the reactive and the activist state, the United States is traditionally posited closer to the reactive state than most states on the European continent. Collectivistic ideologies, such as the political theories of Rousseau and Marx, were influential in early Continental constitutional doctrine. In the United States, these collectivistic theories had little influence. The classical liberalism of John Locke deeply influenced U.S. constitutional doctrine. Government intervention in economic and social life has gradually increased on the European continent since the 19th century. Since the emergence of the welfare state after the Second World War, almost all areas of human life are in one way or another affected by government policy.

5 Damaska 1986, p. 71-94.
6 Cappelletti 1970 and Klein 1901.

Although government intervention also has become more common in a number of policy areas in the United States, most would agree that, even in recent times of financial turmoil, labels like 'antistatism', 'individualism' and 'laissez faire' describe the attitude of average Americans towards the state.[7] It is remarkable for Continental lawyers to see that policy on important economic and social issues is not actively developed by the government. In the United States, civil litigation serves as an alternative policy making mechanism.[8] As De Tocqueville noted, 'scarcely any political question arises in the United States that is not resolved, sooner or later, into a judicial question'.[9] It is the individual, rather than a government agency, who by means of a lawsuit, can serve the common interest by pursuing his own interests.[10] Class actions, treble damages and other legal instruments serve as mechanisms to ensure that private litigants have an incentive to initiate litigation. The shareholders' derivative suit, rather than governmental oversight, was regarded by the Supreme Court as 'the chief regulator of corporate management'.[11] American courts, much more than European courts, are thereby required to create law and policy on a case by case basis.

Different Functions of the Procedural System

The function of civil justice systems in a reactive state differs from the function of the justice system in an activist state. Within a reactive state, the court system is designed to resolve conflicts between individuals. The objectives of the reactive state are very modest. The state has no interest or preference for a particular solution that resolves the dispute. The state is only interested in preserving peace between the individuals that constitute society. A 1951 American introduction to civil procedure states it as follows:

> '(...) it is a primary function of government to settle private disputes between individuals arising out of their conflicting interests. If the government fails in the performing of such function, the individuals involved in such disputes will sooner or later inevitably seek a settlement of their difficulties in some form of private warfare in which the aggrieved party seeks vengeance against the alleged wrongdoer. Lynch law has sometimes prevailed where the law enforcing agencies have failed to operate to the satisfaction of the given community. To avoid such undesirable results and to prevent individuals from taking the law into their own hands, the state has organized tribunals

7 Chase 2005, p. 50. Chase describes 'American Culture' and argues it is linked with procedural law.

8 Robert Kagan has referred used the term 'adversarial legalism' to denote the distinctive way in which government policies are made and implemented through civil law suits, Kagan 2003.

9 De Tocqueville 1899, Chapter 16.

10 See for instance the 1862 False Claims Act, also known as 'Lincoln's Law' allowing citizens to maintain a case on behalf of the United States in fraud cases and to receive part of the damages awarded. Today the 1986 version of the Act provides treble damages for defrauding the United States whereby 15-25% of recovered money is to be paid to the individual that initiated the action.

11 *Cohen v. Beneficial Indus. Loan Corp.*, 337 U.S. 541, 547-8 (1949), discussed by Kötz 2003.

> to which individuals engaged in disputes are encouraged to resort for the adjudication of their differences'.[12]

In a reactive state it is important that the procedure and the outcome are such that these will effectively solve the dispute between the litigants. Thus, the substantive rules and norms applied should preferably be those rules that are considered fair and acceptable to the litigants. In a reactive state, the courts might therefore preferably refer to 'customary law' or 'the common law of the people' rather than to rules imposed upon the litigants.

The civil justice system within an activist state is generally also concerned with the resolution of disputes but strives for other objectives at the same time. The activist state is not satisfied if the dispute has been adequately resolved in the eyes of the litigants. Activist states, much more than reactive states, are concerned with the outcome of legal process. An activist state requires that each decision is in line with the policy and substantive rules imposed by the government. The court system within an activist state primarily serves to implement and enforce government policies. The enforcement of substantive law is of great importance in an activist state. Substantive law, in turn, is believed to 'improve' society.

Fact-finding: the Pursuit of Truth and the Principle of Party-Presentation

In a reactive state, procedures serve to resolve disputes. The reactive state is never inquisitive about the true state of affairs. The pursuit of truth is only seen as a means to resolve a dispute in a way satisfactory to both parties.[13] In a reactive state, parties determine the scope of their conflict and are therefore responsible to gather facts and allege and present proof.[14] Parties may freely determine that certain factual matters are irrelevant. Factual matters that are not disputed by the parties should not be subject to further inquiry. Within a reactive state the gathering and presentation of facts is done in accordance with the adversarial system, or, to use the German terminology: in a reactive state the principle of party-presentation *(Verhandlungsmaxime)* prevails.

During the heyday of laissez-faire liberalism, western Continental systems strongly adhered to the adversarial system. The 1877 German Code of Civil Procedure was constructed on the premise that civil litigation was a private matter. Parties would conduct litigation in an effective and efficient manner if left free to pursue their own interests.[15] According to Adolf Wach, a leading German proceduralist at the beginning of the previous century, the pursuit of truth itself was not an end of civil litigation. The parties were to determine the scope and purpose of litigation. Viewed from this perspective, the pursuit of truth could only be

12 Reppy 1954, p. 1.

13 The pursuit of truth is generally seen as the object of evidence law and procedural law. But it may be a means to a more remote end. Also see Goldman 2005, p. 164.

14 Damaska 1986, p. 123.

15 Verkijk 2010.

relevant as a means to protect the private rights of the parties.[16] Hence, the 1877 Code of Civil Procedure adhered to the principle of party-presentation, which Wach considered to be the principle that 'expressed that the State had no interest in the dispute between the parties'.[17]

In the Netherlands, the adversarial principle was also undisputed throughout the 19th century.[18] It was held that, in the realm of private law, the judge could not *ex officio* allege facts not presented by the parties.[19] If a fact adduced by one party was acknowledged or not denied by the other party, the judge had to establish the facts as adduced and could not order the production of evidence.[20] It was commonly accepted that in the realm of private law the 'formal truth' (i.e. the facts as alleged by the parties) rather than the 'substantive truth' (i.e. the 'real' truth) should serve as a basis for the court's decision. Van Boneval Faure put it as follows:

> 'In order to make the administration of justice possible, it is necessary that the judge is satisfied with the formal truth with respect to the facts of the case, even though he tries as much as possible to discover the substantive truth. (...) In civil cases the formal truth is all the more of importance, as the nature of civil rights requires that enforcement of these rights depends upon the parties and likewise the acceptance and denial of fact, on which the existence of rights depends, as well as, to a certain degree, the presentation of evidence, depends upon the parties'.[21]

In the Dutch legal system, the principle of 'party autonomy' is still widely regarded as one of the main restrictions to the pursuit of truth in civil litigation.[22]

The Belgian Judicial Code of 1967 provides a more recent example of a Continental jurisdiction in which the parties 'lead the process of litigation'.[23] The Belgian attorney Van Reepinghen defended his draft for a new Judicial Code in 1963. He argued that the Belgian system had always respected the autonomy of the

16 Wach 1914, p. 26: ,Die Ermittlung der Wahrheit von Tatsachen um ihrer selbst willen ist nie Zweck des Zivilprozesses, ihre Feststellung niemals Urteilswirkung. Sie hat nur Bedeutung als Mittel zum Zwecke des Rechtsschutzes. Wie dieser um der Parteien willen ist, wie sie als die Sachinteressenten die domini litis sund und bleiben werden, daher den Gegenstand und das Ziel des Prozesses durch ihren Willen bestimmen, so hat die Ermittlung des Sachverhalts nur in dieser Relation Wert und Sinn'.

17 Wach 1872, p. 40. as cited by Leipold 1982, p. 443: 'Sie (d.h. die Verhandlungsmaxime) ist der Grundsatz der staatlichen Interesselosigkeit an der Streitsache (...)'.

18 Bosch-Boesjes 1991, p. 23; Dammingh 2009, p. 10-12 and Anonymous 1891, p. 384.

19 HR 20 June 1845, W. 626; Van Emden 1876, p. 16 and Smith 2004, p. 21.

20 Article 48 of the 1838 Dutch Code of Civil Procedure. See Chapter 2.

21 Van Boneval Faure 1896, §94: '(…) noodzakelijk is het om eene werkelijke rechtspraak mogelijk te maken, dat de rechter zich met formeele waarheid ten aanzien van het bestaan der feiten tevreden stelt, al tracht hij ook zoveel mogelijk de materieele waarheid te ontdekken (…). In het burgerlijk geding heeft de formeele waarheid te meer gezag omdat, gelijk de aard der burgerlijke rechten medebrengt dat hunnen handhaving afhankelijk is van partijen, dit evenzeer met het aannemen en het betwisten van feiten waarvan het bestaan der rechten afhankelijk is, ja zelfs tot op eene zekere hoogte met het aanwenden van bewijsmiddelen het geval is'.

22 Asser 2009, p. 34-35.

23 Verslag van Reepinghen, Parl. St. Senaat, 1963-64, No. 60. p. 157: 'De leiding van het geding door de partijen is een postulaat van ons Gerechtelijk Recht'.

parties in civil cases and that the starting point for procedural reform should be to improve the existing system rather than to commit oneself to tempting sophisticated theories.[24] A little later, Van Reepinghen compared the Belgian system with that of other states, arguing that socialist states such as Poland, 'refuted the postulate of a neutral judiciary'.[25] The Belgian Parliament eventually accepted a Code that adhered more rigorously to the principle of party-presentation than the Codes of most other western European jurisdictions.

Although procedural rules have granted American judges wide discretionary powers, American jurisdictions are characterized as 'adversarial'. The adversarial system is sometimes argued to be superior in establishing facts correctly. Primarily however, it serves to resolve disputes. As Landsman argued: 'the American system (...) tends to commit the adversary system to the objective of resolving disputes rather than searching for material truth'.[26] Similarly, Damaska argued that '(...) it is the primacy of the conflict-resolving vision that explains why the competitive fact-finding style appears acceptable - or even desirable - in Anglo-American countries, despite the departures it entails from ordinary fact-finding practices'.[27] Morgan, who drafted the 1942 Model Code of Evidence, stated: 'A lawsuit is not a means of making a scientific investigation for the ascertainment of truth; it is a proceeding for the orderly settlement of a controversy between litigants'.[28]

Within an activist state, which embraces a model of a good society and implements policies accordingly, procedure serves to enforce substantive laws. In such a system, it is of great importance that the facts are established correctly, as a truthful decision on matters of fact is needed to enforce substantive law.[29] The pursuit of truth is a central tenet of litigation in an activist state. Representatives of the state, such as the judge or the state attorney, are expected to actively uncover the truth beyond and behind the statements of the litigants. The adversarial system can obstruct the pursuit of truth. An illustration thereof is provided by 19th century Dutch divorce law. Section 263 of the 1838 Dutch Civil Code explicitly specified that mutual consent divorce was not permitted. Case law of the Supreme Court however held that Article 1962 of the Civil Code was applicable in family law cases.[30] This procedural provision held that facts stated by one party and acknowledged (or not denied) by the other party, provided full proof. If both spouses agreed that the wife would state and the husband would not deny that the husband had committed adultery, the rule required the judge to establish that adultery had been committed. This 'adversarial' procedural rule rendered ineffective the policy and laws of the legislator that forbade mutual consent divorce. Hence, it is not surprising that the

24 Verslag van Reepinghen, Parl. St. Senaat, 1963-64, nr. 60. p. 158: 'Hieraan is het dat men meet hoe het vertrekpunt van een goede hervorming van de rechtspleging te vinden is 'in de beredeneerde verbetering van het stelsel dat in zwang is en niet in het aannemen van vernuftige theorieën die misschien verleidelijk zijn ...'.

25 Verslag van Reepinghen, Parl. St. Senaat, 1963-64, No. 60. p. 160.

26 Landsman 1988, p. 3.

27 Damaska 1986, p. 124.

28 Morgan 1941, p. 539.

29 Damaska 1986, p. 119 *et seq.*

30 Dutch Court of Cassation, 22 June 1883, W. 4924.

principle of party-presentation has been criticized by those who favored a more active role of the state in society and wished to enforce government policy. Since the late 19th century, socialists, national socialists and proponents of utilitarian doctrines all constructed forms of procedure based on a collectivist ideology rather than on classical liberalism.

The Austrian Code of 1895 provides an early and successful example of a codification designed to enforce the policies of an activist state. The 1895 Code of Civil Procedure aimed to enforce substantive law. Substantive law in turn aimed to improve the overall welfare in society. Even though the Austrian model is authoritarian, its ideology fits well in the modern welfare state that has been predominant in a number of Western European states from the early 20th century onwards. The Austrian Code of Civil Procedure, concerned with the implementation of utilitarian policies, clearly stressed the importance of the pursuit of truth and rejected the principle of party-presentation.

Socialist doctrine has generally not regarded both litigants as equal and free citizens but stressed the inequality between the litigants. Anton Menger, a 19th century Austrian socialist academic, argued that the adversarial systems of Austria and Germany were a means to oppress the poor.[31] The adversarial system in which the judge was extremely passive created the need for litigants to hire expensive legal advisors. This afforded the rich an advantage over those who had no means to afford a lawyer. Socialists hoped to reverse the social order and considered legislation as an instrument to implement policies aimed to advance towards a socialist state. Lawsuits were not regarded as a contest between opposing interests, but placed in a broader social context. Civil procedural law and substantive private law were thereby ultimately absorbed by public law.[32] One distinctive feature of socialist law was that it gave the State Attorney wide powers to intervene in every civil lawsuit.[33]

The 1964 Code of Civil Procedure of the Russian Socialist Federal Republic, which served as a model for other socialist jurisdictions, provides the best known example of a Code that refuted the principle of party-presentation and required the judge to ascertain the truth behind and beyond the allegations of the parties.[34] The Russian legislation also refuted the principle of party-disposition (*Dispositionsmaxime*), *inter alia* by empowering the state attorney (*Prokurutura)* to initiate a civil action on behalf of an individual and by allowing the court to grant

31 Leipold 1982, Section III.

32 Quigley 1989 and Cappelletti 1970, p. 884.

33 State Attorneys in other jurisdictions had more restrictive powers to intervene in civil lawsuits. Former Article 324 of the 1838 Dutch Code of Civil Procedure limited the powers of the Dutch State Attorney (*Openbaar Ministerie*) to specific categories of cases, mainly those where the public interest was involved. Similarly, Article 42 of the present Dutch Code of Civil Procedure empowers the State Attorney to attend court hearings, to give its opinion and inspect case related documents. The Dutch State Attorney may not adduce facts, present evidence or initiate a normal remedy on behalf of a litigant.

34 Van Caenegem 1971, p. 100 and Cappelletti 1970, p. 877.

the plaintiff something he had not asked for.[35] The 1975 Code of Civil Procedure of the Democratic Republic of Germany provides another example of socialist procedural legislation.[36] The Code is best described by quoting at length from the first seven provisions describing its general principles:

> 'Section 2 The role of the Court
> (1) The courts have a duty, to protect the socialist state and the order within the community, to protect and enforce the rights and interests that have been recognized by law, such that an effective legal process may contribute to further develop socialist relations within the community of citizens.
> (2) The courts are required, in a concentrated and swift process, to clarify factual issues relevant to the case, to establish the facts truthfully and to decide in accordance with the law. The courts are responsible for the enforcement of their judgments.
> (3) The courts should inform the litigants about their rights and duties and should assist the litigants to ensure that their rights and duties are identified and taken into account.
> (4) The courts have to use their influence to ensure that socialist law is enforced and applied. The courts should, by critically assessing their own work, through guidelines and recommendations, or by other suitable means, strife to avoid the violation of laws that have been identified in proceedings and to resolve the causes of litigation.
>
> Section 3 Rights and Duties of the Parties
> (1) (...) The parties have the right and the duty to participate in the proceeding, most particularly in the process of fact finding. They have a duty, when they are heard to clarify the issues, to provide a complete and truthful representation of all matters of fact.
> (2-4) (…)
>
> Section 7 Participation of the State Attorney
> The state attorney may, to fulfill his duty to protect the socialist legal order, in order to secure the socialist state and the order within the community or to protect socialist property and the rights of citizens, participate in every proceeding, request a remedy or - in those cases identified by law - initiate an action'.[37]

35 Cappelletti 1970, p. 876 and Damaska 1986, p. 160, p. 169 and p. 202. Article 41 Code of Civil Procedure (1964-2002), provided that the State Attorney could 'apply to court in defence of rights (…) of other persons or intervene in the dispute at any stage of the proceedings, where this was required for the protection of the interests of the state or the society or the rights (…) of citizens'. Also see in this respect Article 27 sub 4 of the Law on the Prokuratura.

36 Gesetz über das gerichtliche Verfahren in Zivil-, Familien- und Arbeitsrechtssachen, Zivilprozessordnung of the 19th of June 1975, (*Official State Journal* (GBl) I Nr. 29 S. 533). See Leipold 1982, Part IV.

37 '§2 *Aufgaben der Gerichte* (1) Die Gerichte haben die Aufgabe, die sozialistische Staats- und Gesellschaftsordnung zu schützen, gesetzlich garantierte Rechte und Interessen zu wahren und durchzusetzen sowie durch eine hohe Wirksamheit des gerichtlichen Verfahrens dazu beizutragen, sozialistische Beziehungen im gesellschaftlichen Zusammenleben der Bürger zu fördern. (2) Die Gerichte sind verpflichtet, in einem konzentrierten und zügigen Verfahren die für die Entscheidung erheblichen Tatsachen aufzuklären, wahrheitsgemäss festzustellen und nach den Rechtsvorschriften zu entscheiden. Sie sind für die Vollstreckung ihrer Entscheidung verantwortlich. (3) Die Gerichte haben den am Verfahren Beteiligten ihre Rechte und Pflichten zu erläutern und sie bei deren Wahrnehmung zu unterstützen. (4) Die →

The general principles of the 1975 Code of Civil Procedure summarize all the basic tenets of an activist state. The more detailed provisions of the Code have been designed in line with the leading principles. For example, specific provisions empowered the state attorney to comment on evidence, to request a court to reopen a case and to request the Supreme Court to quash a decision on behalf of the state.[38] Some provisions commonly found in *laissez-faire* codifications, were not part of the 1975 German Code. There were no rules on default judgments that required the court to rule on matters of fact in favor of the plaintiff if the defendant did not defend his case.[39]

The law and ideology of Nazi Germany provides a third example of a collectivist approach to civil litigation. Academics who wrote on the precise form of National Socialist court procedures rejected the existing 1877 German Code of Civil Procedure as representing the ideals of classical liberalism. A Nazi Code of Civil Procedure would have to take the 'German people' rather than the individual as a starting point.[40] The central aim of civil litigation was not conflict resolution, but policy implementation.[41]

Those arguing for Nazi reform generally proposed to abolish the principle of party-presentation as a leading procedural principle.[42] At the same time, National Socialist doctrine endorsed a strong role for the judiciary.[43] A new Code of Civil Procedure was never enacted in Nazi Germany. The Act on the Participation of the State Attorney in Civil Cases of 15 July 1941 provides an example of legislation that

Gerichte haben auf die bewusste Einhaltung und Verwirklichung des sozialistischen Rechts Einfluss zu nehmen. Sie sollen durch Gerichtskritik, Hinweise und Empfehlungen oder in anderer geeigneter Weise darauf hinwirken, dass Rechtsverletzungen, die im Verfahren festgestellt wurden, sowie Ursachen und Bedingungen des Rechtsstreits beseitigt werden.
§3 *Rechte und Pflichten der Prozessparteien* (1) (...) Die Prozessparteien haben das Recht und die Pflicht, am Verfahren teilzunehmen, insbesondere bei der Feststellung des Sachverhalts mitzuwirken. Sie sind verpflichtet, in ihren Erklärungen und Aussagen den Sachverhalt vollständig und wahrheitsgemäss darzulegen.
§7 *Mitwirkung des Staatsanwalts* Der Staatsanwalt kann in Erfüllung seiner Aufgaben zur Wahrung der sozialistischen Gesetzlichkeit, zur Sicherung der sozialistischen Staats- und Gesellschaftsordnung, zum Schutz des sozialistischen Eigentums und der Rechte der Bürger in jedem Verfahren mitwirken, Rechtsmittel einlegen und in den in Rechtsvorschriften vorgesehenen Fällen Klage einreichen'.

38 Sections 64, 160 and 163 Code of Civil Procedure Democratic Republic of Germany. The request to the Supreme Court to quash a decision had to be made by the 'Generalstaatsanwalt', who, according to Article 98 of the Constitution of the German Democratic Republic, was in charge of the office of the state attorney.

39 Sections 66-67 Code of Civil Procedure Democratic Republic of Germany.

40 Leipold 1982, Part V. Leipold *inter alia* describes the works of Hans Otto de Boor, who argued: 'Die liberale Auffassung, die hinter der ZPO steht, sieht den Prozess vom Einzelfall her, die Prozessrechtslehre des Nationalsozialismus sieht ihn von der Volksgemeinschaft aus'. Also See Böhm 1990, p. 159-160.

41 De Boor denied that the courts only had a 'Schlichtungsfunktion'. See the views of De Boor as discussed by Böhm 1990, p. 158.

42 Leipold 1982, Part V.

43 Böhm 1990, p. 165.

refuted the principle of party-presentation and the principle of party-disposition.[44] The Act allowed the State Attorney to reopen cases in the public interest.[45] Most explicit was the first paragraph of Section 1 of the Act, which read:

> 'Section 1 (1) In civil cases before the ordinary courts the state attorney is entitled to participate in order to present, from the perspective of the interest of the German people in the proceeding, those issues that should be considered when a judgment is rendered. Thereto the state attorney is entitled to participate in all oral hearings, to adduce matters of fact, to present evidence and to provide an advice on the judgment that will be rendered'.[46]

The Austrian Code of 1895 was much less radical than the legislation enacted by socialists and national socialists. Nevertheless, there is a close resemblance in jurisprudence between the socialist, national socialist and the Austrian legislation. These similarities are no coincidence, as there have been frequent examples of cross influences. Franz Klein was inspired by the socialist Anton Menger.[47] Similarly, many eastern European countries had adopted a Code of Civil Procedure based on the Austrian Code before the adoption of socialist ideology.[48] A third example of cross influences is that the National Socialist Act on the Participation of the State Attorney, ironically enough published 23 days after the commencement of *Unternehmen Barbarossa* (i.e. the invasion of the Soviet Union), was inspired by legislation on the role of the *Prokutura* in the Soviet Republics.

In post-modern Europe, which has allegedly witnessed the bankruptcy of the big meta-narratives and ideologies, the influence of ideological differences on modern systems of civil procedure should not be overemphasized. Since the fall of the iron curtain, ideological features of socialist procedural legislation have been removed.[49] Perhaps the influences of ideology have always been much smaller in legal practice than one would infer on the basis of the ideological language used in procedural legislation.[50] Modern Continental systems have largely sought to strike a balance between the procedural doctrines associated with competing ideological doctrines. For example, German civil procedural law has been a battleground of

44 Gesetz über die Mitwirkung des Staatsanwalts in bürgerlichen Rechtssachen (GMSBR). Vom 15. Juli 1941, Reichsgesetzblatt 1941 I, No. 77, p. 383.

45 Sections 2-6 GMSBR.

46 'In bürgerlichen Rechtssachen der ordentlichen Gerichte ist der Staatsanwalt zur Mitwirkung befugt, um die vom Standpunkt der Volksgemeinschaft im Verfahren und bei der Entscheidung zu berücksichtigenden Umstände geltend zu machen. Hierzu kann der Staatsanwalt an allen Verhandlungen teilnehmen, Tatsachen und Beweismittel vorbringen und sich über die zu erlassende Entscheidung gutachtlich äussern'.

47 See Chapters 2 and 7.

48 Klein's ideology has been termed a first step in the direction of socialist legislation. See on the historic link between Austrian and Socialist procedural law: Jelinek 1991, p. 83-86.

49 See for example Weitz 2006, for the changes in Poland since 1989.

50 Uzelac 2010: '(...) the socialist lawyers were never fully "socialist" in essence, they were only putting a thin layer of ideological justification on their actions in order to assure their own ideological legitimacy in the eyes of the political regime'.

political ideologies.[51] The *bürgerlich liberalen* Code of Civil Procedure of 1877, still in force today, underwent a number of revisions mostly inspired by the Austrian Code of 1895. During the same time Germany has been affected by socialist and National Socialist procedural doctrine and legislation. In Austria in addition, judges often are less pro-active than Franz Klein had envisaged. In practice, the differences between the Dutch and German system and the Austrian system are rather small. A giant ideological leap in the political arena may at the same time be an insignificant step in legal practice.

Although differences should not be overdrawn, the different theoretical starting points of modern systems of civil litigation can explain some differences that currently exist. One example is the degree in which legal systems allow the parties to deviate by contract from procedural rules on fact-gathering and evidence. In the Netherlands, the parties are in principle free to make a binding contract on matters of evidence.[52] The Dutch Code enables parties to engage in contracts that shift the burden of proof, specify that documents provide full proof or that evidence by means of witness statements will not be admissible. Although exceptions exist in matters of family law, such contracts in Dutch law are generally enforceable and bind the court.[53] The Austrian Code of 1895 abandoned the principle of party-presentation; in principle, therefore, contracts between the parties concerning evidence do not bind the Austrian judge.[54] The Austrian Supreme Court has decided that contracts which require the judge to award full proof to a certain document or contracts that limit the evidential value of a means of proof are not enforceable.[55]

Role of the Court and the Role of Private Practitioners

Public courts are governmental organizations that generally share the operation of the system of public justice with private professionals such as lawyers and bailiffs. In a *laissez-faire* reactive state, government intervention in society is preferably very limited. In addition, the public justice system in a reactive state fulfills only the relatively modest function of resolving disputes. Accordingly, the courts tend to leave a greater share of the operation of the public justice system to private

51 See in general Verkijk 2010.

52 Similarly, in the United States, FRCP Rule 29 allows parties to deviate from discovery rules by stipulation.

53 Article 153 Code of Civil Procedure reads: 'Contract in which parties deviate from the rules of evidence, are not enforceable if they are related to matters of fact parties cannot freely dispose of and if they are not enforceable according to the Civil Code'. See Hidma & Rutgers 2004, Chapter 2, §5, also see Section 2.3.2.2.

54 Fasching 1990, No. 890-891.

55 Austrian Supreme Court, 7 October 2003, 4 Ob 188/03f: 'Beweisverträge, insbesondere solche Verträge zwischen den Prozessparteien, mit denen sie sich verpflichten, dem Gericht eine bestimmte Beweiswürdigung vorzuschreiben oder den Beweismitteln einen bestimmten Beweiswert zuzugestehen, sind unwirksam; sie können weder erzwungen noch kann ihre Verletzung im laufenden Rechtsstreit selbst geltend gemacht werden'. Courts have recognized that parties can make binding agreements that shift the burden of proof to the other party. See Rechberger in Fasching & Konecny 2002-2005, vor §266, Nos. 38-39.

practitioners. The courts mainly serve to make a final decision. Therefore the court, being a part of a reactive state, will also be 'reactive'.

In an activist state, the government actively develops policies. The public justice system functions not only to resolve disputes but also to do so in accordance with these policies. Often government policies require the court to be more actively involved in the system of public justice. If it would make the public justice system more effective, efficient or fair, an activist state could consider active involvement in serving documents, gathering facts or in providing legal assistance to the parties.

In the United States, many of the tasks in the public justice system have been delegated to lawyers. A clear example set out in greater detail in Chapter 3, is the gradual privatization of the process of fact gathering. After the introduction of the 1938 Federal Rules of Civil Procedure, (FRCP) the centre of gravity in the fact-finding process shifted from trials to discovery and thereby from the courtroom to the lawyer's office. Witnesses once primarily heard in courtrooms are now generally deposed in lawyers' offices. Depositions are generally not followed by a further examination at trial. The 1938 FRCP put into place a system that allows a thorough search for the facts with a minimum of government intervention.[56]

The Prussian Judicial Ordinance of 1781 and 1793 is often mentioned as an example of a Code that had almost fully put the operation of the justice system in the hands of public officers.[57] It was based on the premise that it was the duty of the court to establish *ex officio* the veracity of facts in civil litigation by directly communicating with the litigants. The Code abolished the role of private practitioners in civil litigation and introduced new government officials to provide the parties with legal assistance.[58] Similar radical approaches could be found in socialist countries. The Russian Socialist Federal Republic had abolished the bar and reorganized it on a collective basis.[59] In Albania, the introduction of socialism was first followed by legislation that required attorneys to assist the courts in fulfilling their duties.[60] Subsequently, by decree of the 20th of June 1967 lawyers and notaries were replaced by newly introduced offices of legal assistance.[61] Legal specialists that worked for the offices of legal assistance were appointed by the High Court of Justice and provided legal assistance to individuals and state organs.

In Continental jurisdictions today, the process of fact-gathering has in general not been fully delegated to lawyers. As described above, the court is often actively involved in the early stages of litigation. Differences between Continental countries do exist. The role of the Austrian court is very extensive.[62] The court is responsible for serving almost all procedural documents, including the complaint.[63] In other

56 Yeazell 2004, p. 965.

57 Engelmann 1927, p. 590 *et seq.*

58 See on the role of lawyers Ledford 1996, p. 32-33 and Damaska 1986, p. 202.

59 Cappelletti 1970, p. 876.

60 Çuri, P., 2002, E drejta avokatore shqiptare, p. 520. Article 2 of the Law No. 345, 20.11.1946 'Mbi avokatët'; Article 1 Law No. 3350, 3.10.1961 'Mbi avokatinë'.

61 Decree No. 4277, 20.6.1967 'Mbi krijimin e zyrave të ndihmës juridike'.

62 In Austria the applicable terminology is 'Gerichtsbetrieb'. See Klein & Engel 1927, Chapter 6, p. 170.

63 Section 87 Austrian Code of Civil Procedure.

countries, such as the Netherlands, the plaintiff is held responsible for hiring a qualified bailiff who subsequently serves the complaint on the defendant.[64] Similarly, the responsibility for the enforcement of legal decisions is allocated differently throughout jurisdictions.[65] In the Netherlands, the enforcement of judgments has been largely privatized. In Austria however, the courts are responsible for the enforcement of judgments.[66]

Figures on the number of judges and attorneys per 100.000 inhabitants reflect the large differences between the roles which attorneys and judges play in the administration of justice. The numbers should be interpreted with care, because the data *inter alia* include both civil, criminal and administrative cases. Also it should be considered that the figures below ignore differences that exist in the numbers of legal professionals other than lawyers and judges (such as law clerks, magistrate judges, public notaries etc.). The figures do indicate that the number of attorneys per professional judge varies greatly between jurisdictions.

Table 9.1. Legal professions, 2006 Data[67]

	Number of professional judges, fte, per 100.000 inhabitants	Number of lawyers per 100.000 inhabitants
Germany	24.5	168
Austria	20.2	84
The Netherlands	12.7	92
England and Wales	7.0	262[68]
United States	10.2 state court judges[69] 0.4 federal judges[70]	373[71]

Conclusion

We may conclude that in an activist state the forms of procedure differ fundamentally from the forms of procedure in a reactive state. The comparison made between both political perspectives on the role of the state in society and their impact on the form of the justice system is summarized in Table 9.2.

64 See e.g. Articles 111 and 45 Dutch Code of Civil Procedure.

65 For a comparative overview, see CEPEJ 2007.

66 Hess 2005, p. 32, p. 34-35.

67 See CEPEJ 2008, Tables 51 and 104.

68 CEPEJ 2008, Table 104. For England, the Table includes both barristers and solicitors.

69 This figure, the average number of state court judges in the United States per 100.000 inhabitants, is based on data from Court Statistics Project, *State Court Caseload Statistics 2007* (National Center for State Courts 2008), available at <www.ncsc.org>, last consulted in February 2010. Figure G. There were 356 judges at the Courts of last resort, 985 judges at Courts of Appeal, 11,349 General Jurisdiction Courts and 18,161 Special Jurisdiction Courts. The population in the United States in 2006 was 302,681 million.

70 The number of judgeships at the U.S. District Courts in 2006 equaled 678, the number of bankruptcy judgeships 324, the number of judgeships at the Courts of Appeal was 167. The number of Supreme Court Judges is 9. Duff 2008, Table 1, p. 19 and Table 3, p. 22. The total number of judges is 1,178.

71 According to the ABA there were 1,128,729 active attorneys in the United States in 2006, see <www.abanet.org>, last consulted in February 2010.

Table 9.2. The reactive and the activist state

	Activist State	Reactive State
A Good Society	State has a conception of a good society	The state has no preset conception of a good society
Aims of Process	Enforcement of Government Policy	Dispute Resolution
Fact-finding	Pursuit of Truth	*Verhandlungsmaxime*/ Adversarialism
Division of Labor	Emphasis on the Court/ *Amtsbetrieb*	Emphasis on Private Practitioners/ *Parteibetrieb*

It must be noted that a distinction between pure activist states and pure reactive states can only be made in the abstract. The jurisdictions discussed above tend to provide solutions between these theoretical extremes.

3. Democracy, Rules and the Organization of Institutions

Two Different Means to ensure the Democratic Legitimacy of the Legal Process
Western European and American states claim to be 'democratic'. Rendering justice in civil cases is one of the most important functions of the state. Hence it is important that the administration of justice has some form of democratic legitimacy. Two techniques to ensure democratic legitimacy are most common. First, most legal systems provide for rules that ensure that the Code of Civil Procedure is enacted by democratically chosen representatives of the people. The constitutions of most jurisdictions have empowered the legislature to make rules that regulate the legal process. Second, many jurisdictions have ensured the democratic legitimacy of the decision maker. Judges are sometimes elected and 'the people' are sometimes involved directly in the legal process as jurors. Whereas the first technique focuses on the legitimacy of the rules that regulate the legal process, the second technique focuses on the democratic legitimacy of the decision maker.

Many legal systems, mostly Continental ones, have chosen to ascertain the democratic legitimacy of the legal process by making use of the first technique only. Judges and attorneys are expected to apply the rules in the spirit of the legislator such that the legal process itself has democratic legitimacy. In such legal systems, the Acts of Parliament are considered to be the primary and supreme source of law. In line with the views of Montesquieu, judges are only required to be 'the mouths of the law'.[72]

Judicial procedure is more than the whole of legal rules found in a Code of Civil Procedure.[73] Customs and law often diverge; rules in the Code are often neglected and common practices might not be prescribed by the law. Practices can vary between regions, between courts and even between individual judges. The judicial process is not always primarily shaped by the law of procedure, but by the habit of mind of those who apply the law. For the proper functioning of the judicial process, the mindset and practices of the individuals that run the system is of

72 Montesquieu 1748, Livre XI, Ch. 6.
73 On the relationship between custom and law, see Calamandrei 1956, p. 10-15.

greater significance than the technical perfection of the Code of Civil Procedure.[74] To conclude, legal procedures do not exist in the abstract. As Langbein put it: '(t)here is a deep relationship between *how* we proceed and *who* does the proceeding'.[75]

Procedure is not only about rules but also about the individuals that apply the rules. The view that democratic values are sufficiently preserved as long as Parliament has been involved in the drafting of rules may therefore be mistaken.[76] Many jurisdictions have therefore ensured that the actors that have a decisive role in the legal process have direct democratic legitimacy.

The Relationship between Democracy and Bureaucracy

That some form of democratic legitimacy of the legal process is desirable goes unquestioned. Democratic legitimacy is widely considered to be essential to ensure that procedures before the court are sensible and acceptable in the eyes of the public. Nevertheless, democratic values often need to be weighed against other values. In this Section it will be argued that a civil justice system will have to strike a balance between democratic values and conflicting considerations of cost and time efficiency. It will be argued that democratic processes and modes of decision making are generally opposed to bureaucratic processes and modes of decision making.

It is common to contrast democratic processes with bureaucratic processes. U.S. President Andrew Jackson believed that democracy and rotation in office would prevent the development of a corrupt bureaucracy.[77] Max Weber noted that democratic principles of adjudication are clearly not identical with what he regarded to be a rational, and formalistic mode of adjudication.[78]

According to Weber, a central characteristic of a bureaucracy is that it offers 'the optimal possibility for the realization of the principle of division of labor in administration according to purely technical considerations, allocating individual tasks to functionaries who are trained as specialists and who continuously add to their experience by constant practice'.[79] Bureaucracies are generally implemented in order to enable governments to fulfill specific tasks efficiently. As Weber put it:[80]

> 'A fully developed bureaucratic administration stands in the same relationship to non-bureaucratic forms as machinery to non-mechanical modes of production. Precision, speed, consistency, availability of records, continuity, possibility of secrecy, unity,

74 Klein 1891, p. 7: 'Das Gesetz gibt eine Menge Regeln und Vorschriften, die für sich und in ihrer Komposition, rein wissenschaftlich beurteilt, den besten Prozess darstellen. Aber was aus ihnen in Wirklichkeit wird, darüber entscheiden Jene, welche das Gesetz anwenden: Richter und Anwälte'.

75 Langbein 1995, p. 551.

76 Also see Smits 2008a.

77 See Andrew Jackson's First Annual Message, December 8, 1829. Available at <www.presidency.ucsb.edu/ws/index.php?pid=29471>, last consulted in February 2010.

78 Weber 1954, p. 351.

79 Weber 1954, p. 350.

80 Weber 1954, p. 349, Chapter XIV.

> rigorous coordination and mineralization of friction and of expense for materials and personnel are achieved in a strictly bureaucratized, especially in a monocratically organized, administration conducted by trained officials to an extent incomparably greater than in any collegial form of administration or in any conducted by honoratoires or part-time administrators'.

Whereas the principles of specialization and division of labor are central to the bureaucratic process, democratic processes operate differently. The democratic logic may oppose specialization and division of labor. In a direct democracy, decisions are made by 'the people' rather than by trained specialists. In democratic systems where representatives of the people fulfill vital governmental functions, specialized training is not required before one is eligible to run for office. Specialization through continuous training is limited for those that have been democratically elected. After all, democracy generally requires rotation of office. Rotation of office implies that government officials serve for limited terms. The logic of modern democratic systems is also often at odds with a strict division of labor. Political accountability requires that presidents, ministers or secretaries of state are politically responsible for a broad policy field. In most legal systems, the Members of Parliament are required to vote on legislative proposals covering all policy areas.

Table 9.3. Democratic and bureaucratic models

	Pure Democratic Model	Pure Bureaucratic Model
Rulemaking	By (Representatives of) the People (e.g. Parliament)	By Experts (e.g. judges and court auditors)
Involvement of Lay People	With Lay Arbiters (e.g. Civil Jury)	No Lay Arbiters
Court Personnel	Rotation of Office for elected Judges and Paralegal Staff	Career Judges and career Clerks
Specialization	No Specialized Courts and no Specialization within the Court.	Specialized Courts and Specialization within the Courts

In a pure democratic model procedural rules are made by (representatives of) the people. The members of the judiciary in a pure democratic model are elected. Similarly, in the pure democratic model, lay people are directly involved as arbiters in the legal process. Within a pure democratic model, there is less room for specialized training and a strict division of labor. The degree in which democratic elements have been implemented will therefore affect the ability to implement bureaucratic elements.[81]

In a pure bureaucratic model, a body of specialized bureaucrats will draft procedural rules. The judicial process in a pure bureaucratic model is operated by career judges and career clerks. The judicial apparatus is hierarchically ordered into Sections and Subsections, each specialized in a certain step in the legal process or a

81 The distinction made here between democratic and bureaucratic models has similarieties with the distinction between what Damaska coined the 'coordinate ideal' and the 'hierarchical ideal'. See Damaska 1986.

certain category of cases. A bureaucratic judicial apparatus should function like a modern computer, much faster and much more efficient than an old fashioned typewriter.

Democracy and Rulemaking
In most jurisdictions, the power to make and amend a Code of Civil Procedure is vested in democratically chosen representatives of the people. Especially in many Continental countries, it is believed to be of utmost importance that the procedural rules should be enacted by Parliament.[82] It is argued that important areas of the law - such as civil procedural law - ought to be codified by the representatives of 'the people'. Rousseau's philosophy provided the philosophical foundation and democratic justification for the national codification movements in a number of countries.[83] The first 'Dutch' constitution, *de Staatssregeling voor het Bataafse Volk* (1798), was clearly inspired by Rousseau's works and explicitly specified that the law was 'the expression of the will of the people, as expressed by the majority of citizens or its representatives'.[84] Article 28 of this constitution specified that codifications, including a Code of Civil Procedure, had to be enacted for the whole republic within two years.[85] The provision was retained in other early constitutions.[86] The present Dutch Constitution still specifies that the legislator should regulate the forms of civil procedure by formal act in a general Code of Civil Procedure.[87] In the Netherlands, the formal legislative process is the only way in which changes are made to the Code of Civil Procedure. The Dutch rulemaking process is democratic. At the same time it limits the use of efficient bureaucratic methods. Members of Dutch Parliament that ultimately decide on procedural rules are generally not specialists in the administration of the civil justice system. Parliament often simply approves legislation drafted by specialists of the Ministry of Justice, if however legislation is subject to debate in Parliament, the Dutch process of rulemaking will consume a fair amount of resources.

In most American jurisdictions, the power to promulgate rules is vested in a parliamentary body. There is however a long Anglo-American tradition in which

82 Gourevitch 2004, p. 67, The Social Contract, Chapter 6.

83 This conception of democracy is in line with Rousseau's philosophy. Rousseau believed that 'the people' should enact statutes for 'the people'. Only statutes that were 'acts of the general will' could properly be referred to as laws. Rousseau had set out his views on codification in his 'Considérations sur le gouvernement de Pologne'. See Lokin & Zwalve 2001, p. 41.

84 Article 5 of the *Staatsregeling voor het Bataafse Volk* read: 'De wet is de wil van het geheele maatschappylyk lichaam, uitgedrukt door de meerderheid of der burgeren of van derzelver vertegenwoordigers (...)'.

85 '28. Er zal een wetboek gemaakt worden zoo wel van burgerlyke als van lyfstraflyke wetten te gelyk met de wyze van regtsvordering op gronden door de staatsregeling verzekerd en algemeen voor de gansche republiek. Deszelfs invoering zal zyn uiterlyk binnen twee Jaaren na de invoering der staatsregeling'.

86 See Article 100 of the 1814 Dutch Constitution and Article 163 of the 1815 Dutch Constitution. The two year time limit was not retained.

87 Article 107: '1. De wet regelt het burgerlijk recht, het strafrecht en het burgerlijk en strafprocesrecht in algemene wetboeken, behoudens de bevoegdheid tot regeling van bepaalde onderwerpen in afzonderlijke wetten'.

legislators have delegated the power to make rules to courts.[88] The Process Acts of 1792 and 1828 specified that the procedure in federal courts would normally adjust to the procedure in state courts subject to alterations and additions set by the U.S. courts and the U.S. Supreme Court.[89] The Supreme Court had promulgated Federal Rules of Equity as early as 1822 on the basis of the aforementioned process act of 1792. Present codifications, such as the FRCP and the FRE are also largely created by the Judiciary. Under the 1934 Rules Enabling Act, much of the rulemaking powers of Congress were delegated to the United States Supreme Court.[90] Although Congress retained the powers to 'step in', rulemaking is currently largely left to the U.S. Supreme Court.[91] The current process of amending the FRE or the FRCP is slightly less democratic than rulemaking by Congress itself. At the same time, the Federal American practice of rulemaking is more bureaucratic and probably more efficient. This is because the rules are generally drafted and amended by specialists, mostly judges, who generally involve other (specialist) stakeholders in the drafting process.

The State of Michigan provides an example of a system that went even further in empowering a court to enact rules. The seven Michigan Supreme Court judges have been empowered to enact rules of procedure pursuant to Article 6 §5 of the Michigan Constitution.[92] As these Supreme Court judges are elected in non-partisan elections, the rulemaking process still has democratic legitimacy. Subchapter 1.200 of the Michigan Court Rules provides for an administrative procedure which enables other stakeholders, such as the members of the bar, to be heard on proposed amendments to the Rules. The Michigan rules provide an example of rulemaking by specialists that have democratic legitimacy.

The precise process that determines how the rules of procedure are made may influence the content and form of the rules, including those on fact-finding. Because the Dutch Parliamentary process is fairly cumbersome and Parliament is overburdened, changes in style alone to the Dutch Code of Civil Procedure are infrequent. If rules are largely drafted by the judges, it is likely that the perspective of the courts will prevail more often than the perspective of the litigants or attorneys.

Democracy and Lay Arbiters: The American Civil Jury

History provides a rich source of examples of procedural systems that have made use of lay arbiters. In the Russian Socialist Federal Republic, lay people were involved in the judicial process.[93] Similarly, the Constitution of the German

88 Hepburn 1907, p. 683.

89 Millar 1952, p. 58.

90 U.S.C. 28 §§2071-2077. In 1988 Congress further regulated the federal rulemaking process, see U.S.C. 28 §§2072-2074, as amended by Pub. L. 100-702, Title IV, §401(a), 102 Stat. 4648 (1988).

91 Congress stepped in prior to the promulgation of the FRE, see Saltzburg, Martin & Capra 1998, p. 3.

92 Michigan Constitution of 1963, Article 6, paragraph 2. Article VI of the 1850 Michigan Constitution had already granted the court rights to draft rules, see Honigman 1959, p. 16.

93 Cappelletti 1970, p. 876.

Democratic Republic prescribed the use of lay judges (*Schöffen*) who had the same legal powers as professional judges.[94] Modern European Continental systems usually do not make use of lay judges in civil cases.

In the United States, the general distrust of governmental organizations has led to the large scale involvement of lay people in the justice system. In early colonial days there were various experiments involving lay people in the resolution of disputes. The Pennsylvanian laws of 1682 distrusted formal litigation and specified that disputes were to be resolved by three lay peacemakers. The arbitration by these peacemakers was declared to be as valid as a judgment by a Court of Justice. Similar experiments that prescribed arbitration by lay people were seen elsewhere.[95]

The civil jury is the best known example of the involvement of lay people in the administration of justice. As described in Chapter 8, the civil jury provides for the direct participation of citizens in matters of government. The civil jury thereby is a classic example of 'government by the people' and constitutes a forum for deliberative democracy.[96] The involvement of lay jurors in the legal process, as is common in the United States, is diametrically opposed to the specialization and division of labor that is central to a bureaucratic organization of the justice system.[97] The American jury is a bulwark of democracy; at the same time the civil jury makes it impossible to create a system that reaps the fruits of specialization. Even the greatest supporters of the jury system admit that it is inferior in terms of costs and delay to a professional judiciary.[98]

The use of lay jurors has a large impact on the modes and forms of procedure. As I have argued in Chapter 8, many American rules of procedure and evidence, such as the exclusionary rules of evidence, the presentation of all evidence at a single uninterrupted trial, discovery and the emphasis on the oral presentation of evidence, exist to accommodate for the civil jury. As a consequence, the existence of the civil jury provides an important explanation for diverging modes of fact-gathering and fact-finding in different jurisdictions.[99]

Democracy and the Judiciary

Democratically chosen officials often play an important role in appointing judges. The United States Supreme Court judges are nominated by the President and appointed 'with the advice and consent of the Senate'.[100] Even on the European

94 Article 96 of the Constitution of the German Democratic Republic, see Fernhout 1981, Part 3.5.

95 Friedman 1985, p. 45.

96 Landsman 1992, p. 599 and Carrington 2003, p. 83.

97 Weber 1954, p. 318. Weber considered the civil jury to be 'irrational'.

98 See e.g. Landsman 1992, Part IV.

99 The gradual disappearance of the English jury has also gradually led to the abandonnement of many of the rules accommodating the civil jury, other rules have remained as 'vestiges' of the old system. See Andrews 2003a, p. 774.

100 Article II of the U.S. Constitution.

continent, political institutions with democratic legitimacy are involved in the appointment of judges of Constitutional Courts.[101]

A more direct method to exercise democratic control over the judiciary is to elect judges. On the European continent, former socialist states such as the Russian Socialist Federal Republic and the German Democratic Republic had elected judges through popular elections.[102] Currently, the popular election of judges is not common in modern European jurisdictions. The practices in a number of Swiss cantons are a notable exception. From a European perspective, the widespread American practices of electing judges are therefore exceptional.[103] In 2006, 89% of all state judges in the United States are elected one way or the other. Non-partisan, partisan and retention election are the most common ways to elect judges.[104] The election or political appointment of judges impacts the organization of the judiciary, the career of a judge and, subsequently, the ordinary forms of procedure.

The election or political appointment of judges has a very large impact on the career path of judges. The popular election of judges requires rotation of office as the people should be able to remove an ill-functioning judge. In many American states, the position of the judge and judicial staff is shaped by a Jacksonian image of public office whereby 'rotation' is the rule rather than the exception.[105] This model not only affects judges that face re-elections. Law clerks and other supportive staff are often exclusively assigned to a single judge. Sometimes paralegal staff is required to leave office if a new judge is elected. Even Federal judges, appointed for life under Article III of the U.S. Constitution, are generally not career judges. Being a federal judge is considered to be an honorable position. It is typically a 'second career' that is pursued only after one has practiced law for a decade or two. We may conclude that the democratic election and political appointment of judges has led to a system designed on the premise that judges (and sometimes paralegals) serve for short and fixed terms.

In Continental systems, judges are not chosen or appointed because of their personal characteristics. They are often selected before the age of thirty and trained to become anonymous experts. Judges are typically appointed for life. Many judges on the European continent have worked almost their entire career in the judiciary. It is common in the United States to speak of the 'legal profession'. On the European Continent, in contrast, it is common to speak of 'the legal professions'.[106] Shifting from one profession to the other on the European Continent generally requires additional training.

101 See for a comparative overview: Russel 2001.

102 Cappelletti 1970, p. 876. Articles 58, 94 and 95 of the former Constitution of the German Democratic Republic prescribed that judges and lay judges would be elected in popular elections or would be appointed by representatives of the people.

103 Liptek 2008.

104 Warren 2006, p. 4-5. For an overview per state, see <http://www.judicialselection.us>, last consulted in February 2010.

105 See Andrew Jackson's First Annual Message, 8 December 1829. Available at <www.presidency.ucsb.edu/ws/index.php?pid=29471>, last consulted in February 2010.

106 Chase, Herschkoff, Silberman, Taniguchi & Varano 2007, Chapter 2, Sections III-V.

The election or political appointment of judges also impacts the organization of the judiciary. As judges are elected by the people or appointed by the President for their personal characteristics, it is difficult to require the judge to be 'squeezed' into a larger bureaucratic machine. The democratic legitimacy of a judge provides a powerful argument for American judges to resist hierarchical subordination. The political accountability of judges set limitations on bureaucratization. In order to be accountable, judges should be enabled to some extent to determine for themselves how to perform their job. The standardization of work methods and the division of labor within a bureaucracy offers too many opportunities for individuals to disclaim responsibility and accountability. If a judge is only responsible for a small step in the administration of justice, an individual judge alone cannot be held accountable for deficiencies in the system.[107]

Courts in the United States are generally not organized along bureaucratic lines.[108] Often U.S. District Courts have a few judges only.[109] If the courts are larger, each judge runs his own 'small court' within the court. U.S. District Court judges in the larger courts typically have their own personal courtroom and their own chambers. It is common that cases are randomly distributed amongst the judges of a U.S. District Court. Judges often decide a criminal case in the morning and hear a civil case in the afternoon. Each judge has a relatively large degree of freedom to determine his or her own mode of handling cases. The important point is that, in the United States, the popular election or presidential appointment of judges hinders bureaucratization. Democratic legitimacy opposes hierarchical subordination. Political accountability is at odds with specialization.

On the continent, courts may be organized as bureaucratic organizations.[110] In Austria, Klein had argued in favor of an efficient allocation of labor, specialization and a bureaucratic organization of the judiciary (see Section 7.1). Continental judges do generally not have their own court room and chambers. Supportive staff is mostly not exclusively assigned to a single judge. The prevailing constitutional doctrine holds that judges ought to apply law rather than create it.[111] In cases in which a panel of judges makes a decision, no dissenting opinions will be given. It is the court that renders a decision, rather than an individual judge. In the Netherlands, courts are presently to a relatively large degree organized along bureaucratic lines.[112] Specialization primarily takes place within the courts.[113] In the

107 Calamandrei 1956, p. 32.

108 Specialized administrative courts and tribunals exist in the United States (e.g. the United States Tax Court). Judges in these courts or tribunals are mostly not judges under Article III of the U.S. Constitution.

109 In 2008, there were 678 authorized District Court judges and 94 District Courts.

110 Damaska 1986, p. 29-38. Damaska argues that from the 11th century onwards, the Church was increasingly organized along bureaucratic lines, a development that also affected the judiciary in the Canonical courts.

111 Montesquieu 1748, Livre XI, Ch. 6: 'Les juges ne sont que la bouche qui pronounce les paroles de la loi, des êtres inanimés qui n'en peuvent modérer ni la force, ni la rigeur'.

112 There currently is a trend towards more specialization. See Jurgens & Tromp 2009.

average Dutch District Court, there are a number of departments.[114] A Civil Law Section of the court generally handles larger civil cases.[115] In practice, the Civil Law Section is often again split up in smaller divisions, such as a bankruptcy, a family law and a commercial division. Within the smaller divisions, a senior judge usually allots the cases to the judges within the division (*Kamervoorzitter*). Judges certainly do not handle a criminal case before and a civil case after lunch. Dutch judges form a part of a larger bureaucratic apparatus.

We may conclude that democratic values affect the career path of judges and the organization of the justice system.[116] This in turn affects the ordinary procedures (of fact-finding) before the courts. Let me illustrate this by means of three examples. First, American judges have generally worked as attorneys for years. American judges therefore are probably more capable than Continental judges of understanding the lawyer's perspective on a case. One American judge explained that she seldom interrupted the cross-examination of counsel, as she recalled she did not appreciate it when she was interrupted when cross-examining a witness herself.[117] A second example illustrates that the re-election of judges impacts the judge's decisions. Huber and Gordon showed, on the basis of sentencing data from 22,095 Pennsylvania criminal cases, that judges give higher sanctions as reelection nears.[118] Third, the fact that judges on the European continent usually specialize will probably have a large influence on their role in the legal process. A specialist judge who has in depth knowledge of the substantive law in his area of specialization is not likely to rely as much on the legal arguments provided by counsel. Such a judge can be proactive during a court hearing to decide on questions of law and to identify the relevant factual issues. It is more difficult for a judge who is not specialized to play a pro-active role in the litigation process. The adversarial system hence fits well into a system in which judges are not specialized.

Conclusion

Western procedural systems are influenced by democratic values. Democratic values may affect the way in which the procedural rules are created and may affect the way in which the decision maker in the legal process is selected. The two different ways in which democratic values can influence litigation are interrelated. It is not surprising that the delegation of rulemaking powers takes place in American rather than Continental jurisdictions. On the continent such a delegation of rulemaking powers would create a democratic deficit.

113 In the Netherlands the Court of Appeal in The Hague is specialized in patent cases, whereas the Court in Leeuwarden is specialized in handling violations of traffic regulations etc. See in general: Tromp, Jurgens, De Groot-van Leeuwen & Bovend'Eert 2006.

114 Article 47 Act on the Judicial Organization (*Wet RO*).

115 On the Dutch Judicial Organization, see Bovend'Eert & Kortmann 2008, Chapter 4.

116 Whether or not judges are elected also has a massive effect on the perception of ordinary citizens of the judiciary. Benesh 2006, p. 704, argues that citizens that live in states in which judges are elected have less confidence in the judiciary than citizens that live in states in which judges are appointed.

117 This observation is based on a private conversation with a judge in a state court.

118 Huber & Gordon 2004.

All modern western jurisdictions tend to have some form of democratic control over the procedural rules that govern the forms of litigation. The biggest difference between modern legal systems is whether or not the actors in the legal process have democratic legitimacy. In the United States, the actors in the legal process generally have democratic legitimacy. On the European continent judges have limited or no democratic legitimacy.

Democratic input limits the degree to which bureaucratization can take place. Most relevant in this respect is that the election and political appointment of judges and the existence of the civil jury hinder the division of labor and specialization. The procedural rules and practices in a system operated by lay people and officers that serve for limited terms is likely to differ from the rules and practices in a system run by career judges and career clerks. I believe these differences have a large impact on the ordinary process of fact-finding. Bureaucratization certainly affects the efficiency of the process of fact-finding. In addition, as explained in Chapter 8, the existence of a civil jury explains many distinctive American procedural rules on fact-finding.

4. Political Ideology, Democracy and the Forms of Procedure

The differences between the procedures before the civil courts of different jurisdictions are well documented. A distinction between common law and civil law systems is often made.[119] Although such crude categories between legal systems lead to oversimplification and unjustified generalizations, these categories are generally useful. Two main differences are most commonly mentioned between the rules in Continental and common law jurisdictions.[120] First, there are differences with respect to the role of the court. In civil law jurisdictions, the court has a greater responsibility for gathering information and evidence. The different approaches to expert evidence in the United States and on the continent, discussed in Chapter 5, well illustrates this general distinction between the common law and the Continental traditions. A second difference between both traditions is that the common law system is based on the distinction between a pretrial stage and a trial stage. On the European continent proceedings have no such preset structure; the procedure usually consists of a sequence of hearings.

In the previous Sections, I have argued that these main differences between the legal systems flow from different political and theoretical starting points of legal systems. Essential to the forms of process are: 1) the different views on the role of the state in society and 2) the way in which democratic ideals have affected the institutions that operate the litigation process. On the basis of this analysis, one could make a distinction between four ideal types of civil procedure. These ideal

119 See e.g. Zekoll 2006 and Van Rhee & Verkerk 2006.

120 See e.g. Langbein 1985, p. 826.

types are mentioned in the grid below, along with legal systems that have largely been constructed along the lines of these ideal types.[121]

Table 9.4. Four procedural models

Role of the State\Democracy	Democratic Institutions operate the Justice System	No Democratic Institutions operate the Justice System
The Activist State and Policy Implementation	System of the former German Democratic Republic	Austrian Code of 1895 The Prussian Code of 1781
The Reactive State and Dispute Resolution	Federal Legal System of the United States	19th century Dutch and German Procedural Systems

Although the four ideal types identified above are depicted as logically separable, the differing views of the role of the state and the role of democracy in the legal system are interrelated. The combination of an activist state and democratic institutions is difficult to implement. Democratically elected judges, chosen by the people for their personal characteristics, skills and reasonableness, could obstruct the policies of other branches of government. To the extent lay people are involved in the administration of justice, they could have difficulties applying the often complex body of substantive law. Within activist states, the courts have generally played a submissive role and the separation of powers was generally rejected. Within the Nazi state, for example, the *Führerprinzip* was a leading constitutional principle that led to the rejection of the separation of powers and the independence of the judiciary. High ranking Nazi official Hans Frank, minister of Justice in Bavaria (1933-1934) and President of the Academy of German Law from 1933 onwards, argued that the judge was to complete the work of the legislator and function as a bridge between the will of the legislator and reality.[122] The judge according to Frank, was never allowed to infringe upon the leading principles of the National Socialist program. In Soviet Russia, courts were expected to seek guidance from party officials in specific matters.[123] In the German Democratic Republic, the Constitution specified that the Supreme Court was accountable to the legislative branches of government: the *Volkskammer* and the *Staatsrat*. Article 6 of the Code of Procedure of the German Democratic Republic had resolved possible tensions between government and the lower courts by requesting mutual cooperation.

It is much easier to combine the ideal of a reactive state with democratic institutions. In the reactive state, there is no government policy in civil law matters and hence the government has no interest in how the dispute is resolved. One democratic institution perhaps best fits the ideals of a reactive state: the civil jury.[124]

121 The grid has similarities to models identified by Damaska, Damaska 1986, p. 181.
122 Frank, 'Rechtsgrundlegung des nationalsozialistischen Füherstaates', quoted by Böhm 1990, p. 153.
123 Damaska 1986, p. 173.
124 Damaska 1986, p. 135.

PART IV

THE (IN)EFFICIENCY OF ADVERSARIAL JUSTICE

Chapter 10

THE (IN)EFFICIENCY OF ADVERSARIAL JUSTICE

A comparison between legal systems can be enhanced and enriched by enlisting economic models. Modern jurisdictions are all adversarial in the sense that parties are primarily responsible for adducing facts and producing evidence. It will be argued that in an adversarial model there are incentives to overspend on fact-finding. Many procedural rules may be rationalized as attempts to avoid excessive expenditure on fact-finding. The combination of procedural rules within a jurisdiction determines whether parties and lawyers are induced to allocate resources efficiently from a social perspective. It will be argued that in some jurisdictions, such as the Federal American system, there are incentives for parties to spend a large amount of resources on fact-finding. In other jurisdictions, such as Austria, there are incentives to spend little on fact-finding.

1. Introduction: How Simple Cases become Complex Cases

Fact-finding procedures before the courts typically consist of three stages. In the first stage, the genuinely disputed issues are identified. In the second stage, parties present evidence to convince the trier of fact that their version of the facts is the most plausible. In the third stage, a decision is rendered. In order to resolve even a simple case, there can be a number of disputed facts and it can be cumbersome or expensive to provide evidence for each of them. At first sight, most cases are remarkably simple. But once a case begins to unfold, issues get fuzzy. Lawyers are trained to ask questions and to invoke a multitude of legal rules. The construction of new legal arguments requires that additional facts be adduced. Simple cases may become complex cases, as is illustrated by the following fictitious medical malpractice case that takes place in a fictitious jurisdiction.

John wrote a letter demanding damages from his doctor Mary, claiming that her medical malpractice caused a serious leg injury. Mary refused to pay: she argued that John had been treated well and that complications can occur in patients with John's condition, even with adequate treatment. At first, the case seemed remarkably simple to both Mary and John. There was only a single decisive factual question: did Mary treat John as any competent doctor would have treated John?

Before John and Mary decided to turn to professional lawyers, they were confident that their dispute could be resolved within a short time.

John's lawyer decided to serve Mary with a complaint, in which he demanded damages for maltreatment, claiming that Mary had not acted in accordance with protocol A. In addition, it is claimed that John would not have undergone the treatment if Mary had properly informed John of the risks involved.

Mary's lawyer was eager to protect his client from 'frivolous claims'. In the written answer he claimed that protocol A was not suitable to treat John and that the non-application of protocol A could not have caused John's leg injury. Furthermore, Mary denied that she had not informed John, claiming that she had briefed John on the matter before treatment. In addition, Mary claimed she gave John a brochure that contained all relevant information. In addition, Mary noted that the treatment was absolutely necessary from a medical point of view; given the very small odds of complications, no sensible well-informed person would have declined to undergo the treatment. The written answer furthermore raised the possibility that the injury was caused by another event. Mary's lawyer claimed that witness C saw John play rugby and jog only one week after the treatment, even though he had been explicitly instructed to refrain from all such activities for two months. The closing paragraph of the answer stated that 'the amount of damages claimed is outrageous'.

As the exchange of pleadings revealed many unresolved issues, the judge allowed both parties to file additional pleadings and granted leave for the discovery of relevant information. Both parties actively continued their discussion, supporting their previous arguments and raising new ones.

John's lawyer firmly denied that John had been involved in a game of rugby and added that even if John had played rugby, it could not explain John's injury. On the issue of 'informed consent', John's lawyer maintained that John had not been properly informed about the risks of the treatment. The 150-page brochure that John had received was incomprehensible and only mentioned possible complications in a footnote.

During the discovery phase, John's lawyer gained access to an electronic file in which all details of the treatment had been logged. He found that Mary had administered medicine B to John. John's lawyer claimed that the doctor knew or should have known that John was allergic to some of the ingredients of medicine B. When Mary was interrogated, she denied that she was or should have been aware of the allergy, but acknowledged that it would have been better if she had not administered medicine B. Mary claimed that there had been no allergic reaction and that the issue was certainly not related to John's injury.

As the case unfolded other legal arguments were raised and many additional facts proved to be in dispute. Once disputed factual issues were identified, evidence had to be adduced to resolve these. The judge determined that 'trial was a search for truth' and that no relevant evidence should be concealed. On the issue of whether John had played a game of rugby, it was sensible to summon all players he had allegedly played rugby with as witnesses. Expert evidence had to be examined to determine if the injury could have been caused by a game of rugby. On the precise impact of both Protocol A and Medicine B at least two experts would have to provide an opinion. The assessment of damages was another issue that certainly had to be thoroughly examined. In addition, the parties were allowed to challenge the testimony of the (expert) witnesses and to present rebuttal. John was allowed to summon witnesses who could testify that witness C, who allegedly saw him play rugby, is a notorious liar.

A case that may be simple to a lay person at first glance, may turn into an enormously complex vehicle of litigation. Figure 10.1 contains an oversimplified graphical representation of the factual debate. The aim of this Figure is only to illustrate how a lawsuit may develop. Of course it is possible to use a more formal method of analysis.[1] Many details have been left out for reasons of simplicity. In Figure 10.1, the boxes represent disputed facts, the possible means of evidence are made bold. Much like a tree that develops new branches, a legal dispute can almost endlessly be subdivided into smaller problems that potentially are all relevant to solve the case.

Figure 10.1, Disputed Facts and Evidence, a Graphical Representation

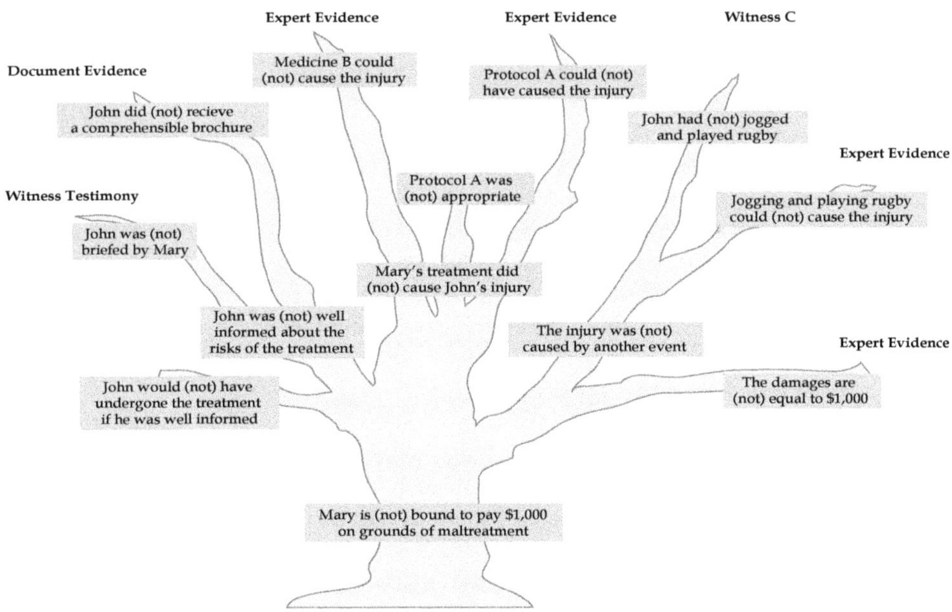

[1] See e.g. the Chart Method of Analysis as developed by Wigmore 1937, §§340-352 for an example of a more formalized method of analysis.

All legal systems, at least in theory, agree that the time and resources spent to resolve (factual) issues should be proportional to the importance and stakes of the case. One should neither employ too much nor too few resources for the process of fact-finding.

John could happen to be John Terry, the captain of Chelsea F.C. and an important player in the English national football squad. The transfer value of a football player of his stature is in the millions of pounds. The damages associated with an abrupt termination of his career could be massive. The injuries of great football players, as well as the law suits they are involved in, are generally covered by most major newspapers. If John's last name were Terry, we could possibly appreciate the litigation procedure described in the example above as being 'thorough'. We could applaud the zealousness of lawyers and would respect the emphasis of the court on the pursuit of truth.

With the last name of Doe, we might have second thoughts about the procedure described above. John Doe's damages amount to $10,000 or $1,000 and his injury is less serious and ultimately curable. The burden of too many legal arguments, too many disputed facts and too much adverse evidence might cause John to abandon his lawsuit before a decision is reached. The prospect of getting involved in procedures as described above could hamper honest and hardworking doctors in freely performing their profession. John Doe and Mary could be so disappointed in the process of litigation, that they would rather solve future conflicts by a coin toss.

In the subsequent Sections, I will: 1) describe a theoretical framework that could help us to determine the optimal level of resources that should be used to resolve factual questions; 2) explain how in an adversarial setting the parties are inclined to spend too many resources to resolve factual issues and 3) explain how procedural legislation can be understood as an attempt to curb the costs of litigation. These insights may be of use 4) to understand why some procedural systems are more thorough and more expensive than other systems.

2. Efficient Fact-Finding Processes

In analyzing civil procedural rules, Richard A. Posner has argued that the purpose of legal procedure is to minimize the sum of two types of costs: 'error costs' (the social costs generated when a judicial system fails to carry out the allocative or other social functions assigned to it) and 'direct costs' (the costs of operating the machinery of justice, i.e. lawyer fees, costs of the courts etc.).[2] The essence of the economic approach is that all possible objectives and aims of the litigation process are best understood as factors that affect either the error costs or the direct costs of litigation.[3] In this approach, the maximization of welfare of the society at large,

2 Posner 1973, p. 399-400.

3 Posner 1999, p. 1485. This does require one to stretch the notion of 'error costs', possibly rendering the term meaningless.

rather than interests or rights of individuals, is the implicit ultimate end of the litigation process. The economic approach is difficult to apply, *inter alia* because it is very difficult to quantify, measure and predict error costs. For the remainder of this Chapter, I assume that accuracy of the fact-finding process is amongst the main factors that has an impact on error costs. One procedure can be said to be more accurate than another procedure if there is a higher probability that the procedure leads to a correct final decision on all relevant matters of fact.

Fact-finding in civil litigation may be modeled as a 'search model'.[4] Searching for additional information will increase the accuracy of the fact-finding process and will also increase the direct costs. If the facts are established with greater accuracy, the error costs will be lower. The procedure applied in the case of John and Mary was accurate in the sense that many (if not all) relevant facts were identified and all available relevant evidence was considered. As the example illustrated, greater accuracy is obtained at higher costs. The construction of each new legal argument, the discussion of each additional material fact and the examination of each additional witness will add to the direct costs of litigation.

If we accept a number of initial assumptions, we can at least in theory identify optimal numbers of legal arguments, genuinely disputed facts and expenses on evidence. This point can be clarified by means of a simple example on the optimum number of witnesses needed to prove a matter of fact. Let us assume that two vehicles collided at the crossing of 5th Avenue and 34th Street. Within a law suit arising from this accident, it is disputed whether or not one of the vehicles had been speeding prior to the collision. Assume that 35 pedestrians were present at the crossing when the accident occurred and that no other evidence is available in order to determine whether or not the vehicle exceeded the speed limit. It is well known that witness memory is far from perfect and the ability of individuals to estimate the speed of a vehicle is limited.[5] Therefore the testimony of each witness, although useful, is by itself insufficient to determine the issue with sufficient certainty. The first witness will provide a lot of useful new information, hearing a second or third witness will also yield valuable information. The point is that once a certain number of witnesses is heard, it is less likely that hearing another witness will reveal new factual details. Every witness is expected to increase the likelihood that a correct decision will be rendered, but not by the same amount. The hearing of the 23rd witness will probably only increase the accuracy of the fact-finding process by a minute amount. Put differently: there is a diminishing (expected) marginal utility of summoning one additional witness. This effect is even greater if we take into account that one would first examine those witnesses who are most likely to provide useful information. In Figure 10.2 we have plotted the increased accuracy (i.e. the probability that the facts will be established correctly) of the fact finding process as a function of the number of witnesses examined. For each additional witness that is examined the accuracy of the process of fact-finding increases, which in turn will lead to a decrease of the error costs of litigation. As the marginal utility

4 Posner 1999, p. 1481.

5 For a psychological overview on studies on the reliability of witnesses, see Wolters 2002.

of hearing additional witnesses diminishes, we may assume that the marginal decrease in the error costs of the litigation process also diminishes.

Figure 10.2, An Example: The Expected Accuracy of the Process of Fact-finding as a Function of the Number of Witnesses Examined

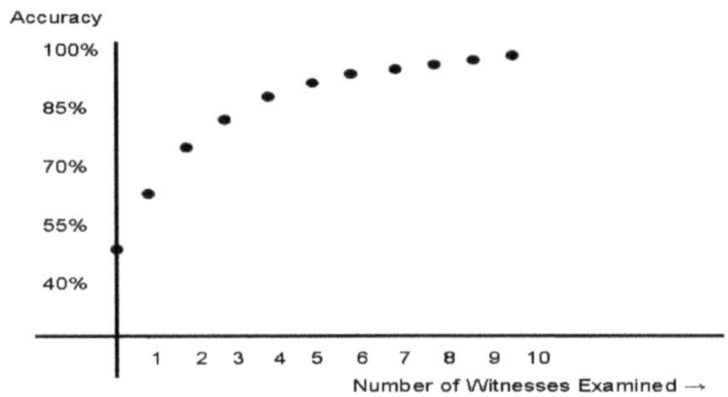

Although the additional value of each additional witness decreases, there is no reason to believe that the additional direct costs of hearing additional witnesses beyond the first would diminish at the same rate. It is reasonable to assume that the marginal costs of hearing additional witnesses are fixed or at least not diminishing as quickly as the marginal benefits of examining witnesses. If we plot the marginal direct costs and the marginal benefits of hearing witnesses, it becomes apparent what the optimal number of witnesses is in theory.[6] Figure 10.3, illustrates that hearing the first witness would cost 600 Euro, but would save 1,200 Euro worth of error costs. Similarly, the benefits of hearing witnesses two through five would decrease the sum of error costs and direct costs. Hearing the seventh witness would not be efficient and such would increase the direct costs by 600 Euro and decrease the error costs 500 Euro. The optimal number of witnesses is five or six. It must be noted that Figures 10.2 and 10.3 merely serve to clarify the theoretical argument. In reality it is difficult to calculate direct costs and even more difficult to estimate the accuracy of the fact-finding process and the error costs.

Figure 10.3, An Example: The Marginal Costs and Benefits of Examining Witnesses

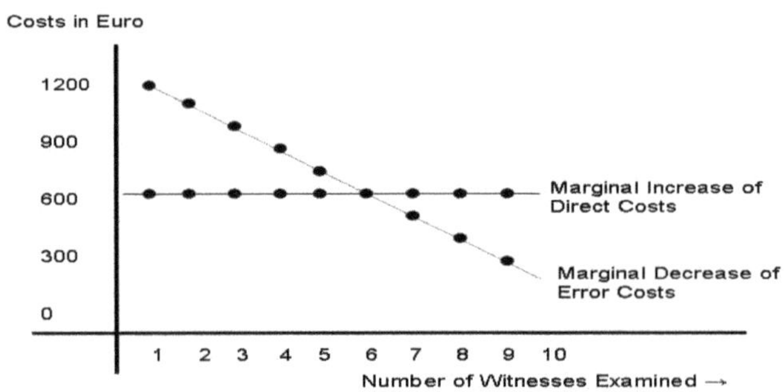

6 Posner 1973, p. 435-438.

The simple model used to determine the optimum number of witnesses can easily be applied to other stages in the litigation process. One could argue that (at least in theory) there is an optimum number of legal arguments that should be constructed to resolve a case adequately. Similarly, there is an optimum amount of resources that should be invested in searching for facts that are potentially relevant to the case. And as illustrated by the example above, there is also an optimum amount of resources that should be invested in examining all relevant evidence. Therefore in theory, we could identify an optimal number of pleadings, an optimal number of interrogatories, an optimal number of depositions, an optimal number of expert witnesses etc. It must be recalled that this approach aims to minimize the costs of litigation to society at large, not merely the costs incurred by the litigants. It might well be the case that the optimal solution for society at large is suboptimal from the perspective of the litigants or the courts.

The benefits of the fact-finding process depend on the marginal decrease of the error costs. It is likely that the benefits of hearing additional witnesses or experts are larger in more important high stake cases. It is therefore reasonable to assume that the benefits of conducting a more thorough search for the facts are larger in the case brought by John Terry than in the case brought by John Doe. In an important case, with high stakes, the optimal number of witnesses, experts and interrogatories will probably be larger than in a similar less significant case.

3. Adversarialism and Inefficiencies in Civil Litigation

Complaints about the inefficiency of litigation are numerous and widely heard in virtually all jurisdictions.[7] Limiting excessive delay and costs have always been amongst the prime challenges to those that regulate the justice system. While the causes of such inefficiencies are numerous, one particular source of delay will be addressed in this Section: numerous participants in an adversarial legal process have an incentive to spend a more than socially optimal amount resources on the process of fact-finding. To clarify my analysis, I will exaggerate in order to make the argument that adversarialism promotes inefficiencies. I will slightly downplay the degree in which parties and lawyers will be induced to seek mutual cooperation. In Section 10.4, I will provide a more nuanced view and argue that a proper framework of procedural rules may induce the parties in an adversarial system to allocate resources on the process of fact-finding efficiently.

3.1. *Adversarialism*

My aim is to show that an adversarial system, in which the parties are entitled to decide whether legal arguments may be raised, facts may be adduced or discovery may be had, is likely to lead to an excessive expenditure on fact-finding. Central to my analysis is that transaction costs in civil litigation are generally high. After all, in an economically perfect world with rational people, no transaction costs, perfect

7 See *inter alia* Zuckerman 1999, p. 23; Woolf 1996, p. 356 and Van Rhee 2004.

information, clear and perfect laws, everyone would settle disputes and no one would ever go to court. Many cases do not settle before they are brought to court due to information asymmetries, the high emotional costs of settlement or because of the strategic behavior of the parties. Even during litigation, many parties remain unwilling to cooperate. In the absence of cooperation and trust, aggressive competition is common amongst the litigants. I shall argue that in a competitive system, in which negative externalities are numerous, inefficiencies arise. Too often, litigants dwell in the nasty world of Nash rather than the cozy world of Coase.

In Chapter 8, I have argued that the most convincing rationale for the adversarial system is that it may contribute to the fairness of the procedure and to the neutrality of the trier of fact. The choice for the adversarial system however also impacts the effectiveness and efficiency of the litigation process. From the perspective of efficiency, it is generally believed to be sensible to ask the parties to adduce facts and suggest evidence. After all, the parties are often best acquainted with the factual basis of their dispute.

Proponents of the adversarial system proclaim that it assures a thorough factual investigation of the disputed facts.[8] The U.S. Court of Appeals for the Fourth Circuit stated: '(o)ur adversary system for the resolution of disputes rests on the unshakable foundation that truth is the object of the system's process which is designed for the purpose of dispensing justice'.[9] In this context, two arguments are commonly put forward in support of the adversarial system. The adversarial system attributes the responsibility for the presentation of facts to those that have an incentive to find all facts and evidence favorable to their case. Judges tend to have no or few incentives to establish the facts truthfully.[10] As rules of procedure aim to make all materials equally available to both parties, the adversarial system creates incentives that stimulate the parties to allege all relevant facts and evidence. Hence, the adversarial system expands the pool of information which is available to the fact-finder.[11] Also, it is frequently argued that a 'free competition' of theories will ultimately be the best method to separate the good theories on matters of fact from the bad ones.[12] This argument suggests that the full force of an argument cannot be understood by the adjudicator unless it is presented with partisan zeal by one party and vigorously challenged by the opposing party.[13] To summarize it bluntly: 'the

8 See Belliotti 1988, p. 23. Very famous in this respect is the often quoted phrase of Wigmore: 'cross-examination is beyond any doubt the greatest legal engine ever invented for the discovery of truth'. The phrase has often been quoted by American courts, such as the U.S. Supreme Court. See for instance *Watkins v. Sowders*, 449 U.S. 341 (1981) 'Yet, under our adversary system of justice, cross-examination has always been considered a most effective way to ascertain truth'.

9 *United States v. Shaffer Equip. Co.*, 11 F.3d 450 (1993), *U.S. App. LEXIS 32040.*

10 Fucik 1998.

11 Landsman 1988, p. 25.

12 There is a similarity between this argument and the economical theory of Adam Smith. Both display faith in social harmony through the free play of the pursuit of self interest, Frankel 1980, p. 53.

13 Fuller 1961, p. 31.

truth (...) will be best arrived at by granting the competing parties, with help of an advocate, an opportunity to fight as hard as possible'.[14]

These alleged merits of the adversarial system are disputed. Many legal scholars have doubted whether such a polarization and the passivity of the adjudicator will indeed improve the accuracy of the process of fact-finding.[15] Studies that aimed to empirically assess the effectiveness of adversarial fact-finding arrangements have generally been defective in terms of methodology or inconclusive in terms of their findings.[16] The question of the effectiveness of the adversarial system is perhaps too broad and too general, and needs to be subdivided into more precise questions.[17]

3.2. *Adversarial Fact-Finding as a Competitive Game*

Adversarialism and Externalities

Parties and their lawyers generally decide themselves to adduce new arguments, to allege additional facts or to summon an additional witnesses. When parties and their lawyers take such decisions, they tend to ignore the costs and benefits to others (i.e. externalities).

A decision taken by one party will affect the costs and benefits of the other party. Arguments and factual statements in the pleadings will need to be adequately addressed by opposing counsel. Depositions must be defended and experts require opposing experts. Witnesses should be cross-examined or impeached. Requests for the production of documents require that these documents be produced or that the request is objected to. In short: any decision to adduce facts, search for facts or to provide evidence to prove facts is likely to impose costs on the other party.

Economists such as Parker have argued that the costs of the process of fact-finding are only incurred by the parties.[18] I believe such a view is incomplete. The decisions of the parties to adduce facts or present evidence also affects the court. Every motion raised in the litigation process and every witness summoned requires the courts to invest resources. The time invested by judges and paralegal staff in managing and deciding one case cannot be invested in other cases.

14 Johnston & Lufrano 2001, p. 147.

15 Damaska 1997a, p. 96, p. 98.

16 See e.g. Block, Parker, Vyborna & Dusek 2000 and Boudreau & McCubbins 2006. Both studies are examples of laboratory studies that simplify reality to such an extent, that I would be hesitant to attach much value to their outcomes.

17 Also see Sections 4.2.3, 6.2.1 and 11.4.

18 See e.g. Parker 1995, p. 55. 'Whatever its vices, adversarial presentation of evidence has the signal virtue of internalizing the costs and benefits of fact-finding to the immediate parties, much as substantive property rights do in the contracting process. While litigation, given its coercive aspect, is not entirely analogous to contracting, it comes closest in the context of fact-finding in a particular case where the social interest in the particular outcome approaches zero. Much of the criticism of the adversarial system in recent years seems to ignore this point'.

Additionally, the decisions of the parties often affect third parties such as witnesses, jurors, experts or those who possess documents that are relevant to the case. Witnesses are often bound to testify, even if they do not wish to do so. If witnesses have to invest time in giving testimony, they cannot use that time differently.

It could also be argued that society at large has an interest in the effective and efficient operation of the justice system. The choices made by the parties certainly affect the efficiency of the operation of justice in their case. Every time courts effectively and efficiently enforce legal rights, this has a (very small) influence on the citizen's perception of the justice system. An efficient, effective and accurate process of fact-finding may deter citizens from breaching the law.[19] Cheap and effective procedures enhance access to justice.[20] Good procedures create positive externalities.

Excessive Fact-finding

The existence of externalities will lead each litigant to ignore the costs incurred by the opposing party, the court and third parties. This creates incentives for a party to overspend on fact-finding. Consider the decision of a party to file interrogatories. A party that sends written questions to his adversary will do so in order to find useful information that will either save him costs or will enhance his chances of winning. The main social benefit of interrogatories is that they ensure that relevant information becomes known to both parties. Thus it becomes more likely that the final decision in a case will be based on all relevant facts, which in turn has a positive effect on the error costs. The benefits of interrogatories for the larger part accrue to the party that files these interrogatories. Often, the answering of interrogatories takes more time and effort than filing interrogatories. In Massachusetts in the 1920s, printed forms with interrogatories were used in automobile accident cases. These forms contained hundreds of interrogatories and were not designed for a particular case but could serve as a 'standard list' of questions. Thus it was very cheap for one party to file 400 interrogatories. Obviously, it was extremely expensive for the other party to answer these. It was also reported that the interrogatory practice was burdensome for the court.[21]

The parties will render a decision on the number of interrogatories filed based on their own marginal costs and their own marginal benefits for filing each additional interrogatory. Figure 10.4 is a simplified graphical representation of the marginal costs and benefits of interrogatories. Again, it only serves to clarify the theoretical argument. It shows that the marginal benefits of each additional interrogatory beyond the first are diminishing. These benefits primarily accrue to the interrogating party. The costs of each interrogatory are shared between both parties (and the court). From a social perspective taking into account all costs, it is

19 On the relationship between fact-finding and deterrence, see Posner 1999, p. 1483.

20 Weissel 1998.

21 George Ragland, 'Discovery Before Trial', 1932, p. 93-94 as quoted by Subrin 1997, p. 707.

optimal that a litigant only files 30 interrogatories.[22] The party that files interrogatories often only takes into account the marginal costs of filing an additional interrogatory and ignores the costs of the court and the other party. A 'rational' interrogating party will file 50 interrogatories.

Figure 10.4, Marginal Costs and Benefits of Interrogatories

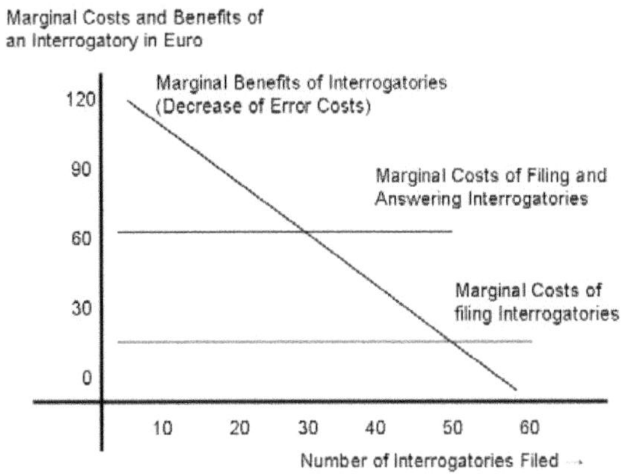

What holds true for the number of interrogatories filed, also holds true for the number of facts and legal arguments adduced in the pleadings, the number of depositions noticed, the number of document requests and the number of witnesses summoned by each party. In general, each party will be inclined to overspend in each stage of the dispute. Adversarial fact-finding processes will lead to lengthy pleadings, too many legal arguments, too many factual allegations, too much discovery and too much evidence.

The Prisoner's Dilemma, A Cournot Model or a One Dollar Auction

An over-expenditure on fact-finding has a negative effect on the court, third persons and the litigants. Often the litigants gain very little from a substantial investment in fact-finding. There are different ways to model the competitive strategic behavior of the parties. These essentially lead to the same conclusion: adversarial fact-finding creates incentives for both parties to make choices that are not in their joint interest.

Parties generally are interested in the satisfactory resolution of their dispute (i.e. winning) rather than the accuracy of the process of fact-finding. Thus, each side is inclined to invest a large amount of resources into the fact-finding process. To each of the parties, the choice for excessive fact-finding is a dominant strategy to enhance the odds of winning. If both parties overspend on fact-finding, their respective benefits may cancel out. To use the terminology of game theory: the Nash

22 Obviously, if one would like to apply economic models, there are enormous difficulties to determine the decrease of the error costs.

equilibrium is not a Pareto efficient solution. The parties are placed in a prisoner's dilemma.[23]

Suppose Mary and John are quarrelling over $50,000. After both have invested a small amount of money to explore the factual basis of the dispute, the odds of winning equal 50% for both parties. Both have an expected payoff of $25,000. Both may decide to spend more money on fact-finding (i.e. additional discovery). As the costs are generally shared between the parties, both will incur costs of $2,000 each if one of the parties decides to spend more money on discovery. If only one party opts for additional discovery, this increases that parties' odds of winning by 20%. As shown in Table 10.1, it is a dominant strategy for both to invest in additional discovery.

Table 10.1. Litigation as a prisoner's dilemma, investment choices and expected payoffs.

		Mary	
		Low Investments	High Investments
John	Low Investments	John: $25,000 Mary: $25,000	John: $13,000 Mary: $33,000
	High Investments	John: $33,000 Mary: $13,000	John: $21,000 Mary: $21,000

One could make the model slightly more sophisticated by allowing both parties to determine independently the amount of resources they wish to invest in the litigation process. The model deviates from the above as it allows the parties to choose any level of investment rather than choosing between high and low levels of investment. Akin to the Cournot duopoly model, one could assume that the odds of winning the case are a function of the amount of money both parties are willing to invest in fact-finding. This requires the parties to guess the amount of resources their opponent is going to invest in fact-finding. An example of an oversimplified model along such lines is shown below. The conclusion based on such a simple model is that parties will overspend and that the competitive equilibrium will not be (Pareto) efficient.

23 On the prisoner dilemma in general see Keith Murnighan 1992. For an early application of such game theoretic concepts in the area of civil litigation see Setaer 1989.

Example 10.1, Litigation and investment, a simplified model

Suppose that the gains of both parties (G1 and G2), as denoted in the formulae below, are a function of the odds of winning the case (p for the plaintiff and (1-p) for the defendant), the amount of money at stake (S) and the amount of resources the parties are willing to invest in litigation ($c1, c2 > 0$).

$$G1 = p * S - c1$$
$$G2 = (1-p) * S - c2$$

Let us assume that the odds of winning the case are a function of the amount of money invested in litigation: $p = c1/(c1 + c2)$.
The plaintiff and the defendant will invest an amount of money that will maximize their expected gains. The plaintiff will invest an amount of $c1 = - c2 + \sqrt{Sc2}$, the defendant will invest $c2 = - c1 + \sqrt{Sc1}$. It can be calculated that the Cournot Nash equilibrium to this problem is $c1 = c2 = S/4$.[24] This solution is not Pareto optimal.

So far, we have assumed that the parties only choose once whether or not they wish to invest additional resources into the process of fact-finding. It might be the case that parties are allowed to make additional investments during the process of litigation. The problem could become akin to a 'one dollar auction' game.[25] In theory, if the game of litigation is played out in a number of stages, the parties' expenditures on litigation could then easily exceed the stakes of litigation.

Suppose that $100,000 is at stake in the case between John and Mary. Suppose further that litigation is a turn-based game in which the parties may in turn decide to invest additional money on expert evidence, scientific jury selection or discovery of documents. At the outset of litigation, John and Mary could be convinced that the odds of winning are 50% for both of them. Round 1: John believes that if he invests $5,000, his chances of winning increase from 50% to 65%. The investment increases his expected payoff by $10,000, so John will make the investment. Round 2: Mary believes that her odds of winning have been reduced to 35% due to the investments made by John. If she invests $5,000 however, she could probably increase her chances of winning to 50%. The investment increases her expected payoff by $10,000. Round 3: John realizes that Mary's investment decreases his odds of winning. He believes that if he invests $5,000 more, his chances of winning increase from 50% to 65%. The investment increases his expected payoff by $10,000, so John will make the investment. Each round beyond round 3 may be a repetition of rounds two and three. In theory therefore, we could have hundreds of rounds and the parties could spend an infinite amount of resources on litigation.

It should be noted that if litigation is not a game played once, it is more likely that parties will opt for different strategies. The fear of retaliation may withhold parties from imposing great costs on their opponent. Similarly, if two lawyers know that they are likely to litigate against each other at future occasions, both sides

24 On Cournot Nash equilibria in general see Gravelle & Rees 1998, p. 300-304.

25 On one dollar auctions in general see Keith Murnighan 1992, Chapter 9. For a similar description of litigation also see Posner 1992, §21.8, p. 566. 'Because of the sequential character of expenditures on litigation, it is not possible to exclude the possibility that the parties' combined expenditures will exceed the stakes'.

might be inclined to avoid the most aggressive and costly tactics (i.e. choose a *tit for tat* strategy).[26] If litigation no longer is 'a game played once', it is possible that strategic considerations will diminish the problem of excessive expenditures.

Assessment of Damages, Estimates of Probabilities and the Role of Lawyers
One could further expand competitive models in many ways. It would make sense not to model the stakes of the case as given (i.e. as an exogenous variable). Decisions on damages are amongst the most important decisions taken within the legal process. Therefore, it could certainly be rewarding for litigants like John and Mary to invest in paralegal staff, expert witnesses or methods to improve the jury selection process. Empirical studies have shown that expert witness testimony has a substantial impact on the decisions of juries on damages. A study by Raitz *et al.* showed that claims awarded by mock jurors were significantly higher if expert witnesses had testified and that about half of the mock jurors reached a verdict on damages that was exactly equal to the amount provided by one of the experts.[27] Greene *et al.* found that mock juries award higher damages if only the plaintiff presented an economic expert witness compared to cases in which both parties or neither party presented an economic witness.[28] These findings indicate that parties may well be caught in a prisoner's dilemma that causes them to both hire expert witnesses to assess damages. The additional amounts that parties spend on the assessment of damages will probably create little social value. It has been argued by Kaplow and Shavell that the parties' costs on the assessment of damages are likely to outweigh the social benefits.[29]

Another way to expand the model is to take into account the fact that both parties make a different estimate of their chances of winning the case. Psychological research indicates that litigants typically are prone to a self-serving bias which leads them to overestimate the chances of a favorable judgment.[30] Similarly, lawyers are likely to overestimate the probability of winning.[31] These factors decrease parties' willingness to settle and increases their willingness to invest in litigation. The effect of such an over-estimation is probably particularly strong in litigation. Conflicts in which parties have a too rosy picture of their position are less likely to settle prior to litigation. An over estimation of one's probability of winning is more likely to occur in those cases pending before the courts of justice.[32] In short: the tendency to overestimate exacerbates the problem of an over-expenditure on fact finding.

It also seems sensible not to identify the lawyer with his or her client. If parties are represented by a lawyer, additional incentives for excessive spending on fact-

26 On tit for tat strategies, see Axelrod 1984, Chapters 2 and 3.

27 Raitz, Greene, Goodman and Loftus 1990.

28 Greene, Downey & Goodman 1999.

29 See Kaplow & Shavell 1996.

30 See for instance for a recent empirical study: Gilliland & Dunn 2008.

31 According to M. Malsch, *Advocaten voorspellen de uitkomst van hun zaken*, Amsterdam, Swets & Zeitlinger, p. 42, as discussed by Richter 1991, p. 98-100. Dutch lawyers overestimate their chances of winning by on average 11%.

32 Hay 1995 and Priest & Klein 1984.

finding may be in place. The relationship between a client and his lawyer could be modeled as a principal agent problem.[33] The lawyer's interests may deviate from those of his client. Lawyers have a financial interest in procedures that create a greater demand for their services. Additional motions, frequent discovery requests, long pleadings and large numbers of witnesses all require more attorney time. Lawyers may therefore have a preference for procedures that are more formalistic, more complex and more technical than socially optimal.[34] In addition, the fear of being involved in professional liability litigation, further induces lawyers to prefer an overly thorough search for facts. Although lawyers may have many reasons not to promote an over-expenditure on litigation (i.e. reputation, Bar regulations or moral considerations), it seems that (procedural) rules primarily induce lawyers to overspend on fact-finding. In fact, a 2008 survey showed that only 11% of trial lawyers believes that clients, rather than attorneys, drive excessive discovery.[35]

3.3. *Adversarialism and Incentives to Obstruct the Pursuit of Truth*

From a social perspective the adversarial system may lead not only to an over-expenditure on fact-finding but also to counter-productive combat for combat's sake. Often resources may be used to hinder the accurate reconstruction of the facts of the case. Parties may ultimately be interested in winning, not in the accuracy of the process of fact-finding. In order to win, parties are induced to deliberately 'throw pepper in the eyes of the surgeon'.[36] Generally speaking, there is always one party that has an interest in ensuring that a relevant fact remains hidden and is not properly valued by the trier of fact. By adducing facts, arguments and theories that confuse the trier of fact, parties may create smoke screens to conceal the issues that are of true significance to the case.

Both parties may put a lot of effort in evading the attempts of the other party to discover information.[37] Often when a party is requested to answer an interrogatory, he can either choose to give a perfectly legal - yet evasive - answer to the question or he can provide the information he or she knows the other party is searching for. It probably is a dominant strategy to provide the evasive answer. Complaints about evasive answers to interrogatories are indeed common in legal practice.[38] If both parties file interrogatories, both will provide evasive answers. In the end, it might cause lawyers to put a lot of effort in not improving the accuracy of the fact-finding process. Again, parties are caught in a prisoner's dilemma in which the dominant strategy of evasion is possibly to the detriment of both.

The presentation of evidence in an adversarial system is also likely to negatively affect the reliability of evidence. Witnesses and expert witnesses may be induced to give a biased testimony. The resources that lawyers invest in the

33 Kobayashi & Parker 2000, p. 13 and Note 1982, p. 357-358.
34 Ogus 2002.
35 ACTL & IAALS 2008, A-4.
36 See Langbein 1993.
37 Farnsworth 2007, p. 103-104.
38 See e.g. Brazil 1980 p. 825, p. 829. For a more detailed discussion see Section 3.3.2.

preparation of witnesses and discussing the case with experts may very well cause the witnesses to become biased.[39] Although the preparation of (expert) witness testimony might in some cases have a positive impact on the accuracy of the fact-finding process, there is ample evidence that the costly preparation of witnesses may hamper the pursuit of truth.[40]

A third way in which parties in an adversarial setting may be induced to obstruct the process of fact-finding is to abuse the financial position of a poorer opponent. As the costs of litigation are largely symmetrical, the adversarial system induces rich parties to threaten to drive poorer opponents into bankruptcy.[41] This may lead a party to file a motion for a dismissal of the complaint for no other reason than to impose costs on an opponent. To any rich party, such a harassment strategy could prove to be a dominant strategy to force the opponent into an unfair settlement.[42] From a social perspective, such strategies are hurtful.

4. Understanding Procedural Legislation

The adversarial system creates incentives for over-expenditure and counter-productive behavior. Nevertheless, these problems may not always be pervasive in legal practice. Research has abundantly shown that people are generally willing to cooperate even if they are placed in a competitive environment.[43] In a large proportion of cases pending before the courts, the parties and their lawyers are cooperative and the costs are not disproportional.[44] Nevertheless, there are good reasons to believe the problems described in the previous Sections are genuine problems in at least a small proportion of cases. Litigants often do not cooperate in their joint interest and commonly courts become the battleground where the conflict continues, rather than the forum where conflicts are peacefully resolved. The adversarial system in which lawyers are supposed to be zealous and partisan may even exacerbate competition.

Legislators have often attempted to enact legislation to avoid inefficiencies in litigation. Procedural rules may provide a framework in which the parties have incentives to take decisions that are efficient from a social point of view. Regulatory frameworks generally exist out of a mix of rules that: 1) deter abuse; 2) internalize externalities; 3) encourage agreements between the parties; 4) limit the possibilities to spend and 5) provide judges with powers to intervene. If a proper regulatory

39 See e.g. Sheppard & Vidmar 1980. See for more detail the discussion in Section 6.2.

40 See the studies discussed and quoted in Chapters 5 and 6 of this book.

41 See e.g. Note 1982, p. 370-371 and the discussion on discovery abuse in Chapter 3.

42 The idea that inequality hampers fairness is not merely a theoretical problem. Surveys show that a huge majority of the U.S. population believes that courts treat rich people better than poor ones, see for a nice overview of (early) surveys on the attitudes towards courts: Sarat 1976, Appendix, Table 3.

43 A fascinating illustration is the cooperative behaviour between soldiers of both sides in the First World War, See Axelrod 1984, Chapter 4. Also see De Waal 2009.

44 See e.g. the studies quoted in Section 6.2.1.

framework is in place, the adversarial system may lead to an efficient allocation of resources.

Rules that deter Abuse and Punish Vexatious Behavior

In most jurisdictions, behavior that frustrates rather than promotes the accuracy of the fact-finding process is regarded as abusive and therefore forbidden. Courts may impose sanctions to deter the litigants from behaving abusively. Severe criminal sanctions exist to deter litigants from the most serious forms of obstructing the legal process, such as forgery or perjury.[45] Similarly, lawyers may face disciplinary sanctions if they deliberately lie to the court. Procedural codifications often empower the court to impose sanctions to avoid other specific forms of abuse. In Austria, for example, a party who knows that a document is genuine but nevertheless argues it is not, may be fined by the judge.[46] Similarly, if parties fail to comply with a discovery order given by a judge in a U.S. District Court, this may be treated as contempt of court. In addition, most jurisdictions seem to apply general standards and broad legal concepts that enable courts to sanction behavior that frustrates the process of fact-finding, even if the behavior is not specifically forbidden by statute.[47] The duty imposed on the litigants in most Continental countries to provide a truthful and complete account of the facts provides one example of such a broad norm against counter-productive behavior.

It must be noted that abusive behavior is hard to detect and often not sanctioned. The odds of getting convicted for perjury are incredibly low.[48] It is therefore doubtful whether the mere existence of legal sanctions suffices to deter abuse.

Rules on Costs and Fees that may Internalize Externalities

The cost regime is likely to affect many aspects of the litigation process, including the willingness of parties to invest in the process of fact-finding.[49] A carefully designed system on fees and costs may be an effective way to internalize externalities and to increase the efficiency of the fact-finding process.

There is empirical evidence that shows that fee structures affect the behavior of lawyers.[50] Lawyer fee structures may create incentives for lawyers to devote more or less time to fact-finding. If a lawyer receives an hourly fee, she has an incentive to

45 See for instance the 21st Chapter Austrian Criminal Code (*Strafgesetzbuch*, StGB).

46 Sections 313 and 220 Austrian Code of Civil Procedure.

47 See for instance Hazard 1999, p. 49. In the Netherlands courts often use the broad concepts such as 'abuse of rights' (Article 3:13 Civil Code) and 'good faith'. See Van der Wiel 2004, No. 188 and Lindijer 2006. In Austria the phrase 'Treu und Glauben' is commonly used, see Fasching 1990, No. 135.

48 See e.g. Nagel 1951.

49 The literature on cost regimes is abundant. See Kritzer 2001; Faure, Hartlief & Philipsen 2006 and Posner 1973, p. 437.

50 A 1997 national survey in the United States, for instance, hourly billing (as opposed to a contingent fee or some other method) associated with increased times from filing to disposition Willging, Stienstra, Shaphard & Miletich 1998, p. 541. For an overview of empirical research see Kritzer 2001.

spend more hours on the case than is optimal for her client. However, if the lawyer receives a percentage of the amount awarded to her client (*quota pars litis*), the lawyer will have an incentive to spend less on litigation than would be optimal for her client. Equally, if lawyers receive a fixed regulated lump sum fee for each step in the litigation process, lawyers have an incentive to under-prepare for each of these steps.[51]

The existence of different sorts of cost shifting rules also impacts the willingness of parties to invest in the process of fact-finding. In theory, costs could be internalized by requiring parties who allege facts, discover information or adduce evidence, to compensate for costs incurred by the other party and the court.[52] An example of a rule that would internalize such externalities would be a rule that specifies that the party that requests the discovery of documents should pay the costs of producing these documents.[53] In contrast, a cost-shifting rule that requires the losing party to compensate the prevailing party (i.e. the 'English Rule') effectively increases the stakes of litigation. Such a cost-shifting rule creates an incentive for the parties to increase their investment in fact-finding.

The court fee system may also serve to internalize externalities. In some jurisdictions, one or both parties are requested to pay a fixed fee. In other systems, the court fee depends on the services rendered.[54] In Scotland, a 'pay as you go' system is implemented in which the parties pay a fee each time the court renders a service. The fees for services in this regime are often dependent on the length of the court hearing or the number of pages typed or copied.[55] A 'pay as you go system' rather than a system with fixed fees may be used - just like Pigouvian taxation - as a means to internalize the costs incurred by the courts and third parties. Thus, it would take away an incentive for the parties to overspend on fact-finding.

Rules Promoting Cooperation in Civil Litigation

If transaction costs are low, economic theory predicts that the parties to a lawsuit will engage in a contract that will be efficient to both parties. In reality, parties often reach agreements to ensure that the process of fact-finding is not unnecessarily cumbersome. Empirical studies in the United States have revealed that it is very common - even in contentious cases - for attorneys to informally exchange information.[56] Similarly, lawyers are often cooperative in granting each other extensions of time to file pleadings or (responses to) motions. If the parties cooperate and engage in agreements on factual matters, it is possible for them to avoid a prisoner's dilemma. Parties could for instance voluntarily narrow down the

51 Adams 1998.
52 Cooter & Rubinfeld 1995.
53 See e.g Article 843a Dutch Code of Civil Procedure.
54 See in general for a comparative study on court fees, Faure & Moerland 2006.
55 Faure & Moerland 2006, Chapter 7.
56 In cases where there was some disclosure or discovery, 62% of the attorneys also engaged in informal exchange of information. Such cooperative behavior mostly took place in non-contentious litigation (64%). In very contentious cases 46% of the attorneys that also engaged in formal discovery or disclosure informally exchanged information. Willging, Stienstra, Shaphard & Miletich 1998, p. 146.

issues, agree to appoint a single expert and reach an agreement to limit the number of witnesses each side presents. Thereby parties could reduce the scope of the factual debate (compare Figures 10.1 and 10.5).

In many cases transaction costs are very high and parties will not make a reasonable agreement to cut litigation costs. Both sides will disagree on questions of law or will be hostile to each other and may therefore not be willing to settle their case. Legislators have deliberately enacted provisions that promote cooperation and remove impediments to private agreements.[57] During court hearings and pretrial conferences, judges commonly encourage both parties to reach an agreement on the further course of the litigation process.[58] Rule 29 of the U.S. FRCP allows the parties to stipulate that 'procedures governing or limiting discovery be modified'. Similarly, Article 153 Dutch Code of Civil Procedures enables the parties in most Dutch civil cases to make binding agreements that deviate from the rules of evidence.[59]

Capping Rules

There is a broad category of what I call 'capping rules', that limit either: 1) the number of phases of the dispute; 2) the length of these phases or 3) the arsenal of procedural weapons available to the parties. These rules effectively restrict the freedom of the parties to invest endlessly in the process of fact-finding. Without such rules, a lawsuit may grow and expand at an exponential rate.

Many 'capping rules' set different kinds of numerical limits on what parties may do. Examples include: rules that set a presumptive numerical limit on the number of interrogatories parties may file[60] or the number of witnesses who may be summoned.[61] Such rules may limit the degree in which parties can overspend on litigation, if the limit is properly set. Rule makers have also enacted rules on the maximum length of pleadings and the maximum time a deposition may take.[62] In international arbitration, chess clocks are sometimes used to limit the speaking time of both sides. Strict deadlines for the completion of a pleading or discovery stage also serve to avoid lengthy debates.

Other typical capping rules are those that limit the number of stages in the litigation process. Many legal systems typically do not allow each party to file more than a single written pleading in ordinary cases.[63] Most legal systems seem to favor the presentation of evidence at a single concentrated hearing. Such rules on the concentration of the procedure effectively limit the number of rounds in the

57 On the (normative) Coase Theorem, see Cooter & Ulen 2004, Chapter 4.

58 See in this respect Section 3.3.

59 See Section 9.2.

60 E.g. in 1929, in Massachusetts, the maximum number of interrogatories was 30. See Subrin 1997, p. 707.

61 Before the Great Council of Malines, in the 16th century, the number of witnesses per disputed fact was limited to ten, Van Rhee 1997, p. 152.

62 Federal Rules of Appellate Procedure Rule 27(d)(2) sets a presumptive 20 page limit for motions.

63 Such is for instance the case in Austria, the Netherlands and the Federal U.S. system, see Chapter 4.

litigation process. These rules prevent the sequential investments of the parties turning litigation into the everlasting one dollar auction described above.

Another very effective way to limit the scope of the argument is to put a cap on the number of factual or legal arguments a party may raise. A classic example is the old system of common law pleading, which did not allow either one of the parties to raise more than a single argument. Common law pleading thereby aimed to narrow down the issues to a single factual or legal question (see Section 3.1).

Procedural rules that prohibit the parties from adducing certain facts, arguments or means of proof are more radical devices to narrow down the issues. Some systems have refused to consider facts if these were adduced too late. Similarly, legislators have held that certain categories of evidence are inadmissible because the evidence is considered to be irrelevant, misleading or unreliable.[64] The rules of evidence that restrict the use of character evidence (i.e. evidence showing that witness C is a notorious liar) prevent an endless discussion on the reliability of evidence already examined. The hearsay rule as well as the rules on relevance may prevent 'bad quality evidence' from being examined.

Judicial Intervention

Another common strategy to narrow down the issues is to empower the judge to actively manage the process of fact-finding. Much like a gardener who prunes roses, a judge may actively see to it that a law suit does not meander widely in all directions. In an adversarial setting, judicial intervention generally does not lead the court to adduce facts or suggest the most suitable means of proof. Judges in this setting usually have four main instruments at their disposal to manage the efficient resolution of disputes.

First, judges may take early decisions on legal questions, such that it becomes clear at an early point in time which facts are relevant and which facts are not relevant.

In addition, the judge may help the parties to identify the key issues. The judge may discuss the case with the parties and ask them to identify the core issues. Most legal systems have empowered judges to identify issues that require evidence. Judges may subsequently render summary judgments that narrow down the issues.

Furthermore, most legal systems have empowered the judge to determine the order in which issues are resolved. Thereby judges can, for instance, prevent parties from investing large amounts of resources to discuss damages while the question of liability is still unresolved.

Fourth, judges often apply, adjust and interpret capping rules. Procedural legislation sometimes grants parties the right to discover information or allege evidence only with leave of the court. In England, leave of the court is generally needed if the parties wish to present expert evidence (see Section 5.3.1). Judges may refuse additional expenditures on fact-finding if the costs outweigh the benefits.

[64] See for instance Section 275(1) Austrian Code of Civil Procedure, for an overview of the literature on the economic analysis of American rules of admissibility, see: Parker & Kobayashi 2000.

In the example mentioned in the introduction to this Chapter, John and Mary were involved in a dispute in which the judge had not been active in narrowing down the issues. Especially in the case of John Doe, an active judge would have handled this case differently. For example: the judge could decide as a matter of law that providing a patient with a 150 page brochure is by itself insufficient to properly inform a patient. The judge could further determine that the damages were not genuinely disputed by the defendant. The judge would discuss the case with the parties to identify core issues. It could be concluded that there are in essence two main factual issues that have to be resolved: 1) 'What is the cause of John's injury?' and 2) 'Was John sufficiently informed by Mary on the risks of the treatment?' An active judge will indicate who has the burden of proof on each of these two issue, decide that the cause of the injury will be addressed first and determine that no more than one expert would be consulted to provide an opinion on the cause of the injury. Judicial intervention (as well as agreements between the parties) may narrow down the scope of the dispute (see Graph 10.5). This may reduce the complexity of the fact-finding process (compare Figures 10.1 and 10.5). Such judicial intervention has a positive effect on the costs of the fact-finding process. It may however have a negative impact on the accuracy of the fact-finding process. If experts are not consulted to help assess damages, the decision on damages is probably less accurate.

Figure 10.5, Judicial Intervention: Narrowing down the Issues, a Graphical Representation

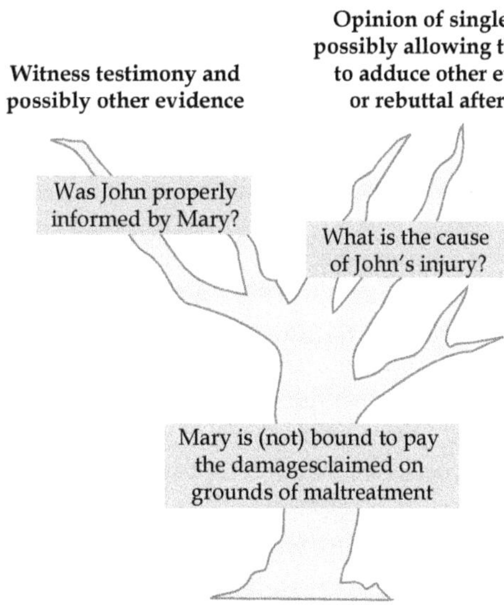

Whether judges have an incentive to use their discretionary powers in the interest of efficiency is a different question. Judges might be induced to take into account different issues when deciding a case, such as whether they will be able to finish their work before Friday afternoon. Judges may also prefer to spend time on an interesting bankruptcy case rather than dealing with the case of John Doe. Equally, judges may worry about their career perspectives.[65] Effective judicial intervention may require a range of policy measures that induce judges to use their discretion in the public interest.

Conclusion
Adversarial systems tend to create incentives for the parties to overspend on evidence. Many procedural rules may be rationalized or justified as attempts to avoid an inefficient over-expenditure on fact-finding. If a proper regulatory framework exists, the adversarial system may be efficient. Such a regulatory framework should exist out of a right mix of rules that internalize externalities, encourage agreements between the parties, deter abuse, limit the possibilities to spend and provide judges with powers to intervene. However, the application and enforcement of such procedural rules may be costly. Rules that require the judge to grant leave for the presentation of expert evidence, for example, do require the court to make a (costly) assessment of the expected costs and benefits of expertise.

5. Efficient Fact-finding: Comparative Remarks

Comparative Mixes
Many debates in comparative procedural literature revolve around the question whether specific jurisdictions provide incentives that lead to an efficient allocation of resources. Often the differences between jurisdictions are relatively small. Rules that punish vexatious behavior can be found in all jurisdictions.[66] In other respects, the differences between jurisdictions are considerable. In the subsequent Sections I aim to point out some of the most remarkable features of the Austrian, Dutch and the U.S. federal legal system. Each of these systems has chosen a different mix of legal mechanisms that may curb the expenditure on fact-finding.

The Austrian legal system has few rules that explicitly encourage parties to cooperate and jointly reach an agreement on matters of fact. Some Austrian rules create incentives for the parties to spend a lot on litigation, such as the rules that allow for the shifting of attorney costs incurred by the winning party.[67] Nevertheless, there are a broad range of mechanisms in the Austrian system that reduces the incentives of parties to overspend on fact-finding.

More than in the United States or the Netherlands, the Austrian system aims for a concentrated judicial process in which the judgment is ideally only preceded by the exchange of a single set of written pleadings, a preparatory hearing and an

65 See for a critical perspective on the role of judges Macey 1994 and Posner 1993.

66 The most significant difference seems to be that legal sanctions in the United States tend to be more severe than on the continent. In the United States oath taking seems to be much more common than in Austria and the Netherlands (see Chapter 6.2). This implies that criminal sanctions apply more widely. Similarly, the sanctions mentioned in FRCP, Rule 37 seem to be more severe than those mentioned in for instance the Dutch Code of Civil Procedure.

67 Section 41 *et seq.* Austrian Code of Civil Procedure and Rechberger & Simotta 2009, p. 222-224.

evidentiary hearing.[68] The plaintiff is encouraged to make a request for the production of documents in his complaint and to present his interrogatories at the (preparatory) oral hearing rather than filing separate requests.[69]

In the Austrian legal system, much more than in other modern jurisdictions, judicial intervention is considered the main instrument to ensure the efficiency and accuracy of the process of fact-finding (Chapters 2 and 7). Klein was convinced that the best way to prevent abuse was to empower a judge to actively discuss the case with the parties at an oral hearing. Discovery is not available without leave of the court. A well-substantiated request for the production of each document should be examined by the court before the production of a document is ordered. Similarly, questions may be put to the opposing party at an oral hearing, but the court may set aside interrogatories that it believes to be irrelevant.[70] Compared to other jurisdictions, the Austrian judge also has wide powers regarding the presentation of evidence. Judges tend to identify the issues that require evidence at an early point in time.[71] The court may refuse to examine expert evidence against the will of the parties. The court may also refuse presentation of evidence if it would undoubtedly lead to delay.[72] Judicial intervention is therefore regarded as an important tool to narrow down the dispute (compare Figure 10.1 and 10.5).

In Austria, a lawyer and a client are free to choose between different lawyer fee structures. It seems to be very common that a statutory lump sum fee is used to reward lawyers for each activity performed in the litigation process.[73] The Austrian regulated fee system awards lawyers a fixed amount of money for each written submission and an hourly fee for attending court hearings. The most problematic side effect of the Austrian regulated fee scheme is that lawyers are induced to under-prepare for the drafting of written pleadings and the oral hearings. The lump sum fee that is awarded for each activity performed, does not encourage attorneys to devote resources to search for additional facts if it does not lead to additional procedural activities. The fee system may cause lawyers to benefit from filing deficient pleadings or from not adequately preparing for the court hearing. Under preparation may cause a court hearing to take half an hour longer.

The Dutch fact-finding arrangements are in some regards similar to those in Austria. As in Austria, there is a strong preference for a concentrated procedure, especially in the first stages of the litigation process.[74] More so than the Austrian system, the Dutch system removes impediments for the parties to make an agreement on matters of fact. In the Netherlands, the procedural system increasingly provides for judicial intervention to render quick decisions on points of

68 See Section 4.1.

69 Sections 184, 229 Austrian Code of Civil Procedure.

70 Sections 184 and 303 Austrian Code of Civil Procedure.

71 See Sections 4.1 and 2.3.

72 Section 275 Austrian Code of Civil Procedure.

73 See the Austrian *Rechtsanwaltstarifgesetz*, *Official State Journal* (BGBl) No. 189/1969. Also see Section 2.3.1. It has been observed that the rates provided by this Act are predominantly used in Austrian practice. See Oberhammer & Domej 2010. Unfortunately I have not found empirical studies that confirm this observation.

74 See Section 4.1.

law or to identify key issues. Some have argued that a 'funnel model' is used in the Dutch procedural practice (*trechtermodel)* Once the case is filed it sort of enters the conical mouth of the funnel: a wide number of issues may be addressed at the outset of litigation. As the case proceeds, a subset of these facts is further examined. Once the case reaches the evidence phase (i.e. the funnel's narrow stem), only a couple of core factual issues remain.

On the other hand, there are several factors in the Netherlands that induce parties and lawyers to invest large amounts of money in fact-finding. Lawyers commonly bill by the hour. If a lawyer may charge per stone, a lawyer has a strong incentive to leave no stone unturned.

A problematic feature seems to be the wide availability of *de novo* review on appeal, with full reconsideration of all factual matters. On appeal, a Dutch plaintiff may amend his claim, the defendant may raise new defenses and both parties may adduce evidence they had not adduced at first instance.[75] Parties may even plead facts in an appeal that are inconsistent with the facts they pleaded at first instance.[76] The basic premise is that litigants gain a second chance to correct all the mistakes they made at first instance. Dutch appeal procedures provide the parties with ample opportunities to continue spending on fact-finding on appeal. Such lenient rules may also cause litigants to litigate carelessly at the court of first instance. It seems that *de novo* appeal increases the costs of litigation considerably without necessarily significantly improving the accuracy of the fact-finding process. As *de novo* appeal is also available in less significant cases, it may allow for a disproportionate spending on fact-finding. *De novo* appeal does not exist in Austria and the United States.[77]

Another distinctive feature of the Dutch system is that the rules on (document) discovery in the Netherlands are historically very restrictive and do not allow the parties to engage in a broad search for facts. Although the Dutch rules limit the costs of litigation, this may seriously hamper the accuracy of the process of fact-finding.

One of the distinctive features of the U.S. federal system is the availability of broad and liberal discovery rules that operate largely extra judicially. These rules, that have come to form the centre of gravity in the U.S. legal process, allow the parties to search for information without prior leave of the court. Ample empirical and anecdotal evidence suggests that parties tend to overspend on discovery in at least a significant proportion of cases.[78] Visiting U.S. law firms, I was struck to see the large quantities of discovered documents and the lengthy transcripts of depositions and fascinated to see lawyers using carts and trolleys to take these

75 Hugenholtz 2006, No. 143. Recent case law does show that there are some restrictions on the course of the proceeding in appeal: Court of Cassation 20 June 2008, *LJN* BC 4959.

76 Dutch Court of Cassation, 1 March 2002, *NJ* 2003, 355.

77 In Austria, for example, the 'Neuerungsverbot' forbids parties to allege new claims or facts on appeal, Section 482 Austrian Code of Civil Procedure; Rechberger & Simotta 2003, No. 425 and Baur 1970, p. 445-449. In the United States findings on matters of fact may be overturned on appeal only if these are clearly erroneous, see Yeazell 2008, p. 655-665.

78 Section 3.3.2 and Cooter & Rubinfeld 1995, p. 66-68.

documents with them to trial.[79] The problem of curbing excessive expenditures on discovery has been one of the main aims of legislative reform. Two strategies have been remarkable from a comparative perspective. More than in the Netherlands and Austria, the Federal Rules of Civil Procedure require the parties to confer. Since 1993, formal discovery can generally not take place until the parties have conferred to jointly construct a 'discovery plan'.[80] Similarly, parties are required to try to resolve possible discovery disputes in good faith, before filing a motion with the court. A second strategy to curb excessive expenditure has been the wide use of capping rules. There are rules that limit how often specific discovery devices can be used and rules that limit the time that parties have for the completion of discovery.[81]

A second related distinctive feature of the Federal American system is that judicial intervention aimed at narrowing down the dispute is often absent or takes place at a relatively late point in time. In Austria and the Netherlands, the dispute is narrowed down soon after the defendant filed his answer. In the U.S., the parties engage in a broad search for facts after the answer is filed. Summary judgments are typically rendered only after the discovery process is concluded. Within the U.S. federal system, specious allegations and poor defenses might be explored in great detail. Judges often allow branches to grow in all directions before these are pruned.[82] The issues are only narrowed down after the case has reached full growth. In the United States, witnesses may have been deposed and documents been discovered on issues not genuinely disputed (compare Figures 10.1 and 10.5). The lack of court intervention in the process of fact-gathering seems to have a second negative consequence. Vexatious behavior may take place more frequently and largely remains unpunished. U.S. lawyers generally believe that a greater availability of judges is needed to avoid discovery abuse.[83]

A third distinctive feature of the American system is the existence of the civil jury and the single uninterrupted jury trial. The civil jury may have many potential economic benefits.[84] Nevertheless, it primarily is a source of inefficiencies. In the United States, the single uninterrupted jury trial precludes the judge from determining that issues need to be resolved in a specific order; thus lawyers are forced to investigate the entire case.[85] Both sides may spend large amounts of money on economic experts that are prepared to testify on the damages. If the defendant is not held liable at trial for the damages incurred by the plaintiff, these investments have been futile. Moreover, the existence of jury trials prevents the merging of the investigative and evidential phases of litigation. This often implies that witnesses and experts need to be examined twice. Judges may need to examine

79 On deposition transcripts, see Section 6.2.2.

80 FRCP Rule 26(d).

81 Section 3.3.

82 The point that common law systems often fail to narrow down the issues and identify key issues at an early stage of the litigation process has also been made by Cannon 2006.

83 See the empirical studies discussed in Sections 3.3.2 and 3.3.3.

84 For a too rosy account of the economic benefits of the jury, see for instance Posner 1999, p. 1493.

85 Langbein 1985, p. 831.

expert evidence to determine whether it is admissible and the jury may have to examine the same evidence in order to determine whether or not it is credible (see Sections 5.2 and 6.2.3). On the continent, the investigatory function of discovery and the evidence presenting function of trial are generally merged; experts and witnesses are generally heard only once.[86] Also, the direct costs of the jury are fairly large. The whole process of jury selection, most notably the availability of three preemptive strikes and the use of scientific jury selection techniques, is an expensive process that is not likely to produce many social benefits.

The fee structure of the American system has some features that create incentives for an over-expenditure on fact-finding. The fact that American lawyers are increasingly billing by the hour has led to a 'pleasing convergence' of the professional urge of lawyers to be thorough and their economic interest in increasing the number of billable hours.[87] Other elements of the fee and cost regime in the United States induce the lawyers and parties to limit their expenditure, more so than in Austria and the Netherlands. The use of contingency fees as well as the absence of rules that require the losing party to compensate the attorney fees of the prevailing party are the clearest examples.

Comparative Conclusions

Adversarial fact-finding processes may induce parties to make efficient choices if the right legislative framework is in place. There are large differences in the degree to which jurisdictions have managed to create a right mix of rules that internalize externalities, encourage agreements between the parties, deter abuse, limit the possibilities to spend and provide judges with powers to intervene. In the previous paragraphs some of the differences between the Dutch, Austrian and federal American systems have been highlighted.

Different systems seem to have chosen different rules that aim to avoid excessive expenditure on fact-finding. In Austria and the Netherlands, judicial intervention plays a pivotal role. In the U.S., parties are encouraged to jointly agree upon an efficient allocation of resources. Some proceduralists have hinted that Continental jurisdictions like France or Germany have designed systems that lead litigants to invest too little in fact-finding, whereas the American system would induce the parties to overspend on fact-finding.[88] This general observation seems correct. The Austrian system in particular seems to be designed to curb the possibilities of overspending on fact-finding. Especially in cases in which lawyers receive a fixed fee per activity performed, it could even be the case that the Austrian system creates incentives to spend too few resources on fact-finding. In the United States, the existence of the single uninterrupted trial and the limited judicial intervention in the early stages of litigation seem to lead to a situation in which there are too few mechanisms to narrow down the issues. American litigants are

86 Adams 1998, p. 247.

87 Rosenberg & King 1981, p. 582.

88 See Adams 1998 and Miller 1997, p. 907, respectively comparing American procedural arrangements with German and French regulations.

more likely than litigants in the Netherlands and Austria to end up with too many legal arguments, too many facts and too much evidence.

Chapter 11

SUMMARY AND CONCLUSION

In order to determine whether a plaintiff in a civil case is entitled to her claim, the underlying facts are often decisive. This book discussed the rules on fact-finding. These rules regulate how information is gathered, evidence is presented and how a decision on matters of fact is made.

1. Historical Trends in the Process of Fact-finding

Austria and the Netherlands: Historical Trends in the Process of Fact-finding

The common point of departure, for both the Austrian and Dutch system of Civil Procedure is the Romano-Canonical model (Section 2.1). In this model, the pleadings and the admission or denial of facts under oath served as the main instruments to gather facts. There were hardly any instruments for the discovery of information. The role of the court was limited in the Romano-Canonical model. The judge was passive during the process of fact-gathering, had little influence over the taking of evidence and could not freely evaluate evidence. A set of technical rules determined the course of the proceeding. Evidence was presented during a sequence of hearings. Procedural rules prescribed the way in which evidence was presented and weighed. To a large extent, the procedure was a written procedure.

The Romano-Canonical model was largely developed in the 12th and 13th centuries. In medieval and early modern times, local variations of this model were adopted in courts throughout Europe. Many courts in Austrian lands and the Low Countries were also strongly influenced by the Romano-Canonical model (Section 2.1.2). Codifications that were enacted to create uniform procedural rules within national jurisdictions generally retained elements of the learned procedure. Early codifications, such as the French Royal Ordinance of 1667, the 1781 Austrian General Judicial Ordinance and the 1838 Dutch Code of Civil Procedure, contained numerous provisions directly derived from the learned procedure (Section 2.2). If one compares several early Continental codifications, one finds many similarities (See e.g. Section 6.1.3).

From the late 19th century onwards, procedural rules and practices were adopted that departed from the general principles of the Romano-Canonical model.

Generally, it was argued that new rules could improve both the accuracy and efficiency of the process of fact-finding. The fact-finding arrangements of the Austrian Code of Civil Procedure of 1895 brought about many changes in Austria. The Code embraced orality, immediacy, the free evaluation of evidence and judicial intervention. In essence, the fundamentals of the Austrian rules on fact-finding have not changed since 1895. The Austrian Code would prove to be influential in many other Continental jurisdictions (Section 2.3).

The Dutch system was subject to gradual reform. Changes that were adopted in Austria in the late 19th century were only recently made in the Netherlands. The 1988 Civil Evidence Act and the 2002 Reform Act made the most significant amendments to the rules on fact-finding. It is likely that new changes will be made in the near future. Empirical studies have been conducted assessing the effects of recent changes.

The developments in the Netherlands and Austria largely pointed in the same direction. Table 11.1 summarizes the main developments in Austria and the Netherlands. Four main developments that were identified in Section 2.4 are discussed below.

First, the structure of the proceedings changed in both Austria and the Netherlands. This had important implications for the process of fact-gathering. Presently, the parties generally file one written pleading each. After the pleadings have been exchanged, an Austrian or Dutch judge will schedule a personal appearance of the parties. This preparatory hearing *inter alia* serves to discuss the subject matter of the case. The preparatory oral hearing is currently the most important stage in the process of fact-gathering. Dutch empirical research indicates that the increased use of these preparatory hearings reduced the time to disposition and positively affected the perceived fairness of the procedure (see Sections 2.4 and 6.1).

Second, Continental systems have increasingly required the parties to disclose information and have widened the possibilities for party-driven discovery. Rules were introduced to prevent parties from withholding relevant information. Parties in Austria and the Netherlands are required to provide a complete and truthful account of the facts. Judges are likely to draw adverse inferences if parties withhold information or insufficiently substantiate their factual allegations. Parties are also required to disclose in their pleadings the evidence they intend to use in support of their factual allegations. Judges have gained more powers to order the parties to produce evidence. The Austrian Code of 1895 introduced party-driven discovery regulations inspired by the English rules. In the Netherlands, rules on discovery have been slightly widened since the 1950s. Nevertheless the Dutch rules on discovery are still relatively restrictive.

Third, the law of evidence has been 'deformalized'. The theory of formal proof that prevailed in Medieval times was considered unnecessarily complex. Rules that declared evidence inadmissible have virtually all been abolished in both Austria and the Netherlands. Most restrictions on the free evaluation of evidence have been abolished in both countries as well.

The last development in the Netherlands and Austria is that there has been a shift in the roles of parties, lawyers and judges in the process of fact-finding. Judges in Austria and the Netherlands currently have legal powers to actively participate in the process of fact-finding. Currently, judges in both Austria and the Netherlands are actively involved in clarifying the issues. They identify the facts that require evidence and are actively involved in the presentation of evidence.

Table 11.1. Main Developments in the Austrian and Dutch Fact-finding Processes

	Romano-Canonical Model	Modern Continental Systems
Pleadings	Possibly multiple pleadings for each party.	Generally each party files one written pleading only.
Preparatory hearings	No preparatory hearings, only the affirmation or denial of facts under oath.	A discussion of factual issues at a preparatory hearing.
Discovery	Rules only provide for very limited discovery.	Discovery is more widely available, but only used to a limited extent.
Admissibility of Evidence	There are many restrictions on the admissibility of (witness) evidence.	Virtually all relevant evidence is admissible.
Presentation of Evidence	The procedure is written and party-driven.	The procedure is oral and partly court-driven.
Evaluation of Evidence	There are numerous regulations on the evaluation of evidence.	The free evaluation of all relevant evidence is the general rule.

The United States: Historical Trends in the Process of Fact-finding

The present U.S. fact-finding arrangements are not rooted in one, but in (at least) two distinct English procedural regimes: common law and equity. Each of these two systems had their own procedure to resolve factual questions. The differences between these systems have been discussed in Section 3.1 and are summarized in the table below.

Table 11.2. Fact-finding Arrangements of the Common Law and Equity Procedure

	Common Law	Equity
Pleadings	Common law pleading produced a single issue.	Pleadings did not reduce the dispute to one issue.
Discovery	No discovery was available.	Limited means of discovery were available.
Presentation of evidence	Witnesses were heard in open court	Witnesses were heard in secrecy.
Roles of attorneys and judges	from the 17th century onwards, the procedure was increasingly more adversarial.	The role of the court was prominent in the presentation of evidence.
Decision maker on factual matters	Civil jury	Professional judge

The fundamentals of the English rules on fact-finding were adopted in many North American colonies. After the Revolution, a system based on the English common law was also adopted at the federal level. The right to a jury trial in common law cases was enshrined in the U.S. Constitution. The fundamentals of English procedure also influenced territories of the Union that were acquired at a later point in time.

The fact-finding arrangements in Angelo-American jurisdictions changed radically in the late 18th and the 19th century. One important development was that the adversarial system became increasingly important.

Moreover, important changes were made to the rules of evidence (Section 3.1.2.3). Some rules that had previously existed, such as those that disqualified specific categories of witnesses, were abolished. Many evidence rules that one finds in modern American codifications were newly developed in the late 18th and the 19th century. Rules were introduced to ensure that the jury would remain passive and independent. In addition, exclusionary rules of evidence, such as the hearsay rule, were developed.

A third important development was the adoption of the 1848 New York Field Code in a large number of state jurisdictions (Section 3.2). The Code contributed to the codification of procedural law and had important implications for the process of fact-finding. The Code simplified procedural law by merging the common law and equity procedures. A single unified system of rules applied to all civil cases. In addition, the Field Code abolished the older forms of pleading and introduced a less formalistic system of 'fact pleading'.

More recently, the American fact-finding arrangements have gone through another host of changes. The introduction of the 1938 Federal Rules of Civil Procedure (FRCP) would radically reform the procedural regime. The FRCP merged the procedures of law and equity in the federal courts. In Section 3.4 it was argued that there had been four significant developments since the introduction of the 1938 FRCP.

First, the 1938 FRCP embraced the notion of 'notice pleading'. The underlying idea was that the written pleadings primarily serve to give notice to the court and the opponent about the pleader's case. Pleading rules did not require a party to provide a detailed account of the facts. An important implication was that pleadings were no longer used as a means to narrow down the factual issues.

Second, a new middle phase in the process of litigation was created pursuant to the introduction of the 1938 FRCP. The new rules on discovery aimed to prepare for trial and to ensure that all relevant information was available to both parties. These rules enabled the parties to conduct a broad search for facts with little court intervention. By the 1970s, discovery was the new centre stage in the U.S. process of fact-gathering. Interrogatories, depositions and requests for the discovery of documents are currently used in a large proportion of cases. Empirical data indicate that discovery consumes a large proportion of the time and resources allotted to litigation. In addition, summary judgments became more widely available to dispose of (parts of) the dispute before trial. Increasingly, lawyers and judges put effort in arguing and deciding motions for summary judgments. Summary judgments often provide decisions on matters of fact.

In the recent decades, trials have become rare. There has been a sharp decline in the number of cases that reach the trial stage in both state courts and federal courts. The decline in the number of trials is caused by the multitude of factors, including the increased workload of judges and the creation of the new middle phase in the litigation process.

The developments above have led to a fourth general trend in U.S. litigation: a gradual shift in the roles of parties, lawyers and judges in the process of fact-finding. The role of the court in American civil litigation was at the heart of legislative reform. Since 1938, judges were granted more and wider discretionary powers to manage the litigation process. Judges presently issue scheduling orders, monitor the progress of litigation and render summary judgments. Nevertheless, the process of fact-finding became increasingly lawyer driven. As discovery became more important, the system of fact-gathering was effectively delegated to the bar. At the same time, the number of trials declined. This led to the evisceration of the roles of the civil jury and the judge as decision-makers. Despite wider judicial powers, a system has emerged in which the process of fact-finding is largely privatized. The American process of fact-gathering presently operates with a minimum of court intervention.

Diverging modes of Fact-finding

In Chapter 4, it was concluded that procedural rules have frequently been transplanted from one jurisdiction into another. Those that draft procedural legislation generally adopt rules and principles that were used, tried and tested elsewhere. The fact-finding arrangements of the Austrian Code of 1895 were inspired by numerous regulations of Austrian, English, German and French origin. Similarly, those that drafted the Federal Rules of Civil Procedure were inspired by the Federal Equity Rules and legislation enacted in state jurisdictions. Sometimes, changes brought about in one jurisdiction are adopted in a large number of other jurisdictions. One clear example is the abolition of the rule that disqualified parties from testifying (Chapter 6). The rule was first abolished in Connecticut and England. This example was soon followed by all other American jurisdictions. The English example also inspired developments in Austria as early as 1873. Subsequently, changes in Austria and England inspired other Continental jurisdictions to lift the ban on party witnesses.

There have been many examples of cross-influences between Anglo-American and Continental European jurisdictions. Often these cross-influences contributed to a gradual approximation of procedural systems. The pleading rules introduced by the 1848 New York Field Code were similar to those on the Continent. At the same time, the hearing of witnesses in open court and the free evaluation of evidence became leading principles in Continental systems. However, since the 1930s, there have been very few instances whereby Continental rules have been adopted in the U.S. Since the introduction of the FRCP, American developments have not been influenced by those on the Continent. Moreover, many new differences emerged since the 1930s. The introduction of very liberal party-driven discovery rules in the U.S. provides the clearest example. The broad and extra-judicial American rules on depositions and the discovery of (electronic) documents are alien to Continental lawyers.

Since the late 19th century, judicial intervention became increasingly important in most Continental jurisdictions. In the Netherlands and Austria, the personal appearance of the parties in the presence of the judge is currently the most significant phase in the process of fact-gathering. Despite the growing importance of international trade and transnational litigation, Continental and U.S. fact-finding arrangements grew further apart since the 1930s.

2. Different Fact Finding Rules and Practices

The differences between the Austrian, Dutch and U.S. federal black letter rules on fact-finding in civil cases are numerous. In addition, there are many differences in the way in which the laws are applied. In Chapter 4, the differences in the ordinary course of a lawsuit have been discussed. In the Netherlands and Austria, the process of fact-gathering is concentrated, whereas the presentation of evidence may take place at a number of dispersed court sessions. In the United States there may be many procedural steps in the pretrial stage of litigation. At the same time, evidence will be presented to the trier of fact during a single uninterrupted hearing. In discussing the differences between legal systems, it is important to distinguish between 'black letter law' and 'law in action'.

Often the written rules in one system differ greatly from those in other systems. Out of court depositions are important within the U.S. system of fact-gathering but unavailable in both the Netherlands and Austria (Section 6.1). The Austrian Code of Civil Procedure does not recognize or regulate party-appointed experts (Section 5.2). Rules on party-appointed experts are available in the Netherlands and the United States. Similarly, exclusionary rules of evidence exist in the United States but are virtually unknown in Austria and the Netherlands (Sections 3.2, 8.2 and 8.3). Jury trials, to provide a last example, are unavailable in Austria and the Netherlands and generally available in the United States (Section 8.3).

Most of the time, differences between American, Dutch and Austrian fact-finding procedures are not a matter of law. Often the laws are more or less similar while the legal practice differs greatly. In Austria, the Netherlands and the U.S., the law empowers the court to appoint experts. Austrian and Dutch judges frequently use these powers whereas empirical data show that judges in the U.S. seldom appoint experts (Section 5.3.3). In Chapter 4, I argued that the pleading rules in the Netherlands, Austria and the United States are more or less similar, but that there are reasons to assume that these operate differently in each of these jurisdictions. Moreover, judges in all jurisdictions may take time to discuss factual matters with the parties and their lawyers at a preparatory hearing. In Austria and the Netherlands judges do so more extensively than in the United States (Section 6.1). In all jurisdictions, the laws allow both judges and attorneys to question witnesses. On the European Continent, judges often put questions to witnesses. In the United States the witnesses are primarily cross-examined by counsel (Sections 3.1, 6.2.2 and 8.2).

Most of the time the fact-finding rules in Austria are roughly similar to those in the Netherlands. Both systems were initially influenced by the Romano-Canonical model. In more recent times, central tenets of the Austrian Code of Civil Procedure were also adopted in the Netherlands. Both systems were jointly contrasted with Anglo-American systems. Nevertheless, important differences do exist. In general, the role of the Austrian court is more extensive than the role of the Dutch court. In the Netherlands, the principle of party-presentation is weakened but not abolished as was the case in Austria (Section 2.3). The pursuit of truth has not played a pivotal role in the Dutch system either. Another significant difference is that the provisions on discovery in Austria are more extensive than those in the Netherlands.

The main differences between Dutch, Austrian and U.S. fact-finding arrangements and practices are summarized in Table 11.3.

Table 11.3. Fact-finding Processes: Main Differences

Stages in the Process of Fact-finding		Main Differences between Austria, the Netherlands and the United States
Fact-gathering	Pleading	Pleadings are more significant in Continental practice than in the U.S. practice as a means to clarify the facts and to narrow down the issues (Chapter 4).
	Disclosure	All systems require the parties to disclose information *sua sponte* but many small differences exist.
	Discovery	In the U.S., more so than on the Continent, discovery is widely available and used extensively. In the U.S., discovery operates extra-judicially.
	Preparatory Hearings	On the Continent, more so than in American practice, courts use preparatory hearings to discuss factual issues with the parties.
	Summary Judgments	On the Continent, judges generally render a decision at an early point in time to narrow down the issues. In the U.S., summary judgments are usually rendered after discovery is concluded.
Presentation of Evidence	Exclusionary Rules	Exclusionary rules exist in the U.S. but are virtually all abolished in Austria and the Netherlands.
	Witness Examination	In the U.S., witnesses are primarily cross-examined by counsel. In Austria and the Netherlands, the judge plays a more prominent role.
	Expertise	On the Continent, judges frequently appoint experts. In the U.S., party-appointed expert witnesses primarily testify at trial.
Decision Making	Decision Maker	Austrian and Dutch cases are virtually all tried by professional judges. In the U.S., trial by jury is the normal mode of trial.
	Rules on the Evaluation of Evidence	In the U.S. evidence is traditionally freely evaluated. On the Continent, most restrictions on the free evaluation of evidence have been abolished.
	Reasons for a decision	In the U.S., juries do not provide reasons for their verdicts. Continental judges are generally required to give reasons for their judgment.

In Sections 6.2.3, 8.2 and 8.3, I have argued that the differences between the Austrian, Dutch and U.S. black letter rules on fact-finding, as well as the differences in practice, are interrelated. I have argued that these differences flow from two fundamental differences: the different roles of judges and attorneys in the process of fact-finding and the (non) use of civil juries.

3. Understanding Differences: Procedural Models and Rules

Understanding the System of Rules
Rules should not be considered in isolation. In most jurisdictions, the rules on fact-finding constitute a carefully designed system. The drafters of procedural legislation commonly 1) identify the objectives of rules on fact-finding and 2) make assumptions about the effects that rules will have in legal practice. In Chapters 7, 8 and 9 I have aimed to answer the following questions: 'What are the main objectives and principles of the fact-finding process in both Austria and the United States?' and 'What is the rationale behind the objectives and principles of the process of fact-finding in Austria and the United States?'

In Chapters 7, I have aimed to describe the objectives and assumptions underlying the Austrian Code of Civil Procedure. In Chapter 8, I have made a 'rational reconstruction' of the U.S. rules on fact-finding and have identified their underlying objectives and assumptions. It was argued that underlying theories and objectives clarify and justify more specific rules of procedure in both Austria and the United States.

The Objectives of the Fact-Finding Process
It is commonly believed that the pursuit of truth is the primary end of the process of fact-finding. However, the pursuit of truth is not an end in itself, but a means directed towards a more remote end. A technical or pure epistemological perspective does not suffice to understand the fact-finding arrangements of legal systems. The pursuit of truth is believed to be of importance to promote settlement, reach a correct decision, level the playing field and to make the court's decision acceptable in the eyes of the litigants and the public. In order to understand the process of fact-finding, it is relevant to identify the final ends of the litigation process.

In Chapter 9, I have argued that political theory provides an adequate framework to understand and explain differences between jurisdictions. I have argued that the prevailing views on democracy and the role of the state in society impact the main objectives of the fact-finding process. First, a theoretical distinction was made between activist states and reactive states. The reactive state embraces the ideals of *laissez faire* classical liberalism. In a reactive state, individuals pursue their own ends and the state merely provides a forum to resolve conflicts that arise between individuals. Within a reactive state, fact-finding processes serve the satisfactory resolution of disputes. The litigants' perception that the procedure was fair is of great significance in a reactive state.

In an activist state, the government embraces a conception of an 'ideal society'. It implements policies that aim to advance towards creating such an ideal society. Although courts in an activist state resolve disputes, dispute resolution is not the primary aim of the litigation process. Within an activist state, civil litigation serves to implement and enforce government policies. The objective of the process of fact-finding is to establish the facts correctly, such that it is possible to enforce substantive law.

Second, it was argued that democratic values affect the way in which the decision maker in the legal process is selected (Chapter 9). Civil juries and elected judges enhance the democratic legitimacy of the litigation process. However, such a democratic input sets limits to the degree in which specialization and bureaucratization can take place. Democratic fact-finding procedures are likely to be less efficient (Chapters 8-10).

Virtually all legal systems are concerned with the rectitude of the final decision, fairness, efficiency and (democratic) legitimacy of the legal process (Table 11.4). Some of these (conflicting) ends of the litigation process have been explicitly codified. For example, FRCP Rule 1 states that the federal rules 'should be construed and administered to secure the just, speedy and inexpensive determination of every action'. If these primary ends of the litigation process are attained, the judicial process may create positive externalities. The positive side effects of the litigation process may be identified as (collateral) ends of the justice system. It is undisputed that the legal process should be designed in such a way that it enhances access to justice.

Table 11.4. What constitutes a Good Fact-finding Procedure?

Rectitude of the Decision, Correct Outcomes	Fairness of the Litigation Process	Efficiency of the Litigation Process	Legitimacy of the Litigation Process
Have legal rules been applied correctly? Is the decision based on 'true' facts?	Could the parties voice their opinion and were they treated with dignity? Was the decision maker neutral and impartial?	Have the costs of litigation been reasonable? Is the lawsuit resolved within reasonable time?	Do the rules of procedure have (democratic) legitimacy? Does the decision maker have (democratic) legitimacy?

The Austrian Model

Different jurisdictions emphasize different ends of the process of fact-finding. In Chapter 7, the Austrian model of civil litigation was discussed. The Austrian model takes the community as a starting point. In essence, the model is both collectivistic and utilitarian. The Austrian model embraced features of an activist state. According to Franz Klein, procedural law served to enforce substantive law. In addition, he was concerned with the efficiency of the justice system. In order to promote efficiency, Klein favored specialization and the division of labor. He proposed to organize the judiciary along bureaucratic lines. In the Austrian system, the trier of fact has no democratic legitimacy. We may conclude that in the Austrian model of fact-finding, the rectitude of the final decision and the efficiency of the legal process were the most important objectives.

Many specific Austrian fact-finding rules should be understood as an attempt to create a system that would produce good outcomes at low costs. Rules on fact-finding were designed to establish the facts correctly. The pursuit of truth was hence of great importance. Courts have a duty to establish the facts correctly, parties ought to be truthful. Procedural rules empower both the court and the parties to search for relevant information and evidence. The most innovative feature of the 1895 Code of Civil Procedure was that it strengthened the role of the judge. Active judicial intervention was pivotal in the Austrian model. Klein assumed that by strengthening the role of the court, it was possible to enforce substantive law effectively and efficiently.

The U.S. Model

In Chapter 8, it was argued that two distinctive features of the U.S. fact-finding process are most prominent: 1) the civil jury and 2) the adversarial system. The main justification for the civil jury is that it provides for democratic legitimacy. Several arguments exist to opt for an adversarial procedural model. In my opinion, two arguments are most compelling. First, the adversarial system is able to avoid premature decision-making by the trier of fact and thereby serves to ensure that the trier of fact remains unbiased and impartial. Furthermore, the adversarial system provides both parties with sufficient opportunities to voice their opinion. If parties are heard, this positively affects the litigant's perception of procedural fairness.

The U.S. federal system has features of a reactive state. It seems to be more concerned with the resolution of disputes than the enforcement of government policies. In addition, it provides the trier of fact with democratic legitimacy. We may conclude that the federal U.S. process of fact-finding primarily aims for the fair and legitimate resolution of disputes (see Chapter 9).

Specific U.S. rules on fact-finding either serve to accommodate the civil jury or are needed to implement an adversarial system. Typical U.S. rules on the structure of American litigation, the oral presentation of evidence, the exclusion of evidence and the use of direct sanctions against parties are all needed to accommodate the civil jury. Rules on pretrial discovery, the presentation of evidence and the exclusion of evidence all fit well within the adversarial system.

4. Understanding Differences: Fact-finding Processes in Action

Those that draft procedural rules generally strive to attain specific objectives and make assumptions about the effects that rules will have in legal practice. Rules are normally designed and adopted to promote the efficiency, legitimacy, accuracy or fairness of the process of fact-finding.

In the preceding Chapters, many factors have been identified that affect the success of fact-finding rules. Sometimes rules are adequate, but other factors needed to attain the acquired results are lacking. At other times, the empirical assumptions underlying the legislative model were inaccurate or incorrect. Empirical research that predicts or evaluates the effects of legislative changes has only been used recently. In the preceding chapters, examples of successful and unsuccessful policies have been discussed.

Rules are often ineffective because judges or attorneys are unwilling or unable to apply the rules. This dissertation listed many less successful examples of legislative attempts to increase the role of the judiciary in the process of fact-finding. Austrian judges have not always been willing to search for the truth beyond and behind the allegations of the parties (Section 2.3). Similarly, New York judges were generally not positive towards the innovations brought about by the 1848 Field Code (Section 3.2). U.S. District Court judges have often been overburdened. Therefore, they have not been able to take sufficient time to make use of their discretionary powers (Section 3.4.3). More successful examples have also been discussed, such as the Austrian and Dutch attempts to encourage the judge to discuss the facts of the case with the parties during an oral preparatory hearing. Both in Austria and the Netherlands, legislative changes went hand-in-hand with an increase in the number of judges. An obvious conclusion is that procedural rules may prove to be ineffective if professionals are unwilling or unable to apply them.

Often a legal system functions differently than intended by the legislature because the effects of legislation were not foreseen. The introduction of broad and liberal rules on discovery in the United States aimed to enhance the mutual knowledge of relevant facts (Section 3.2.2). The rules successfully managed to ensure that information was properly exchanged. The rules also had numerous (positive and negative) side-effects that were largely unforeseen. The drafters of the FRCP could not foresee in 1938 how rules on the discovery of documents would operate in a world in which Xerox machines, faxes, computers and digital databases are part of everyday life. Many other effects may have been unforeseen. Discovery rules have been abused in ways that are diametrically opposed to the objectives of the FRCP (see Section 3.3.2). In addition, I argued that the introduction of broad rules on discovery has contributed to a sharp decline in the number of trials (see Section 3.4.3).

It was concluded in Sections 7.4 and 8.4 that Austrian and U.S. fact-finding rules do not always operate as intended. Legal systems do not always succeed in providing for an effective, fair, legitimate and efficient process of fact-finding. To understand how the rules on fact-finding operate in legal practice, references to empirical studies have been made throughout the previous chapters. It is difficult to make conclusive comparative judgments. Nevertheless, some remarks will be made on the degree in which the main objectives and models underlying procedural legislation are congruent with the actual fact-finding processes before the courts.

Fairness of the Process of Fact-finding

The American system, more so than the Austrian system, emphasizes the role of parties and lawyers in litigation. I have argued that the main reason to opt for an adversarial system is that it may enhance the fairness of the legal process. Moreover, I have argued that there are good reasons to assume that an American civil jury is less likely to make premature decisions than a professional Continental judge (Chapter 8). In addition, there have been fears that Continental litigants may feel that their views are insufficiently taken into account when expert evidence is evaluated (Section 5.1.4).

It is however difficult to make conclusive comparative judgments on the fairness of the procedure. Laboratory studies generally do not enable us to draw firm conclusions about real life procedures (Chapter 8). Similarly, it is difficult to compare the available studies that have measured litigant satisfaction and litigants' perceptions of fairness. In Chapter 6, several studies that measured the litigants' perception of fairness were discussed. Different questionnaires, scales, and research questions have been used in different countries, which makes it difficult to compare data across borders. The available data do not provide strong reasons to believe that litigants would perceive a procedure in the U.S. as fairer than the procedure in the Netherlands or *vice versa*. It is possible to draw more specific conclusions. On the basis of empirical studies conducted in the Netherlands, one may for instance conclude that scheduling a personal appearance of the parties positively affects the litigant's perception of the fairness of the procedure (Section 6.2.1).

The Accuracy of the Process of Fact-finding

Austrian academics have indicated that rules that aimed to promote the pursuit of truth may not have been very successful in legal practice (see Section 2.3.1.4). Austrian judges have not always been inclined to search for facts beyond and behind the allegations of the parties. In addition, the Austrian system does not correctly align incentives. The analysis of the Austrian procedural rules and the prevailing cost regime in Chapter 10 showed that Austrian lawyers are not always induced to prepare their cases thoroughly.

There are also reasons to doubt whether the American adversarial system is capable of establishing the facts correctly. As argued in Chapter 3 and 10, the American system induces the parties to conduct a thorough search for facts. On the other hand, parties also have an incentive to distort or conceal the truth or to exploit the financial inequality between the parties.

In Chapter 5, the effectiveness of different approaches to expertise was addressed. On the Continent, it often seems difficult to identify mistakes made by experts and to oppose the findings of court appointed experts. It is often said that judges insufficiently scrutinize the findings of the expert. In the United States, expert witnesses are induced to do their work thoroughly. Findings of an expert are likely to be scrutinized by another expert. However, there is reason to doubt the reliability and objectivity of party-appointed expert witnesses. In an American setting, it is more likely that expert witnesses provide an unreliable and biased testimony.

In Section 6.2.1.2, surveys of litigants and lawyers were discussed. American surveys show that discovery successfully enhances the mutual knowledge of the case and manages to avoid surprise at trial. Similarly, Dutch surveys indicate that a majority of litigants and lawyers are of the opinion that relevant information had been adduced after the personal appearance of the parties was concluded.

Democratic Legitimacy of the Fact-finding Process

Much more than on the Continent, the actors in the U.S. system of litigation have democratic legitimacy. In the federal system, the civil jury is the most important vehicle to involve the people in the litigation process. In addition, judges are directly elected by the people in many American state jurisdictions. It is fair to say that the American process of fact-finding is more democratic. Nevertheless, it must be noted that the sharp decline in the number of trials effectively eviscerated the democratic legitimacy of the American judicial process. Today, only a very small share of all cases is tried by a civil jury. In addition, it is very doubtful whether the popular election of judges improves the public perception of legitimacy.

Efficiency of Litigation

The resources (money and time) allocated to the process of fact-finding should be proportional to the needs of the case. One can spend too much or too little money on fact-finding processes in litigation (Chapter 10). In practice, complaints about the high costs of litigation are most common.

It is difficult to compare available data on the efficiency of the justice system. It is for example hard to make conclusive comparative judgments on the degree in which national jurisdictions are able to curb delay (Chapter 4). The time to disposition differs greatly between jurisdictions. There are however many factors that determine the time needed to resolve civil cases. Cases handled by Austrian County Courts have different case characteristics than those handled by U.S. District Courts. It is extremely tough to correct for all such differences. On the basis of the available data, no comparative conclusions could be drawn. It is possible to analyze more specific changes within jurisdictions and their impact on the (median) time to disposition (see for example Section 2.4).

Although there are compelling reasons to believe that the Austrian approach to expert evidence is less costly than the American approach to expertise, there are no conclusive data to confirm this hypothesis (Chapter 5). I argued that mixed models, such as the system presently used in England, provide a promising alternative that may lead to a proportional allocation of resources. In a mixed model, the Continental approach is used in the majority of relatively simple and small cases. The use of party -appointed experts may provide an added value in specific categories of (complex) cases.

The use of civil juries has a negative impact on the costs of litigation (Chapter 8 and 10). There are two main reasons for this observation. First, it is clear that the employment of twelve additional lay jurors adds to the direct costs of litigation. Second, the jury has an impact on the course of litigation. The divide between the pretrial and the trial stage of litigation is needed to accommodate for the civil jury. This may in turn lead to the duplication of work. As explained in Chapter 5, experts may be heard multiple times: they may be deposed, may be heard during a *Daubert* hearing and may provide a testimony at trial. In Continental systems, these hearings can be merged.

In Chapter 10, I made use of economic theory to analyze the incentives for the litigants and lawyers within the Austrian, Dutch and U.S. procedural systems. Legal incentives are likely to affect the effectiveness and efficiency of the process of fact-finding. I argued that adversarial systems may induce parties to overspend on fact-finding unless a proper legal framework is in place. It was argued that in the U.S.

federal system, there are many incentives for parties to spend large amounts of resources on fact-finding. The U.S. federal system induces the parties to be very thorough, probably too thorough. In other jurisdictions, such as Austria, there might be incentives for the parties to spend very few resources on fact-finding. The analysis supports the complaints often heard in comparative literature that U.S. litigation is more expensive.

5. Concluding Remarks

The procedures that are used to resolve factual questions in Austrian and Dutch courts differs greatly from those used in American courts. This book aimed to enhance our understanding of these differences and aimed to show how these differences evolved throughout time. Often, procedural rules are implemented that were tried and tested elsewhere. A remarkable conclusion is that the differences between the fact-finding arrangements in Continental and American jurisdiction are larger today than they were a century ago.

This book showed that fact-finding arrangements do not exist in the abstract. Procedural rules constitute a system that should be studied as a single whole. It has been argued that political theories and ideologies shape the language and content of the law. How procedural rules operate in practice depends on a multitude of factors, such as the mindset of judges and attorneys and the court's budget.

Over the last decades, there has been an increased focus on empirical studies and methods to predict and evaluate the effects of legislative change. These studies are of great value in predicting under what circumstances available legal solutions may produce positive effects.

I believe comparative law may serve as a useful tool to generate possible legal solutions to pressing procedural problems. In addition, experiences in other jurisdictions may be of use to asses the possible effects of legislative change. These may be of help to identify under what conditions legal rules may flourish. This book has mainly been descriptive. Nevertheless, I hope this book may serve as an accessible starting point to generate viable legal solutions that may improve existing systems. For example, Austrian experiences may provide a source of inspiration for proposals to widen the Dutch rules on document discovery. Similarly, Continental jurisdictions that are faced with new challenges to utilize party appointed experts may consider adopting rules inspired by the American rules. Rules on the admissibility of party appointed experts and the disclosure of mandatory expert reports may prove to be useful in a Continental setting.

SAMENVATTING. HET ONDERZOEK NAAR DE FEITEN IN HET CIVIELE PROCES, EEN RECHTSVERGELIJKEND PERSPECTIEF

In veel civiele procedures voert de gedaagde verweer tegen de vordering die door de eiser is ingesteld. Om te bepalen of de vordering moet worden toegewezen, is behalve het toepasselijke recht ook de juistheid van de door partijen gestelde feiten van belang. Dit proefschrift handelt over het onderzoek naar de feiten in de procedure. Het onderzoek naar de feiten in het civiele proces bestaat uit drie fasen. In de eerste fase worden feiten verzameld, hoofd en bijzaken worden onderscheiden en de daadwerkelijke twistpunten worden geïdentificeerd. In de tweede fase worden de partijen in de gelegenheid gesteld bewijs aan te dragen. In de laatste fase wordt er een beslissing genomen ten aanzien van de feiten. Het doel van deze dissertatie is om de procesrechtelijke regels ten aanzien van elk van deze fasen inzichtelijk te maken door deze te contrasteren met buitenlandse regelgeving. Daartoe worden de regels die in Nederland gelden met name vergeleken met de regelgeving in Oostenrijk en de Verenigde Staten. Allereerst wordt ingegaan op de historische achtergrond van het procesrecht. Vervolgens worden de huidige verschillen tussen voornoemde jurisdicties in kaart gebracht. Tot slot volgt een theoretische beschouwing over de doelen en beginselen van het onderzoek naar de feiten in het civiele proces.

Feiten in het civiele proces: de herkomst van de regels

Het procesrecht in veel moderne Europese staten, waaronder Oostenrijk en Nederland, is terug te voeren op het geleerde Romano-Canonieke recht dat hoofdzakelijk in de 11e tot en met de 13e eeuw ontwikkeld werd. Hoewel er lokale varianten bestonden, werden elementen van het Romano-Canonieke model op den duur in vele rechtbanken in Europa gebruikt. Het middeleeuwse *ius commune* heeft uiteindelijk een grote invloed gehad op 18e en 19e eeuwse nationale codificaties (hoofdstuk 2). In het geleerde model werd het onderzoek naar de feiten in groot detail gereguleerd. De procedure was voornamelijk schriftelijk en gaf de rechter weinig discretionaire bevoegdheden. Dit procesmodel werd aan het einde van de 19e eeuw sterk bekritiseerd. Dit leidde in Oostenrijk in 1895 tot de invoering van een nieuwe *Zivilprozessordnung*. Veel regels die als onnodig formalistisch werden getypeerd werden afgeschaft. Het wetboek benadrukte de mondelinge behandeling van de zaak, kende de rechter veel bevoegdheden toe en verwachtte van partijen dat zij zich coöperatief zouden opstellen. Het Oostenrijkse voorbeeld werd door vele jurisdicties op het Europese continent gevolgd. De meeste Nederlandse wetswijzigingen van de laatste decennia lijken sterk op veranderingen die in Oostenrijk een eeuw eerder werden doorgevoerd.

De huidige Amerikaanse regeling omtrent het verzamelen, bewijzen en vaststellen van de feiten is geworteld in het middeleeuwse Engelse rechtssysteem (hoofdstuk 3). Traditioneel waren er in Engeland meerdere procesrechtelijke systemen. In de *common law* rechtbanken werd gebruik gemaakt van een procedure die bestond uit twee stadia. In de eerste (schriftelijke) ronde werden de partijen gedwongen om hun geschil terug te brengen tot één enkel feitelijk of juridisch twistpunt (*common law pleading*). Was het twistpunt feitelijk van aard, dan konden partijen in de tweede fase meestal bewijs presenteren voor de jury (*jury trial*). Andere rechtbanken die eveneens bevoegd waren over civielrechtelijk geschillen te oordelen, zoals de *Court of Chancery,* hanteerden een geheel andere procedure die meestal sterker leek op de procedure op het Europese Continent. Het Engelse recht werd in hoofdlijnen ook toegepast in de Engelse koloniën. Na de Amerikaanse onafhankelijkheid bleef het Engelse recht lang richtinggevend. Het recht van partijen op een *trial by jury* werd zelfs in de grondwet verankerd. Het procesrecht was in sterke mate rechtersrecht. Daarnaast was het sterk gefragmenteerd. De vorm van het proces hing nauw samen met het materiële recht; de vordering bepaalde doorgaans het precieze verloop van de procedure (*forms of action*). Daarnaast hanteerden veel Amerikaanse koloniën aparte procedures voor *equity* zaken. Aan de versnippering van het procesrecht kwam een einde doordat in de 19e en de 20e eeuw het procesrecht, en later ook het bewijsrecht, gecodificeerd werden. De *New York Code of Procedure* van 1848 (Field Code) en de *Federal Rules of Civil Procedure* (1938, FRCP) bleken de meest invloedrijke Amerikaanse codificaties. Geleidelijk ontstond er een nieuwe procedure die uiteindelijk op veel punten af zou wijken van het oude *common law* systeem.

Veel invloedrijke wetboeken, zoals de Oostenrijkse *Zivilprozessordnung* van 1895 en de Amerikaanse FRCP van 1938 bestaan voor een heel groot deel uit wettelijke bepalingen die vrijwel letterlijk zijn overgenomen uit andere jurisdicties. Nieuwe wetboeken zijn zoals nieuwe recepten: ze presenteren een nieuwe mix van bekende ingrediënten. Zo was het Wetboek van New York van 1848 onder meer beïnvloed door de Engelse *common law* en *equity* procedures en wetgeving uit Louisiana en Frankrijk. Evenzo was het Nederlandse Wetboek van 1838 hoofdzakelijk een variatie op een bekend recept: de Franse *Code de Procédure Civile* van 1806. De geringe wederzijdse beïnvloeding door jurisdicties aan weerszijden van de Atlantische Oceaan is opmerkelijk. Wanneer men de ontwikkelingen op het Europese Continent en in de Verenigde Staten beziet valt op dat regels aangaande het verzamelen, bewijzen en vaststellen van de feiten nu sterker van elkaar verschillen dan in 1930.

Verschillen tussen het Oostenrijkse, Amerikaanse en Nederlandse proces
Op dit moment zijn er grote verschillen tussen jurisdicties ten aanzien van de wijze waarop binnen civiele procedures de feiten verzameld, bewezen en vastgesteld worden. Soms zijn deze verschillen een gevolg van verschillende rechtsregels. In andere gevallen zijn de regels vergelijkbaar maar zijn er grote verschillen in de rechtspraktijk waarneembaar.

In de eerste fase van de procedure worden de feiten verzameld en de belangrijkste twistpunten geïdentificeerd. Mede doordat de Field Code van 1848 geïnspireerd was op Franse wetgeving is er wel enige gelijkenis tussen de Amerikaanse en continentale regels aangaande de voorbereidende schriftelijke ronde. In elk van de besproken jurisdicties wordt in beginsel aan beide partijen eenmaal de gelegenheid geboden schriftelijk hun zienswijze kenbaar te maken en feiten aan te dragen. Hoewel de regels enigszins vergelijkbaar zijn, lijkt het belang van de inleidende schriftelijk stukken in Nederland en Oostenrijk groter te zijn dan in de Verenigde Staten (zie hoofdstuk 3.4.1 en 4.2.2).

In Nederland en Oostenrijk is de mondelinge behandeling van de zaak onder leiding van de rechter het belangrijkste middel om het feitencomplex op te helderen (hoofdstuk 6). In Oostenrijk is de mondelinge behandeling van de zaak al sinds 1895 de belangrijkste fase in het civiele proces. In Nederland was het wettelijk al jaren mogelijk om de (feiten van de) zaak mondeling te bespreken (comparitie van partijen). Pas in de laatste decennia wordt er door de rechtbanken op grote schaal gebruik gemaakt van comparities nadat de gedaagde schriftelijk voor antwoord geconcludeerd heeft. Tijdens de comparitie wordt doorgaans (veel) tijd besteed aan het verhelderen van de (feitelijke) geschilpunten. Meestal is de rechter actief tijdens de zitting.

Hoewel de Amerikaanse rechter eveneens bevoegd is om de zaak inhoudelijk met de partijen te bespreken ter zitting, gebeurt dit in de praktijk zelden. In de Verenigde Staten ligt in de eerste fase van het proces heel sterk de nadruk op het verzamelen van de feiten door middel van *discovery*. Opvallend vanuit rechtsvergelijkend en historisch perspectief is dat de FRCP de partijen ruime mogelijkheden biedt om de wederpartij of derden te dwingen informatie te verstrekken. Voorts valt op dat *discovery* zich doorgaans volledig buiten de rechter om voltrekt. Uit empirische studies blijkt dat *discovery* steeds meer het zwaartepunt in de Amerikaanse procedure is geworden. Met name wordt er in de rechtspraktijk gebruik gemaakt van *interrogatories* (het voorleggen van schriftelijke vragen aan de wederpartij), *depositions* (het 'voorlopige' verhoor van partijen of getuigen buiten de rechter en de rechtbank om) en *requests for the discovery of documents* (verzoek aan de wederpartij tot overleggen van documenten). Ook worden de partijen sinds de jaren 90 verplicht uit zichzelf informatie te verstrekken aan de wederpartij, onder andere ten aanzien van het bewijs dat ze uiteindelijk willen gebruiken (*disclosure*).

In Nederland zijn er minder juridische mogelijkheden voor de partijen om de wederpartij te dwingen informatie beschikbaar te stellen. Zo zijn naar Nederlands recht de mogelijkheden om relevante documenten van de wederpartij op te vragen beperkt. De Oostenrijkse regeling is in dit opzicht ruimer. Zij biedt partijen de mogelijkheid de wederpartij vragen te stellen of bewijsmiddelen op te vragen. In geen van beide landen opereren de beschikbare *discovery* regels echter volledig buiten de rechter om. Wel zijn in Nederland en Oostenrijk ten gevolge van procesrechthervormingen de partijen meer en meer verplicht alle relevante informatie aan te dragen. Daarnaast heeft ook de rechtbank bevoegdheden om partijen ambtshalve te bevelen informatie of bewijs te verstrekken.

In zowel Oostenrijk, Nederland als de V.S. is het niet ongewoon dat de rechtbank (door middel van een tussenvonnis) een beslissing neemt waarin zij de betwiste feiten identificeert. Belangrijk verschil is dat in Nederland en Oostenrijk de beslissing meestal wordt genomen tijdens of snel na de eerste mondelinge behandeling van de zaak. In de V.S. wordt een *summary judgment* vaak pas gewezen na de *discovery* fase.

Nadat alle relevante informatie verzameld en besproken is, wordt de partijen in de tweede fase van het proces de mogelijkheid geboden om bewijs te leveren. Uitgangspunt in Oostenrijk, Nederland en de V.S. is dat al het relevante bewijs in beginsel toelaatbaar is (vrije bewijsleer). In Oostenrijk en Nederland zijn er vrijwel geen uitzonderingen op deze regel. In de V.S. zijn er meer uitzonderingen op de toelaatbaarheid van het bewijs. Bewijs van horen zeggen (*de auditu*) en onbetrouwbaar deskundigen bewijs mogen niet ter zitting als bewijs gepresenteerd worden. In Nederland en Oostenrijk is dergelijk bewijs toelaatbaar, maar kan een rechter bijvoorbeeld aan een *de auditu* verklaring minder bewijskracht toekennen.

Voorts zijn er grote verschillen in de rechtspraktijk aangaande de wijze waarop bewijs gepresenteerd wordt. In Nederland en Oostenrijk zijn rechters vaak actief betrokken bij de presentatie van het bewijs. Zo benoemen rechters regelmatig zelf deskundigen. In de Verenigde Staten zijn rechters weliswaar bevoegd om deskundigen te benoemen maar doen zij dit zelden. Doorgaans selecteren de partijen zelf elk hun eigen deskundigen die ter zitting een verklaring kunnen geven. Daarnaast zijn rechters in Oostenrijk en Nederland veelal actiever op de zitting waar bewijs gepresenteerd wordt dan hun Amerikaanse ambtsgenoten. Zo worden op het continent getuigen hoofdzakelijk door de rechter verhoord terwijl zij in de V.S. onder de invloed van het *adversarial system* voornamelijk onderhevig zijn aan *cross-examination* door de advocaten.

Tot slot moet opgemerkt worden dat in de V.S. het bewijs in civiele zaken op één zitting gepresenteerd wordt aan de jury of aan de rechter (*trial*). Hoewel een *trial* soms meerdere dagen duurt, zijn vrijwel alle trials binnen één week beëindigd. In Nederland (en in mindere mate ook in Oostenrijk) is het niet ongebruikelijk dat eerst getuigen gehoord worden die door eiser zijn opgeroepen en dat het tegenbewijs van gedaagde een maand later geleverd wordt. In ingewikkelde zaken is het mogelijk dat bewijs geleverd wordt op drie of vier zittingsdagen, soms verspreid over enkele maanden.

Een ander in het oog springend verschil tussen jurisdicties in de V.S. enerzijds en Nederland en Oostenrijk anderzijds is dat in de V.S. het recht op een *trial by jury* grondwettelijk verankerd is. Juryrechtspraak is de gebruikelijke manier om te beslissen over het door partijen naar voren gebrachte bewijs. De jury mag het bewijs vrij waarderen en geeft geen redenen voor haar oordeel. In Oostenrijk en Nederland wordt de eindbeslissing altijd door de rechter genomen. De meeste beperkingen op de vrije waardering van het bewijs in Oostenrijk en Nederland zijn inmiddels afgeschaft. Rechters hebben in beginsel de (beperkte) plicht hun beslissing te motiveren.

De verschillen tussen de federale Amerikaanse traditie en die van Nederland en Oostenrijk vloeien voort uit twee meer fundamentele uitgangspunten (hoofdstuk 8). Deze verschillen hangen samen met de verschillende rollen van advocaten en rechters in het civiele proces en met het gebruik van lekenrechtspraak.

In Oostenrijk en Nederland is een (geleidelijke) verandering opgetreden in de rollen van rechters en advocaten in het civiele proces (hoofdstuk 2.4.4). De meer prominente rol van de mondelinge behandeling van de zaak, de grotere bevoegdheid van de rechter om de afgifte van bewijsstukken te vorderen en de afschaffing van formele regels aangaande de bewijswaardering hebben ertoe geleid dat de rechter actiever betrokken is bij het verzamelen, bewijzen en vaststellen van de feiten. Hoewel de Nederlandse rechter zich nog immer lijdelijk op dient te stellen, is de rol van de rechter in de rechtspraktijk belangrijker geworden. In Oostenrijk is de leer van de lijdelijkheid van de rechter in grote mate verlaten.

Rechters in de Verenigde Staten hebben steeds meer bevoegdheden gekregen om als 'casemanager' op te treden (hoofdstuk 3.3.3). Toch is de rechter in de Amerikaanse rechtspraktijk nu veel minder betrokken bij het verzamelen, bewijzen en vaststellen van de feiten dan vóór de introductie van de FRCP. Omdat *discovery* zich vrijwel geheel buiten de rechter om afspeelt, is met name het verzamelen van de feiten en van het bewijs nu volledig aan advocaten en partijen overgelaten. In zekere zin kan men spreken van een toegenomen 'privatisering' van de overheidsrechtspraak in de V.S. sinds 1938 (hoofdstuk 3.4.4).

Kort samengevat kan men stellen dat in de continentale rechtspraktijk de rechter actiever betrokken is bij het verzamelen, bewijzen en vaststellen van de feiten. Veel Amerikaanse regels en gewoonten passen binnen een procescultuur die gedomineerd wordt door het *adversarial system*. De Amerikaanse regels ten aanzien van bewijsuitsluiting en *discovery* alsmede het verhoor van getuigen door *cross-examination* vloeien voort uit dit beginsel. Veel regels in Nederland en Oostenrijk passen op hun beurt binnen een procestraditie waarin de rechter zich actiever opstelt in het onderzoek naar de feiten.

Ook het gebruik van de jury in civiele zaken heeft een grote impact op het procesrecht en de procespraktijk. Veel Amerikaanse regels dienen vooral om de rechtspraak door 12 leken mogelijk te maken. De nadruk op de mondelinge presentatie van bewijs, het onderscheid tussen een *trial* en een *pretrial* fase en het gebruik van directe sancties tegen procespartijen zijn met name te rechtvaardigen binnen een systeem waarin recht wordt gesproken door een jury.

Het feitelijk debat en de doelen van het civiele proces

De regels over het verzamelen, bewijzen en vaststellen van de feiten dienen doorgaans de waarheidsvinding. Toch is waarheidsvinding in het civiele proces niet een doel op zichzelf, maar eerder een middel om andere doelen te verwezenlijken. Waarheidsvinding is onder meer van belang om te komen tot een juiste beslissing, schikkingen te bevorderen en om de ongelijkheid tussen partijen op te heffen. Een puur kentheoretisch perspectief op het onderzoek naar de feiten volstaat daarom niet om de regels over het verzamelen, bewijzen en vaststellen van de feiten te begrijpen. Om het onderzoek naar de feiten te begrijpen is het van belang om de uiteindelijke doelen van het civiele proces te identificeren. Vier belangrijke doelen van het civiele proces zijn hieronder weergegeven (Tabel 12.1). In iedere jurisdictie wordt het belang van een juiste uitkomst, een eerlijk proces, efficiëntie en legitimiteit onderkent. Het gewicht dat wordt toegekend aan deze afzonderlijke doelen verschilt echter sterk.

Tabel 12.1 Vier doelen van het civiele proces

De uitkomst van het proces is correct	Het proces is eerlijk	Het proces is efficiënt	Het proces is legitiem
Zijn de juiste (materiële) rechtsregels toegepast? Zijn de feiten waarheidsgetrouw vastgesteld?	Zijn de partijen gehoord? Zijn de partijen met respect behandeld? Is de beslisser neutraal en onpartijdig?	Waren de kosten en de duur van de procedure gezien het belang van de zaak redelijk?	Zijn de regels van het proces democratisch tot stand gekomen? Is de beslisser (democratisch) gelegitimeerd?

De visie op de rol van de staat in de samenleving en de visie op democratie bepalen in sterke mate de doelen van het civiele proces (hoofdstuk 9). Politieke opvattingen over de belangrijkste doelen van het proces werken door in de vaststelling van regels over het verzamelen, bewijzen en vaststellen van de feiten.

Allereerst werd in hoofdstuk 9, in navolging van Damaska, een onderscheid gemaakt tussen twee theoretische uitersten: activistische en reactieve staten. Een reactieve staat heeft geen opvatting over hoe de maatschappij eruit zou moeten zien. Het is aan de burgers hun eigen doelen na te streven. De reactieve staat voert een klassiek liberaal *laissez faire* beleid. Wanneer individuen betrokken raken in een conflict, heeft de staat geen voorkeur voor een specifieke oplossing. In de reactieve staat is het enkel van belang om wanorde en chaos te voorkomen. Geschiloplossing is het dan ook het enige doel van het civiele proces. In een reactieve staat is waarheidsvinding enkel van belang wanneer dit aan de geschiloplossing bijdraagt.

De activistische staat daarentegen, heeft een duidelijke opvatting over wat goed is voor de maatschappij en voor de burgers. Zij voert een actief beleid op vele terreinen van het leven om de maatschappij volgens deze maatstaven te verbeteren. Hoewel geschiloplossing ook van belang is in de activistische staat, dient procesrecht vooral om het overheidsbeleid te implementeren. In een activistische staat is het procesrecht dienstbaar aan het materiële recht: rechtshandhaving is haar primaire functie. Om recht te kunnen handhaven is waarheidsvinding van groot belang. In de activistische staat dienen de feiten correct vastgesteld te worden. De rechter, die namens de staat optreedt, heeft de plicht de feiten zoveel als mogelijk naar waarheid vast te stellen.

Naast de visie op staatsinrichting hebben ook de opvattingen over democratie een grote invloed op het procesrecht. In de meeste landen worden de procesrechtelijke regels vastgesteld door de volksvertegenwoordiging. Sommige jurisdicties gaan een stap verder. Met name in Amerikaanse jurisdicties zijn rechters vaak direct gekozen of politiek benoemd. Daarnaast komt jury rechtspraak op grote schaal voor in de V.S. Dit betekent dat de beslissing ten aanzien van de feiten (direct) democratisch gelegitimeerd is. Met name het gebruik van jury's in civiele zaken heeft een enorme impact op de regels aangaande het verzamelen, bewijzen en vaststellen van de feiten. Lekenrechtspraak heeft tevens grote gevolgen voor de efficiëntie van het burgerlijk proces. Deze vorm van rechtspraak staat namelijk haaks op specialisatie. Het verkiezen van rechters heeft voorts tot gevolg dat het moeilijk is de rechterlijke macht bureaucratisch te organiseren. De democratische rechtsgang beperkt de mogelijkheden om het proces efficiënt te organiseren.

De wetgever streeft er meestal naar regels te ontwerpen die ertoe bijdragen dat het onderzoek naar de feiten legitiem is en tevens efficiënt, eerlijk en accuraat verloopt. Dit beoogde resultaat wordt niet altijd bereikt. Soms zijn de regels weliswaar adequaat, maar laat de implementatie te wensen over. Op andere momenten worden de doelstellingen niet gehaald omdat de beleidstheorie waarop de regelgeving is gebaseerd onjuist of onvolledig is.

Het gebruik van empirische studies teneinde de effecten van regelgeving te voorspellen of te evalueren neemt de laatste decennia toe. Dit maakt het mogelijk de effecten van interventies - zoals de introductie van de comparitie na antwoord in Nederland - te meten. Het is veel moeilijker om aan de hand van de beschikbare gegevens een vergelijkend oordeel te vellen over de procesrechtelijke regels in verschillende jurisdicties. Het is bijvoorbeeld erg moeilijk te bepalen welk systeem van regels leidt tot een snellere afhandeling van zaken (zie hoofdstuk 4). Evenzo is het lastig te beoordelen welk procesrechtelijk systeem door de procespartijen als eerlijker ervaren wordt (zie hoofdstuk. 8.2.2, 5.1.4 en 6.2.1).

In het Oostenrijkse procesmodel ligt de nadruk op de uitkomst van het proces en de efficiency van de procedure. Het Oostenrijkse procesmodel werd ontwikkeld door Frans Klein aan het eind van de 19e eeuw. Dit model is in essentie gebaseerd op een collectivistisch en utilistisch maatschappijbeeld. Het Oostenrijkse model neemt de gemeenschap als uitgangspunt en stelt dat de staat er zorg voor dient te dragen dat de welvaart van de burgers vergroot wordt. Het Oostenrijks model bevat elementen van het procesmodel van de 'activistische staat'. Franz Klein betoogde dat procesrecht ertoe dient om het materiële recht te handhaven. Daarnaast hechtte hij veel waarde aan het efficiënt afhandelen van zaken. Om die reden toonde Klein zich een voorstander van specialisatie. Voorts was hij van mening dat de rechterlijke macht bureaucratisch georganiseerd dient te worden. In Oostenrijk wordt geen gebruik gemaakt van lekenrechtspraak in civiele zaken en heeft de rechter geen directe democratische legitimatie.

Specifieke Oostenrijkse regels aangaande het verzamelen, bewijzen en vaststellen van de feiten kunnen gezien worden als het resultaat van een poging om een systeem te ontwerpen dat op efficiënte wijze leidt tot een juiste vaststelling van de feiten. Waarheidsvinding is van groot belang in het Oostenrijkse rechtssysteem. Rechters zijn verplicht de feiten zoveel mogelijk naar waarheid vast te stellen en partijen zijn verplicht de feiten volledig en naar waarheid aan te voeren. Rechters en partijen zijn bevoegd om zich toegang te verschaffen tot relevante informatie en beschikbare bewijsmiddelen. Bij de invoering van de *Zivilprozessordnung* werd de versterking van de rol van de rechter in het civiele proces gezien als het belangrijkste middel om te komen tot een efficiënte en correcte afhandeling van geschillen. De Oostenrijkse rechter dient vanaf het begin van de procedure actief betrokken te zijn bij de zaak.

De Nederlandse procesrechttraditie is in de laatste decennia meer in de richting geschoven van het Oostenrijkse procesmodel. Toch zijn de beginselen van het Nederlands procesrecht gematigder. In Nederland ligt de nadruk veel minder op waarheidsvinding dan in Oostenrijk. Daarnaast is de lijdelijkheid van de rechter nog altijd een van de uitgangspunten van het Nederlands procesrecht. Wel is gedurende de laatste decennia veel meer aandacht voor de kosten en de duur van de procedure.

Tot op zekere hoogte is (de implementatie van) het procesrecht in haar huidige vorm in Nederland en Oostenrijk effectief gebleken. In het algemeen worden de meeste zaken in Nederland en Oostenrijk snel afgehandeld. Daarnaast heb ik betoogd dat er gegronde redenen zijn om aan te nemen dat het Oostenrijkse proces (en in mindere mate ook het Nederlandse proces) betrekkelijk kostenefficiënt is (zie o.m. hoofdstuk 10.5). Een belangrijke aanname van het Oostenrijkse procesmodel is dat de actieve rechter een positieve invloed zou hebben op een effectieve en efficiënte afhandeling van zaken. Recente Nederlandse studies hebben aangetoond dat procedures waarin de rechter actief deelneemt (o.m. doordat een comparitie gehouden wordt) sneller afgehandeld worden. Daarnaast was Franz Klein van mening dat een actieve rechter zou voorkomen dat partijen en advocaten zich te kwader trouw zouden gedragen. Er is wel enige steun voor deze aanname. Zo zijn de meeste Amerikaanse advocaten van mening dat Amerikaanse rechters actiever dienen op te treden om misbruik van procesrecht te voorkomen.

Andere aspecten van het Oostenrijkse recht lijken minder succesvol. Het is met name de vraag of waarheidsvinding in de Oostenrijkse procespraktijk goed uit de verf is gekomen. Er zijn weinig prikkels voor advocaten en rechters om echt op zoek te gaan naar de onderliggende feiten (hoofdstuk 10.5). Oostenrijkse rechters zijn tevens huiverig gebleken om buiten het partijdebat te treden teneinde de feiten juist vast te stellen (hoofdstuk 2.3.1.4).

Eerder is betoogd dat het (federale) Amerikaanse procesrecht twee fundamentele kenmerken heeft: 1) jury rechtspraak en 2) het *adversarial system*. De civiele jury moet bovenal gezien worden als een democratische instelling. Zij is het toonbeeld van volkssoevereiniteit en een waarborg tegen rechterlijke willekeur.

Het *adversarial system* vergt dat de rechter en de jury zich afzijdig opstellen in de procedure. Dit uitgangspunt kan met name door huidige psychologische inzichten gelegitimeerd worden. Doordat degene die de beslissing over de feiten neemt zich in het proces lijdelijk opstelt, kan worden voorkomen dat er vroegtijdig een beslissing wordt genomen die gebaseerd is op onvolledige informatie. Door zich afzijdig op te stellen is het mogelijk dat de beslisser zich niet laat leiden door vooroordelen en daadwerkelijk onpartijdig blijft. Voorts biedt een systeem waarin de rechter zich afzijdig houdt de partijen voldoende ruimte om gehoord te worden.

Het federale Amerikaanse systeem heeft kenmerken van de reactieve staat en blijkt voornamelijk gericht te zijn op het oplossen van geschillen. Daarnaast is het procesrecht in de V.S. in grotere mate dan in andere landen democratisch gelegitimeerd. Het verzamelen, bewijzen en vaststellen van de feiten dient hoofdzakelijk om te komen tot een legitieme en eerlijke manier van geschiloplossing.

Het Amerikaanse proces kan gekenmerkt worden als democratisch. Veel rechters worden verkozen of politiek benoemd. De lekenrechtspraak geniet bovendien groot aanzien. Toch dienen er wel enige kanttekeningen geplaatst te worden. Ten eerste is het zeer de vraag of het verkiezen of politiek benoemen van rechters tot gevolg heeft dat burgers de rechtspraak als legitiem ervaren. Daarnaast is het aantal trials de laatste decennia sterk afgenomen. In de Federale rechtbanken wordt in slechts 1% van alle aangebrachte zaken een jury samengesteld.

Er is geen empirisch bewijs dat aantoont dat het Amerikaanse *adversarial system* tot gevolg heeft dat het Amerikaanse systeem door de procespartijen als eerlijker wordt gezien dan de Nederlandse en Oostenrijkse systemen. Nederlandse en Amerikaanse studies laten zelfs zien dat het optreden van de rechter door advocaten en procespartijen vaak gewaardeerd wordt.

Het is zeer de vraag of het *adversarial system* ertoe bijdraagt om te komen tot een correcte vaststelling van de feiten. Enerzijds worden de partijen geprikkeld om de feiten grondig te onderzoeken. Anderzijds hebben de partijen er ook belang bij ongunstige informatie te verhullen. Daarnaast is er gegronde reden om aan te nemen dat het *adversarial system* in de V.S. negatieve gevolgen heeft voor de onafhankelijkheid van getuigen en deskundigen.

Hoewel empirische vergelijkende studies niet beschikbaar zijn, is er gegronde reden om aan te nemen dat procederen in de V.S. duurder is dan in Oostenrijk en Nederland. Zo leidt het gebruik van jury's tot hoge kosten. Daarnaast hebben de ruime *discovery* regels tot gevolg dat de omvang van een geschil eerder toe- dan af neemt. In hoofdstuk 10 heb ik betoogd dat in het Amerikaanse systeem partijen geprikkeld worden om te veel geld te besteden aan het verzamelen en bewijzen van feiten.

Afsluitende opmerkingen

Er zijn grote verschillen in de wijze waarop de feiten in het proces verzameld, bewezen en vastgesteld worden. Dit boek heeft tot doel gehad deze verschillen in kaart te brengen. Tevens hoop ik dat dit boek een bijdrage heeft geleverd aan het begrijpen van deze verschillen. Ik heb betoogd dat afzonderlijke regels in samenhang bestudeerd dienen te worden. Daarnaast is aangegeven hoe men vanuit een historische, ideologische of economische invalshoek procesrecht regels kan begrijpen. Aan de hand van het beschikbare empirische materiaal is ook aangegeven hoe het onderzoek naar de feiten in de rechtspraktijk verloopt.

Hoewel dit boek hoofdzakelijk beschrijvend van aard is, kan rechtsvergelijkend onderzoek tevens bijzonder nuttig zijn om inspiratie op te doen teneinde een bestaand procesmodel te verbeteren. Empirisch onderzoek dat in één land is verricht, kan mogelijk ook inzichten opleveren die elders gebruikt kunnen worden. In zekere zin is de wereld één groot juridisch laboratorium waar op grote schaal geëxperimenteerd wordt. Ik hoop dat dit boek tevens van waarde mag zijn om bestaande systemen te verbeteren. Zo kunnen de Oostenrijkse bepalingen inzake *discovery* en de Amerikaanse bepalingen aangaande het vrijgeven van een *mandatory expert report* dienen als bron van inspiratie om het Nederlandse rechtssysteem te verbeteren.

BIBLIOGRAPHY

Note: this bibliography lists the short titles with prepositions in alfabetical order. This implies that Van Boneval Faure 1893 is listed under the V and De Groot 2004 under the D.

ACTL & IAALS 2008
Interim Report on the joint project of the American College of Trial Lawyers task force on discovery and the Institute for the Advancement of the American Legal System, August 2008, available at <www.actl.com>, last consulted in February 2010.

Adams 1998
Adams, M.A., 'Civil Procedure in the USA and Civil Law Countries', in: P. Newman (ed.), *The New Palgrave Dictionary of Economics and the Law,* London: MacMillan Reference Ltd, 1998, p. 245-250.

Adviescommissie Burgerlijk Procesrecht 2008
Adviescommissie Burgerlijk Procesrecht, 'Advies over gegevensverstrekking in burgerlijke zaken ('discovery')', 16 *TCR,* 2008, p. 123-130.

Allen 1997
Allen, C.J.W., *The Law of Evidence in Victorian England,* Cambridge Studies in Legal History, Cambridge: Cambridge University Press, 1997.

American Law Institute 1942
American Law Institute, *Model Code of Evidence,* Philadelphia: American Law Institute, 1942.

American Law Institute & Unidroit 2006
American Law Institute, and Unidroit, *Principles of Transnational Civil Procedure,* Cambridge: Cambridge University Press, 2006.

Andrews 1995
Andrews, N., 'The Adversarial Principle: Fairness and Efficiency: Reflections on the Recommendations of the Woolf Report', in: A.A.S. Zuckerman and R. Cranston (eds.), *Reform of Civil Procedure,* Oxford: Clarendon Press, 1995, p. 169-183.

Andrews 2003a
Andrews, N., *English Civil Procedure, Fundamentals of the New Civil Justice System,* Oxford: Oxford University Press, 2003.

Anema 1940
Anema, A., *Mr. C. Asser's Handleiding tot de Beoefening van het Nederlandsch Burgerlijk Recht, Vijfde Deel, van Bewijs,* 4e dr., Zwolle: W.E.J. Tjeenk Willink, 1940.

Anonymous 1891
Anonymous, 'De lijdelijkheid des rechters', 52 *Themis, Verzameling van bijdragen tot de kennis van het Publiek- en Privaatrecht,* 1891, p. 381-398.

Anonymous 1898
Anonymous, 'Burgerlijk Procesrecht', 59 *Themis, Verzameling van bijdragen tot de kennis van het Publiek- en Privaatrecht,* 1898, p. 321-400.

Ariens 1992
Ariens, M., 'Progress is our only Product: Legal Reform and the Codification of Evidence', 17 *Law and Social Inquiry,* 1992, p. 213-257.

Asser 2002
Asser, W.D.H., 'Bewijsrecht in de nieuwe wet', 4 *Praktisch Procederen,* 2002, p. 26-30.

Asser 2009
Asser, W.D.H., 'Burgerlijk (proces)recht: bewijs in het spanningsveld tussen rechter en partijen', in: W.D.H. Asser, J.F. Nijboer & Y.E. Schuurmans, *Bewijsrecht: het bewijs geregeld? Preadvies voor de Nederlandse Vereniging Voor Rechtsvergelijking,* Nijmegen: Wolf Legal Publishers, p. 11-60.

Asser & Vranken 1999
Asser, W.D.H. & Vranken, J.B.M., *Verantwoordelijk procederen, gedachten over fundamentele vernieuwing van het procesrecht, preadvies voor de Nederlandse Vereniging van Procesrecht,* Den Haag: Boom Juridische uitgevers, 1999.

Asser, Groen, Vranken & Tzankova 2003
Asser, W.D.H., Groen, H.A., Vranken, J.B.M. & Tzankova, I.N., *Een nieuwe balans, interimrapport fundamentele herbezinning Nederlands burgerlijk procesrecht,* Den Haag: Boom Juridische uitgevers, 2003.

Asser, Groen, Vranken & Tzankova 2006
Asser, W.D.H., Groen, H.A., Vranken, J.B.M. & Tzankova, I.N., *Uitgebalanceerd, eindrapport fundamentele herbezinning Nederlands burgerlijk procesrecht,* Den Haag: Boom Juridische uitgevers, 2006.

Axelrod 1984
Axelrod, R., *The Evolution of Cooperation,* rev. ed.., Basic Books, 1984 (reprint 2006).

Bahrick, Hall & Berger 1996
Bahrick, H.P., Hall, L.K. & Berger, St.A., 'Accuracy and Distortion In Memory For High School Grades', 7(5) *Psychological Science,* 1996, p. 265-271.

Bajons 2003
Bajons, E.M., 'Österreich', in: H. Nagel & E.M. Bajons (eds.), *Beweis-Preuve-Evidence,* Baden: Nomos Verlagsgesellschaft, 2003, p. 427-475.

Bajons 2005
Bajons, E.M., 'Civil Procedure for Austria Revisited. An Outline of recent Austrian Civil Procedure Reforms', in: N. Trocker & V. Varano (eds.), *The Reforms of Civil Procedure in Comparative Perspective,* Torino: G. Giappichelli Editore, 2005, p. 115-129.

Baker 2002
Baker, J.H., *An introduction to English legal history,* 4th ed., London: Butterworths LexisNexis, 2002.

Ballon 2004
Ballon, O.J., *Einführung in das österreichische Zivilprozessrecht – Streitiges Verfahren,* 10. Aufl., Graz: Leykam, 2004.

Barendrecht & Van Den Reek 1994
Barendrecht, J.M. & Van Den Reek, W.A.J.P., 'Exhibitieplicht en bewijsbeslag', 6155 *WPNR,* 1994, p. 739-745.

Baumgartner 2009
Baumgartner, S.P., 'Civil Procedure Reform in Switzerland and the Role of Legal Transplants', *Paper presented at the Conference of the International Association of Procedural Law,* 2009.

Baur 1970
Baur, F., 'Zeit- und Geistesströmungen im Prozeß', *JBl,* 1970, p. 445-453.

Becker 2005
Becker, H.G.G., *Procesgids, De Etstoel van Drenthe,* Hilversum: Verloren, 2005.

Beekhuis 1960
Beekhuis, C.H., 'Het nieuwe ontwerp bewijsrecht', 121 *RM Themis,* 1960, p. 573-600.

Beekhuis 1970
Beekhuis, C.H., 'Het nieuwe Nederlandse wetsontwerp voor het bewijsrecht', *Tijdschrift voor het privaatrecht*, 1970, p. 83-147.

Belliotti 1988
Belliotti, R.A., 'Our Adversary System: In Search for a Foundation', 1(1) *Canadian Journal of Law and Jurisprudence*, 1988, p. 19-34.

Benesh 2006
Benesh, S.C., 'Understanding Public Confidence in American Courts', 68(3) *The Journal of Politics*, 2006, p. 697-707.

Bentham 1781
Bentham, J., *Introduction to the Principles of Morals and Legislation*, 1781.

Bentham 1827
Bentham, J., *Rationale of Judicial Evidence (Reprint)*, New York: Garland Publishing, 1827/1978.

Bentham 1838
Bentham, J., 'Principles of Judicial Procedure, With the Outlines of a Procedure Code', in: J. Bowring (ed.), *The Works of Jeremy Bentham, Volume II*, Edinburgh: Simpkin, Marshall & Co., 1843, p. 1838-1843.

Bentham 1843
Bentham, J., 'General View of a Complete Code of Law', in: J. Bowring (ed.), *The Works of Jeremy Bentham*, Edinburgh: Simpkin, Marshall & Co., 1843, Vol. III.

Berkvens 2006
Berkvens, A.M.J.A., ''Zur Abkurtzung unnötiger Processualweitläufigkeiten', Een bijdrage over de geschiedenis van het Hof van Appel te Thorn 1718-1795', 74(1-2) *The Legal History Review*, 2006, p. 121-148.

Berkvens 2010a
Berkvens, A.M.J.A., *Procesgids Overkwartier*, Hilversum: Verloren, 2010 (forthcoming).

Berkvens 2010b
Berkvens, A.M.J.A., *Procesgids Maastricht*, Hilversum: Verloren, 2010 (forthcoming).

Berman 1961
Berman, H.J., 'The Historical Background of American Law', in: H.J. Berman (ed.), *Talks on American Law*, New York: Vintage Books, 1961, p. 1-17.

Bernstein 1987
Bernstein, H.L., 'Whose Advantage After All? A Comment on the Comparison of Civil Justice Systems', 21 *U.C. Davis L. Rev.*, 1987-1988, p. 587-603.

Best 2004
Best, A., *2004-2 Cumulative Supplement to Wigmore on Evidence*, New York: Aspen Publishers, 2004.

Biden 1992
Biden, J.R., 'Equal, Accessible, Affordable Justice Under Law: The Civil Justice Reform Act of 1990', 1 *Cornell J. L. and Pub. Pol'y*, 1992, p. 1-24.

Bienert-Nießl 2003
Bienert-Nießl, R., *Materiellrechtliche Auskunftpflichten im Zivilprozeß*, Juristische Schriftenreihe Band 196; Wien: Verlag Österreich, 2003.

Birks 1996
Birks, P., 'Equity in Modern Law', 26 *Western Australian Law Review*, 1996, p. 1-99.

Blackstone 1768
Blackstone, W., *Commentaries on the Laws of England*, Oxford: Clarendon Press, 1768.

Block, Parker, Vyborna & Dusek 2000
Block, M.K., Parker, J.S., Vyborna, O. & Dusek, L., 'An Experimental Comparison of Adversarial versus Inquisitorial Procedural Regimes', 2(1) *American Law and Economics Review*, 2000, p. 170-194.

Bloemers 1948
Bloemers, J.H.F., 'Het Onderzoek naar de Feiten in het Burgerlijk Proces', 22(30) *NJB*, 1948, p. 554-557.

Blume 1965
Blume, W.W., 'Adoption in California of the Field Code of Civil Procedure: A Chapter in American Legal History', 17 *Hastings L.J.*, 1965-1966, p. 701-726.

Boccaccini 2002
Boccaccini, M.A., 'What Do We Really Know about Witness Preparation', 20 *Behavioral Sciences and the Law*, 2002, p. 161-189.

Bodanksy 1981
Bodansky, J.N., 'The Abolition of the Party-Witness Disqualification: An Historical Survey', 70 *Ky. L. Rev*, 1981-1982, p. 91-130.

Böhm 1978
Böhm, P., 'Der Streit um die Verhandlungsmaxime', in: H. Coing (ed.), *Ius Commune, Veröffentlichen des Max-Planck-Instituts für Europäische Rechtsgeschichte*, Frankfurt am Main: Vittorio Klostermann, 1978, VII, p. 136-159.

Böhm 1990
Böhm, P., 'Zivilprozess und Ideologie im nationalsozialistischen Staat', in: U. Davy (ed.), *Nationalsozialismus und Recht,* Wien: Wirtschaftsverlag Dr. Anton Orac, 1990, p. 149-172.

Bosch-Boesjes 1991
Bosch-Boesjes, J.E., *Lijdelijkheid in geding,* Deventer: Kluwer, 1991.

Boudreau & McCubbins 2006
Boudreau, C. & Mccubbins, M.D., 'The Battle for Truth: Theory and Experiments Regarding Competition and the Adversarial System', (Research Paper No. 07-63) *SSRN,* <http://ssrn.com/abstract=929546>, 2006.

Bourcier & De Bonis 1999
Bourcier, D. & De Bonis, M., *Les Paradoxes de l'Expertise,* Le Plessis-Robinson: Institut Synthethélabo, 1999.

Bourdeaux 1937
Bourdeaux, M.H., *Code de Procédure Civile, Petite Collection Dalloz,* Paris: Jurisprudence Générale Dalloz, 1937.

Bovend'Eert & Kortmann 2008
Bovend'Eert, P.P.T. & Kortmann, C.A.J.M., *Rechterlijke organisatie, rechters en rechtspraak,* Alphen aan de Rijn: Kluwer, 2008.

Brazil 1980
Brazil, W.D., 'Civil Discovery: Lawyers' Views of Its Effectiveness, Its Principle Problems and Abuses', *Am. B. Found. Res. J.,* 1980, p. 787-902.

Broers 2000
Broers, E.J.M.F.C., *Procesgids Staatse Raad van Brabant,* Hilversum: Verloren, 2000.

Bundesministerium 2009
The Austrian Judicial System, Vienna: Bundesministerium für Justiz (<http://www.justiz.gv.at>), 2009.

Burbank 1997
Burbank, St.B. & Silberman, L.J., 'Civil Procedure Reform in Comparative Context: The United States of America', 45 *Am. J. Comp. L.,* 1997, p. 675-704.

Burbank 2004
Burbank, St.B., 'Judgment in Federal Civil Cases: Drifting Toward Bethlehem or Gomorrah?', 1(3) *Journal of Empirical Legal Studies,* 2004, p. 591-626.

Burnham 2006
Burnham, W., *Introduction to the Law and Legal System of the United States,* 4th ed., St. Paul: West Group, 2006.

Cadiet 2005
Cadiet, L., 'The New French Code of Civil Procedure', in: C.H. van Rhee (ed.), *European Traditions in Civil Procedure,* Antwerp: Intersentia, 2005, p. 49-68.

Calamandrei 1956
Calamandrei, P., *Procedure and Democracy,* New York: New York University Press, 1956.

Cannon 2006
Cannon, A.J., 'Effective Fact-finding', 25 *Civil Justice Quaterly,* 2006, p. 327-348.

Cappelletti 1970
Cappelletti, M., 'Social and Political Aspects of Civil Procedure - Reforms and Trends in Western and Eastern Europe', 69 *Mich. L. Rev.,* 1970-1971, p. 847-886.

Carey-Miller & Beaumont 1993
Carey-Miller, D.L. & Beaumont, P.R. (eds.), *The Option Of Litigating In Europe,* London: The United Kingdom National Committee of Comparative Law, 1993.

Caroli 1907
Caroli, J.P.A.N., 'In hoever behooren de hoofdbeginselen waarop de burgerlijke procedure in eersten aanleg berust te worden gewijzigd?', *HNJV,* 1907, p. 1-125.

Carpi & Cartells 2008
Carpi, F. & Cartells, M. (eds.), *Oral and Written Proceedings: Efficiency in Civil Procedure,* Valencia: University of Valencia, 2008.

Carrington 2003
Carrington, P.D., 'The Civil Jury and American Democracy', 13 *Duke J. Comp. & Int'l L.,* 2003, p. 79-94.

Cecil & Willging 1994
Cecil, J.S. & Willging, T.E., 'Accepting Daubert's Invitation: Defining a Role for Court-Appointed Experts in Assessing Scientific Validity', 43 *Emory Law J.,* 1994, p. 995-1070.

Cecil, Miletich & Cort 2001
Cecil, J.S., Miletich, D.P. & Cort, G., *Trends in Summary Judgment Practice: A Preliminary Analysis,* Fed. Judicial Ctr., 2001.

CEPEJ 2007
Cepej, *Enforcement of Court Decisions in Europe,* available at <http://www.coe.int>, 2007.

CEPEJ 2008
European Commission for the Efficiency of Justice (Cepej), *European Judicial Systems (2006 data),* Council of Europe (<http://www.coe.int/>), 2008.

Chase 2005
Chase, O.G., *Law, Culture, and Ritual, Disputing Systems in Cross-Cultural Context*, New York: New York University Press, 2005.

Chase, Herschkoff, Silberman, Taniguchi & Varano 2007
Chase, O.G., Herschkoff, H., Silberman, L., Taniguchi, Y. & Varano, V., *Civil Litigation in Comparative Context*, Thomson West, 2007.

Claessens 2008
Claessens, S., *Free Movement of Lawyers in the European Union*, Nijmegen: Wolf Legal Publishers, 2008.

Clark 1935
Clark, Ch.E., 'A New Federal Civil Procedure II', 44 *Yale L.J.*, 1935, p. 1291-1310.

Clark 1947
Clark, Ch.E., *Handbook of the Law of Code Pleading*, Hornbook Series; St. Paul, Minn.: West Publishing, 1947.

Clark 1951
Clark, Ch.E., 'The Summary Judgment', 36 *Minnesota Law Review*, 1951-1952, p. 567-579.

Clark 1958
Clark, Ch.E., 'The Federal Rules of Civil Procedure: 1938-1958', 58 *Colum. L. Rev.*, 1958, p. 435-451.

Clark 1961
Clark, Ch.E., 'Federal Procedural Reform and States' Rights; to a More Perfect Union', 40 *Tex. L. Rev.*, 1961, p. 211-229.

Clark 1993
Clark, D.S., 'The Civil Law Influence on David Dudley Field's Code of Civil Procedure', in: M. Reimann (ed.), *The Reception of Continental Ideas in the Common Law World 1820-1920*, Berlin: Duncker & Humblot, 1993, p. 63-87.

Clemenz & Gugler 1998
Clemenz, G. & Gugler, K., 'Gesamtwirtschaftliche Entwicklung und Prozeß-verhalten', in: P. Lewisch & W.H. Rechberger (eds.), *100 Jahre ZPO, Ökonomische Analyse des Zivilprozesses*, Wien: Manz, 1998, p. 23-37.

Coe & Morse 1941
Coe, M.V. & Morse, L.W., 'Chronology of the Development of the David Dudley Field Code', 27 *Cornell L. Q.*, 1941-1942, p. 238-245.

Colquit 2001
Colquitt, J.A., 'On the Dimensionality of Organizational Justice: A Construct Validation of a Measure', 86(3) *Journal of Applied Psychology*, 2001, p. 386-399.

Cooter & Rubinfeld 1995
Cooter, R.D. & Rubinfeld, D.L., 'Reforming the New Discovery Rules', 84 *Geo. L. J.*, 1995-1996, p. 61-89.

Cooter & Ulen 2004
Cooter, R. & Ulen, Th., *Law & Economics*, Prentice Hall, 2004.

Cousy 2008
Cousy, H., 'Civil liability of the (forensic) expert: a problem or a non-issue', in: G.G. Hesen, S.D. Lindenbergh & G.E. van Maanen (eds.), *Schadevaststelling en de rol van de deskundige*, Deventer: Kluwer, 2008, p. 261-268.

Cowan 2003
Cowan, J.D., 'What attorneys think of jury trial innovations', 86(4) *Judicature*, 2003, p. 192-199.

Coxe 1901
Coxe, A.C., 'The Trials of Jury Trials', 1 *Columbia Law Review*, 1901, p. 286-297.

Crèvecouer 1975
Crèvecouer, B., 'Partij- en getuigeverklaringen in een nieuw bewijsrecht', 49(39) *NJB*, 1975, p. 1271-1277.

Crombag 2006
Crombag, H.F.M., 'Over tunnelvisie', 29 *Trema*, 2006, p. 273-279.

Damaska 1986
Damaska, M.R., *The Faces of Justice and State Authority*, New Haven/London: Yale University Press, 1986.

Damaska 1991
Damaska, M.R., 'On Hearsay and its Analogues', 76 *Minnesota Law Review*, 1991-1992, p. 425-459.

Damaska 1997a
Damaska, M.R., *Evidence Law Adrift*, New Haven/London: Yale University Press, 1997.

Damaska 1997b
Damaska, M.R., 'The Uncertain Fate of Evidentiary Transplants: Anglo-American and Continental Experiments', 45 *Am. J. Comp. L.*, 1997, p. 839-852.

Dammingh 2009
Dammingh, J.J., 'De veranderende rol van de rechter in het civiele proces', in: L.E. De Groot-van Leeuwen, P.H.P.H.M.C. van Kempen, C.J.M. Klaassen & R.J.N. Schlössels (eds.), *Eén procesrecht? Over convergentie en divergentie van het burgerlijk, straf- en bestuursprocesrecht*, Deventer: Kluwer, 2009, p. 9-22.

Damrau 1988
Damrau, J., 'Der Einfluß der Ideen Franz Kleins auf den Deutschen Zivilprozeß', in: H. Hofmeister (ed.), *Forschungsband Franz Klein*, Wien: Manz, 1988, p. 158-171.

De Damhouder 1626
De Damhouder, J., *Practyke in Civile Saeken*, 's Gravenhage, 1626.

De Groot 2004
De Groot, G., 'De rechter contracteert niet', 12 *TCR*, 2004, p. 79-86.

De Groot 2008
De Groot, G., *Het Deskundigenadvies in de Civiele Procedure*, Deventer: Kluwer, 2008.

De Hartogh 1965
De Hartogh, S.L.F., 'Partijen als getuigen', 39 *NJB*, 1965, p. 367-368.

De Hoop 1989
De Hoop, J.L., 'Het voorlopig getuigenverhoor, het voorlopig deskundigenbericht en het deskundigenbericht', 5938 *WPNR*, 1989, p. 714-720.

De Tocqueville 1899
De Tocqueville, A., *Democracy in America*, <http://xroads.virginia.edu/~HYPER/DETOC/toc_indx.html>, last consulted in August 2007, 1899.

De Tombe-Grootenhuis 1993
De Tombe-Grootenhuis, M., *De Partij-Getuigenverklaring in het Burgerlijk Procesrecht*, Arnhem: Gouda Quint, 1993.

De Vrieze 1943
De Vrieze, J., 'Werking van den decisoiren eed', 17(12) *NJB*, 1943, p. 113-118.

De Waal 2009
De Waal, F., *The Age of Empathy*, New York: Harmony Books, 2009.

Deixler-Hübner 1992
Deixler-Hübner, A., 'Fortschreitender Einsatz von Sachverständigen, Notwendigkeit und Gefahr?', *Österreichische Richterzeitung*, 1992, p. 251.

Denijs 1936
Denijs, K., 'Kan het verhoor op vraagpunten niet uit zijn nutteloosheid worden opgeheven?', 10(33) *NJB*, 1936, p. 741-747.

Devine, Clayton, Dunford, Seying & Pryce 2001
Devine, D.J., Clayton, L.D., Dunford, B.B., Seying, R. & Pryce, J., 'Jury Decision Making, 45 years of Empirical Research on Deliberating Groups', 7(3) *Psychology, Public Policy, and Law*, 2001, p. 622-727.

Diephuis, Eshuis & De Heer-De Lange 2010
Diephuis, B.J., Eshuis, R.J.J., & De Heer-De Lange, N.E., *Rechtspleging Civiel en Bestuur 2008*, The Hague: Raad voor de Rechtspraak, WODC, 2010, available at <www.wodc.nl>, last consulted in April 2010.

Dietrich 1913
Dietrich, F.S., 'The New Federal General Equity Rules', 76 *Central Law Journal*, 1913, p. 281-287.

Dilcher 1959
Dilcher, H., 'Die prozessuale Verwendungsbefugnis, ein Beitrag zur Lehre vom "rechtswidrigen" Beweismittel', 158 *AcP*, 1959, p. 469-503.

Dirkzwager 1960
Dirkzwager, D.P., 'Rapport aan de Algemene Raad inzake het Ontwerp Bewijsrecht', 40 *Advocatenblad*, 1960, p. 184-207.

Dixon & Gill 2002
Dixon, L. & Gill, B., *Changes in the Standards for Admitting Expert Evidence in Federal Civil Cases Since the Daubert Decision*, Santa Monica: RAND Institute for Civil Justice, 2002.

Djankov, La Porta, Lopez-de-Silanes & Shleifer 2003
Djankov, S., La Porta, R., Lopez-De-Silanes, F. & Shleifer, A., 'Courts', 117 *The Quarterly Journal of Economics*, 2003, p. 453-517.

Dobie 1938
Dobie, A.M., 'The Federal Rules of Civil Procedure', 25(3) *Virginia Law Review*, 1938-1939, p. 261-315.

Drabbe 1962
Drabbe, L.W.M.M., 'Een voorlopig partij-verhoor?', 36 *NJB*, 1962, p. 973-980.

Drabbe 1965
Drabbe, L.W.M.M., 'Partijen als getuigen', 39 *NJB*, 1965, p. 297-306.

Dubinsky 2008
Dubinsky, P.R., 'Is Transnational Litigation a Distinct Field? The Persistence of Exceptionalism in American Procedural Law', 44(1) *Stan. J. Int'l L.*, 2008, p. 1-56.

Duff 2008
Duff, J.C., *2007 Annual Report of the Director: Judicial Business of the United States Courts*, Washington D.C.: Government Printing Office, 2008.

Duin, Warnaar & Leijten 1990
Duin, S.C., Warnaar, C.M. & Leijten, J.P., 'Het rendement van de ambtshalve bevolen comparitie na antwoord', 13 *Trema*, 1990, p. 401-407.

Dwyer 2004
Dwyer, D.M., 'Changing Approaches to Expert Evidence in England and Italy', 2(4) *International Commentary on Evidence*, 2004, Article 4.

Dwyer 2007a
Dwyer, D.M., 'The Effective Management of Bias in Civil Expert Evidence', 26(1) *Civil Justice Quaterly*, 2007, p. 57-78.

Dwyer 2007b
Dwyer, D.M., 'Expert Evidence in English Civil Courts, 1550-1800', 28(1) *The Journal of Legal History*, 2007, p. 93-118.

Dwyer 2008
Dwyer, D.M., 'Legal Remedies for the Negligent Expert', 12 *International Journal of Evidence and Proof*, 2008, p. 93-115.

Eckardt 2008
Eckardt, M., 'Explaining Legal Change from an Evolutionary Economics Perspective', 9(4) *German Law Journal*, 2008, p. 437-464.

Edmond 2003
Edmond, G., 'After Objectivity: Expert Evidence and Procedural Reform', 25 *Sydney Law Review*, 2003, p. 131-164.

Ekelmans 2005
Ekelmans, J., 'De exhibitieplicht in de praktijk: de ruime mogelijkheden tot opvragen van bescheiden', 13 *TCR*, 2005, p. 59-67.

Ekelmans 2007
Ekelmans, J., *De exhibitieplicht in kort bestek*, Zutphen: Paris, 2007.

Endemann 1891
Endemann, W., 'Civilprozessverfahren nach der kanonistischen Lehre', 15 *ZZP*, 1891, p. 179-330.

Engelmann 1927
Engelmann, A., *History of Continental Civil Procedure*, Translated and edited by R.W. Millar, Boston: Little, Brown and Company, 1927.

Van Erkelens & Jungmann 1892
Van Erkelens, W. & Jungmann, J.A., *Verslag der Handelingen van de Staten-Generaal gedurende de zitting van 1832-1833*, 's Gravenhage: Martinus Nijhoff, 1892.

Ervo, Gräns & Jokela 2009
Ervo, L., Gräns, M. & Jokela, A. (eds.), *Europeanization of Procedural Law*, Groningen: Europa Law Publishing, 2009.

Eshuis 1998
Eshuis, R.J.J., *Een kwestie van tijd*, Onderzoek en Beleid, 171, Den Haag: WODC, 1998.

Eshuis 2007
Eshuis, R.J.J., *Het Recht in Betere Tijden*, Onderzoek en Beleid, 254, Meppel: Boom, 2007.

Eshuis 2009
Eshuis, R.J.J., *De daad bij het woord, Het naleven van rechterlijke uitspraken en schikkingsafspraken*, SDU, Raad voor de Rechtspraak, WODC, Research Memoranda 1, 2009.

Ewald 1994
Ewald, W., 'Comparative Jurisprudence (I): What was it Like to Try a Rat', 143 *U. Pa. L. Rev.*, 1994-1995, p. 1889-2147.

Ewald 1995
Ewald, W., 'Comparative Jurisprudence (II): The Logic of Legal Transplants', 43 *Am. J. Comp. L.*, 1995, p. 489-510.

Farnsworth 2007
Farnsworth, W., *The Legal Analist*, Chicago: University of Chicago Press, 2007.

Fasching 1982
Fasching, H.W., 'Die Zivilverfahrensnovelle 1981', 104(3-4) *JBl*, 1982, p. 68-79, p. 121-131.

Fasching 1988
Fasching, H.W., 'Weiterentwicklung des österreichischen Zivilprozeßrechts im Lichte der Ideen Franz Kleins', in: H. Hofmeister (ed.), *Forschungsband Franz Klein*, Wien: Manz, 1988, p. 97-117.

Fasching 1990
Fasching, H.W., *Lehrbuch des österreichischen Zivilprozeßrechts*, 2. Aufl., Wien: Manz, 1990.

Fasching 1998
Fasching, H.W., '100 Jahre österreichische Zivilprozeßgesetze', in: P.G Mayr (ed.), *100 Jahre österreichische Zivilprozeßgesetze,* Wien: Verlag Österreich, 1998, p. 17-32.

Fasching & Konecny 2002-2005
Fasching, H.W. & Konecny, A. (eds.), *Kommentar zu den Zivilprozessgesetzen*, Wien: Manz, 2002/2003/2004/2005.

Faure & Moerland 2006
Faure, M.G. & Moerland, C.A.R., *Griffierechten*, Meppel: Boom Juridische uitgevers, 2006.

Faure, Hartlief & Philipsen 2006
Faure, M.G., Hartlief, T. & Philipsen, N.J., *Resultaatgerelateerde beloningssystemen voor advocaten Een vergelijkende beschrijving van beloningssystemen voor advocaten in een aantal landen van de Europese Unie en Hong Kong,* Den Haag/Maastricht: WODC METRO, 2006.

Feith 1892
Feith, R., *De Decisoire Eed,* Leiden: S.C. van Doesburgh, 1892.

Feith Committee 1901
Feith Committee, *Ontwerp tot herziening van de eerste zes Titels van het Vierde Boek van het Burgerlijk Wetboek,* 's Gravenhage: Gebr. Belinfante, 1901.

Fernhout 1981
Fernhout, F.J., *Een Korte Beschrijving van het Staatsrecht van de Duitse Democratische Republiek,* Groningen: Doctoraal Scriptie, 1981.

Fernhout 2005
Fernhout, F.J., 'N partijgetuigen = 0 getuigen', 85 *Advocatenblad,* 2005, p. 482-484.

Field 1891
Field, D.D., 'Law Reform in the United States and Its Influence Abroad', 25 *The American Law Review,* 1891, p. 515-535.

Field Code 1850
The Code of Civil Procedure of the State of New-York, (Reprint of the Complete Code of 1850), New Jersey: The Lawbook Exchange Ltd., 1998.

Finman 1962
Finman, T., 'The Request For Admissions in Federal Civil Procedure', 71(3) *The Yale Law Journal*, 1962, p. 371-436.

Flanders 1978
Flanders, S., 'Case Management in Federal Courts, Some Controversies and Some Results', 4 *Just. Sys. J.*, 1978-1979, p. 147-165.

Frank 2004
Frank, M.J., 'Florida's Request for Admission Rule: 150 Years on the Road to Inconsistency, Ineffectiveness and Appellate Nullification', 6 *Fla. Coastal L. Rev.*, 2004, p. 255-330.

Frankel 1980
Frankel, M.E., 'Partisan Justice (selected fragments)', in: S. Landsman (ed.), *Readings on Adversarial Justice: The American Approach to Adjudication,* St. Paul: West Publishing, 1980, p. 53-59.

Friedenthal, Kane & Miller 2005
Friedenthal, J.H., Kane, M.K. & Miller, A.R., *Civil Procedure,* 4th ed., Hornbook Series, St. Paul: Thomson West, 2005.

Friedman 1985
Friedman, L.M., *A History of American Law,* 2nd ed., New York: Simon and Schuster/Touchstone Books, 1985.

Friedman 1998
Friedman, L.M., 'Some notes on the Civil Jury in Historical Perspective', 48 *DePaul Law Review*, 1998, p. 201-220.

Friedman 2002
Friedman, R.D., 'No Link: The Jury and the Origins of the Confrontation Right and the Hearsay Rule', in: J.W. Cairns & G. McLeod (eds.), *The Dearest Birth Right of the People of England, The Jury in the History of the Common Law,* Oxford: Hart, 2002, p. 93-100.

Friedman 2008
Friedman, L.M., 'The Litigation Revolution', in: M. Grossberg & C. Tomlins (eds.), *The Cambridge History of Law in America,* Cambridge: Cambridge University Press, 2008, Vol. 3, p. 175-194.

Froeb & Kobayashi 2001
Froeb, L.M. & Kobayashi, B.H., 'Evidence Production in Adversarial vs. Inquisitorial Regimes', 70 *Economic Letters*, 2001, p. 267-272.

Fucik 1998
Fucik, R., 'Die Rolle des Richters in der ZPO. Eine Ökonomische Analyse', in: P. Lewisch & W.H. Rechberger (eds.), *100 Jahre ZPO, Ökonomische Analyse des Zivilprozesses,* Wien: Manz, 1998, p. 191-202.

Füger Von Rechtborn 1865
Füger Von Rechtborn, M., *Der Beweis durch Eide im Civilprocesse: Nach allgemeinen Grundsätzen der Beweistheorie mit Erl. diesfälligen Bestimmungen der Gerichtsordnungen Oesterreichs,* Wien: Lechner, 1865.

Fuller 1961
Fuller, L.L., 'The Adversary System', in: H.J. Berman (ed.), *Talks on American Law,* New York: Vintage Books, 1961, p. 30-44.

Fuller 1978
Fuller, L.L., 'The Forms and Limits of Adjudication', 92 *Harvard Law Review,* 1978, p. 353-409.

Funke 1986
Funke, A.P., 'Enige notities inzake wetsontwerp 10 377, Nieuwe Regeling Bewijsrecht', 60 *NJB,* 1986, p. 964-965.

Galanter 2004
Galanter, M., 'The Vanishing Trial: An Examination of Trials and Related Matters in Federal and State Courts', 1(3) *Journal of Empirical Legal Studies,* 2004, p. 459-570.

Genn 1999
Genn, H., *Paths to Justice: What People Do and Think About Going to Law,* Oxford: Hart Publishing, 1999.

Giesen 1999
Giesen, I., *Bewijslastverdeling bij beroepsaansprakelijkheid,* Deventer: W.E.J. Tjeenk Willink, 1999.

Gilliland & Dunn 2008
Gilliland, V. & Dunn, J.C., 'Decision making in Civil Disputes: The Effects of Legal Role, Frame, and Perceived Chance of Winning', 3(7) *Judgment and Decision Making,* 2008, p. 512-527.

Ginsburg 1965
Ginsburg, R.B., 'Civil Procedure - Basic Features of the Swedish System', 14 *American Journal of Comparative Law,* 1965-1966, p. 336-346.

Glaser 1859
Glaser, J., *Über Friedensgerichte und das Verfahren in geringfügigen Rechtssachen,* Wien: Tandler, 1859.

Glaser 1968
Glaser, W.A., *Pretrial Discovery and the Adversary System*, New York: Russell Sage Foundation, 1968.

Goldman 2005
Goldman, A.I., 'Legal Evidence', in: M.P. Golding & W.A. Edmundson (eds.), *The Blackwell Guide to the Philosophy of Law and Legal Theory*, Oxford: Blackwell Publishing, 2005, p. 163-175.

Goriely, Moorhead & Abrams 2002
Goriely, T., Moorhead, R. & Abrams, P., *More Civil Justice? The Impact of the Woolf Reforms on Pre-action Behaviour*, Research Study 43: The Law Society and Civil Justice Council, 2002.

Gourevitch 2004
Gourevitch, V. (ed.), *Rousseau, The Social Contract and other later Political Writings*, Cambridge: Cambridge University Press, 2004.

Government Draft 1907
Government Draft, *Ontwerp van Wet tot herziening van de eerste zes Titels van het Vierde Boek van het Burgerlijk Wetboek, Invoeringswet, 1ste Aflevering*, 's Gravenhage: Gebr. Belinfante, 1907.

Gras & Wiersema 1986
Gras, E. & Wiersema, H.W., 'Het nieuwe bewijsrecht - W.O. 10377 - nadert de eindstreep', 60 *NJB*, 1986, p. 520-523.

Gratama Committee 1921a
Gratama Committee, *Ontwerp tot Vaststelling van een Wetboek van Burgerlijke Rechtsvordering, I (Wetboek)*, 's Gravenhage: Gebr. Belinfante, 1921.

Gratama Committee 1921b
Gratama Committee, *Ontwerp tot Vaststelling van een Wetboek van Burgerlijke Rechtsvordering, II (Toelichting)*, 's Gravenhage: Gebr. Belinfante, 1921.

Gravelle & Rees 1998
Gravelle, H. & Rees, R., *Microeconomics*, 2nd ed., London: Longman, 1998.

Greene, Downey & Goodman 1999
Greene, E., Downey, C. & Goodman, J., 'Juror Decisions about Damages in Employment Discrimination Cases', 17 *Behavioral Sciences and the Law*, 1999, p. 107-121.

Groeneveld & Klijn 2002
Groeneveld, J.P. & Klijn, A., *Nieuwe Burgerlijke Rechtsvordering*, Amsterdam: NIPO, 2002.

Gross 1986
Gross, S.R., 'The American Advantage: The Value of Inefficient Litigation', 85 *Mich. L. Rev.*, 1986-1987, p. 734-755.

Gross 1991
Gross, S.R., 'Expert Evidence', *Wis. L. Rev.*, 1991, p. 1114-1231.

Haardt 1949
Haardt, W.L., 'Boekbeschouwingen', 110 *RM Themis*, 1949, p. 315-320.

Haardt 1951
Haardt, W.L., 'De beginselen van het burgerlijk bewijs', *HNJV*, 1951, p. 51-107.

Haardt 1959
Haardt, W.L., 'Het Ontwerp Bewijsrecht', 33(23) *NJB*, 1959, p. 465-502.

Hale 1713
Hale, M., *The History and Analysis of the Common Law of England*, New Jersey: The Lawbook Exchange (Reprint in 2000), 1713.

Hamilton, Madison & Jay 1788
Hamilton, A., Madison, J. & Jay, J., *The Federalist or The New Constitution*, New York: J. and A. McLean, 1788.

Hanly 2005
Hanly, C., 'The Decline of Civil Jury Trial in Nineteenth-Century England', 26(3) *The Journal of Legal History*, 2005, p. 253-278.

Hans & Albertson 2003
Hans, V.P. & Albertson, S., 'Empirical Research and Civil Jury Reform', 78 *Notre Dame L. Rev*, 2003, p. 1497-1523.

Hansen 2000
Hansen, M., 'Expertise to Go', 86 *ABA J*, 2000, p. 44-52.

Harrison 2001
Harrison, J.L., 'Reconceptualising the Expert Witness: Social Costs, Current Controls and Proposed Responses', 18 *Yale J. on Reg.*, 2001, p. 253-314.

Hartzfeld 1907
Hartzfeld, C.A.J., 'In hoever behooren de hoofdbeginselen waarop de burgerlijke procedure in eersten aanleg berust te worden gewijzigd? (Deel 1)', *HNJV*, 1907, p. 126-194.

Hay 1995
Hay, B.L., 'Effort, Information, Settlement, Trial', 24 *J. Legal Stud.*, 1995, p. 29-62.

Hazard 1997
Hazard, G.C., 'From Whom No Secrets Are Hid', 76 *Tex. L. Rev.*, 1997-1998, p. 1665-1694.

Hazard 1999
Hazard, G.C., 'Abuse of Rights: A Summary View of the Common Law Systems', in: M. Taruffo (ed.), *Abuse of Procedural Rights, Comparative Standards of Procedural Fairness*, The Hague/London/Boston: Kluwer Law International, 1999, p. 35-107.

Hebly 1992
Hebly, J.M., *The Netherlands Civil Evidence Act 1988 and Related Provisions of the Netherlands Law of Evidence*, Deventer: Kluwer, 1992.

Heimerl 1857
Heimerl, F., *Darstellung der gesetzlichen Bestimmungen über die Parteien und deren Stellvertreter im civilgerichtlichen Verfahren in Oesterreich*, Wien, 1857.

Helmholz 2004
Helmholz, R.H., *The Oxford History of the Laws of England, Volume 1, The Canon Law and Ecclesiastical Jurisdiction from 597 to th 1640s*, Oxford: Oxford University Press, 2004.

Hempenius-Van Dijk 2004
Hempenius-Van Dijk, B.S., *Hof van Friesland, de hoofdlijnen van het procederen in civiele zaken voor het Hof van Friesland zowel in eerste instantie als in appel*, Procesgidsen; Hilversum: Verloren, 2004.

Hepburn 1907
Hepburn, Ch. Mcguffy, 'The Historical Development of Code Pleading in America and England', in: Association of American Law Schools (ed.), *Select Essays in Anglo-American Legal History*, Boston: Little, Brown and company, 1907-1909, Chapter 39, p. 643-690.

Herman 2008
Herman, S., 'The Louisiana Code of Practice (1825): A Civilian Essai Among Anglo-American Sources', 12(1) *EJCL*, 2008, p. 1-25.

Herrmann 1995
Herrmann, F.R., 'The Establishment of a Rule Against Hearsay in Romano-Canonical Procedure', 36 *Va. J. Int'l L.*, 1995-1996, p. 1-52.

Herzog 1967
Herzog, P., *Civil Procedure in France*, Columbia University School of Law Project on International Procedure; The Hague: Martinus Nijhoff, 1967.

Hess 1999
Hess, B., 'Abuse of Procedural Rights in Germany and Austria', in: M. Taruffo (ed.), *Abuse of Procedural Rights: Comparative Standards of Procedural Fairness,* The Hague/ London/Boston: Kluwer Law International, 1999, p. 151-180.

Hess 2005
Hess, B., 'Comparative Analysis of the National Reports', in: M. Andenas, B. Hess & P. Oberhammer (eds.), *Enforcement Agency Practice in Europe,* London: British Institute of International and Comparative Law, 2005, p. 25-46.

Heuer & Penrod 1994
Heuer, L. & Penrod, S., 'Trial Complexity: A Field Investigation of Its Meaning and Its Effects', 18 *Law & Hum.Behav.*, 1994, p. 29-51.

Heuer & Penrod 1996
Heuer, L. & Penrod, S., 'Increasing Juror Participation in Trials through Note taking and Question asking', 79(5) *Judicature*, 1996, p. 256-262.

Hidma 1981
Hidma, T.R., 'Nog iets over de getuige eed', 55 *NJB*, 1981, p. 1054-1056.

Hidma & Rutgers 2004
Hidma, T.R. & Rutgers, G.R., *Bewijs*, 8th ed., Pitlo, Het Nederlands Burgerlijk Recht; Deventer: Kluwer, 2004.

Higginbotham 2002
Higginbotham, P.E., 'So Why Do We Call Them Trial Courts?', 55 *SMU L. Rev.*, 2002, p. 1405-1426.

Holdsworth 1907
Holdsworth, W.S., 'The Development of Written and Oral Pleading', in: Association of American Law Schools (ed.), *Select Essays in Angelo-American Legal History,* Boston: Little, Brown and company, 1907-1909, p. 614-642, Chapter 38.

Honigman 1959
Honigman, J.L., 'Edson R. Sunderland's Role in Michigan Procedure', 58 *Mich. L. Rev.*, 1959-1960, p. 13-19.

Hoogenbergh 1938
Hoogenbergh, P.H.M., 'Proceshervorming', 12(41) *NJB*, 1938, p. 931-941.

Hopf 2004
Hopf, G., 'Das Zivilrechts-Mediations-Gesetz', *ÖJZ*, 2004, p. 41-51.

Hough 1918
Hough, Ch.M., 'Due Process of Law To-Day', 32 *Harv. L. Rev.*, 1918-1919, p. 218-233.

Huang 2003
Huang, K.-Ch., *Introducing Discovery into Civil Law*, Durham: Carolina Academic Press, 2003.

Huber & Gordon 2004
Huber, G.A. & Gordon, S.C., 'Accountability and Coercion: Is Justice Blind when It Runs for Office?', 48(2) *American Journal of Political Science*, 2004, p. 247-263.

Hugenholtz 2006
Hugenholtz, W. & Heemskerk, W.H., *Hoofdlijnen van Nederlands Burgerlijk Procesrecht*, 21st ed., Den Haag: Elsevier, 2006.

Ingelse 2004
Ingelse, P. (ed.), *Commentaren op fundamentele herbezinning*, Nijmegen: Ars Aequi Libri, 2004.

Israel 2004
Israel, S.M., *Taking and Defending Depositions*, Philidelphia: ALI ABA, 2004.

Issacharoff 1995
Issacharoff, S., *Should there be Rules of Procedure?*, Leiden: Leiden University Institute of Anglo-American Law, 1995.

Jaarverslag 2006
De Rechtspraak, *Jaarverslag 2006*, available at <www.rechtspraak.nl>, last consulted in February 2010.

Jaarverslag 2008
De Rechtspraak, *Jaarverslag 2008*, available at <www.rechtspraak.nl>, last consulted in February 2010.

Jacob 1982
Jacob, J.I.H., *The Reform of Civil Procedural Law and other Essays in Civil Procedure*, London: Sweet and Maxwell, 1982.

Jacob 2004
Jacob, Sir R., 'Court-appointed Experts v Party Experts: Which is Better?', 23 *Civil Justice Quaterly*, 2004, p. 400-407.

Jacobs 1955
Jacobs, N.L., 'The Uniform Rules of Evidence', 10(3) *Rutgers L. Rev*, 1955, p. 485-500.

Jelinek 1991
Jelinek, W., 'Einflüsse des österreichischen Zivilprozessrechts auf andere Rechtsordnungen', in: W.J. Habscheid (ed.), *Das deutsche Zivilprozessrecht und seine Ausstrahlung auf andere Rechtsordnungen: Grundlagen- und Landesberichte*, Bielefeld: Gieseking-Verlag, 1991, p. 41-89.

Jenks 1949
Jenks, E., *A Short History of English Law*, 6th ed., London: Methuen & Co. Ltd., 1949.

Johnston & Lufrano 2001
Johnston, R.G. & Lufrano, S., 'The Adversary System as a Means of Seeking Truth and Justice', 35 *J. Marshall L. Rev.*, 2001-2002, p. 147-161.

Jolowicz 2000
Jolowicz, J.A., *On Civil Procedure*, Cambridge: Cambridge University Press, 2000.

Jolowicz 2003
Jolowicz, J.A., 'Adversarial and Inquisitorial Models of Civil Procedure', 52 *International and Comparative Law Quarterly*, 2003, p. 281-295.

Jongbloed 2002
Jongbloed, A.W., *Inleiding nieuw burgerlijk procesrecht*, Den Haag: Boom Juridische uitgevers, 2002.

Jongbloed 2005
Jongbloed, A.W., 'The Netherlands, 1838-2005', in: C.H. van Rhee (ed.), *European Traditions in Civil Procedure*, Antwerp: Intersentia, 2005, p. 69-95.

Joseph 2002
Joseph, G.P., 'Expert Approaches', 28(4) *Litigation*, 2002, p. 20-25.

Jurgens & Tromp 2009
Jurgens, M. & Tromp, J.W.M., 'Minister en Raad vor de rechtspraak: bezint eer ge begint! Is concentratie van rechtspraak bij de gerechten in eerste aanleg noodzakelijk?', 32(5) *Trema*, 2009, p. 182-188.

Kagan 2003
Kagan, R.A., *Adversarial Legalism, the American Way of Law*, Cambridge: Harvard University Press, 2003.

Kahn-Freud 1974
Kahn-Freund, O., 'On Uses and Misuses of Comparative Law', 37(1) *Mod. L. Rev.*, 1974, p. 1-27.

Kakalik, Dunworth, Hill, McCaffrey, Oshiro, Pace & Vaiana 1996
Kakalik, J.S., Dunworth, T., Hill, L.A., McCaffrey, D., Oshiro, M., Pace, N.M. & Vaiana, M.E., *Just, Speedy, and Inexpensive? An Evaluation of Judicial Case Management Under the Civil Justice Reform Act*, RAND Monograph Report; RAND Corporation, 1996.

Kakalik, Hensler, McCaffrey, Oshiro, Pace & Vaiana 1996
Kakalik, J.S., Hensler, D.R., McCaffrey, D.F., Oshiro, M., Pace, N.M. & Vaiana, M.E. (eds.), *Discovery Management, Further Analysis of the Civil Justice Reform Act Evaluation Data*, RAND Monograph Report; RAND Corporation, 1996.

Kalven 1964
Kalven, H., 'The Dignity of the Civil Jury', 50 *Virginia Law Review*, 1964, p. 1055-1075.

Kalven & Zeisel 1971
Kalven, H. & Zeisel, H., *The American Jury*, Phoenix Edn., Chicago: The University of Chicago Press, 1971.

Kane 1964
Kane, R.F., 'The Work-Product Doctrine - Cornerstone of The Adversary System', 31 *Ins. Counsel J.*, 1964, p. 130-134.

Kaplan 1961
Kaplan, B., 'Trial by Jury', in: H.J. Berman (ed.), *Talks on American Law*, New York: Vintage Books, 1961, p. 44-54.

Kaplow & Shavell 1996
Kaplow, L. & Shavell, S., 'Accuracy in the Assessment of Damages', 39 *J. L. & Econ*, 1996, p. 191-210.

Kaser & Hackl 1996
Kaser, M. & Hackl, K., *Das Römische Zivilprozessrecht*, 2nd ed., München: C.H. Beck, 1996.

Katzenmeier 2002
Katzenmeier, C., 'Aufklärungs-/Mitwerkungspflicht der nicht beweislasteten Partei', 57 *JZ*, 2002, p. 533-540.

Keith Murnighan 1992
Keith Murnighan, J., *Bargaining Games*, New York: William Morrow, 1992.

Kessler 2004
Kessler, A.D., 'Our Inquisitorial Tradition', 90 *Cornell L. Rev.*, 2004-2005, p. 1181-1276.

Klaassen 2002
Klaassen, C.J.M., 'Spreken is zilver, zwijgen is fout, De waarheidsplicht van artikel 21 NRv', 76(30) *NJB*, 2002, p. 1450-1458.

Klaassen 2009
Klaassen, C.J.M., 'Feitengaring en bewijslevering in de civiele procedure', in: L.E. De Groot-van Leeuwen, P.H.P.H.M.C. van Kempen, C.J.M. Klaassen & R.J.N. Schlössels (eds.), *Eén procesrecht? Over convergentie en divergentie van het burgerlijk, straf- en bestuursprocesrecht*, Deventer: Kluwer, 2009, p. 57-85.

Klang 1948
Klang, H., 'Der Zivilprozeßgesetze in der Praxis. Errinerungen eines alten Richters', in: J. Gerö (ed.), *Festschrift zur Fünfzigjahrfeier der Österreichischen Zivilprozessordnung*, Wien: Manz, 1948, p. 84-108.

Klein 1885
Klein, F., *Die schuldhafte Parteihandlung: Eine Untersuchung aus dem Civilprocessrechte*, Wien: Toeplitz & Deuticke, 1885.

Klein 1891
Klein, F., *Pro Futuro, Betrachtungen über Probleme der Civilprocessreform in Österreich*, Leipzig/Wien: Franz Deuticke, 1891.

Klein 1900
Klein, F., *Vorlesungen über die Praxis des Civilprocesses*, Wien: Manz, 1900.

Klein 1901
Klein, F., 'Zeit- und Geistesströmungen im Prozesse (Vortrag 1901)', *Reden, Vortragen, Aufsatze, Briefe*, Wien: Manz, 1927, p. 117-138.

Klein & Engel 1927
Klein, F. & Engel, F., *Der Zivilprozess Oesterreichs*, Mannheim: J. Bensheimer, 1927.

Klicka 1992
Klicka, T., 'Aufklärungspflichten der Prozeßparteien im österreichischen Zivilprozeßrecht', 114(4) *JBl*, 1992, p. 231-237.

Klicka 1995
Klicka, T., *Die Beweislastverteilung im Zivilverfahrensrecht*, Wien: Manz, 1995.

Kobayashi & Parker 2000
Kobayashi, B.H. & Parker, J.S., 'Civil Procedure: General', in: B. Bouckaert & G. de Geest (eds.), *Encyclopedia of Law and Economics*,V, Cheltenham: Edward Elgar, 2000, No. 7000, 1-27.

Kodek 2001
Kodek, G.E., 'Die Verwertung rechtswidriger Tonbandaufnahmen und Abhörergebnisse im Zivilverfahren. Zugleich ein Beitrag zur Verwertbarkeit rechtswidrig erlangter Beweismittel', *ÖJZ*, 2001, p. 281-334.

Kohl 1971
Kohl, A., *Procès Civil et Sincérité*, La Haye: Martinus Nijhoff, 1971.

Kohl 1984
Kohl, A., *Roman Law Systems*, International Encyclopedia of Comparative Law, Vol. XVI; Tübingen: J.C.B. Mohr, 1984.

Konecny 1984
Konecny, A., 'Zur Erweiterung der Verbesserungsvorschriften durch die Zivilverfahrens-Novelle 1983', 106(1-2) *JBl*, 1984, p. 13-25, p. 61-72.

König 1982
König, B., 'Bemerkungen zur Regierungsvorlage einer Zivilverfahrens-Novelle', 104(15-16) *JBl*, 1982, p. 406-418.

Koriat & Fiedler 2006
Koriat, A. & Fiedler, K., 'Inflation of Conditional Predictions', 135(3) *Journal of Experimental Psychology*, 2006, p. 429-447.

Koschaker 1953
Koschaker, P., *Europa und das römische Recht*, München: C.H. Beck, 1953.

Köster 1956
Köster, H.K., 'Het Getuigenverhoor in Burgerlijke Zaken', 36 *Advocatenblad*, 1956.

Kötz 2003
Kötz, H., 'Civil Justice Systems in Europe and the United States', 13 *Duke Journal of Comparative & International Law*, 2003, p. 61-77.

Krafka, Dunn, Johnson, Cecil & Miletich 2002
Krafka, C., Dunn, M.A., Johnson, M.T, Cecil, J.S. & Miletich, D., *Judge and Attorney Experiences, Practices, and Concerns Regarding Expert Testimony in Federal Civil Trials*, Federal Judicial Centre, 2002.

Kralik 1988
Kralik, W., 'Die Verwirklichung der Ideen Franz Kleins in der Zivilprozessordnung von 1895', in: H. Hofmeister (ed.), *Forschungsband Franz Klein*, Wien: Manz, 1988, p. 89-96.

Krammer 1990
Krammer, H., *Die "Allmacht" des Sachverständigen*, Schriftenreien Niederösterreichischen Juristische Gesellschaft, Wien: Orac, 1990.

Kremer 1999
Kremer, M., *Onrechtmatig verkregen bewijs in civiele zaken*, Deventer: W.E.J. Tjeenk Willink, 1999.

Kremer 2003
Kremer, M., 'Vooralsnog vooral van symbolische betekenis, de waarheids en volledigheidsplicht onder het vernieuwde civiele procesrecht', 83(8) *Advocatenblad,* 2003, p. 332-337.

Kritzer 2001
Kritzer, H.M., 'Lawyer Fees and Lawyer Behavior in Litigation: What does Empirical Literature Really Say', 80 *Tex. L. Rev.,* 2001-2002, p. 1943-1984.

Kritzer 2004
Kritzer, H.M., 'Disappearing Trials? A Comparative Perspective', 1(3) *Journal of Empirical Legal Studies,* 2004, p. 735-754.

Kuhn, Weinstock & Flaton 1994
Kuhn, D., Weinstock, M. & Flaton, R., 'How Well Do Jurors Reason? Competence Dimensions of Individual Variation in a Juror Reasoning Task', 5(5) *Psychological Science,* 1994, p. 289-296.

Lackner 1983
Lackner, H., 'Die Prozessuale Relevanz außerprozessualer Sachverständigengutachten', *ÖJZ,* 1983, p. 518 ff.

Ladd 1942
Ladd, M., 'A Modern Code of Evidence', in: American Law Institute (ed.), *Model Code of Evidence,* Philadelphia: American Law Institute, 1942.

Landsman 1983
Landsman, S., 'Reforming Adversary Procedure: A Proposal Concerning the Psychology of Memory and the Testimony of Disinterested Witnesses', 45 *U. Pitt. L. Rev.,* 1983-1984, p. 547-624.

Landsman 1988
Landsman, S., *Readings on Adversarial Justice: The American Approach to Adjudication,* St. Paul, Minn.: West Publishing Co., 1988.

Landsman 1990
Landsman, S., 'From Gilbert to Bentham: The Reconceptualization of Evidence Theory', 36 *The Wayne Law Review,* 1990, p. 1149-1186.

Landsman 1992
Landsman, S., 'The Civil Jury in America: Scenes from an Unappreciated History', 44 *Hastings L.J.,* 1992-1993, p. 579-620.

Landsman 1999
Landsman, S., 'The Civil Jury in America', 62 *Law & Contemp. Prob.,* 1999, p. 285-304.

Lane 1932
Lane, W.R., 'Twenty Years Under The Federal Equity Rules', 46 *Harvard Law Review*, 1932-1933, p. 638-675.

Lang 1999
Lang, J., *Die Aufklärungspflicht der Parteien des Zivilprozesses vor dem Hintergrund der europäischen Rechtsvereinheitlichung*, Berlin: Duncker & Humblot, 1999.

Langbein 1974
Langbein, J.H., 'Fact Finding in the English Court of Chancery: A Rebuttal', 83 *Yale L.J.*, 1974, p. 1620-1630.

Langbein 1985
Langbein, J.H., 'The German Advantage in Civil Procedure', 52 *University of Chicago Law Review*, 1985, p. 823-866.

Langbein 1993
Langbein, J.H., 'Why Adversary Justice Fails', 1 *Frank G. Raichle Lecture Series on Law in American Society*, 1993, p. 151-173.

Langbein 1995
Langbein, J.H., 'The Influence of Comparative Procedure in the United States', 43 *Am. J. Comp. L.*, 1995, p. 545-554.

Langbein 1996
Langbein, J.H., 'Historical Foundations of the Law of Evidence: A View from the Ryder Sources', 96(5) *Colum. L. Rev.*, 1996, p. 1168-1202.

Langbein 2003
Langbein, J.H., *The Origins of Adversary Criminal Trial*, Oxford: Oxford University Press, 2003.

Langdell 1907
Langdell, C.C., 'The Development of Equity Pleading from Canon Law Procedure', in: Association of American Law Schools (ed.), *Select Essays in Angelo-American Legal History*, Boston: Little, Brown and company, 1907-1909, Chapter 44, p. 753-778.

Le Bailly & Verhas 2005
Le Bailly, M.-Ch. & Verhas, Chr.M.O., *Procesgids, Hoge Raad van Holland, Zeeland en West-Friesland*, Hilversum: Verloren, 2005.

Learned Hand 1901
Learned Hand, 'Historical and Practical Considerations Regarding Expert Testimony', 15 *Harvard Law Review*, 1901, p. 40-58.

Lebre de Freitas 2004
Lebre De Freitas, J.M. (ed.), *The Law of Evidence in the European Union*, The Hague: Kluwer Law International, 2004.

Ledeboer 1888
Ledeboer, R.B., *Eenige Opmerkingen over de Verplichting tot Overlegging van Schriftelijke Bewijsstukken*, Amsterdam: Holdert & Co., 1888.

Ledford 1996
Ledford, K.F., *From General Estate to Special Interest, German Lawyers 1878-1933*, Cambridge: Cambride University Press, 1996.

Leertouwer, Van Tulder, Diephuis, Folkeringa & Eshuis 2005
Leertouwer, E.C., Van Tulder, F.P., Diephuis, B.J., Folkeringa, M. & Eshuis, R.J.J., *Prognosemodellen Justitiële Ketens: Civiel en Bestuur*, Den Haag: Raad voor de Rechtspraak, WODC, 2005.

Leipold 1982
Leipold, D., 'Zivilprozessrecht und Ideologie, am Beispiel der Verhandlungs-maxime', 37(13) *JZ*, 1982, p. 441-448.

Leonard & Gold 2004
Leonard, D.P. & Gold, V.J., *Evidence. A Structured Approach*, New York: Aspen Publishers, 2004.

Lettow Lerner 2000
Lettow Lerner, R., 'The Transformation of the American Civil Trial: The Silent Judge', 42 *Wm. & Mary L. Rev.*, 2000-2001, p. 195-264.

Levy 1965
Levy, J.P. (ed.), *La Preuve, 2, Moyen Age et Temps Modernes*, Bruxelles: Recueils de la Société Jean Bodin pour l'histoire comparative des institutions, 1965.

Lewisch 1998a
Lewisch, P., 'Der Zivilprozeß: Soziales Übel oder soziale Wohltat?', in: P. Lewisch & W.H. Rechberger (eds.), *100 Jahre ZPO, Ökonomische Analyse des Zivilprozesses*, Wien: Manz, 1998, p. 94-119.

Lilly 1987
Lilly, G.C., *An Introduction to the Law of Evidence*, 2nd ed., St. Paul, Minn.: West Publ. Co., 1987.

Lind 1998
Lind, E.A., 'Procedural Justice, Disputing, and Reactions to Legal Authorities', in: A. Sarat (ed.), *Everyday Practices and Trouble Cases*, Evanston: Northwestern University Press, 1998, p. 177-198.

Lind, Kanfer & Earley 1990
Lind, E.A., Kanfer, R. & Earley, P.C., 'Voice, control, and procedural justice: Instrumental and noninstrumental concerns in fairness judgments', 59(5) *Journal of Personality and Social Psychology*, 1990, p. 952-959.

Lind, Maccoun, Ebener, Felstiner, Hensler, Resnik & Tyler 1990
Lind, E.A, Maccoun, R.J., Ebener, P.A., Felstiner, W.L.F., Hensler, D.R., Resnik, J. & Tyler, T.R., 'In the Eye of the Beholder: Tort Litigants' Evaluations of their Experiences in the Civil Justice System', 24(4) *Law & Society Review*, 1990, p. 953-996.

Lind & Tyler 1988
Lind, E.A. & Tyler, T.R., *The Social Psychology of Procedural Justice*, New York/London: Plenum Press, 1988.

Lind, Walker, Kurtz, Musante & Thibaut 1980
Lind, E.A., Walker, L., Kurtz, S., Musante, L. & Thibaut, J., 'Procedure and Outcome Effects on Reactions to Adjudicated Resolution of Conflicts of Interest', 39(4) *Journal of Personality and Social Psychology*, 1980, p. 643-653.

Lindijer 2006
Lindijer, V.C.A., *De Goede Procesorde*, Deventer: Kluwer, 2006.

Linssen 2009
Linssen, J.G.A., 'Bewijsbeslag', in: A.J. Van Der Meer, J.G.A. Linssen & J.C. van Oven, *De reikwijdte van het beslag*, Den Haag: Boom Juridische uitgevers, 2009, p. 21-33.

Liptek 2008
Liptek, A., 'Rendering Justice, With One Eye on Re-election', *New York Times*, 25 May 2008.

Litewsky 1999
Litewski, W., *Der römisch-kanonische Zivilprozess nach den älteren ordines iudiciarii*, Krakow: Wydawnictwo Uniwersytetu Jagiellonskiego, 1999.

Lobban 2002
Lobban, M., 'The Strange Life of the English Civil Jury, 1837-1914', in: J.W. Cairns & G. McLeod (eds.), *The Dearest Birth Right of the People of England, The Jury in the History of the Common Law*, Oxford: Hart Publishing, 2002, p. 173-216.

Locke 1690
Locke, J., *The Second Treatise of Government*, New Jersey: Prentice Hall, 1690.

Lokin & Zwalve 2001
Lokin, J.H.A. & Zwalve, W.J., *Hoofdstukken uit de Europese Codificatie Geschiedenis*, Deventer: Kluwer, 2001.

Lowenfeld 1997
Lowenfeld, A.F., 'Introduction: The Elements of Procedure: Are They Separately Portable', 45 *Am. J. Comp. L.*, 1997, p. 649-656.

Lynch 1963
Lynch, W.C., 'Pre-Trial Procedures', 39 *North Dakota Law Rev.*, 1963, p. 176.

Lysens 2008
Lysens, T., 'Het Deskundigenonderzoek in het Belgisch Recht', in: G.G. Hesen *et al.* (ed.), *Schadevaststelling en de rol van de deskundige,* Deventer: Kluwer, 2008, p. 207-214.

Macey 1994
Macey, J.R., 'Judicial Preferences, Public Choice, and the Rules of Procedure', 23 *J. Legal Stud.*, 1994, p. 627-646.

Macnair 1999
Macnair, M.R.T., *The Law of Proof in Early Modern Equity,* Berlin: Duncker & Humblot, 1999.

Macnair 2007
Macnair, M.R.T., 'Equity and Conscience', 27(4) *Oxford Journal of Legal Studies,* 2007, p. 659-681.

Maelzer 1931
Maelzer, H., *Vernehmung der Partei und Parteieid im reichsdeutschen, österreichischen und künftigen deutschen Zivilprozeß*, 1, Untersuchungen zur deutsch-österreichischen Rechtsangleichung; Leipzig: Robert Noske, 1931.

Maitland 1909
Maitland, F.W., *The Forms of Action at Common Law*, 1909.

Mark 2004
Mark, G.A., 'Ius commune, practick and civil procedure in the sixteenth-century Court of Session', 72(3-4) *The Legal History Review*, 2004, p. 283-295.

Markesinis 1994
Markesinis, B.S., 'Learning from Europe and Learning in Europe', in: B.S. Markesinis (ed.), *The Gradual Convergence,* Oxford: Clarendon Press, 1994, p. 1-32.

Marx 1926
Marx, A.J., 'Comparitie van Partijen', 1(38) *NJB*, 1926, p. 563-568, p. 579-585.

Materialien 1897
Materialien zu den neuen österreichischen Zivilprozessgesetzen, Wien: Manz, 1897.

Maxeiner 2006
Maxeiner, J.R., 'Legal Indeterminacy Made in America: U.S. Legal Methods and the Rule of Law', 41(2) *Valparaiso University Law Review*, 2006, p. 517-589.

Mayr 2004
Mayr, P.G, 'Das Beweisrecht in Österreich', in: J.M. Lebre de Freita (ed.), *The Law of Evidence in the European Union*, The Hague: Kluwer, 2004, p. 33-64.

McEwan 1998
McEwan, J., *Evidence and the Adversarial Process*, 2nd ed., Oxford: Hart, 1998.

McKenna & Wiggins 1998
McKenna, J.A. & Wiggins, E.C., 'Empirical Research on Discovery', 39 *B.C. L. Rev.*, 1998, p. 785-809.

McMahon 1960
McMahon, H.G., 'The Louisiana Code of Civil Procedure', 21 *La. L. Rev.*, 1960-1961, p. 1-40.

Meier 1986
Meier, P., 'Damned Liars and Expert Witnesses', 81(394) *Journal of the American Statistical Association*, 1986, p. 269-276.

Meijers 1918
Meijers, E.M., 'De Invloed der Praktijk op de Vorming van het Nederlands Procesrecht', 1 *Tijdschrift voor rechtsgeschiedenis*, 1918, p. 146-170.

Mein, Verberk & Vos 2008
Mein, A.G., Verberk, S. & Vos, J.W., *Communiceren met Justitiabelen*, Den Haag: Raad voor de Rechtspraak/B&A Consulting, 2008.

Merryman 1999a
Merryman, J.H., 'On the Convergence (and Divergence) of the Civil Law and the Common Law', in: J.H. Merryman (ed.), *The Loneliness of the Comparative Lawyer*, The Hague: Kluwer Law International, 1999, p. 15-52.

Merryman 1999b
Merryman, J.H., 'Comparative Law and Scientific Explanation', in: J.H. Merryman (ed.), *The Loneliness of the Comparative Lawyer*, The Hague: Kluwer Law International, 1999, p. 476-502.

Michell & Mandhane 2005
Michell, P. & Mandhane, R., 'The Uncertain Duty of the Expert Witness', 42(3) *Alberta Law Review*, 2005, p. 635-675.

Millar 1923
Millar, R.W., 'The Formative Principles of Civil Procedure', 18 *Ill. L. Rev*, 1923-1924, p. 1-36, p. 94-117, p. 150-168.

Millar 1926
Millar, R.W., 'Some Comparative Aspects of Civil Pleading Under Anglo-American and Continental Systems', 12 *A.B.A.J.*, 1926, p. 401-407.

Millar 1936
Millar, R.W., 'The Old Regime and the New in Civil Procedure', 14 *N.Y.U. L.Q. Rev.*, 1936-1937, p. 1-27, p. 197-226.

Millar 1937
Millar, R.W., 'The Mechanisms of Fact-Discovery: A Study in Comparative Civil Procedure', 32 *Ill. L. Rev*, 1937-1938, p. 261-294, p. 424-455.

Millar 1952
Millar, R.W., *Civil Procedure of the Trial Court in Historical Perspective*, New Jersey: Clark, Reprint by The Lawbook Exchange, 1952.

Miller 1997
Miller, G.P., 'The Legal-Economic Analysis of Comparative Civil Procedure', 45 *Am. J. Comp. L.*, 1997, p. 905-918.

Miller 2003
Miller, A.R., 'The Pretrial Rush to Judgment: Are the "Litigation Explosion", "Liability Crisis", and Efficiency Cliches Eroding Our Day in Court and Jury Trial Commitments?', 78 *N.Y.U. L. Rev.*, 2003, p. 982-1134.

Mnookin 2007
Mnookin, J.L., 'Idealizing Science and Demonizing Experts', 52 *Villanova Law Review*, 2007, p. 101-138.

Mondak 1993
Mondak, J.J., 'Institutional Legitimacy and Procedural Justice, Re-examining the Question of Causality', 27 *Law & Society Review*, 1993, p. 599-608.

De Montesquieu 1748
De Montesquieu, Ch., *L'esprit des lois*, 1748.

Moorman van Kappen 1994
Moorman Van Kappen, O., 'Zum Einfluß des Code Civil in den Niederlanden', in: R. Schulze (ed.), *Französisches Zivilrecht in Europa während des 19. Jahrhunderts*, Berlin: Schriften zur Europäischen Rechts- und Verfassungsgeschichte, 1994, 12, p. 177-204.

Morgan 1941
Morgan, E.M., 'The Code of Evidence Proposed by the American Law Institute', 27 *A.B.A.J.*, 1941, p. 539-542.

Morill 1985
Morill, S.S., 'The Illinois Medical Malpractice Reform Act of 1985: A Constitutional Analysis of the Medical Review Panel Procedure', 35 *DePaul Law Review*, 1985-1986, p. 345-390.

Münks 1992
Münks, A., *Vom Parteieid zur Parteivernehmung in der Geschichte des Zivilprozesses*, Heft 85, Prozeßrechtliche Abhandlungen, Köln/Berlin/Bonn/München: Carl Heymanns Verlag KG, 1992.

Mullenix 1993
Mullenix, L.S., 'Discovery in Disarray: The Pervasive Myth of Pervasive Discovery Abuse and the Consequences for Unfounded Rulemaking', 46 *Stan. L. Rev.*, 1993-1994, p. 1393-1446.

Munch-Petersen 1926
Munch-Petersen, H., 'The Social Aspect of Procedure from a European Point of View', 11 *Minnesota Law Review*, 1926-1927, p. 624-635.

Murphy & Tyler 2008
Murphy, K. & Tyler, T.R., 'Procedural Justice and Compliance Behaviour: The Mediating Role of Emotions', 38 *European Journal of Social Psychology*, 2008, p. 652-668.

Murray 1997
Murray, P.L., 'A Comparative Law Experiment', 8(2) *Ind. Int'l Comp. L. Rev.*, 1997-1998, p. 231-260.

Murray 2004
Murray, P.L., 'The Disappearing Massachusetts Civil Jury Trial', 89(2) *Mass. L. Rev.*, 2004, p. 51-61.

Murray 2006
Murray, P.L., 'Die Flucht aus der Ziviljustiz', 11 *ZZPInt*, 2006, p. 295-313.

Murray 2008
Murray, P.L., 'The Privatization of Civil Justice', 91(6) *Judicature*, 2008, p. 272-316.

Murray & Sheldon 2003
Murray, P.L. & Sheldon, J., 'Rethinking the rules of evidentiary admissibility in non-jury trials', 86(5) *Judicature*, 2003, p. 227-231.

Nagel 1951
Nagel, W.H., *De Meineed, strafrechtsociologische beschouwingen*, Amsterdam: De Bezige Bij, 1951.

Nagel & Bajons 2003
Nagel, H. & Bajons, E.M. (eds.), *Beweis, Preuve, Evidence,* Baden: Nomos Verlagsgesellschaft, 2003.

NCES 2006
National Center for Eductaion Statistics, *National Assessment of Adult Literacy, A First Look at the Literacy of America's Adults in the 21st Century*, <http://nces.ed.gov/NAAL/PDF/2006470.PDF> (last consulted in October 2009), 2006.

Nickerson 1998
Nickerson, R.S., 'Confirmation Bias, A Ubiquitous Phenomenon in Many Guises', 2(2) *Review of General Psychology*, 1998, p. 175-220.

Nolen 1941
Nolen, 'De Advocaat en het Proces', 23 *Advocatenblad*, 1941.

Noordziek 1892
Noordziek, J.J.F., *Verslag der handelingen van de Tweede Kamer der Staten-Generaal, gedurende de zitting van 1824-1825*, 's Gravenhage: Martinus Nijhoff, 1892.

Nörr 1973
Nörr, K.W., *Die Literatur Zum Gemeinen Zivilprozess, Erster Band Mittelalter (1100-1500)*, Handbuch der Quellen und literatur der neueren Europäischen Privatrechtsgeschichte, München: C.H. Beck'sche Verlagsbuchhandlung, 1973.

Note 1961
Note, 'Developments In The Law – Discovery', 74 *Harv. L. Rev.*, 1961, p. 940-1072.

Note 1964
Note, 'The Changing Role of the Jury in the Nineteenth Century', 74 *Yale L.J.*, 1964-1965, p. 170-192.

Note 1982
Note, 'Discovery Abuse Under the Federal Rules: Causes and Cures', 92 *Yale L.J.*, 1982-1983, p. 352-375.

Note 1997
Note, 'Developments in the Law: The Civil Jury (I and II)', 110 *Harvard Law Review*, 1997, p. 1408-1443.

Novakovski 2006
Novakovski, T., 'Een functionele substantiëringsplicht: illusie of werkelijkheid?', 167 *RM Themis*, 2006, p. 3-12.

Oberhammer 1993
Oberhammer, P., 'Richtermacht, Wahrheitspflicht und Parteienvertretung, Gesichtspunkte der "Arbeitsgemeinschaft Zivilprozess"', in: W.H. Rechberger & P. Oberhammer (eds.), *Konfliktvermeidung und Konfliktregelung,* Wien: Manz, 1993, p. 31-84.

Oberhammer 1999
Oberhammer, P., 'Parteiaussage, Parteivernehmung und freie Beweiswürdigung am Ende des 20. Jahrhunderts', 113(3) *ZZP*, 1999, p. 295-326.

Oberhammer & Domej 2005
Oberhammer, P. & Domej, T., 'Party Interrogation in Germany, Switzerland and Austria', in: C.H. van Rhee (ed.), *European Traditions in Civil Procedure,* Antwerp: Intersentia, 2005, p. 255-259.

Oberhammer & Domej 2005
Oberhammer, P. & Domej, T., 'Germany, Switzerland and Austria', in: C.H. van Rhee (ed.), *European Traditions in Civil Procedure,* Antwerp: Intersentia, 2005, p. 103-128.

Oberhammer & Domej 2010
Oberhammer, P. & Domej, T., 'Delay in Modern Austrian Civil Procedure and the Legislator's Response', in: C.H. van Rhee (ed.), *Within Reasonable Time: The History of Delay in Civil Procedure,* 2010 (forthcoming).

Ogus 2002
Ogus, A., 'The Economic Basis of Legal Culture: Networks and Monopolization', 22(3) *Oxford Journal of Legal Studies*, 2002, p. 419-434.

Olivier 2000
Olivier, M., 'Modalités pratiques d'application de l'article 278 NCPC', *Gaz. Pal.*, 2000, p. 839-843.

Opzoomer & Levy 1902
Opzoomer, C.W. & Levy, J.A., *Het Burgerlijk Wetboek Verklaard,* 13, 's Gravenhage: Gebr. Belinfante, 1902.

Opzoomer & Levy 1906
Opzoomer, C.W. & Levy, J.A., *Het Burgerlijk Wetboek Verklaard,* 15, 's Gravenhage: Gebr. Belinfante, 1906.

Ostrom, Strickland & Hannaford-Agor 2004
Ostrom, B.J., Strickland, S.M. & Hannaford-Agor, P.L., 'Examining Trial Trends in State Courts: 1976-2002', 1(3) *Journal of Empirical Legal Studies*, 2004, p. 755-788.

Parker 1995
Parker, J.S., 'Daubert's Debut: The Supreme Court, the Economics of Scientific Evidence, and the Adversarial System', 4 *Sup. Ct. Econ. Rev.*, 1995, p. 1-56.

Parker & Kobayashi 2000
Parker, J.S. & Kobayashi, B.H., '7900 Evidence', in: B. Bouckaert & G. de Geest (eds.), *Encyclopedia of Law and Economics*, V, Northhampton: Edward Elgar, 2000.

Parker & Lewisch 1998
Parker, J.S. & Lewisch, P., 'Materielle Wahrheitsfindung im Zivilprozeß', in: P. Lewisch & W.H. Rechberger (eds.), *100 Jahre ZPO, Ökonomische Analyse des Zivilprozesses*, Wien: Manz, 1998, p. 203-223.

Patterson 2005
Patterson, D., 'The When, If, and How of Challenging Expert Testimony in Federal Court', 28 *American J. Trial Advoc.*, 2005-2006, p. 167-197.

Pitlo & Hidma 1981
Pitlo, A. & Hidma, T.R., *Bewijs en Verjaring*, 4, Het Nederlands Burgerlijk Recht, Arnhem: Gouda Quint, 1981.

Plucknett 1956
Plucknett, T.F.T., *A Concise History of the Common Law*, 5th ed., Boston: Little, Brown and Company, 1956.

Pos 1971
Pos, H., 'Pleidooi voor een beperkt partijverhoor onder ede', 46 *NJB*, 1971, p. 193-202.

Posner 1973
Posner, R.A., 'An Economic Approach to Legal Procedure and Judicial Administration', 2(2) *Journal of Legal Studies*, 1973, p. 399-458.

Posner 1992
Posner, R.A., *Economic Analysis of Law*, 4th ed., Boston/Toronto/London: Little, Brown and Company, 1992.

Posner 1993
Posner, R.A., 'What do Judges and Justices Maximize?', 3 *Sup. Ct. Econ. Rev.*, 1993, p. 1-41.

Posner 1999
Posner, R.A., 'An Economic Approach to the Law of Evidence', 51 *Stan. L. Rev.*, 1999, p. 1477-1546.

Post 1907
Post, J.C., 'Bijdrage tot de hervorming van onze burgerlijke rechtsvordering, het Oostenrijkse proces in de praktijk', *Rechtsgeleerd Magazijn Themis*, 1907, p. 369-380.

Pound 1906
Pound, R., 'The Causes of Popular Dissatisfaction with the Administration of Justice', 14 *The American Lawyer*, 1906, p. 445-451.

Poythress 1994
Poythress, N.G., 'Procedural Preferences, Perceptions of Fairness, and Compliance with Outcomes', 18 *Law and Human Behavior*, 1994, p. 361-376.

Priest 1990
Priest, G.L., 'The Role of the Civil Jury in a System of Private Litigation', 1990 *U. Chi. Legal F.*, 1990, p. 161-200.

Priest & Klein 1984
Priest, G.L. & Klein, B., 'The Selection of Disputes For Litigation', 13 *J. Legal Stud.*, 1984, p. 1-55.

Pusey 2000
Pusey, A., 'Judges Rule In Favor Of Juries; Surveys by Morning News', *Dallas Morning News*, 7 May 2000.

Quigley 1989
Quigley, J., 'Socialist Law and the Civil Law Tradition', 37 *Am. J. Comp. L.*, 1989, p. 781-792.

Raitz, Greene, Goodman & Loftus 1990
Raitz, A., Greene, E., Goodman, J. & Loftus, E.F., 'The Influence of Expert Testimony on Juror's Decision Making', 14(4) *Law and Human Behavior*, 1990, p. 385-395.

Ralston 1940
Ralston, E.A., 'Interrogatories on Facts and Articles: A Louisiana Method of Discovery', 15 *Tul. L. Rev.*, 1940-1941, p. 445-155.

Rechberger 1998
Rechberger, W.H., 'Rechtspolitische Ziele und Gestaltungsanliegen der österreichischen Zivilprozeßordnung', in: P. Lewisch & W.H. Rechberger (eds.), *100 Jahre ZPO, Ökonomische Analyse des Zivilprozesses*, Wien: Manz, 1998, p. 53-67.

Rechberger 2000
Rechberger, W.H., *Kommentar zur ZPO*, 2nd ed., Wien: Springer, 2000.

Rechberger 2001
Rechberger, W.H., 'Die Verfahrenskonzentration im Österreichischen Zivilprozess', in: M. Kamil Yildrim (ed.), *Zivilprozessrecht im Lichte der Maxime,* Istanbul: Alkim, 2001, p. 1-14.

Rechberger 2006
Rechberger, W.H., 'Das neue österreichische Schiedsrecht', 119 *ZZP*, 2006, p. 261-278.

Rechberger & Simotta 2003
Rechberger, W.H. & Simotta, D.A., *Grundriss des österreichischen Zivilprocesrechts, Erkenntnisverfahren*, 6., rev. ed., Wien: Manz, 2003.

Rechberger & Simotta 2009
Rechberger, W.H. & Simotta, D.A., *Zivilprozessrecht, Erkenntnisverfahren*, 7th ed., Wien: Manz, 2009.

Reindl 1988
Reindl, P., 'Franz Klein und das Justizministerium', in: H. Hofmeister (ed.), *Forschungsband Franz Klein,* Wien: Manz, 1988, p. 77-88.

Reppy 1954
Reppy, A., *Introduction to Civil Procedure: Actions and Pleading at Common Law,* Buffalo: Dennis & Co, 1954.

Resnik 1982
Resnik, J., 'Managerial Judges', 96 *Harv. L. Rev.*, 1982-1983, p. 374-448.

Resnik 1984
Resnik, J., 'Managerial Judges and Court Delay: the Unproven Assumption', 23 *Judges J.*, 1984, p. 8-11, p. 54-55.

Resnik 1986
Resnik, J., 'Failing Faith: Adjudicatory Procedure in Decline', 53 *U. Chi. L.*, 1986, p. 494-560.

Resnik 1999
Resnik, J., 'Trial as Error, Jurisdiction as Injury: Transforming the Meaning of Article III', 113 *Harv. L. Rev.*, 1999-2000, p. 924-1040.

Resnik 2002
Resnik, J., 'Mediating Preferences: Litigant Preferences for Process and Judicial Preferences for Settlement', *J. Disp. Resol.*, 2002, p. 155-170.

Richter 1991
Richters, H.W., *Schikkingen en Proceskansen*, Rotterdam: Proefschrift, 1991.

Roberts & Hough 2009
Roberts, J.V. & Hough, M., *Public opinion and the jury: an international literature review*, Ministry of Justice Research Series 1/09; <www.justice.gov.uk/publications/research.htm>, 2009.

Rosenberg 1969
Rosenberg, M., 'Changes Ahead in Federal Pretrial Discovery', 45 *F.R.D.*, 1969, p. 479-498.

Rosenberg 1988a
Rosenberg, M., 'The Impact of Procedure - Impact Studies in the Administration of Justice', 51 *Law & Contemp. Prob.*, 1988, p. 13-30.

Rosenberg 1988b
Rosenberg, M., 'Federal Rules of Civil Procedure in Action: Assessing their Impact', 137 *U. Pa. L. Rev.*, 1988, p. 2197-2214.

Rosenberg & King 1981
Rosenberg, M. & King, W.R., 'Curbing Discovery Abuse in Civil Litigation: Enough is Enough', 1981 *BYU L. Rev.*, 1981, p. 579-596.

Rosenberg, Schwab & Gottwald 2004
Rosenberg, L., Schwab, K.H. & Gottwald, P., *Zivilprozessrecht*, 16. Aufl., München: C.H. Beck, 2004.

Russel 2001
Russel, P.H. (ed.), *Judicial Independence in the Age of Democracy: Critical Perspectives from around the World*, Charlottesville: University Press of Virginia, 2001.

Rutgers, Flach & Boon 1988
Rutgers, G.R., Flach, R.J.C. & Boon, G.J., *Parlementaire Geschiedenis van de Nieuwe Regeling van het Bewijsrecht in Burgerlijke Zaken*, Deventer: Kluwer, 1988.

Ruva, McEvoy & Becker Bryant 2007
Ruva, C., McEvoy, C. & Becker Bryant, J., 'Effects of Pre-Trial Publicity and Jury Deliberation on Juror Bias and Source Memory Errors', 21 *Applied Cognitive Psychology*, 2007, p. 45-67.

Salomons 2002
Salomons, F.R., 'Het nieuwe burgerlijk procesrecht', 52 *Ars Aequi*, 2002, p. 347-351.

Saltzburg, Martin & Capra 1998
Saltzburg, S.A., Martin, M.M. & Capra, D.J., *Federal Rules of Evidence Manual*, Charlottesville: Lexis Law Publishing, 1998.

Sarat 1976
Sarat, A., 'Studying American Legal Culture: An Assesment of Survey Evidence', 11 *Law & Socý Rev.*, 1976-1977, p. 427-488.

Satter 1936
Satter, K., 'Das Werk Franz Kleins und sein Einfluss auf die neueren Prozessgesetze', 60 *ZZP*, 1936, p. 272-316.

Schenk 1948
Schenk, W., 'De herziening van het burgerlijk procesrecht', 22 *NJB*, 1948, p. 618-625.

Schmoekel 2000
Schmoekel, M., 'Nikolaus I. und das Beweisrecht im 9. Jahrhundert', in: R.H. Helmholz *et al.* (eds.), *Grundlagen des Rechts,* Paderborn: Ferdinand Schöningh, 2000, p. 53-76.

Schoibl 1987
Schoibl, N.A., *Die Entwicklung des österreichischen Zivilverfahrensrechts*, Frankfurt am Main: Peter Lang GmbH, 1987.

Schünemann & Bandilla 1989
Schünemann, B. & Bandilla, W., 'Perseverance in Courtroom Decisions', in: H. Wegener, F. Lösel & J. Haisch (eds.), *Criminal Behavior and the Justice System, Psychological Perspectives,* New York: Springer Verlag, 1989, p. 181-192.

Schwartz 1898
Schwartz, J.C., *Vierhundert Jahre deutscher Civilproceß-Gesetzgebung,* Berlin: Puttkammer & Mühlbrecht, 1898.

Schwarzer 1989
Schwarzer, W.W., 'The Federal Rules, The Adversary Process, and Discovery Reform', 50 *U. Pitt. L. Rev.*, 1989, p. 703-724.

Schwarzer 1991
Schwarzer, W.W., 'Slaying the Monsters of Cost and Delay: Would Disclosure be More Effective than Discovery?', 74 *Judicature*, 1991, p. 178-183.

Setaer 1989
Setaer, J.K., 'The Barrister and the Bomb: The Dynamics of Cooperation, Nuclear Deterrence, and Discovery Abuse', 69 *B.U. L. Rev.*, 1989, p. 569-657.

Sheppard & Vidmar 1980
Sheppard, B.H. & Vidmar, N., 'Adversary Pretrial Procedures and Testimonial Evidence: Effects of Lawyer's Role and Machiavellianism', 39 *Journal of Personality and Social Psychology*, 1980, p. 320-332.

Shestowsky 2004
Shestowsky, D., 'Procedural Preferences in Alternative Dispute Resolution', 10(3) *Psychology, Public Policy, and Law*, 2004, p. 211-249.

Sijmonsma 2007
Sijmonsma, J.R., *Art. 843a Wetboek van Burgerlijke Rechtsvordering ont(k)leed*, Nijmegen: Ars Aequi Libri, 2007.

Silving 1959
Silving, H., 'The Oath: I', 68(7) *The Yale Law Journal*, 1959, p. 1329-1390.

Smith 2004
Smith, C.E., *Ambtshalve aanvullen van rechtsgronden, Deel 14*, Ars Aequi Cahiers, Privaatrecht, Nijmegen: Ars Aequi Libri, 2004.

Smits 2008a
Smits, J., 'European Private Law and Democracy: a Misunderstood Relationship', in: M. Faure & F. Stephen (eds.), *Essays in the Law and Economics of Regulation in Honour of Anthony Ogus*, Antwerp: Intersentia, 2008, p. 49-59.

Smits 2008b
Smits, J.M., 'Applied Evolutionary Theory: Explaining Legal Change in Transnational and European Private Law', 9(4) *German Law Journal*, 2008, p. 477-491.

Snijders 1996
Snijders, H.J. (ed.), *Access to Civil Procedure Abroad*, The Hague: Kluwer Law International, 1996.

Snijders, Klaassen & Meijer 2007
Snijders, H.J., Klaassen, C.J.M. & Meijer, G.J., *Nederlands Burgerlijk Procesrecht*, 4th rev. ed., Deventer: Kluwer, 2007.

Sofaer 1982
Sofaer, A.D., 'Sanctioning Attorneys for Discovery Abuse Under the New Federal Rules: On The Limited Utility of Punishment', 57 *St. John's L. Rev.*, 1982-1983, p. 680-731.

Sperl 1925
Sperl, H., *Lehrbuch der Bürgerlichen Rechtspflege, 1. Band, 1. Teil*, Wien: Hölder-Pichler-Tempsky U.B., 1925.

Sprung 1976
Sprung, R. & König, B., '"Iura novit curia" und rechtliches Gehör', 98(1) *JBl*, 1976, p. 1-7.

Sprung 1977
Sprung, R., 'Grundlagen des Österreichischen Zivilprozessrechts', 90 *ZZP*, 1977, p. 380-394.

Sprung 1988
Sprung, R., 'Der Lebensweg Franz Kleins', in: H. Hofmeister (ed.), *Forschungsband Franz Klein,* Wien: Manz, 1988, p. 13-78.

Staatscommissie Dorhout Mees 1948
Staatscommissie Dorhout Mees, Report, 'Richtlijnen over de herziening van het burgerlijk procesrecht en de rechterlijke organisatie', 28 *Advocatenblad*, 1948, p. 135-153, p. 186-200.

Stampfer 1998
Stampfer, M., 'Die Zivilprozeßordnung von 1898 vor dem Hintergrund zeitgenössischer sozialer Rechtsgestaltung', in: P. Lewisch & W.H. Rechberger (eds.), *100 Jahre ZPO, Ökonomische Analyse des Zivilprozesses,* Wien: Manz, 1998, p. 69-93.

Star Busmann 1921
Star Busmann, C.W., 'De Nederlandsche Advocatenvereeniging over het Ontwerp-Rechtsvordering', 83/W. 10776 *Weekblad van het Recht*, 1921.

Star Busmann 1938
Star Busmann, C.W., 'Het Burgerlijk Wetboek en het Burgerlijk Proces (Bewijs)', in: P. Scholten & E.M. Meijers (eds.), *Gedenkboek Burgerlijk Wetboek 1838-1938,* Zwolle: Tjeenk-Willink, 1938, p. 611-635.

Star Busmann 1955
Star Busmann, C.W., *Hoofdstukken van Burgerlijke Rechtsvordering,* 2nd rev. ed., Haarlem: De Erven F. Bohn N.V., 1955.

Stein 1970
Stein, P.A., 'Het Wetsontwerp Bewijsrecht', 45 *NJB*, 1970, p. 333-380.

Stein 1987
Stein, H., 'Comparitie na Antwoord', 67(8) *Advocatenblad*, 1987, p. 173-174.

Stein 1988
Stein, P.A., 'Het nieuwe bewijsrecht voor de civiele procedure', 62 *NJB*, 1988, p. 387-395.

Stempel 2001
Stempel, J.W., 'Ullysses Tied to the Generic Whipping Post: the Continuing Odyssey of Discovery "Reform"', 64 *Law & Contemp. Prob.*, 2001, p. 197-252.

Stiefel & Maxeiner 1994
Stiefel, E.C. & Maxeiner, J.R., 'Civil Justice Reform in the United States - Opportunity for Learning from "Civilized" European Procedure Instead of Continued Isolation?', 42 *Am. J. Comp. L.*, 1994, p. 147-162.

Stipanowich 2004
Stipanowich, Th.J., 'ADR and the "Vanishing Trial": The Growth and Impact of "Alternative Dispute Resolution"', 1(3) *Journal of Empirical Legal Studies*, 2004, p. 843-912.

Storme 1994
Storme, M. (ed.), *Rapprochement du droit judiciaire de l'Union européenne/ Approximation of judiciary law in the European Union*, Dordrecht: Nijhoff, 1994.

Striegel 1965
Striegel, L.E., 'Request for Admissions - The Neglected Tool of Discovery', 5 *Washburn L. J.*, 1965, p. 47-61.

Stürner 1976
Stürner, R., *Die Aufklärungspflicht der Parteien des Zivilprozesses*, Tübingen: J.C.B. Mohr, 1976.

Stürner 2001
Stürner, R., 'Transnational Civil Procedure: Discovery and sanctions Against Non-Compliance', 6(4) *Revue de droit Uniforme*, 2001, p. 871-886.

Stürner 2005
Stürner, R., 'The Principles of Transnational Civil Procedure', 69 *Rabels Zeitschrift*, 2005, p. 201-254.

Stürner 2007
Stürner, R., 'Die "Principles of Transnational Civil Procedure"', 11 *ZZP Int*, 2006-2007, p. 381-402.

Subrin 1986
Subrin, S.N., 'How Equity Conquered Common Law: The Federal Rules of Civil Procedure In Historical Perspective', 135 *U. Pa. L. Rev.*, 1986-1987, p. 909-1002.

Subrin 1988
Subrin, S.N., 'David Dudley Field and the Field Code: A Historical Analysis of an Earlier Procedural Vision', 6 *Law and History Review*, 1988, p. 311-373.

Subrin 1994
Subrin, S.N., 'Fudge Points and Thin Ice in Discovery Reform and the Case for Selective Substance-Specific Procedure', 46 *Fla. L. Rev.*, 1994, p. 27-56.

Subrin 1997
Subrin, S.N., 'Fishing Expeditions Allowed: the Historical Background of the 1938 Federal Discovery Rules', 39 *B.C. L. Rev.*, 1997-1998, p. 691-746.

Summers 2000
Summers, R.S., 'Formal Legal Truth and Substantive Truth in Judicial Fact-Finding', in: R.S. Summers (ed.), *Essays in Legal Theory,* Dordrecht: Kluwer, 2000, p. 284-297.

Sunderland 1914
Sunderland, E.R., 'The Inefficiency of the American Jury', 13 *Michigan Law Review,* 1914-1915, p. 302-316.

Sunderland 1916
Sunderland, E.R., 'The Michigan Judicature Act of 1915', 14 *Mich. L. Rev.*, 1916, p. 551-561.

Sunderland 1932
Sunderland, E.R., 'Scope and Method of Discovery Before Trial', 42 *Yale L.J.*, 1932-1933, p. 863-877.

Sunderland 1937
Sunderland, E.R., 'The Theory and Practice of Pre-Trial Procedure', 36 *Mich. L. Rev.*, 1937, p. 215-227.

Sunderland 1938
Sunderland, E.R., 'The New Federal Rules', 45 *W. Va. L. Q.*, 1938-1939, p. 5-30.

Taelman 2003
Taelman, P., 'Het Deskundigenonderzoek in Burgerlijke Zaken', in: G. de Leval *et al.* (eds.), *Gerechtelijk deskundigenonderzoek, de rol van de accountant en de belasting-consulent,* Brugge: die Keure, 2003, p. 61-131.

Taylor 1996
Taylor, R.F., 'A Comparative Study of Expert Testimony in France and the United States: Philosophical Underpinnings, History, Practice and Procedure', 31 *Texas International Law Journal*, 1996, p. 181-213.

Thayer 1898
Thayer, J.B., *Preliminary Treatise on Evidence at the Common Law*, Boston, 1898.

Thibaut & Walker 1975
Thibaut, J. & Walker, L., *Procedural Justice, A Psychological Analysis*, New York: John Wiley & Sons, 1975.

Thibaut & Walker 1978
Thibaut, J. & Walker, L., 'A Theory of Procedure', 66 *Cal. L. Review*, 1978, p. 541-566.

Tissier 1906
Tissier, M.A., 'Le Centenaire du Code de Procédure et Les Projects de Réforme', V *Revue trimestrielle de droit civil*, 1906, p. 625-660.

Tobias 1998
Tobias, C., 'Did the Civil Justice Reform Act of 1990 Actually Expire?', 31 *U. Mich. J. L.*, 1998, p. 887-899.

Tomlin & Cooper 2006
Tomlin, J.T. & Cooper, D., 'When Should Judges Appoint Experts? A Law and Economics Perspective', (bepress Legal Series Paper 1699) <http://law.bepress.com/expresso/eps/1699>, 2006, p. 1-36.

Trenité 1914
Nolst Trenité, J.G.L., 'Proceshervormings-Plannen', 33 *Rechtsgeleerd Magazijn*, 1914, p. 293-296.

Tromp, Jurgens, De Groot-Van Leeuwen & Bovend'Eert 2006
Tromp, J.W.M., Jurgens, M., De Groot-Van Leeuwen, L.E. & Bovend'Eert, P.P.T. (eds.), *Concentratie en specialisatie van rechtspraak: noodzaak of overbodig?*, Deventer: Kluwer, 2006.

Trubek, Sarat, Felstiner, Kritzer & Grossman 1983
Trubek, D.M., Sarat, A., Felstiner, W.L.F., Kritzer, H.M. & Grossman, J.B., 'The Costs of Ordinary Litigation', 31 *UCLA L. Rev*, 1983-1984, p. 72-127.

Twining 2004
Twining, W., 'Diffusion of Law: A Global Perspective', 49 *J. Legal Pluralism & Unofficial L.*, 2004, p. 1-45.

Twining 2006
Twining, W., *Rethinking Evidence, Exploratory Essays*, 2nd ed., Cambridge: Cambridge University Press, 2006.

Tyler 1990
Tyler, T.R., *Why People Obey the Law*, New Haven: Yale University Press, 1990.

Tyler 2001
Tyler, T.R. & Lind, E.A., 'Procedural Justice', in: J. Sanders & V. Lee Hamilton (eds.), *Handbook of Justice Research in Law*, New York: Kluwer Academic/Plenum Publishers, 2001, p. 65-92.

Uzelac 2004
Uzelac, A., 'Accelerating civil proceedings in Croatia', in: C.H. van Rhee (ed.), *The Laws Delay*, Antwerp: Intersentia, 2004, p. 283-314.

Uzelac 2010
Uzelac, A., 'Survival of the Third Legal Tradition?', *Conference Paper International Association of Procedural Law*, 2010 (forthcoming).

Van Bell 1866
Van Bell, C., *Het Bewijs, Volgens het Burgerlijk Regt*, Dordrecht: Blussé en van Braam, 1866.

Van Boneval Faure 1893
Van Boneval Faure, R., *Het Nederlandsche Burgerlijk Procesrecht (1)*, 3rd rev. ed., Leiden: E.J. Brill, 1893.

Van Boneval Faure 1896
Van Boneval Faure, R., *Het Nederlandsche Burgerlijk Procesrecht (4)*, 2nd rev. ed., Leiden: E.J. Brill, 1896.

Van Boneval Faure 1900
Van Boneval Faure, R., *Het Nederlandsche Burgerlijk Procesrecht (2-3)*, 3rd rev. ed., Leiden: E.J. Brill, 1900.

Van Caenegem 1971
Van Caenegem, R.C., 'History of Civil Procedure', in: M. Cappelletti (ed.), *International Encyclopedia of Comparative Law, Volume XVI, Civil Procedure*, Tübingen: J.C.B. Mohr, 1971.

Van Caenegem 2002
Van Caenegem, R.C., *European Law in the Past and the Future*, Cambridge: Cambridge University Press, 2002.

Van Creveld 1940
Van Creveld, I., 'De aanvullende eed alleen partij-eed?', 14(7) *NJB*, 1940, p. 151-154.

Van Creveld 1959
Van Creveld, I., 'Het ontwerp bewijsrecht', 33 *NJB*, 1959, p. 669-675.

Van Deinse 1941
Van Deinse, J.F., 'De wijziging van den procesgang', 15(17) *NJB*, 1941, p. 325-329.

Van den Berg 1997
Van den Berg, B., 'Artikel 2.8.51 en 2.8.53 NRv; invoering van het "eigen deskundigenonderzoek"', 5 *TCR*, 1997, p. 49-55.

Van den Berg 1999
Van den Berg, B., *Deskundigheid in het Geding*, Den Haag: Boom, Juridische uitgevers, 1999.

Van den Bos, Wilke, Lind, & Vermunt 1998
Van den Bos, K., Wilke, H.A.M., Lind, E.A. & Vermunt, R., 'Evaluating Outcomes by Means of the Fair Process Effect: Evidence for Different Processes in Fairness and Satisfaction Judgments', 74(6) *Journal of Personality and Social Psychology*, 1998, p. 1493-1503.

Van den Reek 1997
Van den Reek, W.A.J.P., *Mededelingsplichten in het burgerlijk procesrecht, beschouwingen over de verhouding tussen de rechter en partijen en tussen partijen onderling naar Nedelands en Engels recht*, Deventer: Tjeenk Willink, 1997.

Van der Linden 2008
Van der Linden, J., *Zitten, luisteren en schikken*, Research Memoranda No. 5(4), Raad voor de Rechtspraak, 2008.

Van der Linden 2010
Van der Linden, J., *De civiele zitting centraal: informeren, afstemmen en schikken*, Deventer: Kluwer, 2010.

Van der Linden, Klijn & Van Tulder 2009
Van der Linden, J., Klijn, A. & Van Tulder, F.P., 'Meesterlijk gedrag: leren van compareren', 3 *Rechtstreeks*, 2009, p. 7-45.

Van der S. 1857
Van der S., 'Verschijning van partijen in persoon voor den regter', 4(2) *Themis, Rechtskundig tijdschrift*, 1857, p. 188-198.

Van der Wiel 2004
Van der Wiel, B.T.M., *De rechtsverhouding tussen procespartijen*, Deventer: Kluwer, 2004.

Van Dijk 2007
Van Dijk, Chr.H., 'Hoe te beoordelen of de deskundige deskundig is?', 24(10) *NTBR*, 2007, p. 434-441.

Van Emden 1876
Van Emden, D.S., *Het Wetboek van Burgerlijke Regtsvordering opgehelderd door jurisprudentie van den Hoogen Raad*, Den Haag: Gebr. Belinfante, 1876.

Van Erp 2006
Van Erp, J.G., *Kwantitatieve ontwikkelingen rechtspraak 2000-2005*, WODC Cahier 2006-10, Den Haag: WODC, 2006.

Van Erp, Niemijer, Ter Voert & Meijer 2007
Van Erp, J.G., Niemeijer, E., Ter Voert, M.J. & Meijer, R.F., *Geschilprocedures en rechtspraak in cijfers 2005*, WODC Cahier 2007-8, Den Haag: WODC, 2007.

Van Hooijdonk & Eijsvoogel 2009
Van Hooijdonk, M. & Eijsvoogel, P., *Litigation in the Netherlands*, The Hague: Wolters Kluwer, 2009.

Van Koppen & Malsch 1992
Van Koppen, P.J. & Malsch, M., 'Hoe de verliezer wint', 66 *NJB*, 1992, p. 1101-1104.

Van Koppen & Penrod 2003
Van Koppen, P.J. & Penrod, S. (eds.), *Adversarial versus Inquisitorial Perspectives on Criminal Justice Systems*, Perspectives in Law & Psychology, New York/Dordrecht: Kluwer Academic, 2003.

Van Kuyk 1921
Van Kuyk, J., 'De beteekenis van "gemeen" in de artt. 1922 en 1923 B.W.', 2690 *WPNR*, 1921, p. 301-303.

Van Kuyk 1923
Van Kuyk, J., 'De Nederlandsche Advocaten-Vereeniging over Proceshervorming', (85/W. 11108) *Weekblad van het Recht*, 1923, p. 3-4.

Van Mierlo 1998
Van Mierlo, A.I.M., 'Burgerlijk Procesrecht? Welke commissie had U in gedachten?', 6(2) *TCR*, 1998, p. 21-26.

Van Mierlo & Bart 2002
Van Mierlo, A.I.M. & Bart, F.M., *Parlementaire Geschiedenis Herziening van het Burgerlijk Procesrecht voor Burgerlijke Zaken, in het bijzonder de Wijze van Procederen in Eerste Aanleg*, Deventer: Kluwer, 2002.

Van Mierlo & Van Dam-Lely 2003
Van Mierlo, A.I.M. & Van Dam-Lely, J.H., *Procederen bij dagvaarding in eerste aanleg*, Deventer: Kluwer, 2003.

Van Nispen 1993
Van Nispen, C.J.J.C., *De terloopse hercodificatie van ons burgerlijk procesrecht*, Deventer: Kluwer, 1993.

Van Prooijen, Van den Bos, Lind & Wilke 2006
Van Prooijen, J.W., Van den Bos, K., Lind, E.A. & Wilke, H.A.M., 'How do people react to negative procedures? On the moderating role of authority's biased attitudes', 42 *Journal of Experimental Social Psychology*, 2006, p. 632-645.

Van Rhee 1997
Van Rhee, C.H., *Litigation and Legislation, Civil Procedure at First Instance in the Great Council for the Netherlands in Malines (1522-1559)*, Brussels, 1997.

Van Rhee 1999
Van Rhee, C.H., 'De codificatie van het Burgerlijk Procesrecht in de Verenigde Staten van Amerika', in: J.M. van Buren-Dee *et al.* (eds.), *Privaatrecht en Gros,* Antwerpen/Groningen: 1999, p. 333-342.

Van Rhee 2000a
Van Rhee, C.H., 'Civil Procedure: a European Ius Commune?', 4 *European Review of Private Law,* 2000, p. 589-611.

Van Rhee 2000b
Van Rhee, C.H., 'Ons tegenwoordig sukkelproces', 68(3) *Tijdschrift voor Rechtsgeschiedenis,* 2000, p. 331-346.

Van Rhee 2004
Van Rhee, C.H. (ed.), *The Law's Delay,* Antwerp: Intersentia, 2004.

Van Rhee 2005a
Van Rhee, C.H., 'Der Einfluss des Zivilprozessmodells von Franz Klein in den Niederlanden', in: Bundesministerium für Justiz (ed.), *Franz Klein Symposium. Dokumentation des Symposions zum 150. Geburtstag von Franz Klein am 6. Mai 2004,* Wien: Graz, 2005, p. 19-36.

Van Rhee 2005b
Van Rhee, C.H. (ed.), *European Traditions in Civil Procedure,* Antwerp: Intersentia, 2005.

Van Rhee 2005c
Van Rhee, C.H., 'English Civil Procedure until the Civil Procedure Rules (1998)', in: C.H. van Rhee (ed.), *European Traditions in Civil Procedure,* Antwerp: Intersentia, 2005, p. 129-159.

Van Rhee 2006
Van Rhee, C.H., 'The Influence of the French Code de Procédure Civile(1806) in 19th Century Europe', in: L. Cadiet & G. Canivet (eds.), *De la Commémoration d'un code à l'autre: 200 ans de procédure civile en France,* Paris: LexisNexis/Litec, 2006, p. 129-165.

Van Rhee 2008a
Van Rhee, C.H., 'The Development of Civil Procedural Law in Twentieth Century Europe: From Party Autonomy to Judicial Case Management and Efficiency', in: C.H. van Rhee (ed.), *Judicial Case Management and Efficiency in Civil Litigation,* Antwerp: Intersentia, 2008, p. 11-25.

Van Rhee 2008b
Van Rhee, C.H., 'Dutch Civil Procedural Law in an International Context', in: M. Deguchi & M. Storme (eds.), *The reception and transmission of civil procedural law in the global society,* Antwerp: Maklu, 2008, p. 191-212.

Van Rhee 2008c
Van Rhee, C.H., 'Presumptions in Dutch Private Law (19th and 20th Centuries) within a European Context', in: A.W. Jongbloed (ed.), *The XIIIth World Congress of Procedural Law: The Belgian and Dutch Reports,* Antwerp: Intersentia, 2008, p. 85-101.

Van Rhee & Verkerk 2006
Van Rhee, C.H. & Verkerk, R.R., 'Civil Procedure', in: J. Smits (ed.), *Elgar Encyclopedia of Comparative Law,* Edward Elgar Publishing, 2006, p. 120-134.

Van Rossum 1907
Van Rossum, W., *Het Nederlandsch Wetboek van Burgerlijke Rechtsvordering, verklaard en door formulieren toegelicht,* Groningen: J.B. Wolters, 1907.

Van Tuyll van Serooskerken 1956
Van Tuyll van Serooskerken, M., 'Het Getuigenverhoor in Burgerlijke Zaken', 36 *Advocatenblad,* 1956, p. 317-232.

Veegens 1948
Veegens, J.D., 'Herziening van het procesrecht', 22(29) *NJB,* 1948, p. 485-511.

Veegens & Oppenheim 1921
Veegens, J.D. & Oppenheim, A.S., *Schets van het Nederlandsch Burgerlijk Recht,* 3rd ed., Haarlem: H.D. Tjeenk Willink & Zoon, 1921.

Velthoven & Klein Haarhuis 2010
Velthoven, B.C.J. & Klein Haarhuis, C.M., *Geschilbeslechtingsdelta 2009,* Den Haag: WODC, 2010.

Velthoven & Ter Voert 2004
Velthoven, B.C.J. & Ter Voert, M.J., *Geschilbeslechtingsdelta 2003,* WODC Onderzoek en Beleid, Meppel: Boom, 2004.

Verkerk 2005a
Verkerk, R., 'Powers of the Judge, the Netherlands', in: C.H. van Rhee (ed.), *European Traditions in Civil Procedure,* Antwerp/Oxford: Intersentia, 2005, p. 281-290.

Verkerk 2005b
Verkerk, R.R., 'Powers of the Judge, England and Wales', in: C.H. van Rhee (ed.), *European Traditions in Civil Procedure,* Antwerp/Oxford: Intersentia, 2005, p. 307-315.

Verkerk 2007
Verkerk, R.R., 'Procesrechtelijke waarborgen voor een betrouwbaar deskundigen-onderzoek', 24(10) *NTBR,* 2007, p. 491-500.

Verkerk 2009
Verkerk, R.R., 'Comparative aspects of expert evidence in civil litigation', 13(3) *International Journal of Evidence and Proof,* 2009, p. 167-197.

Verkerk 2010
Verkerk, R.R., 'Fairness and Compliance', in: C.H. van Rhee & A. Uzelac (eds.), *Enforcement and Enforceability - Tradition and Reform*, Antwerp: Intersentia, 2010, (forthcoming).

Verkijk 2010
Verkijk, R., *De advocaat in het burgerlijk process*, (diss. forthcoming), 2010.

Verschoof 2004
Verschoof, R.J., 'De praktijk van de comparitie na antwoord', 27 *Trema*, 2004, p. 339-345.

Vidmar 2003
Vidmar, N., 'The American Civil Jury for Ausländer (Foreigners)', 13 *Duke J. Comp. & Int'l L.*, 2003, p. 95-124.

Von Bethmann-Hollweg 1874
Von Bethmann-Hollweg, M.A., *Der germanisch-romanische Civilprozeß, im Mittelalter*, 6 Civilprozeß des gemeinen Rechts in geschichtlicher Entwicklung, Bonn: Adolph Marcus, 1874.

Von Gönner 1801
Von Gönner, N.T., *Handbuch des deutschen gemeinen Prozesses*, Erlangen: Palm, 1801.

Von Mehren 1982
Von Mehren, A.T., 'The Significance for Procedural Practice and Theory of the Concentrated Trial: Comparative Remarks', in: N. Horn (ed.), *Europäisches Rechtsdenken in Geschichte und Gegenwart*, München: C.H. Beck, 1982, 2, p. 361-371.

Wach 1872
Wach, A., 'Der Entwurf einer Deutschen Civilprozessordnung', 14 *Kritische Vierteljahrsschrift*, 1872, p. 329-373.

Wach 1914
Wach, A., *Grundfragen und Reform des Zivilprozesses*, Berlin: Verlag von Otto Liebmann, 1914.

Warren 2006
Warren, R.K., *State Judicial Elections: the Polarization of America's Courts*, November 2006, available at <http://www.courtinfo.ca.gov>, last consulted in February 2010.

Watson 1978
Watson, A., 'Comparative Law and Legal Change', 37 *Cambridge L.J.*, 1978, p. 313-336.

Watson 1993
Watson, A., *Legal Transplants, An Approach to Comparative Law*, 2nd ed., London: The University of Georgia Press, 1993.

Weber 1954
Weber, M., *Law in Economy and Society*, 20th Century Legal Philosphy Series, Cambridge: Harvard University Press, 1954.

Wedekind 1971
Wedekind, W.G.Ph.E., *Bijdrage tot de kennis van de ontwikkeling van de procesgang in civiele zaken voor het Hof van Holland in de eerste helft van de zestiende eeuw*, Assen: Van Gorcum, 1971.

Wehli 1896
Wehli, A., 'Die Beweislast im neuen Civilprocesse', 25(39-40) *JBl*, 1896, p. 457-487.

Weissel 1998
Weissel, E., 'Der Zugang zum Recht als Wirtschaftliches Gut', in: P. Lewisch & W.H. Rechberger (eds.), *100 Jahre ZPO, Ökonomische Analyse des Zivilprozesses,* Wien: Manz, 1998, p. 121-161.

Weitz 2006
Weitz, K., 'Die Entwicklung des polnischen Zivilprozessrechts nach der politischen Wende im Jahre 1989', 11 *ZZP Int*, 2006, p. 89-116.

Welsch 2003
Welsh, N.A., 'Perceptions of Fairness in Negotiation', 87 *Marq. l. Rev.*, 2003-2004, p. 753-767.

Wesseling-Van Gent 2006
Wesseling-Van Gent, E.M., 'To fish or not to fish, that's the question', in: P.J. van Der Korst *et al.* (eds.), *Het verzamelen van feiten en bewijs: begrenzing versus verruiming, een kruisbestuiving tussen civiel procesrecht en ondernemingsprocesrecht*, Den Haag: Boom, 2006, p. 81-119.

Weve 1878
Weve, F.A.T., 'Iets over behoud, hervorming of vervanging van het verhoor op vraagpunten', 9(3) *Themis, Rechtskundig tijdschrift*, 1878, p. 229-237.

Wieten 2002
Wieten, H.L.G., 'Het nieuwe procesrecht in burgerlijke zaken; een overzicht', 6492 *WPNR*, 2002, p. 413-420.

Wigmore 1937
Wigmore, J.H., *The Science of Judicial Proof*, 3rd ed., Boston: Little, Brown and Company, 1937.

Wigmore 1940
Wigmore, J.H., *A Treatise on the Anglo-American System of Evidence in Trials at Common Law*, 3rd ed., Boston: Little, Brown and Company, 1940.

Wijffels 2005a
Wijffels, A., 'France: Party Interrogation as Evidence', in: C.H. van Rhee (ed.), *European Traditions in Civil Procedure,* Antwerp: Intersentia, 2005, p. 235-243.

Wijffels 2005b
Wijffels, A., 'French Civil Procedure 1806-1975', in: C.H. van Rhee (ed.), *European Traditions in Civil Procedure,* Antwerp: Intersentia, 2005, p. 25-48.

Wijffels 2005c
Wijffels, A., 'France: Powers of the Judge', in: C.H. van Rhee (ed.), *European Traditions in Civil Procedure,* Antwerp: Intersentia, 2005, p. 269-279.

Wijffels 2008
Wijffels, A., 'The Code de procédure civile (1806) in France, Belgium and the Netherlands', in: C.H. van Rhee, D. Heirbout & M. Storme (eds.), *The French Code of Civil Procedure (1806) after 200 years,* Mechelen: Wolters Kluwer, 2008, p. 5-73.

Willging 1986
Willging, T.E., *Court-appointed Experts,* Federal Judicial Center, 1986, available at <www.fjc.gov>, last consulted in February 2010.

Willging, Stienstra, Shaphard & Miletich 1998
Willging, T.E., Stienstra, D., Shaphard, J. & Miletich, D., 'An Empirical Study of Discovery and Disclosure Practice under the 1993 Federal Rule Amendments', 39 *B.C. L. Rev.*, 1998, p. 525-596.

Wollschläger 1998
Wollschläger, Ch., 'Exploring Global Landscapes of Litigation Rates', in: J. Brand & D. Strempel (eds.), *Soziologie des Rechts: Festschrift für Erhard Blankenburg zum 60. Geburtstag,* Baden-Baden: Nomos, 1998, p. 577-588.

Wolters 2002
Wolters, G., 'Herinneringen door getuigen', in: P.J. van Koppen (ed.), *Het recht van binnen, psychologie van het recht,* Deventer: Kluwer, 2002, p. 397-415.

Woolf 1996
Woolf, H., *Access to Justice, Final Report*, London: The Stationairy Office, 1996.

Wrede 1923
Wrede, R.A., 'Die Parteivernehmung im Zivilprozess der nordischen Länder', 12 *Rheinische Zeitschrift für Zivil- und Prozessrecht*, 1923, p. 362-375.

Wright 1959
Wright, Ch.A., 'Procedural Reform in the States', 24 *F.R.D.*, 1959, p. 85-123.

Yeazell 1994
Yeazell, S.C., 'The Misunderstood Consequences of Modern Civil Process', *Wis. L. Rev.*, 1994, p. 631-678.

Yeazell 2004
Yeazell, S.C., 'Getting What We Asked For, Getting What We Paid For, and Not Liking What We Got: The Vanishing Civil Trial', 1(3) *Journal of Empirical Legal Studies*, 2004, p. 943-971.

Yeazell 2008
Yeazell, S.C., *Civil Procedure*, New York: Aspen Publishers, 2008.

Yoshida 2001
Yoshida, M. (ed.), *Die Informationsbeschaffung im Zivilprozeß*, Europäische Hochschulschriften, Frankfurt am Main: Peter Lang, 2001.

Zechner 1986
Zechner, A., 'Der gerichtliche Sachverständige - Privater oder Beweisorgan', 108(13-14) *JBl*, 1986, p. 415-424.

Zekoll 2006
Zekoll, J., 'Comparative Civil Procedure', in: M. Reimann & R. Zimmermann (eds.), *The Oxford Handbook of Comparative Law*, Oxford: Oxford University Press, 2006, p.1327-1363.

Zuckerman 1999
Zuckerman, A.A.S. (ed.), *Civil Justice in Crisis*, Oxford: Oxford University Press, 1999.

Zuckerman 2003
Zuckerman, A.A.S., *Civil Procedure*, London: LexisNexis UK, 2003.

Zweigert & Kötz 1998
Zweigert, K. & Kötz, H., *An Introduction to Comparative Law*, 3rd ed., Oxford: Clarendon Press, 1998.

INDEX

CURRICULUM VITAE

Remme Verkerk was born on 2 May 1980 in Enschede, the Netherlands. He received his primary and secondary education in Eindhoven, Kaohsiung (Taiwan) and Roermond. Remme obtained a master's degree in econometrics (2003) and a master's degree in law (2004) at Maastricht University.

Remme worked shortly as a computer programmer (Phillips, Sittard, the Netherlands, 2003 and Unitrans Pty. Ltd., Gaborone, Botswana, 2002) before working at Maastricht University. During his work at the University he published several articles in the area of civil procedure. He taught courses on legal history, legal philosophy, European integration, civil litigation and political philosophy. In 2005 and 2006 Remme also worked as a clerk at the District Court of Maastricht. As of September 2010, Remme will join the litigation department of Houthoff Buruma in the Hague.

A peer-reviewed book series in which the common foundations of the legal systems of the Member States of the European Community are the central focus.

The *Ius Commune Europaeum* series includes horizontal comparative legal studies as well as studies on the effect of treaties within the national legal systems. All the classic fields of law are covered. The books are published in various European languages under the auspices of METRO, the Institute for Transnational Legal Research at the Maastricht University.

Recently published:

Volume 69: *Vennootschappelijke beleidsbepaling in geval van financiële moeilijkheden; de positie van bestuurders en aandeelhouders*, M. OLAERTS
Volume 70: *Judicial Case Management and Efficiency in Civil Litigation*, C.H. VAN RHEE (ed.)
Volume 71: *Specific Performance in Contract Law: National and Other Perspectives*, J.M. SMITS, D. HAAS and G. HESEN (eds.)
Volume 72: *Environmental Liability in a Federal System. A Law and Economics Analysis*, K. DE SMEDT
Volume 73: *De optimale inrichting van de verkeersboete in België en Nederland vanuit een strafrechtelijk en bestuursrechtelijk perspectief. Een juridische en rechtseconomische analyse*, L. DEBEN
Volume 74: *Civil Justice between Efficiency and Quality: From Ius Commune to the CEPEJ*, C.H. VAN RHEE and A. UZELAC (eds.)
Volume 75: *The Principle of Numerus Clausus in European Property Law*, B. AKKERMANS
Volume 76: *European Cooperation between Financial Supervisory Authorities, Tax Authorities and Judicial Authorities*, M. LUCHTMAN
Volume 77: *Access to Justice and the Judiciary: Towards New European Standards of Affordability, Quality and Efficiency of Civil Adjudication*, A. UZELAC and C.H. VAN RHEE (eds.)
Volume 78: *The European Private Company (SPE): A Critical Analysis of the EU Draft Statute*, D.F.M.M. ZAMAN, C.A. SCHWARZ, M.L. LENNARTS, H.-J. DE KLUIVER and A.F.M. DORRESTEIJN (eds.)
Volume 79: *Constitutions Compared. An Introduction to Comparative Constitutional Law (*2nd edition*)*, A.W. HERINGA and PH. KIIVER
Volume 80: *Rechtsbescherming en overheidsovereenkomsten*, K. WAUTERS
Volume 81: *Derden in het contractenrecht*, I. SAMOY
Volume 82: *The Right to Specific Performance. The Historical Development*, J.H. DONDORP and J.J. HALLEBEEK (eds.)
Volume 83: *Financial Supervision in a Comparative Perspective*, M. POTO
Volume 84: *Enforcement and Enforceability – Tradition and Reform*, C.H. VAN RHEE and A. UZELAC (eds.)
Volume 85: *Fact-Finding in Civil Litigation. A Comparative Perspective*, R.R. VERKERK

www.ingramcontent.com/pod-product-compliance
Ingram Content Group UK Ltd.
Pitfield, Milton Keynes, MK11 3LW, UK
UKHW051925100926
8556IPUK00022B/1370

9 789400 000742